READINGS IN APPLIED ENGLISH LINGUISTICS

READINGS IN APPLIED ENGLISH LINGUISTICS

THIRD
EDITION

HAROLD B. ALLEN
UNIVERSITY OF MINNESOTA, MINNEAPOLIS
(EMERITUS)

MICHAEL D. LINN
UNIVERSITY OF MINNESOTA, DULUTH

ALFRED A. KNOPF  NEW YORK

THIS IS A BORZOI BOOK
PUBLISHED BY ALFRED A. KNOPF, INC.

Third Edition
98765432
Copyright © 1982 by Alfred A. Knopf, Inc.
      © 1958, 1964 by Harold B. Allen

Library of Congress Cataloging in Publication Data

Main entry under title:

Readings in applied English linguistics.

     Includes bibliographical references.
     1. Linguistics—Addresses, essays, lectures. 2. English language—Addresses, essays, lectures. 3. English language—Study and teaching—Addresses, essays, lectures. I. Allen, Harold Byron, 1902–   . II. Linn, Michael D.
P25.R38 1982   410   81–18663
ISBN 0–394–32750–0   AACR2

Manufactured in the United States of America

Book Design: Karin Gerdes-Kincheloe
Cover Design: Claude Martinot
Production: Suzanne Loeb

Like its two predecessors, this book reflects a deep and abiding concern with the English teaching profession and the field of linguistics and, indeed, with the general spread of knowledge about language itself and our own language in particular. Like them, this collection is an attempt to meet the need for making readily available the direct words of writers in the field instead of only a filtered and synthesized treatment in the words of a single textbook author.

The first such collection designed primarily for the teachers and prospective teachers of English as well as for beginning students in linguistics was the senior editor's *Readings in Applied English Linguistics* (Appleton-Century-Crofts, 1958). Within a few years, developments in linguistic theory and applications to the teaching of composition led to a second edition in 1964. Again, the rapid expansion of linguistic research with its implications for English teaching and for an introduction to linguistics called for another edition. But, as preparations for that edition began, the publishing company went out of business.

In the meantime the precedent of the first edition had been followed by the publication of other language anthologies, but none seemed to have an essential component intended for relating the contents to classroom teaching. To meet the continuing need for such a collection, the senior editor enlisted the cooperation of Michael Linn, who as coeditor contributed the benefit of his more recent classroom experience and research.

But already the changes in the field of English linguistics were so great and so numerous that clearly much more than the replacement of a few out-of-date articles was now required in order to form a third edition. Linguistic theory had rejected earlier assumptions, attention had turned to the process by which language is acquired, concern with social variation had become critical, name study had entered the secondary schools, lexicography as such had become the focus of scholarly interest, and recognition was being given to the problem of the English teacher with a few students not having English as a first language. What was required was not a third edition but a new book. This is that book, with only the title and eight time-tried articles retained from the second edition.

The extraordinary multiplication of books and journals has made increasingly difficult a judicious selection of appropriate articles. We have attempted not to provide an overview of any of the several subfields but rather to choose representative articles offering significant insights. One article may be a conspectus or summary, another may stimulate with a critical reaction to a definite point of view, another may report a case study or other specific application, and another may describe research. Any one of the articles may lead a student to take off on his own to explore some subfield in depth. We hope so.

The articles are grouped into related and sometimes overlapping categories. The section on teaching, for instance, inevitably overlaps other sections. The section order is pragmatic, although requirements in a given course may dictate a change in order. Such a change would not be critical, of course.

Because many articles have copious reading references, we have not provided an overall bibliography. A few important references not otherwise mentioned have been cited in the several section introductions. Serious students should be aware of three general bibliographical sources as well. The period from the beginning of printing to the end of 1922 is exhaustively covered by Arthur G. Kennedy's *A Bibliography of Writings on the English Language* (reprinted, Hafner, 1961). The period from 1922 through 1975 is selectively covered by the 3,000 titles in Harold B. Allen's *Linguistics and English Linguistics: A Bibliography* (2nd ed., AHM Publishing Corporation, 1977). An exhaustive annual listing is that of the successive third volumes in the *MLA International Bibliography*, published by the Modern Language Association.

Whatever contribution this book can make to the preparation of teachers of English or to the general understanding of language would have been impossible, of course, without the primary work of the authors who have generously granted permission to reprint. For that consent we are most appreciative. We are grateful as well to the following readers who provided us with many useful comments and suggestions:

John Algeo, University of Georgia
David DeCamp, late of The University of Texas, Austin
Donald Freeman, Temple University
Sidney Greenbaum, University of Wisconsin, Milwaukee
Richard Larson, Lehman College, CUNY
Bruce Pearson, University of South Carolina
Jean Pival, University of Kentucky
Jessica Wirth, University of Wisconsin, Milwaukee

CONTENTS

PART V   LINGUISTICS AND USAGE   295

PART VI   LINGUISTICS AND TEACHING   339

PART VII   LINGUISTICS AND THE DICTIONARY   469

PART VIII   LINGUISTICS AND NAME STUDY   513

PART IX   LINGUISTICS AND LITERATURE   547

PART I

THE BACKGROUND

Although during the 1960s there developed a still current disregard for history, it is a truism that we rise into the future by standing on the shoulders of our predecessors. An understanding of the present requires an understanding of the past.

Specifically, to satisfy an interest in the English language and certainly to teach English on any level, one needs at least a synoptic overview of its history as well as an understanding of its theories. This section attempts to provide such an overview.

If you have ever attended a course in the history of the English language, Kenneth Wilson's opening article will offer an effective review of the main currents of internal and external change since the gradual fusing of the West Germanic dialects of the invaders began a millennium and a half ago. If the background of Modern English is new to you, this article will lay a broad basis for comprehending the really amazing progress of English from a state in which inflectional forms led in importance to today's state in which word-order—syntax—dominates. We hope that you subsequently will be led to search for illustrative support—and thus expand your historical awareness—by going to one of the historical texts Wilson recommends.

Wilson's contribution includes also a historical overview of two related areas, the history of English grammars and the history of English dictionaries. As both of these areas will be treated in depth later in this collection, this article serves as an introduction.

The next three articles, by Karl Dykema, Charles Hartung, and Nelson Francis, form a unit which cogently and concisely traces the variations in grammatical theory from the ancient Greek and Roman philosophers to the recent work of the structural grammarians. Because these authors have different viewpoints, their articles complement one another as they portray the history of grammar. An excellent conspectus of this complex history is that by R. H. Robins, reader in linguistics in the School of Oriental and African Studies at the University of London, in his *Ancient and Mediaeval Grammatical Theory in Europe* (Bell, London, 1951).

Dykema first outlines the Graeco-Latinate origins of the still powerful prescriptive grammatical tradition. Hartung then relates this persistent tradition to the transitional work of the language scholars of two generations ago before he epitomizes the contribution of a great leader in structural linguistics, Charles C. Fries. Not to be slighted in this article is the brief glance at the distinction between morphological and syntactic parts of speech, for example, between ''adjective'' and ''adjectival.'' Recognition of this simple distinction in school textbooks would prevent hours of futile classroom arguments over the arbitrary classification of a word as a given part of speech. Although Hartung attributes this distinction to James Sledd, it actually was first proposed by the late Henry Lee Smith, Jr., professor of linguistics at the University of Buffalo.

Next, Francis's "Revolution in Grammar," a classic short article in the field, successfully combines into a single clear presentation the phonological and syntactic analyses found in three seminal books in English structural grammar: George L. Trager and Henry Lee Smith's *An Outline of English Structure* (Battenberg Press, 1951), Charles C. Fries's *An American English Grammar* (Appleton-Century, 1940), and Fries's *The Structure of English* (Harcourt, Brace, 1952). The high-water mark of the structural approach to language study was reached by Francis's own long-popular textbook *The Structure of American English* (Ronald, 1958) and Archibald A. Hill's *Introduction to Linguistic Structures* (Harcourt, Brace, 1958). It is significant that during the preparation of these two books there should appear Noam Chomsky's *Syntactic Structures* (Mouton, 1957), the short monograph that began a whole new era in the history of linguistic theory and analysis—of all language as well as of English itself.

For a more extensive background of the history of linguistics, including a statement of the relevance of American work to the development of linguistics in Europe, the student will find the following useful:

Aarsleff, Hans. *The Study of Language in England, 1780–1860*. Princeton: Princeton University Press, 1967.

Carroll, John B. *The Study of Language: A Survey of Linguistics and Related Disciplines in America*. Cambridge: Harvard University Press, 1953.

Firth, John R. "A Synopsis of Linguistic Theory, 1930–1950." In *Studies in Linguistic Analysis*. London: Philological Society, 1957. Pp. 1–32.

Hall, Robert A., Jr. "American Linguistics, 1925–50." In *Archivum Linguisticum* 3(1951): 101–125; 4(1952): 1–16.

Mohrmann, Christine, Alf Sommerfelt, and Joshua Whatmough. *Trends in European and American Linguistics, 1930–1960*. Utrecht: Spectrum, 1961.

Pedersen, Holger. *Linguistic Science in the Nineteenth Century*. John W. Spargo, transl. Cambridge: Harvard University Press, 1931. Reprinted as *The Discovery of Language*. Bloomington: Indiana University Press, 1962.

Robins, R. H. *A Short History of Linguistics*. Bloomington: Indiana University Press, 1967.

Finally, Part I includes a key article by the late Benjamin Whorf. Although not mentioned in the preceding three articles, Whorf here propounds a belief that still holds an important, albeit controversial, place in the thinking of descriptivists, especially anthropological linguists. Sometimes identified as the Whorf-Sapir hypothesis because of the share the late Edward Sapir had in its development, this principle of linguistic relativity, this idea that language determines thought, has been rejected by some linguists in its absolute form because of extensive research in Indian languages of the Southwest. But its general thrust toward a recognition of the often powerful influence of words and grammatical forms upon thinking and attitudes is still accepted. We believe the inclusion of this article is well justified. For a perceptive statement of Whorf's linguistic significance, see John B. Carroll's introduction in the collection of Whorf's writings, *Language, Thought, and Reality*, M.I.T. Press, 1956; paperback edition, 1964.

KENNETH G. WILSON

Once a student of Charles Fries and Albert Marckwardt at the University of Michigan, the author is now professor of English and vice president for academic affairs at the University of Connecticut. With Leonard Dean he edited one of the early college texts for the general user, Essays on Language and Usage *(Oxford University Press, 1959, and later revised).*

THE ENGLISH LANGUAGE: PAST AND PRESENT

THE HISTORY OF THE ENGLISH LANGUAGE

Introduction

The English language is usually said to have begun in the sixth and seventh centuries, when the Germanic Angles, Saxons, and Jutes invaded and settled the Celtic island of Britain.[1] With the techniques of historical linguistics and philology, in spite of the lack of written records, we have been able to reconstruct the older forms, sounds, and vocabularies of the invaders' language in remarkable detail, working mainly from later written sources and from our knowledge of linguistic change. The Celtic language, together with most of the Roman linguistic remains, disappeared from England, except for a few place names. The history of English had begun.

The Ancestral History

The shift into a new territory of a large number of speakers of a language, isolated from the homeland and in contact with a new language and culture, sets in motion its own rates and kinds of change, so that although the home language may continue strong and pursue its own life, the two strains—here two strains of a West Germanic language—will develop independently and will eventually become different enough from each other as to be no longer mutually intelligible. As a result there will be two separate languages.

The continental origins are important: there the Germanic languages were already fully formed; they belonged to a family of languages, Indo-European, which was already important in the history of the world, both in influence and in numbers of speakers.

Although we have never heard or seen it, scholars have managed to reconstruct much of Indo-European; from the study of many related languages they have been able to recreate the sounds, the grammar, and the vocabulary of this ur-language from which so many of the modern western and some of the eastern languages have come. The reconstruction itself is a fascinating story, but here we can say only that somewhere in the period 3500 to 2000 B.C., there was a people living probably in northeastern Europe who spoke a language we now call Indo-European. Centuries of migrations, conquests, divisions, and expansions splintered this language (which had itself probably splintered

---

[1] The first section of this article relies heavily on three good histories of English: Baugh (2); Robertson and Cassidy (19); and Pyles (18).

off from another, earlier language) into new languages, some of which in turn spawned still more languages, not regularly or predictably in time, but gradually or spasmodically, as the vagaries of human society drove the people apart. Today we find descendants of the Indo-European language family stretched over almost the entire globe, and we recognize the ancient history of the family in its name. Indo-European languages are native to a wide swath from northern Europe across the eastern Mediterranean into India, and more recently they have been planted in North America, Africa, and Australia.

Through historical linguistic techniques, English can be traced to its origins. It belongs to the Germanic subdivision of a major subgroup of Indo-European. Sound shifts—systematic evolutions in what happened to certain sounds of the Germanic languages only—plus certain grammatical characteristics, such as the loss of nearly all inflectional signs of tense and aspect except the distinction between the present and the preterit, distinguish the Germanic languages. And similar differences distinguish the West Germanic languages from those of the East and North. Thus English traces its history from the West Germanic group to an Anglo-Frisian group and finally to English itself.

The History of the Speakers of English

In the eighth and ninth centuries we begin to find texts in English written by Englishmen; it is then that we begin the documented history of the language. We have some convenient names: Old English or Anglo-Saxon is the language of the early Middle Ages, roughly from the beginnings to 1000 or 1100. Middle English is the language from 1100 or so to the Renaissance, to about 1500 or 1550. Early Modern English is Renaissance English, lasting perhaps until 1700, and Modern English is the language from the beginning of the eighteenth century until today. These "periods" are arbitrary; more often they measure the social history of its speakers rather than characteristic differences in the language itself, although the differences are there: the English of Alfred, of Chaucer, and of Shakespeare differed markedly, just as our own differs from Shakespeare's. Conventional histories of English examine and try to account for the gross differences in the language at each of these periods.

But the history of *what* is the history of English? Certainly the history of its vocabulary, of its words and their meanings, would be a major consideration. But there are other important aspects too.

In some ways, the history of the speakers themselves is the most important part of the history of a language. Who were the people, how did they live, what did they speak about, whom did they meet, and what happened to them? Social history will be reflected above all in the vocabulary, since a people will invent and adapt words and their meanings to fit its daily requirements; as these change, so will the vocabulary change.

To the student of language history, however, there are other kinds of historical study which are equally important: the history of the sounds of the language, and the development of its grammar—the forms of the words, their inflections and the grammatical meanings they contain, and the constantly evolving rules of the syntax—these too can be historically traced. In this brief account we can only offer reminders of the social history and of the military, economic, political, and religious activities of the English people which affected the history of their language.

We must study the effects of the Scandinavian invasions, wherein a similar Germanic people came into close (and eventually submerged) relationship with the English. The Norman invasion and the several centuries of Norman and French domination of government and upper-class life left their marks, as did the migrations of people from the

Low Countries into London in the later Middle Ages. The Renaissance, that time of expansion and invention, inquiry and experiment—political, geographical, social, military, scientific, and religious—affected the quality of English life and left its marks on the language. The development of the Empire in the eighteenth and nineteenth centuries is important: Englishmen began to know the whole world, and the scientific and commercial prowess of the industrial revolution made England the great mercantile and naval power we now think of as Victorian. And then came the great wars of the modern era, with the tremendous social, economic, and political upheaval they left in their wake: all these forces and events have left their marks on the English language.

The American Speakers of English

We need more than a simple footnote, too, to pick up the American version of this social history, which from the seventeenth century on began to run a separate course.[2] Important are the very facts of the arrival of the English on this continent. For example, both the New England and Virginia settlements spoke dialects from the English Home Counties—from the area around London—but different social class dialects; hence the language in these two locations, though essentially Elizabethan at the outset, differed markedly.

And the English encountered other Europeans when they came: in the Great Lakes and Mississippi areas they found the French had been there first, naming the places and animals and tribes, and pronouncing the Indian words in a French that the English could only anglicize. In lower New York, the Dutch had left their mark on the social and topographical order, and in Florida and the Southwest the Spanish had long since named the geographical parts. And everywhere there were the Indians, not many people in all but speaking many dialects and languages. All these facts of social and political history have left their signs on the American varieties of English, just as they have left them on American life itself.

Later history is important too. A nation of immigrants, we owe something to the kinds of people who settled the various sections of the country: to the Germans in Pennsylvania and the lower Ohio Valley, to the Scotch in the lower Midwest and the uplands of the Border States, to the Scandinavians in the upper Midwest, and to the Irish in Boston and the Italians in New York, just to name a few. As the country assumed the role of inspiration to the downtrodden, thousands of the economically and politically ''out'' came from the countries of central and southern Europe. And the Negro deserves our attention: he made little mark on the language at first, so low was his social status; but in recent years his words, his dialects, and his special meanings have made a solid impact—on the life of Americans and the American version of English.

All these contacts had their effects—some major, some trivial. But there is much more. We began by being a rural country, with a frontier which stayed open until the First World War. But now we are a great industrial power, an urban society, and these changes have changed the language too.

Hence one vital part of the history of the language is the history of its speakers—who they were, whom they met, how they lived, and what they did and thought and strove for; these things shape speakers' words and the way they say them and even the way they string them together.

---

[2] The best account is by Marckwardt (14).

The History of the English Vocabulary

When we study the history of the vocabulary, we can see the importance of social history; vocabulary changes most quickly of all the aspects of language. English in the seventh century displays a predominantly Germanic vocabulary. There are a few Roman words dating from continental encounters with the Romans, and there are a few others picked up from the Roman remains the English found in Britain. But the words are mostly Germanic.

Since the English drove out the British Celts, the latter added almost no Celtic words to the language—a few place names and little more. Missionary culture from Britain's conversion to Christianity added Latin names for religious things. But when the Vikings came and settled down, the two Germanic strains borrowed freely from each other. Actually, many of their words were similar, and sometimes the two similar words were both kept, a shift being made in the meaning of one or the other: *shirt* and *skirt* were originally the same Germanic word; both versions were kept, with different meanings (2: 113). Occasionally, the Scandinavian word displaced the English one: *egg* replaced the English *ey*, first in the Northern dialect and then in all English.

With Norman and later massive French influences in the Middle Ages, the English vocabulary changed markedly. It borrowed wholesale from French. With Christianity it had accepted Latin words; now it often borrowed the same words again, this time in their French forms and with their French meanings. It borrowed the names of all sorts of French ideas: words for government, law, dress, food, manners, and the like. Chaucer's fourteenth-century vocabulary looks very different from King Alfred's ninth-century one, mainly because so many of Chaucer's words were borrowed from French.

The Renaissance brought a different sort of change:[3] scholars and writers deliberately added words or made them up from Latin and Greek, and travelers brought back Italian names for exotic things (2: 113). As English explorers, businessmen, and soldiers went farther and farther afield, even some eastern Mediterranean and New World words began to appear in the language.

In this country, immigration had an effect on the vocabulary, though not in proportion to the numbers of immigrants. The Germans were the most numerous of the non-English-speaking immigrants, yet they have left us only many words for food and drink, a few words for educational matters, and surprisingly little else. The Italians illustrate the whole pattern nicely. When in the seventeenth and eighteenth centuries, the English milords began to take the grand tour, Italian words for music and painting and other aspects of art and cultivation were added to English; we cannot discuss music and painting without using borrowed Italian terms. But when the poor Italians came to New York in the early twentieth century, they had little interest for us except as laborers. We did not ape their language except in jest; they hurried instead to learn ours. As a result, American English added the names of a few Italian dishes to its vocabulary from this contact, and little more.

The point is important: when two cultures come into contact, everything seems to depend upon who is master, or at least upon who feels inferior. Hence English borrowed massively from French during the Middle Ages, when French power and culture seemed demonstrably superior. But in the past two centuries, English has borrowed from French

---

[3] The best account is by Baugh (2: 240–305).

only the terms for hairstyles and women's dress and the like, while terms of technology and the names of soft drinks the French have borrowed from us.

The History of the Sounds of English: Phonology

We can also study the history of the *sounds* of English. Using written records from the Middle Ages and the early Renaissance, we can tell from the unfixed spelling a good deal about how the words were pronounced. The histories of English sounds have been elaborately worked out, and the changes are regular, according to generalizable patterns. It is possible to reconstruct these changes, so that we can make reasonable guesses at what Shakespeare's language (or Chaucer's or Alfred's) actually sounded like.

Once the spelling became fixed, we lost a good bit of the information previously provided when each man spelled the way he spoke, but in literature—Hardy's Wessex novels, for example—we find evidence in the author's attempt to suggest or imitate the sounds of the spoken language by unconventional spelling. Mark Twain did this sort of thing well in *Huckleberry Finn.*

With nineteenth- and twentieth-century skills in phonetic notation, and most recently with the development of the phonograph and wire and tape recorders, scholars have learned to record permanently the sound of the language. The history of English sounds before modern times was often a matter of scholarly deduction; henceforth it will be able to rely on accurate recordings.

The History of English Word-Forms: Morphology

We are on even more elaborately detailed ground when we turn to the history of English forms and inflections. Old English was a highly inflected language, as were its Germanic progenitors. It still carried distinctive endings (*a*) for four forms of the verb, (*b*) for number in several parts of speech, (*c*) for case in nouns and adjectives (including both weak and strong declensions in adjectives), and (*d*) for person, number, and case in pronouns. It inflected its demonstratives.

There are useful generalizations we can make about the history of English morphology: we can say first of all that the general trend has been for inflections to disappear and be "replaced" by other means of giving the needed grammatical information. Nouns illustrate the pattern: Alfred's nouns had four cases—nominative, genitive, dative, and accusative. But the case distinctions began to drop off, perhaps partly because the heavy forward stress characteristic of Old English (words tended to be stressed on the first or root syllable) began to make it hard to distinguish among unstressed endings like *–an, –en, –em, –am,* and the like, and partly because other devices began to serve the same purpose. Word order was becoming fixed, so that one looked for nominative case nouns towards the beginning of sentences, and therefore soon one did not require the reassurance of a case ending to know one had a subject before a verb. By Chaucer's time, of case in nouns, only an all-purpose nominative form, a genitive form, and a few relic dative-accusatives were left. Today, although we still have both the "nominative" all-purpose form and the genitive, the datives and accusatives are gone; there are now only two cases in nouns, and for the genitive there is an alternative: a periphrastic construction with *of* which permits us to say *the road's surface* without the genitive inflection, as *the surface of the road.*

Pronouns also show the disappearance of some case inflections since Old English. Middle English still distinguished some of the datives and accusatives: *hine* was accusative, *him*, dative. Now we have coalesced these two into *him*, a form we might logically call a dual-purpose objective case form.

The pattern of deteriorating inflections is felt everywhere: case has disappeared from adjectives, and even some of the signs of tense in verbs are coalescing. Only the third person singular still maintains a distinctive inflection in the present tense: *he swims*, but *I, you, we, you,* and *they* merely *swim*.

Old English had two very different schemes for signalling the past tense and the past participle. The strong verb system had eight distinctive classes of vowel change to signal tense; we see one class pattern reflected in the forms of the Modern English verb *drink, drank, drunk* (OE *drincan, dronc, druncon, druncen*). The strong verb system was very large in Old English; but the weak system, which ended both preterit and past participle with a dental suffix, also included large numbers of verbs, and in the end it has come to dominate. Hundreds of our formerly strong verbs have taken on the weak pattern: *grip, gripped, gripped; gleam, gleamed, gleamed,* and so on. The increasing dominance of the weak pattern is clear in the child's language: he usually says *swimmed* at first, until he learns the older strong form which we now retain as a kind of exception to the trend. And when we make new verbs—*televise*, for example—we make them on the weak system model; the preterit is *televised*, with the dental suffix.

Changes of this sort, reflecting the general replacement of much of the inflectional system by other grammatical devices, might lead us to attempt too hasty a generalization. It is true that inflections have been disappearing, and that distinctive forms like those of the subjunctive have been diminishing in use. But there is another tendency to be considered too: the smaller the number of inflections left, and the higher the frequency of their occurrence in our speech and writing, the more likely we are to retain them. Hence the pronouns retain more of case than do the nouns, and most of those that remain seem fairly strongly entrenched. And while much of the subjunctive is weakening (one seldom hears "If he arrive early" any more), other parts of it seem as strong as ever ("If I were you" and "I asked that he come tomorrow" seem firmly entrenched).

Hence we can see that the history of English morphology does permit generalizations; but it is also clear that students of the language need to realize the importance of looking at individual words and individual grammatical devices in great detail if they would have an accurate appreciation of this aspect of linguistic history.

The History of English Word Order: Syntax

An oversimplified statement of a thousand years of syntactic change might go something like this: Word order and function words (prepositions and conjunctions and the like) were already grammatical devices in Old English, but fewer in number and apparently simpler and less forceful in operation than they are today; by the Middle English period, these devices were beginning to be more powerful and more numerous, and the closer we get to the Modern English period, the more these devices take on the force of overriding signals of grammatical meaning, capable in many instances of canceling out the significance of the inflections that remain.

Case is no longer so important as is the *word order* component of syntax: "Him hit John" is not really ambiguous today; we ignore the small boy's error of case, and we know unquestionably who hit whom. But in Old English, had *John* carried a nominative inflection, the roles of striker and struck would clearly have been reversed.

English syntax has, then, an increasingly complex history; nor are we always entirely sure of the degree of complexity or the true force of word order and function words in Old English. There are many open questions here. But we do know that the subject-verb-object and subject-verb-complement patterns have become very powerful. Positions for modifiers too have developed distinctive patterns, since we must rely on position to tell us which adjective goes with which noun, now that inflections are no longer doing the job.

Our question patterns involve either (*a*) reversal of subject and verb, a pattern more common in Early Modern English and before than it is today (*Rides he to the wars?*), or (*b*) the use of auxiliaries in the reversed position with the verb itself tagging along later (*Can I come too? Does he ever ride?*). We also have a list of question-asking function words which fall into normal subject position, often with a reversal of subject and verb, to make questions: *Whom is he calling? Where are you going? What happened?*

Major patterns of syntax then have developed over the past thousand years of English; they are laws which govern the way we string our words together. When case is gone, we pick out the indirect object in one of two syntactic ways: word order (John gave *his brother* the book) or function word (John gave the book *to his brother*) where the prepositional phrase replaces the indirect object construction.

The history of English syntax illustrates the trend toward fixed patterns in English; it also illustrates two important principles for any language study: (*a*) we must always examine particulars and test the accuracy of generalizations; and (*b*) it helps to understand the English of today or any other day if we can see how the pattern under study evolved over the centuries.

THE HISTORY OF ENGLISH GRAMMARS[4]

Introduction

Prior to the eighteenth century there were no full-dress attempts to describe the structure of English. Since then, grammarians and laymen both have struggled with each other in attempting to understand its structure and to "improve" it. Many of the misunderstandings have arisen from the term *grammar* itself: English grammar is first of all the system of patterns and rules which enables us to use the language. Whether we can describe and state these patterns and rules or not, they do exist: even little children and the mentally defective can speak English; they "know" English grammar even if they cannot tell us what it is they know. But *an* English grammar is also any specific attempt to *describe* the structural system of English. And finally, to confuse the situation further, English grammar in the schools and to the layman has also come to refer simply to points of difficulty and variation, to the choices on which we have placed strong values—in short, to usage. Here we shall concern ourselves solely with the second of these uses of the term *grammar*: the history of attempts to describe the structure of English.

Universal Grammar

Systematic study of the structure of English had to await both the "coming of age of English," when it had gained respectability, and the eighteenth-century zeal for order, regularity, and the power of generalization. Universal grammar was a logical beginning, based as it was on ideas of the similarities (and the classical authority) of Latin and Greek. If English seemed to lack something to be found in this universal grammar, it must be a flaw, and it must be corrected.

---

[4] In this section, I have relied heavily on Gleason (10: 67–87).

Pioneer grammarians like Robert Lowth and Joseph Priestley leaned heavily on universal grammar: Lowth's extremely influential *A Short Introduction to English Grammar* (1762) reported variations between English and Latin constructions, and cited English authorial practices to illustrate the rules for English structure. Everywhere Lowth (like Dr. Johnson in his *Dictionary*, 1755) assumed that universal grammar should be the guide to English grammarians; he sought usually to bring English into line (10: 68–70).

Modern linguistic scholarship had, until a recent reawakening of interest, very largely disproved the old universal grammar. Part of the problem was that of the blind men and the elephant: comparative grammarians had arrived at their conclusions about universal grammar from an examination of many languages—ancient and modern—but as luck would have it, nearly all were Indo-European. Hence, they found so many similarities that principles seemed obvious. But as anthropologists began to describe the languages they encountered in Asia, Africa, and the Pacific, as well as the Indian and Eskimo languages of the Western Hemisphere, almost all the principles of universal grammar turned out to be unsound.

School Grammars

Despite the fact that the most influential of the old school grammars was written in England, school grammars are a peculiarly American phenomenon, fostered by the American zeal for popular education. Lindley Murray's *English Grammar Adapted to the Different Classes of Learners* (1795) was the most widely used and widely imitated of the school grammars. An American who moved to Britain after the Revolution, Murray composed a grammar which was oversimple, dogmatic, and logical at the expense of accurate observation. It laid out "the rules" of English grammar, treating syntax, parts of speech, rules of parsing, spelling, and a number of other topics. It was clear, forceful, and incredibly successful. Gleason remarks:

> Murray frankly appeals to expediency in determining his rules. He recognizes that there are only two case forms in the noun, but considers it easier to teach three, since there are three in the pronoun. His grammar deals almost entirely with words— their classification and forms comprising etymology, and their uses constituting syntax. . . . Almost nothing is said about the order of words (10: 71–72).

Within the tradition of school grammars, others began to try to show graphically the structure of the English sentence. Alonzo Reed and Brainerd Kellogg perfected a scheme for diagraming which combined the analytical features of parsing with earlier and clumsier attempts at graphic display of sentence structure. It too caught on (10: 73–74).

The chief problems with school grammars were that they oversimplified and that they stressed logic at the expense of accuracy. They were teachable grammars, and in the schools they were—and are—used prescriptively. In the effort to be clear and firm, they often obscured complexities and they sometimes falsified the facts of English structure in the effort to be orderly and "complete."

Traditional Grammars

In continental Europe, the nineteenth and early twentieth centuries provided a fine group of scholarly English grammars. Not textbooks, these were fresh, exhaustively detailed examinations of the structure of English. Conservative and careful, the traditional grammarians closely examined the language, especially the written language, classifying meticulously, never glossing over difficulties, always reporting the details that did not seem to fit.

These grammars were traditional in that they were organized around the conventional classifications of parts of speech, elements of the sentence, and types of sentence. Whatever their descriptions lack in power (that is, in strength of generalization) is made up in detail of description. The classics are Poutsma's *A Grammar of Late Modern English,* Kruisinga's *A Handbook of Present-Day English,* and Jespersen's *A Modern English Grammar on Historical Principles.* Jespersen's seven-volume work is both typical and innovative: he was a thoroughly trained historical linguist, and he had the fine ability of the small boy in *The Emperor's Clothes;* he could observe accurately and though he worked within a tradition, he was seldom bound by it (10: 77–78).

The great European reference grammars have flaws. But their quality has never really ceased to be admired, and they have more recently been given new praise by the transformational-generative grammarians, who see in their attention to detail and in their insistence on dealing with total meaning a kindred spirit of investigation into English structure.[5]

Structural Grammars

Structural grammars depend on the work of descriptive linguists, particularly in that they work wholly from real samples of English. The key document is Charles Carpenter Fries' *The Structure of English,* which begins by reclassifying the parts of speech into four form-classes and fifteen groups of function words. Fries makes some good distinctions: for example, he finds that auxiliaries clearly are not like traditionally classified verbs because they neither display the full formal patterns of verb morphology nor do they distribute themselves as traditional verbs do. He concludes that they are function words.

His attempts at more rigorous adherence to schemes of classification based first on form and then on position or function, rather than on all three intermixed, were a major contribution, since they permitted grammars to deal more powerfully with the details observed.

This reassessment of the parts of speech caused much of the furor which Fries' book stirred up, particularly among teachers, but the main thrust of the book was its attempt to deal with syntax, especially with the patterns of English word order (10: 79–80).

Much pedagogy has been developed from combining Fries' close look at real samples of language and his efforts at generalizations about syntax with the strong emphasis on the spoken language which stems from the linguists, especially from the work of Trager and Smith (20). This combination has led to solid attempts at fairly full structural grammars, such as W. Nelson Francis' *The Structure of American English* (8), the most widely used text for the training of English teachers in grammar during the past decade.

The Contributions of American Linguists

Beginning with Leonard Bloomfield, American anthropologically oriented linguists began to apply to the English language the descriptive methods they used in dealing with exotic languages among Pacific islanders, Eskimos, and Indians. What followed was a series of studies, among them the Smith-Trager *An Outline of English Structure* (1951) (20).

---

[5] Gleason cites three modern works in this tradition: Zandvoort (26); Jespersen (13); and Curme (7, 6).

It was the first full treatment of English sound structure—including stress, pitch, and juncture—together with a brief but perceptive account of morphology; it did not go far into syntax (10: 82–84). The spoken language was the key; hence the linguists of the forties and fifties attacked the traditional grammarians for their reliance upon the written language and for dealing with meaning as a whole.

Intonation patterns were seen as components of grammar, and this led to what some linguists call "phonological syntax," the elaboration of the grammar of the spoken language. Archibald Hill's *Introduction to Linguistic Structures* (1958) developed this line of descriptions further, although, like much structural analysis, it was not always well received (12).

Eugene Nida, *A Synopsis of English Syntax* (16), concentrated exclusively on syntax; the scheme of immediate constituent analysis which he employed has been widely modified and developed. Gleason says:

> Each construction was described as consisting of two parts (very rarely three or more) of specific types and in a definable relation. Long sentences are described in terms of many layers of such simple constructions, one within another (10: 85).

In the end we find people like Francis developing fairly comprehensive descriptions, in which the immediate constituent technique is elaborately worked out; and in which four kinds of structure are described: predication, complementation, modification, and coordination (8: 291ff.). Francis and others have polished these approaches for use in teaching; but they have by no means resolved all the problems of describing English structure, particularly syntax.

Transformational-Generative Grammars

Beginning with assumptions by Noam Chomsky and others, a whole series of new schemes for describing the manufacture of English sentences has begun to appear recently. None has actually presented a full grammar as yet, and all differ in detail, in completeness, and in some of their assumptions, but they also have some assumptions in common:

1. That there are some universal principles describing what it is that people know when they know (i.e., use unconsciously) any natural language.
2. That the structure of the language itself can be stated in a detailed hierarchy of rules for making sentences.
3. That such a set of rules will generate *all* English sentences, not just those already available for analysis, but others yet unspoken and unwritten.

Most of the attempts at writing such generative grammars begin from Noam Chomsky's idea that the structure of a language has three parts: (*a*) a small "kernel" of sentence types, or short distinctive formulas involving subjects, verbs, and complements; (*b*) a large number of rules for transforming these types by substitution, reordering, and combining their parts; and a list of morphophonemic rules which will enable us to turn into actual sentences the "structured strings" of terms which result from the application of transformational rules to one or more of the kernel types (4).

The structures revealed by this kind of grammatical description are exceedingly complex, as are the systems of rules, and thus far no complete grammar has been written, although a number of broadly successful efforts have been made at describing the gross patterns and at working out some of the details of specific parts such as the structures involving English nominals, or those which generate English questions.

Conclusion

The history of the attempts to describe English structure has been relatively short but incredibly active in recent years. Since the development of transformational-generative theories, we have seen many revisions, not only of the details but of basic assumptions. Not all grammarians accept the tripartite scheme described above.

Furthermore, the attention given to total meaning by this kind of grammar, in great contrast to the bell-jar atmosphere which structural grammarians try to create in separating grammatical meaning from total meaning, has led to a number of elaborate new schemes of description which are still in the hands of the theorists: *stratificational grammar*, for example, separates "deep structure," or meaning, from "surface structure" or the actual final syntax of the sentence.

What some students of language conclude from this lively recent series of developments is that although we are not yet "home free," we are eventually going to be able to write a full grammar of this language from a transformational-generative point of view. Others disagree, although they admit that in the attempt we will continue to learn much more about how people "know" languages and what the psycholinguistic facts truly are.

Meantime it is clear that teachers of English must know at least three broad schemes of structural analysis—the scholarly traditional, the structural, and the transformational-generative. All give useful information about the structure of English, and all offer methodological advice to those whose job it is to teach English.

THE HISTORY OF ENGLISH LEXICOGRAPHY

The Beginnings

Lexicography, the art of dictionary-making, has always had a very practical purpose, right from the very beginning.[6] From the very first word-books to the wide diversity to be found in the many kinds of modern dictionaries, all have been made primarily as practical tools. The dictionary is not a particularly old idea, moreover; and an examination of some of the practical purposes and of the books that have resulted shows us several threads:

1. Medieval scholars constantly sought to compile treatises which would incorporate all that was known about everything: these encyclopedias grew into alphabetical lists of the names of things, of natural phenomena, and of man's institutions; they often resembled dictionaries, and their development into the modern encyclopedia has at several points intertwined with that of the dictionary.
2. A more direct ancestor of the dictionary is the word-list, the gloss of "hard" or foreign words assembled to help the medieval reader with a difficult text. In Latin manuscripts of important works, English monks wrote marginal glosses

---

[6] A useful summary is found on pages 4–9 of Guralnik (11).

in Latin and English, explaining the meanings of unfamiliar Latin terms. In the fourteenth and fifteenth centuries, collections of these glosses were separately compiled, to help students read important books, and to help the English scholar discover the proper Latin term for an English idea. Hence the *glossarium* was a first in the lineage of modern English dictionaries.

3. During the sixteenth and seventeenth centuries, Englishmen were traveling, exploring, studying, and doing business all over Europe, the Near East, and even the New World, and to help them make their way, experienced people began to put together English–foreign-language phrase books and dictionaries. Some of the earliest and best were for English-French, English-Spanish, and English-Italian.

4. Still another practical book resulted from Renaissance interest in the English vocabulary. Many scholars, irked by the seeming inelegance and imprecision of English, began consciously to manufacture English words on Latin, Greek, Italian, and French models. They borrowed especially from the classical languages: words like *contiguate, splendente, adjuvate,* and *panion* were coined or borrowed in great numbers, and the reader soon needed help. While many of these coinages soon disappeared, others remained in the language, so that today we find it difficult to imagine how strange such words as *relinquish, antique,* and *illustrate* must have looked to sixteenth-century readers. The dictionary of "hard words" was created to help.

5. The wholesale manufacture of new words also contributed to the development of dictionaries indirectly: men of letters were split into two camps during the Renaissance—those who favored and those who hated these coinages. This quarrel over "inkhorn terms" focused attention on the vocabulary and gave impetus to the production of lists and essays from both attackers and defenders. More groundwork was being laid for the production of the modern dictionary.

6. Finally, the rise of the middle class, and later, the industrial revolution produced still other markets for dictionaries—the same practical markets which letter-writers and books of etiquette were serving; somehow they were all to help the new bourgeoisie acquire the gentle patina.

The First Great Modern Dictionaries

We have space here to mention only four of the great dictionaries which first wove together the several threads described above; two were English, two American; all four have shaped the art of lexicography as we know it today.

1. Nathaniel Bailey's *Universal Etymological Dictionary of the English Language* (1721) was the first. It was "the first to pay attention to current usage, the first to feature etymology, the first to syllabify, the first to give illustrative quotations, the first to include illustrations, and the first to indicate pronunciation."[7]

2. Samuel Johnson used Bailey's work and many others when he wrote his own great *Dictionary* (1755). He began his enormous task in the hope of recording, repairing and fixing once and for all the vocabulary of English. When he had finished, he ruefully concluded that change was inexorable; he came to a view

---

[7] Guralnik (11) as reprinted in *Harbrace Guide to Dictionaries* (25: 4).

of the lexicographer's task which is still one of the most accurate—and poignant. He tried to fix orthography, and he used English authors of reputation for his illustrative citations. His work is often idiosyncratic and sometimes erratic, especially in the etymologies. But above all, he made a truly comprehensive dictionary, and he wrote good definitions, avoiding circularity and seeking precision and clarity. His book was the first great "authority," and in its many subsequent editions and imitations, both in Britain and the United States, it came to play the very role of arbiter that Johnson had originally intended but had despaired, in the end, of achieving.

3. In 1828, leaning heavily on Johnson and Bailey, Noah Webster published the first of his "big" dictionaries, *An American Dictionary of The English Language*. In his early dictionaries, Webster too had a program: he sought to distinguish American spelling, pronunciation, and meaning from those of British English. Like Johnson, Webster greatly improved the style of definition-writing, seeking succinct, accurate statements and using American illustrations wherever he could. His later editions were more conservative, and he gave up his spelling reforms, but like his famous spelling book, Webster's later dictionaries became household words, particularly after the Merriam family began to publish them. His name, more than any other, is still synonymous with *dictionary*.

4. One of the main reasons American lexicography pushed forward so rapidly in the nineteenth century was the great commercial rivalry which grew between Webster and Joseph Worcester, whose *Comprehensive Pronouncing Dictionary of the English Language* appeared in 1830. It leaned heavily on Webster's 1828 edition, but, as Harold Whitehall points out, it "was characterized by the additions of new words, a more conservative spelling, brief, well-phrased definitions, full indication of pronunciation by means of diacritics, use of stress marks to divide syllables, and lists of synonyms (24: xxxiii)." From the 1840's on, the Webster and Worcester dictionaries, first edited by the famous men themselves and later by their successors in their names, multiplied and grew in fame. In the end, Webster's successors won out, but not before both dictionaries were placed throughout this westward-marching nation. The frontier brought with it the first popular movements in education, and with the Bible and Webster's "Blue Back Speller" as both the tools and the symbols of this zeal for universal literacy, reliance on "the dictionary" as the arbiter of taste, the judge of meaning, and the authority on spelling and pronunciation was permanently fastened on the American character.

Lexicography Today

English today offers its users the most complete and varied array of dictionaries in the world. We can give here only the briefest account of the variety, but what is most significant is the ready availability of continually updated dictionaries of the very highest quality, and at relatively low cost. We lean heavily on our dictionaries, and competition keeps them good.

We have fine *historical dictionaries;* the *Oxford English Dictionary*[8] is the greatest

---

[8] This dictionary (17), sometimes called the *New English Dictionary,* was published in ten volumes between 1884 and 1927; a corrected reissue with a one-volume supplement was published in 1933.

of these. This ten-volume work prints long entries with dated citations in context for every word in the vocabulary. A work of enormous scholarship, its qualities have become the model for all historical considerations of the vocabulary of English. No lexicographer can work without the *Oxford* at his elbow. Its work on pronunciation is British and minimal and its supplement is dated 1933; but for history it is unmatched. Other historical dictionaries use it as a point of departure: for American English differences from British English, we have the four-volume *A Dictionary of American English on Historical Principles* (5), and Mathews' two-volume *Dictionary of Americanisms* (15). Historical dictionaries of Middle English, Early Modern English, and Scottish are all either being published or prepared. For accurate, detailed, complete information about the history of an English word, these are the works to consult.

Our commercial *unabridged dictionaries* are a unique type. The most famous currently is the Merriam-Webster Third Edition of the *New International* (23). At their best, the great commercial unabridged dictionaries offer incredibly complete information about spellings, pronunciations, meanings, usage, synonyms, and brief etymologies. Some are encyclopedic, like the old *Century* (3) of 1889 and 1909; though badly out of date now, the *Century* is remembered as displaying the highest standard for the quality of its definitions. Most of the commercial houses which make unabridged dictionaries maintain files and revise regularly; almost all produce smaller, abridged dictionaries, based on the big book.

Desk and *collegiate* dictionaries are also uniquely American, one-volume books which are the most widely used of all. Their virtues are their currency and their compactness. Competition keeps their editors revising regularly, and they are noted for excellent definitions, up-to-the-minute information on spelling, pronunciation, and usage, and a surprising amount of encyclopedic information. The current best are probably Merriam-Webster's *Seventh New Collegiate* (21), Funk and Wagnalls' *Standard College Dictionary* (9), the *American College Dictionary* (1), and the college editions of *Webster's New World Dictionary of the American Language* (22) and the Random House dictionary (1). Each has its peculiar virtues and defects, but competition keeps each trying to outdo the others. Sold on the strength of the American need for reassurance, they are a remarkable kind of lexicography.

There are also dozens of other kinds of dictionaries, each for a special purpose: graded school dictionaries abound, many of them of good quality; the dictionaries of usage, which (like the old "hard word" books) deal only with problems which they discuss in little illustrated essays, have multiplied; there are special-vocabulary dictionaries, covering the technical vocabulary of special fields; and there are dictionaries of synonyms, to name only a few.

Conclusion

Not just the usual problems plague the lexicographer today—the selection of entries, the documentation of his findings, the wording of definitions, and the like; he also faces a very basic decision when he sets out to make a dictionary. On the one hand, modern linguistic science has given him clear evidence that the best dictionary is the one which records the language as it is, warts and all. Where the pattern of usage is unclear or divided, he must let his readers know that this is so. On the other hand, however, the layman insists that there must be right answers to his questions about language, and he expects the dictionary to give him these. The lexicographer expects to *describe* standards;

the layman wants him to *set* them, and he uses his dictionary as though it were a law book, not a report of current custom. The quarrel over *Webster III* illustrates this quandary all too clearly: the scholar of language wants full information, wants shade and nuance clearly delineated—not just in meanings, but in every aspect of every entry. He wants as many minority reports as possible. The layman (and many other professional users of language too) insists that the dictionary ought to set a standard to which everyone may adhere.

The lexicographer is not a scientist; he is a writer, an editor, an artist. He must draw conclusions, and even as he tries to distinguish two shades of meaning in a definition, he is creating, not just reporting. Yet he must be careful not to display his personal crotchets about the language he wishes English were, to the detriment of his description of the English we actually have.

To use his dictionaries, therefore, teacher and student alike need full awareness (*a*) of how he works, (*b*) of the information he has to work with, and (*c*) of the problems of choice posed him by limitations of taste, space, and time. Once he has that, any user of dictionaries can use them intelligently, both as a guide to what the world expects of his English, and as a clear picture of how others actually use theirs. Among other things, he will realize that, depending on his purpose, not one, but many dictionaries can help him.

TEACHING LANGUAGE HISTORY IN THE SCHOOLS TODAY

We are having a kind of Renaissance in interest in language history today. As suggested at many points in the discussions above, there are many kinds of history of language and language-related matters, and nearly all can be made interesting to the student.

Two things are happening: first, through the teacher-training programs, summer linguistic institutes, and in-service programs, the English teachers themselves are studying the history of the language, filling themselves with lore. And such study stresses every-where the need both for information and for generalization; it lays emphasis both on trends and on the importance of specific investigations.

Second, the teachers in turn are changing the curriculum. Materials are being developed, texts being written, and lessons being created to introduce pupils at all levels to the various aspects of the history of their language. The curriculum centers in several states are publishing materials to aid the teachers. School libraries are acquiring the dictionaries and reference works. And teachers themselves have come to see what enormous curiosity nearly everyone, properly stimulated, has.

In its own right, and for the kind of social perceptivity we seek to foster in school children, the study is both fascinating and good. And it also directs attention at a major problem of the schools: to manipulate his language well—a major goal of education—the student seems likely to profit a great deal from learning how his language came to be.

BIBLIOGRAPHY

1. *The American College Dictionary*. New York: Random House, 1947 and later printings.
2. Baugh, Albert C. *A History of English Language*. 2d ed. New York: Appleton-Century-Crofts, 1957.

3. *The Century Dictionary*. New York: Century Co., 1889.

4. Chomsky, Noam A. *Syntactic Structures*. Janua Linguarum, Series Minor, No. 4, The Hague: Mouton & Co., 1957.

5. Craigie, Sir William, and Hulbert, James R. (eds). *A Dictionary of American English on Historical Principles*. Chicago: University of Chicago Press, 1938.

6. Curme, G. O. *Parts of Speech and Accidence: A Grammar of the English Language*. Vol. 2. Boston: D. C. Heath & Co., 1953.

7. ———. *Syntax: A Grammar of English Usage*. Vol. 3. Boston: D. C. Heath & Co., 1931.

8. Francis, W. Nelson. *The Structure of American English*. New York: Ronald Press, 1958.

9. *Funk and Wagnalls' Standard College Dictionary*. Text ed. New York: Harcourt, Brace & World, 1963 and later printings.

10. Gleason, H. A. Jr. "English Grammars" in his *Linguistics and English Grammar*, pp. 67–87. New York: Holt, Rinehart & Winston, 1965.

11. Guralnik, David B. *The Making of a New Dictionary*. Cleveland: World Publishing Co., 1953.

12. Hill, Archibald. *Introduction to Linguistic Structures: From Sound to Sentence in English*. New York: Harcourt, Brace & World, 1958.

13. Jespersen, J. O. H. *Essentials of English Grammar*. New York: Henry Holt & Co., 1933.

14. Marckwardt, Albert H. *American English*. New York: Oxford University Press, 1958.

15. Mathews, Mitford M. (ed.). *Dictionary of Americanisms on Historical Principles*. Chicago: University of Chicago Press, 1951.

16. Nida, Eugene. *A Synopsis of English Syntax*. Norman, Okla.: Summer Institute of Linguistics, 1960.

17. *Oxford English Dictionary*. 10 vols. Oxford: Clarendon Press, 1884–1927 (one-volume supplement published in 1933).

18. Pyles, Thomas. *The Origins and Development of the English Language*. New York: Harcourt, Brace & World, 1964.

19. Robertson, Stuart and Cassidy, Frederic G. *The Development of Modern English*. 2d ed. New York: Prentice-Hall, 1954.

20. Trager, George L. and Smith, Henry Lee, Jr. *An Outline of English Structure*. Studies in Linguistics, Occasional Papers, No. 3, reprinted. Washington: American Council of Learned Societies, 1957.

21. *Webster's Seventh New Collegiate Dictionary*. Text. ed. Springfield, Mass.: G. & C. Merriam Co., 1963 and later printings.

22. *Webster's New World Dictionary of the American Language*. College ed. Cleveland: World Publishing Co., 1953 and later printings.

23. *Webster's Third New International Dictionary of the English Language*. Springfield, Mass.: G. & C. Merriam Co., 1966.

24. Whitehall, Harold. "Introduction," *Webster's New World Dictionary of the American Language*. College ed. Cleveland: World Publishing Co., 1960.

25. Wilson, Kenneth G.; Hendrickson, R. H.; and Taylor, Peter Alan. *Harbrace Guide to Dictionaries*. New York: Harcourt, Brace & World, 1963.

26. Zandvoort, R. W. *A Handbook of English Grammar*. London: Longmans, 1957.

DISCUSSION QUESTIONS

1. If the nominative case came to be limited to the beginning of a sentence, what relationship can you find between that circumstance and the development of informal, spoken *It's me* and *Who do you want to see?*

2. In your experience has misunderstanding ever arisen because of mistaking one meaning of *grammar* for another?

3. After finding in your library an eighteenth-century or early-nineteenth-century dictionary, compare in detail its treatment of several words with the corresponding treatment in your college desk dictionary. If your library lacks such early dictionaries, then use the *Oxford English Dictionary* to trace the semantic history of the following words: *knave, wench, churl,* and *gentleman.*

KARL W. DYKEMA

The late Professor Dykema was director of the division of languages and literature at Youngstown University. He had served as chairman of the Conference on College Composition and Communication.

WHERE OUR GRAMMAR CAME FROM

The title of this paper is too brief to be quite accurate. Perhaps with the following subtitle it does not promise too much: A partial account of the origin and development of the attitudes which commonly pass for grammatical in Western culture and particularly in English-speaking societies.

The etymology of *grammar* shows rather sharp changes in meaning: It starts with Greek *gramma, letter* (of the alphabet), itself a development from *graphein, draw* or *write*. The plural *grammata* develops in meaning through *letters* to *alphabet* to the *rudiments of writing,* to *the rudiments of learning.* The adjective form *grammatike* with *techne* meant the art of knowing one's letters. From this form comes the Latin *grammaticus.* The medieval vernacular forms with *r* are something of a mystery, appearing first in Old Provençal as *gramaira* and developing in English with a variety of spellings, often with only one *m* and ending in *er*. One of the more amusing forms is that with the first *r* dissimilated to *l, glamour.*

In present usage at least four senses can be distinguished which have an application to language: (1) The complete structural pattern of a language learned unconsciously by the child as he acquires his native tongue; (2) an attempt to describe objectively and systematically this fundamental structure, usually called descriptive grammar; (3) a partial description of the language based on puristic or pedagogical objectives, usually called prescriptive grammar; (4) a conviction held by a good many people that somewhere there is an authoritative book called a grammar, the conscientious memorization of which will eliminate all difficulties from their use of language. This I call grammar as remedy. It is mainly with the last two of these notions of grammar that I shall concern myself, prescriptive grammar and grammar as remedy, and how the earlier conceptions of grammar were metamorphosed into them.

As the etymology of the word suggests, Western grammar begins with the ancient Greeks. As early as Plato we find in the *Sophist* the statement that a word describing action is a verb (rhema), one which performs the action is a noun (onoma). Aristotle adds conjunctions (syndesmoi), recognizes that sentences have predicates, and is aware of three genders and of inflection (*Rhetoric,* etc.). The Stoics attempted to separate linguistic study from philosophy and made important contributions to the discipline. In their writings we find terms which are approximately equivalent to *noun, verb, conjunction, article, number, gender, case, voice, mood,* and *tense.*[1] But the direct source of most of our widely used grammatical terms is Dionysius Thrax's little *Techne Grammatike,* which

---

[1] R. H. Robins, *Ancient and Medieval Grammatical Theory in Europe* (London, 1951), pp. 20–35.

Gilbert Murray recollects his great-uncle still using at the Merchants Taylors' School in the nineteenth century to learn Greek from.[2]

A few quotations from this little work will illustrate how close many of our school grammars still are to their source of more than 2000 years ago:

> A sentence is a combination of words, either in prose or verse, making complete sense. . . . Of discourse there are eight parts: noun, verb, participle, article, pronoun, preposition, adverb, and conjunction. . . . A noun is a part of discourse having cases, indicating a body (as 'stone') or a thing (as 'education'), and is used in a common and a peculiar way (i.e., is common or proper). . . . A verb is a word without case, admitting tenses, persons, and numbers, and indicating action and passion (i.e., being-acted-upon). . . . A pronoun is a word indicative of definite persons and is used in place of a noun. . . . The adverb is an uninflected part of discourse, used of a verb or subjoined to a verb. . . . The conjunction is a word conjoining or connecting thought in some order and filling a gap in the expression.[3]

The few examples I have given emphasize analysis by meaning, because that is the aspect of classical grammar which our traditional grammar has dwelt upon. But the definitions of noun and verb, it should be observed, begin with formal distinctions—case and tense— and throughout the work there is clearly an awareness of the importance of structure in the functioning of the language. The contribution of the Greeks to linguistics was a great one, as Gilbert Murray and others have pointed out. But for twenty centuries their work was carried on by slavish and unimaginative imitators incapable of developing the work of their predecessors. Especially in the less highly inflected languages like English and French it did not occur to them that the inflectional devices of Latin and Greek must have some counterpart in the structure of the modern language.

Though today there are a few scholars in universities who assert that they pursue grammar for its own sake as an academic discipline, most people conceive of grammar only as a utilitarian thing, as a means of learning to use a language correctly. This notion was certainly completely absent from the thinking of Plato, Aristotle, and the Stoics, and probably from that of Dionysius Thrax. Grammar began as a philosophical inquiry into the nature of language. Now, for most people, it is merely a dogmatic means of achieving correctness. It is this transformation that I am mainly concerned with.

How the transformation took place is not easy to document. Perhaps the most plausible explanation lies in the familiar desire of younger teachers to regurgitate undigested fragments of what they have swallowed in the course of their higher education. All too often a high school teacher just out of college will use his college lecture notes as the foundation of his high school teaching, or a teacher of undergraduates tries to give them exactly what he got in his graduate seminar.

Then there is the fundamental difference between the prevailing purposes of elementary and advanced instruction. Primary education is severely utilitarian; and though it can hardly be denied that, especially in our society, graduate instruction is often infected by utilitarianism, the speculative approach does persist, and inquiry for its own sake plays a major role. The curriculum at all levels of education is and has been determined

---

[2] Gilbert Murray, *Greek Studies* (Oxford, 1964), p. 181.

[3] "The Grammar of Dionysius Thrax," translated . . . by Thos. Davidson, *Journal of Speculative Philosophy*, VIII (1874), 326–339.

partly by tradition, partly by immediate utilitarian objectives, partly by a desire to perpetuate the best elements of the cultural heritage. The application of these criteria is of ascending difficulty. Easiest is to accept without question the practice of one's predecessors; not much harder is to accept a limited practical goal and provide instruction intended to achieve it. Most difficult is to select critically what is most valuable in the cultural heritage, and the Romans weren't up to it.

Because of Greek prestige in the ancient world, less developed cultures borrowed extensively from that of Greece. The influence of Greek art, philosophy, and literature on Rome is familiar, but Greek grammar was quite as influential and became the model not only for grammars of Latin but of Syriac, Armenian, Hebrew, and possibly Arabic as well.

It could not be a good model. The structure of every language is peculiar to itself—though there are, of course, similarities between members of the same linguistic family—and the best description of it derives from a careful examination of the language itself, not from an attempt to fit it into the pattern of another. To be sure, both Greek and Latin are rich in inflections and the Latin of Varro was not much further away from the parent Indo-European than was the Greek of Dionysius Thrax; so the deformation imposed by the model was less distorting than when the same procedure was followed many centuries later and attempts were made to strait-jacket the modern vernaculars of Europe within the model of Latin grammar. For example, Greek had a definite article, Latin had none, though in Varro's *De Lingua Latina,* the term *articuli* is applied to the demonstratives *is* and *hic* (VIII, 45, 51). Latin has more cases but a different tense system and no dual. English has only two inflected active tenses against six for Latin, but many more periphrastic verbal constructions than had Latin.

The attention given to grammar by the ancients seems to have been considerable. Susemihl in his *History of Greek Literature in the Alexandrian Period* discusses over fifty grammarians. One of them, Aristophanes of Byzantium (ca. 257–ca. 180 B.C.), was librarian to Ptolemy Epiphanius, who imprisoned him to prevent the king of Pergamum from hiring him away.

Among the Romans, grammarians were also in demand. The slave Lutatius Daphnis, a grammarian, was bought for 700,000 sesterces, perhaps $35,000, which puts him about in the class of a lesser baseball player. Caesar put this Lutatius Daphnis in charge of the public libraries, though it was not until much later, according to Suetonius, that a regular salary of 100,000 sesterces was paid from the privy purse for Latin and Greek teachers of rhetoric (Suetonius, *Lives of the Caesars,* VIII, xviii). Caesar himself took part in one of the persisting grammatical quarrels of the time, that of the analogists and the anomalists, by producing a work called *De Analogia,* known to us only in fragments. Though he favored the analogists, who demanded complete inflectional consistency, it is significant that he wanted no radical departures from usage.[4] Suetonius also states that Claudius ''invented three new letters and added them to the [Latin] alphabet, maintaining that they were greatly needed; he published a book on their theory when he was still in private life, and when he became emperor had no difficulty in bringing about their general use'' (Suetonius, *Lives of the Caesars,* V, xli). Theodore Roosevelt was less successful when he tried to impose a few spelling reforms on the Government Printing Office; Congress refused to permit the changes.

---

[4] Jean Collart, *Varron, Grammairien Latin* (Paris, 1954), pp. 10, 19, 146; Robins, p. 58.

Though Caesar favored the analogists, he was unwilling to depart from established usage. His position was that of many of his cultivated contemporaries, as it has been of many cultivated people ever since. The appeal of analogy is the appeal of logic, a creation of the Greeks and a tool that has been used with interesting and surprising effects in most areas of Western thought ever since. The foundation of Aristotelian logic is the syllogism. As the analogists applied the syllogism to language it worked like this: The form of the personal pronoun determines the form of the verb of which the pronoun is the subject. The form *you* is plural; therefore the form of the verb *be* which follows it must be plural; hence *you were,* not *you was.* So we have in cultivated English today only *you were.* But the cultivated dare not apply this syllogism to the intensive or reflexive, where the eighteenth-century practice of agreement with the notional number of the pronoun still persists. The eighteenth century had both *you was there yourself* and *you were there yourselves;* while we have *you were there yourselves* when the notional number of *you* is plural, but *you were there yourself* when it is singular.

Language has its own logic, which it is the function of the descriptive grammarian to discover if he can. Whatever it may be, it is not Aristotelian logic. But for two millennia our attitudes toward language have been colored by the assumption that the system of a language can be analyzed and prescribed by an intellectual tool that is inapplicable.

Conformity to a standard, or correctness if you like, is, of course, socially of the greatest importance. There is a long record of the penalties imposed on those who deviate from the standard, the earliest I know of being the account given in *Judges* (12, 4–6) of the forty and two thousand Ephraimites who were slain by the Gileadites because they pronounced *shibboleth sibboleth.* Later examples are less gory. Aristophanes in the *Lysistrata* (lines 81–206) ridicules the dialect of the Spartan women, though they are the allies of the Athenian women in their campaign of sexual frustration. Stephen Runciman in his *Byzantine Civilization* says "the Patriarch Nicetas in the Eleventh Century was laughed at for his Slavonic accent, and the statesman Margarites treated with disrespect in the Thirteenth because he spoke with a rough rustic voice."[5] And Chaucer's nun spoke the provincial French of the Benedictine nunnery of Stratford-Bow, the French of Paris— standard French—being to her unknown.

Conformity to the standard is what matters. But how is the standard to be determined? Quintilian, whom Professor T. W. Baldwin calls "The Supreme Authority" in his *Shakespeare's Small Latine and Lesse Greeke,* provides a most illuminating basis for discussion. In the *Institutes* Quintilian tells us that:

> Language is based on reason, antiquity, authority and usage. Reason finds its chief support in analogy and sometimes in etymology. As for antiquity, it is commended to us by the possession of a certain majesty, I might almost say sanctity. Authority as a rule we derive from orators and historians. For poets, owing to the necessities of metre, are allowed a certain licence. . . . The judgment of a supreme orator is placed on the same level as reason, and even error brings no disgrace, if it results from treading in the footsteps of such distinguished guides. Usage however is the surest pilot in speaking, and we should treat language as currency minted with the public stamp. But in all cases we have need of a critical judgment, . . . (I.vi. 1–3)

---

[5] Stephen Runciman, *Byzantine Civilization* (Meridian Books, New York, 1956), pp. 173, 176.

This is fuller than Horace's neater statement: "Use is the judge, and law, and rule of speech" (*De Arte Poetica, 72: Quem [usus] penes arbitrium est et ius et norma loquendi*) and shows more clearly why we have troubles. Usage "is the surest pilot" but "we have need of a critical judgment."

Quintilian has more to say on the matter:

> Usage remains to be discussed. For it would be almost laughable to prefer the language of the past to that of the present day, and what is ancient speech but ancient usage of speaking? But even here the critical faculty is necessary, and we must make up our minds what we mean by usage. If it be defined merely as the practice of the majority, we shall have a very dangerous rule affecting not merely style but life as well, a far more serious matter. For where is so much good to be found that what is right should please the majority? The practices of depilation, of dressing the hair in tiers, or of drinking to excess at the baths, although they may have thrust their way into society, cannot claim the support of usage, since there is something to blame in all of them (although we have usage on our side when we bathe or have our hair cut or take our meals together). So too in speech we must not accept as a rule of language words and phrases that have become a vicious habit with a number of persons. To say nothing of the language of the uneducated, so we are all of us well aware that whole theatres and the entire crowd of spectators will often commit *barbarisms* in the cries which they utter as one man. I will therefore define usage in speech as the agreed practice of educated men, just as where our way of life is concerned I should define it as the agreed practice of all good men. (I.vi. 43–45)

But Quintilian makes it quite apparent from the many examples he cites that educated men are not entirely agreed on their practice, and that they lean heavily on the authority of Greek usage:

> More recent scholars have instituted the practice of giving Greek nouns their Greek declension, although this is not always possible. Personally I prefer to follow the Latin method, so far as grace of diction will permit. For I should not like to say *Calypsonem* on the analogy of *Iunonem,* although Gaius Caesar in deference to antiquity does adopt this way of declining it. Current practice has however prevailed over his authority. In other words which can be declined in either way without impropriety, those who prefer it can employ the Greek form: they will not be speaking Latin, but will not on the other hand deserve censure. (I.v. 63–64)

A thorough knowledge of Greek, learned from slave-tutors, had long been common among educated Romans, but it was Varro who transferred the entire body of Greek grammatical scholarship to Latin in his *De Lingua Latina,* written between 57 and 45 B.C. Though of the original 25 books of that work only V through X survive relatively intact, we have a fairly good account of what was in the rest because Varro is the source which all later Latin grammarians follow, and they have apparently borrowed from him most faithfully.

Greek grammar, is, then, a development of Greek philosophy, an attempt to treat systematically an important aspect of human behavior. It is a late development which in Alexandrian culture is given a practical application through its use in the editing, elucidation, and interpretation of texts, especially that of Homer; and in the correction of solecisms. Since there was little of the speculative in the Romans, Varro's encyclopedic treatment of Latin language and literature was the ultimate source of a host of school texts.

What has been presented so far is a partial account of the development of philology, though this ancient term has been an ambiguous one for almost as long as it has existed—naturally enough, since it derives from the Greek roots usually translated as *love* and *word*. Some people love words as the means of argument, others because they are the foundation of literature, others still for their forms and relations in discourse. All these senses have been designated by the word since it first appeared in Greek, and in nineteenth-century France and Germany it normally included literary history, textual and literary criticism, and linguistics. (We might well revive the word; it would provide a single term by which we could describe ourselves along with chemists, historians, and the rest; we are philologists.)

The ancients called the various aspects of this study by a variety of names: *philologos, grammatikos, grammatistes, kritikos* in Greek; *philologus, grammaticus, litterator, criticus* in Latin. They were evidently no more certain of exactly what the terms signified than we are today with similar terms. Suetonius writes:

> The term *grammaticus* became prevalent through Greek influence, but at first such men were called *litterati*. Cornelius Nepos, too, in a little book in which he explains the difference between *litteratus* and *eruditus* says that the former is commonly applied to those who can speak or write on any subject accurately, cleverly and with authority; but that it should strictly be used of interpreters of the poets, whom the Greeks call *grammatici*. That these were also called *litteratores* is shown by Messala Corvinus in one of his letters, in which he says, "I am not concerned with Furius Bibaculus, nor with Ticidas either, or with the *litterator* Cato." For he unquestionably refers to Valerius Cato, who was famous both as a poet and as a grammarian. Some however make a distinction between *litteratus* and *litterator*, as the Greeks do between *grammaticus* and *grammatista*, using the former of a master of his subject, the latter of one moderately proficient. Orbilius too supports this view by examples, saying: "In the days of our forefathers, when anyone's slaves were offered for sale, it was not usual except in special cases to advertise any one of them as *litteratus* but rather as *litterator*, implying that he had a smattering of letters, but was not a finished scholar."
>
> The grammarians of early days taught rhetoric as well, and we have treatises from many men on both subjects. It was this custom, I think, which led those of later times also, although the two professions had now become distinct, nevertheless either to retain or to introduce certain kinds of exercises suited to the training of orators, such as problems, paraphrases, addresses, character sketches and similar things; doubtless that they might not turn over their pupils to the rhetoricians wholly ignorant and unprepared. But I observe that such instruction is now given up, because of the lack of application and the youth of some of the pupils; for I do not believe that it is because the subjects are underrated. I remember that at any rate when I was a young man, one of these teachers, Princeps by name, used to declaim and engage in discussion on alternate days; and that sometimes he would give instruction in the morning, and in the afternoon remove his desk and declaim. I used to hear, too, that within the memory of our forefathers some passed directly from the grammar school to the Forum and took their place among the most eminent advocates. (*On Grammarians*, iv)

Another writer who provides evidence on the Roman attitudes toward language is Aulus Gellius in his *Attic Nights*. Gellius represents the aristocrat's conviction that what he himself does must be right coupled with the conservative attitude that older practice is to be preferred:

> Valerius Probus was once asked, as I learned from one of his friends, whether one ought to say *has urbis* or *has urbes* and *hanc turrem* or *hanc turrim*. "If," he replied, "you are either composing verse or writing prose and have to use those words,

pay no attention to the musty, fusty rules of the grammarians, but consult your own ear as to what is to be said in any given place. What it favours will surely be the best.'' Then the one who had asked the question said: ''What do you mean by 'consult my ear'?'' and he told me that Probus answered: ''Just as Vergil did his, when in different passages he had used *urbis* and *urbes,* following the taste and judgement of his ear. For in the first *Georgic,* which,'' said he, ''I have read in a copy corrected by the poet's own hand, he wrote *urbis* with an *i.* . . .

But turn and change it so as to read *urbes,* and somehow you will make it duller and heavier. On the other hand, in the third *Aeneid* he wrote *urbes* with an *e*: . . .

Change this too so as to read *urbis* and the word will be too slender and colourless, so great indeed is the different effect of combination in the harmony of neighbouring sounds. . . .

These words have, I think, a more agreeable lightness than if you should use the form in *e* in both places.'' But the one who had asked the question, a boorish fellow surely and with untrained ear, said: ''I don't just understand why you say that one form is better and more correct in one place and the other in the other.'' Then Probus, now somewhat impatient, retorted: ''Don't trouble then to inquire whether you ought to say *urbis* or *urbes.* For since you are the kind of man that I see you are and err without detriment to yourself, you will lose nothing whichever you say.'' (XIII. xxi. 3–8)

And his attitude towards grammarians is expressed quite as explicitly in this passage:

Within my memory Aelius Melissus held the highest rank among the grammarians of his day at Rome; but in literary criticism he showed greater boastfulness and sophistry than real merit. Besides many other works which he wrote, he made a book which at the time when it was issued seemed to be one of remarkable learning. The title of the book was designed to be especially attractive to readers, for it was called *On Correctness in Speech.* Who, then would suppose that he could speak correctly or with propriety unless he had learned those rules of Melissus?

From that book I take these words: ''*Matrona,* 'a matron,' is a woman who has given birth once; she who has done so more than once is called *mater familias,* 'mother of a fmaily'; just so a sow which has had one litter is called *porcetra;* one which has had more, *scrofa.*'' But to decide whether Melissus thought out this distinction between *matrona* and *mater familias* and that it was his own conjecture, or whether he read what someone else had written, surely requires soothsayers. For with regard to *porcetra* he has, it is true, the authority of Pomponius in the Atellan farce which bears that very title; but that ''matron'' was applied only to a woman who had given birth once, and ''mother of the family'' only to one who had done so more than once, can be proved by the authority of no ancient writer. . . . (XVIII. vi. 1–7)

By the Middle Ages the aristocrats were unlikely to have had much education, and the classical heritage was perpetuated by the grammarians, whose dogmatic victory was complete. Donatus (fl. 400) and Priscian (fl. 500) are the dominating figures. The name of the first, shortened to Donat or Donet, became synonymous with 'grammar' or 'lesson' in Old French and Middle English, and the grammar of the second survives in over a thousand manuscripts.[6] He also has the distinction of being consigned to Hell by Dante (*Inferno,* 15: 110).

---

[6] John Edwin Sandys, *A History of Classical Scholarship* (Cambridge, 1920), vol. 1, p. 230, note; p. 274.

As an example of Priscian, here is the beginning of an analysis of the *Aeneid*—this is not from his big grammar, which was in eighteen books, but from a smaller one, *Partitiones Duodecim Versuum Aeneidos Principalium:*

> Scan the verse, *Arma vi / rumque ca / no Tro / iae qui / primus ab / oris.* How many caesuras does it have? Two. What are they? Semiquinaria (penthemimeral) and semiseptenaria (hephthemimeral). How? The semiquinaria is *arma virumque cano* and the semiseptenaria is *arma virumque cano Troiae.* How many figures are there? Ten. For what reason? Because it consists of three dactyls and two spondees. How many parts of speech has this verse? Nine. How many nouns? Six: *arma, virum, Troiae, qui, primus, oris.* How many verbs? One: *cano.* How many prepositions? One: *ab.* How many conjunctions? One, *que.* Discuss each word; *arma,* what part of speech is it? Noun. Of what sort? Appelative (or common). What is its species? General. Its gender? Neuter. Why neuter? Because all nouns which end in *a* in the plural are unquestionably of neuter gender. Why is the singular not used? Because this noun signifies many and various things. . . .[7]

And this is not the end of the catechism on the opening line of Virgil. Evidently this sort of drill was to accompany the study of the poem from beginning to end, if the end was ever reached.

Increasingly in the Middle Ages the written heritage of Greece and Rome was accepted unquestioningly because literate men did not have a cultural background which would permit them to ask pertinent questions. We learn, for example, that one of the best sources for the text of Diogenes Laertius is a manuscript of about 1200 written by a scribe "who obviously knew no Greek."[8] To be sure, there were sometimes conflicts between the Christian heritage and the classical, usually resolved in favor of the Christian. In a medieval manuscript is a comment: "Concerning the words *scala* (step), and *scopa* (broom), we do not follow Donatus and the others who claim they are plural because we know that the Holy Ghost has ruled that they are singular." And it was comforting when the traditions of classical grammar could be given divine corroboration. For example: "The verb has three persons. This I hold to be divinely inspired, for our belief in the Trinity is thereby manifested in words." Or this: "Some maintain that there are more, some that there are fewer parts of speech. But the world-encircling church has only eight offices [Presumably Ostiariat, Lektorat, Exorzistat, Akolythat, Subdiakonat, Diakonat, Presbyterat, Episkopat]. I am convinced that this is through divine inspiration. Since it is through Latin that those who are chosen come most quickly to a knowledge of the Trinity and under its guidance find their way along the royal road into their heavenly home, it was necessary that the Latin language should be created with eight parts of speech."[9]

On the other hand, St. Boniface's (675–754) "sense of grammatical accuracy was so deeply shocked when he heard an ignorant priest administering the rite of baptism *in*

---

[7] Heinrich Keil, *Grammatici Latini* (Leipzig, 1859), vol. 3, p. 459.

[8] Diogenes Laertius, *Lives of Eminent Philosophers,* with an English translation by R. D. Hicks (Loeb Classical Library) (Cambridge & London, 1925), vol. 1, p. xxxv. (The quotations from Suetonius, Varro, Quintilian, and Aulus Gellius are from the translations in the Loeb Classical Library editions.)

[9] J. J. Baebler, *Beiträge zu einer Geschichte der lateinischen Grammatik im Mittelalter* (Halle a. S., 1885), p. 22/Hans Arens, *Sprachwissenschaft, der Gang ihrer Entwicklung von der Antike bis zur Gegenwart* (Munich, 1955), pp. 30, 31.

nomine Patria et Filia et Spiritus sancti [that is, with complete disregard of the required case endings] that he almost doubted the validity of the rite."[10]

Up to about the twelfth century Donatus and Priscian, whose grammars were based ultimately on classical Latin, were followed unquestioningly except where there seemed to be a conflict with sacred texts. The Vulgate and various theological writings were in a later Latin which might disagree with classical grammar, as in the more frequent use of the personal pronouns.[11]

But in the twelfth century the reintroduction of Greek philosophy had a tremendous impact on medieval thought, as is best illustrated by the Aristotelianism of Aquinas. And St. Thomas, as might be expected, deals with philological matters in the *Summa Theologica,* and again as might be expected through the syllogism:

> It seems that in Holy Writ a word cannot have several senses, historical or literal, allegorical, tropological or moral, and anagogical. For many different senses in one text produce confusion and deception and destroy all force of argument. Hence no argument, but only fallacies, can be deduced from a multiplicity of propositions. But Holy Writ ought to be able to state the truth without any fallacy. Therefore in it there cannot be several senses to a word. (First Part, Question One, Article 10, Objection 1)

A more explicitly grammatical example is this one from the thirteenth century:

> For a complete sentence, two things are necessary, namely a subject and a predicate. The subject is that which is being discussed; it is what determines the person of the verb. The predicate is that which is expressed by the subject. Nouns were invented to provide subjects. . . . Verbs were invented to provide predicates.

This concept of grammar being something created is found in another thirteenth-century writer:

> Was he who invented grammar a grammarian? No, because the creation of grammar cannot be based on teaching since that would presuppose its existence. Grammar was invented. For the invention of grammar must precede grammar. So it was not the grammarian but the philosopher who created grammar, for the philosopher studies the nature of things and recognizes their essential qualities.[12]

The authority of the grammarian was occasionally challenged. In a seventeenth-century German satirical treatment of schoolmasters is this account of a fifteenth-century episode:

> The Emperor Sigismund came to the Council of Constance and said: "Videte patres, ut eradicetis schismam Hussitarium." There sat an old Bohemian pedant in the Council who was convinced that with this box on the ear to Priscian the Emperor had sinned against the Catholic Church as gravely as had John Hus and Hieronymus of Prague. So he said [in Latin]: Most Serene Highness, *schisma* is neuter gender." The emperor said [in German]: "How do you know that?" The old Bohemian pedant answered

---

[10] Sandys, p. 469.
[11] Baebler, p. 22.
[12] Arens, pp. 34, 32.

[now in German]: "Alexander Gallus says so." The emperor said: "Who is Alexander Gallus?" The Bohemian pedant answered: "He is a monk." "Yes," said Sigismund, "I am the Roman emperor, and my word is worth at least that of a monk." (Joh. Balthaser Schupp, *Der Teutsche Schulmeister,* 1663)[13]

It now remains to consider the transfer of these attitudes to the modern vernacular languages. But first a brief review of the three preceding stages. The first is the unique situation in Greece, which differed from that of any of the succeeding cultures in two significant ways: It was essentially a monolingual society, and at least during the period of its greatest intellectual and artistic achievement it knew nothing of formal grammar. Rome differed in both essentials. The cultivated Roman was educated in Greek, and formal grammar was a part of his Latin education, though this does not mean that he learned Greek through formal grammar. In the Middle Ages the two-language requirement for the educated, which was characteristic of Rome, was continued, but with an important difference. Whereas for the Roman, Latin was a respectable language with a respectable literature, for the educated man of the Middle Ages his native vernacular was not respectable and at least at first had no important literature. Also he learned the language of scholarship and literature in a way quite different from that used by the Roman. He learned it with the aid of formal grammar.

Of these three stages, the third, the medieval, is much the longest; in formal education and scholarship it lasts well into the eighteenth century and therefore has a duration of well over a thousand years. Of course during the last two or three hundred of those years a great change had come over Europe, due partly to an intimate reacquaintance with the heritage of Greece and Rome. But in the field of philology this meant largely a return to the attitudes of the ancients. It also meant the transference of the whole philological approach—ancient and medieval—to the modern vernacular languages.

The history of vernacular grammars and of English grammars in particular comes next in this development, but there is no space for it here.

One consequence of this transfer must be illustrated: The ambivalence it has given us toward language. Here are some examples. Trollope in his *Autobiography* writes:

The ordinary talk of ordinary people is carried on in short sharp expressive sentences, which very frequently are never completed,—the language of which even among educated people is often incorrect. The novel-writer in constructing his dialogue must so steer between absolute accuracy of language—which would give to his conversation an air of pedantry, and the slovenly inaccuracy of ordinary talkers, which if closely followed would offend by an appearance of grimace—as to produce upon the ear of his readers a sense of reality. If he be quite real he will seem to attempt to be funny. If he be quite correct he will seem to be unreal.[14]

The nineteenth-century German philologist Wilhelm Scherer, discussing the great dramatist Heinrich Kleist, remarks that "he did distinguished work in all forms. There dwells in his language an individual magic, though he has an uncertain control of German grammar."[15] And in a recent review in the *TLS* is this sentence: "He [Leonard Clark] died after completing the first draft of his book, *Yucatan Adventure,* which would have

---

[13] Baebler, p. 118.

[14] Anthony Trollope, *An Autobiography* (World's Classics, Oxford, 1953), p. 206.

[15] Wilhelm Scherer, *Geschichte der deutschen Literatur* (Knaur, Berlin, n.d.), p. 752.

gained some grammar, while losing some of the punch of its author's virile enthusiasm, if it had been more carefully revised."[16]

In a detective story, Rex Stout has Archie Goodwin make this comment after one of the principal characters has said, "Yes. . . . We shall see.": "But what really settled it was her saying, "We shall see." He [Nero Wolfe] will always stretch a point, within reason, for people who use words as he thinks they should be used."[17] But in another story Wolfe is made to say, "If it's her again. . . ."[18]

And Mark Twain, who took Cooper severely to task for his "ungrammatical" English, did what was perhaps his best work, in *Huckleberry Finn,* by using a narrative device which relieved him of all responsibility for conforming to standard usage.

One of the most eloquent and emphatic in condemnation of the Latin grammatical tradition was Macaulay but, as you might guess, he is much too long to quote here.[19]

I conclude by returning to the four senses of the term grammar outlined at the beginning. Contemporary philologists who specialize in linguistics have, it seems to me, attempted to strip away the accretions of two thousand years and are turning to a rigorously descriptive approach, the seeds of which are to be found in the Greeks. Other philologists have other interests, such as literary history, literary criticism, and, of course, the problem of getting freshmen to write better. As an inescapable burden of their academic heritage, they have to bear the weight of the ancient and medieval grammatical tradition, which survives in the other two senses, prescriptive grammar and grammar as remedy. What I have tried to do is to give some account of how that tradition developed, how it was transmitted, and why much of it is essentially irrelevant to the problems the philologist faces today.[20]

DISCUSSION QUESTIONS

1. How do Dykema's four "grammars" correspond with Wilson's three?

2. If there is some validity in Probus's contrast between *urbis* and *urbes,* would you expect equal validity in a contrast between, say, *attitude* and *aditude, what* and *wot,* and *diphtheria* and *diptheria?* Explain.

3. What insights have you gained from Dykema regarding past attitudes toward language?

[16] *Times Literary Supplement,* March 20, 1959, p. 156.

[17] Rex Stout, "Murder Is No Joke," *And Four to Go, A Nero Wolfe Foursome* (Viking, New York, 1958), p. 155.

[18] Rex Stout, "Too Many Women," *All Aces, A Nero Wolfe Omnibus* (Viking, New York, 1958), p. 237.

[19] T. B. Macaulay, "The London University," Edinburgh Review, February, 1826, in *Critical, Historical and Miscellaneous Essays and Poems* (Porter and Coats, Philadelphia, n.d.), vol. 3, pp. 631–634.

[20] A somewhat shorter version of this paper was read to the Northeastern Ohio College English Group, Akron, 5 November 1960.

CHARLES V. HARTUNG

Professor Hartung has recently retired as emeritus professor of English from the University of California, Los Angeles, to live, he writes, near "one of the most beautiful fishing lakes in America."

THE PERSISTENCE OF TRADITION IN GRAMMAR

Recent proclamations of a "revolution in grammar"[1] have sought to define a sharp break between the traditional grammar and the new linguistics. The basic problems persist, however, and the solutions of traditional grammarians have to be understood and judged before we can see new approaches to grammar in their proper perspective.

Historically, the term *grammar* has referred to both the study and the art of language. The Alexandrian grammarians incorporated in the art of grammar the separate verbal disciplines that we now refer to as philology, literary criticism, rhetoric, and linguistics. The Roman rhetorician Quintilian began the process of specialization. He divided grammar into two main branches—the broad study of literature and the more specialized art of speaking and writing correctly.[2] The latter conception was adopted by European grammarians and prevailed until late in the nineteenth century, when grammar became defined more specifically as the science of the sentence.

But even the most eminent nineteenth-century spokesmen for grammar as a science did not agree about either the scope or the purpose of grammar. We can observe this division in the thinking of the two greatest philologists of the English-speaking world, Henry Sweet and William Dwight Whitney. Sweet recognized the inclusive nature of grammar when he said, "Grammar in the widest sense of the word is . . . both the science and the art of language."[3] But Sweet did not think that study of grammar as a corrective of "what are called 'ungrammatical' expressions" was of much practical value. He also considered this practice theoretically unsound because he thought that rules of grammar have no value except as statements of fact. Consequently, the business of grammar as a science was to observe the facts of language and then to classify and state them methodically.[4] Whitney was also an eminent advocate of grammar as a science. He declared that grammar did not make rules and laws for language, but only reported the facts of good language in an orderly way.[5] But as a reading of Whitney's *Essentials of English Grammar* soon reveals, he judged goodness and orderliness by degree of adherence to the standard rules. The opposing attitudes of Whitney and Sweet may be exemplified briefly by their judgments on *it is me*, a linguistic shibboleth of their time. Whitney says: "Careless and inaccurate speakers . . . often use such expressions as *it is them, it was*

---

[1] See W. Nelson Francis, "Revolution in Grammar," *Quarterly Journal of Speech*, XL (October, 1954), 299–312. [Reprinted in this collection.—Eds.]

[2] *Institutes of Oratory*, trans. J. S. Watson (London, 1907), I, 29 (1. 4. 1–3).

[3] Henry Sweet, *A New English Grammar* (Oxford, 1891), Part I, p. 4.

[4] *Ibid.*, p. 1.

[5] William Dwight Whitney, *Essentials of English Grammar* (Boston, 1877), p. 4.

us, if it were her; and in the case of *it is me* the practice has become so common that it is even regarded as good English by respectable authorities,"[6] Sweet says: "I confine myself to the statement and explanation of facts, without attempting to settle the relative correctness of divergent usages. If an 'ungrammatical' expression such as *it is me* is in general use among educated people, I accept it as such, simply adding that it is avoided in the literary language."[7]

We see in these contrasting attitudes the transition from the ancient prescriptive use of grammar to the modern practice of scientific description. Despite the different ideas Whitney and Sweet had about the purpose of grammar, their methods of analysis were similar. They both followed the traditional practice of classifying words into parts of speech and sentences into kinds of discourse. Although modern scientific grammarians have developed somewhat different approaches, the parts of speech approach is still widely used. C. C. Fries in 1952 produced in his *Structure of English*[8] a scheme of analysis that incorporates modern attitudes and techniques but is nevertheless in basic ways traditional. James Sledd's *A Short Introduction to English Grammar,*[9] published in 1959, has introduced modern techniques while retaining the essential framework of the traditional approach.

Although the traditional parts of speech approach to grammar has been condemned by many modern scientific grammarians, it is still by far the most widely taught and studied system of linguistic methodology. The reasons for this are clear. Parts of speech classification has behind it a tradition of over two thousand years of practical use. During this time it has been subjected to rigorous intellectual examination by some of the best minds in European culture. This examination has not solved the theoretical problems posed by the method, but it has enabled the method to be used in the practical mastery of languages. Greek, Latin, and then the vernacular languages were learned for practical purposes by means of systems of rules devised by prescriptive grammarians. Moreover, throughout the Middle Ages and the Renaissance the study of Greek and Latin grammar was the main agency for keeping alive the cultural heritage of Greece and Rome.

In addition to making these solid contributions, the study of grammar has also served as a basis for the theoretical examination of language. The parts of speech grammarians are open to charges of unsoundness in their speculative efforts, but they have also suggested ways for grammarians to deal with language as a whole. Modern scientific grammarians have developed methods that are more precise and more theoretically consistent than the older methods, but they have often done so by rigidly limiting the scope of linguistic analysis. They still have to find solutions for many basic problems that traditional grammarians have tried for so long to solve.

The major problem in classifying the parts of speech has been that of setting up a logically consistent system of definitions. This problem has arisen largely because grammarians have tried to find distinct classes for all of the functionally different kinds of words used in connected discourse. Because of the inherent complexity of language the classes have been developed through the consideration of four contrasting bases for definition: (1) the lexical meaning of the word apart from its grammatical use; (2) the logical function of the word in the structure of thought; (3) the syntactical position of the

---

[6] *Ibid.,* p. 160.

[7] Sweet, p. xi.

[8] C. C. Fries, *The Structure of English* (New York, 1952).

[9] James Sledd, *A Short Introduction to English Grammar* (Chicago, 1959).

word in connected discourse; and (4) the inflectional capacity of the word to change its form in a system of paradigms.

Aristotle made the first substantial effort to devise a system of parts of speech. The noun he defined as "a sound significant by convention, which has no reference to time, and of which no part is significant apart from the rest."[10] A notable feature of this definition is its concentration on the semantic (i.e., lexical) properties of the word. As a result of this stress on positive semantic value Aristotle denied to the negative term *not-man* the substantival characteristics of the noun. For reasons of logic he also considered only the nominative form to be a noun proper. Case declensions other than the nominative were not to be classed as nouns, for they could not be coupled with finite forms of verbs to form propositions that could be judged to be either true or false. From this logical extension of this definition we infer that Aristotle conceived that a noun must be a complete word unit possessing positive semantic value and logic capable of functioning as the subject of a finite verb.

The verb Aristotle defined as "that which, in addition to its proper meaning, carries with it the notion of time. No part of it has independent meaning, and it is a sign of something said of something else."[11] The verb, then, is similar to the noun in that it has substantival meaning, but it differs from the noun in carrying a notion of present existence. "Health," according to Aristotle, is a noun; "is healthy," a verb. The verb proper in Aristotle's scheme is limited to words indicating present time; words indicating past and future are not verbs proper but tenses of a verb. Moreover, the verb proper is characterized by its capacity for combining with a noun to form a predication.

Since in *De Interpretatione* Aristotle was concerned only with the logically necessary parts of discourse, he defined only the noun and the verb. In *De Poetica*[12] he added definitions of other elements. The conjunction, literally "ligament," is defined as a non-significant sound serving to connect two or more significant sounds; it includes not only the regular connectives recognized by later grammarians but also particles that were later to be classified as prepositions. The article, literally "joint," is defined as a non-significant sound serving to mark the beginning, end, or dividing-point of a sentence; it includes words that were later to be defined as personal and relative pronouns. It is notable that the conjunction and the article are defined purely by reference to their syntactical positions in discourse. Since they have no independent semantic value and serve no necessary logical function, they are not to be considered as parts of speech on the same level as the noun and the verb.

In the definitions of the noun and verb in *De Poetica*, Aristotle does not repeat those parts of his definitions in *De Interpretatione* referring to the complementary logical functions of these two parts of speech. This omission may be due to corruption of the text, but it is more likely that he was limiting discussion to the lexical as opposed to the non-lexical properties of units of discourse. In *De Poetica* he is specifically concerned with diction and therefore centers his attention on lexical matters. His definitions of the noun and verb stress semantic properties. His definitions of the article and conjunction indicate that these words have no semantic significance and serve a purely syntactical

---

[10] See Aristotle, *De Interpretatione*, trans. E. M. Edghill, *The Works of Aristotle*, ed. W. D. Ross (London, 1928), I, 16a.

[11] *Ibid.*, 16b.

[12] See Aristotle, *De Poetica*, trans. Ingram Bywater in *Introduction to Aristotle*, ed. Richard McKeon (New York, 1947), 1456b–58a.

function. Discussions of the various properties of language occur in contexts specifically concerned with matters of logic, rhetoric, and diction. In these various contexts he centers on features relevant to the topic discussed. In none of his extant works is there a systematic discussion of grammar as an autonomous discipline. He had no special occasion to work out a logically consistent scheme of specifically grammatical definitions. As a result of his many-sided approach to grammatical matters, he found some use for all four of the major criteria for defining the parts of speech, lexical, logical, and morphological criteria to define the different properties of the noun and verb, and syntactical criteria for the article and conjunction. Despite the fact that Aristotle provided no systematic treatment of grammar in any one place, his scattered comments do provide a basis for a reasonably comprehensive scheme. Later grammarians were able to base ambitious philosophical treatments of language on his definitions. For example, James Harris,[13] an English grammarian and linguistic theorist of the eighteenth century, found it possible to use Aristotle's definitions of the four parts of speech as a framework for an impressive statement of linguistic theory.

After the death of Aristotle there was much inconclusive discussion of grammar by philosophers of the Athenian world, particularly the Stoics, but the most substantial contributions were made by Alexandrian grammarians. These contributions were summed up in Dionysius Thrax's quintessential *Art of Grammar*,[14] the first comprehensive textbook of Greek grammar and probably the most influential grammar of any language ever published. Gilbert Murray, the English classical scholar, attests that it was used as a basic text in English schools until the second half of the nineteenth century.[15] In keeping with Alexandrian practice, Dionysius conceived the art of grammar quite broadly, including the arts usually assigned to poetics, rhetoric, and philology. Despite this very comprehensive scheme, most of Dionysius's *techne* is concerned with what we now recognize as strictly grammatical matters; definitions of the parts of speech receive the most attention. Since Dionysius was an Analogist, believing in the fundamental regularity of language, he limited his body of data to examples taken from classical literature and constructed a normative grammar.

The major contribution of Dionysius to the methodology of grammar was in analytical procedure. He extended definitions of the parts of speech to eight, using formal criteria to define the pronoun, the participle, the preposition, and the adverb. His scheme of classification is a model of deductive procedure. He begins with a definition of the word as "the smallest part of an ordered sentence," then defines the sentence as a combination of words expressing a thought complete in itself, next lists the eight parts of speech (noun, verb, participle, article, pronoun, preposition, adverb, and conjunction), and finally defines and exemplifies the separate parts of speech by examples taken from the best classical literature. In defining the parts of speech, Dionysius uses formal, lexical, and syntactical criteria but does not attempt to apply the three sets of criteria consistently to all eight parts of speech. He defines the noun and verb by their lexical properties and their capacity for inflection. A noun, for example, indicates a concrete body, "stone,"

---

[13] James Harris, *Hermes or A Philosophical Inquiry Concerning Universal Grammar* [1751], 5th ed. (London, 1794).

[14] "The Grammar of Dionysios Thrax," trans. Thos. Davidson, *Journal of Speculative Philosophy*, VIII (1874), 326–339.

[15] Gilbert Murray, *Greek Studies* (Oxford, 1946), p. 181.

or an abstract thing, "education," and is characterized by case and number. A verb lacks case, admits tense, person, and number, and indicates action and passion. The participle shares the properties of both nouns and verbs with the exception of person and mood. The article is capable of inflection similar to a noun and is distinguished also by its syntactical position preceding the noun. The pronoun indicates definite persons and serves as a substitute for the noun. Prepositions and conjunctions serve syntactical functions as connectives. Adverbs are uninflected parts of speech defined by relations to the verb. As we can see from this summary, Dionysius takes fully into account grammatical matters such as inflection and syntactical position (i.e., form), but he also uses lexical criteria to define words with nominal and verbal properties. He does not refer to such logical relational categories as subject, predicate, and complement.

Dionysius's framework of classification, even though it does apply different criteria to different parts of speech, is admirably designed for describing Greek, the language on which it was based. Because the scheme was so effective, it was later used, with some experimental revisions, to describe other languages. Grammarians of Latin dropped the article, as inapplicable to Latin, and added the interjection. The participle was alternately dropped and added. As late as the nineteenth century Goold Brown's English grammar[16] included both the article and the participle as separate parts of speech. The noun was subdivided by eighteenth-century grammarians into substantive and adjective. But for the most part the scheme of the parts of speech has remained essentially as Dionysius worked it out.

Later changes, such as separation of noun from adjective and dropping of the participle, were foreshadowed by distinctions to be found in his definitions. Even when medieval grammarians modified the standard grammars of Donatus and Priscian to describe medieval instead of classical Latin, they did not find it necessary to make drastic changes in the criteria of classification.[17] The difficulties arising from the use of different bases of definition became acute only when the scheme of Dionysius was applied to languages differing structurally from the classical languages. Before the rise of modern linguistic science European grammarians sought to devise logically consistent systems of grammar. Medieval scholastic philosophers, for example, reintroduced into grammatical analysis the Aristotelean categories; and Arnauld and Lancelot, the grammarians and logicians of Port Royal, made grammar a branch of logic.

The general and philosophical grammar of Port Royal[18] is a full-fledged attempt to define parts of speech by logical categories based on a hierarchy of such mental operations as conception, judgment, and reasoning. Conception is defined as simple apprehension of ideas such as *being* and *God* and of material images such as *circles, dogs,* and *horses*. Judgment is the making of an affirmation that something is or is not so, e.g., *the earth is round*. Reasoning is the use of two judgments to form a third. For example, if we

---

[16] Goold Brown, *Grammar of English Grammars* (New York, 1862).

[17] See Petrus Helyas, *Summa Prisciani* in Vincentius Beluacensis, *Speculum Doctrinale* (Venetiis, 1494).

[18] A. Arnauld and C. Lancelot, *Grammaire générale et raisonnée de Port-Royal* (Paris, 1660). Port Royal was a Cistercian convent near Versailles. It was noted particularly as a center of Jansenism, a doctrine brilliantly defended by Arnauld and Pascal. At Port Royal a school was established for the sons of Jansenist parents. For this school a number of important textbooks were written, including the famous *Logic of Port Royal* and the grammar cited above.

assume that virtues are praiseworthy and patience is a virtue, we must also assume that patience is praiseworthy. In practical grammatical analysis the Port Royal grammarians did not go so far as the third step. They considered the central grammatical process that of forming a proposition by means of stating a judgment. Any proposition they conceived to include two terms, a subject and an attribute. The subject is that about which one makes an affirmation, e.g. *earth*; an attribute is that which one affirms about the subject, e.g. *round*. The link between the two terms is expressed by *is*. Our thoughts may be distinguished into two parts—objects and form or manner. The principal manner is that of making judgments. But we must also take into account such mental processes as combining and separating, and we need to distinguish the structural characteristics of such mental impulses as desires, commands, and questions. Words that signify objects of thought are called nouns (substantives and adjectives), participles, pronouns, particles, prepositions, and adverbs. Those signifying form and manner are verbs, conjunctions, and interjections.

The major assumption of the Port Royal approach is that grammar is essentially logical. In the Port Royal system the purely formal elements of accidence and syntax as well as the lexical properties of words are not considered essential. The verb, for example, is defined as a word whose principal function is to signify affirmation, and definitions based on formal and lexical criteria are dismissed as false. That part of Aristotle's definition referring to the verb as a word significant with tense is considered irrelevant because it does not state what the verb signifies, but merely the means of signification. Definitions based on the inflectional capacity of the verb are dismissed for the same reason. Lexical definitions of the verb as a word signifying action and passion or that which passes are also dismissed as invalid. These definitions are considered logically unsound because they neither fit all of the thing defined nor fit it alone; there are verbs which do not signify action or passion or that which passes, and there are words other than verbs that do signify these meanings. The participle *flowing*, for example, signifies a thing that passes just as well as the finite verb *flows*. By such reasoning the Port Royal grammarians discounted the importance of form and lexical meaning as criteria for defining the parts of speech, and pointed up the importance of the logical relationships of words in the structure of thought.

The Port Royal grammarians had a great influence on the methodology of grammatical analysis, especially on syntax. Their influence was particularly strong in Europe and can be seen in such a comparatively modern grammar as the monumental work of Poutsma,[19] still the most ambitiously executed study of the structure of English. But the Port Royal definitions of the parts of speech were by no means universally accepted. In England the classical tradition of Dionysius and Donatus, as carried on in such a Latin grammar as that of John Lily,[20] maintained its dominance. The reasons are relatively simple. Whereas the Port Royal grammarians were interested primarily in demonstrating the general philosophical functions of linguistic form, practical grammarians were concerned mainly with devising prescriptive rules that would provide a guide to usage. For this reason they preferred simple categorical statements supported by examples of correct and incorrect usage to abstract reasoning based on principles of logic. Bishop Lowth

---

[19] H. Poutsma, *A Grammar of Modern English* (Groningen, 1904–26).
[20] John Lily, *Brevissima Institutio seu Ratio Grammatices cognoscendae* [etc.] (Londini, 1668).

might praise a philosophical grammar such as the *Hermes* of James Harris,[21] which was in the tradition of Aristotle, the Medieval scholastics, and the Port Royal grammarians, but for practical reasons he wrote his own grammar according to the pattern of the most commonly used elementary Latin grammars of his time.

Lowth's definitions of the parts of speech are even more simple than those to be found in the Latin grammars. He explains the reasons for this in the preface to his grammar. Because of the relative simplicity of the English scheme of inflections, Lowth could omit references to inflection in his definitions of the parts of speech. His definitions are made up of rather loosely phrased, simple statements based on lexical and syntactical critera. They make no attempt to account for the morphological or logical properties of parts of speech. They are, in fact, hardly more than labels used for the organization of prescriptive statements. Their limitations are pointed out even by early nineteenth-century prescriptive grammarians such as William Cobbett and Goold Brown.[22] Nevertheless, they did succeed in becoming the standard definitions that are most commonly used even today in school grammars.

For over a hundred years, until Henry Sweet's *A New English Grammar* in 1891, Bishop Lowth dominated linguistic discussion in England. Popularizations of his grammar by such copyists as Lindley Murray and Samuel Kirkham[23] were sold in the millions. As a result of the popularity of such grammars, the nineteenth century has been termed the midsummer madness of grammar. But in the late nineteenth century, Henry Sweet introduced the scientific spirit into English grammar. Sweet adopted the part of speech approach to the methodology of grammar, but his purpose was full analytical description rather than dogmatic prescription. Influenced by the Port Royal approach and by Hermann Paul's demonstration of the logical weaknesses resulting from inconsistent use of the categories of form, function, and meaning,[24] Sweet made a full use of all three criteria in defining the traditionally accepted parts of speech. He not only applied his threefold method of analysis to nouns, verbs, adjectives, and adverbs, but to pronouns, prepositions, and conjunctions, which up until his time had been discussed almost entirely from the standpoint of their syntactical relations.

Although Sweet analyzed the standard parts of speech under the separate headings of form, function, and meaning, he made no consistent effort to keep his categories distinct. Under any one of his headings he introduced analysis that pertained more logically to either or both of his other two categories. Moreover, he did not distinguish the logical properties of discourse from grammatical and semantic properties. For example, he discusses the logical uses of the noun under the heading of form, those of the adjective under the heading of meaning, and those of the verb under the heading of function. Such disregard for consistent analytical procedure was probably due to Sweet's basic evaluation of language. He was fond of saying that language is an imperfect instrument of thought, and he provided numerous examples of the imperfect correspondence between grammatical and logical categories. More basically, however, Sweet considered any sharp distinction

---

[21] Robert Lowth, *A Short Introduction to English Grammar, A New Ed.* (London, 1783), pp. xiii–xiv.

[22] William Cobbett, *A Grammar of the English Language* (London, 1833); Goold Brown cited in n. 16 above.

[23] Lindley Murray, *English Grammar, adapted to the Different Classes of Learners* (New York, 1802); Samuel Kirkham, *English Grammar in Familiar Lectures* (New York, 1857).

[24] Hermann Paul, *Prinzipien der Sprachgeschichte* (Halle, 1880).

between form and meaning artificial. The concern of grammar, he believed, is not with form and meaning separately but with connections between the two. To describe these connections, the grammarian may start either with form or with meaning:

> Syntax may be studied from two points of view. We can either start from the grammatical forms, and explain their uses, as when we describe the meanings and functions of the genitive case, or the subjunctive mood; or we may take a grammatical category, and describe the different forms by which it is expressed, as when we give an account of the different ways in which predication is expressed—by a single verb, by the verb *to be* with an adjective or noun-word, etc. We distinguish these as *formal* and *logical* syntax respectively.[25]

In this passage Sweet explicitly recognizes the distinction between the formal and logical approaches to syntax, and he implies that either approach is legitimate as long as the grammarian accounts for the functional relationship between form and meaning. But Sweet did not always hold to this principle. His contrast of the functions of accidence and syntax is a case in point. Accidence, he wrote, concerns itself as much as possible with form and as little as possible with meaning, whereas syntax ignores formal distinctions as much as possible and concentrates on meaning. For this sharply drawn distinction Sweet was criticized by Otto Jespersen,[26] who thought the grammarian should always keep in mind that form and function are inseparable in the life of language. Actually, Jespersen owed a great deal to Sweet, and the difference between his view and Sweet's is more a matter of degree than of essence. Jespersen merely developed somewhat more rigorously than Sweet the exposition of the dual orientation of language to outer form and inner logical meanings. Specifically, Jespersen worked out with greater precision and detail Sweet's distinction between the contrasting points of view of speaker and hearer. The speaker starts with inner notional categories for which he finds outer verbal forms; the hearer translates outer forms into inner meanings. The middle point in each transaction is that of function, a term used by Jespersen to designate the specific forms of such grammatical categories as number, case, and tense.[27]

Although Jespersen, like Sweet, based his analysis of the parts of speech on the threefold division of form, function, and meaning, he greatly reduced the importance of specific definitions of the parts of speech. He denied, in fact, the possibility of basing a satisfactory classification of words on short and easily applicable definitions. Instead he assumed that there is sufficient empirical evidence to identify word-classes and then examined in detail the arguments for and against certain principles of classification. For instance, he used the word *noun* as a general heading for substantives and adjectives, and then examined in detail such traditional concepts as substance, quality, specialization, and generalization to determine whether these concepts are useful in distinguishing substantives from adjectives. He concluded that there is an element of truth in such logical distinctions, but that ultimately any practical division of one part of speech from another must be determined by formal criteria that differ from one language to another.[28]

Because of the importance Jespersen gave to formal criteria, he saw no point in

---

[25] Sweet, p. 205.

[26] Otto Jespersen, *The Philosophy of Grammar* (London, 1924), p. 40.

[27] *Ibid.*, pp. 39–46.

[28] *Ibid.*, pp. 58–63.

making in English such a distinction as that between dative and accusative.[29] To him this was merely one more instance of the application to English of distinctions that pertain to Latin. For his emphasis on formal criteria that were applicable especially to individual languages, Jespersen was widely criticized by traditional grammarians, who also looked askance at many of his innovations in terminology and analytical techniques. Today we recognize that Jespersen did not depart radically from the traditional approach to grammar; his introduction of new analytical techniques was evidently intended to buttress the traditional parts of speech grammar by providing it with a more resourceful methodology.

Jespersen fully recognized the difficulties inherent in defining parts of speech, but he still felt that there was justification for retaining much of the traditional scheme. He refused to join the ranks of such of his contemporaries as Brunot, De Saussure, Sapir, and Bloomfield,[30] who were sceptical of the utility of the parts of speech approach. Jespersen held that the main difficulty with the approach was a pedagogical one, which could be obviated, particularly at the elementary level, if the teacher depended upon examples rather than brief definitions. In his *Essentials of English Grammar*[31] Jespersen provided a demonstration of how he would reduce the importance of explicit definitions. Under the headings of the parts of speech he lists groups of words with short identifying labels. Substantives such as *God, devil, man, John,* et cetera are labeled parenthetically as living beings and plants; *star, stone, mountain,* et cetera as things; *iron, air, tea,* et cetera as substances; *lightning, death, laughter,* et cetera as happenings, acts, states; *year, inch, bushel,* et cetera as measures, indications of quantity; *beauty, kindness, poverty,* et cetera as qualities. This practice of listing examples with parenthetical labels is followed for the other word-classes—adjectives, verbs, pronouns, and particles. In his class of particles Jespersen included all words that would not fit into his primary classes.

The plan of organization in *Essentials of English Grammar* is evidently designed to keep parts of speech classification in the background. Only one short chapter out of thirty-six is devoted explicitly to defining word-classes, and no chapter is headed by the traditional names of the parts of speech. But this practice is somewhat misleading. Actually, Jespersen has merely abandoned parts of speech classification as an obvious principle of organization. His detailed discussions of grammatical categories and syntactical structures assume the premises and follow in analytical detail the traditional parts of speech methodology. That these discussions have been distributed in a new arrangement may be regarded in some ways as more of a loss than a gain. The richly detailed analyses often lose much of their cogency because they do not fall readily into a systematic framework. The *Philosophy of Grammar* makes clear why Jespersen has tried to reduce the role of parts of speech methodology. With grammatical evidence drawn from many of the same sources as those used by modern linguists, he shows the difficulties of applying the parts of speech approach to languages that exhibit principles of structure different from those of the Indo-European languages.

Jespersen emphasized the need to investigate the inter-relations of form, function, and meaning in defining the parts of speech, but also recognized the particular importance

---

[29] *Ibid.,* p. 174.

[30] F. Brunot, *La pensée et la langue* (Paris, 1922); Ferdinand de Saussure, *Cours de linguistique générale* [1916], 5th ed. (Paris, 1960); Edward Sapir, *Language: an Introduction to the Study of Speech* (New York, 1921); Leonard Bloomfield, *Language* (New York, 1933).

[31] Otto Jespersen, *Essentials of English Grammar* (New York, 1933).

of formal criteria in grammatical analysis. Modern parts of speech grammarians have placed even greater stress on formal criteria for defining the parts of speech. C. C. Fries, in his work on the structure of the sentence,[32] constantly emphasizes form and disassociates his analysis of the parts of speech from the traditional terminology by using such neutral designations as Class 1, Class 2, Class 3, and Class 4 words. James Sledd retains the traditional terms but scrupulously attempts to eliminate semantic and logical criteria from his definitions.[33] Examination of salient points of analysis in the works of these two modern grammarians will reveal the present status of the parts of speech approach.

To Fries "the grammar of a language consists of the devices that signal structural meaning."[34] Structural meaning is to be carefully distinguished from lexical meaning, which is the province of the dictionary rather than of the grammar. The total meaning of any utterance consists, to be sure, of the two kinds of meaning in combination. But the concern of the grammarian is not with the total meaning but with the special contribution of structural elements to the total meaning. He therefore is concerned not with words as lexical units but with the arrangements of words as parts of speech. To identify the parts of speech, the grammarian considers three main sets of structural signals: the forms of individual words, the correlations of these forms, and the order in which the words are arranged.

In *The Structure of English* Fries demonstrates the central importance of a word's position as a clue to determining its class affiliation. By examining many examples and setting up typical frames of positional relations, he shows that in English certain classes of words normally precede or follow other classes of words. When the function word *the* is present, for example, it regularly precedes and marks the presence of a particular word-class, which can be designated as Class 1. A Class 1 word typically occupies certain positional relations to another word-class, which can be designated as Class 2. Other Classes, 3 and 4, can be identified by their relations to Classes 1 and 2. We can see how this positional principle works by examining the lexically meaningless construction Fries has provided: *the vapy koobs dasaked the citar molently.*[35] By applying his typical frames to this construction, Fries can assume that *the* marks the presence of a Class 1 word. But even if there were no *the,* he could still identify the Class 1 word by its positional relations to the other words in the construction. By such clues he can identify *koobs* and *citar* as Class 1 words, *dasaked* as a Class 2 word, *vapy* as a Class 3 word, and *molently* as a Class 4 word. The fact that *vapy* might also occur in Class 1 frames poses no great problem. In this particular instance it is in a Class 3 frame, identifiable as a Class 3 word.

In addition to word position, Fries uses formal correlations among words that help to identify structural functions. He provides a number of ingenious ways to illustrate such correlations, particularly the use of material replete with structural clues but lacking lexical significance. An example is the previously quoted construction: *the vapy koobs dasaked the citar molently.* At the outset we must assume with Fries that this sequence of sounds occurs in an English context, and that the morphemes—minimum meaningful units—have been identified and have indicated the probability that the sounds are divisible into the words that we see on the written page. Since we do not know the lexical meanings of the individual words, we must assign the words to parts of speech by those structural clues that are evident. Each word does by itself provide certain formal clues, but for

---

[32] Fries, p. 56.
[33] Sledd, see n. 9 above.
[34] Fries, p. 56.
[35] *Ibid.,* p. 111.

more certain assignment we must depend on correlation and position. The *s* ending on *koobs*, for example, may be assigned to different morphemes, resulting in different structural meanings. The one we select will depend on how we correlate the word as a unit with other words in the group. One correlation would result in two word groups, *the vapy koobs*, and *dasaked the citar molently*. This correlation allows us to look upon *the vapy koobs* by itself as a grammatically complete utterance. But the other group cannot be so considered with the clues we have available. Of course, if we had a complete phonetic transcription of the cited construction, indications of juncture would indicate immediately the probable construction. We would also have little difficulty if we were given a completely punctuated construction with both structural and lexical meaning. Such a sentence would be "The musty stinks polluted the air completely."

In Fries' grammar positional and correlational data provide the main criteria for identifying word classes. But he also demonstrates in rich detail the ways in which the forms of individual words provide clues to probable structural uses. Words like *arrival, departure, delivery, [acceptance], catcher,* and *applicant,* for example, form regular patterns of contrast with such forms as *arrive, depart, deliver, accept, catch,* and *apply.* Word forms like *bigness, activity, bag, truth,* and *book* contrast regularly with such forms as *big, active, baggy, true,* and *bookish. Way, day,* and *sea* contrast with *away, daily,* and *seaward.* Systematic notation of such similarities and differences in the forms of words provides one set of clues to use as a basis of parts of speech classification. We must keep in mind, however, that in English, the position of the word in relation to other words in the sentence is the most positive clue to its structural use and word-class.

Defining word-classes depends in this system on the structural use of the word in the sentence. Fries, therefore, is faced with the need to find a definition of the sentence as a structural unit. In searching for such a definition he examines and dismisses in turn definitions which are based on semantic, intuitive, psychological, and logical grounds. The first to be dismissed as scientifically inadequate is the traditional definition of the sentence as the expression of a complete thought. Definitions based on logical relations follow in short order. By a process of elimination he finally accepts Bloomfield's definition: "Each sentence is an independent linguistic form, not included by virtue of any grammatical construction in any larger linguistic form."[36]

By applying this definition to his data, transcribed telephone conversations, Fries finds that he can classify utterance units into three kinds: (1) a single minimum free utterance; (2) a single free utterance, not minimum but expanded; (3) a sequence of two or more free utterances. To define the limits of utterance units, Fries accepts Bloomfield's assumption that language consists of speaker-hearer relationships in which both speaker and hearer respond to stimuli in the total situation. As a result of this he classifies utterances according to responses evoked:

Communicative Utterances

    I. Utterances regularly eliciting "oral" responses only:
       A. *Greetings.* B. *Calls.* C. *Questions.*
   II. Utterances regularly eliciting "action" responses, sometimes accompanied by one of a limited list of oral responses: *requests* or *commands.*
  III. Utterances regularly eliciting convention signals of attention to continuous discourse. . . .

---

[36] *Ibid.,* p. 21 (Bloomfield, p. 170).

Non-communicative Utterances

> Utterances characteristic of situations such as surprise, sudden pain, prolonged pain, disgust, anger, laughter, sorrow.[37]

What strikes one about this scheme is the attempt to describe by formal clues linguistic functions that more traditional grammarians have defined in terms of semantic, logical, and formal properties of language. In this scheme Fries has found a place for the traditional terms, *statements, questions,* and *commands.* But for the usual rubric *exclamations* he substitutes the phrase *non-communicative utterances.* This phrase evidently is based upon Bloomfield's conception of language as "the use of sound waves to bridge the gap between two nervous systems."[38] The distinct phases of this process are: (1) a speaker stimulated to produce sounds possessing symbolic value; (2) the speech sounds; (3) a hearer making a practical response to the sounds. This formula obviously does not cover the full range of language situations. The behavioristic assumption that the "meaning" of a speech situation necessarily calls for a practical response in an individual other than speaker fails to account for those instances when communication takes place without an overt response. And most importantly, it fails to account for the speculative and expressive uses of language involving only one person. These semantic limitations do not, however, invalidate Fries' structural analysis of his word groups. Within the limits of his assumptions he has made a solid contribution to the description of the structure of the English sentence. The use of his descriptive methods by such popularizers as Lloyd and Warfel, and Paul Roberts,[39] provides testimony to their effectiveness.

In some ways Sledd's grammar is even more traditional than Fries.[40] It retains, for example, such traditional terms as noun, verb, adverb, adjective, predicate, and complement, although these are redefined to fit structural criteria. The most notable innovation by Sledd is his distinction between parts of speech identified by form and parts of speech identified by position. The parts of speech identified by form are noun, pronoun, verb, adjective, and adverb. The parts of speech identified by position—nominal, verbal, adjectival, and adverbial—are identical with Fries' four primary classes. We can see how the distinction works by examining Sledd's treatment of adjectives.[41] Thus *poor* is always an adjective because it fits into the inflectional series *poor, poorer, poorest.* But whenever any one of these forms occurs in the normal position of a noun, as in the sentence *the poor are always with us,* it is also a nominal. A word like *beautiful* is not considered an adjective because it cannot be fitted into an inflectional series. Instead it is classified as an adjectival. By a similar process of reasoning Sledd distinguishes between the noun and the nominal, the verb and the verbal. The pronoun is identified by its form; by position it is a nominal. For the distinction between the adverb and the adverbial he

---

[37] *Ibid.,* p. 53.

[38] *Ibid.,* p. 33, n. 8. The quotation is Fries' summary of the theory set forth in Leonard Bloomfield's *Language,* chs. 2 and 9, pp. 21–41, 139–157. Fries refers specifically to these pages as the basis for his summary statement.

[39] Donald J. Lloyd and Harry R. Warfel, *American English in Its Cultural Setting* (New York, 1956); Paul Roberts, *Patterns of English* (New York, 1956) and *Understanding English* (New York, 1958).

[40] See Sledd, p. 10, for reasons.

[41] *Ibid.,* p. 81.

introduces a slightly different criterion. He points out that in the traditional scheme many adverbs differ in form from adjectives only by the addition of the suffix –ly, e. g., *quick* and *quickly*. Consequently, he restricts the term adverb to the member of such pairs having the –ly ending. All other words appearing in the position of the adverb are adverbials.

Fries and Sledd seem to have carried structural parts of speech classification to its ultimate stage. It is difficult to see how any future grammarian can add essentially to their results. Any further development in the parts of speech approach would need, it seems, to return to a broader base of classification and find ways to interrelate lexical, logical, and formal criteria more consistently and systematically than grammarians have been able to do in the past. Possibly if Henry Sweet had made a more systematic distinction between the formal and the logical properties of syntax he might have demonstrated more conclusively the possibilities of a comprehensive system for defining word-classes. Some future grammarian may be able to accomplish what Sweet did not. It is more likely, however, that the grammar of the future will develop away from parts of speech analysis toward one of the newer systems. The traditional system of word classification was developed specifically to describe the structure of Indo-European languages and has not proved effective for languages of other family groups. At present the major efforts in linguistic study are being directed toward developing a methodology of analysis that will apply effectively to radically different kinds of languages.

At any rate, the course before the general student of language is clear. He should understand the strengths and limitations of the traditional methodology. He should appreciate what the new methodology is contributing to a solid knowledge of language. Moreover, he should keep in mind that the study of grammar is influenced by the general intellectual climate. In the past it has developed as a normative discipline in close touch with logic and philosophy. In its latest form it is developing as a descriptive science. It is probable that the future study of grammar will be enriched by advancements in the behavioral sciences. In such an event it will again be a broad humanistic study.

DISCUSSION QUESTIONS

1. How does Hartung's analysis of the major problem in classifying parts of speech relate to the classification of *library* as a noun or an adjective in *He got a library job*? What would it be according to the scheme of Dionysius? To that of Sledd?

2. How does Lowth's approach to grammatical categories differ from that of the Port Royal grammarians?

3. What reasons do you think Fries had for rejecting the traditional school definition of a sentence? Have you ever questioned this definition?

4. Find in some current school grammars definitions of a sentence. Are they traditional or Friesian?

| W. NELSON FRANCIS |

While professor of English at Franklin and Marshall College, Francis authored the leading structural grammar textbook, The Structure of American English *(Ronald Press, 1958). In 1962 he moved to Brown University, where he retired in 1976 as emeritus professor of linguistics. As a Fulbright scholar in 1956–1957 he did field work for the Dialect Survey of England.*

This paper was written over twenty-five years ago. During the intervening time, theories of grammar and the views of grammarians, including the author, have changed drastically. But the article reflects faithfully the views of a structural grammarian of its time.

W. Nelson Francis, August, 1980

REVOLUTION IN GRAMMAR

I

A long overdue revolution is at present taking place in the study of English grammar— a revolution as sweeping in its consequences as the Darwinian revolution in biology. It is the result of the application to English of methods of descriptive analysis originally developed for use with languages of primitive people. To anyone at all interested in language, it is challenging; to those concerned with the teaching of English (including parents), it presents the necessity of radically revising both the substance and the methods of their teaching.

A curious paradox exists in regard to grammar. On the one hand it is felt to be the dullest and driest of academic subjects, fit only for those in whose veins the red blood of life has long since turned to ink. On the other, it is a subject upon which people who would scorn to be professional grammarians hold very dogmatic opinions, which they will defend with considerable emotion. Much of this prejudice stems from the usual sources of prejudice—ignorance and confusion. Even highly educated people seldom have a clear idea of what grammarians do, and there is an unfortunate confusion about the meaning of the term ''grammar'' itself.

Hence it would be well to begin with definitions. What do people mean when they use the word ''grammar''? Actually the word is used to refer to three different things, and much of the emotional thinking about matters grammatical arises from confusion among these different meanings.

The first thing we mean by ''grammar'' is ''the set of formal patterns in which the words of a language are arranged in order to convey larger meanings.'' It is not necessary that we be able to discuss these patterns self-consciously in order to be able to use them. In fact, all speakers of a language above the age of five or six know how to use its complex forms of organization with considerable skill; in this sense of the word—call it ''Grammar 1''—they are thoroughly familiar with its grammar.

The second meaning of ''grammar''—call it ''Grammar 2''—is ''the branch of linguistic science which is concerned with the description, analysis, and formulization of formal language patterns." Just as gravity was in full operation before Newton's apple fell, so grammar in the first sense was in full operation before anyone formulated the first rule that began the history of grammar as a study.

The third sense in which people use the word "grammar" is "linguistic etiquette." This we may call "Grammar 3." The word in this sense is often coupled with a derogatory adjective: we say that the expression "he ain't here" is "bad grammar." What we mean is that such an expression is bad linguistic manners in certain circles. From the point of view of "Grammar 1" it is faultless; it conforms just as completely to the structural patterns of English as does "he isn't here." The trouble with it is like the trouble with Prince Hal in Shakespeare's play—it is "bad," not in itself, but in the company it keeps.

As has already been suggested, much confusion arises from mixing these meanings. One hears a good deal of criticism of teachers of English couched in such terms as "they don't teach grammar any more." Criticism of this sort is based on the wholly unproved assumption that teaching Grammar 2 will increase the student's proficiency in Grammar 1 or improve his manners in Grammar 3. Actually, the form of Grammar 2 which is usually taught is a very inaccurate and misleading analysis of the facts of Grammar 1; and it therefore is of highly questionable value in improving a person's ability to handle the structural patterns of his language. It is hardly reasonable to expect that teaching a person some inaccurate grammatical analysis will either improve the effectiveness of his assertions or teach him what expressions are acceptable to use in a given social context.

These, then, are the three meanings of "grammar": Grammar 1, a form of behavior; Grammar 2, a field of study, a science; and Grammar 3, a branch of etiquette.

II

Grammarians have arrived at some basic principles of their science, three of which are fundamental to this discussion. The first is that a language constitutes a set of behavior patterns common to the members of a given community. It is a part of what the anthropologists call the culture of the community. Actually it has complex and intimate relationships with other phases of culture such as myth and ritual. But for purposes of study it may be dealt with as a separate set of phenomena that can be objectively described and analyzed like any other universe of facts. Specifically, its phenomena can be observed, recorded, classified, and compared; and general laws of their behavior can be made by the same inductive process that is used to produce the "laws" of physics, chemistry, and the other sciences.

A second important principle of linguistic science is that each language or dialect has its own unique system of behavior patterns. Parts of this system may show similarities to parts of the systems of other languages, particularly if those languages are genetically related. But different languages solve the problems of expression and communication in different ways, just as the problems of movement through water are solved in different ways by lobsters, fish, seals, and penguins. A couple of corollaries of this principle are important. The first is that there is no such thing as "universal grammar," or at least if there is, it is so general and abstract as to be of little use. The second corollary is that the grammar of each language must be made up on the basis of a study of that particular language—a study that is free from preconceived notions of what a language should contain and how it should operate. The marine biologist does not criticize the octopus for using jet-propulsion to get him through the water instead of the methods of a self-respecting fish. Neither does the linguistic scientist express alarm or distress when he finds a language that seems to get along quite well without any words that correspond to what in English we call verbs.

A third principle on which linguistic science is based is that the analysis and description of a given language must conform to the requirements laid down for any satisfactory scientific theory. These are (1) simplicity, (2) consistency, (3) completeness, and (4) usefulness for predicting the behavior of phenomena not brought under immediate observation when the theory was formed. Linguistic scientists who have recently turned their attention to English have found that, judged by these criteria, the traditional grammar of English is unsatisfactory. It falls down badly on the first two requirements, being unduly complex and glaringly inconsistent within itself. It can be made to work, just as the Ptolemaic earth-centered astronomy can be, but at the cost of great elaboration and complication. The new grammar, like the Copernican sun-centered astronomy, solves the same problems with greater elegance, which is the scientist's word for the simplicity, compactness, and tidiness that characterize a satisfactory theory.

III

A brief look at the history of the traditional grammar of English will make apparent the reasons for its inadequacy. The study of English grammar is actually an outgrowth of the linguistic interest of the Renaissance. It was during the later Middle Ages and early Renaissance that the various vernacular languages of Europe came into their own. They began to be used for many kinds of writing which had previously always been done in Latin. As the vernaculars, in the hands of great writers like Dante and Chaucer, came of age as members of the linguistic family, a concomitant interest in their grammars arose. The earliest important English grammar was written by Shakespeare's contemporary, Ben Jonson.

It is important to observe that not only Ben Jonson himself but also those who followed him in the study of English grammar were men deeply learned in Latin and sometimes in Greek. For all their interest in English, they were conditioned from earliest school days to conceive of the classical languages as superior to the vernaculars. We still sometimes call the elementary school the "grammar school"; historically the term means the school where Latin grammar was taught. By the time the Renaissance or eighteenth-century scholar took his university degree, he was accustomed to use Latin as the normal means of communication with his fellow scholars. Dr. Samuel Johnson, for instance, who had only three years at the university and did not take a degree, wrote poetry in both Latin and Greek. Hence it was natural for these men to take Latin grammar as the norm, and to analyze English in terms of Latin. The grammarians of the seventeenth and eighteenth centuries who formulated the traditional grammar of English looked for the devices and distinctions of Latin grammar in English, and where they did not actually find them they imagined or created them. Of course, since English is a member of the Indo-European family of languages, to which Latin and Greek also belong, it did have many grammatical elements in common with them. But many of these had been obscured or wholly lost as a result of the extensive changes that had taken place in English— changes that the early grammarians inevitably conceived of as degeneration. They felt that it was their function to resist further change, if not to repair the damage already done. So preoccupied were they with the grammar of Latin as the ideal that they overlooked in large part the exceedingly complex and delicate system that English had substituted for the Indo-European grammar it had abandoned. Instead they stretched unhappy English on the Procrustean bed of Latin. It is no wonder that we commonly hear people say, "I didn't really understand grammar until I began to study Latin." This is eloquent testimony to the fact that the grammar "rules" of our present-day textbooks are largely an inheritance from the Latin-based grammar of the eighteenth century.

Meanwhile the extension of linguistic study beyond the Indo-European and Semitic families began to reveal that there are many different ways in which linguistic phenomena are organized—in other words, many different kinds of grammar. The tone-languages of the Orient and of North America, and the complex agglutinative languages of Africa, among others, forced grammarians to abandon the idea of a universal or ideal grammar and to direct their attention more closely to the individual systems employed by the multifarious languages of mankind. With the growth and refinement of the scientific method and its application to the field of anthropology, language came under more rigorous scientific scrutiny. As with anthropology in general, linguistic science at first concerned itself with the primitive. Finally, again following the lead of anthropology, linguistics began to apply its techniques to the old familiar tongues, among them English. Accelerated by the practical need during World War II of teaching languages, including English, to large numbers in a short time, research into the nature of English grammar has moved rapidly in the last fifteen years. The definitive grammar of English is yet to be written, but the results so far achieved are spectacular. It is now as unrealistic to teach "traditional" grammar of English as it is to teach "traditional" (i.e pre-Darwinian) biology or "traditional" (i.e. four-element) chemistry. Yet nearly all certified teachers of English on all levels are doing so. Here is a cultural lag of major proportions.

IV

Before we can proceed to a sketch of what the new grammar of English looks like, we must take account of a few more of the premises of linguistic science. They must be understood and accepted by anyone who wishes to understand the new grammar.

First, the spoken language is primary, at least for the original study of a language. In many of the primitive languages,[1] of course, where writing is unknown, the spoken language is the *only* form. This is in many ways an advantage to the linguist, because the written language may use conventions that obscure its basic structure. The reason for the primary importance of the spoken language is that language originates as speech, and most of the changes and innovations that occur in the history of a given language begin in the spoken tongue.

Secondly, we must take account of the concept of dialect. I suppose most laymen would define a dialect as "a corrupt form of language spoken in a given region by people who don't know any better." This introduces moral judgments which are repulsive to the linguistic scholar. Let us approach the definition of a dialect from the more objective end, through the notion of a speech community. A speech community is merely a group of people who are in pretty constant intercommunication. There are various types of

---

[1] "Primitive languages" here is really an abbreviated statement for "languages used by peoples of relatively primitive culture"; it is not to be taken as implying anything simple or rudimentary about the languages themselves. Many languages included under the term, such as native languages of Africa and Mexico, exhibit grammatical complexities unknown to more "civilized" languages.

speech communities: local ones, like "the people who live in Tidewater Virginia"; class ones, like "the white-collar class"; occupational ones, like "doctors, nurses, and other people who work in hospitals"; social ones, like "clubwomen." In a sense, each of these has its own dialect. Each family may be said to have its own dialect; in fact, in so far as each of us has his own vocabulary and particular quirks of speech, each individual has his own dialect. Also, of course, in so far as he is a member of many speech communities, each individual is more or less master of many dialects and shifts easily and almost unconsciously from one to another as he shifts from one social environment to another.

In the light of this concept of dialects, a language can be defined as a group of dialects which have enough of their sound-system, vocabulary, and grammar (Grammar 1, that is) in common to permit their speakers to be mutually intelligible in the ordinary affairs of life. It usually happens that one of the many dialects that make up a language comes to have more prestige than the others; in modern times it has usually been the dialect of the middle-class residents of the capital, like Parisian French and London English, which is so distinguished. This comes to be thought of as the standard dialect; in fact, its speakers become snobbish and succeed in establishing the belief that it is not a dialect at all, but the only proper form of the language. This causes the speakers of other dialects to become self-conscious and ashamed of their speech, or else aggressive and jingoistic about it—either of which is an acknowledgment of their feelings of inferiority. Thus one of the duties of the educational system comes to be that of teaching the standard dialect to all so as to relieve them of feelings of inferiority, and thus relieve society of linguistic neurotics. This is where Grammar 3, linguistic etiquette, comes into the picture.

A third premise arising from the two just discussed is that the difference between the way educated people talk and the way they write is a dialectal difference. The spread between these two dialects may be very narrow, as in present-day America, or very wide, as in Norway, where people often speak local Norwegian dialects but write in the Dano-Norwegian *Riksmaal*. The extreme is the use by writers of an entirely different language, or at least an ancient and no longer spoken form of the language—like Sanskrit in northern India or Latin in western Europe during the Middle Ages. A corollary of this premise is that anyone setting out to write a grammar must know and make clear whether he is dealing with the spoken or the written dialect. Virtually all current English grammars deal with the written language only; evidence for this is that their rules for the plurals of nouns, for instance, are really spelling rules, which say nothing about pronunciation.

This is not the place to go into any sort of detail about the methods of analysis the linguistic scientist uses. Suffice it to say that he begins by breaking up the flow of speech into minimum sound-units, or phones, which he then groups into families called phonemes, the minimum significant sound-units. Most languages have from twenty to sixty of these. American English has forty-one: nine vowels, twenty-four consonants, four degrees of stress, and four levels of pitch. These phonemes group themselves into minimum meaningful units, called morphemes. These fall into two groups: free morphemes, those that can enter freely into many conbinations with other free morphemes to make phrases and sentences; and bound morphemes, which are always found tied in a close and often indissoluble relationship with other bound or free morphemes. An example of a free morpheme is "dog"; an example of a bound morpheme is "un-" or "ex-." The linguist usually avoids talking about "words" because the term is very inexact. Is "instead of," for instance, to be considered one, two, or three words? This is purely a matter of opinion; but it is a matter of fact that it is made up of three morphemes.

In any case, our analysis has now brought the linguist to the point where he has some notion of the word-stock (he would call it the "lexicon") of his language. He must then go into the question of how the morphemes are grouped into meaningful utterances, which is the field of grammar proper. At this point in the analysis of English, as of many other languages, it becomes apparent that there are three bases upon which classification and analysis may be built: form, function, and meaning. For illustration let us take the word "boys" in the utterance "the boys are here." From the point of view of form, "boys" is a noun with the plural ending "s" (pronounced like "z"), preceded by the noun-determiner "the," and tied by concord to the verb "are," which it precedes. From the point of view of function, "boys" is the subject of the verb "are" and of the sentence. From the point of view of meaning, "boys" points out or names more than one of the male young of the human species, about whom an assertion is being made.

Of these three bases of classification, the one most amenable to objective description and analysis of a rigorously scientific sort is form. In fact, many conclusions about form can be drawn by a person unable to understand or speak the language. Next comes function. But except as it is revealed by form, function is dependent on knowing the meaning. In a telegraphic sentence like "ship sails today"[2] no one can say whether "ship" is the subject of "sails" or an imperative verb with "sails" as its object until he knows what the sentence means. Most shaky of all bases for grammatical analysis is meaning. Attempts have been made to reduce the phenomena of meaning to objective description, but so far they have not succeeded very well. Meaning is such a subjective quality that it is usually omitted entirely from scientific description. The botanist can describe the forms of plants and the functions of their various parts, but he refuses to concern himself with their meaning. It is left to the poet to find symbolic meanings in roses, violets, and lilies.

At this point it is interesting to note that the traditional grammar of English bases some of its key concepts and definitions on this very subjective and shaky foundation of meaning. A recent English grammar defines a sentence as "a group of words which expresses a complete thought through the use of a verb, called its predicate, and a subject, consisting of a noun or pronoun about which the verb has something to say."[3] But what is a complete thought? Actually we do not identify sentences this way at all. If someone says, "I don't know what to do," dropping his voice at the end, and pauses, the hearer will know that it is quite safe for him to make a comment without running the risk of interrupting an unfinished sentence. But if the speaker says the same words and maintains a level pitch at the end, the polite listener will wait for him to finish his sentence. The words are the same, the meaning is the same; the only difference is a slight one in the pitch of the final syllable—a purely formal distinction, which signals that the first utterance is complete, a sentence, while the second is incomplete. In writing we would translate these signals into punctuation: a period or exclamation point at the end of the first, a comma or dash at the end of the second. It is the form of the utterance, not the completeness of the thought, that tells us whether it is a whole sentence or only part of one.

Another favorite definition of the traditional grammar, also based on meaning, is that of "noun" as "the name of a person, place, or thing"; or, as the grammar just quoted has it, "the name of anybody or anything, with or without life, and with or without

---

[2] This example is taken from C. C. Fries, *The Structure of English* (New York, 1952), p. 62. This important book will be discussed below.
[3] Ralph B. Allen, *English Grammar* (New York, 1950), p. 187.

substance or form."[4] Yet we identify nouns, not by asking if they name something, but by their positions in expressions and by the formal marks they carry. In the sentence, "The slithy toves did gyre and gimble in the wabe," any speaker of English knows that "toves" and "wabe" are nouns, though he cannot tell what they name, if indeed they name anything. How does he know? Actually because they have certain formal marks, like their position in relation to "the" as well as the whole arrangement of the sentence. We know from our practical knowledge of English grammar (Grammar 1), which we have had since before we went to school, that if we were to put meaningful words into this sentence, we would have to put nouns in place of "toves" and "wabe," giving something like "The slithy snakes did gyre and gimble in the wood." The pattern of the sentence simply will not allow us to say "The slithy arounds did gyre and gimble in the wooden."

One trouble with the traditional grammar, then, is that it relies heavily on the most subjective element in language, meaning. Another is that it shifts the ground of its classification and produces the elementary logical error of cross-division. A zoologist who divided animals into invertebrates, mammals, and beasts of burden would not get very far before running into trouble. Yet the traditional grammar is guilty of the same error when it defines three parts of speech on the basis of meaning (noun, verb, and interjection), four more on the basis of function (adjective, adverb, pronoun, conjunction), and one partly on function and partly on form (preposition). The result is that in such an expression as "a dog's life" there can be endless futile argument about whether "dog's" is a noun or an adjective. It is, of course, a noun from the point of view of form and an adjective from the point of view of function, and hence falls into both classes, just as a horse is both a mammal and a beast of burden. No wonder students are bewildered in their attempts to master the traditional grammar. Their natural clearness of mind tells them that it is a crazy patchwork violating the elementary principles of logical thought.

V

If the traditional grammar is so bad, what does the new grammar offer in its place?

It offers a description, analysis, and set of definitions and formulas—rules, if you will—based firmly and consistently on the easiest, or at least the most objective, aspect of language, form. Experts can quibble over whether "dog's" in "a dog's life" is a noun or an adjective, but anyone can see that it is spelled with " 's" and hear that it ends with a "z" sound; likewise anyone can tell that it comes in the middle between "a" and "life." Furthermore he can tell that something important has happened if the expression is changed to "the dog's alive," "the live dogs," or "the dogs lived," even if he doesn't know what the words mean and has never heard of such functions as modifier, subject, or attributive genitive. He cannot, of course, get very far into his analysis without either a knowledge of the language or access to someone with such knowledge. He will also need a minimum technical vocabulary describing grammatical functions. Just so the anatomist is better off for knowing physiology. But the grammarian, like the anatomist, must beware of allowing his preconceived notions to lead him into the error of interpreting before he describes—an error which often results in his finding only what he is looking for.

---

[4] *Ibid.*, p. 1.

When the grammarian looks at English objectively, he finds that it conveys its meanings by two broad devices: the denotations and connotations of words separately considered, which the linguist calls "lexical meaning," and the significance of word-forms, word-groups, and arrangements apart from the lexical meanings of the words, which the linguist calls "structural meaning." The first of these is the domain of the lexicographer and the semanticist, and hence is not our present concern. The second, the structural meaning, is the business of the structural linguist, or grammarian. The importance of this second kind of meaning must be emphasized because it is often overlooked. The man in the street tends to think of the meaning of a sentence as being the aggregate of the dictionary meanings of the words that make it up; hence the widespread fallacy of literal translation—the feeling that if you take a French sentence and a French-English dictionary and write down the English equivalent of each French word you will come out with an intelligible English sentence. How ludicrous the results can be, anyone knows who is familiar with Mark Twain's retranslation from the French of his jumping frog story. One sentence reads, "Eh bien! I no saw not that that frog has nothing of better than each frog." Upon which Mark's comment is, "if that isn't grammar gone to seed, then I count myself no judge."[5]

The second point brought out by a formal analysis of English is that it uses four principal devices of form to signal structural meanings:

1. Word order—the sequence in which words and word-groups are arranged.
2. Function-words—words devoid of lexical meaning which indicate relationships among the meaningful words with which they appear.
3. Inflections—alterations in the forms of words themselves to signal changes in meaning and relationship.
4. Formal contrasts—contrasts in the forms of words signaling greater differences in function and meaning. These could also be considered inflections, but it is more convenient for both the lexicographer and the grammarian to consider them separately.

Usually several of these are present in any utterance, but they can be separately illustrated by means of contrasting expressions involving minimum variation—the kind of controlled experiment used in the scientific laboratory.

To illustrate the structural meaning of word order, let us compare the two sentences "man bites dog" and "dog bites man."—The words are identical in lexical meaning and in form; the only difference is in sequence. It is interesting to note that Latin expresses the difference between these two by changes in the form of the words, without necessarily altering the order: "homo canem mordet" or "hominem canis mordet." Latin grammar is worse than useless in understanding this point of English grammar.

Next, compare the sentences "the dog is the friend of man" and "any dog is a friend of that man." Here the words having lexical meaning are "dog," "is," "friend," and "man," which appear in the same form and the same order in both sentences. The formal differences between them are in the substitution of "any" and "a" for "the,"

[5] Mark Twain, "The Jumping Frog; the Original Story in English; the Retranslation Clawed Back from the French, into a Civilized Language Once More, by Patient and Unremunerated Toil," *1601 . . . and Sketches Old and New* (n.p., 1933), p. 50.

and in the insertion of "that." These little words are function-words; they make quite a difference in the meanings of the two sentences, though it is virtually impossible to say what they mean in isolation.

Third, compare the sentences "the dog loves the man" and "the dogs loved the men." Here the words are the same, in the same order, with the same function-words in the same positions. But the forms of the three words having lexical meanings have been changed: "dog" to "dogs," "loves" to "loved," and "man" to "men." These changes are inflections. English has very few of them as compared with Greek, Latin, Russian, or even German. But it still uses them; about one word in four in an ordinary English sentence is inflected.

Fourth, consider the difference between "the dog's friend arrived" and "the dog's friendly arrival." Here the difference lies in the change of "friend" to "friendly," a formal alteration signaling a change of function from subject to modifier, and the change of "arrived" to "arrival," signaling a change of function from predicate to head-word in a noun-modifier group. These changes are of the same formal nature as inflections, but because they produce words of different lexical meaning, classifiable as different parts of speech, it is better to call them formal contrasts than inflections. In other words, it is logically quite defensible to consider "love," "loving," and "loved" as the same word in differing aspects and to consider "friend," "friendly," "friendliness," "friendship," and "befriend" as different words related by formal and semantic similarities. But this is only a matter of convenience of analysis, which permits a more accurate description of English structure. In another language we might find that this kind of distinction is unnecessary but that some other distinction, unnecessary in English, is required. The categories of grammatical description are not sacrosanct; they are as much a part of man's organization of his observations as they are of the nature of things.

If we are considering the spoken variety of English, we must add a fifth device for indicating structural meaning—the various musical and rhythmic patterns which the linguist classifies under juncture, stress, and intonation. Consider the following pairs of sentences:

> Alfred, the alligator is sick
> Alfred the alligator is sick.

These are identical in the four respects discussed above—word order, function-words, inflections, and word-form. Yet they have markedly different meanings, as would be revealed by the intonation if they were spoken aloud. These differences in intonation are to a certain extent indicated in the written language by punctuation—that is, in fact, the primary function of punctuation.

VI

The examples so far given were chosen to illustrate in isolation the various kinds of structural devices in English grammar. Much more commonly the structural meaning of a given sentence is indicated by a combination of two or more of these devices: a sort of margin of safety which permits some of the devices to be missed or done away with without obscuring the structural meaning of the sentence, as indeed anyone knows who has ever written a telegram or a newspaper headline. On the other hand, sentences which do not have enough of these formal devices are inevitably ambiguous. Take the example already given, Fries's "ship sails today." This is ambiguous because there is nothing to indicate which of the first two words is performing a noun function and which a verb function. If we mark the noun by putting the noun-determining function-word "the" in front of it, the ambiguity disappears; we have either "the ship sails today" or "ship the sails today." The ambiguity could just as well be resolved by using other devices: consider "ship sailed today," "ship to sail today," "ship sail today," "shipping sails today," "shipment of sails today," and so on. It is simply a question of having enough formal devices in the sentence to indicate its structural meaning clearly.

How powerful the structural meanings of English are is illustrated by so-called "nonsense." In English, nonsense as a literary form often consists of utterances that have a clear structural meaning but use words that either have no lexical meanings, or whose lexical meanings are inconsistent one with another. This will become apparent if we subject a rather famous bit of English nonsense to formal grammatical analysis:

> All mimsy were the borogoves
> And the mome raths outgrabe.

This passage consists of ten words, five of them words that should have lexical meaning but don't, one standard verb, and four function-words. In so far as it is possible to indicate its abstract structure, it would be this:

> All . . . . y were the . . . . s
> And the . . . . . . s . . . .

Although this is a relatively simple formal organization, it signals some rather complicated meanings. The first thing we observe is that the first line presents a conflict: word order seems to signal one thing, and inflections and function-words something else. Specifically, "mimsy" is in the position normally occupied by the subject, but we know that it is not the subject and that "borogoves" is. We know this because there is an inflectional tie between the form "were" and the "s" ending of "borogoves," because there is the noun-determiner "the" before it, and because the alternative candidate for subject, "mimsy," lacks both of these. It is true that "mimsy" does have the function-word "all" before it, which may indicate a noun; but when it does, the noun is either plural (in which case "mimsy" would most likely end in "s"), or else the noun is what grammarians call a mass-word (like "sugar," "coal," "snow"), in which case the verb would have to be "was," not "were." All these formal considerations are sufficient to counteract the effect of word order and show that the sentence is of the type that may be represented thus:

> All gloomy were the Democrats.

Actually there is one other possibility. If "mimsy" belongs to the small group of nouns which don't use "s" to make the plural, and if "borogoves" has been so implied (but not specifically mentioned) in the context as to justify its appearing with the determiner "the," the sentence would then belong to the following type:

> (In the campaign for funds) all alumni were the canvassers.
> (In the drought last summer) all cattle were the sufferers.

But the odds are so much against this that most of us would be prepared to fight for our belief that "borogoves" are things that can be named, and that at the time referred to they were in a complete state of "mimsyness."

Moving on to the second line, "and the mome raths outgrabe," the first thing we note is that the ''And'' signals another parallel assertion to follow. We are thus prepared to recognize from the noun-determiner ''the,'' the plural infection ''s,'' and the particular positions of ''mome'' and ''outgrabe,'' as well as the continuing influence of the ''were'' of the preceding line, that we are dealing with a sentence of this pattern:

> And the lone rats agreed.

The influence of the ''were'' is particularly important here; it guides us in selecting among several interpretations of the sentence. Specifically, it requires us to identify ''outgrabe'' as a verb in the past tense, and thus a ''strong'' or ''irregular'' verb, since it lacks the characteristic past-tense ending ''d'' or ''ed.'' We do this in spite of the fact that there is another strong candidate for the position of verb: that is, ''raths,'' which bears a regular verb inflection and could be tied with ''mome'' as its subject in the normal noun-verb relationship. In such a case we should have to recognize ''outgrabe'' as either an adverb of the kind not marked by the form-contrast ''ly,'' an adjective, or the past participle of a strong verb. The sentence would then belong to one of the following types:

> And the moon shines above.
> And the man stays aloof.
> And the fool seems outdone.

But we reject all of these—probably they don't even occur to us—because they all have verbs in the present tense, whereas the ''were'' of the first line combines with the ''And'' at the beginning of the second to set the whole in the past.

We might recognize one further possibility for the structural meaning of this second line, particularly in the verse context, since we are used to certain patterns in verse that do not often appear in speech or prose. The ''were'' of the first line could be understood as doing double duty, its ghost or echo appearing between ''raths'' and ''outgrabe.'' Then we would have something like this:

> All gloomy were the Democrats
> And the home folks outraged.

But again the odds are pretty heavy against this. I for one am so sure that ''outgrabe'' is the past tense of a strong verb that I can give its present. In my dialect, at least, it is ''outgribe.''

The reader may not realize it, but in the last four paragraphs I have been discussing grammar from a purely formal point of view. I have not once called a word a noun because it names something (that is, I have not once resorted to meaning), nor have I called any word an adjective because it modifies a noun (that is, resorted to function). Instead I have been working in the opposite direction, from form toward function and meaning. I have used only criteria which are objectively observable, and I have assumed only a working knowledge of certain structural patterns and devices known to all speakers of English over the age of six. I did use some technical terms like ''noun,'' ''verb,'' and ''tense,'' but only to save time; I could have got along without them.

If one clears his mind of the inconsistencies of the traditional grammar (not so easy a process as it might be), he can proceed with a similarly rigorous formal analysis of a sufficient number of representative utterances in English and come out with a descriptive grammar. This is just what Professor Fries did in gathering and studying the material for the analysis he presents in the remarkable book to which I have already referred, *The Structure of English*. What he actually did was to put a tape recorder into action and record about fifty hours of telephone conversation among the good citizens of Ann Arbor,

Michigan. When this material was transcribed, it constituted about a quarter of a million words of perfectly natural speech by educated middle-class Americans. The details of his conclusions cannot be presented here, but they are sufficiently different from the usual grammar to be revolutionary. For instance, he recognizes only four parts of speech among the words with lexical meaning, roughly corresponding to what the traditional grammar calls substantives, verbs, adjectives and adverbs, though to avoid preconceived notions from the traditional grammar Fries calls them Class 1, Class 2, Class 3, and Class 4 words. To these he adds a relatively small group of function-words, 154 in his materials, which he divides into fifteen groups. These must be memorized by anyone learning the language; they are not subject to the same kind of general rules that govern the four parts of speech. Undoubtedly his conclusions will be developed and modified by himself and by other linguistic scholars, but for the present his book remains the most complete treatment extant of English grammar from the point of view of linguistic science.

VII

Two vital questions are raised by this revolution in grammar. The first is, "What is the value of this new system?" In the minds of many who ask it, the implication of this question is, "We have been getting along all these years with traditional grammar, so it can't be so very bad. Why should we go through the painful process of unlearning and relearning grammar just because linguistic scientists have concocted some new theories?"

The first answer to this question is the bravest and most honest. It is that the superseding of vague and sloppy thinking by clear and precise thinking is an exciting experience in and for itself. To acquire insight into the workings of a language, and to recognize the infinitely delicate system of relationship, balance, and interplay that constitutes its grammar, is to become closely acquainted with one of man's most miraculous creations, not unworthy to be set beside the equally beautiful organization of the physical universe. And to find that its most complex effects are produced by the multi-layered organization of relatively simple materials is to bring our thinking about language into accord with modern thought in other fields, which is more and more coming to emphasize the importance of organization—the fact that an organized whole is truly greater than the sum of all its parts.

There are other answers, more practical if less philosophically valid. It is too early to tell, but it seems probable that a realistic, scientific grammar should vastly facilitate the teaching of English, especially as a foreign language. Already results are showing here; it has been found that if intonation contours and other structural patterns are taught quite early, the student has a confidence that allows him to attempt to speak the language much sooner than he otherwise would.

The new grammar can also be of use in improving the native speaker's proficiency in handling the structural devices of his own language. In other words, Grammar 2, if it is accurate and consistent, *can* be of use in improving skill in Grammar 1. An illustration is that famous bugaboo, the dangling participle. Consider a specific instance of it, which once appeared on a college freshman's theme, to the mingled delight and despair of the instructor:

Having eaten our lunch, the steamboat departed.

What is the trouble with this sentence? Clearly there must be something wrong with it, because it makes people laugh, although it was not the intent of the writer to make them laugh. In other words, it produces a completely wrong response, resulting in total breakdown of communication. It is, in fact, "bad grammar" in a much more serious way than are mere dialectal divergences like "he ain't here" or "he never seen none," which produce social reactions but communicate effectively. In the light of the new grammar, the trouble with our dangling participle is that the form, instead of leading to the meaning, is in conflict with it. Into the position which, in this pattern, is reserved for the word naming the eater of the lunch, the writer has inserted the word "steamboat." The resulting tug-of-war between form and meaning is only momentary; meaning quickly wins out, simply because our common sense tells us that steamboats don't eat lunches. But if the pull of the lexical meaning is not given a good deal of help from common sense, the form will conquer the meaning, or the two will remain in ambiguous equilibrium—as, for instance, in "Having eaten our lunch, the passengers boarded the steamboat." Writers will find it easier to avoid such troubles if they know about the forms of English and are taught to use the form to convey the meaning, instead of setting up tensions between form and meaning. This, of course, is what English teachers are already trying to do. The new grammar should be a better weapon in their arsenal than the traditional grammar since it is based on a clear understanding of the realities.

The second and more difficult question is, "How can the change from one grammar to the other be effected?" Here we face obstacles of a formidable nature. When we remember the controversies attending on revolutionary changes in biology and astronomy, we realize what a tenacious hold the race can maintain on anything it has once learned, and the resistance it can offer to new ideas. And remember that neither astronomy nor biology was taught in elementary schools. They were, in fact, rather specialized subjects in advanced education. How then change grammar, which is taught to everybody, from the fifth grade up through college? The vested interest represented by thousands upon thousands of English and Speech teachers who have learned the traditional grammar and taught it for many years is a conservative force comparable to those which keep us still using the chaotic system of English spelling and the unwieldy measuring system of inches and feet, pounds and ounces, quarts, bushels, and acres. Moreover, this army is constantly receiving new recruits. It is possible in my state to become certified to teach English in high school if one has had eighteen credit hours of college English—let us say two semesters of freshman composition (almost all of which is taught by people unfamiliar with the new grammar), two semesters of a survey course in English literature, one semester of Shakespeare, and one semester of the contemporary novel. And since hard-pressed school administrators feel that anyone who can speak English can in a pinch teach it, the result is that many people are called upon to teach grammar whose knowledge of the subject is totally inadequate.

There is, in other words, a battle ahead of the new grammar. It will have to fight not only the apathy of the general public but the ignorance and inertia of those who count themselves competent in the field of grammar. The battle is already on, in fact. Those who try to get the concepts of the new grammar introduced into the curriculum are tagged as "liberal" grammarians—the implication being, I suppose, that one has a free choice between "liberal" and "conservative" grammar, and that the liberals are a bit dangerous, perhaps even a touch subversive. They are accused of undermining standards, of holding that "any way of saying something is just as good as any other," of not teaching the fundamentals of good English. I trust that the readers of this article will see how unfounded these charges are. But the smear campaign is on. So far as I know, neither religion nor patriotism has yet been brought into it. When they are, Professor Fries will have to say to Socrates, Galileo, Darwin, Freud, and the other members of the honorable fraternity of the misunderstood, "Move over, gentlemen, and make room for me."

DISCUSSION QUESTIONS

1. Do you accept Francis's notion of the standard dialect as simply one with social prestige and hence the duty of the schools to teach it so as to reduce feelings of inferiority?

2. In what way does Francis find reliance upon meaning unsatisfactory? Does he exclude meaning altogether from the field of language study?

3. In your past schooling, to which of the five sets of devices signaling structural meaning was your attention directed? How and with what effect?

4. Does Francis's explication of the problem of the dangling participle (*having eaten*) seem adequate? Explain.

BENJAMIN LEE WHORF

In occupation an insurance company executive, the late Benjamin Whorf, a student of Edward Sapir, became also a distinguished anthropologist, with many articles to his credit in the field of American Indian linguistics.

SCIENCE AND LINGUISTICS

Every normal person in the world, past infancy in years, can and does talk. By virtue of that fact, every person—civilized or uncivilized—carries through life certain native but deeply rooted ideas about talking and its relation to thinking. Because of their firm connection with speech habits that have become unconscious and automatic, these notions tend to be rather intolerant of opposition. They are by no means entirely personal and haphazard; their basis is definitely systematic, so that we are justified in calling them a system of natural logic—a term that seems to me preferable to the term common sense, often used for the same thing.

According to natural logic, the fact that every person has talked fluently since infancy makes every man his own authority on the process by which he formulates and communicates. He has merely to consult a common substratum of logic or reason which he and everyone else are supposed to possess. Natural logic says that talking is merely an incidental process concerned strictly with communication, not with formulation of ideas. Talking, or the use of language, is supposed only to "express" what is essentially already formulated nonlinguistically. Formulation is an independent process, called thought or thinking, and is supposed to be largely indifferent to the nature of particular languages. Languages have grammars, which are assumed to be merely norms of conventional and social correctness, but the use of language is supposed to be guided not so much by them as by correct, rational, or intelligent *thinking*.

Thought, in this view, does not depend on grammar but on laws of logic or reason which are supposed to be the same for all observers of the universe—to represent a rationale in the universe that can be "found" independently by all intelligent observers, whether they speak Chinese or Choctaw. In our own culture, the formulations of mathematics and of formal logic have acquired the reputation of dealing with this order of things, i.e., with the realm and laws of pure thought. Natural logic holds that different languages are essentially parallel methods for expressing this one-and-the-same rationale of thought and, hence, differ really in but minor ways which may seem important only because they are seen at close range. It holds that mathematics, symbolic logic, philosophy, and so on, are systems contrasted with language which deal directly with this realm of thought, not that they are themselves specialized extensions of language. The attitude of natural logic is well shown in an old quip about a German grammarian who devoted his whole life to the study of the dative case. From the point of view of natural logic, the dative case and grammar in general are an extremely minor issue. A different attitude is said to have been held by the ancient Arabians: Two princes, so the story goes, quarreled over the honor of putting on the shoes of the most learned grammarian of the realm; whereupon their father, the caliph, is said to have remarked that it was the glory of his kingdom that great grammarians were honored even above kings.

The familiar saying that the exception proves the rule contains a good deal of wisdom, though from the standpoint of formal logic it became an absurdity as soon as "prove" no longer meant "put on trial." The old saw began to be profound psychology from the time it ceased to have standing in logic. What it might well suggest to us today is that if a rule has absolutely no exceptions, it is not recognized as a rule or as anything else; it is then part of the background of experience of which we tend to remain unconscious. Never having experienced anything in contrast to it, we cannot isolate it and formulate it as a rule until we so enlarge our experiences and expand our base of reference that we encounter an interruption of its regularity. The situation is somewhat analogous to that of not missing the water till the well runs dry, or not realizing that we need air till we are choking.

For instance, if a race of people had the physiological defect of being able to see only the color blue, they would hardly be able to formulate the rule that they saw only blue. The term blue would convey no meaning to them, their language would lack color terms, and their words denoting their various sensations of blue would answer to, and translate, our words light, dark, white, black, and so on, not our word blue. In order to formulate the rule or norm of seeing only blue, they would need exceptional moments in which they saw other colors. The phenomenon of gravitation forms a rule without

Figure 1 Languages dissect nature differently. The different isolates of meaning (thoughts) used by English and Shawnee in reporting the same experience, that of cleaning a gun by running the ramrod through it. The pronouns "I" and "it" are not shown by symbols, as they have the same meaning in each case. In Shawnee "ni-" equals "I"; "-a" equals "it."

exceptions; needless to say, the untutored person is utterly unaware of any law of gravitation, for it would never enter his head to conceive of a universe in which bodies behaved otherwise than they do at the earth's surface. Like the color blue with our hypothetical race, the law of gravitation is a part of the untutored individual's background, not something he isolates from that background. The law could not be formulated until bodies that always fell were seen in terms of a wider astronomical world in which bodies moved in orbits or went this way and that.

Similarly, whenever we turn our heads, the image of the scene passes across our retinas exactly as it would if the scene turned around us. But this effect is background, and we do not recognize it; we do not see a room turn around us but are conscious only of having turned our heads in a stationary room. If we observe critically while turning the head or eyes quickly, we shall see, no motion it is true, yet a blurring of the scene between two clear views. Normally we are quite unconscious of this continual blurring but seem to be looking about in an unblurred world. Whenever we walk past a tree or house, its image on the retina changes just as if the tree or house were turning on an axis; yet we do not see trees or houses turn as we travel about at ordinary speeds. Sometimes ill-fitting glasses will reveal queer movements in the scene as we look about, but normally we do not see the relative motion of the environment when we move; our psychic make-up is somehow adjusted to disregard whole realms of phenomena that are so all-pervasive as to be irrelevant to our daily lives and needs.

Natural logic contains two fallacies: First, it does not see that the phenomena of a language are to its own speakers largely of a background character and so are outside the critical consciousness and control of the speaker who is expounding natural logic. Hence, when anyone, as a natural logician, is talking about reason, logic, and the laws of correct thinking, he is apt to be simply marching in step with purely grammatical facts that have somewhat of a background character in his own language or family of languages but are by no means universal in all languages and in no sense a common substratum of reason. Second, natural logic confuses agreement about subject matter, attained through use of language, with knowledge of the linguistic process by which agreement is attained, i.e., with the province of the despised (and to its notion superfluous) grammarian. Two fluent speakers, of English let us say, quickly reach a point of assent about the subject matter of this speech; they agree about what their language refers to. One of them, A, can give directions that will be carried out by the other, B, to A's complete satisfaction. Because they thus understand each other so perfectly, A and B, as natural logicians, suppose they must of course know how it is all done. They think, e.g., that it is simply a matter of choosing words to express thoughts. If you ask A to explain how he got B's agreement so readily, he will simply repeat to you, with more or less elaboration or abbreviation, what he said to B. He has no notion of the process involved. The amazingly complex system of linguistic patterns and classifications which A and B must have in common before they can adjust to each other at all, is all background to A and B.

These background phenomena are the province of the grammarian—or of the linguist, to give him his more modern name as a scientist. The word linguist in common, and especially newspaper, parlance means something entirely different, namely, a person who can quickly attain agreement about subject matter with different people speaking a number of different languages. Such a person is better termed a polyglot or a multilingual. Scientific linguists have long understood that ability to speak a language fluently does not necessarily confer a linguistic knowledge of it, i.e., understanding of its background phenomena and its systematic processes and structure, any more than ability to play a good game of billiards confers or requires any knowledge of the laws of mechanics that operate upon the billiard table.

The situation here is not unlike that in any other field of science. All real scientists have their eyes primarily on background phenomena that cut very little ice, as such, in our daily lives; and yet their studies have a way of bringing out a close relation between these unsuspected realms of fact and such decidedly foreground activities as transporting goods, preparing food, treating the sick, or growing potatoes, which in time may become very much modified simply because of pure scientific investigation in no way concerned with these brute matters themselves. Linguistics is in quite similar case; the background phenomena with which it deals are involved in all our foreground activities of talking and of reaching agreement, in all reasoning and arguing of cases, in all law, arbitration, conciliation, contracts, treaties, public opinion, weighing of scientific theories, formulation of scientific results. Whenever agreement or assent is arrived at in human affairs, and whether or not mathematics or other specialized symbolisms are made part of the procedure, *this agreement is reached by linguistic processes, or else it is not reached.*

As we have seen, an overt knowledge of the linguistic processes by which agreement is attained is not necessary to teaching some sort of agreement, but it is certainly no bar thereto; the more complicated and difficult the matter, the more such knowledge is a distinct aid, till the point may be reached—I suspect the modern world has about arrived at it—when the knowledge becomes not only an aid but a necessity. The situation may be likened to that of navigation. Every boat that sails is in the lap of planetary forces; yet a boy can pilot his small craft around a harbor without benefit of geography, astronomy, mathematics, or international politics. To the captain of an ocean liner, however, some knowledge of all these subjects is essential.

When linguists became able to examine critically and scientifically a large number of languages of widely different patterns, their base of reference was expanded; they experienced an interruption of phenomena hitherto held universal, and a whole new order of significances came into their ken. It was found that the background linguistic system (in other words, the grammar) of each language is not merely a reproducing instrument for voicing ideas but rather is itself the shaper of ideas, the program and guide for the individual's mental activity, for his analysis of impressions, for his synthesis of his mental stock in trade. Formulation of ideas is not an independent process, strictly rational in the old sense, but is part of a particular grammar and differs, from slightly to greatly, as between different grammars. We dissect nature along lines laid down by our native languages. The categories and types that we isolate from the world of phenomena we do not find there because they stare every observer in the face; on the contrary, the world is presented in a kaleidoscopic flux of impressions which has to be organized by our minds—and this means largely by the linguistic systems in our minds. We cut nature up, organize it into concepts, and ascribe significances as we do, largely because we are parties to an agreement to organize it in this way—an agreement that holds throughout our speech community and is codified in the patterns of our language. The agreement is, of course, an implicit and unstated one, *but its terms are absolutely obligatory;* we cannot talk at all except by subscribing to the organization and classification of data which the agreement decrees.

This fact is very significant for modern science, for it means that no individual is free to describe nature with absolute impartiality but is constrained to certain modes of interpretation even while he thinks himself most free. The person most nearly free in such respects would be a linguist familiar with very many widely different linguistic systems. As yet no linguist even is in any such position. We are thus introduced to a new principle of relativity, which holds that all observers are not led by the same physical evidence to the same picture of the universe, unless their linguistic backgrounds are similar, or can in some way be calibrated.

This rather startling conclusion is not so apparent if we compare only our modern European languages, with perhaps Latin and Greek thrown in for good measure. Among these tongues there is a unanimity of major pattern which at first seems to bear out natural logic. But this unanimity exists only because these tongues are all Indo-European dialects cut to the same basic plan, being historically transmitted from what was long ago one speech community; because the modern dialects have long shared in building up a common culture; and because much of this culture, on the more intellectual side, is derived from the linguistic backgrounds of Latin and Greek. Thus this group of languages satisfies the special case of the clause beginning ''unless'' in the statement of the linguistic relativity principle at the end of the preceding paragraph. From this condition follows the unanimity of description of the world in the community of modern scientists. But it must be emphasized that ''all modern Indo-European-speaking observers'' is not the same thing as ''all observers.'' That modern Chinese or Turkish scientists describe the world in the same terms as Western scientists means, of course, only that they have taken over bodily the entire Western system of rationalizations, not that they have corroborated that system from their native posts of observation.

When Semitic, Chinese, Tibetan, or African languages are contrasted with our own, the divergence in analysis of the world becomes more apparent; and when we bring in the native languages of the Americas, where speech communities for many millenniums have gone their ways independently of each other and of the Old World, the fact that languages dissect nature in many different ways becomes patent. The relativity of all conceptual systems, ours included, and their dependence upon language stand revealed. That American Indians speaking only their native tongues are never called upon to act as scientific observers is in no wise to the point. To exclude the evidence which their languages offer as to what the human mind can do is like expecting botanists to study nothing but food plants and hothouse roses and then tell us what the plant world is like!

Let us consider a few examples. In English we divide most of our words into two classes, which have different grammatical and logical properties. Class I we call nouns, e.g., ''house,'' ''man''; Class 2, verbs, e.g., ''hit,'' ''run.'' Many words of one class can act secondarily as of the other class, e.g., ''a hit,'' ''a run,'' or ''to man'' the boat, but on the primary level the division between the classes is absolute. Our language thus gives us a bipolar division of nature. But nature herself is not thus polarized. If it be said that strike, turn, run, are verbs because they denote temporary or short-lasting events, i.e., actions, why then is fist a noun? It also is a temporary event. Why are lightning, spark, wave, eddy, pulsation, flame, storm, phase, cycle, spasm, noise, emotion, nouns? They are temporary events. If man and house are nouns because they are long-lasting and stable events, i.e., things, what then are keep, adhere, extend, project, continue, persist, grow, dwell, and so on, doing among the verbs? If it be objected that possess, adhere, are verbs because they are stable relationships rather than stable percepts, why then should equilibrium, pressure, current, peace, group, nation, society, tribe, sister, or any kinship term, be among the nouns? It will be found that an ''event'' to *us* means ''what our language classes as a verb'' or something analogized therefrom. And it will be found that it is not possible to define event, thing, object, relationship, and so on, from nature, but that to define them always involves a circuitous return to the grammatical categories of the definer's language.

Figure 2. Languages classify items of experience differently. The class corresponding to one word and one thought in language A may be regarded by language B as two or more classes corresponding to two or more words and thoughts.

In the Hopi language, lightning, wave, flame, meteor, puff of smoke, pulsation, are verbs—events of necessarily brief duration cannot be anything but verbs. Cloud and storm are at about the lower limit of duration for nouns. Hopi, you see, actually has a classification of events (or linguistic isolates) by duration type, something strange to our modes of thought. On the other hand, in Nootka, a language of Vancouver Island, all words seem to us to be verbs, but really there are no Classes 1 and 2; we have, as it were, a monistic view of nature that gives us only one class of word for all kinds of events. "A house occurs" or "it houses" is the way of saying "house," exactly like "a flame occurs" or "it burns." These terms seem to us like verbs because they are inflected for durational and temporal nuances, so that the suffixes of the word for house event make it mean long-lasting house, temporary house, future house, house that used to be, what started out to be a house, and so on.

Hopi has a noun that covers every thing or being that flies, with the exception of birds, which class is denoted by another noun. The former noun may be said to denote the class (FC–B)—flying class minus bird. The Hopi actually call insect, airplane, and aviator all by the same word, and feel no difficulty about it. The situation, of course, decides any possible confusion among very disparate members of a broad linguistic class, such as this class (FC–B). This class seems to us too large and inclusive, but so would our class "snow" to an Eskimo. We have the same word for falling snow, snow on the ground, snow packed hard like ice, slushy snow, wind-driven flying snow—whatever the situation may be. To an Eskimo, this all-inclusive word would be almost unthinkable; he would say that falling snow, slushy snow, and so on, are sensuously and operationally different, different things to contend with; he uses different words for them and for other kinds of snow. The Aztecs go even farther than we in the opposite direction, with cold, ice, and snow all represented by the same basic word with different terminations; ice is the noun form; cold, the adjectival form; and for snow, "ice mist."

What surprises most is to find that various grand generalizations of the Western world, such as time, velocity, and matter, are not essential to the construction of a consistent picture of the universe. The psychic experiences that we class under these headings are, of course, not destroyed; rather, categories derived from other kinds of experiences take over the rulership of the cosmology and seem to function just as well. Hopi may be called a timeless language. It recognizes psychological time, which is much like Bergson's "duration," but this "time" is quite unlike the mathematical time, T, used by our physicists. Among the peculiar properties of Hopi time are that it varies with each observer, does not permit of simultaneity, and has zero dimensions, i.e., it cannot be given a number greater than one. The Hopi do not say, "I stayed five days," but "I left on the fifth day." A word referring to this kind of time, like the word day, can have no plural. The puzzle picture in Figure 3 will give mental exercise to anyone who would like to figure out how the Hopi verb gets along without tenses. Actually, the only practical use of our tenses, in one-verb sentences, is to distinguish among five typical situations, which are symbolized in the picture. The timeless Hopi verb does not distinguish between the present, past, and future of the event itself but must always indicate what type of validity the *speaker* intends the statement to have: (a) report of an event (situations 1, 2, 3 in the picture); (b) expectation of an event (situation 4); (c) generalization or law about events (situation 5). Situation 1, where the speaker and listener are in contact with the same objective field, is divided by our language into the two conditions, 1*a* and 1*b*, which it calls present and past, respectively. This division is unnecessary for a language which assures one that the statement is a report.

Hopi grammar, by means of its forms called aspects and modes, also makes it easy to distinguish between momentary, continued, and repeated occurrences, and to indicate the actual sequence of reported events. Thus the universe can be described without recourse to a concept of dimensional time. How would a physics constructed along these lines work, with no T (time) in its equations? Perfectly, as far as I can see, though of course it would require different ideology and perhaps different mathematics. Of course V (velocity) would have to go too. The Hopi language has no word really equivalent to our "speed" or "rapid." What translates these terms is usually a word meaning intense or very, accompanying any verb or motion. Here is a clew to the nature of our new physics. We may have to introduce a new term I, intensity. Every thing and event will have an I, whether we regard the thing or event as moving or as just enduring or being. Perhaps the I of an electric charge will turn out to be its voltage, or potential. We shall use clocks to measure some intensities, or, rather, some *relative* intensities, for the absolute intensity of anything will be meaningless. Our old friend acceleration will still be there but doubtless under a new name. We shall perhaps call it V, meaning not velocity but variation. Perhaps all growths and accumulations will be regarded as V's. We should not have the concept of rate in the temporal sense, since, like velocity, rate introduces a mathematical and linguistic time. Of course, we know that all measurements are ratios, but the measurements of intensities made by comparison with the standard intensity of a clock or a planet we do not treat as ratios, any more than we so treat a distance made by comparison with a yardstick.

A scientist from another culture that used time and velocity would have great difficulty in getting us to understand these concepts. We should talk about the intensity of a chemical reaction; he would speak of its velocity or its rate, which words we should at first think were simply words for intensity in his language. Likewise, he at first would think that intensity was simply our own word for velocity. At first we should agree, later we should begin to disagree, and it might dawn upon both sides that different systems of rationalization were being used. He would find it very hard to make us understand what he really meant by velocity of a chemical reaction. We should have no words that would fit. He would try to explain it by likening it to a running horse, to the difference between a good horse and a lazy horse. We should try to show him, with a superior laugh, that his analogy also was a matter of different intensities, aside from which there was little similarity between a horse and a chemical reaction in a beaker. We should point out that a running horse is moving relative to the ground, whereas the material in the beaker is at rest.

One significant contribution to science from the linguistic point of view may be the greater development of our sense of perspective. We shall no longer be able to see a few recent dialects of the Indo-European family, and the rationalizing techniques elaborated from their patterns, as the apex of the evolution of the human mind; nor their present wide spread as due to any survival from fitness or to anything but a few events of history—events that could be called fortunate only from the parochial point of view of the favored parties. They, and our own thought processes with them, can no longer be envisioned as spanning the gamut of reason and knowledge but only as one constellation in a galactic expanse. A fair realization of the incredible degree of diversity of linguistic system that ranges over the globe leaves one with an inescapable feeling that the human spirit is inconceivably old; that the few thousand years of history covered by our written records are no more than the thickness of a pencil mark on the scale that measures our past experience on this planet; that the events of these recent millenniums spell nothing

OBJECTIVE FIELD	SPEAKER (SENDER)	HEARER (RECEIVER)	HANDLING OF TOPIC RUNNING OF THIRD PERSON
SITUATION 1a			ENGLISH—"HE IS RUNNING" HOPI—"WARI" (RUNNING, STATEMENT OF FACT)
SITUATION 1b OBJECTIVE FIELD BLANK DEVOID OF RUNNING			ENGLISH—"HE RAN" HOPI—"WARI" (RUNNING, STATEMENT OF FACT)
SITUATION 2			ENGLISH—"HE IS RUNNING" HOPI—"WARI" (RUNNING, STATEMENT OF FACT)
SITUATION 3 OBJECTIVE FIELD BLANK			ENGLISH—"HE RAN" HOPI—"ERA WARI" (RUN-NING, STATEMENT OF FACT FROM MEMORY
SITUATION 4 OBJECTIVE FIELD BLANK			ENGLISH—"HE WILL RUN" HOPI—"WARIKNI" (RUN-NING, STATEMENT OF EXPECTATION)
SITUATION 5 OBJECTIVE FIELD BLANK			ENGLISH—"HE RUNS" (E.G. ON THE TRACK TEAM) HOPI—"WARIKNGWE" (RUNNING, STATE-MENT OF LAW)

Figure 3. Contrast between a "temporal" language (English) and a "timeless" language (Hopi). What are to English differences of time are to Hopi differences in the kind of validity.

in any evolutionary wise, that the race has taken no sudden spurt, achieved no commanding synthesis during recent millenniums, but has only played a little with a few of the linguistic formulations and views of nature bequeathed from an inexpressibly longer past. Yet neither this feeling nor the sense of precarious dependence of all we know upon linguistic tools which themselves are largely unknown need be discouraging to science but should, rather, foster that humility which accompanies the true scientific spirit, and thus forbid that arrogance of the mind which hinders real scientific curiosity and detachment.

DISCUSSION QUESTIONS

1. Have you ever found some knowledge of the involved linguistic processes helpful in reaching an agreement?

2. Test the familiar school definitions of a noun and a verb by Whorf's criticism. Are these definitions actually operational? Can you use them to find nouns and verbs?

3. When you say, "I like oranges," English requires you to think and use the plural even though number is really irrelevant. Find other examples of linguistic features or words that needlessly channel thought. Is the drive against sexism in language related to Whorf's thesis?

PART II

THE RECENT SCENE

No linguist in recent years has been more influential than Noam Chomsky. His *Syntactic Structures* (*SS*) (Mouton, 1957) began a major linguistic revolution that has been compared to the Copernican revolution in astronomy. Whenn *SS* first appeared, American Structuralism, as represented by the Nelson Francis article "Revolution in Grammar," reprinted here in Part I, was essentially the only active school in American linguistics. This descriptive school of linguistics searched through linguistic data beginning with the phoneme (the smallest element of sound), proceeded to the morpheme (the smallest unit of meaning), and finally examined syntax (the structure of the sentence). In contrast, the transformational-generative school, begun by Chomsky, was a sentence-generating school concerned with abstracting those rules in the head of the native speaker that enabled him to know and use language. The Chomsky selection, "The Current Scene in Linguistics," discusses the history of linguistics in light of two major traditions: philosophical, or formal, linguistics and descriptive linguistics.

From the beginning, Chomsky's major concern has been to determine what it is that people know when they know language and what it is in the human mind that allows essentially all human beings to learn the language spoken in their environment. Chomsky's concern for trying to capture in his theory the intuitions of native speakers about their language has led him to ask questions such as: What is it that allows every native speaker to understand a sentence the first time that he hears it; and, How is it that every native speaker of English is able to know that sentences (1) and (2) have essentially the same meaning, but that sentence (3), even though it has the same words as (1), has a different meaning?

(1) The car hit the man.
(2) The man was hit by the car.
(3) The man hit the car.

However, even by the time that "The Current Scene" was written in 1966, Transformational Grammar had undergone important alterations. Because the recent scene in linguistics has been so dominated by transformational-generative grammar, a brief synopsis of its history and development will be presented in the next few pages.

The *SS* model, also called the classical model, was essentially a phrase-structure grammar (PSG) to which a transformational component had been added. The PSG did two things: (1) it indicated what elements, or constituents, could be combined in any given language, and (2) what the basic order of the constituents must be in order to have a proper sentence. To illustrate how a PSG works, sentences (1) and (2) will be generated in Derivation 1a.

DERIVATION 1a

(i) S[entence] $\longrightarrow$ NP [noun phrase] + VP [verb phrase]

(ii) VP $\longrightarrow$ Verb + (NP)

(iii) Verb $\longrightarrow$ $\begin{Bmatrix} V_t \underline{\hspace{1em}} NP_1 \\ V_i \end{Bmatrix}$ [transitive verb] [intransitive verb]

(iv) NP $\longrightarrow$ Det[erminer] + N

(v) Det $\longrightarrow$ the, a

(vi) N $\longrightarrow$ car, man, tree, etc.

(vii) V_t $\longrightarrow$ hit, kick, go, etc.

(viii) V_i $\longrightarrow$ sleep, work, etc.

In the phrase-structure rules, the arrow indicates that the symbol on the left is to be rewritten as (or is composed of) the symbol or symbols on the right. Thus rule (i) states that a sentence is composed of a noun phrase and a verb phrase. Rules such as (iii) in which the symbol on the left is rewritten as different symbols on the right, depending upon the context, are called context-sensitive phrase-structure rules. Thus rule (iii) states that a verb is categorized as a V_t (transitive) if it is followed by a noun phrase; otherwise, it is categorized as V_i (intransitive). Rules such as (i) where the symbol on the left is always rewritten as the symbol on the right, or in other words where the context does not affect the rule, are called context-free phrase-structure rules. Symbols that are enclosed in parentheses, such as NP in rule (ii), are optional. In other words, rule (ii) states that some verb phrases have objects and some do not.

The phrase structure rules in Derivation 1a produce the phrase-structure tree shown in Derivation 1b.

DERIVATION 1b

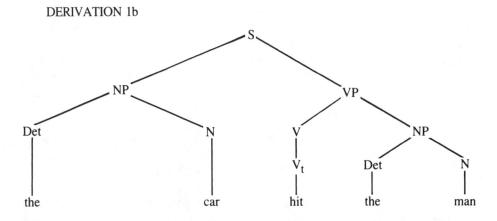

Of course, the same set of phrase-structure rules will produce *the man hit the car*. In fact, with additional vocabulary entries, in rule (vi), this set of rules will account for most simple English sentences that are of the subject-verb-object structure or are of the subject-verb structure.

After the phrase-structure tree is produced, transformational rules can take the phrase-structure tree and rearrange the parts, or constituents, by moving an element, deleting an element, inserting an element, or substituting one for another. For instance, sentence (2), *the man was hit by the car,* results from the passive transformation being applied to the phrase-structure tree in derivation 1b. A simplified example of how the passive transformation operates is shown in Derivation 1c.

DERIVATION 1c

$$NP_1 + V + NP_2 \implies NP_2 + BE + V + by + NP_1$$
$$\text{the car} + \text{hit} + \text{the man} \implies \text{the man} + \text{was} + \text{hit} + \text{by} + \text{the car}$$

As Derivation 1c illustrates, the passive transformation interchanges the subject and object noun phrases, inserts a form of the verb *to be,* and inserts *by* before the NP_1. Thus we can see why sentences (1) and (2) have the same meaning: they have the same phrase structure, including lexical items. Since their difference results only from the passive transformation, and transformations do not change meaning, they have the same meaning. Sentence (3) differs from sentences (1) and (2) because, even though it has the same lexical items as sentence (1), it has a different phrase structure.

In the *SS* model of transformational grammar, a simple sentence such as *the car hit the man* was called a kernel sentence. Compound and complex sentences were formed by combining kernel sentences by transformations. Thus sentence (4) would be the result of joining sentences (5) and (6) by transformations.

(4) Bill, who is my friend, went home.
(5) Bill is my friend.
(6) Bill went home.

The Standard Theory, developed by Chomsky in 1965 in his *Aspects of the Theory of Syntax (ATS),* significantly improved the earlier model. In this model, a distinction was made between surface structure and deep structure. Deep structure was generated by the phrase structure and determined fully the meaning of the sentence. Transformations operated on deep structure, without changing the meaning, to form surface structure, the sentence that we actually hear. Another important modification in the Standard Theory was the introduction of syntactic features that allowed lexical items (words) to be inserted directly into the phrase structure, thus eliminating context-sensitive phrase-structure rules. Through the use of lexical features, words could be classified in several ways at the same time. For example, *child* would be classified as [+ animate] and [+ human] while *dog* would be classified as [+ animate] and [− human]. Thus both *child* and *dog* could be inserted into a sentence that required an animate subject such as sentence (7) to form either (7a) or (7b), but only *child* can be inserted into sentence (8), which requires a human subject.

(7a) The child ate the steak.
(7b) The dog ate the steak.
(8a) The child read the book.
(8b) *The dog read the book.

Sentences such as (8b) have an * in front of them to show that they are considered deviant or not to be accepted literally in normal conversation.

The use of these features allowed the separation of the lexicon, or vocabulary, from the PSG. The lexicon now, like any dictionary, consisted of a collection of lexical items, each of which fully specified the syntactic, phonological, and semantic properties of that word. Words could be inserted into any constituent where there was no conflict in syntactic features between the word and the constituent into which it was being placed. Thus in our example, (8b) could not be generated because the noun *dog* has the feature [−human] and the verb *read* has the feature [+human]. Also, in the Standard Theory, complex and compound sentences were generated by the PSG rather than being simple sentences joined together by transformations.

In the 1960s, the study of grammar was in a turbulent state. Besides Transformational Grammar, Stratificational Grammar was being developed by Sidney Lamb and his followers. Influenced by glossematics, the theory of the Danish linguist Louis Hjelmslev, and his own work in machine translation, Lamb merged the levels of phonology, morphology, syntax, and semantics in a manner that viewed language as a system of relationships. This system allowed the speaker to use the whole system at once rather than maintain a separation of levels as in Transformational Grammar.

If you wish to examine Stratificational Grammar, consult Lamb's *Outline of Stratificational Grammar* (Yale University Press, 1962) or John Algeo's "Stratificational Grammar" (*Journal of English Linguistics,* 3[1969] 1–7).

Through the early 1960s, Transformational Grammar essentially had a single unified theory, but by the middle of the decade, schisms began to develop. In particular there were problems caused by the condition that meaning resided in deep structure and by the condition that transformations could not change meaning. Chomsky himself was presenting major changes in these areas in his lectures at MIT as early as 1965, the year that *ATS* was published. They led to the Extended Standard Theory (EST) and later to the Revised Extended Standard Theory (REST). These will be discussed a little later in the introduction.

The Generative Semantics School of Transformational Grammar originated during the middle 1960s because, in their work on English syntax, linguists such as Paul Postal, George Lakoff, John Ross, and James D. McCawley were forced into proposing deep structures that were continually coming closer to semantic structures. It was determined that at some level of deep structure verbs and adjectives had to be considered members of the same class, as did personal pronouns and definite articles. (For a thorough discussion of this issue, see Paul Postal's, "On So-Called Pronouns in English," in *The 19th Monograph on Language and Linguistics,* ed. Francis Dineen [Washington, D.C.: Georgetown University Press, 1966], pp. 78–206.)

However, the strongest attacks on the Standard Theory came as the result of the three following conditions: (1) that all lexical items be inserted into the phrase structure at the level of deep structure, (2) that all meaning is contained in the deep structure, and (3) that transformations do not change meaning. It followed from conditions (1) and (2) that if two sentences had the same meaning, then they should have the same deep structure. Thus *John killed Jerry* should have the same deep structure as *John caused Jerry to die.* In other words, one of the two sentences should be transformationally derived from the other. Clearly this presented a problem: *cause to die* does not necessarily mean the same as *kill.* Condition (3) came into serious question when it was discovered that transformed sentences do not always mean the same as those from which they are transformed. For example, active sentences do not always have the same meaning as their passive counterparts, as noted in sentences (9) and (10).

9a. Everyone loves someone.
9b. Someone is loved by everyone.
10a. Beavers build dams.
10b. Dams are built by beavers.

One meaning of (9b) is that there is someone (a single person) such that everyone loves him. Clearly, this is not a meaning of (9a). In (10b), one of the meanings is that all dams are built by beavers. It is clear that this is not one of the meanings of sentence (10a). Examples such as the above demonstrated that deep structure as it was proposed in the Standard Theory would either have to be revised or rejected. Because the solutions proposed by the generative semanticists kept getting closer to semantic structure, they proposed that sentences were generated directly from meaning.

Case Grammar, the second offshoot of the Standard Theory, is associated primarily with the work of Charles Fillmore (see his "The Case for Case" in *Universals in Linguistic Theory*, eds. Emmon Bach and Robert T. Harms [New York: Holt, Rinehart and Winston, 1968], pp. 1–90). This model was a reaction to the failure of the Standard Theory to distinguish the semantic roles of the NPs in relation to their verbs. The term "case" was used in a way similar to its use in Latin and Greek-style declensions which tend to show the different kinds of involvement that a participant (noun) might have in an action (verb). The basic structure of the sentence in Case Grammar consisted of a verb and one or more noun phrases, each associated with the verb in a particular case relationship.

While Fillmore proposed six cases and suggested that more might be needed, the use of three will suffice to illustrate how his grammar works. The cases are agentive, instrumental, and objective. If an animate being was perceived as the instigator of an action, the NP would be in the agentive case; if an inanimate force or object was perceived as causally involved in the action, the NP would be in the instrumental case; and if the role of the NP was identified by the action of the verb, the NP would be in the objective case. Sentences (11) through (14) illustrate how Case Grammar functions:

(11)   John broke the window with a hammer.
(12)   The window was broken by John with a hammer.
(13)   The window was broken.
(14)   John broke the window.
(15)   The hammer broke the window.

In each of the sentences in which *John* appears, (11), (12), and (14), it is in the agentive case. In all of the sentences *window* is in the objective case, and *hammer* is in the instrumental case in sentences (11), (12), and (15).

As sentences (11) through (15) illustrate, there was thought to be a universal ordering of cases. If there were an agent noun in the sentence, it would become its logical subject; if there were no agent, the instrumental case would become the subject; and if there were no instrumental case, the objective case would become the subject.

The model of Transformational Grammar that seems to be the dominant theory at the present time is the Extended Standard Theory (EST), sometimes called the Revised Extended Standard Theory (REST). Like the Standard Theory, it has a phrase-structure grammar that has context-free phrase-structure rules that generate the base, or deep structure, but deep structure only determines thematic relations (similar to Fillmore's use of case). These deep structures are then turned into surface structures by transformations. The deep structure (or "D structure" as it is called to distinguish it from deep structure in the Standard Theory) is "deeper" than the deep structure of the Standard Theory. In fact, surface structure (or "S structure" as it is called in REST) is almost as "deep" as the deep structure in the Standard model. The REST model differs from Generative Semantics in that the semantic element of the sentence is assigned after the transformations have been performed, rather than existing as the starting point. For the advanced student of Transformational Grammar who wishes to study the REST model as developed by Chomsky, *Rules and Representations* (Columbia University Press, 1980) is a good place to begin. The student with no previous knowledge of Transformational Grammar will find Suzette Elgin's *A Primer of Transformational Grammar for Rank Beginners* (NCTE, 1975) helpful. Students interested in the history of Transformational Grammar should read Frederick J. Newmeyer's *Linguistic Theory in America* (Academic Press, 1980).

The second selection in this section, "Knowledge of Language" by Neil Smith and Deirdre Wilson, while based on the theory of Chomsky, is an eclectic approach to Transformational Grammar that illustrates how Chomsky has been able to synthesize his concept on the psychology of man and his concept of the language of man. Elaine Chaika's article "Grammars and Teaching" in Part VI may be profitably read at this time.

While transformationalists were developing their theories of grammar, the tagmemicists, departing from American Structuralism as described by Francis in Part I, offered new techniques and methodologies for gathering and classifying data. The central figure in this school has been Kenneth Pike, who, in *Language in Relation to a Unified Theory of Human Behavior,* portrayed all human activity as being patterned much the same way that language is. However, tagmemics disassociated itself from certain doctrinal precepts of the structuralists, such as the nonmixing of levels. A brief overview of this still flourishing school of linguistics with its emphasis on data gathering is presented by John Algeo. If you wish to pursue tagmemics further, in addition to the references mentioned by Algeo, read Kasimierz Sroka's "A Review of Kenneth Pike, *Language in Relation to a Unified Field Theory of the Structure of Human Behavior*" in *Linguistics* 85 (1972): 72–103.

Although the preceding discussion dealt primarily with the syntactic component of grammar, we should not overlook the accompanying development of phonological theory. The next article by Adrian Akmajian, Richard Demers, and Robert Harnish presents an eclectic view of phonology that modifies the articulatory phonology used by the American structuralists, the distinctive feature matrix developed by Roman Jakobson, and the generative rules formulated by Chomsky and Morris Halle. For further work on structural phonology, you can begin with H. A. Gleason, Jr.'s *An Introduction to Descriptive Linguistics* (2nd ed., Holt, Rinehart and Winston, 1961). A good starting point for generative phonology is Sanford Schane's *A Generative Phonology* (Prentice-Hall, 1973). Though it is difficult, you should also consult Chomsky and Halle's *The Sound Pattern of English* (Harper and Row, 1968).

The last three articles in this section examine important, but not mainstream or theoretical, topics. In the first, George Lakoff, at a time when most linguists were concentrating on formal or mathematical solutions to linguistic problems, argues that linguists need to expand the scope of their studies beyond problems that lend themselves to formal solutions. He emphasizes that there are symbiotic relationships between linguistics and other disciplines. Michael Linn describes the nature of pidgin and creole languages and demonstrates that language change is often the result of cultural and social change. If you are interested in learning more about pidgin and creole languages, consult the bibliography at the end of Linn's article. In the last article in this section, George Miller describes how man communicates with more than just verbal language. You who are interested in nonverbal communication will find the following of value:

Birdwhistell, Ray. *Kinesic and Context: Essays on Body Communication*. Philadelphia: University of Pennsylvania Press, 1970.

Hall, Edward T. *The Silent Language*. Garden City, N.Y.: Doubleday, 1959.

While the aforementioned studies of language were flourishing in the United States, the great scholarly tradition in English grammar, represented by Jespersen, Poutsma, Curme, and Kruisinga, still continued in England under the leadership of Randolph Quirk. For a current view of this comprehensive description of the surface structure of the English language, consult the two following books:

Leech, Geoffrey, and Jan Svartvik. *A Communicative Grammar of English*. London: Longman, 1975.

Quirk, Randolph, Sidney Greenbaum, and Geoffrey Leech. *A Contempory Grammar of English*. New York: Seminar Press, 1973.

NOAM CHOMSKY

The best-known and most influential contemporary American linguist, Chomsky began to formulate the theory of transformational-generative grammar while a student under Zellig Harris at the University of Pennsylvania. As Institute professor of linguistics and philosophy at the Massachusetts Institute of Technology he continues to publish dynamic articles and books challenging traditional views in linguistics and psycholinguistics and offering expansions and modifications of transformational theory.

THE CURRENT SCENE IN LINGUISTICS: PRESENT DIRECTIONS

The title of this paper may suggest something more than can be provided. It would be foolhardy to attempt to forecast the development of linguistics or any other field, even in general terms and in the short run. There is no way to anticipate ideas and insights that may, at any time, direct research in new directions or reopen traditional problems that had been too difficult or too unclear to provide a fruitful challenge. The most that one can hope to do is to arrive at a clear appraisal of the present situation in linguistic research, and an accurate understanding of historical tendencies. It would not be realistic to attempt to project such tendencies into the future.

Two major traditions can be distinguished in modern linguistic theory: one is the tradition of "universal" or "philosophical grammar," which flourished in the seventeenth and eighteenth centuries; the second is the tradition of structural or descriptive linguistics, which reached the high point of its development perhaps fifteen or twenty years ago. I think that a synthesis of these two major traditions is possible, and that it is, to some extent, being achieved in current work. Before approaching the problem of synthesis, I would like to sketch briefly—and, necessarily, with some oversimplification—what seem to me to be the most significant features in these two traditions.

As the name indicates, universal grammar was concerned with general features of language structure rather than with particular idiosyncrasies. Particularly in France, universal grammar developed in part in reaction to an earlier descriptivist tradition which held that the only proper task for the grammarian was to present data, to give a kind of "natural history" of language (specifically, of the "cultivated usage" of the court and the best writers). In contrast, universal grammarians urged that the study of language should be elevated from the level of "natural history" to that of "natural philosophy"; hence the term "philosophical grammar," "philosophical" being used, of course, in essentially the sense of our term "scientific." Grammar should not be merely a record of the data of usage, but, rather, should offer an explanation for such data. It should establish general principles, applicable to all languages and based ultimately on intrinsic properties of the mind, which would explain how language is used and why it has the particular properties to which the descriptive grammarian chooses, irrationally, to restrict his attention.

Universal grammarians did not content themselves with merely stating this goal. In fact, many generations of scholars proceeded to develop a rich and far-reaching account of the general principles of language structure, supported by whatever detailed evidence they could find from the linguistic materials available to them. On the basis of these principles, they attempted to explain many particular facts, and to develop a psychological theory dealing with certain aspects of language use, with the production and comprehension of sentences.

The tradition of universal grammar came to an abrupt end in the nineteenth century, for reasons that I will discuss directly. Furthermore, its achievements were very rapidly forgotten, and an interesting mythology developed concerning its limitations and excesses. It has now become something of a cliché among linguists that universal grammar suffered from the following defects: (1) it was not concerned with the sounds of speech, but only with writing; (2) it was based primarily on a Latin model, and was, in some sense "prescriptive"; (3) its assumptions about language structure have been refuted by modern "anthropological linguistics." In addition, many linguists, though not all, would hold that universal grammar was misguided in principle in its attempt to provide explanations rather than mere description of usage, the latter being all that can be contemplated by the "sober scientist."

The first two criticisms are quite easy to refute; the third and fourth are more interesting. Even a cursory glance at the texts will show that phonetics was a major concern of universal grammarians, and that their phonetic theories were not very different from our own. Nor have I been able to discover any confusion of speech and writing. The belief that universal grammar was based on a Latin model is rather curious. In fact, the earliest studies of universal grammar, in France, were a part of the movement to raise the status of the vernacular, and are concerned with details of French that often do not even have any Latin analogue.

As to the belief that modern "anthropological linguistics" has refuted the assumptions of universal grammar, this is not only untrue, but, for a rather important reason, could not be true. The reason is that universal grammar made a sharp distinction between what we may call "deep structure" and "surface structure." The deep structure of a sentence is the abstract underlying form which determines the meaning of the sentence; it is present in the mind but not necessarily represented directly in the physical signal. The surface structure of a sentence is the actual organization of the physical signal into phrases of varying size, into words of various categories, with certain particles, inflections, arrangement, and so on. The fundamental assumption of the universal grammarians was that languages scarcely differ at the level of deep structure—which reflects the basic properties of thought and conception—but that they may vary widely at the much less interesting level of surface structure. But modern anthropological linguistics does not attempt to deal with deep structure and its relations to surface structure. Rather, its attention is limited to surface structure—to the phonetic form of an utterance and its organization into units of varying size. Consequently, the information that it provides has no direct bearing on the hypotheses concerning deep structure postulated by the universal grammarians. And, in fact, it seems to me that what information is now available to us suggests not that they went too far in assuming universality of underlying structure, but that they may have been much too cautious and restrained in what they proposed.

The fourth criticism of universal grammar—namely, that it was misguided in seeking explanations in the first place—I will not discuss. It seems to me that this criticism is based on a misunderstanding of the nature of all rational inquiry. There is particular irony in the fact that this criticism should be advanced with the avowed intention of making linguistics "scientific." It is hardly open to question that the natural sciences are concerned precisely with the problem of explaining phenomena, and have little use for accurate description that is unrelated to problems of explanation.

I think that we have much to learn from a careful study of what was achieved by the universal grammarians of the seventeenth and eighteenth centuries. It seems to me, in fact, that contemporary linguistics would do well to take their concept of language as a point of departure for current work. Not only do they make a fairly clear and well-founded distinction between deep and surface structure, but they also go on to study the nature of deep structure and to provide valuable hints and insights concerning the rules that relate the abstract underlying mental structures to surface form, the rules that we would now call "grammatical transformations." What is more, universal grammar developed as part of a general philosophical tradition that provided deep and important insights, also largely forgotten, into the use and acquisition of language, and furthermore, into problems of perception and acquisition of knowledge in general. These insights can be exploited and developed. The idea that the study of language should proceed within the framework of what we might nowadays call "cognitive psychology" is sound. There is much truth in the traditional view that language provides the most effective means for studying the nature and mechanisms of the human mind, and that only within this context can we perceive the larger issues that determine the directions in which the study of language should develop.

The tradition of universal grammar came to an end more than a century ago. Several factors combined to lead to its decline. For one thing, the problems posed were beyond the scope of the technique and understanding then available. The problem of formulating the rules that determine deep structures and relate them to surface structures, and the deeper problem of determining the general abstract characteristics of these rules, could not be studied with any precision, and discussion therefore remained at the level of hints, examples, and vaguely formulated intentions. In particular, the problem of rule-governed creativity in language simply could not be formulated with sufficient precision to permit research to proceed very far. A second reason for the decline of traditional linguistic theory lies in the remarkable successes of Indo-European comparative linguistics in the nineteenth century. These achievements appeared to dwarf the accomplishments of universal grammar, and led many linguists to scoff at the "metaphysical" and "airy pronouncements" of those who were attempting to deal with a much wider range of problems—and at that particular stage of the development of linguistic theory, were discussing these topics in a highly inconclusive fashion. Looking back now, we can see quite clearly that the concept of language employed by the Indo-European comparativists was an extremely primitive one. It was, however, well-suited to the tasks at hand. It is, therefore, not too surprising that this concept of language, which was then extended and developed by the structural and descriptive linguists of the twentieth century, became almost completely dominant, and that the older tradition of linguistic theory was largely swept aside and forgotten. This is hardly a unique instance in intellectual history.

Structural linguistics is a direct outgrowth of the concepts that emerged in Indo-European comparative study, which was primarily concerned with language as a system of phonological units that undergo systematic modification in phonetically determined contexts. Structural linguistics reinterpreted this concept for a fixed state of a language, investigated the relations among such units and the patterns they form, and attempted, with varying success, to extend the same kind of analysis to "higher levels" of linguistic structure. Its fundamental assumption is that procedures of segmentation and classification, applied to data in a systematic way, can isolate and identify all types of elements that function in a particular language along with the constraints that they obey. A catalogue of these elements, their relations, and their restrictions of "distribution," would, in most structuralist views, constitute a full grammar of the language.

Structural linguistics has very real accomplishments to its credit. To me, it seems that its major achievement is to have provided a factual and a methodological basis that makes it possible to return to the problems that occupied the traditional universal grammarians with some hope of extending and deepening their theory of language structure and language use. Modern descriptive linguistics has enormously enriched the range of factual material available, and has provided entirely new standards of clarity and objectivity. Given this advance in precision and objectivity, it becomes possible to return, with new hope for success, to the problem of constructing the theory of a particular language— its grammar—and to the still more ambitious study of the general theory of language. On the other hand, it seems to me that the substantive contributions to the theory of language structure are few, and that, to a large extent, the concepts of modern linguistics constitute a retrogression as compared with universal grammar. One real advance has been in universal phonetics—I refer here particularly to the work of Jakobson. Other new and important insights might also be cited. But in general, the major contributions of structural linguistics seem to me to be methodological rather than substantive. These methodological contributions are not limited to a raising of the standards of precision. In a more subtle way, the idea that language can be studied as a formal system, a notion which is developed with force and effectiveness in the work of Harris and Hockett, is of particular significance. It is, in fact, this general insight and the techniques that emerged as it developed that have made it possible, in the last few years, to approach the traditional problems once again. Specifically, it is now possible to study the problem of rule-governed creativity in natural language, the problem of constructing grammars that explicitly generate deep and surface structures and express the relations between them, and the deeper problem of determining the universal conditions that limit the form and organization of rules in the grammar of a human language. When these problems are clearly formulated and studied, we are led to a conception of language not unlike that suggested in universal grammar. Furthermore, I think that we are led to conclusions regarding mental processes of very much the sort that were developed, with care and insight, in the rationalist philosophy of mind that provided the intellectual background for universal grammar. It is in this sense that I think we can look forward to a productive synthesis of the two major traditions of linguistic research.

If this point of view is correct in essentials, we can proceed to outline the problems facing the linguist in the following way. He is, first of all, concerned to report data accurately. What is less obvious, but nonetheless correct, is that the data will not be of particular interest to him in itself, but rather only insofar as it sheds light on the grammar of the language from which it is drawn, where by the "grammar of a language" I mean the theory that deals with the mechanisms of sentence construction, which establish a sound-meaning relation in this language. At the next level of study, the linguist is concerned to give a factually accurate formulation of this grammar, that is, a correct formulation of the rules that generate deep and surface structures and interrelate them, and the rules that give a phonetic interpretation of surface structures and a semantic interpretation of deep structures. But, once again, this correct statement of the grammatical principles of a language is not primarily of interest in itself, but only insofar as it sheds light on the more general question of the nature of language; that is, the nature of universal grammar. The primary interest of a correct grammar is that it provides the basis for substantiating or refuting a general theory of linguistic structure which establishes general principles concerning the form of grammar.

Continuing one step higher in level of abstraction, a universal grammar—a general theory of linguistic structure that determines the form of grammar—is primarily of interest for the information it provides concerning innate intellectual structure. Specifically, a general theory of this sort itself must provide a hypothesis concerning innate intellectual structure of sufficient richness to account for the fact that the child acquires a given grammar on the basis of the data available to him. More generally, both a grammar of a particular language and a general theory of language are of interest primarily because of the insight they provide concerning the nature of mental processes, the mechanisms of perception and production and the mechanisms by which knowledge is acquired. There can be little doubt that both specific theories of particular languages and the general theory of linguistic structure provide very relevant evidence for anyone concerned with these matters; to me it seems quite obvious that it is within this general framework that linguistic research finds its intellectual justification.

At every level of abstraction, the linguist is concerned with explanation, not merely with stating facts in one form or another. He tries to construct a grammar which explains particular data on the basis of general principles that govern the language in question. He is interested in explaining these general principles themselves, by showing how they are derived from still more general and abstract postulates drawn from universal grammar. And he would ultimately have to find a way to account for universal grammar on the basis of still more general principles of human mental structure. Finally, although this goal is too remote to be seriously considered, he might envision the prospect that the kind of evidence he can provide may lead to a physiological explanation for this entire range of phenomena.

I should stress that what I have sketched is a logical, not a temporal order of tasks of increasing abstractness. For example, it is not necessary to delay the study of general linguistic theory until particular grammars are available for many languages. Quite the contrary. The study of paticular grammars will be fruitful only insofar as it is based on a precisely articulated theory of linguistic structure, just as the study of particular facts is worth undertaking only when it is guided by some general assumptions about the grammar of the language from which these observations are drawn.

All of this is rather abstract. Let me try to bring the discussion down to earth by mentioning a few particular problems, in the grammar of English, that point to the need for explanatory hypotheses of the sort I have been discussing.

Consider the comparative construction in English; in particular, such sentences as:

>   (1) I have never seen a man taller than John.
>   (2) I have never seen a taller man than John.

Sentences (1) and (2), along with innumerable others, suggest that there should be a rule of English that permits a sentence containing a Noun followed by a Comparative Adjective to be transformed into the corresponding sentence containing the sequence: Comparative Adjective–Noun. This rule would then appear as a special case of the very general rule that forms such Adjective-Noun constructions as "the tall man" from the underlying form "the man who is tall," and so on.

But now consider the sentence:

>   (3) I have never seen a man taller than Mary.

This is perfectly analogous to (1); but we cannot use the rule just mentioned to form

(4) I have never seen a taller man than Mary.

In fact, the sentence (4) is certainly not synonymous with (3), although (2) appears to be synonymous with (1). Sentence (4) implies that Mary is a man although (3) does not. Clearly either the proposed analysis is incorrect, despite the very considerable support one can find for it, or there is some specific condition in English grammar that explains why the rule in question can be used to form (2) but not (4). In either case, a serious explanation is lacking; there is some principle of English grammar, now unknown, for which we must search to explain these facts. The facts are quite clear. They are of no particular interest in themselves, but if they can bring to light some general principle of English grammar, they will be of real significance.

Furthermore, we must ask how every speaker of English comes to acquire this still unknown principle of English grammar. We must, in other words, try to determine what general concept of linguistic structure he employs that leads him to the conclusion that the grammar of English treats (1) and (2) as paraphrases but not the superficially similar pair (3) and (4). This still unknown principle of English grammar may lead us to discover the relevant abstract principle of linguistic structure. It is this hope, of course, that motivates the search for the relevant principle of English grammar.

Innumerable examples can be given of this sort. I will mention just one more. Consider the synonymous sentences (5) and (6):

(5) It would be difficult for him to understand *this*.
(6) For him to understand *this* would be difficult.

Corresponding to (5), we can form relative clauses and questions such as (7):

(7) (i) something which it would be difficult for him to understand
    (ii) what would it be difficult for him to understand?

But there is some principle that prevents the formation of the corresponding constructions of (8), formed in the analogous way from (6):

(8) (i) something which for him to understand would be difficult
    (ii) what would for him to understand be difficult?

The nonsentences of (8) are formed from (6) by exactly the same process that forms the correct sentences of (7) from (5); namely, pronominalization in the position occupied by "this," and a reordering operation. But in the case of (6), something blocks the operation of the rules for forming relative clauses and interrogatives. Again, the facts are interesting because they indicate that some general principle of English grammar must be functioning, unconsciously; and, at the next level of abstraction, they raise the question what general concept of linguistic structure is used by the person learning the language to enable him to acquire the particular principle that explains the difference between (7) and (8).

Notice that there is nothing particularly esoteric about these examples. The processes that form comparative, relative, and interrogative constructions are among the simplest and most obvious in English grammar. Every normal speaker has mastered these processes at an early age. But when we take a really careful look, we find much that is mysterious in these very elementary processes of grammar.

Whatever aspect of a language one studies, problems of this sort abound. There are very few well-supported answers, either at the level of particular or universal grammar.

The linguist who is content merely to record and organize phenomena, and to devise appropriate terminologies, will never come face to face with these problems. They only arise when he attempts to construct a precise system of rules that generate deep structures and relate them to corresponding surface structures. But this is just another way of saying that "pure descriptivism" is not fruitful, that progress in linguistics, as in any other field of inquiry, requires that at every stage of our knowledge and understanding we pursue the search for a deeper explanatory theory.

I would like to conclude with just a few remarks about two problems that are of direct concern to teachers of English. The first is the problem of which grammar to teach, the second, the problem why grammar should be taught at all.

If one thinks of a grammar of English as a theory of English structure, then the question which grammar to teach is no different in principle from the problem facing the biologist who has to decide which of several competing theories to teach. The answer, in either case, is that he should teach the one which appears to be true, given the evidence presently available. Where the evidence does not justify a clear decision, this should be brought to the student's attention and he should be presented with the case for the various alternatives. But in the case of teaching grammar, the issue is often confused by a pseudo-problem, which I think deserves some further discussion.

To facilitate this discussion, let me introduce some terminology. I will use the term "generative grammar" to refer to a theory of language in the sense described above, that is, a system of rules that determine the deep and surface structures of the language in question, the relation between them, the semantic interpretation of the deep structures and the phonetic interpretation of the surface structures. The generative grammar of a language, then, is the system of rules which establishes the relation between sound and meaning in this language. Suppose that the teacher is faced with the question: which generative grammar of English shall I teach? The answer is straightforward in principle, however difficult the problem may be to settle in practice. The answer is, simply: teach the one that is correct.

But generally the problem is posed in rather different terms. There has been a great deal of discussion of the choice not between competing generative grammars, but between a generative grammar and a "descriptive grammar." A "descriptive grammar" is not a theory of the language in the sense described above; it is not, in other words, a system of rules that establishes the sound-meaning correspondence in the language, insofar as this can be precisely expressed. Rather, it is an inventory of elements of various kinds that play a role in the language. For example, a descriptive grammar of English might contain an inventory of phonetic units, of phonemes, of morphemes, of words, of lexical categories, and of phrases or phrase types. Of course the inventory of phrases or phrase types cannot be completed since it is infinite, but let us put aside this difficulty.

It is clear, however, that the choice between a generative grammar and a descriptive grammar is not a genuine one. Actually, a descriptive grammar can be immediately derived from a generative grammar, but not conversely. Given a generative grammar, we can derive the inventories of elements that appear at various levels. The descriptive grammar, in the sense just outlined, is simply one aspect of the full generative grammar. It is an epiphenomenon, derivable from the full system of rules and principles that constitutes the generative grammar. The choice, then, is not between two competing grammars, but between a grammar and one particular aspect of this grammar. To me it seems obvious how this choice should be resolved, since the particular aspect that is isolated in the descriptive grammar seems to be of little independent importance. Surely the principles that determine the inventory, and much else, are more important than the inventory itself. In any event, the nature of the choice is clear; it is not a choice between competing systems, but rather a choice between the whole and a part.

Although I think what I have just said is literally correct, it is still somewhat misleading. I have characterized a descriptive grammar as one particular aspect of a full generative grammar, but actually the concept "descriptive grammar" arose in modern linguistics in a rather different way. A descriptive grammar was itself regarded as a full account of the language. It was, in other words, assumed that the inventory of elements exhausts the grammatical description of the language. Once we have listed the phones, phonemes, etc., we have given a full description of grammatical structure. The grammar is, simply, the collection of these various inventories.

This observation suggests a way of formulating the difference between generative and descriptive grammars in terms of a factual assumption about the nature of language. Let us suppose that a theory of language will consist of a definition of the notion "grammar," as well as definitions of various kinds of units (e.g., phonological units, morphological units, etc.). When we apply such a general theory to data, we use the definitions to find a particular grammar and a particular collection of units. Consider now two theories of this sort that differ in the following way. In one, the units of various kinds are defined independently of the notion "grammar"; the grammar, then, is simply the collection of the various kinds of unit. For example, we define "phoneme," "morpheme," etc., in terms of certain analytic procedures, and define the "grammar" to be the collection of units derived by applying these procedures. In the other theory, the situation is reversed. The notion "grammar" is defined independently of the various kinds of unit; the grammar is a system of such-and-such a kind. The units of various kinds are defined in terms of the logically prior concept "grammar." They are whatever appears in the grammar at such-and-such a level of functioning.

The difference between these two kinds of theory is quite an important one. It is a difference of factual assumption. The intuition that lies behind descriptive grammar is that the units are logically prior to the grammar, which is merely a collection of units. The intuition that lies behind the development of generative grammar is the opposite; it is that the grammar is logically prior to the units, which are merely the elements that appear at a particular stage in the functioning of grammatical processes. We can interpret this controversy in terms of its implications as to the nature of language acquisition. One who accepts the point of view of descriptive grammar will expect language acquisition to be a process of accretion, marked by gradual growth in the size of inventories, the elements of the inventories being developed by some sort of analytic or inductive procedures. One who accepts the underlying point of view of generative grammar will expect, rather, that the process of language acquisition must be more like that of selecting a particular hypothesis from a restricted class of possible hypotheses, on the basis of limited data. The selected hypothesis is the grammar; once accepted, it determines a system of relations among elements and inventories of various sorts. There will, of course, be growth of inventory, but it will be a rather peripheral and "external" matter. Once the child has selected a certain grammar, he will "know" whatever is predicted by this selected hypothesis. He will, in other words, know a great deal about sentences to which he has never been exposed. This is, of course, the characteristic fact about human language.

I have outlined the difference between two theories of grammar in rather vague terms. It can be made quite precise, and the question of choice between them becomes a matter of fact, not decision. My own view is that no descriptivist theory can be reconciled with the known facts about the nature and use of language. This, however, is a matter that goes beyond the scope of this discussion.

To summarize, as the problem is usually put, the choice between generative and descriptive grammars is not a genuine one. It is a choice between a system of principles and one, rather marginal selection of consequences of these principles. But there is a deeper and ultimately factual question, to be resolved not by decision but by sharpening the assumptions and confronting them with facts.

Finally, I would like to say just a word about the matter of the teaching of grammar in the schools. My impression is that grammar is generally taught as an essentially closed and finished system, and in a rather mechanical way. What is taught is a system of terminology, a set of techniques for diagramming sentences, and so on. I do not doubt that this has its function, that the student must have a way of talking about language and its properties. But it seems to me that a great opportunity is lost when the teaching of grammar is limited in this way. I think it is important for students to realize how little we know about the rules that determine the relation of sound and meaning in English, about the general properties of human language, about the matter of how the incredibly complex system of rules that constitutes a grammar is acquired or put to use. Few students are aware of the fact that in their normal, everyday life they are constantly creating new linguistic structures that are immediately understood, despite their novelty, by those to whom they speak or write. They are never brought to the realization of how amazing an accomplishment this is, and of how limited is our comprehension of what makes it possible. Nor do they acquire any insight into the remarkable intricacy of the grammar that they use unconsciously, even insofar as this system is understood and can be explicitly presented. Consequently, they miss both the challenge and the accomplishments of the study of language. This seems to me a pity, because both are very real. Perhaps as the study of language returns gradually to the full scope and scale of its rich tradition, some way will be found to introduce students to the tantalizing problems that language has always posed for those who are puzzled and intrigued by the mysteries of human intelligence.

DISCUSSION QUESTIONS

1. What are the major contributions of the two principal traditions in linguistics?

2. What does Chomsky consider the job of the linguist to be? Compare and contrast his views with those of Francis and Algeo.

3. Do you think explanation in the Chomskian sense is a necessary part of linguistics?

4. What type of grammar do you feel would be the most beneficial for students to study in elementary school, high school, college? Why?

NEIL SMITH and DEIRDRE WILSON

Both Deirdre Wilson and Neil Smith are British linguists. The former, a graduate of both Somerville College of Oxford University and Nuffield College in the city of Oxford, obtained the doctorate in linguistics from Massachusetts Institute of Technology and is now a lecturer in linguistics at University College, London. Her research interest is in rhetoric and pragmatics. Smith, a graduate of Trinity College of Cambridge University and of University College of London University, is currently reader in linguistics and head of the linguistics section at University College, London. He has spent nearly two years at Massachusetts Institute of Technology and at the University of California, Los Angeles, as a Harkness Fellow, and has published in the field of language acquisition. Besides his present interest in language typology he reports that he is happiest when playing with his two children.

KNOWLEDGE OF LANGUAGE

[Here] we attempt to clarify the relation between knowledge and language from two quite different directions. First, we want to distinguish between two types of knowledge, linguistic and non-linguistic (and hence between two types of rules, linguistic and non-linguistic); second, we want to distinguish between knowledge of rules and the exercise of that knowledge (and hence, between knowing a language and speaking or understanding it). Our main purpose is to give a general idea of the range and type of facts which fall within the domain of a grammar: of the facts that can be handled by linguistic rule, and those that cannot.

LINGUISTIC AND NON-LINGUISTIC KNOWLEDGE

Granted that a human being can have knowledge at all, it seems obvious that this knowledge can be classified in various ways. One such classification would involve separating linguistic from non-linguistic knowledge. Following Chomsky, we want to argue that such a classification is not only possible but correct: that it is not just imposed by the analyst, but has a basis in human mental organization. In other words, language, though only one among many cognitive systems, has its own principles and rules, which are different in kind from those governing other cognitive systems, and for this reason must be studied separately.

This is one of the claims which most sharply distinguishes Chomsky from others who have thought seriously about the nature of language. While it is a commonplace to say that language is specific to humans, part of the human essence, what crucially distinguishes man from beast, most linguistic theorists have been extremely cautious about concluding from this that humans must have a specific genetic endowment for language-learning. They attempt instead to explain the acquisition of language in terms of whatever general learning theory they espouse. If they believe that knowledge in general is acquired by observation and generalization, then they will claim the same for language. If they believe that knowledge is generally acquired by some form of conditioning, then they will claim the same for language. If they think that knowledge is best analysed as a disposition to behave in certain ways, then they will claim that knowledge of language is best analysed as a disposition to behave linguistically in certain ways. Language will thus be seen as acquired in the course of general intellectual development, and no language-specific endowment, apart from general intelligence and the ability to learn, will be needed for its acquisition. It is clear, though, that there is an alternative to this position. Language may be *sui generis*, different in kind from other cognitive systems, requiring different learning strategies and different genetic programming. The two claims reinforce each other: if linguistic knowledge is different in kind from non-linguistic knowledge, then it is more likely that we need special programming to learn it; and if we have such special programming, then it is more likely that the result of language-learning *will* be different in kind from other systems not so programmed.

There are a number of rather obvious points that support the special-programming view of language acquisition, and disconfirm the general-intellectual-ability approach. If we measure general intellectual development in terms of logical, mathematical and abstract-reasoning powers, these powers are still increasing at puberty, when the ability to acquire native fluency in a language is decreasing rapidly. A child of eight who can beat an eighteen-year-old at chess is something of a prodigy; if an eighteen-year-old acquires native fluency in a language as quickly as an eight-year-old, simply by being exposed to it, and without any formal training, it is the eighteen-year-old, not the eight-year-old, who is the prodigy. If it is thought unfair to compare linguistic skills with powers of abstract reasoning in this way, the point has already been granted: there is a difference between mathematical and linguistic abilities: linguistic knowledge can be distinguished from other types of knowledge, which depend on different intellectual endowments, and are acquired at different rates.

Particularly striking evidence for this mismatch between linguistic and general cognitive abilities comes from the case of the American girl Genie. Genie was discovered in Los Angeles in 1970, at the age of thirteen; she had been kept locked up in conditions of severe sensory deprivation from infancy. In particular, she had heard virtually no speech throughout the period in which children normally learn their first language. Despite this horrifying background, Genie's intelligence turned out to be within normal limits in essential respects, and thus her progress with language learning provides a useful basis for comparison with the language acquisition of more ordinary children. Her early language acquisition was typical of all children in that it passed through stages of one-word, two-word, three-word and then four-word utterances; however, Genie's three- and four-word utterances typically displayed a cognitive complexity not found in the early speech of normal children, and her vocabulary was much larger than that of children at the same stage of syntactic development. In general, her ability to store *lists* of words is very good, but her ability to learn and manipulate rules has been minimal. This is reflected in the fact that whereas the 'two-word' stage lasts for about two to six weeks with normal children, with Genie it lasted over five months:

e.g. Doctor hurt.
Like mirror.

Moreover, the kind of early negative structures which most two-to-three-year-old children use for a few weeks, where the negative element is initial in the sentence, still persisted with Genie some one and a half *years* after she had first learned to use negatives:

> e.g. No more ear hurt.
> No stay hospital.
> Not have orange record.

Indeed, no syntactic rule which is normally taken to involve the *movement* of a word or phrase from one point in a sentence to another . . . has been consistently mastered by Genie as yet. But in contrast with this slow and partial linguistic progress, Genie's intellectual development appears to be progressing extremely rapidly, and to be approaching the normal for her age.

It seems, then, that language-learning abilities are not only different in kind from other intellectual abilities, but that they also become considerably impaired at a time when other intellectual abilities are still increasing. People who retain these language-learning abilities after puberty are as rare as infant mathematical prodigies. One reason for being interested in linguistic knowledge is thus for the light it might shed on human linguistic programming. If it is reasonable to suspect that such programming exists, then one obvious way of investigating it would be to examine the result of language acquisition—linguistic knowledge—and work out what principles would be needed to acquire it. And since the argument works two ways, someone who is not convinced that any linguistic programming exists might become convinced of its necessity simply by examining the contents of linguistic knowledge and asking himself how they could have been arrived at: could they have been acquired by 'general intellectual reasoning' or all-purpose learning strategies?

One common objection to this programme is that it is not always obvious where the line between linguistic and non-linguistic knowledge should be drawn. In fact some people would want to argue that no such line exists: that all knowledge involves both linguistic and non-linguistic aspects. For example, in order to know that children enjoy games—clearly not the sort of knowledge we would want to record in a grammar—one might nevertheless have to know the meanings of the words *children, enjoy* and *games,* and how to combine them into a meaningful sentence. On the other hand, in order to know that *giraffe* is a noun—clearly an item of knowledge that we would want to record in a grammar—one might nevertheless have to have some exposure to the use of English in general; and it is not, practically speaking, possible to acquire such knowledge without having some knowledge of the outside world. Hence, the argument goes, there is no clear-cut division between linguistic and non-linguistic knowledge, or between knowledge of a grammar and knowledge of the world.

This argument is not really sound. It is perfectly possible to distinguish the contents of knowledge from the preconditions for acquiring it. Thus, in order to know the laws of physics, one must be able to breathe: it does not follow that physics cannot be distinguished from human biology. There may be linguistic preconditions for acquiring knowledge of the world, and non-linguistic preconditions for learning a language: this in no way shows that knowledge of language cannot be distinguished from knowledge of the world.

In fact the notion of linguistic knowledge that we shall adopt is a quite narrow and exclusive one, in the sense that not even all knowledge about language is to count as linguistic knowledge. The principle behind this decision is as follows: knowledge about language which is merely a special case of some wider generalization about human beings does not count as linguistic knowledge. Knowledge about language which does *not* emerge as a special case of some wider generalization about human beings is the only knowledge that we are prepared to call linguistic. This of course makes the theoretical distinction between linguistic and non-linguistic knowledge—the claim that language is *sui generis*—true by definition; however, it still leaves open the empirical question of whether anything actually satisfies our definition of linguistic knowledge.

As an example of knowledge about language which does not count as linguistic knowledge in our sense, consider the following. Most linguists have a stock of odd items of knowledge about various languages: that Japanese has the verb in sentence-final position, that Turkish exhibits vowel-harmony, that Latin has no definite article, and so on. This knowledge seems rather clearly to be encyclopedic, of the same type as knowledge that France is a republic, that the capital of Italy is Rome, and that elephants are found in India. Given the capacity to acquire the latter type of knowledge, one should automatically be able to acquire the former; no special abilities would be required.

Similar remarks apply to certain types of knowledge that native speakers have about their own language. For example, most native speakers of English can recognize the social or regional origins of others on the basis of linguistic cues such as accent, intonation, choice of words and syntactic constructions. They can also recognize such things as colloquial, formal, deferential and authoritarian styles of speech, they can tell whether a particular remark is socially or factually appropriate, literally, sarcastically, humorously or otherwise figuratively intended. Although there are certainly rules and principles which make such judgements possible, and which deserve investigation in their own right, we do not want to say that these judgements are evidence of linguistic knowledge, in our sense. The reason for this is that each such principle seems to be a special case of a more general principle which applies to human non-linguistic behaviour too. For example, one can often tell someone's national, regional or social origins by the way he walks, or his gestures, or his clothes, or his facial expressions, as well as by the way he speaks. There are formal, deferential and authoritarian styles of behaviour as well as speech— and like language they vary from culture to culture. There are constraints of appropriateness, sincerity, politeness, clownishness and so on on behaviour, as well as speech. In general, then, we would expect the principles behind all these aspects of language-use to fall together with other human social and behavioural principles, and to be in no way *sui generis*.

Strictly linguistic knowledge, then, will reduce to knowledge of those principles of sentence-construction and interpretation which do not fall together with wider generalizations about human non-linguistic behaviour. Consider, for example, the claim already mentioned, that children pass through regular stages in learning a language. This would be explained on the assumption—which is not specific to language-learning—that there are degrees of complexity in the material to be learned, and that the simplest material is learned first. What *is* specifically linguistic is not the assumption that the learning process passes through successively more complex stages: it is the definition of linguistic complexity itself. Thus there is no generally observable reason why *Not Johnny go* is simpler than *Johnny not go*. The fact that children tend to learn the former before the latter indicates quite strongly that there is a notion of linguistic complexity which does not follow from general cognitive principles—which is specific to language alone and therefore part of linguistic knowledge as we are defining it. The remainder of this chapter . . . is devoted to giving further examples of strictly linguistic knowledge, and to discussing techniques for studying it.

INTUITIONS

A native speaker of English has at his disposal a vast amount of fairly uncontroversially linguistic knowledge. For example, he knows when two words rhyme; he knows when two sentences are paraphrases; when a single sentence has two different meanings; when a change in word order results in a change of meaning, and when it merely results in ungrammaticality. We have argued that the aim of writing grammars is to give a full account of all these facets of linguistic knowledge. How do we go about doing this?

Because, as we have already seen, linguistic knowledge lies well below the level of consciousness, direct questioning of speakers of a language is likely to yield little reliable information about their linguistic knowledge. If we approach a native speaker of English and ask him whether (1) and (2) have the same syntactic structure, there is not the slightest chance of predicting what he will say:

> (1) I'm leaving, for he makes me nervous.
> (2) I'm leaving, because he makes me nervous.

He may have his own consciously worked out grammatical theory or he may have no conscious idea of syntactic structure at all. In either case, there is no particular reason for believing the answer that he actually gives us, and his knowledge of language will have to be investigated by rather more indirect means.

Whatever their conscious views on grammatical theory, most native speakers will be able to provide us with evidence of the following kind: they will be able to tell us that each of the following sentence pairs has one grammatical member and one ungrammatical one:

> (3) a. It was because he was nervous that he left.
> b. *It was for he was nervous that he left.
> (4) a. Because he makes me nervous, I'm leaving.
> b. *For he makes me nervous, I'm leaving.
> (5) a. Did you leave because he made you nervous?
> b. *Did you leave for he made you nervous?
> (6) a. I left, because I was nervous and because I wanted to go.
> b. *I left, for I was nervous and for I wanted to go.
> (7) a. Maria, who left because I made her nervous, is returning today.
> b. *Maria, who left for I made her nervous, is returning today.

The native speaker of English clearly has some linguistic knowledge which enables him to distinguish *for*-clauses from *because*-clauses, in spite of their similarity in meaning. An adequate grammar must provide some way of replicating this linguistic knowledge. For our present purposes it is not the actual rules which explain the speaker's linguistic judgements that are of interest. What *is* interesting is that such judgements give us good ground for imputing a particular type of linguistic knowledge to the speaker: in this case, knowledge of syntactic structure.[1]

---

[1] In fact, the relevant distinction seems to be that between subordinate and co-ordinate clauses. *For, and* and *but* all link co-ordinate clauses, of roughly equal importance. *Because, although* and *when* introduce subordinate clauses which are in some sense dependent on the main clause which precedes or follows them. It is the fact that co-ordinate clauses have very limited freedom of movement, compared with subordinate clauses, which explains the differential patterns in (3)–(7).

What we have just been suggesting is that one good way of investigating linguistic knowledge is to ask the native speaker for judgements about the sentences of his language: not directly, by asking 'Which of these is a subordinate clause construction?', but indirectly, by eliciting a range of judgements about, say, grammaticality, ungrammaticality, paraphrase and ambiguity, and then constructing a set of rules which will account for these judgements. The relevant judgements are generally called *intuitions*. It is often felt, by both philosophers and linguists, that reliance on native-speaker intuitions is an extremely suspect part of Chomskyan theory: intuitions are 'unscientific,' not amenable to direct observation, variable and untrustworthy. It seems to us that this is not a valid theoretical objection: discovering linguistic rules seems to us exactly analogous to discovering the rules of an invented, uncodified children's game by asking the children concerned whether certain moves are permissible or not, good moves or not, dangerous or not, and so on. How else would one go about discovering unwritten rules?

This is not to say that there are not considerable practical difficulties in deciding how much reliance should be placed on native-speaker intuitions on any given occasion. Consider, for example, a fairly uncomplicated sentence with more than one meaning:

(8) I like Indians without reservations.

A speaker presented with a questionnaire in which he sees (8) divorced from any context, and given a limited amount of time to decide how many meanings it has, might well be unable to produce more than the following two:

(9) a. I have no reservations in my liking for Indians.
    b. I like Indians who don't live on reservations.

Given more time, and perhaps some contextual guidance, he might have noticed that there is a further possible interpretation along the following lines:

(9) c. I like Indians without reservations (about appearing in cowboy films).

Or he might have noticed another alternative:

(9) d. I like Indians without reservations (for seats on the first scheduled flight to the moon).

And there may be still more possibilities. While this indicates that any judgement that (8) has only two interpretations must certainly be set aside, it does not indicate the total unreliability of intuitions. When shown the interpretations in (9a–d), most speakers of English would indeed agree that each was a possible interpretation of (8), and given a suitable context of utterance, most speakers would probably arrive at these interpretations for themselves. In other words, these examples merely indicate that the use of questionnaires is not likely to be a very reliable method of studying linguistic knowledge.

In a similar way, initial judgements about grammaticality, or about the literal interpretation of unambiguous sentences, may well have to be set aside in the light of further investigation. For example, quite often a sentence like (10) will be either judged ungrammatical or wrongly interpreted when heard out of context, even by perfectly competent speakers of English:

(10) The train left at midnight crashed.

Where it is wrongly interpreted, it will be taken to mean the same as (11) or (12):

(11) The train which left at midnight crashed.
(12) The train left at midnight and crashed.

A little thought or prompting, however, should lead to a reevaluation. First, (10) is perfectly grammatical. Second, it means not (11) or (12) but (13):

(13) The train which was left at midnight crashed.

An exactly parallel structure which presents no difficulties of interpretation would be (14):

(14) The baby abandoned at midnight cried.

We would thus, on consideration, not want to write a grammar which would disallow (10), or interpret it as (11) or (12), even though we can elicit speakers' judgements which would initially support this treatment.

Examples like (10) seem to show that the relation between knowing the grammar of a language and actually producing or understanding utterances may be rather indirect. The grammar of the language, and the speaker of the language on mature consideration, associate (10) with the meaning in (13). However, the speaker's first reaction when presented with (10) out of context, is to associate it with the meaning in (11) or (12). This seems to indicate that the speaker who misunderstands (10) has used something other than the rules of his grammar in arriving at his interpretation. Again, as long as he can be brought to see the correct interpretation, there is no reason why this sort of case should lead to scepticism about the validity of intuitions as a guide to linguistic knowledge: but it does emphasize that intuitions do not give us direct insight into the form of linguistic knowledge, and should be treated with corresponding caution.

The reason why (10) causes difficulties of interpretation, while (14) does not, seems to be that in (10) the sequence *the train left at midnight* could itself stand as a complete (and plausible) sentence, and is initially perceived and interpreted accordingly, with wrong results. The corresponding sequence in (14), *the baby abandoned at midnight,* could not itself be a complete sentence, so that (14) is not misleading in the same way. In other words, speakers of English seem to use the following strategy for analysing complex sentences: 'Take the first sequence of words which sounds like a complete (and plausible) sentence, and interpret it *as* a complete sentence.' This strategy leads, as we have seen, to a misanalysis of (10). Now though this strategy seems to play a genuine part in the interpretation of utterances, we would not want to call it a rule of grammar, since it can so clearly lead to wrong results. What this suggests is that speakers invent short-cuts to the analysis of utterances, by-passing the rules of grammar which they also know, gaining speed but occasionally losing accuracy as a result. Such short cuts are occasionally referred to as *perceptual strategies*: strategies used in the perception (understanding) of utterances; we shall have more to say about them in the next section.

The well-known and deceptively innocent reviewer's comment in (15) is another case where the English speaker's initial interpretation turns out, on closer examination, to be incorrect:

(15) This is a book you must not fail to miss.

At first sight, one is tempted to equate it with (16):

(16) This is a book you must not fail to read.

It is only on closer inspection that it turns out to mean (17):

(17) This is a book you must on no account read.

The problem here seems to be not syntactic, as with (10), but rather semantic or logical: sentences containing a combination of semantically 'negative' items are notoriously difficult to understand, and (15) contains *not, fail* and *miss,* in the space of four words. It is arguable that people who hear sentences like (15) and (16) do not give them a serious linguistic analysis at all: they simply guess what the speaker would be most likely to want to say, and interpret accordingly. In the absence of clues to the speaker's intentions, the process of working out what has actually been said is an exceedingly laborious one, often involving paper and pencil analysis, as the reader of (18) may check for himself:

(18)   Common courtesy is a virtue that few people would fail to forget unless not specifically forbidden to do otherwise.

Again, this argues for caution in dealing with initial interpretations of certain types of sentence, and for a distinction between the speaker's perceptual or understanding abilities and his actual knowledge of the language. It is to this latter distinction between knowledge of a language and the exercise of that knowledge that we turn in the next section.

COMPETENCE AND PERFORMANCE

Many of the examples we have used have required assessment on two quite different levels. First, do they conform to the principles for correct sentence-formation in standard English: are they *grammatical*? Second, on an actual occasion of utterance, how appropriate, felicitous or comprehensible would they be: are they *acceptable*? The first level of assessment is a purely linguistic one: the second involves knowledge and abilities that go well beyond the purely linguistic. Within Chomskyan theory, the first is called the level of *competence*, the speaker's knowledge of language, and the second is called the level of *performance*, the speaker's use of language. The study of competence, then, is the study of grammars which are psychologically real, and which contain all the linguistic knowledge, whether innate or acquired, possessed by a given speaker of the language. Such grammars are often referred to as *competence models*. The study of performance, by contrast, is concerned with the principles which govern language use: here such dimensions as appropriateness to context, ease of comprehension, sincerity, truth and stylistic euphony all play a part. Moreover, a *performance model* would have to include, as a competence model would not, some account of the principles by which sentences are actually produced and understood—and hence occasionally misproduced or misunderstood. Like the notion of intuition, the competence–performance distinction seems to us a theoretically valid one, although like the notion of intuition, it raises certain practical difficulties.

Up till now, we have been able to refer indifferently to the objects of linguistic investigation as either *sentences* or *utterances*. In fact, along with the distinction between competence and performance, grammaticality and acceptability, comes a parallel distinction between sentence and utterance. Sentences fall within the domain of competence models; utterances within the domain of performance models. Sentences are abstract objects which are not tied to a particular context, speaker or time of utterance. Utterances, on the other hand, are datable events, tied to a particular speaker, occasion and context. By contrast, sentences are tied to particular grammars, in the sense that a sentence is not grammatical in the absolute, but only with respect to the rules of a certain grammar; utterances, however, may cross the bounds of particular grammars and incorporate words or constructions from many different languages, or from no language at all. Given a bilingual English-French speaker and hearer, (19) might be a perfectly acceptable utterance, although it could never be a grammatical sentence:

(19)   [*]John's being a real idiot—I suppose cela va sans dire.

In other words, acceptable utterances need not be the realization of fully grammatical sentences.

There are also grammatical sentences which can never be realized as fully acceptable utterances. This may be because of their semantic, syntactic or phonological content. Thus (20) would be unacceptable in most contexts because it would patently label its speaker as insincere:

(20) Your hat's on fire, though I don't believe it.

It is perfectly easy to see what this sentence is claiming: it is not even claiming anything contradictory, since it is perfectly possible for people to make assertions which they do not in fact believe. What is not legitimate, as a matter of human behaviour, is to behave insincerely while explicitly drawing one's audience's attention to the fact. In other words, the oddity in (20) is a performance matter rather than a fact of language. (21) would also be unacceptable in most contexts, this time because of its extreme syntactic complexity:

(21) If because when Mary came in John left Harry cried, I'd be surprised.

It is possible, on closer examination, to see that (21) is quite regularly formed according to standard principles of English.[2] However, its syntactic complexity is such that normal speakers would have some difficulty in unravelling its message. Again, this indicates that the oddity in (21) is a performance matter, traceable to whatever principles hearers use in utterance comprehension, rather than a matter of linguistic competence. Finally, (22) would also be unacceptable to many hearers, this time for phonological reasons:

(22) We finally sent an Edinburgh man, for for four Forfar men to go would have seemed like favouritism.

There is nothing wrong with the syntax or semantics of (22): it is just that the accidental accumulation of *for* sounds makes it seem like a joke or a play on words, and diverts attention from the intended message.

To say that there is a distinction between competence and performance is not to deny that there is an intimate connection between the two. Perceptual strategies are often based on rules of grammar, and, if they are used often enough, may themselves actually *become* rules of grammar. For example, the perceptual strategy mentioned in the last section: 'Treat the first string of words that *could* be interpreted as a sentence, as being a sentence, and interpret accordingly', is ultimately based on the organization of English grammar. English has a number of ways of showing the start of a subordinate clause: the relative pronouns *who* and *which*, and the complementizer *that*, are the most common. Where these devices are used, the perceptual strategy just mentioned will be inoperative, as in (23):

(23) The train which left at midnight crashed.

Thus, when the subordinate devices are omitted, the hearer has a certain right to assume that no subordinate clause is involved: hence the existence of the perceptual strategy. As we have seen, the principles of English grammar are such that this perceptual strategy will occasionally lead to a misinterpretation; nonetheless it is the principles of English grammar which originally gave rise to the perceptual strategy itself.

Conversely, what started out as a perceptual strategy may become so entrenched

---

[2] The structure of (21) is as follows: If A happened, I'd be surprised. A = Because B happened, Harry cried. B = When Mary came in, John left.

in the use of language that it gives rise to a rule of grammar. For example, the complementizer *that* which marks the start of a subordinate clause may optionally be omitted in a great many cases, as shown in (24) and (25):

> (24) a. I believe that John left.
>   b. I believe John left.
> (25) a. I told Mary that Bill was sorry.
>   b. I told Mary Bill was sorry.

One of the few places where it may never be omitted is when it introduces a subordinate clause at the very beginning of a sentence: compare (26a) and (26b):

> (26) a. That John should have left upset me.
>   b. *John should have left upset me.

There seems to be no doubt that (26b) is actually ungrammatical, and that English therefore contains a rule of grammar which forbids deletion of a sentence-initial *that*. Returning now to our perceptual strategy, notice that it would invariably lead to a misanalysis of (26b), since the string of words *John should have left* can stand as a sentence on its own, and would thus be taken as the main clause of (26b). Forbidding the deletion of the *that* in (26a) thus guarantees that there will be no wrong application of the perceptual strategy in this case: *That John should have left* cannot stand as a sentence on its own, and hence cannot be treated by the perceptual strategy mentioned. In this case, the rule of grammar is based on the existence of the perceptual strategy, and is designed to prevent its misapplication. Thus there is a clear interaction between rules of grammar and perceptual strategies, either one being capable of giving rise to the other.

   Given that there is such a close connection between rules of competence and perceptual strategies, there have been those who are prepared to argue that any clear-cut distinction between the two is impossible to draw. For example, it might be possible to argue that there is not a distinction between competence models and performance models, but merely between more and less abstract rules of performance, each of which has its part to play in the full production and understanding of utterances. And in general, it might be possible to argue that the difference between linguistic and other principles, or linguistic and other rules, is not one of kind, but merely one of degree.

   While this is a perfectly reasonable alternative to the view of language that we have been, and shall be, presenting, it is not one we shall pursue ourselves. Our main reason for this is that we have never seen a fully coherent outline of a theory based on a single notion of performance, which could account in an adequate way for the facts which can be accounted for in terms of this competence–performance distinction. . . . [We] have argued that, however easy it is to produce and understand, (27) is actually ungrammatical: it is not formed according to established principles of English grammar:

> (27) *This is the sort of book that, having once read it, you feel you want
>   to give it to all your friends.

If we incorporated the principles used to form (27) into English grammar, they would immediately give rise to the clear ungrammaticality of (28):

> (28) *This is a book which I gave it to my friend.

In other words, whatever it is that makes (27) sound natural, it is not, and cannot be, a linguistic rule. It seems to us important that linguistic theory should be able to make this sort of distinction, and we see no way of drawing it without making use of a distinction between competence and performance, language knowledge and language use.

What we have tried to do in this chapter is present a particular view of how knowledge of linguistic rules interacts, on the one hand, with other types of knowledge, and on the other hand with principles of utterance-production and comprehension. The picture that emerges is complex. Firstly, presented with a particular item of knowledge, we must be prepared to argue about how it should be classified, and we have outlined some arguments which might be used. Where the knowledge can be classified as linguistic, then we claim that it forms part of a grammar—a competence grammar—which incorporates linguistic rules. Secondly, presented with a set of judgements about a sentence— how it should be interpreted, how it relates to other sentences, how it is pronounced— we must be prepared to argue about whether these judgements give direct insight into the competence grammar, or whether the judgements themselves must be set aside, or treated as evidence about performance models rather than grammar. Again, we have outlined some arguments which might be used. Where the judgements do not give direct insight into the competence grammar, we may find that they give us clues to the sort of principles used in utterance-comprehension, which are themselves valid objects of study. However, in general it seems to be both correct and interesting to regard the rules of language as separate from those of other cognitive systems, and to regard knowledge of these rules as only indirectly reflected in linguistic behaviour.

DISCUSSION QUESTIONS

1. What role do intuitions play in the study of grammar?

2. If linguistic knowledge is different in kind from other knowledge, does it seem reasonable that it be acquired in a different manner? How does the work on child language support this innateness hypothesis? See the articles by Brown and Moskowitz in Part III.

3. What is the significance of the distinction between competence and performance? Which is most likely to be studied in school? Why?

JOHN ALGEO

The author is professor of English at the University of Georgia and, from 1970 to 1981, served as editor of American Speech, *the journal of the American Dialect Society. This essay resulted from his summer study at the University of Michigan in 1969, with Kenneth Pike, originator of tagmemic grammar.*

TAGMEMICS: A BRIEF OVERVIEW

At a time when linguistic theorizing is a glamorous enterprise that outdazzles the drabber efforts of mere description and taxonomy, the tagmemic theory of Kenneth Pike has one clear distinction. Pike and his associates have not scrupled to dirty their hands with the commoner forms of linguistic labor. Willie Stark, in Robert Penn Warren's *All the King's Men,* observed that you cannot build hospitals without bricks and that "somebody has to paddle in the mud to make 'em." Willie was talking about morality in politics, but the metaphor is applicable also to field work in linguistics, and as such, can be taken (without any further equation of linguistics and populism) as a fair representation of the stance that tagmemicists have assumed: you cannot build theories without facts and somebody has to paddle in the empirical mud to find them. The tagmemic school has indeed sought to develop theory and praxis to an equal degree. It is thus no accident that Pike's *Language in Relation to a Unified Theory . . .* should be balanced (symbolically, not in weight) by Longacre's *Grammar Discovery Procedures* as comprehensive statements of tagmemic theory and practice. To be sure, all theoreticians must occasionally soil themselves with data, but the tendency has been to take readily available facts about well-known languages and to redescribe them according to the favorite theory. The distinction of the tagmemicists is that they have gone on collecting new data about ill-known languages, with unconcern for the low prestige of data-gathering in our time.

In addition to a strongly empirical and pragmatic orientation, tagmemics has a number of characteristics that help to differentiate it from other current forms of linguistics. The most significant of these is indicated by the full title of Pike's major work: *Language in Relation to a Unified Theory of the Structure of Human Behavior.* Pike aims at accounting for language, not as a *sui generis* phenomenon, but as an integral part of the whole of man's life. Language is to be studied, not as an isolated structure, but as a system set off only by indeterminate bounds from a context that expands in time and space and complexity to include ultimately whatever forms a part of man's experience. Pike's aim in the study of behavior is analogous to Einstein's in physics. His linguistic theory is not specifically a theory of language, but is rather a special case of a general unified theory that accounts for all cultural behavior, of which language is itself only a special case.

There is in this tagmemic insistence that language can be adequately studied only as a part of man's total behavior, an apparent contradiction with much of post-Saussurian linguistics, for example, Hjelmslev's view that "linguistics must attempt to grasp language, not as a conglomerate of non-linguistic (*e.g.*, physical, physiological, psychological, logical, sociological) phenomena, but as a self-sufficient totality, a structure *sui generis*." (*Prolegomena to a Theory of Language,* tr. F. J. Whitfield, Madison, 1963, pp. 5–6). The contradiction is, however, more apparent than real. Hjelmslev's concern was to assert the right of the linguist to consider language as an end of investigation, not merely a means. Pike's concern is to affirm that language cannot be adequately investigated apart from the rest of human behavior. Thus their positions are not really in conflict, Hjelmslev being concerned with ends and Pike with scope.

The tagmemic insistence that language be viewed as part of the whole of human behavior and that there be a unified theory to account for the whole can be seen clearly in two ideas: that behavior, including language, can be described from both emic and etic standpoints, and that behavior, again including language, is trimodally structured.

First, the difference between an etic description and an emic one is the difference between what we might expect an alien observer to see and what we would expect of a native. A noncardplayer observing a game of bridge will see different things than a bridge-player will. The noncardplayer, who is an "alien" in this situation, may notice that the cards are handled and passed around, that the players pick up the cards in front of them and carry on a short conversation in cryptic phrases, that one player then puts all of his cards on the table while the other three put theirs down one by one as this player or that pulls little piles of cards in front of him, that a conversation goes on sporadically during the play, and finally that the cards are put together again before the process is repeated. What the bridge-player sees as a "native" to the game is a distinct unit called a "hand," consisting of the deal, the bidding, the play, and the scoring. The noncardplayer observes a number of etic facts, some of which fit into the emic categories of the bridge-player and some of which are irrelevant. Furthermore, the etic observer may have altogether missed some emically significant events, like the scoring. To know which events at the card table are significant for the game, which are not, and how the significant events are related to one another, one must know the rules of the game—that is, one must know the events emically.

The etic and emic standpoints are alternate ways of viewing the same reality. The etic standpoint is a view from outside, either random in its selectivity or with a set of presuppositions that have only a chance relationship to the scene being described. The emic standpoint is a view from within that notices just those features of the scene that are marked as significant by internal criteria.

For speech, a sound spectrogram is a good example of etic description. So is a narrow phonetic recording of a language the transcriber has never heard before. In both cases, some things that are emically relevant to the phonology of the language will almost certainly be missed, whereas a good many quite irrelevant features will be recorded. Such a record of English speech may show the irrelevant voicelessness and friction of the r in *try*, but fail to record the emically significant differences between a colorless 3–1 intonation contour and a 2–2 pattern that means, when given to the isolated word *try*, 'but you probably won't succeed.' On the other hand, a phonemic transcription, whether it consists of "autonomous" or of "systematic" phonemes, is an emic description of speech. So also, an etic description would note the variation in sequence between *He put the book up* and *He put up the book* although it is of no emic relevance to the grammar. The distinction is a familiar one, but Pike was the coiner of the terms and the one who has most clearly pointed out that the concepts are applicable to all of man's activities.

The belief that human behavior is structured in three modes is another aspect of tagmemic theory which emphasizes the continuity of language and nonlinguistic culture. Every unit of behavior can be described in three ways, first according to those features that identify it as a distinct unit and that contrast it with all other distinct units of behavior (feature mode). Second, the unit can be described according to the range of variations by which it is manifested (manifestation mode). And third, the unit can be described according to its distribution relative to other units: whether as a member of a class, a component of a combination, or a cell in a matrix (distribution mode).

For example, in a bridge game a given bid relates to the whole game through all three modes. In its feature mode, a bid of "three clubs" is identified and contrasted with other possible bids by two features—the suit ("clubs") and the number of tricks ("three"). In the manifestation mode, the bid can have a number of variations: "Three clubs," "I bid three clubs," "Well, well, well, thr-r-ree clubby-dubs," "Three clubs?"— although the last especially lacks propriety. In the distribution mode, the bid is an opener, an overcall, or a raise; a free bid, a forced bid, or a jump bid; a preemptive bid, a cue bid, or a normal bid; and so forth, depending on its relationship to the preceding bids in the hand.

The three modes are reflected in language as a whole by its three hierarchies: the feature mode in the lexicon, the manifestation mode in the phonology, and the distribution mode in the grammar. In a general way lexical units are the features of language, phonology its manifestation, and grammar its distribution. But each of the hierarchies can also be analyzed according to the three modes. For example, in the feature mode of phonology, the phoneme unit /m/ is identified and contrasted with all other units by the features of labiality and nasality. In the manifestation mode, /m/ can be bilabial as in *empire* or labiodental as in *emphasize,* and it can be fully voiced as in *mile* or partially devoiced as in *smile.* In the distribution mode, /m/ belongs to the classes of segments that can occur initially (like /h/), finally (like /ŋ/), and as a syllabic (like /ə/).

So also in the feature mode of the lexicon, the morpheme unit *wife* is identified and contrasted with other units by its morphophonemic features /wīf/, it is syntactic feature 'noun,' and its semantic features 'female spouse.' In the manifestation mode it can be /waif/ or /waiv/ (as in *wives*) or /wa :f/ (as in some parts of the South). In the distribution mode, *wife* has its place in the system of kinship terms and belongs to the class of items that can occur as subject of *hope* and as antecedent of *who* and *she.*

In the grammatical hierarchy, there is a basic unit called the tagmeme. The concept of the tagmeme, from which the entire theory is named, was evolved by Pike to fill the need he felt for a basic grammatical unit parallel to the phoneme as a phonological unit and the morpheme as a lexical one. The term comes from Bloomfield's *Language,* where it was used, however, in quite a different sense. Nowhere other than in linguistics is T.S. Eliot's observation truer that words "slip, slide . . . will not stay in place, will not stay still," so we must make do with technical terms that change their meaning with almost every user. As Pike has defined *tagmeme,* it refers to the correlation between a "slot," or grammatical function, and the class of items that can fill that slot. Thus in the clause construction *Men talk,* there is a functional slot of actor-subject with the filler class of nouns represented by *men* and a functional slot of action-predicator with the filler class of intransitive verbs represented by *talk.* The two categories of functional slot and of filler class are defined correlatively, each by the other, together making up the grammatical unit of the tagmeme. In the feature mode of the grammar, the tagmemic unit "noun as actor-subject" contrasts with other units by the features of its functional slot "actor-subject" and its filler class "noun." In the manifestation mode, it can be a large number of morphemes (*men, parrots, money*). In the distribution mode, the tagmeme has a place in various clause structures.

Each of the modes can be seen as reflecting a dominant characteristic: particle, wave, or field theories of structure. Thus the feature mode tends to reflect the unit as a discrete particle with its own identity and contrasting with all other discrete particles— phonemes, morphemes, or tagmemes. The manifestation mode tends to reflect the unit as a continuous wave of activity, without discrete boundaries. For example, allophones in the pronunciation of *woe* overlap and blend into one another in a way that makes segmentation partly arbitrary; similarly there is wavelike overlapping of allomorphs in *whacka want* in which it is difficult to segment neatly the morphemes *what, do,* and *you;* and there is an overlapping of tagmemes in *He saw Xanthippe emptying her pot,* in which *Xanthippe* represents both the object tagmeme after *saw* and the subject tagmeme before *emptying.* The distribution mode tends to reflect the unit as a position in a field or a cell in a matrix. So a phoneme can be located in the traditional articulation chart; psychologists like Osgood can plot morphemes on a graph as they are measured by a semantic differential scale; and tagmemes can be located in a field in which they are transformationally related. Language, and indeed all human behavior can be viewed as particle, wave, or field, as a part of its general trimodal structure.

Once the principle of trimodality is accepted, it begins to expand its applications. Everything can be seen as consisting of contrastive features, with variant manifestations and distributional relations. Lexicon, phonology, and grammar analogize not only with particle, wave, and field; but also with segment, hierarchy, and matrix; with item, process, and relation; with stasis, dynamics, and function; with point, line, and space; with science, art, and philosophy; and even with the true, the beautiful, and the good. We tremble on the verge of a Father-feature, Son-manifestation, and Holy Ghost-distribution that would make proto-tagmemicists out of the conciliar fathers of Nicaea.

We may begin to wonder whether this world and the next are really trimodally structured or whether tagmemics has not slipped a pair of trifocals on us. Are all these triplicities objectively present in the material being studied, or are they a product of the theory on which the study is based? The foregoing question is merely a special case of that dichotomy named by Fred Householder "God's Truth" versus "Hocus Pocus." A God's-Truth man believes that language has a pattern which it is the task of the linguist to discover and account for. The Hocus-Pocus man, on the contrary, holds that language has a pattern which is not directly amenable to description, so that the linguist must invent systems to stand for the data, though these systems can never be uniquely correct representations of the data.

There are no rational grounds for choosing between these two positions. One or the other must be accepted on faith. On the whole, Pike is a God's-Truther who talks about " the discovery of the phoneme," somewhat ironically in view of the attitude of some other proponents of God's Truth, like Noam Chomsky. Yet it is not altogether fair to align Pike wholly with either party in the quarrel. In his usual ecumenical fashion, Pike has attempted to provide for both sides of the dichotomy. For him, etic descriptions are Hocus Pocus because invented and imposed upon the data by the observer; emic descriptions are God's Truth—or at least aim at it—because they are discovered within the data itself. Trimodality for the tagmemicist falls in the latter category; it is an emic fact about the nature of human things and thus represents a significant statement about the universe. Of all modern linguistic theories, it is perhaps only tagmemics that opens its scientific windows onto such mystical landscapes.

Pike, playing upon the etymology of the word *theory,* through which it is connected with the Greek verb *theasthai* 'look at, contemplate,' has likened theories to windows through which we view reality, the view we get depending on the kind of window we look through (*Language,* p. 70). Put so, tagmemics is less a single window than a bank of them, differing in shape, size, and quality. Of all modern theories, tagmemics is probably the most open to influences from outside, the most eclectic. Furthermore, the eclecticism would appear to be by design rather than accident. A God's-Truther, unless he is of one of the more intolerant persuasions, must conclude that whatever light some other theory is capable of shedding on the linguistic data must be the light of God's own sun and thus must be accepted and somehow incorporated into the larger theory. Consequently, what Pike has aimed at is a "unified theory" not only in the sense that it unifies the treatment of language and nonlinguistic behavior, but also in the sense that it tries to unify whatever is useful in other theories. "Whatsoever things are true, whatsoever things are honorable, whatsoever things are just, whatsoever things are pure, whatsoever things are lovely, whatsoever things are of good report; if there be any virtue, and if there be any praise, think on these things," the apostle Paul wrote to the Philippians, but the tagmemicists heard him.

One of the reasons tagmemics can absorb notions from other theories with relative ease is that it is itself not very tight-knit. It is less pure theory than a combination of some theoretical ideas about language in general and a set of procedures for analyzing particular languages. Its strongly heuristic orientation helps it to remain open to influences from other theories, the only requirement being that new approaches must help in the description of a language. In spite of its God's-Truth orientation, tagmemics is on the whole a more tolerant theory than most.

It is possible to see in tagmemics broad correlations with other current approaches to language study. Thus, the tagmemic postulate of three simultaneous and parallel hierarchies in language—the phonological, lexical, and grammatical—has strong affinities with the stratificational view of language as comprising three main kinds of structure. The earlier kind of meaningful transformation, found for example in Chomsky's *Syntactic Structures,* is rejected by tagmemics in favor of its own concept of the matrix, which relates structures with formal and semantic parallels, such as active and passive clauses or statements and questions. The later kind of transformation, however, which serves to derive one level of structure from another in the generative process, does appear in Longacre's tagmemics as "rewrite operations" (*Grammar Discovery Procedures,* pp. 24–34).

The theory with which tagmemics has the greatest affinities, however, is the systemic or scale-and-category grammar of M. A. K. Halliday. On a very general level, Halliday's concern with the situational context of language is reminiscent of Pike's desire to relate language to the totality of human behavior; and Halliday's three levels of phonology, lexis, and grammar parallel quite closely Pike's three hierarchies. More specifically, Halliday's four grammatical categories can be identified in tagmemics: Halliday's unit can be identified with Pike's constructional level (in both theories there are five—sentence, clause, phrase, word, and morpheme). Halliday's elements, which are organized into the category of structure, can be identified with Pike's tagmemes, which are organized into constructions or syntagmemes. Halliday's classes are identical with Pike's distributional classes; and Halliday's system is essentially what Pike seeks to describe with his concept of matrix—a closed set of items that can be related to one another along various dimensions. Furthermore Halliday's three scales have their tagmemic correspondence: rank scale appears as hierarchical level; delicacy corresponds to etic continuum or variable focus; and exponence has been borrowed by Longacre from Halliday (*Grammar Discovery Procedures,* pp. 27–28).

Some believe that there is no possibility of a synthesis among the linguistic theories that compete for our attention today, since they believe that these theories, or some of them, are incompatible in their basic assumptions and aims. It may be so, but to the extent that a synthesis can be made, tagmemicists would appear to have made more progress on the way than any other group. One thing is certain—if the internecine warfare that characterizes much of current linguistics is ever to give way to an age of peace, the insights of tagmemic theory will have to find their place in the new age. But tagmemics will have, perhaps, a better claim on the attention of the next generation of linguists than its mere presence on the field of battle.

Dwight Bolinger has suggested in *Aspects of Language* (New York, 1968; pp. 208–212) that each new movement in linguistics has tended to emphasize most what was most neglected by the preceding movement. It seems clear, as Bolinger points out and as this paper began by assuming, that what is most neglected today is the collection and analysis of raw data. But that is exactly the area in which tagmemicists are most effective. It has been widely assumed among theoretical linguists that data-gathering is a form of arrested development and that those who do it are much like a tribe of food-gatherers living on the edges of a technologically advanced culture. But what if data-gatherers should turn out to be, not a remnant of the past, but instead a wave of the future?

DISCUSSION QUESTIONS

1. Do you think that tagmemics is in the "God's Truth" or the "Hocus Pocus" tradition? What about Chomsky's Transformational Grammar?

2. Since tagmemics is primarily concerned with data gathering, would you expect it to have the tightness that Chomsky desires for his theory? Why?

3. Describe the difference between *emic* and *etic* and give some linguistic and some nonlinguistic examples.

ADRIAN AKMAJIAN, RICHARD A. DEMERS, and ROBERT M. HARNISH

Akmajian, Demers (author of this particular chapter in the book where it appears), and Harnish are members of the department of linguistics at the University of Arizona. All have written in the area of theoretical linguistics as well as in language and communication. Demers also has done research in Lummi and Navaho, American Indian languages.

PHONOLOGY: THE STRUCTURE OF SOUNDS

1. SOME BACKGROUND CONCEPTS

A grammar of a language can be viewed as a system of rules relating sound and meaning; that portion of a grammar that describes the sounds, and the rules governing the distribution of the sounds, is the *phonological component* (or simply, the *phonology*). Among the basic phonological units of all human language sound systems are discrete elements called *phonemes* (the contrasting speech sounds of a language). The pronunciation of the phonemes is highly structured; even our so-called casual pronunciation of words is governed by regular, but abstract, principles.

For an illustration of the structural conditions that govern pronunciation, we begin by considering the following pairs of words, each consisting of a verb and its corresponding agentive noun.

(1)	Verb	Agentive Noun
	(to) write	writer
	(to) shout	shouter
	(to) bat	batter
	(to) hit	hitter

The words in the left column end in a "t" sound. In the related words in the agentive column, the *t* (or *tt*) is regularly pronounced as a "d" sound by most speakers of American (but not British) English. Because of the rapidity of the articulation of the "d" sound, it is referred to as a *flap*. Thus, the "t" sounds in the words on the left in (1) correspond to the flapped "d" sounds in the words on the right.

Rules Governing the Pronunciation of the Sounds of Language

Two important questions immediately arise: What is the nature of the relation between the "t" and flapped "d" sounds? And if there is a relation, how is it to be expressed? Perhaps the simplest account would be that there is *no* relation between the two sounds. Speakers of American English may have simply memorized the different pronunciations of the words in the separate columns and any relation between the members of the pairs is in terms of meaning only. If this were true, however, how could we account for the fact that words we have never encountered before will exhibit the same pattern of distribution of sounds as the examples in (1)? Consider the nonsense words in (2):

(2)	Verb	Agentive Noun
	(to) grite	griter
	(to) bloyt	bloyter
	(to) plat	platter

If you pronounced a flapped *d* in the agentive forms in (1), then you will automatically and unconsciously pronounce a flapped *d* in the agentive forms of the nonsense words in (2). This rule of pronunciation in American English is only one of many rules governing the pronunciation of our words. Given that pronunciation is rule-governed, we must now ask how these rules are stated.

* * *

2. THE PHONEMES OF AMERICAN ENGLISH

In our discussion we will present a special set of symbols to represent the sounds of American English, since they are not adequately represented by the contemporary orthography (spelling system). The letter *t*, for example, can represent a "t" sound (*tin*), a "sh" sound (*nation*), and, as we saw in section 1, a flapped "d" sound (*batter*). On the other hand, various letters other than *j* can represent the first sound in *jug: dge* in *bridge* and *g* in *logic*. Many features of the current orthography are based on the way English was pronounced hundreds of years ago; because English has changed, a different alphabet is required to represent the contemporary pronunciation. We will use a set of symbols that is in general use by American linguists.

American English Vowels

There are two major classes of American English vowels; they have been characterized as *short* versus *long,* or *lax* versus *tense,* respectively.

Short (Lax) Vowels of English

If we imagine that Figure 1 is superimposed on a cross section of the vocal tract, then the relative positions of the vowels represent the relative positions that the tongue assumes

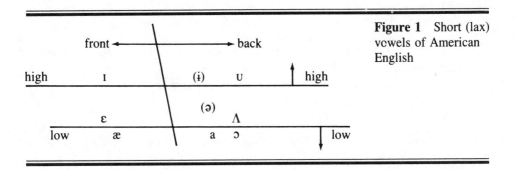

Figure 1   Short (lax) vowels of American English

in forming these vowels (with the mouth on the left). The oral cross section is divided into subsections; in describing the English vowels, linguists frequently cross-classify the vowels in terms of their position in one of the six sections in Figure 1. Thus, /ɪ/ is a high, front vowel, and /ɛ/ is a mid (nonhigh and nonlow) front vowel. The set of symbols we now present is often referred to as a phonemic alphabet. These symbols accurately represent the *major* features of articulation of American English, but do not represent finer phonetic details.

/ɪ/   A high front lax vowel. Typical words exhibiting this vowel are *sin* /sɪn/ and *big* /bɪg/. (Note that orthographic forms are in italics, phonemic forms are enclosed in slashes.)

/ɛ/   A mid front lax vowel. It is found in words such as *get* /gɛt/ and *mend* /mɛnd/.

/æ/   A low front lax vowel. This vowel is called *ash* by many linguists, and in fact it is the vowel sound in the word *ash* /æš/.

/ʌ/   A mid central unrounded lax vowel. It occurs in words such as *putt* /pʌt/ and *luck* /lʌk/.

/ʊ/   A high back slightly rounded lax vowel. It is found in words such as *put* /pʊt/ and *book* /bʊk/.

/a/, /ɔ/   Low back lax vowels. These two vowels show considerable variation of occurrence in American English; it will be up to your instructor to let you know which variant(s) you have in your speech. Some diagnostic words can enable you to determine whether you have both of these vowels in your speech: If you make a phonetic distinction between *cot* and *caught,* you probably will have the vowels represented by /kat/ and /kɔt/, respectively. (If you're from New York City, all bets are off.) You may have more than these two low lax vowels in your speech, especially if you have three different vowels in *father, cot* and *caught.* Many, if not most, Americans in the western United States have a single low back vowel; linguists use either /a/ or /ɔ/ to represent this sound.

Reduced Vowels

There are two vowels in English called reduced vowels; they are shown in parentheses in figure 1. The most common reduced vowel is called schwa and is written as an upside down *e* /ə/. It is the first vowel sound in *about* /əbawt/ and sounds very much like /ʌ/ (some linguists, in fact, use the same symbol for both sounds). The two are slightly different, however, in that ʌ is at least somewhat longer than ə. Say the word *abut* /əbʌt/ a few times to try to hear the difference. The /ə/ is called a reduced vowel because it is frequently a reduction of a regular vowel. Note the different vowels in the word *democrat* /dɛ́məkræt/ and in the word *democracy* /dəmákrəsiy/. The /ɛ/ in /dɛ́məkræt/ corresponds to the first unstressed /ə in /dəmákrəsiy/.

The other reduced vowel is /ɨ/ and is referred to as *barred i* by linguists. It is the vowel sound in the second syllable of *children* /čɪldrɨn/. The reduced vowels of English occur only in unstressed positions (in unemphasized syllables in a word).

Long (Tense) Vowels and Diphthongs

The long vowels of English differ from their short vowel counterparts not only in terms of length but in the place of articulation. If one compares the two vowel sounds in *beat* and *bit,* one will notice that the vowel in *beat* is not only longer, it even sounds higher in pitch. In addition, all of the long vowels of Modern English are diphthongal, which means that these vowel sounds can be divided into two parts: a vowel part that carries the main stress (emphasis), and an offglide, /y/ or /w/. For example, in pronouncing the word *tie,* note that at first the tongue is low (as in the vowel /a/) and gradually rises into a front *ee* /iy/ sound. (Even the vowel in English *beat* /biyt/, which is already a high vowel, rises slightly toward the end.) Hence, a common practice is to represent all the long vowels and diphthongs as clusters of vowels and offglides as follows:

(3)

iy	uw
ey	ow
ay	aw
oy	

/iy/   A high front vowel, with a slightly rising offglide represented by /y/. It occurs in words such as *beat* /biyt/ and *three* /θriy/.

/ey/   A mid front vowel with an accompanying high front offglide. Words such as *clay* /kley/ and *weigh* /wey/ exhibit this sound.

/ay/   Begins as a low back vowel, followed by a rising front offglide. It is found in *my* /may/ and *thigh* /θay/.

/oy/   A sequence of a back rounded vowel followed by a rising front offglide. It is found in words such as *boy* /boy/ and *Floyd* /floyd/.

/uw/   A sequence of a high back rounded vowel followed by a slightly rising back offglide, represented by *w.* It occurs in words such as *boot* /buwt/ and *screw* /skruw/.

/ow/   A mid back rounded vowel followed by a rising back offglide. It occurs in *boat* /bowt/ and *toe* /tow/.

/aw/   A low back unrounded vowel followed by a back offglide. It occurs in *cow* /kaw/ and *plough* /plaw/.

Consonants and Glides

Table 1 displays the consonants of English according to the two major categories of description, manner and place of articulation. The consonant sounds represented by the symbols in Table 1 can be described in terms of the articulatory features discussed in section 1.

Stops

/p/   A voiceless bilabial stop. It is the initial sound in the word *pin* /pɪn/.

/b/   A voiced bilabial stop. It occurs twice in *Bob* /bab/.

/t/   A voiceless alveolar stop. It is the initial sound in *tin* /tɪn/.

/d/   A voiced alveolar stop. It occurs twice in the word *dad* /dæd/.

/k/   A voiceless velar stop. The position of *k* will vary along the roof of the mouth, depending on what vowels precede or follow it. Thus, the /k/ in *keep* /kiyp/ is articulated in a more forward position than the /k/ in *cool* /kuwl/.

/g/   A voiced velar stop. It occurs twice in the word *gig* /gɪg/.

/ʔ/   A glottal stop. It is formed by blocking the passage of air through the vocal tract by means of closing the vocal cords. The American English pronunciation of *button* /bʌʔən/ frequently contains a glottal stop in place of /t/. Also, every word that appears to begin with a vowel actually begins with a glottal stop (/ʔæpəl/ *apple*).

Constrictives (Fricatives)

/f/   A voiceless labiodental constrictive. An /f/ is found in initial position in the word *fish* /fɪš/.

/v/   A voiced labiodental constrictive. It is the initial sound in *vine* /vayn/.

/θ/   A voiceless interdental constrictive. It is usually spelled in English as *th*. It is the initial sound in *theta* /θeytə/, and its symbol is called *theta*.

/ð/   A voiced interdental constrictive. This symbol is also represented by *th* in English spelling. The difference between /ð/ and /θ/ can be easily heard if one says *then* and *thin* slowly. You will hear (or feel) the voicing that accompanies *then* /ðɛn/ and the lack of voicing at the beginning of *thin* /θɪn/.

/s/   A voiceless alveolar constrictive. It is the initial sound in the word *sit* /sɪt/.

/z/   A voiced alveolar constrictive. It is the initial sound in the name *Zeke* /ziyk/.

/š/   A voiceless palatal constrictive. It is pronounced further back in the mouth and with a greater tongue area than the sound /s/. It is the initial sound in the word *ship* /šɪp/.

/ž/   A voiced palatal constrictive. It is the second sound in the word *azure* /æžər/.

/h/   Has many variants. In front of high front vowels it is actually a palatal constrictive as in the word *he*. Before other vowels it is a whispered (voiceless) variant of that vowel with an accompanying constriction in the glottal region. It is the initial sound in *hop* /hap/.

Table 1   The consonants of English

	Voicing	*Bilabial*	*Labiodental*	*Interdental*	*Alveolar*	*Palatal*	*Velar*	*Glottal*
Stops	voiceless	p			t		k	ʔ
	voiced	b			d		g	
Constrictives	voiceless		f	θ	s	š		h
	voiced		v	ð	z	ž		
Affricates	voiceless					č		
	voiced					ǰ		
Nasals		m			n		ŋ	
Liquids					r, l			
Glides		w				y		

Affricates

/č/   A voiceless palatal affricate. The term affricate indicates that friction (constriction) is part of the articulation of this sound. As already noted, an affricate is analyzed as a stop with a secondary release into a constrictive. A /č/ is the last sound in the word *crutch* /krʌč/.

/ǰ/   A voiced palatal affricate. It is found twice in the word *judge* /ǰʌǰ/.

Nasals

/m/   A bilabial nasal stop. The nasal stops are analogous to the voiced stops discussed earlier. When the nasal passages are opened by lowering the velum as a /b/ is being articulated, an /m/ will be produced. An /m/ is the initial sound in *mice* /mays/.

/n/   An alveolar nasal stop. An /n/ is the initial sound in *nice* /nays/.

/ŋ/   A velar nasal stop. As /b/ is to /m/ and as /d/ is to /n/, so /g/ is to /ŋ/. The /ŋ/ is called an *engwa* by many linguists. The normal English spelling for this sound is *ng,* although not all /ŋ/s are represented by *ng,* and not all *ng*'s represent an engwa. For example, there is a difference between *singer* /sɪŋər/ and *finger* /fɪŋgər/. The *ng* in *congress* is the velar nasal, but the *n* in *congressional* is an alveolar /n/ for many speakers of English.

Liquids

/r/   An alveolar liquid in which the tongue tip approaches the alveolar ridge. American English /r/ has concomitant lip rounding (labialization) and some degree of pharyngeal constriction.

/l/   A lateral alveolar liquid. The term *lateral* indicates that the air flows past both sides of the tongue during the articulation of this sound. It is the first sound in *luck* /lʌk/.

Glides

/y/   A high front glide. It occurs only before and after vowels. It is the initial sound in *yes* /yɛs/.

/w/   A high back glide. As in the case with y, w only occurs before and after vowels. It is the initial sound in *wet* /wɛt/.

Phonetic Feature Analysis of Phonemes

Refer again to Figure 1 and list (3), showing the English vowels, and to the table of consonants (table 1). Notice that there is a regularity in the distribution of phonemes. The phonemes in these displays are not random lists but are grouped into systematic classes. In talking about the sound structures of different languages, linguists frequently refer to groupings of phonemes as *series* of sounds. Thus, in table 1 the reader can identify the series of voiced /b, d, g/ and voiceless /p, t, k/ stops. Similarly, one can talk about the series of high vowels /ɪ, ɨ, ʊ/ or the front vowels /ɪ, ɛ, æ/. These groupings are not accidental; they are a reflection of a deeper organizational principle governing the sound system of human language. That is, it is not the phonemes themselves but a more basic set of phonetic features that are the fundamental units of phonological systems. Not only are the phonemes of a language grouped into systematic classes according to phonetic features; but as we will see in section 3, these systematic classes of sounds play a crucial role in the description of the phonological regularities found in human languages.

The next question to be asked, then, is what are *phonetic features*? One view of phonetic features is that for the most part they represent the individually controllable aspects of the pronunciation of the phonemes of a language. Just as we break the continuous stream of sound down into words and words into discrete phonemes, we analyze each phoneme into smaller discrete units called phonetic features. Phonemes can be viewed, then, as simultaneous bundles of phonetic features. We now turn to a discussion of the phonetic features of English, but the reader should keep in mind that the principles we discuss are applicable to the phonological systems of all human languages.

Phonetic Feature Characterization of English Vowels

The phonetic features used in this text are, for the most part, based on a proposal made by Chomsky and Halle in their book, *The Sound Pattern of English* (1968). In Table 2 we present a list of syllabic phonemes (vowels) of English with their respective phonetic feature specifications. The features in the chart represent a breakdown of the vowel sounds in terms of the various vocal tract shapes that produce these sounds.

Table 2   Phonetic feature composition of English vowels

	i (iy)	ɪ	e (ey)	ɛ	æ	u (uw)	ʊ	ʌ	o (ow)	ɔ	a	ə	ɨ
syllabic	+	+	+	+	+	+	+	+	+	+	+	+	+
high	+	+	-	-	-	+	+	-	-	-	-	-	+
back	-	-	-	-	-	+	+	+	+	+	+	+	+
low	-	-	-	-	+	-	-	-	-	+	+	-	-
round	-	-	-	-	-	+·	+	-	+	+	-	-	-
long (tense)	+	-	+	-	-	+	-	-	+	-	-	-	-
reduced	-	-	-	-	-	-	-	-	-	-	-	+	+

At the top of the table we have listed the English vowels and on the left the phonetic features that characterize them. Every plus mark indicates that a vowel has a certain feature, and every minus indicates the lack of this feature. For example, /i/ has the feature *high* but lacks the feature *round,* whereas /u/, which also has the feature *high,* possesses the feature *round.* In other words, the features allow us to distinguish all the vowels, while at the same time allowing us to cross-categorize them into classes. The vowels /i, ɪ, u, ʊ, ɨ/ are members of the class of high vowels.

Let us examine each of the phonetic features of Table 2. The terms *high, low,* and *back* refer to the relative positions the tongue may have in the mouth. These terms have already been used in the description of the vowels in Figure 1. The term *round* refers to the rounding of the lips (also called labialization), which is a feature of English back vowels such as /uw, ʊ, ow and ɔ/. The term *long* is used to distinguish /ɛ/ and /ey/, although we have already noted that there is more than a length difference between these vowels: the /ey/ phoneme begins in a higher position in the mouth than the /ɛ/ phoneme, and the /ey/ also has a high offglide. We have therefore listed the long vowels /iy, ey, uw, ow/ in terms of the features of their first segment. The remaining diphthongs /ay, aw, oy/ are not listed in Table 2; they are to be analyzed as clusters of two phonemes: for example, /ay/ = /a/ + /y/. Finally, *reduced* is a tentative term used to indicate that relatively less effort is used in the articulation of the vowels /ə/ and /i/. Table 2 should be used to find the feature specification for vowels needed to do the exercises.

Phonetic Feature Description of English Consonants

The phonetic feature compositions of English consonants are listed in Table 3. Some of the phonetic features used to describe vowels are also used for consonants. The consonant /k/, for example, requires that the back of the tongue be raised toward the roof of the mouth; /k/ thus has the feature description [+high] and [+back]. Because some of the terms have not been used up to now, we will describe each of the features in Table 3. As you will see, most of them are described in articulatory terms already encountered in section 1.

Table 3 Phonetic feature composition of English consonants

	p	b	m	t	d	n	k	g	ŋ	f	v	s	z	θ	ð	š	ž	č	ǰ	l	r	w	y	h	ʔ
consonant	+	+	+	+	+	+	+	+	+	+	+	+	+	+	+	+	+	+	+	+	+	−	−	−	−
voiced	−	+	+	−	+	+	−	+	+	−	+	−	+	−	+	−	+	−	+	+	+	+	+	−	−
nasal	−	−	+	−	−	+	−	−	+	−	−	−	−	−	−	−	−	−	−	−	−	−	−	−	−
stop	+	+	+	+	+	+	+	+	+	−	−	−	−	−	−	−	−	+	+	−	−	−	−	−	+
affricate	−	−	−	−	−	−	−	−	−	−	−	−	−	−	−	−	−	+	+	−	−	−	−	−	−
sibilant	−	−	−	−	−	−	−	−	−	−	−	+	+	−	−	+	+	+	+	−	−	−	−	−	−
labial	+	+	+	−	−	−	−	−	−	+	+	−	−	−	−	−	−	−	−	−	−	+	−	−	−
interdental	−	−	−	−	−	−	−	−	−	−	−	−	−	+	+	−	−	−	−	−	−	−	−	−	−
glottal	−	−	−	−	−	−	−	−	−	−	−	−	−	−	−	−	−	−	−	−	−	−	−	+	+
sonorant	−	−	+	−	−	+	−	−	+	−	−	−	−	−	−	−	−	−	−	+	+	+	+	+	+
high	−	−	−	−	−	−	+	+	+	−	−	−	−	−	−	+	+	+	+	−	−	+	+	−	−
back	−	−	−	−	−	−	+	+	+	−	−	−	−	−	−	−	−	−	−	−	−	+	−	−	−
low	−	−	−	−	−	−	−	−	−	−	−	−	−	−	−	−	−	−	−	−	−	−	−	+	+
coronal	−	−	−	+	+	+	−	−	−	−	−	+	+	+	+	+	+	+	+	+	+	−	−	−	−
lateral	−	−	−	−	−	−	−	−	−	−	−	−	−	−	−	−	−	−	−	+	−	−	−	−	−
distributed	−	−	−	−	−	−	−	−	−	−	−	−	−	−	−	+	+	+	+	−	−	−	−	−	−

Voiced.   Recall that vibration in the vocal cords can accompany the articulation of various sounds. Examples: /b, g, ǰ/.

Nasal.   In nasal sounds the velum is lowered to activate resonances in the nasal cavity. Examples: /m, n, ŋ/.

Stop.   The air stream through the vocal tract is completely stopped. Examples: /b, m, t/.

Affricate.   The air stream is stopped temporarily, but the stop releases into a constrictive. The release into the constrictive is secondary, and the sequence of stop plus constrictive is actually a single sound. Examples: /č, ǰ/.

Sibilant.   The class of sibilants in English contains sounds with a high degree of friction noise (''hissing''). Examples: /s, š, ǰ/.

Labial.   Articulation involves the lips. Examples: /p, m, b/.

Interdental.   The tongue is pushed forward between the teeth, forming a constrictive sound as the air passes between the upper teeth and the tongue. Examples: /ð, θ/.

Glottal.   The vocal cords constrict or stop the flow of the air. Examples: /h, ʔ/.

Sonorant.   Sonorant sounds are those produced when the vocal tract is open to the extent that spontaneous vibration of the vocal cords occurs (see Chomsky and Halle 1968, 300). Sonorants are consonants and vowels produced in such a way that the degree of constriction in the upper vocal tract is not sufficient to prohibit spontaneous voicing. Examples: /r, l, m/. Sounds made with greater degree of constriction, such that spontaneous voicing is impossible, are called nonsonorants, or, more commonly, *obstruents*.

High.   The body of the tongue is raised toward the roof of the mouth. Examples: /č, g/.

Back.   The body of the tongue remains in its normal back position. Examples: /w, g/. The tongue root can also move forward to a nonback or front position. Examples: /č, ǰ/.

Low.   The tongue is lowered to the bottom of the mouth. Examples: /ʔ, h/.

Coronal.   The blade of the tongue moves up toward the teeth and teeth ridge. Dental, alveolar, and palatal stops are coronal. Examples: /θ, d, ǰ/.

Lateral.   If the tip of the tongue is partially blocking the air stream but the air is allowed to pass along both sides of the tongue, the sound is called lateral. Example: /l/.

Distributed.   This term refers to the relative amount of contact that the tongue makes along the roof of the mouth. The tongue has a relatively longer point of contact in /š/ than in /s/; thus /š/ is distributed and /s/ is nondistributed.

.   As one can see, individual phonetic features are, in general, related to specific shapes of the vocal tract which produce the consonants and vowels found in human language. Each feature is also related to a specific group of controllable muscles in the vocal tract. Figure 2 illustrates this in an oversimplified schematic manner, ignoring certain subtleties.

Suppose we have listed on the left of Figure 2 all the hundred or so that we have just discussed, and on the right all of the phonemes of English. The important relationship is this: each feature is an abstract cover term for a grouping of muscle gestures, and each phoneme, in turn, is made up of a group of features. In this way the features are abstract units of muscle organization, which act in an intermediate position between the muscles involved in speech and the phonemes. For example, let us suppose that feature 1 is the feature *labial,* and feature 2 is the feature *nasal*. In our diagram we have connected feature 1 to a set of muscles that we have arbitrarily labeled 1, 2, 4, and 11. These could

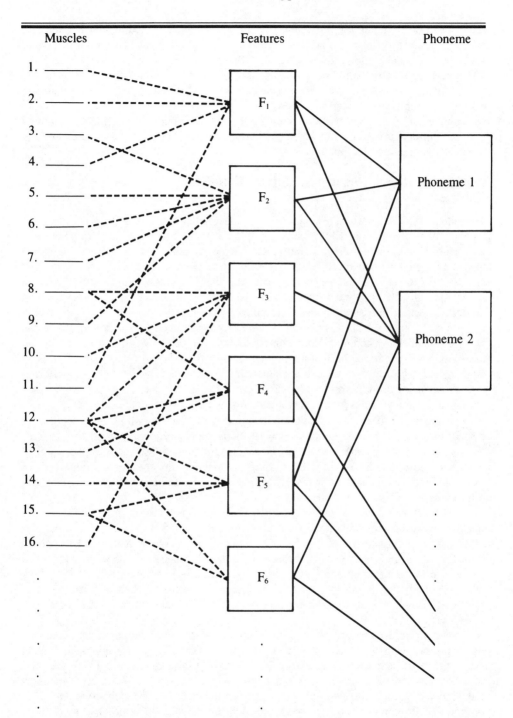

Figure 2   Phonetic features in an intermediate position between muscles and phonemes.

stand for muscles in the jaw, lips, and so forth. We have connected feature 2 to another group of arbitrarily labeled muscles, which could represent the muscles involved in lowering and raising the velum. The chart thus shows both the similarities and the differences in the articulation of /p/ versus /m/. To say that the two phonemes share the feature *labial* is to say that the same muscle groups are involved as part of the articulation of these two consonants. On the other hand, since feature 2 (*nasal*) is associated only with phoneme 2 (/m/), and not with phoneme 1 (/p/), only phoneme 2 will be articulated with the muscles involved in lowering the velum. In sum, the phonetic features link the muscle groupings and the phonemes.

Phonetic Features, Phonemes, and the Notion of Contrast

The phonemes of the world's languages are constructed from differing subsets of the universally available set of phonetic features. Although all languages draw from the same universal set of phonetic features, individual languages can differ in the sets of features that make up their phonemes. The features *coronal, lateral, affricated,* and *distributed* are all found in English, but they never occur together in a single phoneme. By contrast, in Navajo (as well as in many other North American Indian languages), these features do occur together in a single consonant, called a lateral affricate; the Navajo word *ƚah* ("ointment") begins with this phoneme, which is represented by two letters (tł) in the Navajo alphabet. Different feature combinations also occur in vowels. English, for example, does not have the feature of rounding in front vowels, but many European languages do (French, German, and Finnish among others). Thus, the widely differing sounds occurring in the world's languages are actually based in large part on various combinations drawn from a relatively small, restricted set of phonetic features.

A crucial property of phonetic features is that they are not all of equal value with respect to each other in particular languages. It is necessary, at this time, to introduce the distinction between phoneme and phone, since this is an important one in phonological theory. Up to this point we have been using a phonemic alphabet for writing words of English. Linguists have at their disposal a more precise alphabet, however, frequently referred to as a phonetic alphabet.

The nature of the relation between a phonemic and a phonetic alphabet can be made clear with some examples. Just as phonemes are analyzed as simultaneous bundles of phonetic features, phones are likewise bundles of phonetic features, but phones represent much finer phonetic detail than do phonemes. In English the *phones* [tʰ], [t˺], and [t] are varying pronunciations (or simply, variations of) the phoneme /t/. We follow here the traditional practice of writing phonemes in slash lines and phones in square brackets. The phones of /t/ all share the features listed in table 2 for /t/; that is, all are voiceless, coronal stops.

The differences in the phones, however, are as follows: the phone [tʰ], found in initial position in words such as *tin* [tʰɪn], is a stop whose release is accompanied by an extra puff of air, referred to as aspiration (indicated by a raised *h* with the *t*). The presence of aspiration can be observed if one dangles a piece of paper close in front of one's mouth when saying the word *tin*. The paper will move immediately after the /t/ is pronounced. In contrast, no such movement will be noticed when the /t/ follows an /s/ in a word such as *sting:* voiceless stops following /s/ in word-initial position are never aspirated in English.

The phone [t˺] is an unreleased *t*. For example, many speakers of American English do not release the final /t/ of *write*—the tongue remains touching the alveolar ridge. In contrast, the phone [t] is released, but not aspirated. For many speakers, then, a physical difference exists between the final /t/ of *print* and the final /t/ of *write*. Phonetically, the word *print* ends in [t], and the word *write* may end in [tʼ]. There are thus several phonetic variations of the phoneme /t/ in English; these variants are referred to as different *phones*.

The phones of a phoneme bear certain relations to each other. For instance, since each of the three phones of the phoneme /t/ [tʰ, tʼ, t] (also called *allophones* of the phoneme /t/) can occur in final position in a word, more or less freely, they are said to occur in *free variation* in that position. By contrast, the aspirated and unreleased phones [tʰ, tʼ] can never appear after word-initial /s/, though the released, unaspirated phone [t] can. The two phones [tʰ, tʼ] are therefore said to be in *complementary distribution* with [t] after word-initial /s/: [tʰ, tʼ] never appear in that position; [t] does. Thus the phones of a phoneme are generally describable as being in either complementary distribution or in free variation with each other.

The phones [tʰ] and [tʼ] can now be compared to the phone [d], the latter being a phone of the phoneme /d/. These three phones are phonetically (physically) distinguishable, yet the difference between [tʰ] and [d] and between [tʼ] and [d] is not of the same nature as the difference between [tʰ] and [tʼ]. The pair [d] and [tʰ] functions as a contrasting pair in English words and so do [d] and [tʼ], whereas [tʰ] and [tʼ] do not. That is to say, words will differ in meaning by the mere substitution of [tʰ] for [d]: in English, *tin* [tʰɪn] is a different word from *din* [dɪn]. Moreover, even in nonsense words—for example, *plit*—replacing a [tʰ] with a [d] creates a different word, in this case *plid*. Similar facts do not hold for [tʰ] and [tʼ]. Replacing one of these sounds by the other does not yield a new English word. Whether one pronounces a final voiceless coronal stop /t/ with aspiration or without aspiration, a native speaker of English will perceive the word as ending with the same consonant. Thus, *write* pronounced as [raytʰ] or as [raytʼ] is still the same word. Hence one can say that the phonetic difference between [tʰ] and [tʼ], aspiration, is nondistinctive. In general, the feature of voicing (which distinguishes /d/ from /tʰ/ functions *distinctively* (or *phonemically*) in English, whereas, aspiration functions nondistinctively (or nonphonemically).

Languages differ as to what features function distinctively. In Hindi, a language of India, the feature of aspiration functions distinctively in voiceless stops. For speakers of Hindi, the consonants [kʰ] (aspirated) and [k] (nonaspirated) are perceived as two different consonants. For example, *khiil* means "parched grain" whereas *kiil* means "nail."

In sum, if a phonetic feature functions distinctively—that is, if it can be used to distinguish one word from another—then it may be called a *distinctive feature*. All of the phonetic features discussed in this chapter are often called distinctive features because of the phonemic (or distinctive) role that these features play in the sound systems of human languages.

3. PHONOLOGICAL RULES, NATURAL CLASSES, AND THE SPEAKER'S KNOWLEDGE OF PHONOLOGY

The Role of Phonetic Features in the Expression of Phonological Rules

As we have seen, speech sounds can be described in terms of small units that represent very fine and detailed aspects of the articulation of each sound. It is these phonetic features—and not the phonemes themselves—that underlie the phonological regularities (rules) of natural language. We illustrate some phonological regularities with three examples, of increasing complexity.

Example 1: English

In section 1 we discussed some cases of verb and agentive noun pairs:

(4)   Verb   Agentive Noun

(to) write	writer
(to) shout	shouter
(to) bat	batter
(to) hit	hitter

As we noted, for most Americans the final dental stop in the verb *write* is voiceless but appears as a voiced flap (which we now write as [D]) in the agentive noun. We can now describe this phenomenon of the appearance of the [t] and the [D] more precisely, in terms of phonetic features.

Recall that the occurrence of the [D] is not random but rather results from a principle of pronunciation of contemporary American English. Words we have never encountered before will exhibit the same variation between [t] and [D]. Linguists refer to the differing corresponding phonological segments in related words as phonological alternations. The final [t] in *write* [rayt] is said to alternate with the medial [D] in *writer* [rayDər].

Note that the alternation might have a direction and could go either of two ways. Either the [D] must be pronounced as a [t] when it occurs in final position; or, conversely, a [t] must be pronounced as a [D] when it occurs before the /-ər/ agentive suffix. We might formulate the first possibility as follows: Whenever an agentive noun with a [D] is used as a verb, the [D] becomes a [t]. This cannot be correct, however, since the medial [D] of *rider* [rayDər] does not become a final [t] in *ride* [rayd]. Thus the rule seems to be that alveolar stops [t, d] must be pronounced as [D] if preceded by the stressed vowels /áy, í/, and so on, and if followed by /-ər/. This rule is expressed schematically in (5).

(5)

$$
\begin{bmatrix} t \\ d \end{bmatrix} \rightarrow D\ /
\begin{array}{ll}
\text{áy}\!-\!-\!\text{ər} & \text{(writer)} \\
\text{í}\!-\!-\!\text{ər} & \text{(kidder)} \\
\text{æ}\!-\!-\!\text{ər} & \text{(batter)} \\
\text{áw}\!-\!-\!\text{ər} & \text{(powder)} \\
\text{éy}\!-\!-\!\text{ər} & \text{(later)}
\end{array}
$$

In rule (5) the arrow indicates the direction of the change ([t] and [d] become [D]), the slash means "in the environment of," and the dash indicates where the change occurs. Thus the rule in (5) expresses that a [t] or a [d] becomes a [D] between /áy/ and /ər/, between /í/ and /ər/, between /æ/ and /ər/, and so on.

At this point we can hypothesize that our theory of phonology must consist of a description of the phonemes and a set of conditions describing aspects of the occurrence of these phonemes.

Theory 1
The phonological system of a natural language consists of (i) a set of phonemes and (ii) a set of conditions (rules) that define aspects of the pronunciation of those phonemes. The rules that account for phonological alternations are stated by listing the phonemes that condition the phonological change.

Rule (5) will, in fact, cover all the examples mentioned so far. However, it does not account for additional cases of the [t] → [D] alternation. Consider the examples in (6):

(6) Verb   Agentive noun

(to) butt	butter	(ʌ́——ər)
(to) bait	baiter	(éy——ər)
(to) beat	beater	(íy——ər)
(to) exploit	exploiter	(óy——ər)
. . .	. . .	

Rule (5) fails to generalize to these cases, since the stressed vowels listed in (5) are not found in the words in (6). Indeed, the ellipses points in (6) indicte that *any* preceding stressed English vowel can condition the change of [t] to [D]; a list completely fails to express this generalization. The correct statement for the alternation between [t] and [D] is that an alveolar stop will be pronounced as a flap when it occurs between *any* vowels if the left (preceding) vowel bears primary stress. This leads us to our next theory.

Theory 2
The phonological system of a natural language consists of (i) a set of phonemes, and (ii) a set of conditions (rules) that define aspects of the pronunciation of those segments. The rules account for phonological alternations by referring to phonetic features, not by listing phonemes.

Following Theory 2 we will write the rule that expresses the alternation between [t, d] and [D] in English in terms of the phonetic features introduced earlier.

(7) Flap Rule

$$\begin{bmatrix} + \text{coronal} \\ + \text{stop} \\ - \text{affricate} \\ - \text{sonorant} \end{bmatrix} \rightarrow \begin{bmatrix} + \text{voice} \\ + \text{flap} \end{bmatrix} / \begin{bmatrix} + \text{syllabic} \\ + \text{stress} \end{bmatrix} \text{——} [+ \text{syllabic}]$$

$$\text{(d, t)} \quad \rightarrow \quad D \quad / \quad \acute{V} \quad \text{——} \quad V$$

The Flap rule (7) states that a nonaffricate coronal stop ([V́, V]) must be pronounced as a voiced flap ([D]) whenever it occurs between vowels, if the first vowel is stressed. The feature [+stress] is necessary because a coronal stop remains voiceless if the preceding syllable does not bear the main stress of the word (as witness the final [t] in *rapidity* [rəpíDɨtiy]).

Example 1 illustrated that phonological systems are not organized according to whole phonemes. Rather, each phoneme is made up of phonetic features, and phonological rules sensitive to these *features* govern our pronunciation. If the Flap rule were to be expressed in terms of phonemes, all of the English vowels would have to be listed in the rule. However, the feature notation allows us to capture the generalization that any syllabic segment will provide the conditioning environment for rule (7). This is a good illustration of how classes of sounds (here the class of all vowels) play a role in phonological descriptions.

Rule (7) is typical of the rules one finds in the phonological systems of natural language. Languages may differ in the types of rule they have, or even in the number they have, but phonological regularities are describable by rules formulated in phonetic features such as (7). Rule (7), moreover, is not limited to the dental stops in agentive nouns. Forms such as *nutty* [nʌDiy], *beating* [bíyDɨŋ], and *butter* [bʌDər], all satisfy the conditions expressed in rule (7). Any English speaker who has the flap [D] in the agentives in (1) will also have a flap in any word in which the conditions specified in rule (7) are satisfied.

* * *

Interaction of Phonological Rules in English

The theory of phonology outlined so far consists of two major parts: a set of segments (phonemes or phones) and a set of rules. The phonological segments are specified in terms of sets of phonetic features. The rules express regularities of pronunciation. For example, we discussed a rule in which an unvoiced alveolar stop must be pronounced as a voiced flap between vowels when the first vowel is stressed (rule (7)). Standard American English has a large number of rules of this type.

Another rule that affects medial /t/ (that is, /t/ inside a word) is the Glottal Stop rule, which has the following form [Rules 8–11 have been omitted.]:

(12)

Glottal Stop Rule: t → ʔ / V̆——ṇ

This rule indicates that /t/ becomes a glottal stop /ʔ/ when it occurs after a stressed vowel and before a syllabic /n/, which accounts for the typical American pronunciation of *button* [bʌʔṇ]. (Recall that a glottal stop is produced by blocking the airstream by closing the vocal cords, something English speakers consistently do in the middle of the phrase *oh oh* [ówʔow].) In other words the point of closure is shifted from the alveolar region where /t/ is produced to the glottal region resulting in /ʔ/.

The /n/ following the glottal stop is referred to as a syllabic nasal, represented by [ṇ]. The term *syllabic* is used to describe the [ṇ] because in many ways this nasal element functions as an independent syllable. To see this, first note that the word *button* is bisyllabic (has two syllables) and carries the normal bisyllabic stress and tone contour of English nouns—that is, the major emphasis is on the first syllable. Second, the segment following the glottal stop is nasal throughout: it is not possible to isolate any nonnasal vowel between the glottal stop and the nasal. Hence the nasal itself functions as the second syllable.

So far we have discussed the phonological rules as isolated and indeed autonomous from other phonological rules. Now notice that the Glottal Stop rule (12) interacts in interesting ways with the Flap rule (7) in normal American English. Consider the two words *beating* and *beading*. In casual speech a final *-ing* ending can be reduced to a syllabic nasal /-ṇ/, and rules (7) and (12) give us different results depending on whether the ending is /ɨŋ/ or /ṇ/:

(13)

	Formal Speech		Casual Speech	
	beating	beading	beatin'	beadin'
	biyt-ɨŋ	biyd-ɨŋ	biyt-ṇ	biyd-ṇ
Flap Rule (7)	biyD-ɨŋ	biyD-ɨŋ	———	———
Glottal Stop Rule (12)	———	———	biyʔ-ṇ	———
Pronunciation	[biyDɨŋ]	[biyDɨŋ]	[biyʔṇ]	[biydṇ]

Given the rules represented in this section, we see that in more formal speech *beating* and *beading* are pronounced in the same way, but in casual speech the forms end up differently. For some speakers the sentence /ðə reyn ɨz biyDɨŋ an ðə wɪndow/ is ambiguous. It can mean either "The rain is beating on the window," or "The rain is beading on the window."

Ordered Rules? (optional section)

Must the order in which certain rules apply be specified? As matters now stand, the Flap rule (7) would apply to the form /biyt-ṇ/ because the /t/ occurs between syllabics, thus satisfying the conditions for the application of the rule. But that would derive an incorrect form. In order to derive the correct forms for casual speech with our current rules, we would have to specify that rule (12) must apply *before* rule (7) in order to prevent the application of rule (7). However, the question of ordering does not arise if the feature [-nasal] is added to the feature specification [+ syllabic] on the right side of the environment in which the Flap rule (7) applies. With this form, rule (7) and the Glottal Stop rule (12) would apply in mutually exclusive environments.

The Speaker's Knowledge of Phonology: "Possible Words"

When Madison Avenue advertisers want to create a brand name for a new product, they must follow the constraint that the name they invent must be a possible English word. *Possible word* here means a word that does not actually exist in English but that English speakers will readily claim sounds like an English word. Speakers have unconsciously extracted principles as to which sequences of sounds are possible English, and which are not. The soap product names *Fab* and *Biz* were excellent candidates for brand-name status, while hypothetical names such as *Vlk* or *Psulth* would not stand a good chance of being successful. Although all of the individual phonemes in *Vlk* occur in English, they cannot appear in this sequence.

The conditions on the possible sequences of phonemes in a given language are part of a study called *phonotactics*. For example, in English words beginning with three consonants, the first must be an /s/. If /p/ is the second consonant, then /r/, /l/, or /y/ can follow (*spread, spleen,* and *spew*). If the second consonant is /t/, then only /r/ can follow for most dialects of English (*stream*), though some dialects of English allow a /y/ after /st/ sequences if the phoneme /uw/ follows. (Thus, for *stew* one finds the pronunciation /styuw/ as well as the more common /stuw/.) If the second consonant is /k/, then /r/, /l/, /w/, or /y/ can follow (*scream, sclerosis, square,* and *skew*).

Native English speakers can easily recognize that made-up words like *Vlk* violate the sequential constraints on initial phonemes; the strangeness of such words is immediately apparent. It is unlikely that speakers check each new word they encounter against every other word in their vocabulary to judge whether or not it conforms to the patterns of the other words. The judgment is, instead, instantaneous and strongly suggests that speakers have internalized abstract principles that characterize the conditions on pronunciation of their language.

The Speaker's Knowledge of Phonology: Stress Patterns

One of the more remarkable features of the English speaker's knowledge has to do with the stress contours in words. It can be shown that the position of main stress (or emphasis) within a word is in part regular and predictable and is based on the phonological, morphological, and syntactic properties of the word. In this section we will discuss the rules for stress placement in nouns; we will test the validity of the rules by demonstrating how stress is assigned in words that have never been encountered before.

The position of main stress in bisyllabic (two-syllable) nouns is usually on the first syllable (the left one):

(14)

móther	árgyle
móuntain	cóntents
tórrent	tórment

In words with three or more syllables the position of the main stress can vary. It is either on the second syllable from the right (the penultimate syllable) or on the third from the right (the antepenultimate), as shown in (15):

(15) Penultimate	Antepenultimate
contrálto	América
Arizóna	vánity
eléctric	géneral

The difference in stress placement in these words is not random. Rather, stress will be on the penultimate syllable if that syllable consists of either a long vowel (as in *Arizona* /ærɨzównə/) or any vowel followed by at least two consonants (*electric* /əléktrɨk/). These two types of syllables are both designated as *strong* syllables. A *weak* syllable, on the other hand, consists of a short (or lax) vowel followed by at most one consonant; for example, all of the syllables in *America* /əmérɨkə/ are weak. One can state, then, that in words of at least three syllables the stress will be on the penultimate syllable unless that syllable is weak. If the penultimate syllable is weak, stress will be on the next syllable to the left, the antepenultimate syllable.

The English language is constantly acquiring new acronyms (words formed by combining the first letter (or letters) of the words in a descriptive phrase, like *Sunoco* from **Sun Oil Co**mpany), and English speakers automatically stress these novel words according to principles based on syllable strength. Some typical examples follow:

(16) Penultimate Stress	Antepenultimate Stress
Nabísco	Únicef
Unésco	Cónoco
Sunóco	Téxaco

In each of the words with penultimate stress the stressed syllable is strong. In all words with antepenultimate stress the penultimate syllable is weak. An interesting comparison can be made with the two acronyms *Sunóco* and *Cónoco* (**Con**tinental **Oil** Company). On the east coast, where Sunoco stations are found, stress is on the penultimate syllable [sənówkow]. The stress on *Conoco,* the name of a West coast company, is on the antepenultimate syllable /kánəkow/. These two different stress patterns are not counterexamples to the claim that stress placement is determined by regular rules, but rather this difference is consistent with the principles of English stress. In the word *Sunoco* the second syllable is strong because the /o/ is long (/ow/), and thus we have /sənówkow/. In *Conoco,* however, the penultimate syllable is weak /kánəkow/. Many readers may have "incorrectly" stressed the word *Conoco* in the penultimate syllable and pronounced the name as /kənówkow/. Note that in this case the second syllable is now pronounced with a long vowel, and thus stress is ultimately assigned based on whether or not the speaker decides that the penultimate syllable is weak or strong. If the penultimate vowel is interpreted as long, it will be stressed. It is important to note that it is not the stress itself that *causes* a syllable to be strong. In the noun *America,* for example, the stress is on the *e* (pronounced /ɛ/); nevertheless, that vowel is not long. There is, of course, an interaction between vowel length and stress placement, but once one decides the vowel length in the penultimate syllable of *Sunoco* or *Conoco,* the stress placement will follow automatically.

In sum, a theory of phonology can be viewed as a theory that represents native speakers' knowledge of the sounds and regularities of their language. The currently most promising theory of phonology is the following: for all human languages the knowledge of the native speaker is represented in the form of (a) a set of phonemes and (b) a set of phonological rules formulated in terms of phonetic features. The ability of a child to master a phonological system is part of the child's biologically inherited disposition to acquire a spoken language.

DISCUSSION QUESTIONS

1. The authors describe phonemes in two ways. What advantages has each of the ways?

2. Is there symmetry among stops—in other words, do the voiceless stops /p, k/ have the same distribution as /t/? What about voiced stops /b, d, g/? Test yourself with a piece of paper.

3. Can you hear phonemes?

4. Do you find the evidence convincing that phonology is rule-governed? Why could you predict that English might someday have *blick* as a word, but not *nlick?*

GEORGE LAKOFF

After receiving his Ph.D. from Indiana University, Lakoff worked in the Computation Laboratory at Harvard University and began his teaching career at the University of Michigan. Now professor of linguistics at the University of California, Berkeley, he is a leader in the field of Generative Semantics. With Mark Johnson he has recently published Metaphors We Live By *(University of Chicago Press, 1980).*

HUMANISTIC LINGUISTICS

I would like to contrast two approaches to the study of linguistics, what I will call the Nuts-and-Bolts approach and the Humanistic approach. Fields of study are characterized by (i) questions that researchers seek to answer and (ii) tools, both technological and conceptual, that are available and socially acceptable. The Nuts-and-Bolts linguist views research in his field as an attempt to answer the question:

(N-B)   What formal principles, both language-particular and universal, are necessary and sufficient to characterize the distribution of and relationships among linguistic elements in each of the languages of the world?

The Humanist linguist asks a very different question, namely:

(H)   What can the study of language tell us about human beings?

The Humanistic approach is obviously the broader one, since it incorporates the Nuts-and-Bolts approach as a proper subpart: one of the many things that the study of language can tell us about a human being is which formal principles characterize the grammar of the language he speaks. But Humanistic Linguistics is properly concerned with far more than merely grammars and the theory of grammar. Let me start off with just a short list of a few of the things I would take to be part of Humanistic linguistics.

1. The study of the human conceptual apparatus—what is thought? What are concepts? What is human reasoning?
2. The study of what goes on in people's minds. Not just what goes on in the comprehension of language, or production, or acquisition, but what people are thinking and feeling, consciously and unconsciously, as it is revealed by the language they use.
3. The study of personality—how the use of language can tell us what people are like.
4. The study of social interaction and social organization, as it is revealed by the use of language, not just the study of social groups and dialects, but also everyday social interaction.
5. The use of language in political, legal, and social reform.
6. The use of language in literature, the arts, and journalism.

The list can be easily extended, but I think you get the idea.

American linguistics in the Bloomfield-Chomsky era was mostly concerned with Nuts-and-Bolts, although there were important exceptions which will be discussed below. Within the past five years, however, there has been an important swing toward humanistic linguistics. It is important to increase the momentum of this movement and to give it as much intellectual content as possible. Which brings us to the heart of the matter— intellectual content. The typical nuts-and-bolts reaction would be something like: 'Gee, it would be nice to be able to get some insight into people and society by studying language, but given how little we now know, most of that would be just bull.' And given much of the popular literature about language and linguistics, one can only grant that such pitfalls exist. But what is all too often forgotten is that nuts-and-bolts linguistics has within it just as much potential for bull, potential that is constantly being realized. Only in nuts-and-bolts linguistics, it is hidden by empty formalism, and one has to know a lot about formal linguistics to separate it out. Classical transformational grammar is rife with examples. Take the *Syntactic Structures* analysis of the auxiliary in English, which was for years taken to be a classic example of a great result in Nuts-and-Bolts Linguistics. I was one of those who was impressed by that analysis in the early sixties. Here were these very impressive-looking formal rules that seemed to be able to spit out all the morphemes in the right order. I thought there must be something very deep about those rules that enabled them to do that. It seemed to me at the time that there must be something profound about those symbols, AUX, M, TNS, EN, that I did not yet understand but that with study I could someday come to appreciate. What happened was exactly opposite. The more deeply I got into nuts-and-bolts transformational grammar, the more superficial that analysis became. When people like Postal, Ross, Robin Lakoff, myself, and others started really looking into the details of that analysis, the whole thing went up in smoke. In the first place, the morphemes didn't really come out in the right order. Postal noticed that the analysis incorrectly predicted that '*Has John a book?' was the past tense of the question 'Has John a book?' Ross observed that if 'need' and 'dare' were treated as members of the category M, then the analysis claims that the 'need' in 'Need you open the window?' and the 'need' in 'Do you need to open the window?' have nothing whatever to do with each other. Ross also observed that the analysis could not account for the pronominalization possibilities in cases like (1):

(1) Will Sam have been slicing the salami, which Max says he will (have (been))?

Once we started looking at the details, it became clear that the analysis was just plain wrong. In case after case after case. And on reflection it became clear why it was wrong. The analysis told one nothing whatever about the function of tenses and auxiliaries so far as meaning and the use of language is concerned. One need only look at J. McCawley's 'Tense and Time Reference in English' (1971) to see that auxiliaries have a semantic function that is reflected in syntax, or at Robin Lakoff's 'The Pragmatics of Modality' (1972) and 'Tense and Its Relation to Participants' (1970) to see that auxiliaries have a pragmatic function that is reflected in their syntax. Symbols like AUX, M, TNS, etc. are ways of disguising bull. They are not profound. They give little if any insight into the nature of verbal auxiliaries.

The case of the *Syntactic Structures* auxiliary analysis points up the kind of danger that plagues not only Linguistics but other academic fields as well: Formal research tends to drive out nonformal research. The subject matter of the field becomes reduced to the subject matter that can be dealt with by the available conceptual and technological tools. In the heyday of transformational grammar, linguistics became defined by the conceptual tools that Chomsky had made available. The job of the linguist was thought of as investigating how language could be described using transformational grammars. At MIT, the course on other approaches to linguistics became known as 'Bad Guys'. It has been largely through the work of Dwight Bolinger, Charles Fillmore, Robin Lakoff, William Labov, and their followers that linguistics has begun to transcend the nuts-and-bolts approach in a way that has intellectual content. And equally important, it is largely through their work that real intellectual content has begun to be given to Nuts-and-Bolts Linguistics.

Now, I am primarily known as a nuts-and-bolts linguist. And for good reason. I have worked at things like the theory of exceptions, pronominalization constraints, correspondence grammars, global rules, transderivational rules, the logic of fuzzy concepts, the formalization of presuppositions, etc. Chances are that I will continue to do this sort of nuts-and-bolts work on a day-to-day basis. But my perception of what nuts-and-bolts linguistics is about—what good it is and why it is worth the bother—has changed considerably in, say, the past five years. What has brought about this change has been the nonformal writings of Dwight Bolinger, Charles Fillmore, and Robin Lakoff. In paper after paper, these nonformal grammarians have taken up and insightfully discussed problems that are beyond, often far beyond, formal description in any contemporary theories. Their writings are informed by the results of transformational grammar, generative semantics, and other contemporary approaches. Consequently, they know that there is no point in trying to write formal rules for what they are interested in, since there are no theories that work. They have not permitted their interests to be defined by the pitifully inadequate linguistic theories that happen to be available. Yet their papers are insightful and interesting, usually more so than papers on formal linguistics, an alarmingly large percentage of which have fallen into the symbol manipulation syndrome and are no more revealing than the *Syntactic Structures* analysis of the auxiliary. The writings of the nonformal grammarians, together with the recent work by Haj Ross on squishes, reveal the complexity of language in all its glory and the inadequacy of contemporary linguistic theories in all their poverty. They not only show that no theories now work; they show that no theories are going to come close to working in the foreseeable future. They give us an inkling that current theories cannot handle 10 percent, or even 5 percent, or even 1 percent, of what we know about language—a better estimate would be more like .000000000000023 percent!

But if this is so, why bother doing formal linguistics at all? What are nuts and bolts good for if you can't build anything with them?! What sense does it make to talk about ADVANCES IN LINGUISTIC THEORY if we know so little? How can one teach a course in linguistic theory with a straight face? Or justify continuing to patch up inadequate theories with Band-aids and Scotch tape? There are, I think, answers to such questions, though not straightforward and obvious ones.

To begin with, Humanistic Linguistics (currently embodied mostly in the writings of the nonformal grammarians) is in a symbiotic relationship with Nuts-and-Bolts Linguistics. Each gives intellectual content to the other. The writings on formal linguistics, particularly those in transformational grammar and generative semantics, have at least in a negative way shaped the interests of the nonformal grammarians. Nonformal grammarians tend to get interested in what they write about largely because those topics are beyond the scope of contemporary formal linguistics. And formal linguists, at least those working in Generative Semantics, choose the directions in which to extend their theories because nonformal grammarians have pointed out inadequacies. In fact, the so-called 'results' in formal linguistics are far and away more negative than positive. Most of the time, we show you cannot handle such-and-such a phenomenon with such-and-such conceptual apparatus. For example, take the following notion of 'semantic representation':

> A 'semantic representation' is a structure (say a tree structure) made up of symbols (semantic markers in one theory, predicates, arguments, etc. in another) that can adequately represent all aspects of the meaning of a sentence.

One of the important results in recent formal linguistics which grew out of nonformal observations is that semantic representations in this sense do not exist: finite structures made up of symbols cannot adequately represent many aspects of the meaning of a sentence. In fact, once you think about it, this 'result' is obvious. Let's start with a fact about hedges which was noted by Dwight Bolinger in his classic book *Degree Words* (1972). Bolinger observed that words like *regular* and *real* map connotations into literal meanings. Consider (2):

> (2) John's a regular Henry Kissinger.

Depending on context, (2) might mean that John is diplomatic, or that he is a ladies' man, or that he is a manipulative advisor, or that he is professorial, or that he is an opportunist, or that he is jovial, or that he is a war criminal. The point is that connotations are context dependent; and if there are an infinite number of possible contexts, there are an infinite number of connotations for proper names. In short, (2) has an infinite range of possible meanings, each of them dependent on context. But to fans of Paul Grice this will hardly be a surprise. Grice's study of implicature indicates that most sentences have an infinite range of indirectly conveyed meanings, depending on context. In fact, Grice believes that any sentence can mean anything, given the right context. An important recent result in nonformal grammar is that this is not true. For example

> (3) John ran away.
> (4) Away ran John.

(3) can be a request for help, while (4) cannot. Similarly,

> (5) Sam sliced the salami carefully.
> (6) Carefully, Sam sliced the salami.

(5) can be a request to be lenient on Sam, while (6) cannot. The point here is that certain syntactic constructions are limited in the meanings they can convey. Interestingly enough, they are the exceptions rather than the rule. The inadequacy of semantic representations as descriptions of meaning is also shown by hedges like *sort of, rather, pretty (much)*, etc., which, as Zadeh and I have shown, require algebraic functions in any adequate account of their meaning. Such hedges require a model-theoretical approach to meaning; combinatorial structures just cannot do the job.

The nonformal observations that initially revealed such inadequacies in the notion of semantic representation have led to formal theories in which such facts can be handled. Current generative semantics depends very much on model-theoretical interpretations of logical structures. These permit both an account of hedges and an account of implicatures in terms of entailments in context.

Over the past five years, nonformal linguists have pulled formal linguists working on generative semantics more and more into the area of pragmatics, that is, into the study of how language is organized in terms of the assumptions and intentions of participants in a discourse. Robin Lakoff's informal discussion of the function of conjunction in 'If's and's and but's about conjunction', for example, forced me into a realization that entailments in contexts played a central role in grammar, and led directly to the development of transderivational rules. Another example is Ann Borkin's work (1971) showing that the distribution of polarity items depends upon conveyed meaning. Such results, in turn, have led to the further use of model theory in generative semantics, for the purpose of distinguishing between the literal meaning of a sentence and those aspects of meaning that are entailed in a context. Over the past five years, the constant challenge of the nonformal grammarians has led us to more and more theoretical innovations in the area of pragmatics.

At the same time such formal developments have helped to clarify the intuitions of grammarians who were straightjacketed by transformational grammar. For example, take the discussion of tag-questions in Robin Lakoff's 'A syntactic argument for negative transportation' (1969). She considers sentences such as (7)

(7) I don't suppose the Giants will win, will they?

She accounts for the positive tag in terms of negative transportation and claims that tags in general agree with the subject and first auxiliary of the sentential complement of verbs like *suppose, think,* and *believe,* which she refers to as kinds of 'performative' verbs, even though these, strictly speaking, were not performative in the same sense as *state, order,* etc. The intuition behind this description was that the function of tags was to convey a hedged assertion and ask for confirmation. But in 1969, there was no way to express this formally. Given present conceptions of indirect speech acts and transderivational rules, one can express more precisely what that intuition was. Verbs like *suppose, think,* and *believe* can be used to indirectly convey hedged assertions. Tag questions (at least of this type) function to ask for confirmation of what is being hesitantly asserted, which is why they agree with the complements of verbs such as *suppose, think,* and *believe.* The tag is not simply introduced transformationally, but is reduced from the corresponding full question. The tag-construction is an amalgram (see G. Lakoff 1974) of the hedged assertion and the full question; the amalgamation is constrained by the pragmatic conditions described above. Of course, such an analysis is beyond the conceptual resources of transformational grammar; it requires a theory of contextually conditioned indirect speech acts plus a theory of transderivational rules. The point here is that, even to provide a nonformal description of what is going on, as we just have, one requires conceptual resources far beyond transformational grammar. Just as intuitive grammar can guide the formation of theories, so theories can explicate unformalized intuitive descriptions. Nonformal grammar and nuts-and-bolts grammar are mutually supportive.

I would like to suggest that the recent nuts-and-bolts developments in the area of pragmatics, particularly the use of model theory in the study of context and transderivational rules—together with the mode of inquiry developed by the nonformal grammarians—make possible the development of a humanistic linguistics with real content. A good example is Robin Lakoff's essay 'Language and Woman's Place' (1973). Humanistic linguistics would, of course, overlap in subject matter with a number of other disciplines, especially psychology, philosophy of language, logic, anthropology, sociology, literature, education, even law.

At this point I would like to discuss very briefly what I think the most interesting aspects of this overlap between humanistic linguistics and other disciplines will be. Let's start with philosophy. First, the obvious—at least so far as linguists are concerned. It has been noted by many people, e.g. Harman, Davidson, Katz, McCawley, myself, etc., that to the extent that philosophical analysis depends on linguistic analysis, philosophical analysis is an empirical study. This is very slowly beginning to be comprehended by philosophers, but there is a long way to go. I am not talking merely about the philosophy of language. Take the philosophy of action, for example. As Ross (1972) and Vendler (1967) have shown, there is a wealth of linguistic evidence bearing on the analysis of actions. Or take causation. Philosophers almost invariably talk about causation as a relation between events. But sentences like (8) show that causation can relate states and states, states and events, and events and states as well.

(8a) Being poor has prevented me from being happy.
(8b) Being poor made John go mad.
(8c) Sam's hitting Bill made John unhappy.

Or take the philosophy of logic. Logic was originally conceived of as the study of human reasoning in general. Now the study of human reasoning is, or should be, an empirical matter. But since Frege and Russell, logic has been largely an a priori study, and in recent years it has become a highly developed branch of mathematics, which has little to do with human reasoning—except for the subfield of intensional logic, which has been growing rapidly and slowly converging with linguistics. Unfortunately, there is still relatively little empirical research done by intensional logicians. It is here that the work of nonformal linguists can be especially helpful in providing challenging problems that known logics cannot deal with. I have discussed such problems in a number of publications (G. Lakoff 1972a, 1972b, 1973). For now, let me take up just one—the analysis of proper names, a problem which is also of interest in the philosophy of language.

Logicians usually treat proper names as constants, which function as what Kripke calls 'rigid designators.' Typical examples of what logicians mean by proper names are the names of numbers, like '2' and '37,' which (rigidly) designate the numbers two and thirty-seven in all possible worlds. By the same token, 'The Eiffel Tower' would always designate the Eiffel Tower. Another implicit property of proper names as logicians conceive of them is that they are undecomposable. Even a cursory nonformal look at proper names in English reveals that they are rather different than logicians conceive of them as being.

First, they yield ambiguities in opaque contexts.

(9) Sam Schwartz told his girlfriend that his name was Henry Kissinger, and so she believes that she has been dating Henry Kissinger.

(9) has two readings—one where she thinks he is *the* Henry Kissinger and one where she thinks he is merely *a* Henry Kissinger—which leads to:

(10) Sarah is dating *a* Henry Kissinger, not *the* Henry Kissinger.

The use of articles with a proper name has to be accounted for. There is also a mysterious use of the number *one* with proper names.

(11a) One Henry Kissinger was arrested last night in Hyattsville, Md.
(11b) *One Henry Kissinger is fat.

In (11), the 'one' is unstressed. What is it doing there? What is its function? Even stranger for the logician's view of proper names is the fact that parts of them can be quantified over.

(12a) Every Kennedy is jinxed.
(12b) Therefore, Teddy Kennedy is jinxed.
(13a) Every person with the surname Kennedy is jinxed.
(13b) Therefore, Menachem Kennedy is jinxed.

Clearly, this is a matter for logic. What is the internal logical structure of proper names? Why does 'every Kennedy' in (12a) pick out only members of a certain well-known Kennedy family instead of everyone with that surname? Moreover, parts of names can be questioned (as Chris Smeall has observed):

(14a) John who?
(14b) *Who Smith?
(14c) *John Which?
(14d) Which Smith?

Last names are questioned with *who,* and the rest of the name with *which?* Note that when there is a middle name, *which* can question both first and middle name, but not just the first name.

(15a) John Robert Ross.
(15b) *Which Robert Ross?
(15c) Which Ross?

In addition, parts of names can be referred to by pronouns.

(16) Teddy Kennedy would never have been elected if *that* hadn't been his last name.

Then there are cases (pointed out by Henry Thompson) where names can refer to their phonetics, their spelling, or just themselves in the abstract.

(17a) Sally Cherowski is a funny-looking name.
(17b) Lillian LaVerne is a lovely sounding name.
(17c) The aspiring jet-setters dropped two Henry Kissingers and a Jill St. John within five minutes.

Then, there are the host of cases (pointed out to me by Berkeley students) where the name picks out a property.

(18a) Harry is a regular Henry Kissinger.
(18b) It's the Richard Nixons of this world who got us into this mess.
(18c) Paris wouldn't be Paris without the Eiffel Tower.

(18d) There are two New Yorks—
- daytime and night-time New York.
- black New York and white New York.
- the East Side and the West Side.
- the New York before 1800 and the New York after 1800.

(18e) Chomsky is the DeGaulle of Linguistics.
(18f) John is Leonardo-esque.
(18g) Henry Kissinger-types bug me.
(18h) John is a cross between Kissinger and Bismarck.

Simply by using the methodology of nonformal grammar, we have isolated a number of challenges to various philosophical conceptions of proper names. It is my feeling that the real impact of linguistics on philosophy will be in such empirical domains. At the same time, so-called philosophical problems, like opacity, have become linguistic problems, and the subject matter of the fields overlaps.

It will not be long before philosophy will have to confront a host of empirical issues of this sort. That will be a real relief from the kind of relationship conceived of between the fields in the mid-1960's, when the inconclusive and, in my view, relatively boring version of the empiricism-rationalism issue was raging. The debate was mostly hot air. It was not the traditional knowledge-by-experience-only versus some-innate-knowledge argument: the kind of 'knowledge' involved was rather different—the capacity to learn one's native language. Nor were the positions as different as one might be led to believe. The empiricists were not tabula rasa types: they accepted the idea that man has all sorts of innate capacities: an innate capacity to acquire reasoning ability, innate memory and processing capacities, and an innate general learning mechanism. They claimed that all that innate apparatus—whatever it would turn out to be like—should be enough to account for the ability to learn language. Chomsky said it wasn't, and that innate equipment to acquire syntax was also needed. What the debate comes down to was the issue of whether the capacity to acquire syntax was a consequence of the other above-mentioned innate capacities. Hardly the present-day incarnation of the rationalism-empiricism debate. Not that the issue is uninteresting—it just isn't earthshaking, and moreover there was (and remains today) no solid evidence on either side. Each side claimed the burden of proof was on the other—a debating ploy. Nothing conclusive has come of it, except perhaps publicity. In the future, the overlap between linguistics and philosophy will hopefully have some real empirical content.

What about psychology? In 1967, Fodor and Garrett declared 'The most profound problem in psycholinguistics is perhaps to specify the nature of the relation between the grammar and the recognition routine.' That attitude, if not dead, is dying fast. It is my opinion that in the future, such studies will occupy a minor corner of the field. There are simply more interesting problem areas worthy of the name 'psycholinguistics', areas that will become part of a humanistic linguistics. They are:

1. Cognitive Structure.   What can the study of language tell you about the nature of thought, of concepts? The introduction of model-theoretical methods into linguistics has given us a means of studying the human conceptual system in a formal way. Logicians mostly look at model theory as a technical tool for doing completeness proofs. But, when applied to the study of natural language concepts, it turns out to be a way of probing into the mind. Of course, as in all endeavors in formal linguistics, the results are largely negative: the more one formally describes a concept model theoretically, the more we learn we don't know. What is particularly impressive to me is the extent and nature of the complexities of concepts whose simplicity has previously been taken for granted. A good example is the complexity of fuzzy and scalar concepts, as studied by Hans Kamp, Kit Fine, myself, and others. Another example is causation, as it has begun to be analyzed by David Lewis. Once one sees what is really involved in understanding even supposedly simple concepts, the cognitive capacities of children become awe-inspiring. It is ironic that such work at present is being done exclusively by logicians and linguists, and not by psychologists. I believe that in the future the three fields will converge in this area.

Model theory aside, however, the study of cognitive structure has become, in influential circles, an integral part of psycholinguistics. In the study of language acquisition, for example, more and more investigators, especially among current students, seem to be primarily interested in the semantic and pragmatic aspects of language learning, while syntax is being down-played. That is, students of acquisition have been asking not what is the grammar of the child's short utterances (which doesn't seem to give much insight), but rather what does a child know, understand, and intend. Here also, the early results indicate that children know much more than they are given credit for. I have in mind the work of Gelman and Schatz on the communicative capacity of 4-year-olds. Gelman has found, not surprisingly, at least to me, that 4-year-olds have mastered a wide variety of conversational principles, use them skillfully, and moreover, use them very differently in addressing adults versus 2-year-olds. She claims this challenges the view that children of that age are completely egocentric and lack the ability to reason logically. If implicatures are indeed entailments in context, then it would seem that the 4-year-olds she has studied have mastered an incredibly complex logical system. Not being a psychologist, I am not in a position to tell whether she is right. But as a parent who has to daily engage in losing battles with a linguistically cunning 3-year-old, I would feel very dumb indeed to be told that he is incapable of reasoning.[1]

2. Personality and Personal Interaction.   When you meet someone for the first time, you can learn a lot about him by talking to him for a few minutes, discussing any random topic at all, and paying attention to the way he uses language. In any conversation, participants reveal presuppositions, hedge in some cases but not in others, use politeness principles in some places but not others, use various indirect speech acts instead of direct speech acts, etc. What you find out about a person in a random conversation is very largely determined by these pragmatic factors—and these are just the kinds of things that are being studied insightfully today, and to some small extent being formalized. To the extent that they can be formalized, we find out what we do and do not understand about them—mostly the latter. Moreover, the methods of the nonformal grammarians, which are being developed into high art, should enable us to begin to analyze what it is about the use of language that enables us to gain insight into personality through the observation of language use. Moreover, such studies should provide a gold mine of important data that humanistic linguistic theory must come to grips with.

3. Mental Disorders.   There are good clinical psychologists who can listen to a tape of a family conversation, with the child absent, and tell with a high degree of success whether the child is schizophrenic, delinquent, or normal. Moreover there are talented analysts who can diagnose mental disorders accurately by listening to patients' use of language. How are they able to do this? At least partly by looking at the revealed presuppositions, hedges, indirect vs. direct speech acts, etc. Here again humanistic

---

[1] So far as I can tell, the Gelman-Schatz results do not contradict Piaget's results, as they suggest, but rather supplement them. Piaget has shown that children at age four and above behave egocentrically with respect to certain types of tasks. Gelman and Schatz show that in very different (non-Piagetian) situations, they behave, at least in part, non-egocentrically. Their results suggest to me that egocentrism is overcome at different times in different spheres of behavior, which does not seem to me to contradict any Piagetian claims. The same is true of reasoning. If the use of complex conversational principles constitutes reasoning, it is certainly not the conscious, manipulative reasoning of the sort Piaget has tested for. The Gelman-Schatz research seems to raise the question of what counts as egocentrism and reasoning in non-Piagetian tasks and how can their development be traced in ways that supplement Piagetian results.

linguistics overlaps in subject matter with something of interest and concern to all of us. By the way, linguistic work in this area has begun in the research of William Labov on therapeutic discourse and Robin Lakoff on schizophrenic speech.

In addition, much that was thought to be part of performance—for example, hesitations, repetitions, and especially corrections in mid-sentence—have been shown to be an intimate part of grammar. See the classic studies by James (1972, 1973a, 1973b) and DuBois (1974). Again subject matter that was taken to be in the province of psychology has found itself as part of a broadened Linguistics.

Psycholinguistics, as it developed in the sixties, was very much a nuts-and-bolts discipline. The nuts-and-bolts are well-known experimental techniques: clock location, galvanic skin response, eye movement, pupil dilation, sentence paraphrasing, and time measurements for a variety of tasks. It was unfortunate that psycholinguistics, like linguistics proper, fell into the trap of letting the field be defined by the available technological and conceptual tools that were socially acceptable within the field. The alternative, which is now beginning to be realized, is to ask fundamental questions, for example, what can you learn about the mind by studying language, and vice versa?

Let me now turn very briefly to sociolinguistics and anthropological linguistics. The study of presuppositions, speech acts, and implicatures has forced contemporary linguistics into the study of social interaction and culture. The reason is that there are linguistic principles that depend on social and cultural concepts. For example, Robin Lakoff has shown that principles of politeness enter into rules of grammar. Unfortunately, there was no adequate analysis of politeness given in sociology on which those rules could be based. What she did was to get an informal first approximation to those principles by studying linguistics. On the other hand, there is at least one case where a nonobvious sociological concept, Goffman's 'free goods,' plays a role in grammar, namely, constructions with 'may I ask,' which requires the assumption that what is being asked for is not free goods. Also, Eleanor Keenan has shown that conversational principles that Grice took to be universal vary from culture to culture, and that these in part define a culture, and can be gotten at through the study of language. In such areas, linguistics can have a bearing on social theory, and vice versa.

In the study of speech acts, implicatures, and presuppositions, linguistics has come to overlap in subject matter with psychology, philosophy, sociology, and anthropology. It is in this area that I think most progress will be made in establishing linguistics not as the study of the distribution of linguistic elements, but rather as the study of man through language.

REFERENCES

1. Bolinger, Dwight. 1972. Degree words. The Hague, Mouton.

2. Borkin, A. 1971. Polarity items in questions. Chicago Linguistic Society 7.

3. DuBois, J. 1974. Selc-forrection—I mean, Self-correction. CLA paper.

4. Gelman, R. and C. Schatz. 1973. The development of communication skills: Modifications in the speech of young children as a function of listener. Monograph of the Society for Research in Child Development 38.5.

5. Grice, H. P. 1967. Logic and conversation. Unpublished.

6. James, D. 1972. Some aspects of the syntax and semantics of interjections. In: CLS 8. 162–172.

7. ———. 1973a. Another look at, say, some grammatical constraints on, oh, interjections and hesitations. In: CLS 9.

8. ———. 1973b. Aspects of the syntax and semantics of interjections in English. Unpublished Ph.D. dissertation, University of Michigan.

9. Lakoff, George. 1972a. Linguistics in natural logic. In: Semantics of natural language. Edited by Davidson and Harman. Dordrecht, D. Reidel.

10. ———. 1972b. Hedges. In: CLS 8. 183–228.

11. ———. 1973. Hedges. Journal of Philosophical Logic. [Revised version of Lakoff 1972b].

12. ———. 1974. Syntactic amalgams. In: CLS 10.

13. Lakoff, Robin. 1971. A syntactic argument for negative transportation. In: CLS 5. 140–147.

14. ———. 1970. Tense and its relation to participants. Language 46.4:838–849.

15. ———. 1972. The pragmatics of modality. In: CLS 8. 229–246.

16. ———. 1973. Language and woman's place. Language and society.

17. McCawley, James. 1969. Tense and time reference in English. In: Studies in linguistic semantics. Edited by Fillmore and Langendoen. New York, Holt, Rinehart and Winston. 97–114.

18. Ross, John R. 1969. Auxiliaries as main verbs. Journal of Philosophical Linguistics.

19. ———. 1972. Act. In: Semantics of natural language. Edited by Davidson and Harman. Dordrecht, D. Reidel.

20. Vendler, Z. 1967. Linguistics in philosophy. Ithaca, New York, Cornell University Press.

DISCUSSION QUESTIONS

1. Do you agree with Lakoff that "nuts-and-bolts" linguistics and humanistic linguistics can contribute to each other? How?

2. The first two articles in this section are in the "nuts-and-bolts" tradition and the last two are in the humanistic tradition. How do they differ in approach?

3. What are some of the advantages and problems with the "nuts-and-bolts" approach? With the humanistic approach?

MICHAEL D. LINN

After receiving his doctorate from the University of Minnesota, the author taught for several years at Virginia Commonwealth University before moving to the University of Minnesota—Duluth, where as associate professor of English he is currently investigating the speech of the Iron Range. His article originated in an NEH seminar, "Language Change: The Evidence from English," conducted by Wayne O'Neil at MIT in the summer of 1978.

LANGUAGE CHANGE AS REFLECTED IN PIDGINS AND CREOLES

Only recently have pidgins and creoles engaged serious scholarly attention. The dominant attitude—one still popularly accepted—had been that they were merely corruptions of the standard languages. It was held that such corruptions resulted from imperfect learning by subordinates who somehow lacked the capacity to master "complicated" European languages. The persistence of this view probably says more about its believers than it does about pidgins and creoles and, indeed, points to social problems relevant to these language varieties. Both the social problems and the linguistic problems are now, however, attracting serious study by theoretical linguists and sociolinguists interested in language change.

DEFINITION OF PIDGIN AND CREOLE

In traditional etymology, *pidgin* comes from English *pigeon,* with the meaning *business* in expressions such as "That's my pigeon! (*i.e.* that's my own private affair)" (Decamp 7, p. 15), which is still used in Chinese pidgin. While the term was first applied to Chinese pidgin, it is now used to refer to any language that is a contact vernacular and not a native language of any of its speakers. A pidgin's primary function is that of a trading language or plantation language used for communication among people who do not share a common language. Because of the social situation and the need to communicate, a pidgin is a simplified language in that it lacks an extensive vocabulary and grammatical devices such as number and gender. Also, it tends to have invariant morphological form rather than inflectional or declensional forms and hence must rely on word order. It tends to maximize ease of comprehension by minimizing the knowledge that a speaker needs to encode a message and that a listener needs to decode a message. A pidgin is an extreme example of a language that is easy to learn, yet not easy to use.

Because a pidgin is restricted in its use, it either remains a second language or develops into a creole. "The term *creole* (from Portuguese *crioulo via* Spanish and French) originally meant 'white man of European descent born and raised in a tropical or semitropical colony' " (Decamp 7, p. 15). Later the term was applied to nonwhites, particularly African slaves, and finally to particular Caribbean, West African, and East Indian natives. A creole develops from a pidgin that becomes the native language of a group of people who, because of communication needs, extend the domain, use, and expressive functions of the pidgin.

THE ORIGIN OF EUROPEAN-BASED PIDGINS AND CREOLES

No aspect of pidgin and creole studies seems as fraught with controversy as do the hypotheses concerning their origins. Most of the controversy has revolved around three general theories: (1) the polygenetic theory, (2) the monogenetic theory, (3) the hybridization theory. The polygenetic theory, in essence, argues that every pidgin and creole has a separate creation. The monogenetic theory argues that all pidgins and creoles have a common genetic ancestor from which they all developed. In the hybridization theory, Whinnom (21) argues that two or more substratum speakers, none of whom knows each other's language, are involved.

Hall (9, 10) was one of the first to embrace a polygenetic theory. He holds that each pidgin and creole began as a sort of "baby talk" used by the masters, plantation owners, and others in command situations to communicate with their servants or slaves. In using such baby talk, the Europeans deliberately mutilated the standard language by eliminating grammatical inflections, reducing vocabulary, and simplifying phonological and syntactic patterns. The baby-talk theory is the one theory that has been totally refuted. Cassidy points out how the whites learned the creole from the Africans rather than the other way around:

> That the Negroes should have learned English incompletely was only to be expected under the circumstances; that a large influence from their native African should be felt in such English as they learned, goes almost without saying. That the resulting blend should also become to a greater or less degree the speech of the creole whites was the result of conditions of life on the plantation.
>
> (Cassidy 5, p. 21)

Here it should be mentioned that Cassidy uses *creole* to mean simply "island born" and includes both masters and slaves as its speakers. Further refutation of the baby-talk theory results from its inability to account for the fact that the typological similarities shared by creole French, Spanish, English, and the other creole languages are too great for coincidence.

The need to account for this similarity between the various creoles led to the monogenetic theory of creole origin. Most monogeneticists trace the creoles back to a Portuguese pidgin that was based upon Sabir. During the sixteenth century this trade language replaced Arabic and Malay as the trade language in the Far East. Whinnom (21) argues that the Asian Spanish creoles are not simply "restructured Spanish" and the English creoles are not simply restructured English, but that both were relexified pidgin Portuguese. Naro (14) traces the development (with a plethora of documented evidence) to Portugal, where Africans enslaved by Prince Henry the Navigator had been brought to learn Portuguese and thus become translators. Because of the wide variety of languages spoken on the West Coast of Africa, the Portuguese were not able to have a translator for every language, but when the Portuguese developed settlements, many of the settlers came knowing the Portuguese creole. While there is ample evidence for Naro's thesis, he does not feel that the Portuguese creole is the only basis for all other creoles. He suggests, while rejecting Hall's baby-talk thesis, that some creoles might have developed from the Portuguese, but that others developed in different ways. Hancock (11) points out that the relexification hypothesis cannot explain why "so few traces of Portuguese remain in these languages today. The grammatical structure shared by these creoles is no closer to Portuguese than to any other European language; Krio and Gullah have less than one percent and Sranan four percent of their known vocabularies clearly traceable to Portuguese'' (p. 288). He goes on to insist that basic words such as *man, woman, eat,* and *hell* would not be replaced wholesale in so short a time.

What led Whinnom (21) to postulate the hybridization theory for the origin of creoles was his observation that the tourist and his guide are not the people that use pidgins. In his analysis of Chinese pidgin he points out that the pidgin is not spoken by foreigners nor even primarily by the speakers of Chinese who are in a dominant position. It is spoken by Chinese in subordinate positions who do not share a common language among themselves. Here it should be observed that the major dialects of Chinese are not mutually intelligible. It is because the different Chinese speakers are under the domination of English speakers that the pidgin contains a good deal of English. He goes on to hypothesize that pidgins do not develop where two languages are in contact, but that there must be three or more languages in contact. (If speakers are from only two languages and a bilingual situation does not develop, the languages of the dominant social class will be learned.) To capsulize his hypothesis, Whinnom gives the following formula:

$$\frac{\text{Target language}}{\text{Substrate languages A} \times \text{B} (\times \text{C}_n)}.$$

(Whinnom 21, p. 106)

Using Whinnom's formula, a language such as Jamaican creole would result from

$$\frac{\text{English}}{\text{African language 1, African language 2, \ldots African language}_n}.$$

Thus a variety of English was learned because all or most of the slaves had become at least somewhat acquainted with it, and they did not share a common African language. Because English was learned as a second language by slaves with no formal instruction from other slaves, they developed a version that differed from that of their masters. When the original pidgin was being formulated, the English of each slave must have been influenced by his native language so that the pidgin differed from speaker to speaker. Thus the English of a Mandingo would be influenced by Mandingo and the English of a Temne would be influenced by Temne. As the language developed from pidgin to creole, these individual pidgin differences atrophied so that a common creole developed.

The possibility that the hybridization theory accounts for the origin of creoles is strengthened further by examining the reasons for a pidgin to expand into a creole. Because a creole functions as a native language, it must be learned very early in an individual's life—often as the first language. When slaves were first imported to plantations, adults could express complicated ideas in a language that they learned in Africa with those few other slaves that spoke, often imperfectly as a second language, the same language. The pidgin was used primarily as a work language and in large groups where a common language was not shared. Bickerton (1, 2) has demonstrated how pidgin speakers can be differentiated by their native language. It is when the children on the plantation at an early age (often under a year) are placed in a common nursery and need to devise a language for their nursery intragroup communication that a creole arises. While it is theoretically possible that a single parent language could have given rise to the literally dozens of creole languages scattered around the globe, it seems doubtful (particularly since some of them would have to be relexified) that these children would all adopt the same competing language. Likewise, it seems doubtful that they would borrow the same syntactic features from the same competing languages. Remember that these children, unlike those in a normal language learning situation, probably had no one (or at least no adult) correcting their creole language use, because the adults were using pidgin or their native language.

The existence of Hawaiian Creole English makes remote the possibility of a common ancestor or the possibility of common selected borrowings. The other creoles have been spoken for generations by people of African descent. In contrast, Hawaiian creole, which originated only in the early 1900s, involved not African slave populations, but rather immigrant fieldhands from China, Korea, and the Philippines, as well as native Hawaiians. It shares similar structures with African-based creoles probably, we might say, because of similar wiring in the child language acquisition device. If the language device is genetically determined and preverbal children are in similar situations, the languages created by them should share similar syntactic properties.

AN EXAMINATION OF INDIVIDUAL PIDGINS AND CREOLES

To illustrate the process of language change in pidgins and creoles, three languages will be examined briefly. Hawaiian English extends all the way from the original pidgin to standard English. Jamaican Creole extends from the creole through a post-creole continuum. American Black English demonstrates a language that has decreolized, but still contains some remnants of the original creole. Thus these three languages illustrate the beginning, middle, and end of the pidgin-to-creole-to-standard-language process. But it is not necessary to assume that all pidgins and creoles go or will go through the entire process. The language process may end anywhere along the continuum or even stop and become active again.

Hawaiian English

Hawaiian English has undergone three phases: (1) 1778–1876, the *hapa hole* period when the only residents of Hawaii were native speakers of either Hawaiian or English; (2) 1876–1900, the early plantation period when a simplified version of Hawaiian was used; and (3) 1900–the present, when the decline in the Hawaiian language led to its replacement by English. Since Hawaiian pidgin came into existence in the present century, all the phases of its development can be examined.

Tsuzaki believes that the basic issue involving Hawaiian English (HE) is whether it is a pidgin, a creole, or a dialect of English. The positions taken on this question have ranged all the way from considering it to be, exclusively, a pidgin to considering it to be a variety of standard English. Tsuzaki attributes the difference of opinion to two factors:

1) the relatively wide range or latitude of variation found in the structure of HE, apparently in all stages of its development including the present, and
2) the general failure on the part of many analysts and observers to keep synchronic aspects of HE separate from the diachronic.

(Tsuzaki 17, p. 325)

Tsuzaki solves this problem by positing the concept of coexistent systems. He feels there are three coexistent basic systems: (1) an English-based pidgin (HPE), (2) an English-based creole English (HCE), and (3) a dialect of English which in turn is divided into nonstandard and standard. HPE is greatly simplified in comparison to English and has no native speakers, since those who use it have other native languages, primarily Chinese, Hawaiian, Japanese, Korean, and the Philippine languages. In addition, HPE exhibits characteristics common to other pidgins of the world. Tsuzaki lists the following representative features:

(i) Copulaless equational clauses (*e.g. Me/I too much happy* "I am/was very happy")

(ii) Juxtaposition of nouns without the possessive suffix or the preposition *of* (*My husband house kaukau no good* "The food at my husband's house is not good")

(iii) Lack of the definite or indefinite articles (*Outside door me/I see my husband* "Outside the door I see/saw my husband")

(iv) The generalized third person pronoun *em* as direct object of the verb (*No can fool em* "One cannot fool him/her/it/them")

(v) Lack of inflectional suffixes, which makes for an extremely simple morphological system (*One day me/I see some mountain* "One day I see/saw some mountains")

(Tsuzaki 17, p. 330)

The features that HCE shares with the other creoles seem to be most pronounced in the verbal system. Tsuzaki lists seven verb categories followed by their markers, which he calls particles, in parentheses. They occur in the following order:

(i) Negative (no/never)
(ii) Auxiliary (can/might[?]/must[?]/etc.)
(iii) Past tense (been/went/had)
(iv) Future or contingent mood (go)
(v) Progressive aspect (stay)
(vi) Habitual aspect ($\emptyset$ = [unmarked stem])
(vii) Verb stem, nucleus, or base

(Tsuzaki 17, p. 332–333)

In addition, Tsuzaki points out how the prestem particles do not seem to occur within a single verbal construction, a fact that indicates there might be co-occurrence restrictions. "For example, (i) (*never*) and (iii) (past tense) are usually mutually exclusive, since *never*, which is usually used as a past negator, indicates past time. Similarly, categories (ii) and (iii), (iv) and (v) are usually mutually exclusive" (Tsuzaki 17, p. 333). He goes on to indicate that the use of up to three preposed particles in a given verbal construction is common, that four is possible but unusual, and that five seems to be ungrammatical. The following examples are taken from his article.

(1) I no eat	I don't eat
(2) I no go eat	I am not going to eat
(3) I no go stay eat	I am not going to be eating I will not be eating
(4) I no been go stay eat	I (wasn't/hadn't been) eating
*(5) I no could been go stay eat	

The ungrammaticality of sentence (5) illustrates a common characteristic of pidgins and creoles: What makes the languages easy to learn inhibits its use.

From here, Tsuzaki goes on to posit that HCE provides a "base from which on the one hand a pidgin variety of HE, *i.e.* HPE, could be established and a dialect on the other" (p. 333). On the one hand, HPE relies almost exclusively on lexical items to signal the semantics of the verb, although it can use the system of preposed particles just given. Hawaiian nonstandard English, on the other hand, uses a version of the creole system in the direction of standard English. He gives the following two sets of sentences, each set a representative of alternate ways of saying the same thing:

> (6a) Me/I kaukau/eat
> (6b) I stay eat/kaukau
> (6c) I stay eating
> (6d) I eating
> (7a) Me/I kaukau/eat
> (7b) I been eat/kaukau
> (7c) I ate
> (7d) I ate
>   a = HPE
>   b = HCE
>   c = Nonstandard HE
>   d = Standard He
>   (p. 333)

Thus one can see that in the development from HPE to nonstandard HE the change is one from a series of particles preposed to the verb stem to a series of inflectional endings. (Such a process seems common in this type of language change. Bickerton (4) documents in great detail how it occurs in Guyanese English.) At the point where two systems merge, speakers often use phrases such as *stay eating* where *stay* is from HPE and *eating* is from HCE. As one would expect, HPE differs most radically from the other two because it has no native speakers and so has sacrificed its expressive ability for ease of learning. In fact, it is the only variety which does not seem to be mutually intelligible with other dialects of English.

Bickerton (4) basically agrees with Tsuzaki, but he feels the HE picture has been oversimplified. He argues convincingly that, instead of three separate systems, there is a continuum with pidgin at one end and standard English at the other. (This is essentially the same position that he assumes for Guyanese English (Bickerton 2), for which he writes a set of grammatical rules showing the changes in the verbal system as a speaker progresses through the continuum.) In addition, he points out how the pidgin is not a totally unified system, but one that shows the influence of the speaker's native language. The first of these points is demonstrated by the following examples from a single Japanese speaker and the second is illustrated by an example from a Filipino speaker.

> (8) *as kerosin, plaenteishan, wan mans, fo gaelan giv,* "The plantation gave us four gallons of kerosene a month."
> (9) *aemerikan pipl mun preis go, mun preis fularaun, enikain kam hom, aeswai gad ga maed nattekara,* "The American people went to the moon, fooled around there and got back somehow, that's why God became angry" (explaining present-day deterioration in the climate).

(10) *sore kara kech shite kara pulap*
   and after catch do + past after pull-up (*sic*)
   "When I'd caught the turtle I pulled it in."

The Filipino speaker:

(11) *ai it tokak. yu sabe tokak? pfrawg. gud, dae wan, da pfrawg,* "I eat
   tokak. You know what *tokak* means? Frog. Frogs are very good to eat."
(12) *hi kam gro da paemili,* "The family was beginning to grow up."
(13) *hi haelp da medisin,* "The medicine helps."

(Bickerton 1, p. 53)

In the speech of the first speaker, one notices that even a pidgin speaker moves up and down the continuum. Bickerton emphasizes that it is free of the Japanese lexicon, but it is still heavily influenced by the Japanese SOV structure. Yet we can see the influence of Japanese in both lexicon and syntax as we go from sentence (8) to (10): all three sentences are from the same speaker shows a movement up and down the continuum. In contrast, the Filipino speakers (11–13) show little native lexicon; and when they do, such as *tokak,* they explain it. While we do get English SVO sentences in the Filipino speaker, we also see the verb appearing first and a subject-final sentence order, a reflection of their Filipino (primarily Ilocano) background. Bickerton (2, p. 54) states that one never finds this type of sentence spoken by the Japanese pidgin speakers. The pidgin speakers usually remain near one end of the continuum; their children, in the process of creolization, are strung out across the continuum between native creole and the target English, much as second-language learners are. Bickerton feels that this is because of the variety of English that the individual speakers target upon.

Jamaican Creole

Jamaican Creole (JC) illustrates the typical creole evolution toward standard languages. "At one end of this spectrum is a very conservative, countrified, socially isolated form of speech, a true creole, preserving the best evidence of pidgin connections" (Cassidy 6, p. 204), and at the other end is standard English. Cassidy mentions, and Decamp (8) concurs, that speakers are distributed at every point along the continuum. In this sense, Jamaican Creole differs from "true creoles" such as Surinam, Sranan, or Haitian Creole, all of which differ significantly from the national standard languages. Jamaican Creole, of course, is not identical to British Received Standard, but the differences are those of dialect varieties. Decamp has coined the term *post-creole continuum* to distinguish JC from the other creoles that have not decreolized. He feels that two conditions must be present for such a change to take place:

1) First, the dominant official language of the community must be the standard language corresponding to the creole . . .
2) The formerly rigid social stratification must have *partially* (not completely) broken down [his emphasis].

(p. 351)

Cassidy adds two other conditions concerning the continuum development of JC. First, that when it came into existence, the slaves were brought in "such numbers so rapidly, and from so many places that they could neither preserve a functioning African language nor English fully'' (Cassidy 5, p. 12). The second condition that he finds necessary for the development of a creole continuum (he uses the term ''spectrum,'' but it is clearly the same thing) is that the creole becomes so fully established that it could function adequately alongside the British Standard. Cassidy (pp. 10–26) gives ample evidence that this was the case in Jamaica. While there has been a gradual assimilation of JC into the standard, ''The profound social changes of the past thirty years have accentuated this further'' (Decamp's number 2 condition). The result is that the gradual restructuring of JC under the influence of standard Jamaican English is now giving way to the displacement of the creole by the standard.

American Black English

When one studies the development of JC, the similarities in structure and in social and historical developments between JC and American Black English (BE) are obvious. Both developed from a slave plantation system where slaves speaking the same native African language were deliberately kept apart from one another, and in each situation there were many more slaves than Europeans. Also, in both situations there was a continuous supply of new slaves brought from Africa. According to Turner (18), American slave owners' fear of revolt led them to prefer Africans to New World blacks. In neither case was movement from slave to freeman common. The social history of both groups, along with the manner in which creoles are created (Whinnom 21, previously discussed), leads one to consider the possibility that modern BE is the end product of a decreolization process and is now being incorporated in the standard language.

Linguistic Similarities of BE and Other English-Based Creoles

It seems undeniable that Gullah, the language spoken by the Geechee on the sea islands off the Georgia and South Carolina coasts, is a creole with all the ''classical features of other English creoles: serial verbs, locative *de,* habitual/continuation *da*'' (Rickford 15, p. 198).

In addition, BE does have a number of creole characteristics, both in phonology and syntax:

Phonology
_____

    (1) Consonant cluster simplification

        couldn't   couldn

        child   chile

    (2) Loss of initial voiced stop in auxiliaries

              don't   ont or on

    (3) Creole intonation patterns

        bad as [bǽd]

Syntax
_____

    (1) Invariant *be*

        In BE *be* can be used to mean intermittent action. Thus *she be late* means that she is late every day.

    (2) Copula absent

        John tall.

(3) *They* as a possessive pronoun
They hat on the table.

(4) Lack of underlying s in third person singular
(For a discussion of this feature, see Labov *et al.* 13. This report has extensive coverage of BE.)
All of the following are possible sentences:
He go home.
He wants home.
He had gones home.

(5) Stressed *bin*
This is similar to anterior in Guyanese. (See Bickerton's (2) discussion of this feature in a creole continuum.)
She bin tell me that.
This means that the telling was completed a long time ago.

(6) Durative *done*
This has the sense of having started in the distant past and still continuing.
I done been married.
This means "I was married a long time ago and am still married."

These features of BE shared by other English creoles indicate that BE developed from a pidgin through the creole stage and then decreolized. It must have originally been much like the other plantation languages. Support for this position has been generated by the work of black linguists such as Geneva Smitherman (16), who traces the origin of BE back to a pidgin, and Richard Wright (23), who is working at establishing the features of a standard BE. While BE must be viewed as a continuum much like JC, it has been carried a step further. Yet BE cannot be expected to lose its individuality until there is an amalgamation of blacks and whites into a general American culture.

Examination of pidgins and creoles, although a recent phenomenon, has already shed a great deal of light on the nature of language and how it changes. It is important that these two types of languages be recognized for what they are: a second language and a native language with the full range of features necessary for the communication of its speakers. When the communication needs change, then the language changes to meet these needs.

BIBLIOGRAPHY

1. Bickerton, Derek. "Beginnings." In K. Hill, ed., *The Genesis of Language*. Ann Arbor: Karoma Publishers, 1979.

2. ———. Dynamics of a Creole System. London: Cambridge University Press, 1975.

3. ———. "Pidgin and Creole Studies." *Annual Review of Anthropology* 5 (1976).

4. ———. "Pidginization and Creolization: Language Acquisition and Language Universals." In A. Valdman, ed., *Pidgin and Creole Linguistics*. Bloomington: Indiana University Press, 1977.

5. Cassidy, Frederic G. *Jamaica Talk: Three Hundred Years of the English Language in Jamaica*. New York: Macmillan, 1961.

6. ———. "Tracing the Pidgin Element in Jamaican Creole." In D. Hymes, ed., *Pidginization and Creolization of Languages*. London: Cambridge University Press, 1971.

7. Decamp, David. "Introduction: The Study of Pidgin and Creole Languages." In D. Hymes, ed., *Pidginization and Creolization of Languages*. London: Cambridge University Press, 1971.

8. ———. "Toward a Generative Analysis of a Post-Creole Continuum." In D. Hymes, ed., *Pidginization and Creolization of Languages*. London: Cambridge University Press, 1971.

9. Hall, Robert. "Creolized Languages and Genetic Relationship." *Word* 14 (1958): 367–373.

10. ———. *Pidgin and Creole Languages*. Ithaca: Cornell University Press, 1966.

11. Hancock, Ian. "English-Derived Atlantic Creoles." In D. Hymes, ed., *Pidginization and Creolization of Languages*. London: Cambridge University Press, 1971.

12. Hymes, Dell, ed. *Pidginization and Creolization of Languages*. London: Cambridge University Press, 1971.

13. Labov, W., Cohen, P., Robins, C., and Lewis, J. *A Study of the Non-Standard English of Negro and Puerto Rican Speakers in New York City*. Philadelphia: U.S. Regional Survey, 1968.

14. Naro, Anthony. "A Study of Pidginization." *Language* 54 (1978): 314–347.

15. Rickford, John. "The Question of Prior Creolization in Black English." In A. Valdman, ed., *Pidgin and Creole Linguistics*. Bloomington: Indiana University Press, 1977.

16. Smitherman, Geneva. *Talkin and Testifyin: The Language of Black America*. Boston: Houghton Mifflin, 1977.

17. Tsuzaki, Stanley. "Coexistent Systems in Language Variation." In D. Hymes, ed., *Pidginization and Creolization of Languages*. London: Cambridge University Press, 1971.

18. Turner, Lorenzo. *Africanisms in the Gullah Dialect*. Chicago: University of Chicago Press, 1949.

19. Valdman, Albert, ed. *Pidgin and Creole Linguistics*. Bloomington: Indiana University Press, 1977.

20. Voorhoeve, Jan. "Historical and Linguistic Evidence in Favour of the Relexification Theory in the Formation of Creoles." *Language in Society* 2(1973): 133–145.

21. Whinnom, Keith, "Linguistic Hybridization and the Special Case of Pidgins and Creoles." In D. Hymes, ed., *Pidginization and Creolization of Languages*. London: Cambridge University Press, 1971.

22. ———. "The Origin of the European-based Creoles and Pidgins." *Orbis* 14 (1965): 509–527.

23. Wright, Richard. "Extended Review of Robbins Burling, *English in Black and White*, and William Labov, *Language in the Inner City*." *Language in Society* 4 (1975): 185–256.

DISCUSSION QUESTIONS

1. Which of the commonly held theories of the origins of pidgin and creole languages do you find the most plausible?

2. Considering the social relations among the speakers of Hawaiian pidgin, creole, and standard Hawaiian English, do you think it likely that anyone could be fluent in all three?

3. How does the work in pidgins and creole languages combine the formal and descriptive traditions in linguistics?

GEORGE A. MILLER

After holding professorial posts at Harvard and Rockefeller universities, in 1979 Miller became professor of psychology at Princeton University. He has been president of the American Psychological Association and has numerous books and articles to his credit.

NONVERBAL COMMUNICATION

When the German philosopher Nietzsche said that "success is the greatest liar," he meant that a successful person seems especially worthy to us even when his success is due to nothing more than good luck. But Nietzsche's observation can be interpreted more broadly.

People communicate in many different ways. One of the most important ways, of course, is through language. Moreover, when language is written it can be completely isolated from the context in which it occurs; it can be treated as if it were an independent and self-contained process. We have been so successful in using and describing and analyzing this special kind of communication that we sometimes act as if language were the *only* kind of communication that can occur between people. When we act that way, of course, we have been deceived by success, the greatest liar of them all.

Like all animals, people communicate by their actions as well as by the noises they make. It is a sort of biological anomaly of man—something like the giraffe's neck, or the pelican's beak—that our vocal noises have so far outgrown in importance and frequency all our other methods of signaling to one another. Language is obviously essential for human beings, but it is not the whole story of human communication. Not by a long shot.

Consider the following familiar fact. When leaders in one of the less well developed countries decide that they are ready to introduce some technology that is already highly advanced in another country, they do not simply buy all the books that have been written about that technology and have their students read them. The books may exist and they may be very good, but just reading about the technology is not enough. The students must be sent to study in a country where the technology is already flourishing, where they can see it first hand. Once they have been exposed to it in person and experienced it as part of their own lives, they are ready to understand and put to use the information that is in the books. But the verbal message, without the personal experience to back it up, is of little value.

Now what is it that the students learn by participating in a technology that they cannot learn by just reading about it? It seems obvious that they are learning something important, and that whatever it is they are learning is something that we don't know how to put into our verbal descriptions. There is a kind of nonverbal communication that occurs when students are personally involved in the technology and when they interact with people who are using and developing it.

Pictures are one kind of nonverbal communication, of course, and moving pictures can communicate some of the information that is difficult to capture in words. Pictures also have many of the properties that make language so useful—they can be taken in one situation at one time and viewed in an entirely different situation at any later time. Now that we have television satellites, pictures can be transmitted instantaneously all over the world, just as our words can be transmitted by radio. Perhaps the students who are trying to learn how to create a new technology in their own country could supplement their reading by watching moving pictures of people at work in the developed industry. Certainly the pictures would be a help, but they would be very expensive. And we don't really know whether words and pictures together would capture everything the students would be able to learn by going to a more advanced country and participating directly in the technology.

Let me take another familiar example. There are many different cultures in the world, and in each of them the children must learn a great many things that are expected of everyone who participates effectively in that culture. These things are taken for granted by everyone who shares the culture. When I say they are taken for granted, I mean that nobody needs to describe them or write them down or try self-consciously to teach them to children. Indeed, the children begin to learn them before their linguistic skills are far enough developed to understand a verbal description of what they are learning. This kind of learning has sometimes been called "imitation," but that is much too simple an explanation for the complex processes that go on when a child learns what is normal and expected in his own community. Most of the norms are communicated to the child nonverbally, and he internalizes them as if no other possibilities existed. They are as much a part of him as his own body; he would no more question them than he would question the fact that he has two hands and two feet, but only one head.

These cultural norms can be described verbally, of course. Anthropologists who are interested in describing the differences among the many cultures of the world have developed a special sensitivity to cultural norms and have described them at length in their scholarly books. But if a child had to read those books in order to learn what was expected of him, he would never become an effective member of his own community.

What is an example of the sort of thing that children learn nonverbally? One of the simplest examples to observe and analyze and discuss is the way people use clothing and bodily ornamentation to communicate. At any particular time in any particular culture there is an accepted and normal way to dress and to arrange the hair and to paint the face and to wear one's jewelry. By adopting those conventions for dressing himself, a person communicates to the world that he wants to be treated according to the standards of the culture for which they are appropriate. When a black person in America rejects the normal American dress and puts on African clothing, he is communicating to the world that he wants to be treated as an Afro-American. When a white man lets his hair and beard grow, wears very informal clothing, and puts beads around his neck, he is communicating to the world that he rejects many of the traditional values of Western culture. On the surface, dressing up in unusual costumes would seem to be one of the more innocent forms of dissent that a person could express, but in fact it is deeply resented by many people who still feel bound by the traditional conventions of their culture and who become fearful or angry when those norms are violated. The nonverbal message that such a costume communicates is "I reject your culture and your values," and those who resent this message can be violent in their response.

The use of clothing as an avenue of communication is relatively obvious, of course. A somewhat subtler kind of communication occurs in the way people use their eyes. We are remarkably accurate in judging the direction of another person's gaze; psychologists have done experiments that have measured just how accurate such judgments are. From an observation of where a person is looking we can infer what he is looking at, and from knowing what he is looking at we can guess what he is interested in, and from what he is interested in and the general situation we can usually make a fairly good guess about what he is going to do. Thus eye movements can be a rich and important channel of nonverbal communication.

Most personal interaction is initiated by a short period during which two people look directly at one another. Direct eye contact is a signal that each has the other's attention, and that some further form of interaction can follow. In Western cultures, to look directly into another person's eyes is equivalent to saying, ''I am open to you—let the action begin.'' Everyone knows how much lovers can communicate by their eyes, but aggressive eye contact can also be extremely informative.

In large cities, where people are crowded in together with others they neither know nor care about, many people develop a deliberate strategy of avoiding eye contacts. They want to mind their own business, they don't have time to interact with everyone they pass, and they communicate this fact by refusing to look at other people's faces. It is one of the things that make newcomers to the city feel that it is a hostile and unfriendly place.

Eye contact also has an important role in regulating conversational interactions. In America, a typical pattern is for the listener to signal that he is paying attention by looking at the talker's mouth or eyes. Since direct eye contact is often too intimate, the talker may let his eyes wander elsewhere. As the moment arrives for the talker to become a listener, and for his partner to begin talking, there will often be a preliminary eye signal. The talker will often look toward the listener, and the listener will signal that he is ready to talk by glancing away.

Such eye signals will vary, of course, depending on what the people are talking about and what the personal relation is between them. But whatever the pattern of eye signals that two people are using, they use them unconsciously. If you try to become aware of your own eye movements while you are talking to someone, you will find it extremely frustrating. As soon as you try to think self-consciously about your own eye movements, you do not know where you should be looking. If you want to study how the eyes communicate, therefore, you should do it by observing other people, not yourself. But if you watch other people too intently, of course, you may disturb them or make them angry. So be careful!

Even the pupils of your eyes communicate. When a person becomes excited or interested in something, the pupils of his eyes increase in size. In order to test whether we are sensitive to these changes in pupil size, a psychologist showed people two pictures of the face of a pretty girl. The two pictures were completely identical except that in one picture the girl's pupil was constricted, whereas in the other picture her pupil was dilated. The people were asked to say which picture they liked better, and they voted in favor of the picture with the large pupil. Many of the judges did not even realize consciously what the difference was, but apparently they were sensitive to the difference and preferred the eyes that communicated excitement and interest.

Eye communication seems to be particularly important for Americans. It is part of the American culture that people should be kept at a distance, and that contact with another person's body should be avoided in all but the most intimate situations. Because of this social convention of dealing with others at a distance, Americans have to place much reliance on their distance receptors, their eyes and ears, for personal communication. In other cultures, however, people normally come closer together and bodily contact between conversational partners is as normal as eye contact is in America. In the Eastern

Mediterranean cultures, for example, both the touch and the smell of the other person are expected.

The anthropologist Edward T. Hall has studied the spatial relations that seem appropriate to various kinds of interactions. They vary with intimacy, they depend on the possibility of eye contact, and they are different in different cultures. In America, for example, two strangers will converse impersonally at a distance of about four feet. If one moves closer, the other will back away. In a waiting room, strangers will keep apart, but friends will sit together, and members of a family may actually touch one another.

Other cultures have different spatial norms. In Latin America, for example, impersonal discussion normally occurs at a distance of two or three feet, which is the distance that is appropriate for personal discussion in North America. Consequently, it is impossible for a North and a South American both to be comfortable when they talk to one another unless one can adopt the zones that are normal for the other. If the South American advances to a distance that is comfortable for him, it will be too close for the North American, and he will withdraw, and one can chase the other all around the room unless something intervenes to end the conversation. The North American seems aloof and unfriendly to the South American. The South American seems hostile or oversexed to the North American. Hall mentions that North Americans sometimes cope with this difference by barricading themselves behind desks or tables, and that South Americans have been known literally to climb over these barriers in order to attain a comfortable distance at which to talk.

Within one's own culture these spatial signals are perfectly understood. If two North Americans are talking at a distance of one foot or less, you know that what they are saying is highly confidential. At a distance of two to three feet it will be some personal subject matter. At four or five feet it is impersonal, and if they are conversing at a distance of seven or eight feet, we know that they expect others to be listening to what they are saying. When talking to a group, a distance of ten to twenty feet is normal, and at greater distances only greetings are exchanged. These conventions are unconscious but highly reliable. For example, if you are having a personal conversation with a North American at a distance of two feet, you can shift it to an impersonal conversation by the simple procedure of moving back to a distance of four or five feet. If he can't follow you, he will find it quite impossible to maintain a personal discussion at that distance.

These examples should be enough to convince you—if you needed convincing— that we communicate a great deal of information that is not expressed in the words we utter. And I have not even mentioned yet the interesting kind of communication that occurs by means of gestures. A gesture is an expressive motion or action, usually made with the hands and arms, but also with the head or even the whole body. Gestures can occur with or without speech. As a part of the speech act, they usually emphasize what the person is saying, but they may occur without any speech at all. Some gestures are spontaneous, some are highly ritualized and have very specific meaning. And they differ enormously from one culture to another.

Misunderstanding of nonverbal communication is one of the most distressing and unnecessary sources of international friction. For example, few Americans understand how much the Chinese hate to be touched, or slapped on the back, or even to shake hands. How easy it would be for an American to avoid giving offense simply by avoiding these particular gestures that, to him, signify intimacy and friendliness. Or, to take another example, when Khrushchev placed his hands together over his head and shook them, most Americans interpreted it as an arrogant gesture of triumph, the sort of gesture a victorious prize fighter would make, even though Khrushchev seems to have intended it as a friendly gesture of international brotherhood. Sticking out the tongue and quickly drawing it back can be a gesture of self-castigation in one culture, an admission of a social mistake, but someone from another culture might interpret it as a gesture of ridicule or contempt, and in the Eskimo culture it would not be a gesture at all, but the conventional way of directing a current of air when blowing out a candle. Just a little better communication on the nonverbal level might go a long way toward improving international relations.

Ritualized gestures—the bow, the shrug, the smile, the wink, the military salute, the pointed finger, the thumbed nose, sticking out the tongue, and so on—are not really nonverbal communication, because such gestures are just a substitute for the verbal meanings that are associated with them. There are, however, many spontaneous gestures and actions that are unconscious, but communicate a great deal. If you take a moving picture of someone who is deeply engrossed in a conversation, and later show it to him, he will be quite surprised to see many of the gestures he used and the subtle effects they produced. Sometimes what a person is saying unconsciously by his actions may directly contradict what he is saying consciously with his words. Anthropologists have tried to develop a way to write down a description of these nonverbal actions, something like the notation that choreographers use to record the movements of a ballet dancer, but it is difficult to know exactly what the significance of these actions really is, or what the important features are that should be recorded. We can record them photographically, of course, but we still are not agreed on how the photographic record should be analyzed.

Finally, there is a whole spectrum of communication that is vocal, but not really verbal. The most obvious examples are spontaneous gasps of surprise or cries of pain. I suspect this kind of vocal communication is very similar for both man and animal. But our use of vocal signals goes far beyond such grunts and groans. It is a commonplace observation that the way you say something is as important as what you say, and often more important for telling the listener what your real intentions are. Exactly the same words may convey directly opposite messages according to the way they are said. For example, I can say, "Oh, isn't that WONderful" so that I sound enthusiastic, or I can say, "Oh, isn't THAT wonderful" in a sarcastic tone so that you know I don't think it is wonderful at all. Because the actual words uttered are often misleading, lawyers and judges in the courtroom have learned that it is sometimes important to have an actual recording and not just a written transcript of what a person is supposed to have said.

Rapid and highly inflected speech usually communicates excitement, extremely distinct speech usually communicates anger, very loud speech usually communicates pomposity, and a slow monotone usually communicates boredom. The emotional clues that are provided by the way a person talks are extremely subtle, and accomplished actors must practice for many years to bring them under conscious control.

A person's pronunciation also tells a great deal about him. If he has a foreign accent, a sensitive listener can generally tell where he was born. If he speaks with a local dialect, we can often guess what his social origins were and how much education he has had. Often a person will have several different styles of speaking, and will use them to communicate which social role he happens to be playing at the moment. This is such a rich source of social and psychological information, in fact, that a whole new field has recently developed to study it, a field called "sociology of language.". . .

One of the most significant signals that is vocal but nonverbal is the ungrammatical pause. . . . In careful speech most of our pauses are grammatical. That is to say, our pauses occur at the boundaries of grammatical segments, and serve as a kind of audible punctuation. By calling them "grammatical pauses" we imply that they are a normal part of the verbal message. An ungrammatical pause, however, is not part of the verbal message. For example, when I . . . uh . . . pause within a . . . uh . . . grammatical unit, you cannot regard the pause as part of my verbal message. These ungrammatical pauses are better regarded as the places where the speaker is thinking, is searching for words, and is planning how to continue his utterance. For a linguist, of course, the grammatical pause is most interesting, since it reveals something about the structure of the verbal message. For a psychologist, however, the ungrammatical pause is more interesting, because it reveals something about the thought processes of the speaker.

When a skilled person reads a prepared text, there are few ungrammatical pauses. But spontaneous speech is a highly fragmented and discontinuous activity. Indeed, ungrammatical pausing is a reliable signal of spontaneity in speech. The pauses tend to occur at choice points in the message, and particularly before words that are rare or unusual and words that are chosen with particular care. An actor who wanted to make his rehearsed speech sound spontaneous would deliberately introduce ungrammatical pauses at these critical points.

Verbal communication uses only one of the many kinds of signals that people can exchange; for a balanced view of the communication process we should always keep in mind the great variety of other signals that can reinforce or contradict the verbal message. These subtleties are especially important in psychotherapy, where a patient tries to communicate his emotional troubles to a doctor, but may find it difficult or impossible to express in words the real source of his distress. Under such circumstances, a good therapist learns to listen for more than words, and to rely on nonverbal signals to help him interpret the verbal signals. For this reason, many psychologists have been persistently interested in nonverbal communication, and have perhaps been less likely than linguists to fall into the mistaken belief that language is the only way we can communicate.

The price of opening up one's attention to this wider range of events, however, is a certain vagueness about the kind of communication that is occurring—about what it means and how to study it. We have no dictionaries or grammars to help us analyze nonverbal communication, and there is much work that will have to be done in many cultures before we can formulate and test any interesting scientific theories about nonverbal communication. Nevertheless, the obvious fact that so much communication does occur nonverbally should persuade us not to give up, and not to be misled by our success in analyzing verbal messages.

Recognizing the great variety of communication channels that are available is probably only the first step toward a broader conception of communication as a psychological process. Not only must we study what a person says and how he says it, but we must try to understand why he says it. If we concentrate primarily on the words that people say, we are likely to think that the only purpose of language is to exchange information. That is one of its purposes, of course, but certainly not the only one. People exchange many things. Not only do they exchange information, but they also exchange money, goods, services, love, and status. In any particular interaction, a person may give one of these social commodities in exchange for another. He may give information in exchange for money, or give services in exchange for status or love. Perhaps we should first characterize communication acts in terms of what people are trying to give and gain in their social interactions. Then, within that broader frame of reference, we might see better that verbal messages are more appropriate for some exchanges and nonverbal messages for others, and that both have their natural and complementary roles to play in the vast tapestry we call human society.

DISCUSSION QUESTIONS

1. Do you think that nonverbal communication might be preprogrammed as Chomsky claims language is? What kind of evidence would you need to support your point of view?

2. Describe the difference between the dress of the campus conservative and that of the campus radical. What about their respective hair length? Can you think of any corresponding contrasts in their language?

3. In the Ojibwa culture, looking directly at another during conversation is considered a matter of disrespect or even hostility. As a result, the speaker and listener often look at their feet. What problems might this cause for them in school?

PART III

ACQUIRING LANGUAGE

Man has often been defined as the talking animal. Certainly the power of speech is a distinguishing characteristic of mankind. Every human being without neurological damage learns the community language in a relatively short time—an amazing accomplishment in light of the almost infinite complexity of language. Not only do children go from one-word holophrastic utterances to full sentences complete with embedded structures, but by the time they enter school they have learned most of the internal grammar of their native language. In addition, they may expand their vocabulary from about 50 words at eighteen months to about 14,000 at age six. Such an increase means that a child is likely to learn about eight words a day during this formative period—approximately one word every hour of the waking day.

As most parents can testify, watching children develop their language faculty is interesting and rewarding. Yet the scholarly study of child language acquisition is relatively recent. The oldest extant study is Diedrich Tiedmann's diary of infant behavior, written in 1787. Such diaries recording the behavior of one's own children became rather popular in the nineteenth century. Charles Darwin kept one. You will find excerpts from some of them in Aaron Bar-Adon and Werner F. Leopold's *Child Language: A Book of Readings* (Prentice-Hall, 1971).

During the first half of this century most psychologists and students of language apparently concurred in believing that children learned language through imitating their parents' speech. It was then through analogy that the basic syntactic patterns were expanded for use in new situations. A corollary was that the proper way to teach language to young children was through constant pattern drills, a corollary that, of course, was not actually accepted in practice by mothers with infants learning to produce their first words. Phonology, morphology, and syntax at this time were more or less quietly accepted as the province of the linguists; semantics and pragmatics, as that of the psychologists. Probably the major work of this period was Werner Leopold's *Speech Development of a Bilingual Child* (Northwestern University Press, 1939, 1947, 1949). Although slightly on one side in that it concerned the acquisition of two languages by the same child, Leopold's three-volume work minutely described his daughter's acquisition of vocabulary, phonology, and syntax in German and English over a two-year period.

But most serious attempts to study child language acquisition began after the publication of Noam Chomsky's *Syntactic Structures* (Mouton, 1957). His theory of generative grammar made syntax a fruitful area for collaboration between linguists and psychologists, a collaboration from which emerged the rapidly proliferating discipline of psycholinguistics. Chomsky hypothesized that, since children acquire language too rapidly for it to be assumed that they do so by imitation alone, there had to be posited some kind of innate language acquisition device. He further came to hold that, since children extend their language to fit novel situations for which they have no model from previous experience, this extension likewise could not have resulted only from analogy. You will find detailed material on the resulting controversy in Chomsky's celebrated review of B. F. Skinner's *Verbal Behavior* (*Language* 35(1959): 25–58).

Particularly significant for the study of child language was the Chomskyan distinction between competence, the internalized knowledge by which a native speaker is enabled to use his language, and performance, the actual use of that language in a social context. Initially, psychologists rather religiously accepted this distinction, but more recently they have begun to question Chomsky's early transformational models although without rejecting the concept of deep structure. They discovered that a child's early speech is not an abbreviated or imperfect version of an adult grammar but rather is the result of the operation of the child's own set of rules.

The first two articles in this section, by Roger Brown and Breyne Moskowitz, offer complementary accounts of how children acquire language. Both start with the assumption that children are genetically endowed with a language-learning capacity. Recently this assumption has led researchers to explore the possibility that at least the beginning of such an endowment may be found in other animals. From a mass of literature reporting such research we have selected the present essay by Edward Klima and Ursula Bellugi, who raise the question with respect to apes. But the question "Are the apes in a pre-evolutionary stage before language-learning as such can occur?" can as yet be answered only tentatively in the light of the preliminary nature of the research.

You will find extended treatment of this subject in these works:

Brown, Roger. *A First Language: The Early Stages.* Cambridge: Harvard University Press, 1973. This contains a section on ape linguistics, as well as on child language acquisition.

Carey, Susan. "The Child as Word Learner." In *Linguistic Theory and Psychological Reality,* eds. Morris Halle, Joan Bresnan, and George Miller. Cambridge: M.I.T. Press, 1979. Pp. 264–291.

Chomsky, Carol. *The Acquisition of Syntax in Children from 5 to 8.* Cambridge: M.I.T. Press, 1969.

Dale, Philip S. *Language Development: Structure and Function,* 2nd ed. New York: Holt, Rinehart and Winston, 1976.

Laird, Charlton. "A Nonhuman Being Can Learn Language." In *College Composition and Communication* 23 (May 1972): 142–154.

Smith, Frank, and George A. Miller, eds. *The Genesis of Language: A Psycholinguistic Approach.* Cambridge: M.I.T. Press, 1966. There is a section on ape communication.

ROGER BROWN

A graduate of the University of Michigan, since 1952 Brown has taught at the Massachusetts Institute of Technology and at Harvard University, where he is John Lindsley professor of psychology. He has written outstanding articles and textbooks in the field of child language and language acquisition.

DEVELOPMENT OF THE FIRST LANGUAGE IN THE HUMAN SPECIES

The fact that one dare set down the above title, with considerable exaggeration but not perhaps with more than is pardonable, reflects the most interesting development in the study of child speech in the past few years. All over the world the first sentences of small children are being as painstakingly taped, transcribed, and analyzed as if they were the last sayings of great sages. Which is a surprising fate for the likes of "That doggie," "No more milk," and "Hit ball." Reports already made, in progress, or projected for the near future sample development in children not only from many parts of the United States, England, Scotland, France, and Germany, but also development in children learning Luo (central East Africa), Samoan, Finnish, Hebrew, Japanese, Korean, Serbo-Croatian, Swedish, Turkish, Cakchiquel (Mayan-Guatemala), Tzeltal (Mayan-Mexico), American Sign Language in the case of a deaf child, and many other languages. The count you make of the number of studies now available for comparative analysis depends on how much you require in terms of standardized procedure, the full report of data, explicit criteria of acquisition, and so on. Brown (1973), whose methods demand a good deal, finds he can use some 33 reports of 12 languages. Slobin (1971), less interested in proving a small number of generalizations than in setting down a large number of interesting hypotheses suggested by what is known, finds he can use many more studies of some 30 languages from 10 different language families. Of course, this is still only about a 1% sample of the world's languages, but in a field like psycholinguistics, in which "universals" sometimes have been postulated on the basis of one or two languages, 30 languages represent a notable empirical advance. The credit for inspiring this extensive field work on language development belongs chiefly to Slobin at Berkeley, whose vision of a universal developmental sequence has inspired research workers everywhere. The quite surprising degree to which results to date support this vision has sustained the researcher when he gets a bit tired of writing down Luo, Samoan, or Finnish equivalents of "That doggie" and "No more milk."

It has, of course, taken some years to accumulate data on a wide variety of languages and even now, as we shall see, the variety is limited largely to just the first period of sentence construction (what is called Stage I). However, the study of first-language development in the preschool years began to be appreciated as a central topic in psycholinguistics in the early 1960s. The initial impetus came fairly directly from Chomsky's (1957) *Syntactic Structures* and, really, from one particular emphasis in that book and in transformational, generative grammar generally. The emphasis is, to put it simply, that in acquiring a first language, one cannot possibly be said simply to acquire a repertoire of sentences, however large that repertoire is imagined to be, but must instead be said to acquire a rule system that makes it possible to generate a literally infinite variety of sentences, most of them never heard from anyone else. It is not a rare thing for a person to compose a new sentence that is understood within his community; rather, it is really a very ordinary linguistic event. Of course, *Syntactic Structures* was not the first book to picture first-language learning as a largely creative process; it may be doubted if any serious linguist has ever thought otherwise. It was the central role Chomsky gave to creativity that made the difference, plus, of course, the fact that he was able to put into explicit, unified notation a certain number of the basic rules of English.

In saying that a child acquires construction rules, one cannot of course mean that he acquires them in any explicit form; the preschool child cannot tell you any linguistic rules at all. And the chances are that his parents cannot tell you very many either, and they obviously do not attempt to teach the mother tongue by the formulation of rules of sentence construction. One must suppose that what happens is that the preschool child is able to extract from the speech he hears a set of construction rules, many of them exceedingly abstract, which neither he nor his parents know in explicit form. This is saying more than that the child generalizes or forms analogies insofar as the generalizations he manifests conform closely to rules that have been made explicit in linguistic science.

That something of the sort described goes on has always been obvious to everyone for languages like Finnish or Russian which have elaborate rules of word formation, or morphology, rules that seem to cause children to make very numerous systematic errors of a kind that parents and casual observers notice. In English, morphology is fairly simple, and errors that parents notice are correspondingly less common. Nevertheless they do exist, and it is precisely in these errors that one glimpses from time to time that largely hidden but presumably general process. Most American children learning English use the form *hisself* rather than *himself* when they are about four years old. How do they come by it? It actually has been in the language since Middle English and is still in use among some adults, though called, for no good reason, a "substandard" form. It can be shown, however, that children use it when they have never heard it from anyone else, and so presumably they make it up or construct it. Why do they invent something that is, from the standard adult point of view, a mistake? To answer that we must recall the set of words most similar to the reflexive pronoun *himself*. They are such other reflexive pronouns as *myself, yourself,* and *herself*. But all of these others, we see, are constructed by combining the possessive pronoun, *my, your,* or *her* with *self*. The masculine possessive pronoun is *his* and, if the English language were consistent at this point, the reflexive would be *hisself*. As it happens, standard English is not consistent at this point but is, rather, irregular, as all languages are at some points, and the preferred form is *himself*. Children, by inventing *hisself* and often insisting on it for quite a period, "iron out" or correct the irregularity of the language. And, incidentally, they reveal to us the fact that what they are learning are general rules of construction—not just the words and phrases they hear.

Close examination of the speech of children learning English shows that it is often replete with errors of syntax or sentence construction as well as morphology (e.g., "Where Daddy went"). But for some reason, errors of word formation are noticed regularly by parents, whereas they are commonly quite unconscious of errors of syntax. And so it happens that even casual observers of languages with a well-developed morphology are aware of the creative construction process, whereas casual observers of English find it possible seriously to believe that language learning is simply a process of memorizing what has been heard.

The extraction of a finite structure with an infinite generative potential which furthermore is accomplished in large part, though not completely, by the beginning of the school years (see Chomsky, 1969, for certain exceptions and no doubt there are others), all without explicit tuition, was not something any learning theory was prepared to explain, though some were prepared to "handle" it, whatever "handle" means. And so it appeared that first-language acquisition was a major challenge to psychology.

While the first studies of language acquisition were inspired by transformational linguistics, nevertheless, they really were not approved of by the transformational linguists. This was because the studies took the child's spontaneous speech performance, taped and transcribed at home on some regular schedule, for their basic data, and undertook to follow the changes in these data with age. At about the same time in the early 1960s, three studies of, roughly, this sort were begun independently: Martin Braine's (1963) in Maryland, Roger Brown's (Brown & Bellugi, 1964) at Harvard with his associates Ursula Bellugi (now Bellugi-Klima) and Colin Fraser (Brown & Fraser, 1963), and Susan Ervin (now Ervin-Tripp) with Wick Miller (Miller & Ervin, 1964) at Berkeley. The attempt to discover constructional knowledge from "mere performance" seemed quite hopeless to the MIT linguists (e.g., Chomsky, 1964; Lees, 1964). It was at the opposite extreme from the linguist's own method, which was to present candidate-sentences to his own intuition for judgment as grammatical or not. In cases of extreme uncertainty, I suppose he may also have stepped next door to ask the opinion of a colleague.

In retrospect, I think they were partly right and partly wrong about our early methods. They were absolutely right in thinking that no sample of spontaneous speech, however large, would alone enable one to write a fully determinate set of construction rules. I learned that fact over a period of years in which I made the attempt 15 times, for three children at five points of development. There were always, and are always, many things the corpus alone cannot settle. The linguists were wrong, I think, in two ways. First, in supposing that because one cannot learn everything about a child's construction knowledge, one cannot learn anything. One can, in fact, learn quite a lot, and one of the discoveries of the past decade is the variety of ways in which spontaneous running discourse can be "milked" for knowledge of linguistic structure; a great deal of the best evidence lies not simply in the child's own sentences but in the exchanges with others on the level of discourse. I do not think that transformational linguists should have "pronounced" on all of this with such discouraging confidence since they had never, in fact, tried. The other way in which I think the linguists were wrong was in their gross exaggeration of the degree to which spontaneous speech is ungrammatical, a kind of hodgepodge of false starts, incomplete sentences, and so on. Except for talk at learned conferences, even adult speech, allowing for some simple rules of editing and ellipses, seems to be mostly quite grammatical (Labov, 1970). For children and for the speech of parents to children this is even more obviously the case.

The first empirical studies of the 1960s gave rise to various descriptive characterizations, of which "telegraphic speech" (Brown & Fraser, 1963) and "Pivot Grammar" (Braine, 1963) are the best known. These did not lead anywhere very interesting, but they were unchallenged long enough to get into most introductory psychology textbooks where they probably will survive for a few years even though their numerous inadequacies are now well established. Bloom (1970), Schlesinger (1971), and Bowerman (1970) made the most telling criticisms both theoretical and empirical, and Brown (1973) has put the whole, now overwhelmingly negative, case together. It seems to be clear enough to workers in this field that telegraphic speech and Pivot Grammar are false leads that we need not even bother to describe.

However, along with their attacks, especially on Pivot Grammar, Bloom (1970) and Schlesinger (1971) made a positive contribution that has turned out to be the second major impetus to the field. For reasons which must seem very strange to the outsider not immersed in the linguistics of the 1960s, the first analyses of child sentences in this period were in terms of pure syntax, in abstraction from semantics, with no real attention paid to what the children might intend to communicate. Lois Bloom added to her transcriptions of child speech a systematic running account of the nonlinguistic context. And in these contexts she found evidence that the child intends to express certain meanings with even his earliest sentences, meanings that go beyond the simple naming in succession of various aspects of a complex situation, and that actually assert the existence of, or request the creation of, particular relations.

The justification for attributing relational semantic intentions to very small children comprises a complex and not fully satisfying argument. At its strongest, it involves the following sort of experimental procedure. With toys that the child can name available to him he is, on one occasion, asked to "Make the truck hit the car," and on another occasion"Make the car hit the truck." Both sentences involve the same objects and action, but the contrast of word order in English indicates which object is to be in the role of agent (hitter) and which in the role of object (the thing hit). If the child acts out the two events in ways appropriate to the contrasting word orders, he may be said to understand the differences in the semantic relations involved. Similar kinds of contrasts can be set up for possessives ("Show me the Mommy's baby" versus "Show me the baby's Mommy") and prepositions ("Put the pencil on the matches" versus "Put the matches on the pencil"). The evidence to date, of which there is a fairly considerable amount collected in America and Britain (Bever, Mehler, & Valian, 1973; de Villiers & de Villiers, 1973a; Fraser, Bellugi & Brown, 1963; Lovell & Dixon, 1965), indicates that, by late Stage I, children learning English can do these things correctly (experiments on the prepositions are still in a trial stage). By late Stage I, children learning English also are often producing what the nonlinguistic context suggests are intended as relations of possession, location, and agent-action-object. For noncontrastive word orders in English and for languages that do not utilize contrastive word order in these ways, the evidence for relational intentions is essentially the nonlinguistic context. Which context is also, of course, what parents use as an aid to figuring out what their children mean when they speak.

It is, I think, worth a paragraph of digression to point out that another experimental method, a method of judgment and correction of word sequence and so a method nearer that of the transformational linguist himself, yields a quite different outcome. Peter and Jill de Villiers (1972) asked children to observe a dragon puppet who sometimes spoke correctly with respect to word order (e.g., "Drive your car") and sometimes incorrectly (e.g., "Cup the fill"). A second dragon puppet responded to the first when the first spoke correctly by saying "right" and repeating the sentence. When the first puppet spoke incorrectly, the second, tutorial puppet, said "wrong," and corrected the sentence (e.g., "Fill the cup"). After observing a number of such sequences, the child was invited to play the role of the tutorial puppet, and new sentences, correct and incorrect, were supplied. In effect, this is a complicated way of asking the child to make judgments of syntactic well-formedness, supplying corrections as necessary. The instruction is not given easily in words, but by role-playing examples de Villiers and de Villiers found they could get the idea across. While there are many interesting results in their study, the most important is that the children did not make correct word-order judgments 50% of the time until after what we call Stage V, and only the most advanced child successfully corrected wrong orders over half the time. This small but important study suggests that construction rules do not emerge all at once on the levels of spontaneous use, discriminating response, and judgment. The last of these, the linguist's favorite, is, after all, not simply a pipeline to competence but a metalinguistic performance of considerable complexity.

In spite of the fact that the justification for attributing semantic intentions of a relational nature to the child when he first begins composing sentences is not fully satisfactory, the practice, often called the method of "rich interpretation," by contrast with the "lean" behavioral interpretation that preceded it, is by now well justified simply because it has helped expose remarkable developmental universals that formerly had gone unremarked. There are now, I think, three reasonably well-established developmental series in which constructions and the meanings they express appear in a nearly invariant order.

The first of these, and still the only one to have been shown to have validity for many different languages, concerns Stage I. Stage I has been defined rather arbitrarily as the period when the average length of the child's utterances in morphemes (mean length of utterance or *MLU*) first rises above 1.0—in short, the time when combinations of words or morphemes first occur at all—until the *MLU* is 2.0, at which time utterances occasionally will attain as great a length as 7 morphemes. The most obvious superficial fact about child sentences is that they grow longer as the child grows older. Leaning on this fact, modern investigators have devised a set of standard rules for calculating *MLU*, rules partially well motivated and partially arbitrary. Whether the rules are exactly the right ones, and it is already clear that they are not, is almost immaterial because their only function is a temporary one: to render children in one study and in different studies initially comparable in terms of some index superior to chronological age, and this *MLU* does. It has been shown (Brown, 1973) that while individual children vary enormously in rate of linguistic development, and so in what they know at a given chronological age, their constructional and semantic knowledge is fairly uniform at a given *MLU*. It is common, in the literature, to identify five stages, with those above Stage I defined by increments of .50 to the *MLU*.

By definition, then, Stage I children in any language are going to be producing sentences of from 1 to 7 morphemes long with the average steadily increasing across Stage I. What is not true by definition, but is true in fact for all of the languages so far studied, is that the constructions in Stage I are limited semantically to a single rather small set of relations and, furthermore, the complications that occur in the course of the Stage are also everywhere the same. Finally, in Stage I, the only syntactic or expressive devices employed are the combinations of the semantically related forms under one sentence contour and, where relevant in the model language, correct word order. It is important to recognize that there are many other things that *could* happen in Stage I, many ways of increasing *MLU* besides those actually used in Stage I. In Stage I, *MLU* goes up because simple two-term relations begin to be combined into three-term and four-term relations of the same type but occurring in one sentence. In later stages, *MLU*, always sensitive to increases of knowledge, rises in value for quite different reasons; for instance, originally missing obligatory function forms like inflections begin to be supplied, later on the embedding of two or more simple sentences begins, and eventually the coordination of simple sentences.

What are the semantic relations that seem universally to be the subject matter of Stage I speech? In brief, it may be said that they are either relations or propositions concerning the sensory-motor world, and seem to represent the linguistic expression of the sensory-motor intelligence which the work of the great developmental psychologist, Jean Piaget, has described as the principal acquisition of the first 18 months of life. The Stage I relations also correspond very closely with the set of "cases" which Charles Fillmore (1968) has postulated as the universal semantic deep structures of language. This is surprising since Fillmore did not set out to say anything at all about child speech but simply to provide a universal framework for adult grammar.

In actual fact, there is no absolutely fixed list of Stage I relations. A short list of 11 will account for about 75% of Stage I utterances in almost all language samples collected. A longer list of about 18 will come close to accounting for 100%. What are some of the relations? There is, in the first place, a closed semantic set having to do with reference. These include the nominative (e.g., "That ball"), expressions of recurrence (e.g., "More ball"), and expressions of disappearance or nonexistence (e.g., "All gone ball"). Then there is the possessive (e.g., "Daddy chair"), two sorts of locative (e.g., "Book table" and "Go store") and the attributive (e.g., "Big house"). Finally, there are two-term relations comprising portions of a major sort of declarative sentence: agent-action (e.g., "Daddy hit"); action-object (e.g., "Hit ball"); and, surprisingly from the point of view of the adult language, agent-object (e.g., "Daddy ball"). Less frequent relations which do not appear in all samples but which one would want to add to a longer list include: experiencer-state (e.g., "I hear"); datives of indirect object (e.g., "Give Mommy"); comitatives (e.g., "Walk Mommy"); instrumentals (e.g., "Sweep broom"); and just a few others. From all of these constructions, it may be noticed that in English, and in all languages, "obligatory" functional morphemes like inflections, case endings, articles, and prepositions are missing in Stage I. This is, of course, the observation that gave rise to the still roughly accurate descriptive term *telegraphic speech*. The function forms are thought to be absent because of some combination of such variables as their slight phonetic substance and minimal stress, their varying but generally considerable grammatical complexity, and the subtlety of the semantic modulations they express (number, time, aspect, specificity of reference, exact spatial relations, etc.).

Stage I speech seems to be almost perfectly restricted to these two-term relations, expressed, at the least, by subordination to a single sentence contour and often by appropriate word order, until the *MLU* is about 1.50. From here on, complications which lengthen the utterance begin, but they are, remarkably enough, complications of just the same two types in all languages studied so far. The first type involves three-term relations, like agent-action-object; agent-action-locative; and action-object-locative which, in effect, combine sequentially two of the simple relations found before an *MLU* of 1.50 without repeating the term that would appear twice if the two-term relations simply were strung together. In other words, something like agent-action-object (e.g., "Adam hit ball") is made up *as if* the relations agent-action ("Adam hit") and action-object ("Hit ball") had been strung together in sequence with one redundant occurrence of the action ("hit") deleted.

The second type of complication involves the retention of the basic line of the two-term relation with one term, always a noun-phrase, "expanding" as a relation in its own right. Thus, there is development from such forms as "Sit chair" (action-locative) to "Sit Daddy chair" which is an action-locative, such that the locative itself is expanded as a possessive. The forms expanded in this kind of construction are, in all languages so far studied, the same three types: expressions of attribution, possession, and recurrence. Near the very end of Stage I, there are further complications into four-term relations of exactly the same two types described. All of this, of course, gives a very "biological" impression, almost as if semantic cells of a finite set of types were dividing and combining and then redividing and recombining in ways common to the species.

The remaining two best established invariances of order in acquisition have not been studied in a variety of languages but only for American children and, in one case, only for the three unacquainted children in Brown's longitudinal study—the children called, in the literature, Adam, Eve, and Sarah. The full results appear in Stage II of Brown (1973) and in Brown and Hanlon (1970). Stage II in Brown (1973) focuses on 14 functional morphemes including the English noun and verb inflections, the copula *be*, the progressive auxiliary *be*, the prepositions *in* and *on*, and the articles *a* and *the*. For just these forms in English it is possible to define a criterion that is considerably superior to the simple occurrence-or-not used in Stage I and to the semiarbitrary frequency levels used in the remaining sequence to be described. In very many sentence contexts, one or another of the 14 morphemes can be said to be "obligatory" from the point of view of the adult language. Thus in a nomination sentence accompanied by pointing, such as "That book," an article is obligatory; in a sentence like "Here two book," a plural inflection on the noun is obligatory; in "I running," the auxiliary *am* inflected for person, number, and tense is obligatory. It is possible to treat each such sentence frame as a kind of test item in which the obligatory form either appears or is omitted. Brown defined as his criterion of acquisition, presence in 90% of obligatory contexts in six consecutive sampling hours.

There are in the detailed report many surprising and suggestive outcomes. For instance, "acquisition" of these forms turns out never to be a sudden all-or-none affair such as categorical linguistic rules might suggest it should be. It is rather a matter of a slowly increasing probability of presence, varying in rate from morpheme to morpheme, but extending in some cases over several years. The most striking single outcome is that for these three children, with spontaneous speech scored in the fashion described, the order of acquisition of the morphemes approaches invariance, with rank-order correlations between pairs of children all at about .86. This does not say that acquisition of a morpheme is invariant with respect to chronological age: the variation of rate of development even among three children is tremendous. But the order, that is, which construction follows which, is almost constant, and Brown (1973) shows that it is not predicted by morpheme frequency in adult speech, but is well predicted by relative semantic and grammatical complexity. Of course, in languages other than English, the same universal sequence cannot possibly be found because grammatical and semantic differences are too great to yield commensurable data, as they are not with the fundamental relations or cases of Stage I. However, if the 14 particular morphemes are reconceived as particular conjunctions of perceptual salience and degrees of grammatical and semantic complexity, we may find laws of succession which have cross-linguistic validity (see Slobin, 1971).

Until the spring of 1972, Brown was the only researcher who had coded data in terms of presence in, or absence from, obligatory contexts, but then Jill and Peter de Villiers (1973) did the job on a fairly large scale. They made a cross-sectional study from speech samples of 21 English-speaking American children aged between 16 and 40 months. The de Villiers scored the 14 morphemes Brown scored; they used his coding rules to identify obligatory contexts and calculated the children's individual *MLU* values according to his rules.

Two different criteria of morpheme acquisition were used in the analyses of data. Both constituted well-rationalized adaptations to a cross-sectional study of the 90% correct criterion used in Brown's longitudinal study; we will refer to the two orders here simply as 1 and 2. To compare with the de Villiers' two orders there is a single rank order (3) for the three children, Adam, Eve, and Sarah, which was obtained by averaging the orders of the three children.

There are then three rank orders for the same 14 morphemes scored in the same way and using closely similar criteria of acquisition. The degree of invariance is, even to one who expected a substantial similarity, amazing. The rank-order correlations are: between 1 and 2, .84; between 2 and 3, .78; between 1 and 3, .87. These relations are only very slightly below those among Adam, Eve, and Sarah themselves. Thanks to the de Villiers, it has been made clear that we have a developmental phenomenon of substantial generality.

There are numerous other interesting outcomes in the de Villiers' study. The rank-order correlation between age and Order 2 is .68, while that between *MLU* and the same order is .92, very close to perfect. So *MLU* is a better predictor than age in their study, as in ours of morpheme acquisition. In fact, with age partialed out, using a Kendall partial correlation procedure, the original figure of .92 is only reduced to .85, suggesting that age adds little or nothing to the predictive power of *MLU*.

The third sequence, demonstrated only for English by Brown and Hanlon (1970), takes advantage of the fact that what are called tag questions are in English very complex grammatically, though semantically they are rather simple. In many other languages tags are invariant in form (e.g., *n'est-ce pas,* French; *nicht wahr,* German), and so are grammatically simple; but in English, the form of the tag, and there are hundreds of forms, varies in a completely determinate way with the structure of the declarative sentence to which it is appended and for which it asks confirmation. Thus:

> "John will be late, won't he?"
> "Mary can't drive, can she?"

And so on. The little question at the end is short enough, as far as superficial length is concerned, to be produced by the end of Stage I. We know, furthermore, that the semantic of the tag, a request for confirmation, lies within the competence of the Stage I child since he occasionally produces such invariant and simple equivalents as "right?" or "huh?" Nevertheless, Brown and Hanlon (1970) have shown that the production of a full range of well-formed tags is not to be found until after Stage V, sometimes several years after. Until that time, there are, typically, no well-formed tags at all. What accounts for the long delay? Brown and Hanlon present evidence that it is the complexity of the grammatical knowledge that tags entail.

Consider such a declarative sentence as "His wife can drive." How might one develop from this the tag "can't she?" It is, in the first place, necessary to make a pronoun of the subject. The subject is *his wife,* and so the pronoun must be feminine, third person, and since it is a subject, the nominative case—in fact, *she.* Another step is to make the tag negative. In English this is done by adding *not* or the contraction *n't* to the auxiliary verb *can;* hence *can't.* Another step is to make the tag interrogative, since it is a question, and in English that is done by a permutation of order—placing the auxiliary verb ahead of the subject. Still another step is to delete all of the predicate of the base sentence, except the first member of the auxiliary, and that at last yields *can't she?* as a derivative of *His wife can drive.* While this description reads a little bit like a program simulating the process by which tags actually are produced by human beings, it is not intended as anything of the sort. The point is simply that there seems to be no way at all by which a human could produce the right tag for each declarative without *somehow* utilizing all of the grammatical knowledge described, just how no one knows. But memorization is excluded completely by the fact that, while tags themselves are numerous but not infinitely so, the problem is to fit the one right tag to each declarative, and declaratives are infinitely numerous.

In English all of the single constructions, and also all of the pairs, which entail the knowledge involved in tag creation, themselves exist as independent sentences in their own right, for example, interrogatives, negatives, ellipses, negative-ellipses, and so on. One can, therefore, make an ordering of constructions in terms of complexity of grammatical knowledge (in precise fact, only a partial ordering) and ask whether more complex forms are always preceded in child speech by less complex forms. This is what Brown and Hanlon (1970) did for Adam, Eve, and Sarah, and the result was resoundingly affirmative. In this study, then, we have evidence that grammatical complexity as such, when it can be disentangled, as it often cannot, from semantic complexity, is itself a determinant of order of acquisition.

Of course, the question about the mother tongue that we should really like answered is, How is it possible to learn a first language at all? On that question, which ultimately motivates the whole research enterprise, I have nothing to offer that is not negative. But perhaps it is worth while making these negatives explicit since they are still widely supposed to be affirmatives, and indeed to provide a large part of the answer to the question. What I have to say is not primarily addressed to the question, How does the child come to talk at all? since there seem to be fairly obvious utilities in saying a few words in order to express more exactly what he wants, does not want, wonders about, or wishes to share with others. The more exact question on which we have a little information that serves only to make the question more puzzling is, How does the child come to *improve* upon his language, moving steadily in the direction of the adult model? It probably seems surprising that there should be any mystery about the forces impelling improvement, since it is just this aspect of the process that most people imagine that they understand. Surely the improvement is a response to selective social pressures of various kinds; ill-formed or incomplete utterances must be less effective than well-formed and complete utterances in accomplishing the child's intent; parents probably approve of well-formed utterances and disapprove or correct the ill-formed. These ideas sound sensible and may be correct, but the still-scant evidence available does not support them.

At the end of Stage I, the child's constructions are characterized by, in addition to the things we have mentioned, a seemingly lawless oscillating omission of every sort of major constituent including sometimes subjects, objects, verbs, locatives, and so on. The important point about these oscillating omissions is that they seldom seem to impede communication; the other person, usually the mother, being in the same situation and familiar with the child's stock of knowledge, usually understands, so far as one can judge, even the incomplete utterance. Brown (1973) has suggested the Stage I child's speech is well adapted to his purpose, but that, as a speaker, he is very *narrowly* adapted. We may suppose that in speaking to strangers or of new experiences he will have to learn to express obligatory constituents if he wants to get his message across. And that may be the answer: The social pressures to communicate may chiefly operate outside the usual sampling situation, which is that of the child at home with family members.

In Stage II, Brown (1973) found that all of the 14 grammatical morphemes were at first missing, then occasionally present in obligatory contexts, and after varying and often long periods of time, always present in such contexts. What makes the probability of supplying the requisite morpheme rise with time? It is surprisingly difficult to find cases in which omission results in incomprehension or misunderstanding. With respect to the definite and nondefinite articles, it even looks as if listeners almost never really need them, and yet child speakers learn to operate with the exceedingly intricate rules governing their usage. Adult Japanese, speaking English as a second language, do not seem to learn how to operate with the articles as we might expect they would if listeners needed them. Perhaps it is the case that the child automatically does this kind of learning but that adults do not. Second-language learning may be responsive to familiar sorts of learning variables, and first-language learning may not. The two, often thought to be similar processes, may be profoundly and ineradicably different.

Consider the Stage I child's invariably uninflected generic verbs. In Stage II, American parents regularly gloss these verbs in one of four ways: as imperatives, past tense forms, present progressives, or imminent-intentional futures. It is an interesting fact, of course, that these are just the four modulations of the verb that the child then goes on, first, to learn to express. For years we have thought it possible that glosses or expansions of this type might be a major force impelling the child to improve his speech. However, all the evidence available, both naturalistic and experimental (it is summarized in Brown, Cazden, & Bellugi, 1969), offers no support at all for this notion. Cazden (1965), for instance, carried out an experiment testing for the effect on young children's speech of deliberately interpolated "expansions" (the supplying of obligatory functional morphemes), introduced for a period on every preschool day for three months. She obtained no significant effect whatever. It is possible, I think, that such an experiment done now, with the information Stage II makes available, and expanding only by providing morphemes of a complexity for which the child was "ready," rather than as in Cazden's original experiment expanding in all possible ways, would show an effect. But no such experiment has been done, and so no impelling effect of expansion has been demonstrated.

Suppose we look at the facts of the parental glossing of Stage I generic verbs not, as we have done above, as a possible tutorial device but rather, as Slobin (1971) has done, as evidence that the children already intended the meanings their parents attributed to them. In short, think of the parental glosses as veridical readings of the child's thought. From this point of view, the child has been understood correctly, even though his utterances are incomplete. In that case there is no selection pressure. Why does he learn to say more if what he already knows how to say works quite well?

To these observations of the seeming efficacy of the child's incomplete utterances, at least at home with the family, we should add the results of a study reported in Brown and Hanlon (1970). Here it was not primarily a question of the omission of obligatory forms but of the contrast between ill-formed primitive constructions and well-formed mature versions. For certain constructions, *yes-no* questions, tag questions, negatives, and *wh-* questions, Brown and Hanlon (1970) identified periods when Adam, Eve, and Sarah were producing both primitive and mature versions, sometimes the one, sometimes the other. The question was, Did the mature version communicate more successfully than the primitive version? They first identified all instances of primitive and mature versions, and then coded the adult responses for comprehending follow-up, calling comprehending responses "sequiturs" and uncomprehending or irrelevant responses "nonsequiturs." They found no evidence whatever of a difference in communicative efficacy, and so once again, no selection pressure. Why, one asks oneself, should the child learn the complex apparatus of tag questions when "right?" or "huh?" seems to do just the same job? Again one notes that adults learning English as a second language often do not learn tag questions, and the possibility again comes to mind that children operate on language in a way that adults do not.

Brown and Hanlon (1970) have done one other study that bears on the search for selection pressures. Once again it was syntactic well-formedness versus ill-formedness that was in question rather than completeness or incompleteness. This time Brown and Hanlon started with two kinds of adult responses to child utterances: "approval," directed at an antecedent child utterance, and "disapproval," directed at such an antecedent. The question then was, did the two sets of antecedents differ in syntactic correctness? Approving and disapproving responses are, certainly, very reasonable candidates for the respective roles "positive reinforcer" and "punishment." Of course, they do not necessarily qualify as such because reinforcers and punishments are defined by their effects on performance (Skinner, 1953); they have no necessary, independent, nonfunctional properties. Still, of course, they often are put forward as plausible determinants of performance and are thought, generally, to function as such. In order differentially to affect the child's syntax, approval and disapproval must, at a minimum, be governed selectively by correct and incorrect syntax. If they should be so governed, further data still would be needed to show that they affect performance. If they are not so governed, they cannot be a selective force working for correct speech. And Brown and Hanlon found that they are not. In general, the parents seemed to pay no attention to bad syntax nor did they even seem to be aware of it. They approved or disapproved an utterance usually on the grounds of the truth value of the proposition which the parents supposed the child intended to assert. This is a surprising outcome to most middle-class parents, since they are generally under the impression that they do correct the child's speech. From inquiry and observation I find that what parents generally correct is pronunciation, "naughty" words, and regularized irregular allomorphs liked *digged* or *goed*. These facts of the child's speech seem to penetrate parental awareness. But syntax—the child saying, for instance, "Why the dog won't eat?" instead of "Why won't the dog eat?"—seems to be set right automatically in the parent's mind, with the mistake never registering as such.

In sum, then, we presently do not have evidence that there are selective social pressures of any kind operating on children to impel them to bring their speech into line with adult models. It is, however, entirely possible that such pressures do operate in situations unlike the situations we have sampled, for instance, away from home or with strangers. A radically different possibility is that children work out rules for the speech they hear, passing from levels of lesser to greater complexity, simply because the human species is programmed at a certain period in its life to operate in this fashion on linguistic input. Linguistic input would be defined by the universal properties of language. And the period of progressive rule extraction would correspond to Lenneberg's (1967 and elsewhere) proposed "critical period." It may be chiefly adults who learn a new, a second, language in terms of selective social pressures. Comparison of the kinds of errors made by adult second-language learners of English with the kinds made by child first-language learners of English should be enlightening.

If automatic internal programs of structure extraction provide the generally correct sort of answer to how a first language is learned, then, of course, our inquiries into external communication pressures simply are misguided. They look for the answer in the wrong place. That, of course, does not mean that we are anywhere close to having the right answer. It only remains to specify the kinds of programs that would produce the result regularly obtained.

REFERENCES

1. Bever, T. G., Mehler, J. R., & Valian, V. V. Linguistic capacity of very young children. In T. G. Bever & W. Weksel (Eds.), *The acquisition of structure*. New York: Holt, Rinehart & Winston, 1973.

2. Bloom, L. *Language development: Form and function in emerging grammars*. Cambridge: M.I.T. Press, 1970.

3. Bowerman, M. Learning to talk: A cross-linguistic study of early syntactic development with special reference to Finnish. Unpublished doctoral dissertation, Harvard University, 1970.

4. Braine, M.D.S. The ontogeny of English phrase structure: The first phase. *Language*, 1963, **39**, 1–14.

5. Brown, R. *A first language; The early stages*. Cambridge: Harvard University Press, 1973.

6. Brown, R., & Bellugi, U. Three processes in the acquisition of syntax. *Harvard Educational Review*, 1964, **34**, 133–151.

7. Brown, R., Cazden, C., & Bellugi, U. The child's grammar from I to III. In J. P. Hill (Ed.), *Minnesota symposium on child psychology*. Vol. 2. Minneapolis: University of Minnesota Press, 1969.

8. Brown, R., & Fraser, C. The acquisition of syntax. In C. N. Cofer & B.S. Musgrave (Eds.), *Verbal behavior and learning: Problems and processes*. New York: McGraw-Hill, 1963.

9. Brown, R., & Hanlon, C. Derivational complexity and order of acquisition in child speech. In J. R. Hayes (Ed.), *Cognition and the development of language*. New York: Wiley, 1970.

10. Cazden, C. B. Environmental assistance to the child's acquisition of grammar. Unpublished doctoral dissertation, Harvard University, 1965.

11. Chomsky, C. *The acquisition of syntax in children from 5 to 10*. Cambridge: M.I.T. Press, 1969.

12. Chomsky, N. *Syntactic structures*. The Hague: Mouton, 1957.

13. Chomsky, N. Formal discussion of Wick Miller and Susan Ervin. The development of grammar in child language. In U. Bellugi & R. Brown (Eds.), The acquisition of language, *Monographs of the Society for Research in Child Development*, 1964, **29**(1), 35–40.

14. De Villiers, J. G., & de Villiers, P. A. A cross-sectional study of the development of grammatical morphemes in child speech. *Journal of Psycholinguistic Research*, 1973, **2**, 267–268.

15. De Villiers, J. G., & de Villiers, P. A. Development of the use of order in comprehension. *Journal of Psycholinguistic Research*, 1973a, **2**, 331–341.

16. De Villiers, P. A., & de Villiers, J. G. Early judgments of semantic and syntactic acceptability by children. *Journal of Psycholinguistic Research*, 1972, **1**, 299–310.

17. Fillmore, C. J. The case for case. In E. Bach & R. T. Harms (Eds.), *Universals in linguistic theory*. New York: Holt, Rinehart & Winston, 1968.

18. Fraser, C., Bellugi, U., & Brown, R. Control of grammar in imitation, comprehension, and production. *Journal of Verbal Learning and Verbal Behavior*, 1963, **2**, 121–135.

19. Labov, W. The study of language in its social context. *Stadium Generale*, 1970, **23**, 30–87.

20. Lees, R. Formal discussion of Roger Brown and Colin Fraser. The acquisition of syntax. And of Roger Brown, Colin Fraser, and Ursula Bellugi. Explorations in grammar evaluation. In U. Bellugi & R. Brown (Eds.), The acquisition of language. *Monographs of the Society for Research in Child Development*, 1964, **29**(1), 92–98.

21. Lenneberg, E. H. *Biological foundations of language*. New York: Wiley, 1967.

22. Lovell, K., & Dixon, E. M. The growth of grammar in imitation, comprehension, and production. *Journal of Child Psychology and Psychiatry*, 1965, **5**, 1–9.

23. Miller, W., & Ervin, S. The development of grammar in child language. In U. Bellugi & R. Brown (Eds.), The acquisition of language. *Monographs of the Society for Research in Child Development,* 1964, **29**(1), 9–34.

24. Schlesinger, I. M. Production of utterances and language acquisition. In D. I. Slobin (Ed.), *The ontogenesis of grammar.* New York: Academic Press, 1971.

25. Skinner, B. F. *Science and human behavior.* New York: Macmillan, 1953.

26. Slobin, D. I. Developmental psycholinguistics. In W. O. Dingwall (Ed.), *A survey of linguistic science.* College Park: Linguistics Program, University of Maryland, 1971.

DISCUSSION QUESTIONS

1. How does work in child language support or refute Chomsky's thesis that man is genetically endowed to learn language?

2. What evidence is there that children acquire a first language in a manner different from that in which adults acquire a second one. See Bernard Spolsky's article in Part VI.

3. In Stage II, why doesn't the absence of grammatical morphemes (articles, prepositions, inflections, auxiliaries, verbs, and conjunctions) lead to communication breakdowns between mother and child? What correlation with the development of pidgins and creoles can you find? See Michael Linn's article in Part II.

4. Brown observes: "What parents generally correct is pronunciation, 'naughty' words, and regularized irregular allomorphs like *digger* or *goed,*" rather than syntax. Speculate as to why this is so.

BREYNE ARLENE MOSKOWITZ

The author did undergraduate work at the University of Pennsylvania and received her doctorate from the University of California, Berkeley, in 1971. Since 1972 she has taught in the department of linguistics of the University of California, Los Angeles.

THE ACQUISITION OF LANGUAGE

An adult who finds herself in a group of people speaking an unfamiliar foreign language may feel quite uncomfortable. The strange language sounds like gibberish: mysterious strings of sound, rising and falling in unpredictable patterns. Each person speaking the language knows when to speak, how to construct strings and how to interpret other people's strings, but the individual who does not know anything about the language cannot pick out separate words or sounds, let alone discern meanings. She may feel overwhelmed, ignorant and even childlike. It is possible that she is returning to a vague memory from her very early childhood, because the experience of an adult listening to a foreign language comes close to duplicating the experience of an infant listening to the "foreign" language spoken by everyone around her. Like the adult, the child is confronted with the task of learning a language about which she knows nothing.

The task of acquiring language is one for which the adult has lost most of her aptitude but one the child will perform with remarkable skill. Within a short span of time and with almost no direct instruction the child will analyze the language completely. In fact, although many subtle refinements are added between the ages of five and 10, most children have completed the greater part of the basic language-acquisition process by the age of five. By that time a child will have dissected the language into its minimal separable units of sound and meaning; she will have discovered the rules for recombining sounds into words, the meanings of individual words and the rules for recombining words into meaningful sentences, and she will have internalized the intricate patterns of taking turns in dialogue. All in all she will have established herself linguistically as a full-fledged member of a social community, informed about the most subtle details of her native language as it is spoken in a wide variety of situations.

The speed with which children accomplish the complex process of language acquisition is particularly impressive. Ten linguists working full time for 10 years to analyze the structure of the English language could not program a computer with the ability for language acquired by an average child in the first 10 or even five years of life. In spite of the scale of the task and even in spite of adverse conditions—emotional instability, physical disability and so on—children learn to speak. How do they go about it? By what process does a child learn language?

WHAT IS LANGUAGE?

In order to understand how language is learned it is necessary to understand what language is. The issue is confused by two factors. First, language is learned in early childhood, and adults have few memories of the intense effort that went into the learning process, just as they do not remember the process of learning to walk. Second, adults do have conscious memories of being taught the few grammatical rules that are prescribed as "correct" usage, or the norms of "standard" language. It is difficult for adults to dissociate their memories of school lessons from those of true language learning, but the rules learned in school are only the conventions of an educated society. They are arbitrary finishing touches of embroidery on a thick fabric of language that each child weaves for herself before arriving in the English teacher's classroom. The fabric is grammar: the set of rules that describe how to structure language.

The grammar of language includes rules of phonology, which describe how to put sounds together to form words; rules of syntax, which describe how to put words together to form sentences; rules of semantics, which describe how to interpret the meaning of words and sentences, and rules of pragmatics, which describe how to participate in a conversation, how to sequence sentences and how to anticipate the information needed by an interlocutor. The internal grammar each adult has constructed is identical with that of every other adult in all but a few superficial details. Therefore each adult can create or understand an infinite number of sentences she has never heard before. She knows what is acceptable as a word or a sentence and what is not acceptable, and her judgments on these issues concur with those of other adults. For example, speakers of English generally agree that the sentence "Ideas green sleep colorless furiously" is ungrammatical and that the sentence "Colorless green ideas sleep furiously" is grammatical but makes no sense semantically. There is similar agreement on the grammatical relations represented by word order. For example, it is clear that the sentences "John hit Mary" and "Mary hit John" have different meanings although they consist of the same words, and that the sentence "Flying planes can be dangerous" has two possible meanings. At the level of individual words all adult speakers can agree that "brick" is an English word, that "blick" is not an English word but could be one (that is, there is an accidental gap in the adult lexicon, or internal vocabulary) and that "bnick" is not an English word and could not be one.

How children go about learning the grammar that makes communication possible has always fascinated adults, particularly parents, psychologists and investigators of language. Until recently diary keeping was the primary method of study in this area. For example, in 1877 Charles Darwin published an account of his son's development that includes notes on language learning. Unfortunately most of the diarists used inconsistent or incomplete notations to record what they heard (or what they thought they heard), and most of the diaries were only partial listings of emerging types of sentences with inadequate information on developing word meanings. Although the very best of them, such as W. F. Leopold's classic *Speech Development of a Bilingual Child* continue to be a rich resource for contemporary investigators, advances in audio and video recording equipment have made modern diaries generally much more valuable. In the 1960's, however, new discoveries inspired linguists and psychologists to approach the study of language acquisition in a new, systematic way, oriented less toward long-term diary keeping and more toward a search for the patterns in a child's speech at any given time.

An event that revolutionized linguistics was the publication in 1957 of Noam Chomsky's *Syntactic Structures*. Chomsky's investigation of the structure of grammars revealed that language systems were far deeper and more complex than had been suspected. And of course if linguistics was more complicated, then language learning had to be more complicated. In the 21 years since the publication of *Syntactic Structures* the disciplines of linguistics and child language have come of age. The study of the acquisition of language has benefited not only from the increasingly sophisticated understanding of linguistics but also from the improved understanding of cognitive development as it is related to language. The improvements in recording technology have made experimentation in this area more reliable and more detailed, so that investigators framing new and deeper questions are able to accurately capture both rare occurrences and developing structures.

The picture that is emerging from the more sophisticated investigations reveals the child as an active language learner, continually analyzing what she hears and proceeding in a methodical, predictable way to put together the jigsaw puzzle of language. Different children learn language in similar ways. It is not known how many processes are involved in language learning, but the few that have been observed appear repeatedly, from child to child and from language to language. All the examples I shall discuss here concern children who are learning English, but identical processes have been observed in children learning French, Russian, Finnish, Chinese, Zulu and many other languages.

Children learn the systems of grammar—phonology, syntax, semantics, lexicon and pragmatics—by breaking each system down into its smallest combinable parts and then developing rules for combining the parts. In the first two years of life a child spends much time working on one part of the task, disassembling the language to find the separate sounds that can be put together to form words and the separate words that can be put together to form sentences. After the age of two the basic process continues to be refined, and many more sounds and words are produced. The other part of language acquisition—developing rules for combining the basic elements of language—is carried out in a very methodical way: the most general rules are hypothesized first, and as time passes they are successively narrowed down by the addition of more precise rules applying to a more restricted set of sentences. The procedure is the same in any area of language learning, whether the child is acquiring syntax or phonology or semantics. For example, at the earliest stage of acquiring negatives a child does not have at her command the same range of negative structures that an adult does. She has constructed only a single very general rule: Attach ''no'' to the beginning of any sentence constructed by the other rules of grammar. At this stage all negative sentences will be formed according to that rule.

Throughout the acquisition process a child continually revises and refines the rules of her internal grammar, learning increasingly detailed subrules until she achieves a set of rules that enables her to create the full array of complex, adult sentences. The process of refinement continues at least until the age of 10 and probably considerably longer for most children. By the time a child is six or seven, however, the changes in her grammar may be so subtle and sophisticated that they go unnoticed. In general children approach language learning economically, devoting their energy to broad issues before dealing with specific ones. They cope with clear-cut questions first and sort out the details later, and they may adopt any one of a variety of methods for circumventing details of a language system they have not yet dealt with.

PREREQUISITES FOR LANGUAGE

Although some children verbalize much more than others and some increase the length of their utterances much faster than others, all children overgeneralize a single rule before learning to apply it more narrowly and before constructing other less widely applicable rules, and all children speak in one-word sentences before they speak in two-word sentences. The similarities in language learning for different children and different languages are so great that many linguists have believed at one time or another that the human brain is preprogrammed for language learning. Some linguists continue to believe language is innate and only the surface details of the particular language spoken in a child's environment need to be learned. The speed with which children learn language gives this view much appeal. As more parallels between language and other areas of cognition are revealed, however, there is greater reason to believe any language specialization that exists in the child is only one aspect of more general cognitive abilities of the brain.

Whatever the built-in properties the brain brings to the task of language learning may be, it is now known that a child who hears no language learns no language, and that a child learns only the language spoken in her environment. Most infants coo and babble during the first six months of life, but congenitally deaf children have been observed to cease babbling after six months, whereas normal infants continue to babble. A child does not learn language, however, simply by hearing it spoken. A boy with normal hearing but with deaf parents who communicated by the American Sign Language was exposed to television every day so that he would learn English. Because the child was asthmatic and was confined to his home he interacted only with people at home, where his family and all their visitors communicated in sign language. By the age of three he was fluent in sign language but neither understood nor spoke English. It appears that in order to learn a language a child must also be able to interact with real people in that language. A television set does not suffice as the sole medium for language learning because, even though it can ask questions, it cannot respond to a child's answers. A child, then, can develop language only if there is language in her environment and if she can employ that language to communicate with other people in her immediate environment.

CARETAKER SPEECH

In constructing a grammar children have only a limited amount of information available to them, namely the language they hear spoken around them. (Until about the age of three a child models her language on that of her parents; afterward the language of her peer group tends to become more important.) There is no question, however, that the language environments children inhabit are restructured, usually unintentionally, by the adults who take care of them. Recent studies show that there are several ways caretakers systematically modify the child's environment, making the task of language acquisition simpler.

Caretaker speech is a distinct speech register that differs from others in its simplified vocabulary, the systematic phonological simplification of some words, higher pitch, exaggerated intonation, short, simple sentences and a higher proportion of questions (among mothers) or imperatives (among fathers). Speech with the first two characteristics is formally designated Baby Talk. Baby Talk is a subsystem of caretaker speech that has been studied over a wide range of languages and cultures. Its characteristics appear to be universal: in languages as diverse as English, Arabic, Comanche and Gilyak (a Paleo-Siberian language) there are simplified vocabulary items for terms relating to food, toys, animals and body functions. Some words are phonologically simplified, frequently by the duplication of syllables, as in "wawa" for "water" and "choo-choo" for "train," or by the reduction of consonant clusters, as in "tummy" for "stomach" and "scambled eggs" for "scrambled eggs." (Many types of phonological simplification seem to mimic the phonological structure of an infant's own early vocabulary.)

Perhaps the most pervasive characteristic of caretaker speech is its syntactic simplification. While a child is still babbling, adults may address long, complex sentences to her, but as soon as she begins to utter meaningful, identifiable words they almost invariably speak to her in very simple sentences. Over the next few years of the child's language development the speech addressed to her by her caretakers may well be describable by a grammar only six months in advance of her own.

The functions of the various language modifications in caretaker speech are not equally apparent. It is possible that higher pitch and exaggerated intonation serve to alert a child to pay attention to what she is hearing. As for Baby Talk, there is no reason to believe the use of phonologically simplified words in any way affects a child's learning of pronunciation. Baby Talk may have only a psychological function, marking speech as being affectionate. On the other hand, syntactic simplification has a clear function. Consider the speech adults address to other adults; it is full of false starts and long, rambling, highly complex sentences. It is not surprising that elaborate theories of innate language ability arose during the years when linguists examined the speech adults addressed to adults and assumed that the speech addressed to children was similar. Indeed it is hard to imagine how a child could derive the rules of language from such input. The wide study of caretaker speech conducted over the past eight years has shown that children do not face this problem. Rather it appears they construct their initial grammars on the basis of the short, simple, grammatical sentences that are addressed to them in the first year or two they speak.

CORRECTING LANGUAGE

Caretakers simplify children's language-analysis task in other ways. For example, adults talk with other adults about complex ideas, but they talk with children about the here and now, minimizing discussion of feelings, displaced events and so on. Adults accept children's syntactic and phonological "errors," which are a normal part of the acquisition process. It is important to understand that when children make such errors, they are not producing flawed or incomplete replicas of adult sentences; they are producing sentences that are correct and grammatical with respect to their own current internalized grammar. Indeed, children's errors are essential data for students of child language because it is the consistent departures from the adult model that indicate the nature of a child's current hypotheses about the grammar of language. There are a number of memorized, unanalyzed sentences in any child's output of language. If a child says, "Nobody likes me," there is no way of knowing whether she has memorized the sentence intact or has figured out the rules for constructing the sentence. On the other hand, a sentence such as "Nobody don't like me" is clearly not a memorized form but one that reflects an intermediate stage of developing grammar.

Since each child's utterances at a particular stage are from her own point of view grammatically correct, it is not surprising that children are fairly impervious to correction of their language by adults, indeed to any attempts to teach them language. Consider the boy who lamented to his mother, "Nobody don't like me." His mother seized the opportunity to correct him, replying, "Nobody likes me." The child repeated his original version and the mother her modified one a total of eight times until in desperation the mother said, "Now listen carefully! Nobody likes me." Finally her son got the idea and dutifully replied, "Oh! Nobody don't likes me." As the example demonstrates, children do not always understand exactly what it is the adult is correcting. The information the adult is trying to impart may be at odds with the information in the child's head, namely the rules the child is postulating for producing language. The surface correction of a sentence does not give the child a clue about how to revise the rule that produced the sentence.

It seems to be virtually impossible to speed up the language-learning process. Experiments conducted by Russian investigators show that it is extremely difficult to teach children a detail of language more than a few days before they would learn it themselves. Adults sometimes do, of course, attempt to teach children rules of language, expecting them to learn by imitation, but Courtney B. Cazden of Harvard University found that children benefit less from frequent adult correction of their errors than from true conversational interaction. Indeed, correcting errors can interrupt that interaction, which is, after all, the function of language. (One way children may try to secure such interaction is by asking "Why?" Children go through a stage of asking a question repeatedly. It serves to keep the conversation going, which may be the child's real aim. For example, a two-and-a-half-year-old named Stanford asked "Why?" and was given the nonsense answer: "Because the moon is made of green cheese." Although the response was not at all germane to the conversation, Stanford was happy with it and again asked "Why?" Many silly answers later the adult had tired of the conversation but Stanford had not. He was clearly not seeking information. What he needed was to practice the form of social conversation before dealing with its function. Asking "Why?" served that purpose well.)

In point of fact adults rarely correct children's ungrammatical sentences. For example, one mother, on hearing "Tommy fall my truck down," turned to Tommy with "Did you fall Stevie's truck down?" Since imitation seems to have little role in the language-acquisition process, however, it is probably just as well that most adults are either too charmed by children's errors or too busy to correct them.

Practice does appear to have an important function in the child's language-learning process. Many children have been observed purposefully practicing language when they are alone, for example in a crib or a playpen. Ruth H. Weir of Stanford University hid a tape recorder in her son's bedroom and recorded his talk after he was put to bed. She found that he played with words and phrases, stringing together sequences of similar sounds and of variations on a phrase or on the use of a word: "What color . . . what color blanket . . . what color mop . . . what color glass . . . what color TV . . . red ant . . .fire . . . like lipstick . . . blanket . . . now the blue blanket . . . what color TV . . . what color horse . . . then what color table . . . then what color fire . . . here yellow spoon." Children who do not have much opportunity to be alone may use dialogue in a similar fashion. When Weir tried to record the bedtime monologues of her second child, whose room adjoined that of the first, she obtained through-the-wall conversations instead.

THE ONE-WORD STAGE

The first stage of child language is one in which the maximum sentence length is one word; it is followed by a stage in which the maximum sentence length is two words. Early in the one-word stage there are only a few words in a child's vocabulary, but as months go by her lexicon expands with increasing rapidity. The early words are primarily concrete nouns and verbs; more abstract words such as adjectives are acquired later. By the time the child is uttering two-word sentences with some regularity, her lexicon may include hundreds of words.

When a child can say only one word at a time and knows only five words in all, choosing which one to say may not be a complex task. But how does she decide which word to say when she knows 100 words or more? Patricia M. Greenfield of the University of California at Los Angeles and Joshua H. Smith of Stanford have suggested that an important criterion is informativeness, that is, the child selects a word reflecting what is new in a particular situation. Greenfield and Smith also found that a newly acquired word is first used for naming and only later for asking for something.

Superficially the one-word stage seems easy to understand: a child says one word at a time, and so each word is a complete sentence with its own sentence intonation. Ten years ago a child in the one-word stage was thought to be learning word meanings but not syntax. Recently, however, students of child language have seen less of a distinction between the one-word stage as a period of word learning and the subsequent period, beginning with the two-word stage, as one of syntax acquisition. It now seems clear that the infant is engaged in an enormous amount of syntactic analysis in the one-word stage, and indeed that her syntactic abilities are reflected in her utterances and in her accurate perception of multiword sentences addressed to her.

Ronald Scollon of the University of Hawaii and Lois Bloom of Columbia University have pointed out independently that important patterns in word choice in the one-word stage can be found by examining larger segments of children's speech. Scollon observed that a 19-month-old named Brenda was able to use a vertical construction (a series of one-word sentences) to express what an adult might say with a horizontal construction (a multiword sentence). Brenda's pronunciation, which is represented phonetically below, was imperfect and Scollon did not understand her words at the time. Later, when he transcribed the tape of their conversation, he heard the sound of a passing car immediately preceding the conversation and was able to identify Brenda's words as follows:

BRENDA:	"Car [pronounced 'ka']. Car. Car. Car."
SCOLLON:	"What?"
BRENDA:	"Go. Go."
SCOLLON:	[Undecipherable.]
BRENDA:	"Bus [pronounced 'baish']. Bus. Bus. Bus. Bus. Bus. Bus. Bus. Bus."
SCOLLON:	"What? Oh, bicycle? Is that what you said?"
BRENDA:	"Not ['na']."
SCOLLON:	"No?"
BRENDA:	"Not."
SCOLLON:	"No. I got it wrong."

Brenda was not yet able to combine two words syntactically to express "Hearing that car reminds me that we went on the bus yesterday. No, not on a bicycle." She could express that concept, however, by combining words sequentially. Thus the one-word stage is not just a time for learning the meaning of words. In that period a child is developing hypotheses about putting words together in sentences, and she is already putting sentences together in meaningful groups. The next step will be to put two words together to form a single sentence.

THE TWO-WORD STAGE

The two-word stage is a time for experimenting with many binary semantic-syntactic relations such as possessor-possessed ("Mommy sock"), actor-action ("Cat sleeping") and action-object ("Drink soup"). When two-word sentences first began to appear in

Brenda's speech, they were primarily of the following forms: subject noun and verb (as in "Monster go"), verb and object (as in "Read it") and verb or noun and location (as in "Bring home" and "Tree down"). She also continued to use vertical constructions in the two-word stage, providing herself with a means of expressing ideas that were still too advanced for her syntax. Therefore once again a description of Brenda's isolated sentences does not show her full abilities at this point in her linguistic development. Consider a later conversation Scollon had with Brenda:

> BRENDA: "Tape corder. Use it. Use it."
> SCOLLON: "Use it for what?"
> BRENDA: "Talk. Corder talk. Brenda talk."

Brenda's use of vertical constructions to express concepts she is still unable to encode syntactically is just one example of a strategy employed by children in all areas of cognitive development. As Jean Piaget of the University of Geneva and Dan I. Slobin of the University of California at Berkeley put it, new forms are used for old functions and new functions are expressed by old forms. Long before Brenda acquired the complex syntactic form "Use the tape recorder to record me talking" she was able to use her old forms—two-word sentences and vertical construction—to express the new function. Later, when that function was old, she would develop new forms to express it. The controlled dovetailing of form and function can be observed in all areas of language acquisition. For example, before children acquire the past tense they may employ adverbs of time such as "yesterday" with present-tense verbs to express past time, saying "I do it yesterday" before "I dood it."

Bloom has provided a rare view of an intermediate stage between the one-word and the two-word stages in which the two-word construction—a new form—served only an old function. For several weeks Bloom's daughter Alison uttered two-word sentences all of which included the word "wida." Bloom tried hard to find the meaning of "wida" before realizing that it had no meaning. It was, she concluded, simply a placeholder. This case is the clearest ever reported of a new form preceding new functions. The two-word stage is an important time for practicing functions that will later have expanded forms and practicing forms that will later expand their functions.

TELEGRAPHIC SPEECH

There is no three-word stage in child language. For a few years after the end of the two-word stage children do produce rather short sentences, but the almost inviolable length constraints that characterized the first two stages have disappeared. The absence of a three-word stage has not been satisfactorily explained as yet; the answer may have to do with the fact that many basic semantic relations are binary and few are ternary. In any case a great deal is known about the sequential development in the language of the period following the two-word stage. Roger Brown of Harvard has named that language telegraphic speech. (It should be noted that there is no specific age at which a child enters any of these stages of language acquisition and further that there is no particular correlation between intelligence and speed of acquisition.)

Early telegraphic speech is characterized by short, simple sentences made up primarily of content words: words that are rich in semantic content, usually nouns and verbs. The speech is called telegraphic because the sentences lack function "words":

tense endings on verbs and plural endings on nouns, prepositions, conjunctions, articles and so on. As the telegraphic-speech stage progresses, function words are gradually added to sentences. This process has possibly been studied more thoroughly than any other in language acquisition, and a fairly predictable order in the addition of function words has been observed. The same principles that govern the order of acquisition of function words in English have been shown to operate in many other languages, including some, such as Finnish and Russian, that express the same grammatical relations with particularly rich systems of noun and verb suffixes.

In English many grammatical relations are represented by a fixed word order. For example, in the sentence "The dog followed Jamie to school" it is clear it is the dog that did the following. Normal word order in English requires that the subject come before the verb, and so people who speak English recognize "the dog" as the subject of the sentence. In other languages a noun may be marked as a subject not by its position with respect to the other words in the sentence but by a noun suffix, so that in adult sentences word order may be quite flexible. Until children begin to acquire suffixes and other function words, however, they employ fixed word order to express grammatical relations no matter how flexible adult word order may be. In English the strong propensity to follow word order rigidly shows up in children's interpretations of passive sentences such as "Jamie was followed by the dog." At an early age children may interpret some passive sentences correctly, but by age three they begin to ignore the function words such as "was" and "by" in passive sentences and adopt the fixed word-order interpretation. In other words, since "Jamie" appears before the verb, Jamie is assumed to be the actor, or the noun doing the following.

FUNCTION WORDS

In spite of its grammatical dependence on word order, the English language makes use of enough function words to illustrate the basic principles that determine the order in which such words are acquired. The progressive tense ending "-ing," as in "He going," is acquired first, long before the present-tense third-person singular ending "-s," as in "He goes." The "-s" itself is acquired long before the past tense endings, as in "He goed." Once again the child proves to be a sensible linguist, learning first the tense that exhibits the least variation in form. The "-ing" ending is pronounced only one way, regardless of the pronunciation of the verb to which it is attached. The verb endings "-s" and "-ed," however, vary in their pronunciation: compare "cuts(s)," "cuddles (z)," "crushes (əz)," "walked (t)," "played (d)" and "halted (əd)." (The vowel "ə," called "schwa," is pronounced like the unstressed word "a.") Furthermore, present progressive ("-ing") forms are used with greater frequency than any other tense in the speech children hear. Finally, no verb has an irregular "-ing" form, but some verbs do have irregular third-person present-tense singular forms and many have irregular past-tense forms. (The same pattern of learning earliest those forms that exhibit the least variation shows up much more dramatically in languages such as Finnish and Russian, where the paradigms of inflection are much richer.)

The past tense is acquired after the progressive and present tenses, because the relative time it represents is conceptually more difficult. The future tense ("will" and a verb) is formed regularly in English and is as predictable as the progressive tense, but it is a much more abstract concept than the past tense. Therefore it is acquired much later. In the same way the prepositions "in" and "on" appear earlier than any others, at about the same time as "-ing," but prepositions such as "behind" and "in front of," whose correct usage depends on the speaker's frame of reference, are acquired much later.

It is particularly interesting to note that there are three English morphemes that are pronounced identically but are acquired at different times. They are the plural "-s," the possessive "-s" and the third-person singular tense ending "-s," and they are acquired in the order of listing. Roman Jakobson of Harvard has suggested that the explanation of this phenomenon has to do with the complexity of the different relations the morphemes signal: the singular-plural distinction is at the word level, the possessive relates two nouns at the phrase level and the tense ending relates a noun and a verb at the clause level.

The forms of the verb "to be"—"is," "are" and so on—are among the last of the function words to be acquired, particularly in their present-tense forms. Past- and future-tense forms of "to be" carry tense information, of course, but present-tense forms are essentially meaningless, and omitting them is a very sensible strategy for a child who must maximize the information content of a sentence and place priorities on linguistic structures still to be tackled.

PLURALS

When there are competing pronunciations available, as in the case of the plural and past tenses, the process of sorting them out also follows a predictable pattern. Consider the acquisition of the English plural, in which six distinct stages can be observed. In English, as in many other (but not all) languages, nouns have both singular and plural forms. Children usually use the singular forms first, both in situations where the singular form would be appropriate and in situations where the plural form would be appropriate. In instances where the plural form is irregular in the adult model, however, a child may not recognize it as such and may use it in place of the singular or as a free variant of the singular. Thus in the first stage of acquisition, before either the concept of a plural or the linguistic devices for expressing a plural are acquired, a child may say "two cat" or point to "one feet."

When plurals begin to appear regularly, the child forms them according to the most general rule of English plural formation. At this point it is the child's overgeneralization of the rule, resulting in words such as "mans," "foots" or "feets," that shows she has hypothesized the rule: Add the sound /s/ or /z/ to the end of a word to make it plural. (The slashes indicate pronounced sounds, which are not to be confused with the letters used in spelling.)

For many children the overgeneralized forms of the irregular nouns are actually the earliest /s/ and /z/ plurals to appear, preceding "boys," "cats" and other regular forms by hours or days. The period of overgeneralization is considered to be the third stage in the acquisition of plurals because for many children there is an intermediate second stage in which irregular plurals such as "men" actually do appear. Concerned parents may regard the change from the second-stage "men" to the third-stage "mans" as a regression, but in reality it demonstrates progress from an individual memorized item to the application of a general rule.

In the third stage the small number of words that already end in a sound resembling /s/ or /z/, such as "house," "rose" and "bush," are used without any plural ending. Adults normally make such words plural by adding the suffix /əz/. Children usually relegate this detail to the remainder pile, to be dealt with at a later time. When they return to the problem, there is often a short fourth stage of perhaps a day, in which the child delightedly demonstrates her solution by tacking /əz/ endings indiscriminately onto nouns no matter what sound they end in and no matter how many other plural markings they may already have. A child may wake up one morning and throw herself into this stage with all the zeal of a kitten playing with its first ball of string.

Within a few days the novelty wears off and the child enters a less flamboyant fifth stage, in which only irregular plurals still deviate from the model forms. The rapid progression through the fourth stage does not mean that she suddenly focused her attention on the problem of /əz/ plurals. It is more likely that she had the problem at the back of her mind throughout the third stage. She was probably silently formulating hypotheses about the occurrence of /əz/ and testing them against the plurals she was hearing. Finding the right rule required discovering the phonological specification of the class of nouns that take /əz/ plurals.

Arriving at the sixth and final stage in the acquisition of plurals does not require the formulation of any new rules. All that is needed is the simple memorizing of irregular forms. Being rational, the child relegates such minor details to the lowest-priority remainder pile and turns her attention to more interesting linguistic questions. Hence a five-year-old may still not have entered the last stage. In fact, a child in the penultimate stage may not be at all receptive to being taught irregular plurals. For example, a child named Erica pointed to a picture of some "mouses," and her mother corrected her by saying "mice." Erica and her mother each repeated their own version two more times, and then Erica resolved the standoff by turning to a picture of "ducks." She avoided the picture of the mice for several days. Two years later, of course, Erica was perfectly able to say "mice."

NEGATIVE SENTENCES

One of the pioneering language-acquisition studies of the 1960's was undertaken at Harvard by a research group headed by Brown. The group studied the development in the language of three children over a period of several years. Two members of the group, Ursula Bellugi and Edward S. Klima, looked specifically at the changes in the children's negative sentences over the course of the project. They found that negative structures, like other subsystems of the syntactic component of grammar, are acquired in an orderly, rule-governed way.

When the project began, the forms of negative sentences the children employed were quite simple. It appeared that they had incorporated the following rule into their grammar: To make a sentence negative attach "no" or "not" to the beginning of it. On rare occasions, possibly when a child had forgotten to anticipate the negative, "no" could be attached to the end of a sentence, but negative words could not appear inside a sentence.

In the next stage the children continued to follow this rule, but they had also hypothesized and incorporated into their grammars more complex rules that allowed them to generate sentences in which the negatives "no," "not," "can't" and "don't" appeared after the subject and before the verb. These rules constituted quite an advance over attaching a negative word externally to a sentence. Furthermore, some of the primitive imperative sentences constructed at this stage began with "don't" rather than "no." On the other hand, "can't" never appeared at the beginning of a sentence, and neither "can" nor "do" appeared as an auxiliary, as they do in adult speech: "I can do it." These facts suggest that at this point "can't" and "don't" were unanalyzed negative forms rather than contractions of "cannot" and "do not," but that although "can't" and "don't" each seemed to be interchangeable with "no," they were no longer interchangeable with each other.

In the third stage of acquiring negatives many more details of the negative system had appeared in the children's speech. The main feature of the system that still remained to be worked out was the use of pronouns in negative sentences. At this stage the children said "I didn't see something" and "I don't want somebody to wake me up." The pronouns "somebody" and "something" were later replaced with "nobody" and "nothing" and ultimately with the properly concorded forms "anybody" and "anything."

Many features of telegraphic speech were still evident in the thrid stage. The form "is" of the verb "to be" was frequently omitted, as in "This no good." In adult speech the auxiliary "do" often functions as a dummy verb to carry tense and other markings; for example, in "I didn't see it," "do" carries the tense and the negative. In the children's speech at this stage "do" appeared occasionally, but the children had not yet figured out its entire function. Therefore in some sentences the auxiliary "do" was omitted and the negative "not" appeared alone, as in "I not hurt him." In other sentences, such as "I didn't did it," the negative auxiliary form of "do" appears to be correct but is actually an unanalyzed, memorized item; at this stage the tense is regularly marked on the main verb, which in this example happens also to be "do."

Many children acquire negatives in the same way that the children in the Harvard study did, but subsequent investigations have shown that there is more than one way to learn a language. Carol B. Lord of U.C.L.A. identified a quite different strategy employed by a two-year-old named Jennifer. From 24 to 28 months Jennifer used "no" only as a single-word utterance. In order to produce a negative sentence she simply spoke an ordinary sentence with a higher pitch. For example, "I want put it on" spoken with a high pitch meant "I don't want to put it on." Lord noticed that many of the negative sentences adults addressed to Jennifer were spoken with an elevated pitch. Children tend to pay more attention to the beginning and ending of sentences, and in adult speech negative words usually appear in the middle of sentences. With good reason, then, Jennifer seemed to have hypothesized that one makes a sentence negative by uttering it with a higher pitch. Other children have been found to follow the same strategy. There are clearly variations in the hypotheses children make in the process of constructing grammar.

SEMANTICS

Up to this point I have mainly discussed the acquisition of syntactic rules, in part because in the years following the publication of Chomsky's *Syntactic Structures* child-language research in this area flourished. Syntactic rules, which govern the ordering of words in a sentence, are not all a child needs to know about language, however, and after the first flush of excitement over Chomsky's work investigators began to ask questions about other areas of language acquisition. Consider the development of the rules of semantics, which govern the way words are interpreted. Eve V. Clark of Stanford reexamined old diary studies and noticed that the development in the meaning of words during the first several months of the one-word stage seemed to follow a basic pattern.

The first time children in the studies used a word, Clark noted, it seemed to be as a proper noun, as the name of a specific object. Almost immediately, however, the children generalized the word based on some feature of the original object and used it to refer to many other objects. For example, a child named Hildegard first used "tick-tock" as the name for her father's watch, but she quickly broadened the meaning of the word, first to include all clocks, then all watches, then a gas meter, then a firehose wound on a spool and then a bathroom scale with a round dial. Her generalizations appear to be based on her observation of common features of shape: roundness, dials and so on. In general the children in the diary studies overextended meanings based on similarities of movement, texture, size and most frequently, shape.

As the children progressed, the meanings of words were narrowed down until eventually they more or less coincided with the meanings accepted by adult speakers of the language. The narrowing-down process has not been studied intensively, but it seems likely that the process has no fixed end point. Rather it appears that the meanings of words continue to expand and contract through adulthood, long after other types of language acquisition have ceased.

One of the problems encountered in trying to understand the acquisition of semantics is that it is often difficult to determine the precise meaning a child has constructed for a word. Some interesting observations have been made, however, concerning the development of the meanings of the pairs of words that function as opposites in adult language. Margaret Donaldson and George Balfour of the University of Edinburgh asked children from three to five years old which one of two cardboard trees had "more" apples on it. They asked other children of the same age which tree had "less" apples. (Each child was interviewed individually.) Almost all the children in both groups responded by pointing to the tree with more apples on it. Moreover, the children who had been asked to point to the tree with "less" apples showed no hesitation in choosing the tree with more apples. They did not act as though they did not know the meaning of "less"; rather they acted as if they did know the meaning and "less" meant "more."

Subsequent studies have revealed similar systematic error making in the acquisition of other pairs of opposites such as "same" and "different," "big" and "little," "wide" and "narrow" and "tall" and "short." In every case the pattern of learning is the same: one word of the pair is learned first and its meaning is overextended to apply to the other word in the pair. The first word learned is always the unmarked word of the pair, that is, the word adults use when they do not want to indicate either one of the opposites. (For example, in the case of "wide" and "narrow," "wide" is the unmarked word: asking "How wide is the road?" does not suggest that the road is wide, but asking "How narrow is the road?" does suggest that the road is narrow.)

Clark observed a more intricate pattern of error production in the acquisition of the words "before" and "after." Consider the four different types of sentence represented by (1) "He jumped the gate before he patted the dog." (2) "Before he patted the dog he jumped the gate," (3) "He patted the dog after he jumped the gate" and (4) "After he jumped the gate he patted the dog." Clark found that the way the children she observed interpreted sentences such as these could be divided into four stages.

In the first stage the children disregarded the words "before" and "after" in all four of these sentence types and assumed that the event of the first clause took place before the event of the second clause. With this order-of-mention strategy the first and fourth sentence types were interpreted correctly but the second and third sentence types were not. In the second stage sentences using "before" were interpreted correctly but an order-of-mention strategy was still adopted for sentences that used "after." Hence sentences of the fourth type were interpreted correctly but sentences of third type were not. In the next stage both the third and the fourth sentence types were interpreted incorrectly, suggesting that the children had adopted the strategy that "after" actually meant "before." Finally, in the fourth stage both "before" and "after" were interpreted appropriately.

It appears, then, that in learning the meaning of a pair of words such as "more" and "less" or "before" and "after" children acquire first the part of the meaning that is common to both words and only later the part of the meaning that distinguishes the two. Linguists have not yet developed satisfactory ways of separating the components of meaning that make up a single word, but it seems clear that when such components can be identified, it will be established that, for example, "more" and "less" have a large number of components in common and differ only in a single component specifying the pole of the dimension. Beyond the studies of opposites there has been little investigation of the period of semantic acquisition that follows the early period of rampant overgeneralization. How children past the early stage learn the meanings of other kinds of words is still not well understood.

PHONOLOGY

Just as children overgeneralize word meanings and sentence structures, so do they overgeneralize sounds, using sounds they have learned in place of sounds they have not yet acquired. Just as a child may use the word "not" correctly in one sentence but instead of another negative word in a second sentence, so may she correctly contrast /p/ and /b/ at the beginnings of words but employ /p/ at the ends of words, regardless of whether the adult models end with /p/ or /b/. Children also acquire the details of the phonological system in very regular ways. The ways in which they acquire individual sounds, however, are highly idiosyncratic, and so for many years the patterns eluded diarists, who tended to look only at the order in which sounds were acquired. Jakobson made a major advance in this area by suggesting that it was not individual sounds children acquire in an orderly way but the distinctive features of sound, that is, the minimal differences, or contrasts, between sounds. In other words, when a child begins to contrast /p/ and /b/, she also begins to contrast all the other pairs of sounds that, like /p/ and /b/, differ only in the absence or presence of vocal-cord vibration. In English these pairs include /t/ and /d/, and /k/ and the hard /g/. It is the acquisition of this contrast and not of the six individual sounds that is predictable. Jakobson's extensive examination of the diary data for a wide variety of languages supported his theory. Almost all current work in phonological theory rests on the theory of distinctive features that grew out of his work.

My own recent work suggests that phonological units even more basic than the distinctive features play an important part in the early acquisition process. At an early stage, when there are relatively few words in a child's repertory, unanalyzed syllables appear to be the basic unit of the sound system. By designating these syllables as unanalyzed I mean that the child is not able to separate them into their component consonants and vowels. Only later in the acquisition process does such division into smaller units become possible. The gradual discovery of successively smaller units that can form the basis of the phonological system is an important part of the process.

At an even earlier stage, before a child has uttered any words, she is accomplishing a great deal of linguistic learning, working with a unit of phonological organization even more primitive than the syllable. That unit can be defined in terms of pitch contours. By the late babbling period children already control the intonation, or pitch modulation, contours of the language they are learning. At that stage the child sounds as if she is uttering reasonably long sentences, and adult listeners may have the impression they are not quite catching the child's words. There are no words to catch, only random strings of babbled sounds with recognizable, correctly produced question or statement intonation contours. The sounds may accidentally be similar to some of those found in adult English. These sentence-length utterances are called sentence units, and in the phonological system of the child at this stage they are comparable to the consonant-and-vowel segments, syllables and distinctive features that appear in the phonological systems of later stages. The syllables and segments that appear when the period of word learning begins are in no way related to the vast repertory of babbling sounds. Only the intonation contours are carried over from the babbling stage into the later period.

No matter what language environment a child grows up in, the intonation contours characteristic of adult speech in that environment are the linguistic information learned earliest. Some recent studies suggest that it is possible to identify the language environment of a child from her babbling intonation during the second year of life. Other studies suggest that children can be distinguished at an even earlier age on the basis of whether or not their language environment is a tone language, that is, a language in which words spoken with different pitches are identifiable as different words, even though they may have the same sequence of consonants and vowels. To put it another way, "ma" spoken with a high pitch and "ma" spoken with a low pitch can be as different to someone speaking a tone language as "ma" and "pa" are to someone speaking English. (Many African and Asian languages are tone languages.) Tones are learned very early, and entire tone systems are mastered long before other areas of phonology. The extremely early acquisition of pitch patterns may help to explain the difficulty adults have in learning the intonation of a second language.

PHONETICS

There is one significant way in which the acquisition of phonology differs from the acquisition of other language systems. As a child is acquiring the phonological system she must also learn the phonetic realization of the system: the actual details of physiological and acoustic phonetics, which call for the coordination of a complex set of muscle movements. Some children complete the process of learning how to pronounce things earlier than others, but differences of this kind are usually not related to the learning of the phonological system. Brown had what has become a classic conversation with a child who referred to a "fis." Brown repeated "fis," and the child indignantly corrected him, saying "fis." After several such exchanges Brown tried "fish," and the child, finally satisfied, replied, "Yes, fis." It is clear that although the child was still not able to pronounce the distinction between the sounds "s" and "sh," he knew such a systematic phonological distinction existed. Such phonetic muddying of the phonological waters complicates the study of this area of acquisition. Since the child's knowledge of the phonological system may not show up in her speech, it is not easy to determine what a child knows about the system without engaging in complex experimentation and creative hypothesizing.

Children whose phonological system produces only simple words such as "mama" and "papa" actually have a greater phonetic repertory than their utterances suggest. Evidence of that repertory is found in the late babbling stage, when children are working with sentence units and are making a large array of sounds. They do not lose their phonetic ability overnight, but they must constrain it systematically. Going on to the next-higher stage of language learning, the phonological system, is more important to the child than the details of facile pronunciation. Much later, after the phonological system has been acquired, the details of pronunciation receive more attention.

In the period following the babbling period the persisting phonetic facility gets less and less exercise. The vast majority of a child's utterances fail to reflect her real ability to pronounce things accurately; they do, however, reflect her growing ability to pronounce things systematically. (For a child who grows up learning only one language the movements of the muscles of the vocal tract ultimately become so overpracticed that it is difficult to learn new pronunciations during adulthood. On the other hand, people who learn at least two languages in early childhood appear to retain a greater flexibility of the vocal musculature and are more likely to learn to speak an additional language in their adult years without the ''accent'' of their native language.)

In learning to pronounce, then, a child must acquire a sound system that includes the divergent systems of phonology and phonetics. The acquisition of phonology differs from that of phonetics in requiring the creation of a representation of language in the mind of the child. This representation is necessary because of the abstract nature of the units of phonological structure. From only the acoustic signal of adult language the child must derive successively more abstract phonological units: first intonations, then syllables, then distinctive features and finally consonant-and-vowel segments. There are, for example, few clear segment boundaries in the acoustic signal the child receives, and so the consonant-and-vowel units could hardly be derived if the child had no internal representation of language.

At the same time that a child is building a phonological representation of language she is learning to manipulate all the phonetic variations of language, learning to produce each one precisely and automatically. The dual process of phonetics and phonology acquisition is one of the most difficult in all of language learning. Indeed, although a great deal of syntactic and semantic acquisition has yet to take place, it is usually at the completion of the process of learning to pronounce that adults consider a child to be a full-fledged langauge speaker and stop using any form of caretaker speech.

ABNORMAL LANGUAGE DEVELOPMENT

There seems to be little question that the human brain is best suited to language learning before puberty. Foreign languages are certainly learned most easily at that time. Furthermore, it has been observed that people who learn more than one language in childhood have an easier time learning additional languages in later years. It seems to be extremely important for a child to exercise the language-learning faculty. Children who are not exposed to any learnable language during the crucial years, for example children who are deaf before they can speak, generally grow up with the handicap of having little or no language. The handicap is unnecessary: deaf children of deaf parents who communicate by means of the American Sign Language do not grow up without language. They live in an environment where they can make full use of their language-learning abilities, and they are reasonably fluent in sign language by age three, right on the developmental schedule. Deaf children who grow up communicating by means of sign language have a much easier time learning English as a second language than deaf children in oral-speech programs learning English as a first language.

The study of child language acquisition has made important contributions to the study of abnormal speech development. Some investigators of child language have looked at children whose language development is abnormal in the hope of finding the conditions that are necessary and sufficient for normal development; others have looked at the development of language in normal children in the hope of helping children whose language development is abnormal. It now appears that many of the severe language abnormalities found in children can in some way be traced to interruptions of the normal acquisition process. The improved understanding of the normal process is being exploited to create treatment programs for children with such problems. In the past therapeutic methods for children with language problems have emphasized the memorizing of language routines, but methods now being developed would allow a child to work with her own language-learning abilities. For example, the American Sign Language has been taught successfully to several autistic children. Many of these nonverbal and antisocial children have learned in this way to communicate with therapists, in some cases becoming more socially responsive. (Why sign language should be so successful with some autistic children is unclear; it may have to do with the fact that a sign lasts longer than an auditory signal.)

There are still many questions to be answered in the various areas I have discussed, but in general a great deal of progress has been made in understanding child language over the past 20 years. The study of the acquisition of language has come of age. It is now a genuinely interdisciplinary field where psychologists, neurosurgeons and linguists work together to penetrate the mechanisms of perception and cognition as well as the mechanisms of language.

DISCUSSION QUESTIONS

1. In your own words, describe the series of stages that children go through when they learn language.

2. Does the fact that not all children acquire negatives in the same manner refute Chomsky's theory of universals? Support your answer.

3. What evidence is there that the child, even at the one-word stage, is learning syntax and not just word meanings? How does this situation compare with that involving apes? See the following article by Edward Klima and Ursula Bellugi.

4. Determine the unmarked semantic form of these pairs of words: *short—tall*, *thick—thin*, and *strong—weak*. Which member of the pair would you expect a child to learn first? Provide some examples of your own.

5. Taking into account Cazden's findings that "children benefit less from frequent adult correction of their errors than from true conversational interaction," how might you develop a language arts program—particularly one that involves minority children? Would Thomas Kochman approve of such a program? (See his article in Part VI.)

EDWARD S. KLIMA and URSULA BELLUGI

After gaining his doctorate at Harvard University, Klima taught at the Massachusetts Institute of Technology before going to the University of California, San Diego, where since 1967 he has been professor of linguistics. His interests are both psycholinguistics and historical linguistics.

Bellugi also earned her Ph.D. at Harvard, where she taught before becoming the director of the Laboratory for Language and Cognitive Studies in the Salk Institute, La Jolla, California. She has published extensively in the field of cognitive psychology.

TEACHING APES TO COMMUNICATE

Over the past few years, many interesting facts have come to light about the ways animals communicate in their natural state. Certain of these facts suggest properties usually associated only with human language. The bees have a dance whose choreography communicates to the other members of the colony the direction, distance, and richness of the pollen source discovered minutes earlier. Thus in no sense is the bee's message an immediate reaction to its environment of the moment, but more a relating of certain aspects of a past experience. Certain birds, like the white-crowned sparrow, have an elaborate song whose mature shape is determined by the particular dialect it is exposed to at a critical period in its infancy. Thus there are significant aspects of the sparrow song that do not simply go along with being a sparrow, but rather are dependent on early experience. The apes in the wild display an elaborate system of communication combining gestures, facial expressions, and sounds into a composite signal in which the significance of one type of signal—a particular gesture, for example—is dependent on what particular facial expressions and sounds accompany it. The full significance of a signal may, in addition, be determined by the relative social positions of the participants in the communication act. Thus certain aspects, at least, of the system of animal communication do not have a simple one-to-one relationship between unit signal and significance, but depend, rather, on selected aspects of the accompanying signals as well as of the social context.

While too little is known *in detail* about the system of animal communication to provide a deep analysis of its basic elements, the observed complexity of the systems may suggest that they are "languages," similar in principle to human languages but simpler in vocabulary and in the number and complexity of combinations, and, of course, not necessarily vocalized. The assumption that human language is intimately related to the signal systems of the apes and monkeys has appeared especially attractive, since human language could thereby claim the communication system of the nonhuman primates as its evolutionary predecessor.

But, in fact, it is the consensus of opinion among linguists, anthropologists, and psychologists that this is a deceptively loose use of the word "language"—that the natural systems of animal communication are different *in essence* from human language. The scholarly position is expressed plainly by Jane Lancaster when she says:

> The interest in human evolution and in the origin of human language has distorted the study of the communication systems of nonhuman primates. These systems are not steps toward language, and have much more in common with the communication of other mammals than with human language. The more that is known about the communication systems of nonhuman primates the more obvious it is that these systems have little relationship with human language, but much with the ways human beings express emotion through gesture, facial expression, and tone of voice. There is no evidence that human displays expressing emotion, such as laughing, crying, smiling, are any more or less complex than are displays of monkeys and apes or that they differ in form or function.

There is, however, a second question that can be asked about animals and language: a line of inquiry that parallels that of the relationship between animal communication in the wild and human language. The question is: What aspects of human language will a higher animal, like the monkey or the ape, learn under conditions of extended exposure to a language, or even when subjected to intensive training? This, of course, is not a question of the animal's *natural* behavior in its *natural* environment but rather a question of its capabilities in an environment that is manipulated in varyingly *unnatural* ways.

In the last forty years there have been several attempts by American psychologists to raise a chimpanzee in a homelike atmosphere in the hope that given an environment resembling that of a child, another species might be able to learn our language, along with other aspects of human behavior. The Kelloggs raised Gua, a female infant chimpanzee, with their own son Donald who was about the same age, for about nine months. Gua did not learn to speak, but did learn during the course of the training period to respond to more than sixty different English sentences. Some years later, Keith and Cathy Hayes adopted a female chimpanzee, Viki, when she was three days old, and worked with her intensively for six and a half years. Viki learned to make only four sounds that were sometimes recognizable as approximations of English words. These were learned only with the greatest difficulty, and even afterwards there were sometimes confusions and inappropriate uses.

These experiences make it seem that a vocal language is not appropriate for a chimpanzee. We know that there are distinct differences between the articulatory apparatus of the nonhuman primates and that of man, most recently from the work of Philip Lieberman at Haskins Laboratory. Lieberman argued that the vocal mechanisms of the nonprimates are not capable of producing human speech sounds, a result of an anatomical lack of tongue mobility, among other things. It seems that nonhuman primates cannot change the shape of their vocal tract to control the necessary variety of sounds, the way human beings can for the thousands of languages of the world.

From field reports of anthropologists like Jane Goodall, we learn that chimpanzees vocalize primarily under conditions of great excitement in their natural habitat. Perhaps this adds to the difficulty of attempting to train them to control their vocalizations. But does this necessarily mean that it is next to impossible to teach them to communicate with us? It has seemed so, until the past few years when two psychologists at the University of Nevada, Allen and Beatrice Gardner, decided to take a fresh approach to the question of teaching language to a home-raised chimpanzee. They reasoned that the use of the hands is a prominent feature in the behavior of chimpanzees, who have a rich repertoire of gestures both in the wild and in captivity. They undertook to teach an infant chimpanzee a language based on gesture, the American Sign Language of the deaf. They obtained a chimpanzee (Washoe) from the wild when she was about a year old, and worked with her for more than three years. By comparison with the four words that Viki learned to speak, Washoe's progress in sign language is spectacular. By about four years of age, she had learned to make reliably more than eighty different signs. One estimate suggests that she can respond appropriately to more than five hundred different utterances in sign language—a remarkable achievement for a chimpanzee. The Gardners, and all those who were with the chimpanzee, used only signs to communicate with her. They learned signs largely from a dictionary of American Sign Language. They used gestures and manual configurations to represent the concepts in sign language and avoided the use of finger spelling as much as possible.

The sign for *flower,* for example, is made by holding the fingers of one hand extended and brought together at the tip as if holding a flower, and touching this first to one nostril and then to the other. This is a gesture we might use in smelling a flower. The sign for *girl* is made with a closed fist and the thumb extended upward from the fist. Keeping this hand position, the thumb is placed about the middle of the cheek but a few inches away and moved downward to the lower part of the cheek, still maintaining the same distance. On seeing the sign for the first time, it would be difficult to guess its meaning; historically, it derives from an old French sign for *girl,* which was made with two hands, the thumbs on either side of the face outlining the strings of a French girl's bonnet.

The Gardners have made intensive and deliberate attempts to teach Washoe a great number of signs, but they also sign to her in sentences as they prepare her meals, dress her, and play with her in the same way that parents chatter to their children. The signed sequences produced by the Gardners, who are not native signers, are like English sentences with certain elements left out (articles, inflection, auxiliary verbs). A literal translation into English of some of the Gardners' utterances to Washoe might be: *What you want? You not yet hide, You catch me,* and *Me catch you.*

It seems clear from this experiment that Washoe not only has learned to make manual gestures, but makes them in ways that clearly refer to aspects of her external environment. Her ability to name has a development that in many respects is similar to that of a young child. She first learned the sign for *open* with a particular door. She then extended the use of that sign far beyond the original training, first to all closed doors, then to closed containers such as the refrigerator, cupboards, drawers, briefcases, boxes, and jars. Eventually she spontaneously used the sign for *open* to request opening of the water faucet and of a closed bottle of soda pop. She learned a sign for *cat* and a sign for *dog,* originally with pictures of each, and she used the signs appropriately while looking through magazines or books as well as for real cats and dogs. She made the sign for *dog* even when someone drew a caricature of a dog for her, and also when she heard a dog that she could not see barking in the distance.

She sometimes overextends the use of signs in ways that resemble children's early overextensions. Washoe learned the sign for *listen* for an alarm clock which signals meal time. She used the sign for other bells, for the sounds of people walking outside her trailer door, and for watches and clocks. She signed *listen* spontaneously when she found a broken watchband, and then when she saw a flashlight that blinks on and off. Washoe has a sign for *hurt* which she learned first with scratches or bruises. Later she used the sign also for red stains, for a decal on the back of a person's hand, and the first time she saw a person's navel.

Washoe first learned the sign for *flower*, which we have already described, and eventually made it apply to a large variety of flowers and pictures of flowers. As the flower sign became more frequent, the Gardners noticed that she made the sign in several inappropriate contexts which all seemed to include smells—when opening a tobacco pouch, or entering a kitchen filled with cooking smells. They introduced a new sign to her for *smell*, and gradually she began to use it in the contexts where she had formerly used the *flower* sign incorrectly. She now partitions the domain of *flowers* and *odors* in the same way that we do. These examples are all characteristic of the range and extensions of words used by children in the process of learning a language.

Washoe has more than eighty signs which she makes reliably. To give some idea of the range of concepts, we can indicate some rough English equivalents of her signs. She has some request signs: *come-gimme, open, tickle, hug, help, ride-wagon, sit-chair;* some signs that are primarily names of objects: *dog, cat, flower, shoes, key, book, banana;* some signs that represent properties of objects: *red, white;* some that indicate direction or location: *up, out, down;* some name-signs of people who are with her often: *Roger, Dr. Gardner, Mrs. Gardner* (and a sign for *Washoe*); and the signs for *you* and *me*, which are made by pointing to the chest of another person or oneself. While these signs represent concepts that are not always bounded in the same way as their English word translation, one can see that this vocabulary is rich enough to allow for communication in a variety of situations.

At first, Washoe used signs singly, like *open* and *more*. Then, as soon as she knew eight or ten signs, the Gardners report that she began using combinations of signs in sequences. They note that it is not too difficult to define what constitutes a sequence for her by observing something like the relaxation of her hands after making several signs. This is like our intonation contours, which make us feel that someone has finished a sentence or stopped speaking. At first, Washoe combined signs only two at a time, but by the time she was four years old (and had been trained for three years) there were sometimes three or more signs in a sequence. The Gardners specifically trained Washoe to make individual signs; they did not train her to make sequences. It should be interesting then to look at the characteristics of the combinations of signs that she makes, without being specifically taught.

But before describing Washoe's combinations, let us give perspective to her accomplishments by comparing her progress with that of a child. Washoe produced her first combination of signs (*gimme sweet*) when she was about twenty months old. After that, the Gardners kept complete records of every new sign combination they observed. Fourteen months afterwards, they had recorded a total of 330 different combinations of signs used by Washoe. We have the same sort of information for one hearing child, Gregory, provided by the psychologist Martin Braine. Gregory first produced an utterance that combined two words when he was eighteen months old, and his parents recorded all new combinations thereafter. Seven months later, he had produced more than 2,500 different combinations; his parents could no longer reasonably keep track. Certainly there is an enormous difference in sheer productivity, but the crucial differences are more profound than this.

A good example of Washoe's combinations involves the sign for *open*, which was one of the first Washoe learned to use, and she used it frequently. When she had learned other signs, she eventually began combining them with *open* and produced the following sequences, for example:

> *open out*   (when standing in front of a trailer door)
> *open flower*   (to be let through the gate to the flower garden)
> *open drink*   (for the water faucet)
> *food open hurry*   (at the refrigerator door)
> *key open please blanket*   (at the bedding cupboard)
> *open key clean*   (at the soap cupboard)

These are all appropriate combinations, relevant to a particular context; some may not be copies of sentences she has seen other people sign, that is, may be original for Washoe. She does produce names that are fitting to a particular situation, and she combines them in sequences—spontaneously.

The Gardners report, however, that most signs occur in many or all orders, that order seems irrelevant in Washoe's signed sequences. For example, she has produced *open drink* and *drink open; key open* and *open key; more open* and *open more;* the three-sign sequence, *please sweet drink,* has been produced in all possible orders. Let us take one example where it is clear that a change in the order of signs usually occurs for different situations, at least in the way the Gardners sign to Washoe. She loves to be tickled and also likes to tickle the people around her. In the sign language Washoe uses, *I* and *me* are made in the same way, so we will use *me* as the English equivalent. The Gardners sign to Washoe *me tickle you* when they are about to tickle her, and *you tickle me* as a request that she perform the action. Washoe instead has used all possible orders of these signs and did not distinguish one situation from the other. Washoe signed *me tickle* when she wanted someone to tickle her and when she was going to tickle someone. She requested tickling by signing either *you tickle* or *tickle you*. Her combinations, from this and other evidence, seem like unordered sequences of names for aspects of a situation. It is rather like a kind of complex naming (signs, in any order and combination, that are appropriate to a context). This does not have the basic characteristics of our sentences—hierarchical organization, internal structure, certain degree of explicitness, and the expression of basic grammatical relations. In addition, there is no evidence that Washoe asks questions or makes any negative statements.

It seems to us that Washoe's meager production of combinations should not be allowed to result in overhasty conclusions about limitations in what she has the ability to communicate. Washoe's impressive performance in learning to assign names to things, or classes of things, comes as a result of specific training designed to teach her that very task. It should be remembered that Washoe did not naturally start signing in the way that children start phonating (or indeed as the children of the deaf start signing). She was induced to make signs, by reward, by modeling, and so forth. The question was not, Would a chimpanzee naturally copy elements of a manual language to which it was regularly exposed? The question was, rather, Could a chimpanzee be taught selective elements of a manual language and then use these productively, that is, for novel instances? The answer turned out affirmatively when the elements taught corresponded to individual wordlike elements—the signs for *flower,* for *tickling,* for *cat.* That Washoe did not spontaneously capture the relationships implicit between the signs in the sentences to which she was exposed should not be surprising. What was demonstrated with Washoe's impressive naming was that she could be taught to associate a visual-manual token with a certain object or event and could subsequently generalize the use of the token to similar objects or events, though, of course, we do not know by precisely what criterion of similarity.

The reason for the interest in Washoe's multi-sign message formations is that this is the context in which the differing roles of the various signs are specified with respect to the total picture. It seems clear that Washoe can be taught to perform simple naming; her own behavior indicates that she can similarly perform complex naming, emit a string of tokens jointly associated with a situation. It is quite another question whether she can be taught to distinguish, in the *form* of the message, between such differing relations as actor versus acted on—the sort of thing that some languages (like English) accomplish with word order in differentiating *John tickles Mary* from *Mary tickles John,* and that other languages accomplish with different formal devices.

Recently Professor David Premack, a psychologist at the University of California, has been pursuing precisely this sort of question, namely, Can a chimpanzee be taught to code differences in relationship between tokens occurring in combination? In an address to the American Psychological Association in September 1969, Professor Premack outlined an experiment underway on a chimpanzee named Sarah. The mode of communication is manual-visual, as with Washoe, but rather than actually forming the signals, Sarah has at her disposal ready-made tokens, in the form of plastic pieces of varying size, shape, and color. She is trained to associate distinct tokens with selected parts of her experience within the narrow object-world of the experiment: a token for *apples,* another for *bananas,* one for *pail,* one for each of four differently colored chips of wood, a token for her own name, and one for each of the three experimenters. A combination of four tokens is associated with Sarah's handing Mary an apple, for example. Included in such a combination are the tokens already associated with apple, Sarah, and Mary. The tokens that are used by Sarah and her experimenter to form a message are placed on a magnetized slate, vertically when a combination of tokens is required. The experimenters have intentionally avoided any physical relationship between the form of the token and what the token is associated with. For example, the tokens with which the differently colored, but otherwise identical, chips of wood are associated are themselves colorless and differ rather in shape. Like Washoe's signs, Sarah's tokens are trained (as opposed to spontaneous) and arbitrary (as opposed to representational). But rather than emphasizing the number of tokens that Sarah can use, as in the Gardner experiment, Professor Premack is exploring the chimpanzee's ability to associate the selection of tokens and their order in combinations with subtler functional differences.

As of August 1969, Sarah had command of sixty different tokens, all used in combinations of three or four tokens. So the total number of different routines in her command is in the hundreds. Let us examine briefly a sample of the training procedure and the chimpanzee's subsequent productive variations on the procedure. After having been familiarized with the tokens individually, Sarah is taught a four-token sequence, like *Sarah-insert-banana-pail,* in a routine in which the chimpanzee constructs the sequence by placing the four tokens in a vertical row on the slate and at another time acts out putting a banana in a pail. Then she is tested for her ability to extend the pattern to tokens already mastered but not explicitly trained in this particular routine. Thus, if she had previously mastered the use of the token for *apple* in the four-token sequence *Mary-give-apple-Jim,* she would subsequently be tested for her ability *creatively* to associate the novel four-token sequence *Sarah-insert-apple-pail* with the situation in which Sarah is inserting an apple in a pail. Similarly, having been trained to associate different tokens with four differently colored cards (blue, green, yellow, red) Sarah is then taught to associate the three-token sequence *Red-on-Green* with a red card on a green card. Then she will be tested on her ability to extend this training *creatively* to new instances, for example *Blue-on-Yellow*.

So far there have been very strict controls imposed on Sarah's behavior in these routines. Once a combination has been taught in a particular routine, a response consisting of a single token—though adequate in terms of communication—is not accepted, that is, not rewarded. Moreover, the choice of tokens put within Sarah's reach for any particular routine has been very strictly limited. Sometimes she has within reach only those tokens that will ultimately form the correct sequence when ordered in the correct way. So there has been a difference more profound in the training of Washoe and Sarah than just emphasis on vocabulary with Washoe and emphasis on functionally significant combinations with Sarah. Washoe, since she herself ultimately forms her signs, has all of them available at any given moment. Her behavior can more nearly be approached as communication, and can hardly be called just collections of learned routines, particularly since she uses her manual signs outside of the training situation. Moreover, Washoe was permitted and even encouraged to let her own inclinations dictate how she would use her signs. This spontaneous, apparently innovative, and often unexpected behavior on the part of Washoe raises fascinating questions above and beyond those of her success in the training routines.

The experiment with Sarah was much more ambitious in the questions that it was designed to answer. It must still be viewed as in its preliminary stages, where the various controls and procedures used in the routines may well have influenced her performance in ways that have not been taken into account. Once the training has progressed to a sufficient degree that the controls can be loosened and the number of tokens available for any single act of combining made large enough so that she must choose among many possibilities, then we can better assess to what degree Sarah's combinations are communication, and what languagelike properties they display. In evaluating the success of attempts to teach animals to communicate, we must recall that, after all, pets and circus animals can be taught, when given signals, to perform a great number of complicated tricks.

In conclusion, let us return to a theme that has emerged several times in the preceding discussion—a theme that has to do with so-called *languagelike* characteristics of the trained visual-manual communication of Washoe and Sarah. The claim is nowhere made that these chimps have been taught a language—but only that what they *have* been taught displays some significantly languagelike characteristics—notably having to do with the productive or creative use of arbitrary signs. Washoe demonstrated that she could use names productively—that is, that having been taught to associate a given sign with particular real examples of an object, property, or process, she would extend the sign to novel instances not found in the training procedure—apparently giving the same name to objects that shared certain properties. The experiment with Sarah, if successful beyond its present preliminary stage, may indicate that she is able to associate differences of function with variations in the order of tokens—and treat these differences in order of tokens *productively;* that is, in novel cases. But it is very important to recognize an *essential* difference between the sort of productivity that we would ascribe to the behavior of Washoe and Sarah and that that appears to be its counterpart in human language. In human language this productivity, though unlimited, is unlimited only within the tight limits set up by a shared system of special constraints—a grammar—which is reflected by our feeling for what counts as a well-formed expression in our native language. The linguistic productivity that we are referring to is not the metaphorical use of words or the invention of new words, nor is it fanciful distortions of syntax; the linguistic productivity we are referring to is that that characterizes our ability to produce indefinitely many sentences never heard before, whose meanings can be understood (as precisely as they are expressed) by anyone else who shares the system; that is, by anyone who knows the language. It is this coupling of *productivity* with interpretability provided precisely by a shared system of grammar that makes human language such a versatile system of communciation—so versatile that not only can we express things that are outside of our immediate experience, we can even express the inconceivable. Not only can we relate past events and predict future ones, not only can we lie and indeed create whole fictitious worlds, but we can even communicate our most irrational fantasies.

DISCUSSION QUESTIONS

1. In your own words, describe the basic difference between Washoe's language and that of a child. See the articles by Roger Brown and Breyne Moskowitz.

2. Would a system of rewards similar to that used with apes speed up child language acquisition? Support your answer.

3. How would the implications of the experiment be different if Washoe had demonstrated rigid word order?

PART IV

REGIONAL AND SOCIAL VARIATION

As long as it was held that contemporary languages were corruptly descended from some remote perfect language, language scholars and philosophers found it beneath their dignity to concern themselves with language varieties that deviated from the variety that they considered to approximate that of perfect language. Although not perfect, Latin and Greek were considered so nearly perfect that in the late Middle Ages even serious use of Italian, French, or English vernacular met strong opposition.

The notion that there was at least in theory a perfect state of any language subsequently blocked scholarly investigation of language features not held to belong to the standard speech. Such language features were, of course, known and recognized as such. Chaucer wrote of northern speech. Shakespeare recognized regional dialects. In 1674 a lexicon appeared by a naturalist, John Ray, who in studying birds throughout England came across so many unusual local terms that he was constrained to publish them in a small book entitled *North Country Words and South Country Words*. Several smaller underworld glossaries preceded the appearance in 1690 of *A Dictionary of the Canting Crew*.

But such variations in language were dealt with as aberrations until in the nineteenth century historical linguistics made it clear that the so-called standard language in any country was simply a regional dialect that had become prestigious for nonlinguistic reasons— geographical, commercial, or political. The way was now free for scholars to study language variation without fear of adverse criticism. In 1878 the compilers of the great dialect atlas of Germany, *Der Deutscher Sprachatlas,* began a decades-long task of gathering by postal questionnaires information about regional speech differences. It was followed between 1904 and 1910 by another great atlas, the French *L'Atlas linguistique de la France,* dialect information for which was collected by a trained field worker interviewing relatively uneducated rural residents in their homes. Atlas studies in other European countries followed, but it was not until 1930 that Hans Kurath began directing the field work for a projected linguistic atlas of the United States and Canada.

Although financial difficulties limited the realized extent of the project to the Atlantic states, two major regional productions resulted. The first, *The Linguistic Atlas of New England,* edited by Hans Kurath, was published as a handbook and six volumes in three parts between 1939 and 1943. It has since been reprinted (AMS Press, 1973). The second project, covering the Middle and South Atlantic states, produced materials now being edited at the University of South Carolina. Its first fascicles appeared in 1980. In the meantime three books, all published by the University of Michigan Press, appeared with synoptic treatment of some findings of the eastern studies: Hans Kurath, *Word Geography of the Eastern States* (1949); Hans Kurath and Raven I. McDavid, Jr., *The Pronunciation of English in the Atlantic States* (1961); and E. Bagby Atwood, *A Survey of Verb Forms in the Eastern United States* (1953). A principal effect of the eastern studies was the establishment of the areas of three main dialects, called by Kurath Northern, Midland, and Southern, with an important intermediate subdialectal region that he called South Midland but that more recently some have preferred to consider Inland Southern.

Kurath's hope that subsequent dialect research would be undertaken by independent but related regional investigations has borne fruit. The first of them to yield a publication was the *Linguistic Atlas of the Upper Midwest,* published by the University of Minnesota Press in three volumes (1973, 1975, and 1976). Already beginning fascicle publication by the University of Chicago Press is the *Linguistic Atlas of the North Central States,* initiated by the late Albert H. Marckwardt and now edited by Raven McDavid, Jr. These two studies confirmed the Midland-Northern division Kurath had found, and extended its dividing line westward across Ohio, extreme northern Indiana and northern Illinois, across the northern third of Iowa, and diagonally across South Dakota northwestward to the Montana border. A major project nearing completion is the "Linguistic Atlas of the Gulf States," directed by Lee Pederson at Emory University. Other field studies ready for final editing and ultimate publication have been undertaken in California and Nevada, the Pacific Northwest, Arkansas, Oklahoma, and Missouri. Articles about their progress and results have appeared in three anthologies: Harold B. Allen and Gary N. Underwood, *Readings in American Dialectology* (Appleton-Century-Crofts, 1971); Juanita Williamson and Virginia Burke, *A Various Language* (Holt, Rinehart & Winston, 1971); and Richard W. Bailey and Jay L. Robinson, *Varieties of Present-day English* (Macmillan, 1973). An additional reference is Carroll E. Reed, *Dialects of American English,* rev. ed. (University of Massachusetts Press, 1977). Two journals specialize in materials about regional English, *American Speech* and *Publication of the American Dialect Society.* A synoptic treatment of dialect speech features in the several states appears in separate articles in the *Worldmark Encyclopedia of the States* (Worldmark Press and Harper & Row, 1981).

The most comprehensive research in regional variation in this country has been not in dialect geography but in lexicography. Under Frederic G. Cassidy at the University of Wisconsin, a mammoth undertaking of collecting all regional terms in the United States, with dated illustrations from speech and writing, and with accompanying recordings, is being completed. This project, the American Dialect Society's "Dictionary of American Regional English," began with field work between 1965 and 1970, continued with computerized processing of the collections from 1970 to 1975, and is now in the final editing stage. Publication is expected to begin in 1982, ultimately to produce four volumes under the imprint of the Belknap Press of Harvard University.

Although many articles on single regional features have appeared since E. Bagby Atwood's study that opens this section, his description of the role played by the *greasy/ greazy* contrast in marking a major dialect boundary remains a classic. Later research reveals that the distinction is weakening in the west, however, as the isogloss, after extending across northern Indiana and Illinois, barely includes the southern tier of Iowa counties and extreme southeastern Nebraska. The /z/ pronunciation, then, seems unlikely to become more widespread.

European dialect geography focused upon regional differences, but in the Italian atlas both uneducated and educated informants were occasionally interviewed in the same community. This practice Kurath systematically adopted for the eastern atlases, with a three-step gradation from grade school through high school to college. Other American atlas projects have followed his lead, so that for the first time data were available to yield information about social and educational contrast as well as regional contrast.

An early prediction of the value of this new source of information for the sociologist came from a leading dialectologist, Raven I. McDavid, Jr., in his article, "Dialect Geography and Social Science Problems" (*Social Forces* 25 [1946], 168–172), which he followed with "Some Social Differences in Pronunciation" (*Language Learning* 4 [1952–1953], 102–116).

In the second selection here, John Fischer, looking at a microcosmic social group, deals in his pioneer study with a possible cause of social variation and thus points a direction for later sociolinguistic research. Harold Allen, using responses of informants in the Upper Midwest as a basis, pursues McDavid's earlier lead by specifying numerous regional variations with social class significance. His article sets a precedent in the utilization of atlas materials for sociolinguistic purposes and may be used as an example for similar application by a class or even by a single student.

It remained, however, for William Labov's groundbreaking 1964 doctoral dissertation, published by the Center for Applied Linguistics in 1967 as *The Social Stratification of English in New York City,* to provide a new research design for ascertaining significant social variation and hence to stimulate many subsequent researchers to produce a spate of articles and books during the past decade.

At the same time a powerful directive stimulus emerged during the 1960s from the political and economic problems attendant upon the presence in the north of speakers of the southern dialect that has come to be called Black English. Blacks seeking job opportunities and Black children competing with white children in northern urban schools experienced difficulties because of the marked contrast between their speech and that of middle-class white employers and teachers.

A number of linguists, some trained in dialect geography and others moving directly into the field, began to study the nature and history of the distinctive features of Black English and to undertake investigations of the social parameters of Black English in mixed school and community situations. The first large-scale study with this focus was that in Detroit by Roger W. Shuy and Ralph Fasold, whose involvement in that project led to subsequent careers marked by the publication of numerous articles and books dealing with Black English in particular and social dialects in general. Other attention has been directed to the status of Black English as an English dialect with a putative background in an eighteenth-century creole and to the precise linguistic characteristics differentiating it from other southern speech.

Four articles in this section reflect various aspects of scholarly concern with Black English. Bruce Fraser finds significant an apparently unconscious racial bias in the inferences about personality traits made by listeners to a complex of vocal features heard in the taped voices of Black and white speakers from North and South. Anthony Kroch finds himself in disagreement with William Labov's conclusions—appearing in several of his publications—about the direction of language change and acceptance, offering in its place a hypothesis that change is initiated in the prestigious professional class. Robbins Burling considers the specific linguistic features of Black English as they contrast with those of standard white speech. Northern speakers may be slightly confused by one of the items he treats, however—that of the contrast he finds between *four* and *for* in Black speech but not in northern speech. Actually this contrast marks both Northern and Southern dialects but is typically absent from Midland. Representative figures are those of informants for the *Linguistic Atlas of the Upper Midwest.* In Northern-speech states Minnesota and North Dakota 77 percent of the speakers distinguish *four* with a mid-back vowel and *for* with a low-back vowel when it is stressed. But in Iowa and Nebraska, with a strong Midland influence, the proportion of speakers who make the distinction drops to 60 percent. Burling touches upon an issue that for some time was the center of a bitter controversy, that of bidialectalism, which will be discussed also by Thomas Kochman in Part VI of this anthology.

Roger Abrahams, drawing upon his personal contacts in the Black ghetto of Philadelphia and upon other resources, offers a quite different approach to Black English through its varied and rich utility in a dynamic oral environment.

Bibliographical references for this field of language variation now recognized as social dialectology or, more broadly, as sociolinguistics, accompany Kroch's article. Recent additional references are two books by Joey Lee Dillard, heavily oriented toward the creole hypothesis, *Perspectives in Black English* (Mouton, 1975) and *Lexicon of Black English* (Seabury, 1977); and one by Geneva Smitherman, *Talkin and Testifyin: The Language of Black America* (Houghton Mifflin, 1977).

Quite in the wider area of sociolinguistics rather than social dialectology is the concluding essay in this section, Mary Key's exploration of the variety of sex differences in language. Although such differences have long been studied in the speech of primitive peoples by cultural anthropologists, not until the recent concern with women's liberation has much attention been devoted to such differences in English. Impinging upon this concern is the issue of sexism in language. While outside the scope of this anthology, the related issues of censorship and language control may be such as to engage your interest. A principal reference is *Sexism and Language* by Alleen Pace Nilsen, Haig Bosmajian, H. Lee Gershuny, and Julia P. Stanley (National Council of Teachers of English, 1977). A negative reaction by Lance Alter appeared in the "Forum," a feature of the *English Journal* (65 [1976], no. 9, pp. 10, 12).

E. BAGBY ATWOOD

Before his death in 1963 Professor Atwood was a member of the department of English at the University of Texas and head of the Texas dialect project, from which emerged The Regional Vocabulary of Texas *(University of Texas Press, 1962). His monograph* A Survey of Verb Forms in the Eastern United States *is a major contribution to dialectology.*

GREASE AND GREASY: A STUDY OF GEOGRAPHICAL VARIATION

The fact that the verb *to grease* and the adjective *greasy* are pronounced by some Americans with [s] and by others with [z] has long been well known even to amateur observers of speech.[1] It has also been pretty well accepted that the incidence of [s] or [z] in the words in question is primarily dependent on the geographical location of the speaker rather than on his social or educational level—that [s] is, in general, "Northern," [z] "Southern."

As early as 1896, George Hempl published a study[2] of these two words, based on a rather widely circulated written questionnaire. His returns enabled him to divide the country into four major areas, according to the percentages of [s] in *to grease* and *greasy* respectively. The "North"[3]—extending from New England to the Dakotas—showed 88 and 82 per cent of [s] pronunciations; the "Midland," comprising a fairly narrow strip extending from New York City to St. Louis,[4] 42 and 34 per cent; the "South,"[5] 12 and 12 per cent; and the "West"—an ever-widening area extending

---

[1] Webster's *New International Dictionary* states that [z] in *grease* is found "esp. Brit. and Southern U.S."; [z] in *greasy* is "perhaps more general in England and the southern U.S. than in the North and East." Kenyon and Knott, *Pronouncing Dictionary* (Springfield, Mass., 1944), give [s] and [z] for the country as a whole, only [z] for the South. *The Century, Funk and Wagnalls New Standard,* and the *American College Dictionary* merely give [s] or [z] for both words. Kenyon and Knott state that "['grizɪ] and [tə griz] are phonetically normal; ['grisɪ] and [tə gris] imitate the noun *grease* [gris]." Certainly many verbs since Middle English times have been distinguished from the corresponding nouns by voicing the final fricative; cf. *house: to house, proof: to prove, wreath: to wreathe, abuse: to abuse*—and with vowel change *bath: to bathe, breath: to breathe, grass: to graze,* etc. This paper will not be concerned with the origin or history of the feature.

The pronunciation of the vowels is of no significance in our study. For convenience I am using the symbol [i] for both stressed and the unstressed vowels in *greasy.*

[2] "*Grease* and *Greasy,*" *Dialect Notes,* I (1896), 438–44.

[3] In addition to New England, this area includes New Brunswick, Quebec, Ontario, New York, Michigan, Wisconsin, North Dakota, South Dakota, Minnesota, and the northern portions of Pennsylvania, Ohio, Indiana, Illinois, and Iowa.

[4] This includes New York City, New Jersey, Delaware, the District of Columbia, southern Pennsylvania, southern Ohio, northern West Virginia, middle Indiana, middle Illinois, and St. Louis, Missouri.

[5] This includes everything to the south of the Midland, as far west as Texas.

westward from St. Louis—56 and 47 per cent. The material which Hempl was able to collect was admittedly "insufficient";[6] moreover, he had no means of selecting strictly representative informants;[7] and the answers may not always have been correct, since, it seems to me, an understanding of the questions would have required a certain degree of linguistic sophistication.[8] Still, in spite of these handicaps, Hempl's study has not been greatly improved upon by later writers. Most authorities content themselves by stating that [z] in *to grease* and *greasy* is predominantly Southern, and that either [s] or [z] may occur elsewhere.[9] Few investigators have gathered material that would enable them to draw clearer lines between [s] and [z] than Hempl was able to do.[10]

The field records that have been gathered for the *Linguistic Atlas of the United States and Canada*[11] provide us with an excellent basis for delimiting the geographical and social spread of speech forms in the eastern United States. A number of features of the *Atlas* methodology[12] are conducive to an accurate picture of native and normal speech. The informants, though relatively few,[13] were carefully chosen, each being both native

---

[6] *Op. cit.*, p. 438.

[7] For example, he urged his colleagues, especially "teachers of English in colleges, normal schools, and young ladies' seminaries" to use the questions as an exercise in English. (*Ibid.*, p. 444.)

[8] Question 45 reads: "In which (if any) of the following does *s* have the sound of *z: 'the grease,' 'to grease,' 'greasy'*?" (Hempl, "American Speech Maps," *Dialect Notes*, I [1896], 317.) Judging from my experience in teaching phonetic transcription to college seniors and graduate students, a considerable proportion of a class would simply not know whether [s] or [z] was used in such words; certainly many students unhesitatingly write [s] in words like *rose* and *has* simply because the *letter s* is used in standard spelling.

[9] See footnote 1. It is sometimes pointed out that the same speaker may use both ['grisi] and ['grizi] with a distinction in meaning. This point will be discussed below.

[10] A. H. Marckwardt was able to draw a fairly clear line through Ohio, Indiana, and Illinois, though on the basis of relatively little data. See "Folk Speech in Indiana and Adjacent States," *Indiana History Bulletin*, XVII (1940), 120–140. Henry L. Smith has long been using the word *greasy* as a test word in his demonstrations of regional variation and to determine the origins of speakers, though he has not published his material. I presume that Dr. Smith's observations are the source of Mario Pei's statement: " 'greazy' . . . would place the speaker south of Philadelphia, while "greassy" would place him north of Trenton." (*The Story of Language* [Philadelphia and New York, 1949], p. 51.) C. K. Thomas considers the word *greasy* in his survey of the regional speech types, but comes to the strange conclusion that "the choice between [s] and [z] in words like *discern, desolate, absorb, absurd,* and *greasy* seems to be more personal than regional." (*An Introduction to the Phonetics of American English* [New York, 1947], p. 154.) G. P. Krapp is likewise at fault when he states that, in *greasy*, "popular usage and, in general, standard speech have only the form with [z]." (*The Pronunciation of Standard English in America* [New York, 1919], p. 119).

[11] The New England materials have been published as the *Linguistic Atlas of New England*, ed. Hans Kurath and Bernard Bloch, 3 vols. (Providence, R.I., 1939–43). Field records for most of the Middle Atlantic and South Atlantic states were gathered by the late Guy S. Lowman; recently (summer, 1949) Dr. Raven I. McDavid, Jr., completed the work for the eastern seaboard. The records, in an unedited but usable state, are filed at the University of Michigan, where they were made available to me through the courtesy of Professor Kurath.

[12] See *Handbook of the Linguistic Geography of New England*, ed. H. Kurath and others (Providence, R.I., 1939), for a complete account of the *Atlas* methodology.

[13] Something like 1600 informants have been interviewed, representing communities from New Brunswick to northern Florida, approximately as far west as Lake Erie.

to and representative of his community. The answers to questions were elicited, so far as possible, in a conversational atmosphere, and thus the occurrence of ungenuine forms was minimized. Finally, the forms were recorded by trained phoneticians, who would be very unlikely to make such errors as to write [s] when the informant actually uttered [z].

A few words should be said regarding the cartographical representation of linguistic atlas data. In such works as the *Atlas Linguistique de la France*,[14] in which each community, or "point" on the map, is represented by a single speaker, it is usually possible to draw lines, or *isoglosses*, separating those communities where a form occurs from those where it does not occur. Often these isoglosses set off a large block of "points," forming a solid area—as, for example, the southern French territory marked by initial [k] in the word *chandelle*.[15] A more complex presentation is sometimes required, as in the case of the northern French occurrences of [k] in this same word: after setting off our solid area we find outside it a number of scattered communities where the feature in question occurs; these must be indicated by additional lines encircling the "points" where the form is found.[16] In still other cases, the communities where a given speech form occurs (for example, *conin* for 'rabbit') are so scattered that it is impossible to connect them; in such cases our iosoglosses must consist merely of scattered circles here and there on the map.[17] When this situation obtains we would probably do better to assign a symbol (say, a cross, a dot, or a triangle) to the scattered form in question, lest the labyrinth of lines becomes too much for the reader to cope with.

Now, in presenting data from the American *Atlas,* we are faced with all these complications, plus others arising from the fact that more than one informant was chosen to represent each community. That is, at nearly every "point" the American field workers recorded the usage of one elderly, poorly educated informant and one younger, more modern informant. In certain key communities, a third type was included—a well educated, or "cultured," speaker who presumably represented the cultivated usage of the area. Thus, at the same point on the map we often find such variants as *sot down* (preterite), representing rustic usage, *set* or *sit down,* representing more modern popular usage, and *sat down,* representing cultivated usage.[18] It is obviously impossible to draw isoglosses separating *sot* from *set* or *sat;* it is even impractical to set off the *sot* areas, since the form occurs in about every other community through considerable areas. In other cases, of course, it is quite easy to mark off an area where a certain form is current. *Holp* (for *helped*), for example, occupies a very clear-cut area south of the Potomac.[19] Yet a line marking off this area would by no means constitute a dividing line between *holp* and *helped,* since most of the younger informants within the *holp* area use the standard form *helped.* My point is that an isogloss based on American *Atlas* materials

---

[14] Ed. J. Gilliéron and E. Edmont, 7 vols. (Paris, 1902–1910).

[15] See Karl Jaberg, "Sprachgeographie," *Siebenunddreissigstes Jahresheft des Vereins Schweiz. Gymnasiallehrer* (Aarau, 1908), pp. 16–42; also Plate III.

[16] *Ibid.,* Plate III.

[17] *Ibid.,* Plate X.

[18] In addition, the same informant often uses more than one form; all of these are of course entered at that point on the map. On at least one occasion McDavid picked up from the same informant, as the preterite of *see, I seen, I seed, I see,* and *I saw.*

[19] This verb, as well as the others mentioned, is treated in my *Survey of Verb Forms in the Eastern United States.* [Ann Arbor, Mich., 1953]

should in all cases be regarded as an outer limit, not as a dividing line between two speech forms.

The examples hitherto adduced have, of course, illustrated the incidence of "non-standard" as against "standard" speech forms. What of those instances of two forms which are equally "standard," each within its area? Kurath's map of *pail* and *bucket* provides an example.[20] Here too we must follow the same principle: we must first draw the outer limit of one form, then that of the other. The two lines will lap over each other at some points, enclosing certain communities of mixed usage.[21] Thus, *a dividing line is a double isogloss,* each line being the outer limit of one of the two speech forms in question. The areas of overlapping between the two lines may be wide or narrow, depending on many social, geographical, and historical considerations.

Let us return to *grease* and *greasy.* The variation between [s] and [z] in these words furnishes an almost ideal example of geographical (as against social) distribution. Consider first the verb *grease.* It is unnecessary to describe in detail the incidence of [s] and [z], since the accompanying map tells its own story. The northern line of the [z]-form, it may be observed, takes in the southwestern corner of Connecticut (west of the Housatonic); from there it passes westward just to the north of New Jersey; then it dips sharply southward to Philadelphia, to the west of which it again rises gradually northward to the northwestern corner of Pennsylvania. The transition area (where both [s] and [z] are used), is relatively narrow to the west of Philadelphia; to the northeast, however, it widens considerably so as to include most of northern New Jersey, as well as New York City and eastern Long Island.

Outside our pair of isoglosses there is a surprisingly small number of "stray" forms. All together, there are only six occurrences of [z] in the [s] area and only six of [s] in the [z] area.[22] (It will be observed, of course, that there is a second area, or island, of [s] along the Ohio River extending northeastward from the vicinity of Marietta, Ohio.) There is no sign whatever of social variation within the solid [s] and [z] areas; cultivated usage is in strict agreement with popular usage.[23] Within the areas of overlapping there is naturally some variation between older and more modern informants—yet the general trend is not at all clear. In the communities of divided usage to the west of Philadelphia the more modern informant uses [s] in six out of eight instances; in such communities to the northeast of Philadelphia the modern preference is for [s] in six instances, for [z] in six others. As for cultured informants within the areas of overlapping, ten use [griz],

---

[20] *A Word Geography of the Eastern United States* (Ann Arbor, Mich., 1949), Figure 66.

[21] Even after drawing the lines we would find a good many scattered, or "stray," occurrences of *pail* within the *bucket* area and vice versa. Kurath's lines, which are all outer limits, do not attempt to indicate the presence of stray forms or small patches which occur outside the main area; however, since he also publishes maps on which each occurrence of each word is recorded by a symbol, the reader can easily check and interpret his isoglosses.

[22] This amounts to less than one per cent of the informants. Most of the informants who show exceptional usage also give the "normal" form; that is, they use both [s] and [z] forms.

[23] Although the preterite form of the verb was not called for in the work sheets, Lowman picked up some five instances of *grez* [grɛz] in the [z] area; and a number of other informants reported having heard this form.

five use [gris], and one offers both [s] and [z] forms. One might state, very tentatively, that cultivated usage has tended to favor [griz], particularly in New York City and northern New Jersey.

For the adjective *greasy*, the pronunciations [grisi] and [grizi] show almost precisely the same isoglosses as those for [gris] and [griz]. The northern limit of [z] pushes further northward at three points in Pennsylvania;[24] correspondingly, the southern limit of [s] retreats northward at one point in Ohio, three in Pennsylvania, and two in northern New Jersey.[25] Within the [s] area, there are ten stray forms with [z], scattered through New England and the Hudson Valley; six of these occur in the cultured type of informant. Within the [z] area, we again find six stray occurrences of [s]; and precisely the same island of [s] occurs along the Ohio River. In short, a few more eastern informants use [z] in *greasy* than in *grease*, though the difference is not great. Within the areas of overlapping we find almost exactly the same social distribution as in the case of *grease*. Cultured informants prefer [grizi] by eleven to four; this fact, together with the six "stray" northern uses of [z] in the cultured type, inclines us to believe that [z] in *greasy* has penetrated into northeastern cultivated speech a little more palpably than in the case of *grease*—though still to a very slight extent.

After describing the incidence of the speech forms in question, we are still faced with a number of questions, to which our data can provide only partial answers.

What becomes of our isoglosses in the areas west of Pennsylvania? The materials being gathered for the Great Lakes atlas (under the direction of Professor A. H. Marckwardt) will undoubtedly provide an answer. I have not been able to examine the latest of these materials; but judging from preliminary information, as well as from a map already published by Professor Marckwardt,[26] the northern limit of [z] in *greasy* passes through central Ohio, then swings northward so as to take in almost the whole of Indiana, then bends southward through central Illinois in the direction of St. Louis. Whether the areas of transition are wide or narrow we can probably not determine with accuracy, since, in general, only one social type (the elderly, or rustic) in included in the Great Lakes survey.

Why should the isoglosses run where they do? The answer, in part, is relatively simple. Of the two sets of variants, the [s] forms are evidently generalized in the New England colonies, the [z] forms in the Middle and South Atlantic colonies. The westward migrations and settlements of the New Englanders covered New York (State), northern Pennsylvania, Michigan, Wisconsin, and the northern portions of Ohio, Indiana, and Illinois.[27] Many speech features mark off this Northern area from the "Midland"—the

---

[24] Lehigh, Columbia, and Lancaster counties.

[25] Columbia, Armstrong, Blair, Cumberland, Hunterdon, and Morris counties.

[26] "Folk Speech of Indiana and Adjacent States," *op cit.*, p. 128. [Editor's note: for a later statement based upon the completed study involving all three types of informants see A. H. Marckwardt: "Principal and Subsidiary Dialect Areas in the North-Central States," *Publication of the American Dialect Society*, No. 27 (April, 1957).

[27] Kurath, *Word Geography*, pp. 1–7; see also Lois K. M. Rosenberry, *The Expansion of New England* (Boston and New York, 1909). Even the island of [s] forms around Marietta, Ohio, is to be explained on the basis of early settlement; this area was first settled by New Englanders as early as the 1780's. See Rosenberry, pp. 175ff.

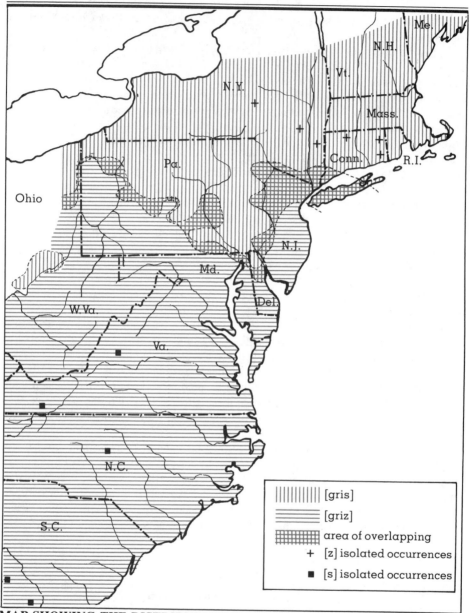

MAP SHOWING THE DISTRIBUTION OF [s] AND [z] IN GREASE (VERB)
Northern Maine and Eastern Georgia (not shown on the map) show the same usage as
the adjoining areas. At the time of this study, no field records were available for Northern
New York.

area occupied primarily by Pennsylvania.[28] Most of the northern lines, to be sure, pass further to the north in Pennsylvania than do those of the [s] in *grease* and *greasy*. Yet the penetration of northern forms to the area of Philadelphia is occasionally to be observed in other instances, for example, the line of Northern *clapboards* (as against Midland and Southern *weatherboards*) dips sharply southward so as to take in Philadelphia and northern Delaware. Another explanation for the prevalence of [gris] and ['grisi] in east central Pennsylvania might be the fact that much of the area was occupied in the early 18th century by Palatine Germans, whose native dialect had no [z] phoneme at all[29] and who may, for this reason, have favored [s] in any English words where variation between [s] and [z] occurred.

What is the British practice with regard to the pronunciation of *grease* and *greasy?* No complete survey has been made; but there seems no doubt that London usage, as well as "Received Standard" usage throughout southern England is mixed.[30] The questionnaires which Hempl circulated in England (for his study cited above) showed that in London only 25 and 33 percent of the informants used [s] in *grease* and *greasy;* but that in England exclusive of London the percentages of [s] were 84 and 74.[31] We have no ground, even yet, for rejecting these figures; but it should be pointed out that folk speech in England, just as in the United States, shows its isoglosses. A survey of the linguistic atlas type conducted by Guy S. Lowman in 1934[32] shows that the [z] in *grease* (I have no information on *greasy*) occupies East Anglia and a small adjoining area; that [s] is universal in the remainder of southern England (we are speaking strictly of the rustic type of speaker). Since the line passes through (or very near) London, it is easy to see why the metropolitan area should show a mixture of usage.

Is there any evidence of a differentiation in meaning between ['grisi] and ['grizi]? The *Atlas* provides no answer to this question, since, in the interest of obtaining comparable data, the words were always called for in the same context ("grease the car, axle, etc." and "my hands are greasy"). In general, such differentiations in meaning are characteristics of areas of mixed usage, not of those where one pronunciation or another is definitely established. The distinction usually given in dictionaries is that ['grisi] may mean literally 'covered with grease,' while ['grizi] may be used with less literal, and

---

[28] Examples of Northern words (from Kurath) are *whiffletree, pail, darning needle* ('dragonfly'), and *co, boss!* (cow call). Verb forms which I have found to have similar distributions are *hadn't ought* ('oughtn't'), *how be you?, clim* ('climbed'), and *see* as a preterite of *to see*. Note that Kurath's definition of "Midland" does not coincide with that of Hempl; the area, according to the former, extends much farther to the south-westward of Pennsylvania than Hempl indicated (See *Word Geography*, pp. 27–37). [Editor's note: see also Atwood's own later study, *A Survey of Verb Forms in the Eastern United States* (University of Michigan Press, Ann Arbor, 1953).]

[29] See Carroll E. Reed, *The Pennsylvania German Dialect Spoken in the Counties of Lehigh and Berks: Phonology and Morphology* (Seattle, Wash., 1949), pp. 20 and 29.

[30] See Daniel Jones, *An English Pronouncing Dictionary*, 9th ed. (London, 1948).

[31] Hempl, *op. cit.*, pp. 442–43.

[32] Lowman's British field records are filed in an unedited state at the University of Michigan.

sometimes unpleasant, connotations.[33] What we can say with confidence is that speakers to the south of our isoglosses do not follow this practice: ['grizi] is universal with the meaning 'covered with grease'; whether or not speakers in the area of overlapping, and to the north of it, would have used ['grizi] had the context been different we are unable to determine.

How should we evaluate the *Atlas* data as a picture of reality? What is most important to realize is that the *Atlas* makes no attempt whatever to record the usage of non-native speakers, or even of those natives who have resided for long periods outside their home communities. Such speakers are rather uncommon in some communities, fairly numerous in others; in a few of the latter, the *Atlas* may even reflect the usage of a minority of old-timers. In view of this, we might be inclined to wonder whether the percentage method might not give a truer picture of prevalent usage than the isogloss method. The proportion of non-native speech forms in a community would, of course, roughly correspond to the proportion of non-native residents; such data would certainly be valuable, though to collect it on a large enough scale (say, 100 or so informants from each county) would be so difficult as to be practically impossible. Few investigators are qualified to make extensive phonetic observations, and those few must take their informants from such captive groups as college classes whose usage may or may not be spontaneous or representative. Another feature of the *Atlas* that must be considered is the preponderance of rather old informants. Since the interviews were conducted several years ago, many of the forms shown to be current among the aged may now be rare or even obsolete; moreover, the *Atlas* records would not reflect the most recent trends, fads, and innovations—some of which are extremely rapid, others extremely slow. It seems unlikely to me that the lines on *grease* and *greasy* have shifted radically in the last few years, yet I have no doubt that usage may have shifted in certain individual communities.[34] All things considered, the *Linguistic Atlas* offers the most reliable body of data as yet assembled, or likely to be assembled in the near future, on American speech; isoglosses based on it reflect the usage of a highly important segment of our population, and they are, moreover, of the highest value in a study of our cultural and settlement history.

---

[33] Daniel Jones, *English Pronouncing Dictionary:* "Some speakers use the forms . . . with a difference of meaning, ['gri:si] having reference merely to the presence of grease and ['gri:zi] having reference to the slipperiness caused by grease." *Webster's NID* states: ". . .many people in all sections use ['grisi] in some connotations and ['grizi] in others, the first esp. in the literal sense, covered with grease." Cf. Kenyon and Knott: "Some distinguish ['grisi] 'covered with grease' from ['grizi] 'slimy' " (*op. cit.*). G. P. Krapp states: "A distinction is sometimes made in the meaning of ['gri:si] and ['gri:zi], the latter being regarded as a word of unpleasant connotation" (*op. cit.*, p. 119). Webster's implies that this distinction is fairly general throughout the country—a very dubious proposition. T. Larsen and F. C. Walker simply prescribe [s] for the meaning 'sticky' and [z] for the meaning 'slippery'—as though this feature were standard and universal. (See *Pronunciation*, Oxford Press, 1931, p. 92.)

[34] Dr. Smith expresses the opinion that the younger generation in New York City has gone over almost entirely to the [s] in *greasy*.

DISCUSSION QUESTIONS

1. What is the significance of a double isogloss?

2. If you have access to a group whose members have mixed geographical backgrounds, determine each member's use of the s/z forms of *greasy* and correlate it with region and education.

3. Make an informal survey of differences in meaning between *greasy* and *greazy*.

4. List what seem to you to be regional variants in speech you have heard recently and find out as much as possible about them in atlases and other resources available to you.

JOHN L. FISCHER

As professor of anthropology at Tulane University, the author has principally engaged in field work in Micronesia, Japan, and New England. In 1979 he held a Fulbright professorship of ethnography in Leningrad State University.

SOCIAL INFLUENCES ON THE CHOICE OF A LINGUISTIC VARIANT

During the year 1954–55 my wife and I were engaged in a study of child-rearing in a semi-rural New England village.[1] In the course of the study I had occasion to record two or more interviews on Audograph discs or tapes, with each of the 24 children of our sample. Previously certain inconsistencies in the children's speech had attracted my attention, especially the variation between *-in* and *-ing* for the present participle ending.[2] Accordingly, in transcribing the discs and tapes, I decided to note the choice of these two variants, and this paper is intended to summarize and discuss this information.

To begin with, all of the 24 children, except three, used both forms to some extent at least. The three exceptions used only the *-ing* form, and since they were less loquacious than most of the other children, it is possible that a larger sample of their speech would have revealed the use of the other variant as well. This may then be regarded as a case of so-called free variation of two linguistic forms within a local speech community, and within the speech of most individual members of our sample community. In general, the choice of one or the other of the variants would not affect the denotation of acts, states, or events by the word.

"Free variation" is of course a label, not an explanation. It does not tell us where the variants came from nor why the speakers use them in differing proportions, but is rather a way of excluding such questions from the scope of immediate inquiry. Historically, I presume that one could investigate the spread of one of these variants into the territory of another through contact and migration, and this would constitute one useful sort of explanation. However, another sort of explanation is possible in terms of current factors which lead a given child in given circumstances to produce one of the variants rather than another, and it is this which I wish to discuss here.

Before discussing the determinants of selection of the variants it will be helpful to understand a little of the general background of the data. The 24 children in our sample consisted of an equal number of boys and girls, both divided into two equal age groups, ages 3–6 and 7–10. By the time the recordings were made my wife and I had been

---

[1] This study was part of a larger cross-cultural study of socialization financed by the Ford Foundation and under the general direction of John Whiting of the Harvard Graduate School of Education and others.

[2] The variation in this dialect between *-in* and *-ing* in the participle ending does not extend to words with a final *-in* in an unstressed syllable in standard speech. This variation is therefore probably best viewed as a case of free alternation of two allomorphs which happen to differ in respect to one phoneme, rather than as a case of phonological free variation.

observing the children periodically for eight to ten months and most of the children were fairly well acquainted with us. Most of the children were interviewed in an office in our house, which was located in the middle of the village. Most of the children had visited our house before, some a number of times. Four younger children who had not were interviewed in their own homes. Three general types of text were obtained:

(1) Protocols for all children for a verbal thematic apperception test (TAT) in which the children were asked to make up stories starting out from short sentences given by the investigator.
(2) For older children only, answers to a formal questionnaire.
(3) For a few of the older children, informal interviews asking them to recount their recent activities.

I shall present first some counts of variants in the TAT protocols, since this test was administered to all the children. As is shown in Table I, a markedly greater number of girls used -ing more frequently, while more boys used more -in.

Table I   Number of children favoring -ing and -in variant suffixes in TAT protocols according to sex

	-ing > -in	-ing < -in	
Boys	5	7	Chi square: 2.84; 05 < P < .1 (by two-tailed test)
Girls	10	2	

This suggests that in this community (and probably others where the choice exists) -ing is regarded as symbolizing female speakers and -in as symbolizing males.

Within each sex, differences in personality are associated with the proportion of frequency of -ing to -in as illustrated in Table II.

Table II   Frequency of use of -ing and -in in TAT protocols of two boys

	-ing	-in	
"Model" boy	38	1	Chi square: 19.67; P < .001
"Typical" boy	10	12	

The first boy was regarded by his teacher and others as a "model" boy. He did his school work well, was popular among his peers, reputed to be thoughtful and considerate. The second boy was generally regarded as a "typical" boy—physically strong, dominating, full of mischief, but disarmingly frank about his transgressions. The "model" boy used almost exclusively the -ing ending here, while the "typical" boy used the -in ending more than half the time, as shown above.

In Table III below, one may also note a slight tendency for the -ing variant to be associated with higher socio-economic status, although this is not statistically significant with a sample of this size. The community studied is fairly small and does not have strong class lines, which is probably why more marked results did not appear.[3]

Table III Number of children favoring -ing and -in endings according to family status

Family Status	-ing > -in	-ing ≤ -in	
Above Median	8	4	Chi square (corrected): 0; P > .9
Below Median	7	5	

Besides asking *who* uses which variant and how much, we may also ask whether there are situational differences in *when* a single speaker uses these variants. One variant in the situation may be described as degree of formality: in the children's terms I would think of this as degree of similarity to a formal classroom recitation. The best child to examine for this variable is the "model" boy of Table II since he was interviewed in all three situations mentioned above and was obligingly talkative in each. As Table IV shows, the frequency of choice of variants changed from an almost exclusive use of -ing in the TAT situation to a predominance of -in in the informal interviews.

TAT	Formal	Informal
	Interview	Interview

Table IV Frequency of -ing and -in in a ten-year-old boy's speech in three situations in order of increasing informality

-ing	38	33	24	Chi square: 37.07 P < .001
-in	1	35	41	

Of course, these three situations should not be regarded as exhaustive of the frequency range of these variants in this boy's speech. In the interviews I myself used the -ing variant consistently and this probably influenced the informant's speech somewhat. Probably in casual conversation with his peers the -in/-ing ratio is even higher than in the informal interview.

Another measure similar in implication to the frequency of variants by type of interview would be differences in frequency between the beginning and later parts of a single interview. Especially in the TAT protocols, which are the most formal texts, I noticed for a number of children that the -ing frequently was higher in the beginning of the interview and later dropped off, presumably as the child became more relaxed and accustomed to the situation. In only one child was the reverse trend noted, and there are

---

[3] Most previous studies of sociological factors connected with linguistic variants have been concerned with linguistic indices of class, caste, or occupational groups. Group boundaries have been regarded, implicitly or explicitly, as barriers to communication analogous to political boundaries, geographical distance, etc. The emphasis in this paper is rather on variations within a face-to-face community whose members are in frequent free communication: variations between social categories of speakers and between individual speakers, and situational variations in the speech of individual speakers. . . .

reasons to believe that this particular child may have become more tense during the administration of the test.

A linguist might ask whether there is any association between the suffix variants and specific verbs. The corpus is not large enough to establish stable frequency indices for the suffixes of individual words, but there is certainly a trend for markedly "formal" verbs to have the -*ing* suffix and markedly "informal" verbs to have the -*in* suffix. The first boy in Table II above, for instance, used -*ing* in *criticizing, correcting, reading, visiting, interesting,* and used -*in* in *punchin, flubbin, swimmin, chewin, hittin.* For some common verbs, however, such as *play, go* and *do* he used both alternatively. Probably only a few verbs are formal or informal enough in their connotations so that the same variant would always be used with them. Of course, the choice of verb vocabulary is itself related to personality and situational factors.

In brief, then, the choice between the -*ing* and the -*in* variants appear to be related to sex, class, personality (aggressive/cooperative), and mood (tense/relaxed) of the speaker,[4] to the formality of the conversation and to the specific verb spoken. While these are "free variants" in the standard type of description of languages in which only grammatical facts and differences in none but "denotative" meanings are taken into account, if we widen our scope of study to include the meaning of these variants to the conversants we might call them "socially conditioned variants," or "socio-symbolic variants," on the grounds that they serve to symbolize things about the relative status of the conversants and their attitudes toward each other, rather than denoting any difference in the universe of primary discourse (the "outer world").[5]

What are the wider implications for linguistics of such an analysis of social factors influencing choice of linguistic variants? For one thing, many linguists have recognized that "free" variation is a logically necessary stage in most or all linguistic change.[6] Less

---

[4] And doubtless of the person spoken to, although this was not investigated.

[5] Uriel Weinreich has suggested to me the term "symptomatic signs," after Karl Bühler, as an alternative for "socio-symbolic variant" which already has a basis in established usage. However, it seems to me that "symptomatic signs" might be in one sense too broad and in another too narrow: too broad in the sense that it might be interpreted to refer to "non-linguistic" features of speech such as general pitch, loudness, timbre, rate, etc., and too narrow in the sense that Bühler appears to regard the symptomatic function as, ideally, purely expressive of the speaker, while I am looking for a broader term which would cover this function but also include expression of the dyadic relationship between the conversants. This cannot simply be taken care of by adding in Bühler's "signal" function which deals with the "appeal" to the listener, since at least some aspects of the relationship do not exist primarily either in speaker or listener but rather *between* them, e.g. relative age, relative rank. See Karl Bühler, *Sprachtheorie,* Jena (1934), esp. p. 28. Whether I should here introduce a term incorporating "symbol" is a further question which I acknowledge but do not discuss here, as it is complex and is not directly relevant to the main argument of the paper.

[6] I find in checking over the literature that this statement seems to be based more on my impressions of conversations with linguists than on published statements. One clear statement of this principle, however, is to be found on p. 367 of Hans Vogt's paper on "Language Contacts," *Word* 10.365–74 (1954). A more general statement applying to any type of cultural element, and by implication linguistic elements, can be found in Ralph Linton's *The Study of Man,* p. 280, N.Y. (1936).

widely appreciated but also recognized by some is another fact: Although the mechanisms of psychic economy are becoming better understood in diachronic phonemics, they are not always sufficient to explain fully the progressive adaption of variant forms, and that people adopt a variant primarily not because it is easier to pronounce (which it most frequently is, but not always), or because it facilitates some important distinction in denotational meaning, but because it expresses how they feel about their relative status versus other conversants.

The clearest and most comprehensive statement of social factors in linguistic change which I have encountered is found in an article by Martin Joos dealing with medieval sibilants.[7] He speaks of "the phonetic drift, which was kept going in the usual way: that is, the dialects and idiolects of higher prestige were more advanced in this direction, and their speakers carried the drift further along so as to maintain the prestige-marking difference against their pursuers. The vanity factor is needed to explain why phonetic drifts tend to continue in the same direction; the 'inertia' sometimes invoked is a label and not an argument." This protracted pursuit of an elite by an envious mass and consequent "flight" of the elite is in my opinion the most important mechanism in linguistic drift, not only in the phonetic drift which Joos discusses, but in syntactic and lexical drift as well.[8]

The study of social factors in linguistic drift is in the field of the sociology of language rather than linguistics proper. However, this study can not reach ultimate fruition without certain linguistic studies by competent linguists. I refer here to studies of individual variations in linguistic forms in small, face-to-face speech communities, and of variations in these forms in the speech of single individuals in a range of social situations. Studies of this sort constitute tasks of respectable magnitude which have, in the main, been neglected.[9]

---

[7] Martin Joos, "The Medieval Sibilants," *Language* 28.222–31 (1952); reprinted in M. Joos (ed.), *Readings in Linguistics,* Washington (1957), pp. 377–8. Others have separately recognized the importance of fashion in linguistic change, especially in the spread of standard dialects, and to a lesser degree have recognized the complementary process of using distinctive linguistic features to emphasize social exclusiveness. J. O. Hertzler in "Toward a Sociology of Language," *Social Forces* 32.109–19 (1953), gives a bibliography including studies of both sorts. Joos's statement however appears to me to be unique in his recognition that the two processes combine to constitute a self-perpetuating cycle. Since Joos is noted for his rigorous definition of the scope of linguistics proper it is perhaps all the more interesting that he should throw in this "sociological"aside.

[8] Incidentally, this flight-pursuit mechanism might be regarded as an explanation of the constant rate of decay of basic "non-cultural" vocabulary postulated by Morris Swadesh's theory of glottochronology. To make it suffice one would also need to assume that all societies possess some form of elite group—if only the "ideal conformist" in some societies— and that mass envy of the elite and ambition to join them are everywhere the same. These assumptions may seem radical and against common sense, but they are not as easy to refute as one might think. Needless to say, one would not assume that the elite is always a property or authority elite. In politically and economically undifferentiated societies, the most important criterion might be technical skill and productivity in consumer goods, admired personality traits, etc.

[9] The classic study in this field is Louis Gauchat's "L'Unité phonétique dans le patois d'une commune," *Aus romanischen Sprachen und Literatur,* Halle, 1905, p. 124. Other references are cited by W. von Wartburg. *Problémes et méthods de la linguistique,* Paris, 1946, p. 33 (footnote). Modern techniques, of course, open entirely new perspectives for research.

A student of social factors in the choice of linguistic variants would wish to know for a fairly large stratified sample of a speech community how often members of a given sub-group used a sizable sample of series of socially significant variants, and for at least some of the sub-groups one would want to know how these frequencies of choice of variants changed under different situations and in the presence of conversants of different social status and personal relationships. A linguist as such would not wish to analyze these social factors in great detail. But it would be well within the scope of linguistics to identify individual informants in a unitary speech community by name or code number and group them according to their similarity or dissimilarity in the use of variants in some standard situation, say, in conversation with the linguist. The psychologist and sociologist could then take these groups and see what sense they made in their terms. In practice, of course, such a rigorous separation between linguistics and the more general social sciences is not required since linguists and other laymen are presumably capable of making a number of distinctions of considerable sociological interest, such as male versus female, etc.

A word about the relation of the proposed study to dialectology is appropriate here. It has generally been the aim of dialectologists to describe linguistic variations between groups which are separated by some communications barrier, especially geography or social class. What I am advocating here is the study of linguistic variations within small groups where there is free and relatively intense communication, so that as far as possible the lack of contact between speakers is not a reason for failure to use the same forms. Of course in a large society such as ours, small closed groups are rare, and some of the variation among the individuals of any group picked for study will be due to the fact that they have different contacts outside the group. But this empirical fact does not reduce the importance of studying variation within the face-to-face community, although it suggests that the best place to study such variation would be on a remote Pacific atoll with a small, long-established population.

What I am proposing might be called comparative idiolectology rather than dialectology. Ideally, a thorough description of a single dialect would be based on the study of a sizable sample of the idiolects in a local speech community, in the same way that a thorough description of a language would be based on the study of a sizable sample of its dialects. In comparative idiolectology one might, as a device of fieldwork, still concentrate on a single informant, but one would want to follow him around with a portable recording machine and note changes in his speech in different settings and situations and with different conversants. Moreover, since phenomenologically language is as much listening as speaking one would be led to analyze what was said comprehensibly to him by others as well as what he said himself.

The untrained listener will not, of course, generally be able to reproduce or identify the differences in the speech of others whom he encounters, unless he is an accomplished mimic. But he does react to these differences by making interpretations about the social situation on the basis of them and will be able to tell when a speaker is talking like a woman, like an upper class person, like a relaxed person, etc., even though he cannot specify all the variant forms on which he bases his judgment.[10] (This is not to deny the

---

[10] The "tape experiment" described by Putnam and O'Hern investigates language and social status in this manner, although the speakers were not members of a single face-to-face community, so the complication of barriers to communication is introduced. See G. N. Putnam and E. M. O'Hern, "The Status Significance of an Isolated Urban Dialect," *Language* 31, Supplement, Language Dissertation, No. 53 (1955).

presence or importance of other ''non-linguistic'' features of speech as well as things entirely unconnected with speech such as dress, physical appearance, gestures, etc., which also serve as cues for judgments of the conversational situation.)

In analyzing socio-symbolic variants there will obviously be a certain amount of association between variant series. In many of the series at least one variant could be distinguished as ''formal,'' and another as ''informal.'' But it is a question for empirical investigation whether this distinction applies to all variant series, and, if so, with how much force. I have suggested above a number of factors which influence the -in/-ing distinction. Conceivably they all bear on formality, that is, compliance, tenseness, femaleness, and high class all make for formal behavior. But even if this is true for these factors in American culture, are they a unitary complex in all cultures, and may there not be other social factors affecting socio-symbolic variants which are independent of the formality complex? Are variants associated with being female always associated as well with formality? In three languages with which I am acquainted, English, Japanese, and Ponapean, I can think of a number of instances where this link is found, but there also appear to be exceptions. In Ponapean, for instance, a minority of women have an unusual allophone for the r phoneme, but this seems to have no relation to the degree of formality. Lisping in English is regarded as feminine, but would indicate little about degree of formality.

Even where the same factor determines the choice of alternants in several series of variants, the breaking point for each series will probably be different. For instance, in the TAT texts discussed above, three of the children used the pronunciation [ey] for the indefinite article a. This pronunciation can be regarded as formal to the point of being artificial and is much more restricted for speakers in this community than the -ing variant of the present participle ending, yet the direction of social symbolism is the same, though not the intensity. In other words, [ey] in itself is more a sign of formality than -ing though both are signs of formality. The ''formality'' index of a given text would be determined by the variant chosen in several series of socio-symbolic variants, each of which would have a different socio-symbolic level with respect to formality. Presumably these series could be ordered in terms of increasingly greater thresholds of formality required to bring about the shift from the informal to the formal form.

I have been stressing here the synchronic implications of socio-symbolic variants. The diachronic implications are at least equally interesting. Obviously the threshold for a given variant does not *necessarily* remain the same, generation after generation. If a particular variant has for whatever reason greater prestige, it will gradually be adopted in more situations by more people: its threshold will be lowered. But as its threshold is lowered and approaches universality in the speech community, its socio-symbolic load is reduced and eventually vanishes. One could hardly convey much of an air of informality, for example, by saying [ə] for the indefinite article, though saying [ey] would be quite stilted. But presumably new series of variants keep arising to replace those which achieve uniformity in this way.

Now what is meant by ''variants of greater prestige''? One could determine which of a pair of variants had the greater prestige by noting which tended to ''spread'' when two conversants who in other situations differed in their choice came together. But the grounds of prestige clearly vary according to individuals and societies. A variant which one man uses because he wants to seem dignified another man would reject because he did not want to seem stiff. Societies likewise have characteristic average value preferences. Using the variable of formality, it is quite possible that one society would show a tendency, at least in some situations, to show a preference for adoption of formal forms of speech, and another in analogous situations show a preference for informal forms. These preferences could in turn be related by persons so inclined to social structure. One would end up with a statement not simply of the direction of linguistic drift, but what this drift meant psychologically and what social changes might check it. It would be very interesting, for instance, to find and examine cognate variants from some related societies with differing descent practices, and see whether the current drift is in the direction of feminization or masculinization. Such data would not only illuminate the mechanism of linguistic drift, but would provide students of social structure with extremely valuable indices of the distribution of envy and cross-segmental identification in the communities speaking the language studied.

DISCUSSION QUESTIONS

1. In your own experience and observation has the adoption of a variant form been due to the speaker's feeling about relative social status versus that of other conversants?

2. Fischer asks, ''Are variants associated with being female always associated with formality?'' What is your answer? Discuss.

3. Fischer says that the grounds of prestige clearly vary according to individuals and society. Do they vary according to age groups?

HAROLD B. ALLEN

A one-time doctoral student of Charles Fries at the University of Michigan, Allen taught there and at San Diego State College. Later he joined the English faculty of the University of Minnesota, from which he retired as professor emeritus of English and linguistics in 1971. He produced The Linguistic Atlas of the Upper Midwest *(University of Minnesota Press, 1973, 1975, 1976) and served as president of both the American Dialect Society and the National Council of Teachers of English.*

THE *LINGUISTIC ATLAS OF THE UPPER MIDWEST* AS A SOURCE OF SOCIOLINGUISTIC INFORMATION[1]

When, nearly fifty years ago, Hans Kurath included a three-point social dimension in the selection of field informants for the Linguistic Atlas of New England, he provided a precedent that increasingly has brought to light significant social variation in American English.[2] The phonological analysis prepared for the third and final volume of the *Linguistic Atlas of the Upper Midwest,*[3] along with the treatment of the lexicon and the grammar in the first two volumes, now adds measurably to the sociolinguistic data available not only to dialectologists but also to students and teachers of usage, to textbook writers, and to sociolinguists themselves.

The *Linguistic Atlas of the Upper Midwest (LAUM)* covers the states of Minnesota, Iowa, North and South Dakota, and Nebraska. Its primary function, like that of other American regional dialect atlases now in progress, is of course the presentation of regional differences in American English. But, also like the other atlases, it follows Kurath's lead in giving information about ascertained social differences as well. It specifies the social range and sometimes even the register of many linguistic items: lexical, grammatical,

---

[1] This is a revised version of a paper orally presented at the regional meeting of the American Dialect Society in St. Louis, Missouri, November 4, 1976.

[2] Although Jakob Jud and Karl Jaberg had incidentally included a few informants from different social classes in their *Sprach und Sachatlas Italiens und der Südschweiss* (1928–1940), Kurath was the first dialectologist to build social range into a systematically surveyed population of a dialect project. As early as 1948 Raven I. McDavid, Jr., drew attention to the significance of the resulting social data for the social scientist. Observation of social contrast appeared in Kurath's *Word Geography of the Eastern United States* (1949) and in his and McDavid's *Pronunciation of English in the Atlantic States* (1961), although it was not detailed and quantified. More detailed statements are in E. Bagby Atwood's *Survey of Verb Forms in the Eastern United States* (1958), a study subsequently extended in two University of Minnesota dissertations by Virginia Glenn McDavid in 1954 (Verb Forms of the North Central States and Upper Midwest) and Jean Malmstrom in 1958 (A Study of the Validity of Textbook Statements about Certain Controversial Grammatical Items in the Light of Evidence from the Linguistic Atlas).

[3] Harold B. Allen. *The Linguistic Atlas of the Upper Midwest.* Volume 1: *Handbook and Lexicon,* 1973. Volume 2: *Grammar,* 1975. Volume 3: *Pronunciation,* 1976. Minneapolis, Minnesota: University of Minnesota Press.

and phonological. The use of the term "range" must not be overlooked. Although the data are presented as summarized frequencies with each of the three informant classes, they are not to be interpreted as absolute frequencies for the classes as such. A frequency distribution of, say, 72% for the relatively uneducated speakers in Type I, of 22% for the better educated high school group of speakers in Type II, and of 6% for the cultivated college group in Type III means simply that there is a fairly sharp decline in the use of a given item or form as one looks at people along the educational ladder, a ladder which at the time of the field work could in the Upper Midwest be reasonably equated with the social ladder.

Two important limitations, then, restrict the interpretation of the data. First, the information is for a particular region, the Upper Midwest, and hence is suggestive and not definitive with respect to other sections of the country, where the distribution might be quite different. It demonstrates principles and procedures only so far as other areas are concerned. Second, the information was gathered at the midcentury point and hence for at least certain items is not to be taken as reflecting the current situation, more than a quarter of a century later. It may be noted, furthermore, that the information is derived from interviews that in themselves offer variation ranging from an occasional fairly formal register to the usual informal and sometimes even casual style. But the language reported is always living English, never the edited variety analyzed in studies of the printed page.

Although within the 800-item corpus of the Upper Midwest worksheets more attention is given specifically to the vocabulary, the lexicon is not very significant in exhibiting social contrast. The selection of vocabulary items was made primarily to reveal differences in everyday words, not levels of personal lexical choice. Yet even with this limitation some vocabulary matters do manifest social range. For example, only a handful of the Type I and Type II informants use bus or railroad *station* exclusively, but 25% of those in Type III use only that word. Its prestige is suggested by the informant who calls *depot* "improper," and by another informant who during the interview corrected himself by saying "station" after he had first replied with "depot," and then commented, "That's the right word." "The sun *rose*" is preferred by all the college graduates and by 83% of the high school group but by a smaller 70% of the Type I informants, with the others choosing *came up*. A slightly higher proportion of the cultivated speakers select *dishcloth* (58%) and a corresponding proportion of the Type I's prefer *dishrag*. Of the 18 informants out of 208 who offer *widow woman* instead of simple *widow,* fourteen are in Type I, four in Type II, and none at all in the college-trained group III. *Relations* instead of *relatives* is preferred by 37% of the least educated, 18% of the high school group, and none of the Type III informants. More than one-third of the Type I speakers use *learn* in the sense of *teach,* but only a few Type II informants do, and none at all in Type III. It may be additionally noted that of the many colorful equivalents of *tired, vomit,* and *jilt,* nearly all are offered by Type I and Type II speakers and only a meager few by those in Type III.

But it is with respect to grammar and pronunciation that the *LAUM* field records are most revelatory of social contrast. Specifically, for more than half a century repeated educational research has found the irregular verbs to be the source of most of the so-called grammatical errors in the writing of school children. It is not surprising that they reveal the greatest social differences in the actual field investigations in the Upper Midwest. Nor is it surprising that, as the not infrequent total of more than 100% indicates, some informants are so insecure that they shift back and forth from one form to another.

Although textbooks and usage manuals usually posit a rather sharp division between the correct and incorrect, the acceptable and the inacceptable, in actual practice the contrast is rather one of varying frequency on a sliding scale or range. Three points on the range can be taken as summaries of sections of the range as a whole. Of the thirty-seven worksheet verb forms listed opposite, for example, only five are not used by at least one college graduate. Thirty-two of them are in use throughout the complete social range, though of course with increasing or decreasing frequency between one end of the range and the other. As social markers, they can be held significant, then, only insofar as they occur with other social markers. Neither the presence nor absence of a given form in the speech of one informant is sufficient evidence to categorize him as a Type I, II, or III speaker.

"He *come* yesterday," for example, though clearly the dominant choice of Type I informants with 75% frequency, still is used in the speech of nearly one-half of the high school group, and by a perhaps surprising 19% of the college-trained informants. Similarly with "He *run* into me," in which the base form *run* appears as a preterit in the speech of 65% of those in Type I, 36% in Type II, and even with 19% again in Type III. Likewise, *give* occurs in a past time context in "He *give* it to me yesterday" for most of the Type I informants but also with decreased incidence in the speech of those in Types II and III. The converse, a preterit form used as past participle, exhibits a similar range in the 59% frequency of "I've never *drove* a horse" among Type I speakers but only 19% among the college informants.

Even "He *done* it" does not turn out to be an entirely illiterate expression if language itself is not used as the criterion. One-fourth of the high school group has it along with one college-trained speaker.

Lie and *lay* are even less inclined to fit into the rigid dichotomy implied in textbook prescriptivism. The distant loss of any *Sprachgefühl* for the special sense and function of preterit causative verbs long ago led to such confusion that today it is a fifty-fifty chance whether an Upper Midwest college graduate will say "She *lay* in bed all morning" or "She *laid* in bed all morning." But Type I speakers are not in doubt as to which is the right form. Eight-five percent of them are confident that it is *laid*. The infinitive is only slightly less a problem to the Type III informants, 81% of whom have the orthodox "I'm going to *lie* down." Of greater value as a social marker is the preterit of the simplex of the analogous verb pair, *sit* and *set*. Although more than one-third of the least educated speakers have *set* as the preterit in "Then they all *set* down," all but one of the Type III group have the standard "They *sat* down." The remaining verbs in the following list likewise offer evidence supporting the existence of a continuous range or continuum along which social contrast is to be measured.

Several of the miscellaneous grammatical items recorded during the interviews provide more positive social markers than do the strong verbs. Concord with *be*, for example, is rigorously observed by the college informants. Not one of them favors the construction accepted by a majority of the Type I speakers, *we was* or *they was*. Nor did any of the college informants use *Here's* followed by a plural subject, such as *your clothes*, although most of the Type I speakers and more than one-half of the Type II's apparently treat *Here's* as an unchangeable formula to be used before either a singular or a plural noun in the predicate.

"I *ain't* going to" is likewise missing in the speech of the college group, although it is in the speech of one-fourth of the Type II's and of one-half of the least educated informants. "I *ain't* done it" is even more clearly a social marker, as it is not only abjured by informants in Type III and used by only nine percent of the high school Type II but is accepted as normal by more than one-third of the Type I's.

Irregular verbs

	Type I %	Type II %	Type III %
bitten	45	81	68
climbed, *pret.*	73	86	100
clum	25	12	0
clim	9	1	0
come, *pret.*	75	41	19
did	57	81	94
done, *pret.*	63	27	6
drank, *ppl.*	92	78	47
drunk	8	27	60
driven	65	80	94
drove, *ppl.*	41	13	6
drowned, *ppl.*	29	8	0
give, *pret.*	52	19	13
gave	66	94	94
lie, *infin.*	60	70	81
lay = lie, *infin.*	52	40	19
laid, *pret.*	77	69	47
lay, *pret.*	15	28	53
ridden	48	82	81
rode, *ppl.*	59	21	19
ran	63	90	100
run, *pret.*	65	36	19
saw	73	82	87
see, *pret.*	42	27	13
sat	60	88	94
set = sat	37	15	6
swam	85	97	100
swum, *pret.*	18	5	0
tore, *ppl.*	42	26	7
torn	60	75	93
threw	77	94	100
throwed, *pret.*	31	9	6
awoke	6	20	19
wakened	6	6	25
woke (up)	84	73	56
written	79	92	100
wrote, *ppl.*	22	9	0

The controversial inverted negative interrogative of *be* offers a different picture. The historically normal phonetic development of *Am not I?* is *Ain't I?*, but the latter has acquired such a pejorative aura that in the Upper Midwest only nine percent of the Type III speakers will use it occasionally in contrast with 45% of the Type II informants and 63% of the Type I's. Conversely, two-thirds of the Type III informants use the stilted *Am I not?* in contrast with only 29% of the Type I speakers, while a surprising 27% of the college group take refuge in the bizarre and illogical *Aren't I?*—although none would seek such consistency as would exist if they should say "I are going too, aren't I?"

Third person *don't* is not so distinctive a social marker as usage manuals would imply. *He don't* is the customary locution not only for almost all the Type I informants and more than one-half of the Type II's but also for nearly one-half of the college-trained group. A similar social gradation appears in the distribution of *way* and *ways*. While *a long way* is preferred by twice as high a proportion of educated informants as by the least educated, the seeming plural *ways* (historically the adverbial genitive in -*es*) is the majority choice of all three types.

Still greater inconsistency appears in the contrast between two locutions in which a numeral precedes a modified noun. Only 15% of the Type I informants and a bare seven percent of the Type II's accept the locution *two pound,* as of flour or sugar; not one college graduate has it. But with the historically parallel *two bushel* the incidence in Type I rises to 62%. Nearly one-half of the Type II speakers have it, as do even 13% of the Type III's. The former is clearly a sharp through minor social marker; the latter, despite its being analogous, is only suggestively so.

Although in the somewhat unusual interview situation nearly one-half of the cultivated informants use the formal *It wasn't I* (preponderantly, the female speakers), only 20% of the Type II informants have it, and only four percent of the Type I's. In all three types the majority say simply *It wasn't me*. When all three types are examined it appears that 80% of those who say *It wasn't I* are women. The relation of this fact to the current concern with sexism in language remains to be studied.

Two syntactic constructions with relative clauses yield variants providing rather sharp social contrast. In the non-restrictive relative clause modifying a noun with the + human feature, as "He's the man REL PRO . . .", more than three-fourths of the Type I speakers select *that,* as do nearly that many of the Type II's; but only one-fourth of the cultivated speakers choose it. Conversely, only one-fifth of Type I select *who,* but three-fourths of those in Type III have it. A minor social marker is the zero or omitted relative as subject, castigated in usage manuals, as in "He's the man brought the furniture." One-tenth of the least educated informants have this construction, as do two percent of the high school group, but none in Type III. The genitive relative pronoun bemuses one-half of the Type I informants. In the possible context "He's the boy whose father . . ." they replace *whose* with *that his* (30%) or *that the* (9%), or with simple *his* and no relative pronoun (9%). Each of the three minor variants is a clear social marker.

A well-known social contrast between *those* and *them* as adjectivals before a plural noun is expectedly attested in the Upper Midwest. *Those boys* is the only locution reported for the college group; *them boys* is used by 60% of the Type I informants and by 22% of the Type II's. Several additional social markers are listed in the following chart, where it is shown that these language matters as well occur with greater frequency in the speech of the least educated: *poison* as a predicate modifier in "Some berries are poison;" *sick at the stomach* and *sick in the stomach; in back of* (the door); *died with* rather than *died from,* and *towards* and *toward*. When in the following chart percentages total more than 100, the indication is simply that an informant uses more than one form.

Grammar miscellany

	Type I	Type II	Type III
We/they was	60%	30%	0%
We/they were	53	76	100
Here are N PL	24	49	100
Here's N PL	81	59	0
I ain't going to	46	26	0
I'm not going to	58	83	100
Ain't I?	63	45	9
Am I not?	29	45	64
Aren't I?	5	15	27
I haven't done it	72	97	100
I ain't done it	38	9	0
He doesn't	26	51	77
He don't	88	60	46
a long) way	24	30	47
a long) ways	86	82	73
two) bushel	62	49	13
two) bushels	43	52	87
two) pound	15	7	0
two) pounds	89	94	100
He's the man that . . .	77	65	27
He's the man who . . .	19	42	73
He's the man Ø	10	2	0
He's a boy whose father . . .	49	79	87
He's a boy that his father . . .	30	11	7
He's a boy that the father . . .	9	5	0
He's a boy his father . . .	9	5	7
Some berries are poisonous	47	67	93
Some berries are poison	55	32	7
those boys	61	90	100
them boys	60	22	0
sick at the stomach	32	26	13
sick in the stomach	13	3	0
sick to the stomach	52	68	94
back of (the door	26	27	31
in back of (the door	8	7	0
behind	71	73	75
toward	40	54	100
towards	63	48	0
died from	31	33	44
died of	45	59	63
died with	29	8	0

Although certain gross matters of pronunciation have sometimes been labeled "incorrect" in the schools, the three-point social range investigated in dialect research provides a sounder description of the social contrasts discernible in phonological variation. While most of the phonological differences revealed in the field records of the Upper Midwest survey are only regionally significant, a number manifest social contrast as well. They occur in several categories.

Stress variation exhibits social correlation in a few words. Among Type I and Type II informants, for instance, the proportion favoring initial stress in the verb *address* is twice as high as among those in Type III. Nearly one-half of the least educated speakers have initial stress in *umbrella,* but only one-fifth of the college group do. One-fourth of the Type I's have primary or secondary stress on the second syllable of *theater,* but only 6% of the Type III's. A conspicuous example is the pronunciation of *genuine.* The least educated speakers strongly favor heavy stress on the final syllable; the cultivated speakers favor zero stress, with corresponding reduction of the vowel to /ɪ/. A similar contrast occurs with *guardian,* with 34% of the Type I informants favoring /gɑrdín/ while all the cultivated speakers have /gɑ́rdìən/.

Stress variation

		Type I	Type II	Type III
address, *vb.*	/ǽdrès/	26%	25%	11%
genuine	/ǰɛ́nyuɪn/	17	47	86
	/ǰɛ́nyuwàɪn/	83	54	14
guardian	/gɑ̀rdín/	34	15	0
theater	/θí-êtɚ/	23	8	6
	/θíətɚ/	64	78	63
	/θɪətɚ/	13	14	31
umbrella	/ə́mbrɛ̀lə/	44	24	19

Vowel variation may create social markers. *LAUM* reports that the pronunciation of *root* as /rut/, although accepted by one-third of the Type I and Type II speakers, is preferred over /rʊt/ by only 13% of the college group. The same checked vowel /ʊ/ in *soot* is the choice of one-half of the least educated speakers but by nine out of ten of the Type III's. None of the latter group has the pronunciation /sət/, the choice of one-third of the Type I speakers. A few of the Type I's have adopted what must be a spelling pronunciation, /sut/. Two variants of *yolk,* /yɛlk/ and /yʊlk/, are favored by Type I speakers over the customary /yok/. The pronunciation /rɛdɪš/ is normal for one-third of the least educated but rare among college-trained speakers. The form /kæg/ for *keg* is a minor social marker, with 15% preference in Type I and no use at all by Type III's. In Minnesota and North Dakota /ɑnt/ and /ænt/ have become social markers, with the former pronunciation of *aunt* preferred by 32% of the Type III speakers and even by 15% of those in Type I. And for speakers stressing the first syllable in *theater* there is a choice of free and checked vowels. More common is /i/, but twice as high a proportion of Type II's selected checked /ɪ/, a pronunciation apparently associated by these informants with the French and British spelling *theatre.*

Vowel variation

		Type I	*Type II*	*Type III*
aunt	/ɑnt/	15%	21%	32%
keg	/kæg/	16	5	0
radish	/rɛdɪš/	33	22	6
root	/rut/	33	35	13
	/rʊt/	76	66	87
soot	/sut/	18	8	13
	/sʊt/	51	73	88
	/sət/	34	18	0
yolk	/yɛlk/ }	31	19	6
	/yʊlk/ }			

Even an unstressed vowel in terminal position manifests socially correlated variations. All the college-educated informants have final /o/ in *minnow* (excepting one with /u/), but the folk speech /mɪni/ is found in the speech of one-fourth of the Type I's. A few of them also have the variation with final /u/. For *meadow* and *widow* a pronunciation with final /ə/ is a minor social marker; for *tomato* it is much more significant, with its use by more than one-half of the Type I speakers.

Terminal reduction Vowel

		Type I	*Type II*	*Type III*
meadow	/mɛdo/	78%	93%	92%
	/mɛdə/	14	2	0
	/mɛdu/	9	8	8
minnow	/mɪni/	25	12	0
	/mɪno/	67	83	100
	/mɪnu/	10	12	6
tomato	/təméto/	46	62	73
	/tərmétə/	54	38	27
widow	/wɪdo/	55	71	82
	/wɪdə/	14	4	0
	/wɪdu/	30	25	18

An apparent epenthetic or anaptyptic vowel exhibits social contrast. It seems to be induced by initial stress in *umbrella,* for the same speakers have both, nearly always in Type I. A similar vowel in *mushroom,* however, is actually historical, as the French etymon is *mousseron* and orthographic variants with medial *e* have persisted since the early 15th century. It is preserved in the speech of one-fourth of the least educated informants, but is rare in the speech of the others. Incidentally, a final *n* instead of *m*, likewise historical, is also preserved largely by Type I speakers, 55% of whom have it beside only 20% of the college group. Another example of the epenthetic schwa may actually be a reduced form of the pronoun *it*. For the injunction *Look here!* 42% of the Type I speakers have either /lʊkəhɪr/ or /lʊkɪthɪr/, with the incidence dropping to one-third in Type II and only 14% in Type III.

A nonhistorical excrescent /t/ is a sharp social feature. It occurs after /s/, with 26% of the Type I informants and 14% of the Type II's adding it to *once* and *across* (but no college graduates), and after /f/, with 18% of the Type I informants and eight percent of the Type II's adding it to *skiff, cliff,* or *trough* (but no college graduates).

Although replacement of terminal velar /ŋ/ by alveolar /n/ is common in the verbal ending *ing*, its presence in the words *nothing* and *something* is much more definitely of social significance. More than one-third of the Type I's say /nə́θɪn/ but only 6% of the Type III's. One-fourth of the Type I's say /sə́mθɪn/ or the assimilated form /sə́mpʔm/, but only 13% of the Type III's.

Addition and replacement

		Type I	Type II	Type III
Look here!	/lʊkəhɪr/			
	/lʊkɪthɪr/	42%	33%	14%
	/lukɪthɪr/			
mushroom	/mə́šrum/	46	75	87
	/mə́šrun/	55	23	20
	/mə́šərun/	23	9	6
nothing	/nə́θɪn/	35	17	6
something	/sə́mθɪn, sə́mpʔm/	25	20	13
umbrella	/ə́mbərèlə/	44	24	19

The historical tendency toward the reduction or simplification of consonant clusters manifests itself with greater strength among the uneducated, except perhaps for the initial cluster /hw/. There the unaspirated variant /w/ is becoming more acceptable to many speakers in Types II and III, as in *wheel, whetstone, white,* and *whip,* though apparently not in *wheat*. Generally Upper Midwest speakers seem to retain initial /h/, especially in Minnesota and North Dakota. But the initial cluster /hy/ has been reduced to simple /y/ for more than one-half of the Type I informants, largely in Iowa and Nebraska, and for one-fifth of the college group.

The final *sts* cluster in several words tends to be retained by cultivated speakers. *Fists,* for instance, is /fɪs·/ or /fɪs·t/ for 75% of the Type I speakers but for only 44% of the Type III's. In two words, *library* and *secretary,* simplification may have been reinforced by the tendency toward dissimilation. *Library* is simply /laibɛri/ for 28% of the Type I informants but for only 12% of the Type III's; and *secretary* is /sɛkɪtɛri/ for 57% of the Type I speakers, and for more than one-fourth of the Type II's, but for only six percent of the Type III's. The cluster /nd/ in *hundred* is reduced to /n/ in the pronunciation /hə́nəʳd/ recorded in the speech of 18% of the Type I and 15% of the Type II informants. No Type III informant was heard to use it.

Cluster simplification

		Type I	*Type II*	*Type III*
fists	/fɪsts/	28%	44%	56%
	/fɪs·t/	19	5	13
	/fɪs·/	56	13	31
humor	/yumɚ/	54	29	20
	/hyumɚ/	43	70	80
hundred	/hʌ́nɚd/	18	15	0
library	/laibrɛri/	70	75	94
	/laibɛri/	28	21	12
secretary	/sɛkrɪtɛri/	39	74	94
	/sɛkɪtɛri/	57	27	6

Spelling pronunciation, the use of the visual form as a guide to the oral form, does not always result from the same factors in yielding a social contrast. The school emphasis upon spelling as the criterion may cause a change in the pronunciation of a familiar word, or sudden encounter with an unfamiliar word may lead to a plausible but nonhistorical pronunciation.

Of the several notable instances in *LAUM*, one, the pronunciation of *mongrel* with visually-suggested /ɑ/ rather than the historical /ə/ otherwise accepted unquestioningly in such words as *money, monkey,* and *wonder,* is usual among college graduates but chosen by but not much more than one-half of the less educated informants. But other examples of spelling pronunciation illustrate a readier acceptance of spelling as a guide by folk speakers. Although one-half of the college informants are sufficiently bemused by the *phth* combination in *diphtheria* to pronounce the obvious first letter and overlook the second, 95% of the Type I informants accept the same solution to the problem with the pronunciation of the first syllable as simple /dɪp/. Nearly one-half of the least educated follow analogous *earth* in their pronunciation of *hearth;* only seven percent of Type III do. One-fourth of the Type I informants have a spelling pronunciation of *palm* with the voiced /l/; only seven percent of the college speakers do. Nearly one-fourth of the Type I's have /s/ in *raspberries* instead of /z/; none of the college informants does.

Although too sporadic to be relied upon as social markers, a number of aberrant pronunciations appear almost exclusively in the speech of Type I informants and hence

Spelling pronunciation

		Type I	*Type II*	*Type III*
diphtheria	/dɪfθɪryə/	5%	18%	50%
	/dɪpθɪryə/	95	82	50
hearth	/hɚθ/	44	26	7
mongrel	/mʌ́ŋgrəl/	43	31	18
	/mɑ́ŋgrəl/	57	69	82
palm	/pɑlm/	25	29	7

do have some value in supporting social categorization. One is the pronunciation /čímbli/ for *chimney;* another is the use of the affricate in either /rɪnč/ or /rɛnč/ for *rinse.* Two lisped pronunciations of /θ/ occur as /f/ in /drauf/ for *drouth* and in /mæfyu/ for *Matthew.* And the Midland preterit or participial ending /t/ rather than /d/ is preserved almost entirely by Type I informants in their versions of *boiled, spoiled,* and *scared.*

Sociologists have quite ignored such data as this article presents in their various attempts to define social classes and subclasses by means of educational and socioeconomic criterions. Sociolinguists have neglected the rich source of relevant data in linguistic atlas field records. In the teaching of English little attention has been placed upon this kind of information. But perhaps now the more readily accessible facts in *LAUM* will be found useful by them in their studies of social mobility and their sometimes imperfect recognition of a range or dimension rather than neatly tiered social classes and usage levels.

DISCUSSION QUESTIONS

1. What factors must be considered in interpreting field data?

2. Why might vocabulary items exhibit little social variation? Is this generally true of vocabulary?

3. Collect and study correlations of socially contrasting forms you have personally encountered.

4. If you are outside the Upper Midwest, do you think the relative figures for the frequency are different for your region? With what items and why?

BRUCE FRASER

With a B.E.E. from Cornell University and a doctorate in linguistics from the Massachusetts Institute of Technology, Fraser is currently professor of education and director of the Program for the Study of Language Behavior at Boston University. Among his many publications is The Verb-Particle Combination in English *(Academic Press, 1976).*

SOME 'UNEXPECTED' REACTIONS TO VARIOUS AMERICAN-ENGLISH DIALECTS[1]

0. INTRODUCTION

There is general agreement that the way a person speaks is often coupled—frequently with little or no justification—with a stereotypic level of education, social status, degree of friendliness, and so forth. Advertising agencies have long recognized this and used it effectively. Imagine the red-neck sheriff in the Dodge commercial speaking like Rod Serling. Or imagine Casey Stengel as the doctor on an aspirin commercial. However, we know little at present about the way(s) in which particular features of speech trigger off a certain stereotype in a different speech group.

The experiment reported on here is a modified version of an experiment designed and carried out by Tucker and Lambert, hereafter T-L. (G. Richard Tucker and Wallace E. Lambert, White and negro listeners' reactions to various American-English dialects, Social Forces, 47(4), June 1969.) The purpose of the T-L experiment and ours as well is to indirectly assess the view that one group holds of a second based solely on the recorded speech of the second group.

> Described briefly, a sample of 'judges' is asked to listen to a series of taped recordings of different speakers reading a standard passage, and to evaluate relevant personality characteristics of each speaker, using only voice characteristics and speech style as cues. The technique appears to expose the listeners' more private feelings and stereotyped attitudes towards a contrasting group or groups whose language, accent, or dialect is distinctive, and it appears to be reliable in that the same profile of reactions emerges on repeated sampling from a particular social group.
>
> (T-L, pp. 463–64)

The T-L experiment was developed to answer two questions: are both black and white subjects able to correctly differentiate between dialects; and if so, does any meaningful pattern emerge? The statistical analysis T-L carried out on their data clearly

---

[1] The work reported here was supported by Ford Foundation Grant No. 700-0656 to the Language Research Foundation. I would like to thank Richard Tucker for making available his tapes of dialect speakers to me, and Mary Selkirk for her valuable assistance in calculating the results.

showed that each group of judges differentiates the various dialects, and that some dialect groups were consistently assessed more favorably than others along the various characteristic continua. Our experiment was intended to verify the original T-L results but also to shed light on the following, third, question: does subject judgment of speaker race correlate with his overall evaluation of the speaker?

1. THE EXPERIMENT

1.1. Rating Scale

The scales of the T-L experiment were chosen to meet two criteria:

> (a) positive ratings should indicate that the listener believes the speakers could attain or have already attained success; and (b) that speakers are 'friendly'. Thus, success should not imply separation from or mobility out of the group represented by the speaker.
>
> (T-L, p. 464)

Pilot work with both black and white college students to determine their criteria for both friendship and success as well as two traits (standardness of speech and good upbringing) added by T-L resulted in a set of 15 criteria. They were: Upbringing, Intelligent, Friendly, Educated, Disposition, Speech, Trustworthy, Ambitious, Faith in God, Talented, Character, Determination, Honest, Personality, and Considerate. Each trait could range from 1 to 8 (arbitrarily chosen); for example, an '8' rating for Educated meant that the subject perceived the speaker as highly educated, while a '2' rating for Honest meant that the speaker was perceived as very dishonest. For our experiment, we eliminated six of the T-L traits: Upbringing, Disposition, Faith in God, Character, Personality, and Considerate. This left us with 9 traits which are numbered sequentially in all presentation of our results.

1.2. Stimulus Voices

The T-L experiment used recordings of 24 speakers: 4 representatives of 6 dialect groups. The groups were:

(1) Radio announcers (Network speakers)
(2) College-educated white southerners (CEWS speakers)
(3) College-educated black southerners (CEBS speakers)
(4) College-educated black speakers from Mississippi presently attending Howard University in Washington, D.C. (HU speakers)
(5) Southern black students from a small all-black southern college in Mississippi (Miss. Peer)
(6) College-educated black southerners presently living in New York City (NY Alumni)

All speakers in groups 1 and 2 were white; all in groups 3–6 were black. Both male and female speakers were chosen for each group except for the CEWS group which, due to an oversight, contained only male speakers. T-L made two tapes: each consisting of a practice speaker followed by 12 speakers, two speakers from each of the six groups. Each speaker read a passage about English composition (45 seconds approximately) followed by a 30-second pause; the next speaker followed this pause. In our experiment, we used only the T-L tape B which had two female speakers from CEBS, HU, and Miss. Peer groups and two male speakers from the CEWS, Network, and NY Alumni groups. In addition, our version of the B tape omitted the second recording of the passage. It was our conclusion that, because we were using only one tape with a fixed order of speakers, it was important to reduce the overall time of the experiment to maintain interest level so that the later speakers would not systematically suffer in the evaluation.

1.3. Subjects

Subjects were 50 male and female students enrolled in T-60, Child Language, at the Harvard Graduate School of Education, Fall, 1971. Of these subjects, four were black. Of these four, two filled out their evaluation forms with all 4's or 8's, so as not to influence the relative evaluation of the speakers by their white co-students.

1.4. Experimental Procedure

The experiment was run in the normal classroom with the 50 subjects plus some auditors and non-subjects. The subjects were asked to listen to the voices on the tape and to rate each speaker from 1–8 in terms of the nine traits listed on the evaluation sheet as well as judge the race of the speaker. A separate rating sheet was provided for the evaluation of each speaker; the order of the traits was the same on each sheet. The practice voice was played, the subjects were asked to make their evaluation in the 30 seconds following, and questions relating to the experimental procedure were then answered. Following that, the modified T-L tape B was played without interruption.

2.0. RESULTS AND DISCUSSION

2.1. Correspondence to the T-L Experiment

The results summarized in Table 1 follow closely the results of the T-L experiment for northern white university students. The mean rating for each group was computed by taking the mean of all 50 subjects for both speakers of that group. For example, one of the Network speakers had a mean of 5.8 for the trait Trustworthy, the second a rating of 4.5. These two, combined, averaged to 5.2, rounding off (always) to the next highest tenth. The figure 5.2 is what is found in Table 1. The second number in each cell is the ranking for that group for that particular trait. For example, the CEWS group was ranked third for the trait Intelligent. When two groups had the same mean rating, they received the same ranking. For example, the NY Alumni and CEWS groups both had a 5.3 rating for Friendly; they were both ranked third. The column marked 'Sum' is the total, for each group, of the ranking for each trait. The sums, in increasing order, indicate a decreasing overall rating of the groups. The column 'T-L Sum' shows the relative ratings found for the equivalent part of the T-L experiment. (Note: the magnitude of the T-L sums is considerably larger because they were using 15 rather than 9 traits.)

The overall ranking of our experiment and the T-L one is the same with the exception of the reversed order of the HU and CEWS groups. In the T-L case, however, the gap between the Network and CEBS groups was considerably larger: the Network to CEBS ratio of rankings was 18:39 while for our experiment, it was 14:20. Whereas the T-L experiment found the main break between the Network and the CEBS groups, we found it between the CEBS and CEWS groups.

Table 1 Mean ratings and ranks of mean ratings of each group

	Trait										
Group	Intelligent	Friendly	Educated	Speech	Trustworthy	Ambitious	Talented	Determination	Honest	Sum	T-L Sum
	1	2	3	4	5	6	7	8	9		
Network	6.3	5.4	6.5	6.8	5.2	5.7	5.5	5.7	5.4	14	18
	[1]	[2]	[1]	[1]	[2]	[2]	[1]	[2]	[2]		
CEBS	5.7	5.3	5.6	5.4	5.1	5.9	5.3	6.1	5.1	20	39
	[2]	[3]	[2]	[2]	[3]	[1]	[2]	[1]	[4]		
Howard	5.6	5.5	5.3	5.0	5.5	5.1	5.1	5.2	5.5	24	48
	[3]	[1]	[4]	[4]	[1]	[3]	[3]	[4]	[1]		
CEWS	5.5	5.1	5.5	5.3	4.9	5.1	4.9	5.3	5.0	33	44
	[4]	[4]	[3]	[3]	[4]	[3]	[4]	[3]	[5]		
NY Alum.	5.0	5.3	4.6	4.3	5.1	5.0	4.8	5.1	5.3	38	80
	[5]	[3]	[5]	[5]	[3]	[4]	[5]	[5]	[3]		
Miss. Peer	5.0	5.1	4.5	4.0	5.1	4.8	4.7	5.0	5.3	44	85
	[5]	[4]	[6]	[6]	[3]	[5]	[6]	[6]	[3]		

Table 2 Comparison of mean ratings for those who misjudged race to the mean ratings for all subjects

	Trait										
Group	Intelligent	Friendly	Educated	Speech	Trustworthy	Ambitious	Talented	Determination	Honest	% Wrong race	T-L % Wrong race
	1	2	3	4	5	6	7	8	9		
Network	6.3	5.4	6.5	6.8	5.2	5.7	5.5	5.7	5.4	1%B	5%B
	—	—	—	—	—	—	—	—	—	—	—
CEBS	5.7	5.3	5.6	5.4	5.1	5.9	5.3	6.1	5.1	28%W	51%W
	4.8	5.0	4.8	5.1	4.7	5.3	4.3	5.5	4.9		
Howard	5.6	5.5	5.3	5.0	5.5	5.1	5.1	5.2	5.5	10%W	14%W
	4.9	4.8	5.0	5.2	4.8	4.3	4.0	4.3	4.3		
CEWS	5.5	5.1	5.5	5.3	4.9	5.1	4.9	5.3	5.0	12%B	13%B
	5.5	4.8	5.5	5.3	4.6	5.1	5.1	5.1	4.6		
NY Alum.	5.0	5.3	4.6	4.3	5.1	5.0	4.8	5.1	5.3	40%W	51%W
	4.8	5.1	4.4	4.4	5.0	4.9	4.7	5.0	5.2		
Miss. Peer	5.0	5.1	4.5	4.0	5.1	4.8	4.7	5.0	5.3	5%W	6%W
	4.5	4.5	4.3	4.0	4.3	4.3	4.4	4.5	4.5		

2.2. New Results

The most interesting result, however, is presented in Table 2. Leaving aside misjudgments for the Network and Mississippi Peer groups because the percentage is so small, we find the following phenomenon: when the speaker was black, and when subjects misjudged the race of the speaker, they tended, in general, to rate the speaker lower in all categories. There are two exceptions: the Speech of the HU and NY Alumni were rated higher when the speaker was judged white. On the other hand, when the speaker was white (the CEWS group) and when the race of the speaker was misjudged, the subjects did not tend, in general, to rate the speaker lower than the average. (They rated the speakers higher in one, the same in four, and lower in four traits.)

Before drawing any conclusions, it is worth considering whether or not these misjudgers are, on the average, just low evaluators. If this were the case, it would explain the relative lower ratings. Table 3 provides a comparison to the average of the mean ratings of those subjects who missed more than one race identification for those cases where they judged correctly—the Network and Mississippi Peer groups.

Table 3 Comparison of mean ratings for subjects who misjudged race to overall mean ratings for Network and Mississippi Peer groups

					Traits				
Group	Intelligent	Friendly	Educated	Speech	Trustworthy	Ambitious	Talented	Determination	Honest
	1	2	3	4	5	6	7	8	9
Network									
Overall mean	6.3	5.4	6.5	6.8	5.2	5.7	5.5	5.7	5.4
Misjudgers' mean	6.2	5.6	6.3	6.7	5.3	5.5	5.5	5.9	5.5
Deviation	− .1	+ .2	− .2	− .1	+ .1	− .2	.0	+ .2	+ .1
Miss. Peer									
Overall mean	5.0	5.1	4.5	4.0	5.1	4.8	4.7	5.0	5.3
Misjudgers' mean	4.7	5.0	4.4	4.2	4.9	4.5	4.4	4.8	5.1
Deviation	− .3	− .1	− .1	+ .2	− .2	− .3	− .3	− .2	− .2

Table 3 shows that those who misjudged the black speakers did not, in general, rate Network speakers lower than the overall average for each trait. (Four were higher, one the same, four lower.) They did tend to rate the Miss. Peer group lower than the average (except for Speech). However, this lower rating, while approximately equal to that in judging the NY Alumni group when they misjudged the race, was nowhere as great as in the CEBS or HU groups, when they also misjudged race.

What, then, explains the data in Table 2? Although there are many hypotheses compatible with the results, the following strikes me as an explanation worth consideration. Assume that for every dialect group, however such a group is to be ultimately defined, has developed a stereotypic pairing function which maps each point on a scale called 'Manner of Speaking' (linguistic features such as pronunciation, syntactic form, choice of words, intonation, rate of speech, voice quality, and so forth) onto a scale for certain character traits, for example, those used in the experiment. For example, the dialect group represented by large northern university graduate students might pair a high degree of 'standardness' of speech (that of the Network group) with a high degree of education but a less high degree of trust. And so forth. Now assume that this pairing is race-dependent. That is, given a level of speech the pairing has one set of values for white speakers, for example, but another for black speakers. If, for a given manner of speaking, this pairing showed higher values for black as opposed to white speakers, this would account for the data in Tables 2 and 3. Stated another way, it wasn't that the misjudgers in the experiment were rating low, but that the correct judgers were rating high. This explanation also accounts for the fact that those who misjudged the race for the CEBS, HU, and NY Alumni groups (cf. Table 2) rated the Speech the same or higher than the overall average while rating other traits lower.

3. CONCLUSION

It is not surprising that the subject group of university graduate students systematically ranked the dialect groups as in the T-L experiment, nor that they characteristically misjudged the race of the CEBS, HU, or NY Alumni groups. What is interesting is the extent to which the rating seems affected by the perceived race of the speaker.

Before one exclaims that here is yet another form of covert racism, I suggest that this phenomenon is hardly rare. We will surely find the same sort of scale-sliding across wide ranges of ethnic groups, regional groups, and, if made obvious, across religious groups. The simple fact is that people will judge differentially on the basis of certain cues—in this case speech alone—because of their experience and certain, albeit inaccurate, stereotypes. No amount of research and breast beating is going to erase these stereotypes, at least in the foreseeable future. However, I suggest that research along the lines discussed above can and should be used to make various (dialect) groups aware of what stereotypes they hold and the ways in which they view other groups, so that they may take steps to counteract this attitude when it is clearly beside the point.

DISCUSSION QUESTIONS

1. Does it seem likely that intelligence, friendliness, and honesty can be accurately correlated with voice characteristics when all the tapes are of the same passage?

2. Fraser suggests that although both Blacks and whites are included here, other groups might be similarly studied. What other groups would you suggest, and why?

3. Have you found yourself making an evaluation of a person on the basis of a telephone conversation? What voice characteristics influenced you? Were you led to change your mind upon meeting the person?

ANTHONY S. KROCH

After completing his doctorate at Massachusetts Institute of Technology in 1974, Kroch began his teaching career at the University of Connecticut. After a brief stint at Temple University he is now in the department of linguistics at the University of Pennsylvania.

TOWARD A THEORY OF SOCIAL DIALECT VARIATION

INTRODUCTION

Over the past ten years the study of language in its social context has become a mature field with a substantial body of method and empirical results.[1] As a result of this work we are arriving at new insights into such classical problems as the origin and diffusion of linguistic change, the nature of stylistic variation in language use, and the effect of class structure on linguistic variation within a speech community. Advances in socio-linguistics have been most evident in the study of co-variation between social context and the sound pattern of speech. The results reported in numerous monographs have laid the basis for substantial theoretical progress in our understanding of the factors that govern dialect variation in stratified communities, at least in its phonological aspect.[2] The formulation of theories of the causes of phonological variation that go beyond guesswork and vague generalities appears at last to be possible. Therefore, we offer the following discussion, based on the material that is now available, as a contribution to the development of an explanatory theory of the mechanisms underlying social dialect variation. Although we shall state our views strongly, we know that they are far from definitive. We present them, not as positions to be defended at all costs, but as stimuli to further theoretical reflection in a field that has been, thus far, descriptively oriented.

The thrust of our proposal can be expressed in the form of the following two-part hypothesis that, while not exhaustive, covers a wide range of recently investigated cases: *First,* the public prestige dialect[3] of the elite in a stratified community differs from the

---

[1] I want to thank the many people, too numerous to mention, who have read and commented on an earlier version of this paper. Special thanks must go to W. Labov, whose comments have been so helpful to me in revising the paper for publication.

[2] This paper directly concerns only the phonological aspect of social dialect variation and, therefore, it cannot hope to present a comprehensive theory of variation. There may well be important parallels between variation and change at the phonological and at other levels; but claims about the one certainly cannot be extended to the others in any direct or automatic way. In our opinion further empirical studies of syntactic and semantic variation will be necessary before it becomes possible to propose substantial theoretical hypotheses in these areas.

[3] The exact relationship between this dialect and the social elite is far from clear at present. For one thing the dialect seems most characteristic not of an economic and/or political ruling class but of the professional representatives of the dominant culture; i.e. the elite in such professions as academia, the law, business management, medicine and the mass media.

dialect(s) of the non-elite strata (working class and other) in at least one phonologically systematic way.[4] In particular, it characteristically resists normal processes of phonetic conditioning (both articulatory and perceptual) that the speech of non-elite strata regularly undergo. This tendency holds both for dynamic processes of linguistic change and for diachronically stable processes of inherent variation.[5] *Second*, the cause of stratified phonological differentiation within a speech community is to be sought not in purely linguistic factors but in ideology. Dominant social groups tend to mark themselves off symbolically as distinct from the groups they dominate and to interpret their symbols of distinctiveness as evidence of superior moral and intellectual qualities. This tendency shows itself not only in speech style but also in such other areas of social symbolism as dress, body carriage, and food. In all these areas dominant groups mark themselves off by introducing elaborated styles and by borrowing from external prestige groups; but in the case of pronunciation they also mark their distinctiveness in a negative way—that is by inhibiting many of the low level, variable processes of phonetic conditioning that characterize spoken language and that underlie regular phonological change. Because these processes are of variable application, they admit readily of non-linguistic influences. Of course, since the different social strata belong to the same speech community, their speech patterns influence one another profoundly. Processes that originate in the popular vernacular infiltrate the prestige dialect and processes of the prestige dialect extend to popular speech. The extent of these mutual influences is variable from case to case, depending on such social factors as the degree of linguistic self-consciousness of the prestige dialect speakers and the strength of their ideological influence on the population as a whole (see Barber 1964). It depends as well on a complex of linguistic, articulatory and perceptual factors.

In the discussion that follows we shall attempt to confirm this hypothesis by investigating, on the one hand, recent descriptions of the phonological differences among social dialects and, on the other hand, the evidence that has become available concerning the ideological motivation for these differences. We shall discover that popular dialects exhibit their greater susceptibility to phonetic conditioning in such features as simplified articulation, replacement or loss of perceptually weak segments, and a greater tendency

---

[4] Our discussion of phonological differentiation must be limited to contexts where there are established prestige dialects. Dialects which are in the process of becoming established, say as standard languages, may easily be less conservative phonetically than the local vernaculars they replace. In the historical process whereby the standard languages of Europe, for example, arose the relationship between prestige and vernacular dialects was quite different from the one we shall be discussing between established prestige dialects and their vernaculars.

[5] This view is, of course, not original with us. For example, H. G. Schogt (1961) says:

Passant maintenant à l'examen des couches sociales d'un seul dialecte géographique, nous constatons deux forces opposées: la langue populaire riche en innovations, qui a pour elle le grand nombre, et la langue des classes aisées, qui est plus conservatrice et qui s'impose par son prestige (p. 91).

[Passing now to the examination of the social strata of a single geographic dialect, we ascertain two opposed forces: the popular language, rich in innovations, which has numbers on its side, and the language of the well-to-do classes, which is more conservative and imposes itself by its prestige.]

The point of our paper is to show that the evidence made available by recent sociolinguistic research can be interpreted so as to support and elaborate this perspective.

to undergo 'natural' vowel shifts.[6] As far as ideology is concerned, we shall see that there is both experimental and historical evidence that prestige dialects require special attention to speech, attention motivated not by the needs of communication but by status consciousness.

CURRENT THEORY OF DIALECT DIFFERENTIATION

Before we proceed with our argument, let us clarify the difference between our hypothesis and others' explanations for social dialect variation. In particular, we must state explicitly the relationship between our views and those of Labov, since his work provides so much of the empirical material available to theoretical reflection. Labov's research has generated considerable evidence for the proposition that working-class speech is more susceptible to the processes of phonetic conditioning than is the prestige dialect. Unfortunately, Labov and other contemporary sociolinguists neither state this principle explicitly nor attempt to provide an explanation for it. Indeed, Labov is not willing to make a clear empirical claim on the linguistic character of social dialect variation. His theoretical statements sometimes point towards our characterization of social dialect differences, but on other occasions he seems to take a position contrary to our proposal.

In the article 'The social setting of linguistic change,' Labov states that ordinary phonological change, what he calls 'change from below the level of conscious awareness,' generally does not originate in the highest status group in a speech community. He says:

> It does sometimes happen that a feature will be introduced by the highest class in the social system, though as a rule this is not an innovating group.
>
> (Labov 1972: 295)

Changes which are introduced by the highest class tend to be conscious attempts to imitate an even more prestigious dialect outside the local area:

> Innovation by the highest-status group is normally a form of borrowing from outside sources, more or less conscious; with some exceptions these will be prestige forms.
>
> (Labov 1972: 290)

In a more recent article, however, he says:

> Dialect differentiation is not confined to uneducated, lower-class people. It is well known that some linguistic changes originate in the upper social groups. Many of these represent the importation of forms from high-prestige foreign languages or classical standards. But some new developments seem to be pushed fa[r]ther and faster among educated speakers, at least until the change becomes noticed and subject to strong social correction.
>
> (Labov 1974: 224)

---

[6] By ' "natural" vowel shifts' we mean regular changes in vowel quality, especially chain shifts, which appear frequently in diverse languages and which seem to have a phonetic motivation, but for which there is as yet no adequate phonetic theory. Thus, we use the term 'natural' in an informal sense to indicate a faith in an eventual substantive (as opposed to formal) explanation of the phenomena, not out of adherence to any theory of naturalness. For systematic exposition of a substantive perspective on phonology see, among others, Lindblom (1971) and Chen & Wang (1975).

In his extensive study of vowel shifts currently in progress in English dialects (Labov, Yaeger & Steiner 1972) Labov does indicate that these shifts seem to originate in the popular vernacular, but elsewhere he explicitly denies the existence of processes of phonetic conditioning in that dialect. For example, he denies that the vernacular differs from the prestige dialect in ease of articulation. In the 'Study of language in its social context,' he says:

> Why don't all people speak the prestige dialect? The usual response is to cite laziness, lack of concern, or isolation from the prestige norm. But there is no foundation for the notion that stigmatized vernacular forms are easier to pronounce.
>
> (Labov 1972: 249)

In this passage, Labov is clearly concerned with discrediting the class-prejudiced notion that the working class vernacular is an inferior or 'lazy' dialect. He is, of course, correct to want to defeat this prejudice; but the proper way to do so is not to deny the fact, obvious from his own research, that non-prestige dialects tend to be articulatorily more economical than the prestige dialect. Defeat of prejudice requires rather that we give a better explanation of this fact than the laziness 'theory' provides. The only evidence Labov gives that vernacular forms are not easier to pronounce is that the vowel shifts in progress in urban working class vernaculars increase the muscular effort needed to pronounce tense vowels over that required in standard English. This point is, however, irrelevant to the existence of a tendency toward ease of articulation because that tendency manifests itself primarily in the consonant system, which Labov does not mention. On another point, Labov's statement explicitly equates ease of pronunciation with 'laziness' and lets the reader believe that if the non-prestige dialect were easier to pronounce, then the charge of laziness would be valid. This is, of course, not so as we shall see in our discussion of the motivation of social dialect differences.

One of the reasons why Labov and other sociolinguists have not seen the link between phonetic conditioning and social dialect variation more clearly is that linguists' traditional attitudes toward this variation are incompatible with the relationship that recent studies have revealed. Because these attitudes, in one form or another, underlie most sociolinguistic theory, including the best and most recent work, the implications of the empirical research have been obscured.

The central assumption of linguists about the origin of dialect variation has been that when sound changes arise in the speech of individuals or small groups, the further spread of these changes depends on the prestige of their users. Under this assumption there is no reason to expect the speech of non-elite groups to be more susceptible to phonetic processes than that of the elite. Indeed, it would lead one to expect either that social dialect variation was phonologically unsystematic or that the speech of the elite showed more phonetic conditioning than that of the common people. The first alternative results if one assumes that sound change is not governed by substantive factors (as in Postal 1968), the second if one assumes that sound change is so governed. A position close to this latter is put forward in Joos (1952) and argued for in Fischer (1964), although neither gives any empirical findings to support his claim. Fischer says (quoting Joos's comment in its entirety):

> The clearest and most comprehensive statement of social factors in linguistic change which I have encountered is found in an article by Martin Joos (1952). . . . He speaks of 'the phonetic drift, which was kept going in the usual way: that is, the dialects and

idiolects of higher prestige were more advanced in this direction, and their speakers carried the drift further along so as to maintain the prestige-marking differences against their pursuers. The vanity factor is needed to explain why phonetic drifts tend to continue in the same direction; the "inertia" sometimes invoked is a label and not an argument.' This protracted pursuit of an elite by an envious mass and the consequent 'flight' of the elite is in my opinion the most important mechanism in linguistic drift, not only in the phonetic drift which Joos discusses, but in syntactic and lexical drifting as well.

(Fischer 1964: 286)

Of course, our view, as put forward in the introduction to this paper, contradicts all approaches that derive sound change from innovation by a prestige group. We are proposing instead that:

1. ordinary unconscious phonological changes are definitely not arbitrary but are, in general, phonetically motivated processes;
2. prestige is a secondary factor in the propagation of phonetically motivated linguistic changes, whose linguistic character is the original basis of their diffusion;
3. the main force of social prestige is to inhibit phonetically conditioned processes, both of change in progress and of stable inherent variation, in the speech of high status groups and those whom they influence.

These three propositions immediately imply that social dialect variation should be systematic and that popular speech should be more 'advanced' than the standard. The evidence which we shall provide in this paper will make it clear that they provide a better basis for sociolinguistic theory than the traditional view.

In view of his empirical work, it is surprising that Labov's theoretical position on the causes of variation and change is in some respects a version of the traditional view as we have outlined it. Labov does criticize Bloomfield and others for their assertion that new forms originate among speakers with the highest social status and are then borrowed by those of lesser status. He says:

Oddly enough, a great deal of the speculative literature on dialect borrowing is based on the notion that all movement of linguistic forms is from the higher-prestige group to the lower.

(Labov 1972: 286)

He then quotes a passage by Bloomfield that puts forward this view and comments:

This is simply a remark, with no more justification than any of the other general observations in Bloomfield's treatment of dialect borrowing. Studies of current sound changes show that a linguistic innovation can begin with any particular group and spread outward and that this is the normal development; that this one group can be the highest-status group, but not necessarily or even frequently so.

(Labov 1972: 286)

But although he rejects the notion that new forms originate at the top of the social hierarchy, he does not abandon the idea that the spread of linguistic innovations depends on the social prestige attached to them. Instead he proposes that popular speech has its own prestige, perhaps as a marker of local identity.[7] He suggests that a change often originates among individuals in a non-elite stratum and is then adopted by their peers, becoming a linguistic symbol of the group's solidarity. This view, which Labov has adapted from Ferguson & Gumperz (1960), we might call 'linguistic pluralism' because it maintains that different social groups within a language community have different prestige norms, much as pluralist social theory claims for those groups different interests and values generally. In this view linguistic variation in the speech of individuals when they switch between more and less formal speech styles is due to the opposition of values between the overall prestige value of the standard and the solidarity value of the popular vernacular.

Labov's linguistic pluralism is certainly less objectionable than earlier views of the popular vernacular as an imperfect imitation of standard speech. Because it still relies on the notion that arbitrary social values are the motive force behind phonological innovation and social dialect variation, however, it cannot adequately account for these phenomena. His theory still gives one no reason to expect the speech of the common people to be more open to phonetic conditioning than that of the elite. In fact, his pluralistic conception of prestige leads one to expect change to originate equally at all social levels and social dialect variation to be, therefore, linguistically random. Thus, the result of Labov's theoretical commitment is that where he notices the greater susceptibility to phonetic conditioning of popular dialects (i.e., in vowel shifting) he can give no explanation for it[8] and that he fails to recognize some of the ways in which this susceptibility manifests itself.

PHONETIC CONDITIONING IN SOCIAL DIALECTS

Having set out our theoretical perspective, we shall now present the evidence by which we justify it. We shall discuss the three main processes of change or inherent variation on which substantial empirical results are available, and we shall see that all three types

---

[7] In one place Labov puts his position as follows:

> A linguistic change begins as a local pattern characteristic of a particular social group, often the result of immigration from another region. It becomes generalized throughout the group, and becomes associated with the social values attributed to that group. It spreads to those neighboring populations which take the first group as a reference group in one way or another. The opposition of the two linguistic forms continues and often comes to symbolize an opposition of social values. These values may rise to the level of social consciousness and become *stereotypes*, subject to irregular social correction, or they may remain below that level as unconscious *markers*. Finally, one or the other of the two forms wins out. There follows a long period when the disappearing form is heard as archaic, a symbol of vanished prestige or stigma, and is used as a source of stereotyped humor until it is extinguished entirely.
>
> (Labov, Yaeger & Steiner 1972: 279)

For another statement of this position see Labov (1974: 250 ff.).

[8] Our analysis of Labov's views on the underlying causes of social dialect variation has the advantage of explaining one striking feature of his work: the contradiction between his empirical results and theoretical statements on sound change. The former universally point to the working class and lower middle class as the originators of sound change in contemporary American English; but the latter claim that sound change can originate in any social stratum.

more readily affect vernacular dialects than standard ones. The processes are: (1) consonantal simplifications, including both articulatory reductions and the loss or replacement of perceptually indistinct segments; (2) vocalic processes of chain shifting; and (3) assimilations of foreign phonemes to a native pattern. Of course, these processes do not exhaust the phonological differences between social dialects nor do they cover all possible kinds of phonetic conditioning in language.[9] Our purpose in presenting the material below is to provide evidence for our basic hypothesis, not to describe exhaustively the range of sociolinguistic phenomena.

Consonantal Simplification

In his study *The Social Stratification of English in New York City*, Labov described the variation of several phonological elements in the city. The consonantal elements were: (1) the initial consonant in words like *thing, theater, thought* (th); (2) the initial consonant in words like *then, the, there* (dh); (3) the final and preconsonantal /r/ in words like *car, bear, card, beard* (r).[10] He discovered that these elements were realized differently by different social classes and by the same social class in different situations. In particular, he found that in casual speech there was a regular correlation between a person's class position and his pronunciation of the elements listed. Lower position in the social hierarchy correlated with: (1) greater use of a lenis stop [t] or the affricate [tth] where standard pronunciation has the fricative [th]; (2) greater use of the voiced stop [d] or affricate [ddh] where standard pronunciation has the voiced affricate [dh]; (3) greater vocalization and dropping of final and preconsonantal /r/.

As far as stylistic variation was concerned, Labov found that in the most formal contexts speakers of all classes shifted their speech away from working class patterns and toward upper middle class norms. Figure 1 illustrates this stylistic and class variation in the dropping of final and preconsonantal /r/.

The data from Labov's study clearly exhibit the greater tendency toward simplification of consonant articulation that we have postulated for non-prestige dialects. The consonantal variables all exhibit articulatory simplification and all involve the loss or modification of perceptually indistinct segments. In the case of final and preconsonantal /r/ the vocalization or dropping of /r/ involves both an articulatory reduction that weakens or eliminates a tongue movement and the loss of a segment that is hard to distinguish from the preceding vowel. Also, the loss of /r/ before a consonant tends to create articulatorily more natural syllable structures in which consonant clusters are shortened or eliminated (Schane 1972). The substitution of stops for the fricatives [th] and [dh] eliminates segments that are at once difficult to articulate[11] and hard to distinguish from other fricatives.

---

[9] In particular it is not the case, nor are we claiming, that regular phonological processes can all be reduced to simplification of some sort. Simplified articulation is just one of the possible manifestations of phonetic conditioning. It happens to be a very common one that covers much of the available data.

[10] The dropping of word final *r* was studied only when the following word began with a consonant. Among white New Yorkers *r* is rarely dropped in the environment r # # V.

[11] The assertion that interdental fricatives are difficult to articulate is supported by a number of facts. Firstly, the sounds are relatively rare to the world's languages. Secondly, children learning to speak English acquire these sounds late. Thirdly, adult speakers learning English as a second language generally have difficulty mastering these sounds.

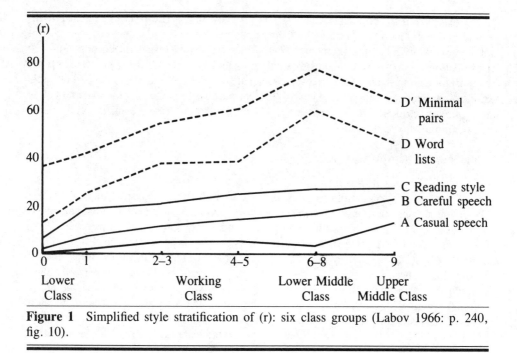

Figure 1 Simplified style stratification of (r): six class groups (Labov 1966: p. 240, fig. 10).

Data comparable to Labov's have been collected on Panamanian Spanish by Henrietta Cedergren (1970), on Brazilian Portuguese by Gregory Guy & Maria Luiza Braga (1976) and on Montreal French by William Kemp & Paul Pupier (1976); and all of them confirm our hypothesis concerning consonant articulation. Cedergren's study involved the following five linguistic variables:

    1. (R):   the devoicing fricativization, pharyngealization, and deletion of syllable-final /r/, with values ranging from 1 to 6 in the direction of these processes.

    2. (PARA):   the alternation of the full form of the preposition *para* with *pa* with values of 1 and 2 respectively.

    3. (ESTA):   alternation of the full form *esta* with *ta,* assigned values of 1 and 2 respectively.

    4. (S):   the syllable final alternation of [s], [h] and [∅] with values of 1, 2 and 3 respectively.

    5. (CH):   palatal versus retroflex and reduced stop onset of /č/, with values of 1 and 2 respectively.

                                             (Quoted in Labov 1972: 293–4.)

The results of Cedergren's study are summarized in Table 1. Each of the five variables shows distinct social variation and in each case the less prestigious social groups use the articulatorily reduced variants more often than does the most prestigious group. That the variants favored by the lower class groups are articulatorily simplified is clear. In the case of (R) and (S) the non-prestige speaker tends to weaken or delete a syllable final consonant. In the case of (PARA) and (ESTA) the non-prestige tendency is to drop an entire syllable. With (CH) no deletion is involved but the tendency is still to replace an energetically pronounced consonant with a weaker one.

Table 1   Social stratification of five Spanish variables in Panama (Cedergren 1970)

| | Social groups | | | |
Variable	I	II	III	IV
(R)	1.62	1.88	2.29	2.29
(PARA)	1.11	1.37	1.39	1.69
(ESTA)	1.26	1.56	1.62	1.71
(S)	2.03	2.24	2.31	2.36
(CH)	1.88	2.24	2.13	2.00

The highest social group is I, the lowest IV.

Guy & Braga (1976) studied the loss of redundant plural markers in Brazilian Portuguese noun phrases like the following:

1. *aqueles rapazes* 'those boys'.
2. *as minhas cadeiras* 'my chairs'.

They found a pronounced tendency for the plural morpheme to be deleted from non-initial elements of the noun phrase, often leaving only one marker of plurality per phrase. This articulatory simplification through the deletion of grammatically redundant consonantal segments was much more pronounced in 'lower class' than in 'middle class' speakers.

Kemp & Pupier (1976) studied consonant cluster reduction in Montreal French and found that in environments where this simplification was possible there was a regular and marked class stratification of simplification in the direction we would predict. Figure 2 summarizes their results.

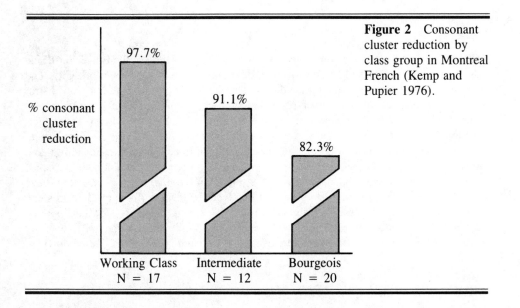

Figure 2   Consonant cluster reduction by class group in Montreal French (Kemp and Pupier 1976).

Aside from the specific consonant changes documented by Labov and others, there is a more general tendency towards simplifying consonantal atriculation that is favored by non-prestige dialects—that is, a tendency to favor the articulatory reductions of rapid speech. An informal pilot survey of eastern Connecticut speech patterns that we conducted indicates that working class casual speech favors some very marked articulatory reductions and assimilations. For example, we frequently found among working class speakers reduced forms like [nʔəm] for 'and them' or [wəsəmaetə] for 'what's the matter?' and assimilations like the palatalized [laešeiyə] for 'last year' or [wəčə duwɪn] for 'what are you doing'; such forms were rarer among middle class speakers.

The processes that go on in rapid or casual speech are perhaps the clearest examples of phonetically conditioned processes that linguists have discussed. Zwicky (1972) points out that:

> Casual speech processes seem to be constrained to be phonetically natural. In the extreme case they can be explained as the inevitable result of increasing speed of speech: the articulators simply cannot achieve their targets in the time available. This is the sort of explanation suggested by Lindblom (1963) for certain vowel reductions in fast speech.
>
> Even when such strong direct explanations are not available, casual speech processes are obviously 'euphonic', serving either ease—assimilation, neutralization, insertion of transitional sounds—or brevity—simplification of geminates, vowel contraction, deletion of weakly articulated segments, monophthongization.
>
> (Zwicky 1972: 608)

He also points out that different speakers use rapid speech forms more or less readily at a given rate of speech. What seems to be true of our informants is not that working class speakers speak more rapidly than middle class speakers but rather that they are more likely to use the reduction processes of rapid speech at a given rate of speech. Indeed, many of the consonantal variations across social class and speech style that have been catalogued could simply be reflexes of the greater openness of non-prestige groups to the euphonic processes of rapid speech.

Vowel Shifts

In addition to its findings on consonantal variables, Labov's study of the Lower East Side also shows that working class and lower middle class speakers in New York City tend to tense and raise low front and back vowels. This raising is part of a general vowel shift currently in progress in a number of American English dialects. Although there are detailed descriptions of vowel shifts in many languages, little is known about their functional effect on phonological systems or the reasons for their widespread occurrence. As Labov points out, ease of articulation does not seem to be a factor in such shifts, and we know too little about how sounds are perceived to know whether perceptual prominence is involved. On the other hand, it seems apparent from the many vowel shifts that have been described that some regular forces are involved for these shifts tend to go in some directions rather than others. In particular, Miller (1972) and Stampe (1972) have pointed out that front and back vowels (which Miller calls 'chromatic' vowels) tend quite generally to raise. There are a number of examples of such raising, perhaps the best known of which is the Great Vowel Shift that occurred from late middle to early modern English.[12] Similar vowel shifts have occurred throughout the Indo-European language family and in other language families as well (see Wolfe 1972; Labov, Yaeger & Steiner 1972).

From the historical evidence Miller and Stampe conclude that the raising of front and back vowels, particularly tense ones, is a natural phonological change; and we can apply their conclusions, at least tentatively, to New York City vowel raising. Since this raising is most prevalent and extreme in working class and lower middle class speech, the New York City data suggest that non-prestige vowel systems may be more open to natural vowel shifting than prestige systems.

This conclusion is greatly strengthened by the empirical work on contemporary vowel shifts reported by Labov, Yaeger and Steiner. They report that the New York City vowel shift is merely one example of an extremely widespread kind of vowel shifting currently in progress in many urban dialects of American and British English. In the more than a score of cities represented in the study, the authors found: (1) that the vowel shifts obey general principles (not very different from the principles of naturalness proposed by Stampe and Miller) and (2) that the vernacular speech of the working class uniformly carries the shifts further than the prestige dialect does.

Phoneme Assimilation

When words are borrowed into one language from another, the phonologically simplest way for this borrowing to occur is for the words to be assimilated to the native sound pattern. This assimilation enables the speaker to use already learned articulations and rules on the borrowed words instead of having to learn new patterns for the sake of a few lexical items. Sometimes, if the borrowing is on a very large scale, features of the phonology of the source language may be borrowed along with the words, as happened

---

[12] The effect of the Great Vowel Shift is illustrated in the following diagram:

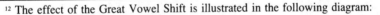
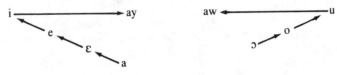

(taken from Wolfe 1972: 1)

Thus we have the following correspondence between early modern English and middle English:

Middle English	Early Modern	Present Day	
[na:me]	[neim]	[neym]	name
[dɛ:d]	[di:d]	[diyd]	deed
[geis]	[gi:s]	[giys]	geese
[wi:n]	[weyn]	[wayn]	wine
[stɔ:n]	[sto:n]	[stown]	stone
[go:s]	[gu:s]	[guws]	goose
[hu:s]	[hows]	[haws]	house

(taken from Bloomfield 1933: 387)

with the Romance Stress Rule in English after the Norman Conquest. This is not, however, the usual case. When we look at social dialects, we discover that prestige dialects often preserve in borrowed words the pronunciation of the source language, or some approximation to it, after the vernacular has completely assimilated the words to the native pattern. The blocking of this assimilation is another example of how prestige dialects inhibit phonetic processes that go on in the vernacular.

Examples of the difference between prestige and vernacular dialects in the assimilation of foreign words are easy to find. Thus, in English many words and phrases borrowed from the French are pronounced variably, with the more learned pronunciation being closer to the French original than is the vernacular one. An excellent example of this sort of variation is described by Bright & Ramanujan (1964) for Tamil, a Dravidian language of India. They compared the borrowing of foreign words into the Brahmin and non-Brahmin dialects of the language and found that the non-Brahmin dialect was more likely to assimilate the pronunciation to the native pattern.

PRESTIGE DIALECTS AND THE SUPPRESSION OF PHONETICALLY CONDITIONED PROCESSES

Linguists have long noticed that prestige dialects tend to preserve archaic forms that are changed or lost in the vernacular. Bloomfield states:

> . . . the standard language, closely tied up with the literary language, tends to become archaic (that is to ignore the changes of the last generations).
>
> (Bloomfield 1964: 393–4)

This same position is put forward by Bright (1964) as regards Tamil and another Dravidian language, Kannada. Bright points out that in these languages the highest caste dialect often preserves phonological characteristics that have undergone change in the non-Brahmin dialect. Thus, he says:

> . . . the non-Brahmin dialect [of Kannada] shows more sound change within native vocabulary; cf. non-Brahmin *ālu* 'milk', Brahmin *hālu* (Medieval *hāl*, Old Kannada *pāl*): non-Brahmin *gombe* 'doll', Brahmin *bombe* (Old Kannada *bombe*).
>
> (Bright 1964: 470)

> Some evidence is available of a similar pattern [to that of Kannada] in the caste dialects of Tamil. For instance Old Tamil had a retroflex fricative which may be transcribed ž; this is preserved in Brahmin dialects but merges with y, ḷ, l or zero in most non-Brahmin dialects.
>
> (Bright 1964: 471)

A similar situation seems to exist in the Indonesian language Javanese with its prestige and non-prestige speech levels (Krama and Ngoko). There is evidence that some of the differences between these levels is due to the retention of archaic phonological features in Krama (White 1972: 26–7).

Facts like these fit quite well with Labov's results on present-day English, as he himself has pointed out (Labov 1972: 297). If we assume that systematic phonological changes resisted by prestige dialects are phonetically conditioned, then the facts fit our position as well. What is still lacking is a clear explanation for the facts. Bloomfield and

Bright both suggest that the central factor retarding phonological change in prestige dialects is literacy. They argue that prestige speakers, being the most educated stratum of society, are more influenced by the literary tradition to resist change. Bright & Ramanujan (1964) suggest that in the non-written Dravidian language Tulu the Brahmin dialect is not phonologically more conservative than the non-Brahmin dialect.

The literacy argument for the tendency of prestige dialects to resist change undoubtedly has some merit. Thus, there are numerous cases in English where the written language has influenced the spoken language, not only by resisting change but also by altering pronunciation in the direction of spelling form (see Barber 1964). We believe, however, that more than the influence of the literary language is involved and also that this influence cannot simply be pointed out but requires an explanation.

Our position, as stated earlier, is that prestige dialects resist phonetically motivated change and inherent variation because prestige speakers seek to mark themselves off as distinct from the common people and because inhibiting phonetic processes is an obvious way to do this. Thus, we are claiming that there is a particular ideological motivation at the origin of social dialect variation. This ideology causes the prestige dialect user to expend more energy in speaking than does the user of the popular vernacular. In addition, there is another reason why prestige dialects would tend to resist phonological change. These dialects are maintained by social elites and such elites are by and large conservative. The use of conservative linguistic forms is for them a symbol of their whole value system. From this standpoint the conservation of the literary language has basically the same source as that of the spoken prestige dialect, since the standards of the literary language are set by the elite. The influence of the literary language on the spoken standard is one manifestation among others of a socially motivated inhibition of linguistic change. This conclusion is reinforced by the fact that prestige dialects not only inhibit changes that violate written forms but also resist changes in such features as vowel quality long before those changes would cause noticeable contradictions between the written and the spoken forms.

Evidence for our explanation of the tendency of prestige dialects to resist phonetic processes can be found in a number of sources. One source of evidence is Labov's documentation of the suppression of change by the upper middle class in New York City (Labov 1966). He found that changes originating in the working class and the lower middle class spread outwards from there to influence the speech of the upper middle class until at a certain point the change has advanced enough linguistically to be noticeable. Then a process of suppression begins in the upper middle class and slowly spreads downward through the social hierarchy. This suppression is associated with definite negative social evaluation of the suppressed feature as 'lower class' (Labov 1972). Thus, Labov's results indicate not only that the social elite suppresses change but also that the motivation for this suppression is a desire to maintain social distinctiveness in speech.

A second source of evidence for our position lies in the attitudes of intellectuals who set standards of usage for the prestige dialects. Such works as Fowler's *A dictionary of modern English usage* (1944) have as their express aim slowing down the rate of change in the language (see Barber 1964: 9). The French Academy is an even more obvious expression of the notion that the standard language should resist change. The guardians of usage view change as degeneration from a past epoch of linguistic and literary greatness; and for them the fact that an innovation arises in the popular vernacular is generally sufficient grounds for excluding it from the prestige dialect.

A third piece of evidence for our view can be found in an extremely interesting experiment conducted by the psychologist George Mahl and analysed linguistically by Labov. Mahl studied the effects of two factors on the speech of 17 middle class college students: (1) blocking a subject's self-monitoring of speech with white noise and (2) blocking his view of the interviewer's face. He collected samples of the subjects' speech under the following four conditions:

1. Facing the interviewer, without masking noise.
2. Facing away (so as not to be able to see the interviewer's face), without masking noise.
3. Facing the interviewer, with masking noise (i.e., wearing earphones through which white noise is administered at sufficient volume to prevent the subject from hearing his own voice).
4. Facing away, with masking noise.

The two alternations of the normal conversational situation introduced by Mahl would both seem to make communication more difficult. Therefore, one would expect that under the abnormal conditions 2–4, subjects would speak more distinctly so as to overcome the interference with communication. Indeed, the masking noise did cause the subjects to speak more loudly, even though the interviewer was not hearing the noise and told the subjects that they need not raise their voices (Mahl 1972: 225).[13]

Interestingly, however, Labov's linguistic analysis found that the subjects shifted toward the vernacular rather than towards prestige pronunciations under the abnormal conditions. Table 2 shows the shift toward replacing interdental fricatives with stops in the speech of one subject.

Table 2   Percentage of 'th' variants in the speech of subject 13 in the 4 conditions (Mahl 1972: 237)

Variants	Facing No noise	Facing away No noise	Facing Noise	Facing away Noise
θ ð (think, that)	86.5	75.9	74.5	68.8
t d (tink, dat)	13.5	24.1	25.5	31.7
	100.0	100.0	100.0	100.0
N (occurrences)	333	261	541	362

The results of Mahl's experiment must be treated as tentative because only a limited body of speech was carefully analysed, but they are nonetheless extremely suggestive. Only if we assume that the use of standard English pronunciation is motivated by social ideology can we explain them. The removal of auditory feedback through masking prevents the speaker from monitoring his speech and so it drops to a more natural level. This demonstrates, as Labov points out (Labov 1972: 97–8), that the prestige dialect

---

[13] The masking noise does not really interfere with communication acoustically since only the subject hears it. The subjects seem to have behaved, however, as though the interviewer was also hearing the noise. The loudness of their speech is one indication of this phenomenon.

requires special attention to be paid to speech. Even more significantly, however, removing the subject's view of the interviewer's face causes just as great a shift toward vernacular forms. This result can only be due to the absence of visual cues lessening the psychological impetus for maintaining an elevated style of speech. If such a small change in the circumstances of conversation causes so significant a shift toward vernacular forms, we can reasonably conclude that social status motivation plays a large part in maintaining the prestige dialect.

Finally, we want to point out that the results of Mahl's experiment are excellent evidence against the 'laziness' theory of vernacular speech. Indeed, under that theory the results would be inexplicable. The laziness theory would certainly predict that under conditions that make communication more difficult, speakers who control both vernacular and prestige forms would favor the latter. However, the results of Mahl's experiment are exactly the reverse: it is precisely under conditions that are less favorable for communication that vernacular features occur more readily. Thus, we can conclude from Mahl's experiment that concern for social status, not concern for communication, is what maintains the prestige dialect.

POSSIBLE COUNTER-EXAMPLES TO THE THEORY

We shall conclude our discussion of social dialect variation with a discussion of some possible counter-examples to the theory we have proposed. The first such case is that of final and preconsonantal /r/ deletion in New York City and the rest of the East Coast (see Labov 1966). Labov says that at the turn of the century the speech of New York City was essentially /r/-less in final and preconsonantal position for all classes. In the 1930s a new prestige norm of /r/ pronunciation arose and this norm became dominant after World War II. This new prestige form (which may be related to the decision by radio and television to adopt a general mid-western pronunciation as the broadcast standard) appeared first in the speech of the upper middle class. Furthermore, even at the time of Labov's study, only the upper middle class used /r/ to any appreciable extent in casual speech. The form appears in working class speech only in formal styles. From our point of view the reintroduction of final and preconsonantal /r/ is a phonetically unmotivated sound change since it revives a perceptually indistinct segment and increases articulatory effort. The change is an excellent example of the tendency, mentioned earlier, of prestige dialects to borrow prestige forms from outside the local area.

Thus far the case of /r/ is unproblematic; but when we turn to the history of final /r/ pronunciation, a possible counter-example to our theory emerges. It has long been known that the /r/-less pronunciation of the eastern United States was originally due to Anglophile sympathies of the upper class. In other words, this consonantal simplification originated as a prestige form and filtered down. Our theory, on the other hand, predicts that such a change would be resisted by the prestige dialect. Further examination of the history of /r/ dropping, however, shows that the case does not pose a real problem for our theory. First of all, there is some evidence (Labov 1972: 287) that the loss of final /r/ originated in England as a lower or lower middle class change later adopted by the upper classes for unknown reasons. When the change was adopted by the English upper classes, it became for upper class eastern Americans, who admired the British aristocracy, a symbol of refinement. Moreover, although the /r/-less pronunciation was originally adopted by the upper classes of the eastern United States, its spread to the other classes is easy to explain. Not only would these groups tend to adopt the pronunciation to the extent that they were influenced by the norms of the dominant social groups, but also the pronunciation would spread throughout the population because of its phonetic motivation. Thus, our theory predicts that the /r/-less pronunciation in nineteenth-century American should be different from other prestige forms. In particular, it should appear in all of the speech styles of the lower and working classes and not be restricted to the formal styles. Also, it should not reflect social stratification due to preferential usage by the dominant class. All the historical data that we have on New York City confirm these predictions (see Labov 1966: 342f., 564).

The second case that might be seen as a counter-example to our theory is the case of the centralization of the syllabic element in the diphthongs /ay/ and /aw/ on the island of Martha's Vineyard, Massachusetts, as described in Labov's article, 'The Social Motivation of a Sound Change' (see Labov 1972: chap. 1). As Labov, Yaeger & Steiner put it:

> The centralization of (ay) and (aw) forms a striking reversal of a general drift in English.
>
> (Labov, Yaeger & Steiner 1972: 309).

In fact, the change violates the principles of vowel shifting that the authors formulate and certainly seems an unnatural one. Moreover, since the change seems to have originated with and is most evident among the fishermen of the rural Chilmark section of the island, one could argue that, according to our theory, the change should have been in a natural direction.

Fortunately, Labov's work on the social context of this change was extremely perceptive and the apparent contradiction with our theory can be resolved. Labov points out that Martha's Vineyard is an archaic dialect area that often preserved linguistic features after they were lost in the rest of New England. Among these features was a somewhat central pronunciation of the syllabic element in /ay/. This pronunciation was characteristic of southern England at the time that Martha's Vineyard was settled (the seventeenth century) but disappeared in one of the last changes of the Great English Vowel Shift. Since the 1930s, Labov showed, the centralization of /ay/ has increased and it has spread by analogy to the parallel diphthong /aw/. The motivation for this change and other strengthening of archaic features that are occurring is an increasing desire on the part of local residents to separate themselves symbolically from invading tourists and to reaffirm local tradition (Labov 1972: 28–32). In other words, the unnatural change in progress on Martha's Vineyard is an attempt to preserve and extend an archaic feature of the local dialect. The tourist economy has given native residents easily understandable reasons for wanting to mark themselves off from the rest of the population. Thus, the particular social situation on Martha's Vineyard explains why a non-prestige group is behaving linguistically in a way otherwise characteristic of elites without invalidating our general position.

Perhaps the most significant problem for our theory in available sociolinguistic studies is the fact, documented by Labov, that the lowest stratum of a community does not initiate phonological change. In his study of the Lower East Side, Labov found that such change originated in the 'working class' and the 'lower middle class' strata but not in the 'lower class'. Moreover, this result has been confirmed in studies of Detroit, Panama City, and Norwich, England (Labov, Yaeger & Steiner 1972: 16). On the other hand, the lower class, while it does not initiate phonological change, is less influenced by the prestige norm than are the working class and lower middle class strata. Thus, when a phonological change that originated in one of these strata is represented by the upper middle class, the lower class ends up using the stigmatized form more frequently than groups above it on the social hierarchy (see, for example, Table 1 *supra* p. 224).

These facts are troublesome to us since we would expect the lower class, being the least influenced by the prestige norm, to also be the most common source of phonological change. Labov himself gives no detailed explanation for the phonomenon in print, but he has suggested that the lower class may less desire the local identity marking that he thinks causes phonological change (Labov, personal communication; also see *supra* footnote 5, p. 228). We would suggest that the explanation may lie rather in the degree to which the lower class is socially and linguistically integrated into the local speech community. For example, if the lower class contains a higher proportion of relatively recent arrivals in the local area or if it is geographically more mobile than working class strata with more stable and better paid employment, then its tendency not to originate sound changes would be explicable. Such changes, while they occur everywhere and have similar linguistic characteristics, differ in detail from one local community to another and would be less likely to arise in a less settled population. In any case, more research is needed not only to resolve the question of the linguistic behavior of the lower class but also to investigate many aspects of social dialect variation that have been as yet little explored. We hope that, in proposing our theoretical model of social dialect variation, we will contribute to making future research in sociolinguistics as fruitful as recent investigations have been.

REFERENCES

1. Barber, C. (1964). *Linguistic change in present-day English*. Birmingham, Alabama: University of Alabama Press.

2. Bloomfield, L. (1933). *Language*. London: George Allen and Unwin.

3. —— (1964). Literature and illiterate speech. In D. Hymes (ed.), *Language in culture and society*. New York: Harper and Row.

4. Bright, W. (1960) Linguistic change in some Indian caste dialects. In C. Ferguson and J. Gumperz (eds), *Linguistic diversity in South Asia*. (Publication of the Research Center in Anthropology, Folklore and Linguistics, No. 13.) Bloomington: Indiana University Press.

5. —— (1964). Social Dialect and Language History. In D. Hymes (ed.), *Language in culture and society*. New York: Harper and Row.

6. Bright, W. & Ramanujan, A. K. (1964). Socio-linguistic variation and language change. In H. Lunt (ed.), *Proceedings of the Ninth International Congress of Linguistics*. The Hague: Mouton.

7. Cedergren, H. (1970) Patterns of free variation: the language variable. Mimeo.

8. Chen, M. & Wang, W. (1975). Sound change: actuation and implementation. *Language* **51**. 225–81.

9. Chomsky, N. & Halle, M. (1968). *The sound pattern of English*. New York: Harper and Row.

10. Ferguson, C. & Gumperz, J. (eds) (1960). *Linguistic diversity in South Asia*. (Publication of the Research Center in Anthropology, Folklore and Linguistics, No. 13). Bloomington: Indiana University Press.

11. Fischer, J. L. (1964). Social influence in the choice of a linguistic variant. In D. Hymes (ed.), *Language in culture and society*. New York: Harper and Row.

12. Fowler, H. W. (1944) *A dictionary of modern English usage*. Oxford University Press.

13. Guy, G. & Braga, M. L. (1976). Number concordance in Brazilian Portuguese. Paper presented at the fifth annual Conference on New Ways of Analyzing Variation in English at Georgetown University, Washington, D.C.

14. Hymes, D. (1964). *Language in Culture and Society*. New York: Harper and Row.

15. Joos, M. (1952). The medieval sibilants. *Language* **28**. 222–31.

16. Kemp, W. & Pupier, P. (1976). Socially based variability in consonant cluster reduction rules. Paper presented at the fifth annual Conference on New Ways of Analyzing Variation in English at Georgetown University, Washington, D.C.

17. Labov, W. (1966) *The social stratification of English in New York City*. Washington, D.C.: Center for Applied Linguistics.

18. ——— (1972). *Sociolinguistic patterns*. Philadelphia: University of Pennsylvania Press.

19. ——— (1974). Language change as a form of communication. In M. Silverstein (ed.), *Human communication: theoretical explorations*. Hillsdale, N.J.: Lawrence Erlbaum Associates.

20. Labov, W., Yaeger, M. & Steiner, R. (1972). *A quantitative study of sound change in progress*. (Report on contract NSF-GS-3287). Philadelphia: University of Pennsylvania.

21. Lieberman, P. (1973). On the evolution of language: a unified view. *Cognition* **2**. 59–94.

22. Lindblom, B. (1963) On vowel reduction. Report 29 of the Speech Transmission Laboratory. Stockholm: Royal Institute of Technology.

23. ——— (1971). Phonetics and the description of language. Mimeo.

24. Mahl, G. (1972). People talking when they can't hear their voices. In P. Siegman and B. Pope (eds), *Studies in dyadic communication*. New York: Pergamon Press.

25. Miller, P. (1972). Vowel neutralization and vowel reduction. In P. Peranteau, J. Levi, and G. Phares (eds.) *Papers from the Eighth Regional Meeting of the Chicago Linguistic Society*. Chicago: Chicago Linguistic Society.

26. Postal, P. (1968). *Aspects of phonological theory*. New York: Harper and Row.

27. Schane, S. (1972). Natural rules in phonology. In R. Stockwell and J. Macaulay (eds), *Linguistic change and generative theory*. Bloomington: Indiana University Press.

28. Schogt, H. G. (1961). La notion de loi dans la phonétique historique. *Lingua* **10**. 72–92.

29. Shuy, R., Wolfram, W. & Riley, W. (1967). *A study of social dialects in Detroit*. Washington, D.C.: Office of Education.

30. Stampe, D. (1972). On the natural history of diphthongs. In P. Peranteau, J. Levi, and G. Phares (eds). *Papers from the Eighth Regional Meeting of the Chicago Linguistic Society*. Chicago: Chicago Linguistic Society.

31. Trudgil, P. (1974). *The social differentiation of English in Norwich*. Cambridge University Press.

32. Weinreich, U., Labov, W. & Herzog, M. (1968). Empirical foundations for a theory of language change. In W. Lehmann and Y. Malkiel (eds), *Directions for historical linguistics*. Austin: University of Texas Press.

33. White, D. (1972). Social dialect formation. Unpublished ms.

34. Wolfe, P. (1972). *Linguistic change and the Great Vowel Shift in English*. Berkeley: University of California Press.

35. Zwicky, A. (1972). On casual speech. In P. Peranteau, J. Levi, and G. Phares (eds.). *Papers from the Eighth Regional Meeting of the Chicago Linguistic Society*. Chicago: Chicago Linguistic Society.

DISCUSSION QUESTIONS

1. What, in your own words, is Kroch's hypothesis? Does your personal experience support it?

2. How does Kroch's hypothesis relate to the views of Labov and Fischer?

3. Does the development of a creole fit with Kroch's hypothesis? See Michael Linn's article in Part II.

4. Look up the variant pronunciations listed in a recent major dictionary for *coupe*, *chassis, detour* (n.), *garage*, and *lingerie*. Which pronunciation do you use? Relate your reply to Kroch's view about the assimilation of foreign words.

ROBBINS BURLING

After receiving his doctorate in anthropology at Harvard University in 1957, Burling taught at the University of Pennsylvania until 1963 and then went to the University of Michigan, where he is currently professor of anthropology. He has done field work in Assam, India and has written and published extensively.

BLACK ENGLISH

ORIGINS OF DIVERSITY

An American who first hears of caste dialects and of the stylistic switching that is so common in India is likely to react with dismay if not outright horror. Polydialectism seems a poor basis upon which to build a unified nation, and the variability of language along caste lines seems downright undemocratic. Yet many of these same phenomena can be found in America too, and indeed, once we recognize how easy it is for linguistic cues to come to symbolize sociological or situational differences, it should be surprising if American social class divisions were not reflected in the way we use language. In particular, we ought to look at our sharpest sociological cleavage—the division between blacks and whites—and ask whether it is not marked by linguistic variables.

Most white Americans probably believe that they could distinguish Negro speakers from white even while blindfolded. Some may imagine that whatever linguistic differences they perceive are simply the result of underlying racial differences. They may suppose that Negro mouths are built differently from white mouths or that Negroes are simply incapable of such clear and accurate articulation as whites. Such racial notions can easily be disproved, for when northern whites are asked to judge taped samples of speech they often mistake a southern white for a Negro, but conversely they will identify the voice of the rather rare Negro who grows up in an otherwise white northern community as belonging to a white speaker. It is unquestionably the experience of the speaker, particularly his experience in early childhood, that determines how he will speak, not his race.

It is easy to dispose of this racist explanation for Negro-white differences, but a contrary linguistic myth is also current among many Americans today that is more difficult to deal with. A good many well-meaning Americans would like to maintain a sort of dogmatic faith that Negro and white speech is in all essentials identical. Many white Americans, who feel deeply that discrimination is wicked and who insist that Negroes be offered all the same opportunities as whites, are eager to deny any difference at all between the two groups, for they are afraid any admission of cultural differences would provide a rationalization for discrimination. But the fear of offending egalitarian ideals should not stand in the way of an investigation of dialectical variability, and when such an investigation is made, it is abundantly clear that most Negroes in the United States today do have features in their speech that separate them from their white neighbors. Indeed, when we remember the history of black Americans and understand the conditions of segregation in which they have lived and continue to live in both the north and the south, it would be startling if important differences were not found. Unfortunately, serious studies of dialects used by Negroes have begun only very recently.

The first and most obvious generalization to make about the English of many Negroes is that it shows abundant characteristics of the southern United States. Throughout the South, where most Negroes once lived, their speech has probably approached in considerable degree the varieties of English spoken by their white neighbors. They need not have spoken identically to these whites, and indeed the segregated conditions of their lives would almost force us to guess that important linguistic differences would separate the speech of the two groups.

In recent decades, as southern Negroes have surged into northern cities, they have brought along their varieties of southern speech. Since they have largely been forced to live in segregated ghettos, often shut off even more completely from association with whites than in their southern homes, their dialects have been perpetuated and passed on to their northern-born children. What had been geographically distinctive features have been converted into ethnic features. Most northern urban Negroes, for instance, fail to distinguish /i/ from /e/ before /n/, so that words like *pin* and *pen* become homonyms. This is characteristic of most southern speech, both black and white, but in a northern city like New York it is hardly found except among Negroes. Most whites do distinguish those two sounds, but only the rare Negro who grows up in a predominantly white neighborhood learns to do so. As a result a New Yorker could guess the race of a fellow New Yorker with a good chance of being correct simply by hearing him pronounce these two words. Many other southern features, besides the collapse of the *i/e* contrast, have no doubt become generalized as ethnic features in the north. Certainly the totality of features is so pervasive that more often than not northern urban Americans can distinguish Negroes from whites simply by hearing them talk.

Not all the special characteristics of northern urban Negro speech are simply southern, however. The ghettos create their own social climate and evoke their unique linguistic signals. The ghettos, after all, draw upon many southern areas, so the migrants do not arrive with a single uniform dialect. Features that have originated from one southern area can be generalized and accepted by other speakers, while other southern features are dropped as people adjust to their new surroundings. As a result, the recent migrant from the South is clearly marked off from older residents by his purer southern traits, and as the years pass, a new and unique dialect, a synthesis of southern and northern forms with some added local innovations, becomes characteristic of many urban Negroes. Instead of a geographically based dialect we can only speak of one that is ethnically based.

It even seems that in some northern cities the speech of Negroes and whites has been becoming more distinct in recent decades. Southern Negroes have been moving north in such large numbers that their speech has tended to swamp out the more northern dialects of their northern Negro predecessors. In Washington, D.C., immigration of whites from the north has tended to shift white dialects in the opposite direction. In some northern cities the differences between black and white speech have now become so clearly marked that radio stations which carry programs and advertising directed toward a Negro audience sometimes use announcers who have recognizably Negro characteristics in their speech. Perhaps this should be no more surprising than the use of Spanish for programs directed to Puerto Ricans in New York or of Navaho for some programs in the Southwest, but the use of Negro English dialects does constitute an almost unique exception to the bland uniformity of most broadcast English in the United States.

A common southern background and a common reaction to ghetto life in the north can account for many of the differences between Negro and white dialects. But it is also worth noting that a number of striking linguistic features, which are not found in either southern or northern white dialects, seem to be common among Negroes in all northern urban areas. Not all the features that tend to set off the kind of English used wherever Negroes are concentrated in large numbers are simply southern. It may be that the seemingly unique character of black English can only be understood as deriving from a long separate history from white English. It may even be that the English of some black Americans still shows the influence of the time when slaves were first imported into this country or even a few traces of their African origin.

When slaves were brought to the Americas, men and women of diverse linguistic background were thrown together with relatively little chance to learn the English of their masters, but with no way of communicating with one another except by means of some approximation to English. The situation would seem to have been ideal for the development of a pidgin language based upon English, and then for its subsequent creolization in the generation that grew up in America knowing no other language but learning to speak by imitating the imperfect English of their parents. A pidgin is a contact language, native to no one, and generally used in a limited range of situations. It may be simple in structure and may show varied influences from the diverse languages of those who use it. When children grow up basing their speech upon such a pidgin, they can be expected to elaborate it and adapt it to all the varied situations of life. But having been filtered through the distortions of the contact period, this newly developed creole, while a full and flexible medium of communication in its own right, can be expected to differ quite markedly from the original language upon which its ancestral pidgin had been based.

A few New World Negro populations continue to speak forms of English that are so divergent as to be recognized as creoles. The only true creole to survive in the United States today is the so-called Gullah dialect spoken along the coast of South Carolina, but others are found in the West Indies and in Surinam on the north coast of South America. It is remarkable that all these creoles seem to resemble each other to some degree, and a few of their features are even reflected in the less deviant English spoken by many Negroes in the United States.

Hints about the characteristics of the English spoken by Negroes over the past two and a half centuries can be found in fragments of dialogue that have periodically appeared in print and purport to reflect the speech of Negroes. It is not uncommon in such dialogue for *me* to be used even as the subject or possessive form of the first person pronoun. A copula is often missing from sentences in which standard English would always have a form of the verb *be,* though *be* itself sometimes appears where it would not be used in standard English. Some words also suggest an avoidance of final consonants or of complex final clusters, either by dropping or simplifying the consonants or by adding vowels at the end, thus shifting the former final consonant into a prevocalic position. These various features appear, among other places, in the dialogue attributed to a Virginia Negro in the play "The Fall of British Tyranny" written by John Leacock of Philadelphia in 1776. A conversation between a certain "kidnapper and the Negro Cudjo" goes as follows

KIDNAPPER	What part did you come from?
CUDJO	Disse brack man, disse one, disse one, disse one, came from Hamton, disse one, disse one, come from Nawfok, me come from Nawfok too.
KIDNAPPER	Very well, what was your master's name?
CUDJO	Me massa name Cunney Tomsee.
KIDNAPPER	Colonel Thompson—eigh?
CUDJO	Eas, massa, Cunney Tomsee.

KIDNAPPER	Well then I'll make you a major—and what's your name?
CUDJO	Me massa cawra me Cudjo.[1]

Similar features appeared in dialogues attributed to Negroes, supposedly coming from the West Indies and Surinam. But, in English-speaking areas of the New World, Negro dialects were never taken seriously enough to be systematically described. We can only infer their characteristics from scattered literary sources. Surinam, however, was ruled by Holland, and here Dutch immigrants had to do their best to communicate with Negroes who spoke an English-based creole. To assist the Dutchmen, grammars of this creole were printed as early as the late 18th century, and these suggest features of the language found all the way north to the United States.

The English spoken by Negroes in the United States today is certainly not a close replica of an 18th century creole, but at least a few details of present day Negro American English may be attributable to an earlier period of pidginization and creolization, followed by persistent modifying influences from standard English. As I will point out, the attrition of final consonants is an important feature of the speech of many Negroes in the United States, and the copula is often missing where it would occur in standard English. One cannot help asking if all forms of New World Negro English might not have a common origin and if centuries of segregation might not have allowed common features to be perpetuated down to the present time. It has even been argued that Negro dialects can be traced all the way to the slave ports of west Africa, where African and European speakers first had to devise makeshift forms of communication. The pidgin English established in these ports would have been carried everywhere in the New World where Africans used English. In subsequent centuries the language would only slowly be modified in proportion to the contact between blacks and speakers of more standard English.

We should even be willing to wonder whether traces of African languages might not have managed to survive the centuries. Certainly African lexical items live on in the more extreme creoles such as Gullah. More tentatively it is tempting to ask if the attrition of final consonants and simplification of final clusters that is so characteristic of much of Negro English is not a distant reflection of the influence of west African languages, for these often have few final consonants. Conceivably this feature of west African languages has even reached out to affect white speakers as well as their Negro neighbors, for in spite of the great status differences dividing blacks from whites in this country, some influences can have gone in both directions. It may not be mere coincidence that certain final consonant clusters are more often simplified in southern white dialects than in those of the north. The *t* of northern pronunciations of the final clusters *-pt* and *-ft* is omitted by some southern white speakers, for instance, with the result that *slept* becomes *slep, stopped* becomes homonymous with *stop* (unless the *t* is reintroduced by analogy with other past tense forms) *left* becomes *lef,* and *loft* becomes *lof.*

Just how important the influence of African languages is in the speech of either Negroes or whites in the United States today must remain an open question until far more has been learned both about the various dialects spoken today and about their antecedents. But it does at least seem clear that many features widely distributed among Negroes today can only be understood as a result of their long and special history.

---

[1] Quoted by William A. Stewart in "Sociolinguistic Factors in the History of American Negro Dialects," *Florida FL Reporter* (Spring 1967), p. 24.

A STIGMATIZED DIALECT

The diverse patterns of English would be no more than linguistic curiosities if they were accepted as the social and cultural equivalent of standard patterns. Americans tend to be relatively tolerant of most regional dialects, but Negro speech patterns have been closely associated with their inferior social position and, like the dialectical specialties of lower-class whites, their patterns have become stigmatized. Many people look upon them not simply as divergent but as inferior. This is true not only of whites. Those Negroes who have themselves struggled for an education and fought to acquire the linguistic symbols associated with education may have little patience with the language of the lower class. Indeed, it is sometimes educated Negro teachers, themselves managing very well with standard English patterns, who most strongly resist any suggestion that the special characteristics of their black students' dialects deserve respect or attention. It may be difficult for some of them to accept the notion that the speech they have worked so hard to suppress is anything but just plain wrong.

To dismiss his speech as simply incorrect or inferior burdens the Negro child who grows up in a northern ghetto with a nearly insuperable problem. To speak naturally with his parents and to compete with his contemporaries on the street, he simply must learn their variety of English. Indeed, if in some miraculous way, he could learn standard English, he would be nothing but an impertinent prig to use it with his parents, and surely his contemporaries would rapidly tease it out of him. The language the child first learns is a rich and flexible medium in its own terms, and it can be used effectively in most of the situations he encounters in daily life. No wonder teachers have only meager success when they try to persuade him to abandon his own easy language in favor of an unnatural—almost foreign—medium. Inevitably, many students simply reject their education and all it stands for.

Years of classroom drilling, exposure to movies and radio, and the brute necessities of trying to get a job do eventually have their effect. While few Negroes from the ghetto fully achieve the middle-class goal of their teachers, many learn to go part way, and many northern Negroes are accomplished dialect switchers. They move toward middle-class standards where that seems to be called for, but they relax into more natural patterns when speaking with their families or close friends, or whenever pretensions would be out of place. They act a bit like speakers in those situations that have been called diglossia. Like Swiss Germans, Negro children first learn a dialect suitable for their home and their close friends. Only in school, if at all, do they learn the standard dialect, which then becomes appropriate for certain kinds of educated discourse, for writing, or for communicating with people outside their own group. Yet in German-speaking Switzerland the two dialects are more clearly recognized as distinct. Each is admired in its own sphere and each can be clearly referred to by its own name. No Swiss, whatever his education, is unwilling to use Swiss German in his home or with close friends. Every Swiss is proud of his dialect, proud of its very distinctiveness from standard German, and no one in Switzerland simply stigmatizes the Swiss dialect as inferior and debased. Although a Swiss switches back and forth as the occasion demands, he is generally clear about his choice, speaking full Swiss German when that is called for but approximating standard German quite closely at other times. He is not likely to glide indecisively between them.

Northern urban Negro dialects are more recent, in more rapid flux, and more consistently despised by speakers of standard English. This has made it difficult for Negroes to develop the pride in their own dialect that the Swiss have in theirs, and most speakers probably slide along more of a continuum than do the Swiss. At one end of the continuum is a speech style close to the standard language and this is the style toward which formal education aims. Students of Negro speech in Washington, D.C., have called this the "acrolect" and have contrasted it with the "basilect" that lies at the opposite and most humble extreme. Ghetto children first hear and speak the basilect, and many Negroes in Washington seem to take it for granted that this is the natural way for small children to talk, just as Javanese expect their children to learn the lowest level of speech first. As children grow older, they learn new or alternative forms and develop more or less skill in switching toward the acrolect.

Consciously or unconsciously, many Negroes learn to slide back and forth along this continuum of styles, though individual speakers vary greatly in the range through which they can switch. The most recent southern migrant, the most severely segregated, the man with the least formal education, may not be able to get far from the basilect. The long-term northern resident, the educated member of the middle class who has daily contact with white speakers of standard English, may use the acrolect easily but be unable to get all the way to the basilect; but many speakers shift over a considerable range. The fluidity of this shifting makes it extremely difficult to make a serious investigation of Negro speech patterns. The middle-class investigator, particularly if he is white, may have great trouble eliciting realistic examples of the more relaxed Negro styles, since the very formality of the investigation encourages informants (whether consciously or not) to shift as far toward the acrolect as they can manage. Where Negroes have adjusted to prejudice and discrimination by accommodating outwardly to the whims of whites, they may be ready to support white stereotypes by guessing at the information the investigator wants and then providing it. They may deliberately conceal the characteristics of their in-group language. Partly for these reasons, though even more through sheer neglect, we have had tragically little reliable knowledge of the speech of lower-class Negroes. By the late 1960s, however, as part of an increasing concern over the fate of segregated Negro children in our educational system, investigations in several cities had finally begun. It is at last possible to sketch a few of the major differences between standard middle-class English and the speech of many urban Negroes. There can be no doubt that the differences extend to every part of language, phonological, grammatical, lexical, and semantic.

PHONOLOGICAL CONTRAST

One set of features that distinguishes the speech of many Negroes is the obscuring of certain phonological contrasts found in standard English, spoken in the northern United States. In final position standard /θ/ often merges with /f/, and standard /ð/ merges with /v/. As a result, words like *Ruth* and *death,* which northern white speakers virtually always pronounce with final interdental fricatives, are often pronounced by Negroes with labiodental fricatives so that they become homonymous with *roof* and *deaf.*

The standard vowels /ay/ and /aw/ as in *find* and *found* may lose their diphthongal qualities and merge with /a/ of *fond,* and all three of these words become homonyms. A number of other vowels may fall together when preceding /l/ or /r/, so that pairs like *boil* and *ball, beer* and *bear, poor* and *pour,* are often homonyms. In all these cases, as in the loss of contrast between the vowels in *pin* and *pen,* many Negroes simply have a few more sets of homonyms in their speech than do most northern whites. Perhaps it is some compensation that a good many southern Negroes do make a distinction between the vowels in *four* and *for,* or *hoarse* and *horse,* which most northern whites confound, though even this distinction tends to be lost by northern migrants.

The existence of these extra homonyms in the speech of Negro children presents them with a few special reading problems, though these should not be insuperable. All English speakers have many homonyms in their speech, and in learning to read English everyone must learn to associate different orthographic sequences with identically pronounced but semantically distinct words. This is one of the barriers we all must overcome in becoming literate. For the most part, a Negro child simply has a somewhat different and larger set of homonyms to cope with. They will give him serious problems only if his teacher fails to understand that these words *are* homonyms in the child's natural speech.

If a student sees the word *death* and reads [def] he is correctly interpreting the written symbols into his natural pronunciation, and he deserves to be congratulated. If his teacher insists on correcting him and telling him to say [deθ], she is pronouncing a sequence of sounds that is quite literally foreign to the child, and he may even have trouble hearing the difference between his own and his teacher's versions. Unwittingly, the teacher is correcting the child's pronunciation instead of his reading skills. The child can only conclude that reading is a mysterious and capricious art. If he has enough experiences of this sort he is all too likely to give up and remain essentially illiterate all his life. It is clearly of the utmost importance for anyone who is teaching such children to understand their system of homonyms and to distinguish cases of nonstandard pronunciations from real reading problems.

In other ways Negro speech often differs more dramatically from that of whites, ways that may pose even more serious barriers to literacy. The most important of these seem to involve the loss of final consonants and the simplification of final clusters. Several related developments are involved in this simplification, and they deserve to be considered individually.

-r

In many Negro dialects (as in some white dialects, of course, both in the north and south) post vocalic and preconsonantal -r tends to be lost. As in some white dialects, this can result in the falling together of such words as *guard* and *god, sore* and *saw, fort* and *fought.* Negro speech, however, may go even further than other r-less dialects by also losing the intervocalic r's that are preserved in most white dialects, certainly in those of the North. For instance, most New Yorkers in a relaxed mood pronounce *four* without r constriction when it occurs finally or before a consonant, as in *fourteen* or *four boys.* But they generally do have r constriction when the same word occurs before a vowel as in *four o'clock.* This gives a white New York child some hint about the orthography he must learn, and it must help to rationalize the spelling of the word for him, even in those positions where he would not actually pronounce the r. To many Negroes, however, these -r's are absent under all conditions. They may say [fɔ'ɔklak] with as little r constriction as they use in [fɔtiyn]. Even an intervocalic r occurring in the middle of the word may be omitted, a pronunciation that has been reflected in dialect spellings such as "inte'ested." The name *Carol* may be pronounced identically to *Cal,* and *Paris* and *terrace* become homonymous with *pass* and *test.* A Negro child who first learns this r-less dialect has no clue in his own speech about why these words should be spelled with an -r, and so he has one extra hurdle to cross if he is to learn to read and write.

-*l*

Although English *l* is phonetically rather like *r*, being similar in its distribution within the syllable and even in its effect upon preceding vowels, it is less often completely lost than -*r*. In most English dialects *l* may be replaced, when preceding a consonant, by a back unrounded glide which amounts to little more than a modification of the preceding vowel, as in the rapid pronunciation of *ball game*. But the complete loss of post vocalic *l* and merger of words spelled with *l* with others that are not are largely Negro phenomena. It is not uncommon for Negroes to fail to make a distinction between such words as *toll* and *toe; tool* and *too; help* and *hep; all* and *awe; fault* and *fought*.

Simplification of Final Clusters

Final clusters may be simplified by losing one of the elements in the cluster. The most common simplification is the loss of the final /t/ or /d/ from such clusters as -*st, -ft, -nt, -nd, -ld, -zd, -md*. Individual speakers vary in the degree and regularity with which these are simplified, and most Americans, both white and black, sometimes simplify them in certain positions (particularly before consonants) or in certain styles of speech, but the tendency toward simplification is more pronounced in the speech of some Negroes. For many Negroes *past* and *pass; meant, mend* and *men; wind* and *wine; hold* and *hole* have become homonyms. Cluster simplification can even be combined with loss of -*l* so that such words as *told, toll* and *toe* may all become homonyms. Clusters with final -*s* or -*z* such as -*ks, -mz, -lz, -dz, -ts* are somewhat less frequently simplified, and these give rise to more complex situations for sometimes it is the first element of the cluster, sometimes the second, that is lost. It is at least possible, however, that the loss of final -*s* or -*z* will reduce such words as *six* and *sick* to homonyms.

It is often difficult to be sure whether the simplified final cluster that we hear really reflects the underlying form of the word as the speaker knows it, or whether we hear only the surface manifestation of a more complex underlying form. One particular case is instructive however: the word *test* seems to be pronounced without the final *t* by many Negroes. Words ending in /t/ in English regularly take an additional /s/ to show the plural, but words ending in /s/ are pluralized by /-iz/. For some Negro speakers the plural of *tests* is [tesiz] and the plural of *ghost* is [gosiz]. This seems to demonstrate conclusively that for these speakers, *test, ghost,* and many other words completely lack any trace of the *t* of our orthography or of the standard pronunciation.

Other Final Consonants

Final -*r*, -*l* and clusters ending in -*t*, -*d*, -*s* and -*z* are those most frequently reduced, but a few Negroes go even further. Final -*t* may be realized as a glottal stop (as in many white dialects), or it may completely disappear. Final -*d* may be devoiced or disappear. Less often -*k* and -*g* may suffer the same fate. Final -*m* and -*n* may be weakened although they usually leave a residue behind in the form of a nasalized vowel. At its most extreme, this reduction in final consonants can go so far that a few individuals seem predominantly to use open syllables, initial consonants followed by a vowel with hardly any final consonants at all. But even for speakers with less extreme reduction, the final parts of words carry a considerably lighter informational load than for speakers of standard English.

LOSS OF SUFFIXES

Even moderate consonant reduction may give speakers rather serious problems in learning the standard language, for it happens that it is the tongue-tip consonants /r,l,t,d,s,z/ that are most often lost. These carry a great semantic burden in standard spoken English, since they are used to form the suffixes. Not only are the plural, possessive, past, and third person singular of the verb shown by one or another of these tongue-tip consonants, but so are most of the colloquial contractions that speakers of the standard use orally, though they write them infrequently. Standard speakers most often indicate the future by a suffixed -ll, as in I'll go, you'll go, where'll he go?, and so on. The colloquial contractions of the copula generally consist of -r, -z, or -s: you're a boy, he's a boy, we're boys, they're boys, the book's good. If a regular phonological rule leads to the loss of these final consonants, then the grammatical constructions would also be in danger of disappearing. This would imply a series of important ways in which the English of some Negroes would deviate from that of most whites. At least some grammatical changes like these seem to have occurred, although the details appear to be very complex, and are so far only partially understood.

That grammatical change has not been simply the automatic consequence of phonological change is shown by the varying treatment of the plural and of the third person singular marker, which, of course, are phonologically identical in standard English. If loss of suffixes were nothing but a simple result of regular phonological change, then we would expect the plural -s and the third person singular -s to have suffered exactly the same fate. In fact, the plural marker is usually as well preserved as any suffix, and it shows little if any tendency to be lost. By contrast, in the speech of many Negroes, the third person singular verb suffix is completely absent. These speakers simply lack this suffix, under all conditions, even in cases in which the usual phonological rule for the loss of -s would not apply. The easiest way to view this situation in historical perspective is to imagine that both suffixes were first lost under the same conditions, particularly when occurring after other consonants where to have retained them would have resulted in an unpronounceable cluster. When either suffix was added to a root, ending in a vowel, it should have been more readily pronounceable. Upon the identical results of this regular phonological rule, divergent analogical processes could then have brought divergent consequences. If the third person singular marker (which, after all, carries a rather meager semantic load) could be skipped in some positions, it might be skipped elsewhere and so dropped by analogy even from verbs that posed no phonological problem. The plural marker carries a far more significant semantic load, and here, perhaps, the plural signs that survived phonological reduction could serve as a model by which plurals could be analogically reintroduced even onto nouns where a difficult consonant cluster would result. The actual historical processes, by which the plural survived but the third person singular was lost, were no doubt a good deal more complex than this simple scheme would suggest, but the results seem understandable only in terms of both phonological and analogical change.

Other suffixes have suffered varied and complex fates. Contracted forms of the copula often fail to be realized in Negro speech, so instead of you're tired or they're tired, some Negroes say you tired and they tired. This much conforms to the regular phonological loss of final -r, but when he's tired appears as he tired, an analogical extension of the missing copula is likely to be involved since loss of final /-z/ when it is not part of a cluster is unusual. Absence of the copula is frequently cited as a characteristic of Negro speech, and this seems to suggest a rather fundamental altering of the organization of tenses. One form of the copula seems not to be lost, however, for the *'m* of *I'm* seems to survive, perhaps because /-m/ has much less tendency for phonological reduction, even than /-z/.

Some possessive pronouns can become identical to the personal pronouns: *your* and *you* may become homonyms as may *their* and *they*. The school child who reads *your brother* as *you bruvver* is actually doing a skillful job of translating the written form into his dialect. Teachers ought to be equally skilled so as to reward rather than to punish such evidence of learning. The noun possessive written *'s* is frequently omitted, even in words ending in a vowel. The possessive forms of some pronouns do survive: *my, our, his, her,* usually remain distinct, and since nobody says *I book* by analogy with the common *they book* and *you book,* the possessive cannot be said to be completely lost even if it is far less frequent than in standard English.

With cluster simplification, the past forms of the verb often became identical to the present forms. *Walked* becomes homonymous with *walk, pass* with *passed, drag* with *dragged,* and similarly for a great many verbs. Nevertheless, the past tense is preserved by irregular verbs, for the loss of the past-present distinction has not been carried by analogy so as to eliminate such distinctions as *tell* from *told*. The irregular verbs, of course, are extremely common in ordinary conversation so the past tense is well preserved in colloquial Negro speech, but the regular verbs are still common enough to reduce the amount of information conveyed by the past tense markers.

The phonological loss of final *-l* is related to a frequent loss of the contracted form of the future. This, of course, does not mean that Negroes are unable to convey notions of future time. Expressions with *going to* are common, for instance, but beyond this, the full and uncontracted form of *will* (perhaps pronounced without a final *-l*) is available and regularly used. A Negro child may be able to say *I go* with an implication of future time, and to be more emphatic, he can say *I will go* or *I wi' go,* but he may never use *I'll go*. For such a child, a reader that uses what appears to a speaker of standard English as the slightly stilted construction "I will go" may be considerably easier to read than a book which uses "I'll go."

GRAMMATICAL CHANGE

It is clear that some dialects spoken by Negroes have come to contrast with the dialects of most whites in many ways: the loss of phonological contrast particularly at the ends of words, the weakening of suffixes, and the analogical extension of the resulting patterns. Similar changes are known to have occurred in many languages. They represent the kinds of processes which have been active in every family of languages whose history is at all well known. It is proper, therefore, to view these dialects as exhibiting entirely normal and understandable historical developments from an earlier form of the language, a form that standard English continues to approximate a bit more closely. Like many historical developments in language, it is possible to look upon some of these modifications of the Negro dialects as though they involved a degree of simplification in the language, but if historical changes could only bring increasing simplicity, then sooner or later languages would simplify themselves out of existence. There must be countervailing mechanisms that reintroduce complexity. Recognizing the apparent simplification of some aspects of the Negro dialects, it is tempting to ask whether there are balancing ways in which those same dialects have become more complex than standard English.

It is impossible to give any confident answer to this question, partly because Negro dialects have been so imperfectly studied but even more because we have such meager means of measuring complexity. Still, one cannot help wondering whether the near disappearance of the possessive *'s* is not compensated for by other devices, if by nothing else but a more consistent use of the possessive with *of*. When the past and future tenses are partially lost and when the copula construction is weakened, one must wonder if other tenses have not appeared to take their place. One set of contrasting constructions that has been recognized as common among Negroes but which is missing from white dialects, is represented by the contrast between *he busy* which means 'he is busy at the moment' and *he be busy* which means 'he is habitually busy.' The use of *be* allows the easy expression of a contrast between momentary and habitual action that can be introduced only by rather cumbersome circumlocutions in standard English. Here is one place where the speech of many blacks has a useful resource surpassing the speech of whites.

Many other constructions, typical of Negro speech, suggest other tenses not found in the standard dialect: *he done told me; it don't all be her fault; I been seen it; I ain't like it; I been washing the car* (which is not simply a reduced form of the standard 'I have been washing the car'); *he be sleeping*. Such sentences surely utilize rules exceeding the limits of standard English. Unquestionably the rules governing them are as orderly and rigid as those of the standard, but they are just as surely different in important ways. From the viewpoint of the standard language, it may look as though these dialects lack certain familiar mechanisms. From the complementary viewpoint of the dialects, other mechanisms seem to be lacking in the standard. Certainly standard rules are not rich enough to generate the examples cited here.

GHETTO EDUCATION

The language of many Negro children of the northern ghettos is divergent enough from standard English to present educators with a terrible dilemma. Everyone agrees that these children deserve an education that is at least as rich as that of the children in the white suburbs. Negro children ought to be able to take pride in their own background and should not be burdened with shame for cultural differences that are not of their making, and which are inferior only in the sense that people with power happen to have different patterns. If black children are to compete successfully with their white suburban contemporaries in the practical if unjust world of the present day United States, they may have to learn the standard language. But if in learning it, they are forced to reject their own native dialect and to accept the dominant society's view that their native language habits are simply inferior, the experience may do them more psychic harm than social good.

Some would argue that Negroes are no worse off today than the generations of children of European immigrants who entered English-speaking schools knowing nothing but Italian, Greek, or Yiddish. These children too were faced with a strange language, which they had to learn to speak and to read. For some, their education may have been traumatic, but many succeeded, and they or their children have been progressively assimilating into the mainstream of American life. Why, it may be asked, are Negroes any worse off? There are at least two reasons.

First, the economic opportunities for a man with a poor knowledge of standard English have declined. Automation has been progressively eliminating unskilled jobs. More than ever before, a man needs an education. But even more than this, the child of the European immigrant spoke a language that both he and his teacher regarded as a real language. It had a literature, it had its own dictionaries, and it had a writing system all its own. These children were not accused of speaking an inferior variety of English; they spoke something entirely different, and their teachers knew they had to start at the beginning with them. It is easy to be deluded into imagining that Negro children simply speak careless English, to conclude that their language patterns are the result of their own laziness, or stupidity, or cussedness. Some of their teachers never realize that they face a situation with similarities to instruction in a foreign language. Even the child may hardly grasp the truth that his own dialect has its own patterns and structure, and he may all too easily accept his teachers' judgment that he is incapable of learning the "proper" way of speaking. In a just world it would seem fairer to ask others to accept Negro speech as a respectable dialect, one that is as valuable and flexible as any other, than to demand that Negroes, already burdened with problems enough, should have to struggle to learn a different dialect. But such a laudable ideal is probably too remote a dream to be taken seriously.

The problems of ghetto education might be clarified if its various objectives were clearly distinguished. The first goal of language teaching is surely to teach children to read, but it is a depressing truth that thousands of Negro children sit through years of school without ever becoming effectively literate. One important reason for their failure is surely the divergence of the language they bring to school from the language of their teachers and from the language reflected in their textbooks. But whatever the defects of the English spelling system, it has at least one virtue: it does not idiosyncratically favor a single English dialect. Northerners, southerners, Americans, and Englishmen read the same written forms, but each pronounces what he reads in his own way. Our written conventions are not identical to any single spoken dialect, so everyone must learn to translate between the written word and his own native speech habits. To the extent that spoken dialects differ, children come to the task of gaining literacy from various vantage points, and it might seem that the task of the Negro child is not much different from that of other children who have also first learned a particular spoken dialect. The Negro child, however, is likely to be seriously handicapped in two ways. First, his spoken dialect is likely to be even further from the written form than is that of most white children, and inevitably this causes him more difficulty when learning to read. Even more important, his teacher may fail to appreciate the children's special dialect. The teachers of most white children speak dialects enough like that of their students to make their learning problems immediately understandable. A teacher readily understands and sympathizes with a northern middle-class child who has trouble remembering when to write *four* and when to write *for*. She does not balk at her students' easy conversion of the written *hit you* into the spoken colloquial [hičuw]. She will probably not be upset when her students uses *'em* when speaking naturally instead of *them*. The same teacher may be utterly mystified by a Negro student's apparent inability to know when to write *toe, toll,* and *told,* or by the apparent capriciousness with which he interprets the past tense, the third person singular, or the possessive suffix. The task of teaching ghetto children to read should benefit greatly from an understanding of what spoken Negro dialects are really like and from reading programs that are specifically designed for speakers of this dialect. One would hope that such a program could avoid stigmatizing the children's own dialect while opening the literate world to them.

Such a reading program will not teach these children standard pronunciation or to speak with standard grammar. That is really a quite separate task, and perhaps it is one that should wait until children are older and until they themselves feel it to be necessary. To try to teach the standard dialect to segregated slum children who have no chance to practice it in their home or on the street, seems to have little more promise of success than the teaching of foreign languages in monolingual America. An older child who has already learned to read and who, from watching television and visiting the movies, has acquired a passive understanding of the standard dialect, may also have both more motivation and more opportunity to escape the restrictions of the ghetto. The prospects may be better for helping him to add active control of the standard to his linguistic repertory, particularly if the curriculum could take realistic account of the language patterns the students start with. What is needed is an instructional program that borrows a few techniques from methods of foreign language instruction and no more than in a foreign language course, need such instruction carry with it the implication that the students' own native language is inferior.

In recent years many of those who have been concerned with education in the ghettoes have come to feel that their realistic goal should be to encourage bidialecticalism, to capitalize upon the skill in dialect switching that many Negroes already have, and to develop ways by which they can learn to do it systematically and well. It is not only arrogant but no doubt utterly useless to ask them to stop speaking with their friends and families in the natural way that they have learned first. They can learn the appropriate time and place for the intimate language and the appropriate time and place for the standard, but they should not have to reject either. The first step in developing such an attitude in students, however, is probably to persuade the thousands of teachers of Negroes that the native dialects of their students have an irreplaceable value to them. These dialects deserve respect and understanding for what they are, not blind and uncompromising opposition.

DISCUSSION QUESTIONS

1. How relevant is this article to Anthony Kroch's hypothesis presented in the preceding article?

2. How valid do you consider the comparison of Black English with Swiss German?

3. Compare Burling's statement about the plural of *test* with Harold Allen's findings about the plural of *fist*.

4. Compare Burling's list of Negro speech features with those listed by Michael Linn as presumably of Creole origin.

ROGER D. ABRAHAMS

Diversely talented as folklorist and educator, the author is a native of Philadelphia, where he became intimately familiar with the Black street life he describes. Former professor of English and anthropology and head of the department of English at the University of Texas, Abrahams now is Keenan professor of anthropology and humanities in the Claremont Colleges, California.

BLACK TALKING ON THE STREETS

Deny the Negro the culture of the land? O.K. He'll brew his own culture—on the street corner. Lock him out from the seats of higher learning? He pays it no nevermind—he'll dream up his own professional doubletalk, from the professions that *are* available to him . . . These boys I ran with at The Corner, breathing half-comic prayers at the Tree of Hope, they were the new sophisticates of the race, the jivers, the sweettalkers, the jawblockers. They spouted at each other like soldiers sharpening their bayonets—what they were sharpening, in all this verbal horseplay, was their wits, the only weapons they had. Their sophistication didn't come out of moldy books and dicty colleges. It came from opening their eyes wide and gunning the world hard.

. . . They were the genius of the people, always on their toes, never missing a trick, asking no favors and taking no guff, not looking for trouble but solid ready for it. Spawned in a social vacuum and hung up in mid-air, they were beginning to build their own culture. Their language was a declaration of independence.

(Mezzrow & Wolfe 1969: 193–4)

Black is . . . : Being so nasty and filthy you cook in all the big downtown restaurants . . . Exploited by the news/Tortured by the blues/breaking the rules/and paying your dues . . . Realizing 'they' all look alike too! . . . Playing the 'dozens!'

(From a Black cocktail napkin)

Blacks do indeed speak differently than whites. Here I do not refer to the phonological and morphological differences much discussed in the literature of Black English, but rather to the ways in which Blacks use talk as part of their daily lives. Whether or not it is sufficient basis for an argument of *cultural* differences (as Mezzrow implies above), it seems clear that Afro-Americans in the United States do constitute a separate *speech community*. That is, they differ from other groups in the varieties of speech they employ and in the ways they use these varieties in carrying out the ritual (predictable) dimension of their personal interactions. Or, to put it in Hymes' terms for speech community, they 'share rules for the conduct and interpretation of speech, and rules for the interpretation of at least one linguistic variety' (Hymes 1972: 54).

We recognize, then, this sense of community in Black speaking in a great many ways—not least of which is the kind and intensity of talk about talk which one encounters in conversations and the special in-group names given by the speakers to ways of talking. Such Black terms for speech events constitute one important dimension of their system of speaking, and focus on speech use in very different ways from the usages of Euro-American discourse. This is not to say that there are not parallel terms or analogous practices in standard American English. Rather, the range, the intensity, the proliferation of terms, and the importance of such events are, as a whole, quite different from the configuration of communicative systems found elsewhere.

The existence of this distinct speaking community is recognized by Blacks (as well as whites) in their lore about themselves. One hears discussions not only about how *bad* or *country* some Blacks talk, but also how *lame* and uninformed whites are at communicating with each other. The Black ability to use words artfully and playfully is often encountered as an explanation of how and why Blacks outwit whites in certain conflict situations. There is thus a ground-level recognition of speaking differences among Blacks that gives the idea of a distinct speaking community a sense of analytic reality. Furthermore, analysis is carried on by the Black speakers themselves in discussions about the effectiveness or ineffectiveness of someone's abilities at using speech on some level of performance.

Perhaps the clearest indication of the distinctiveness of the Black speech community lies in the use of speech in the pursuit of public *playing,* and a parallel use of silence or other verbal restrictions in the more private sectors of the community. That is, attitudes toward work and play differ in Afro- and Euro-American communities. In Black communities, work is essentially a private matter, something learned in the home as part of the respectable and cooperative ideals of home life. Play, on the other hand, is inappropriate for the most part in the home, but rather is regarded as a public kind of phenomenon. Playing, in fact, is an important way in which one distinguishes oneself in public, and engaging in witty verbal exchanges is one important way of playing. (In the Euro-American system, on the other hand, play tends to be regarded as something appropriate for an adult to do in private—certainly something you don't usually want to get caught at, unless you're a member of a team. Work is the way in which one distinguishes oneself, and is therefore properly a public activity.) Thus, one crucial distinction to be made with regard to defining the Black speaking community is between house talk, especially 'around moms,' and street talk. Because active verbal performance in the street is one of the main means of asserting one's presence and place, there are a greater number of terms for street talk than for house talk. In the house, communications often are defined in terms of a Momma's imposed set of restrictions; especially when the speaking is defined as playful (Abrahams 1973). Here the restrictions may be on the subject of discussion, the vocabulary used, the amount of noise generally permitted to emanate from the residents of the house, and the communication relationships pursued in that ambience. There are, of course, numerous modes of talk, especially in the area of conversation, which are shared in both worlds. But the distinctions between the two are dramatic, for in the street world certain kinds of play are regarded as a norm—and valued as such—which are out of place for the most part in the house.

In general women—and especially female heads of households and older women—speak differently than men. Women are expected to be more restrained in their talk, less loud, less public, and much less abandoned. Parents attempt to instill this in the girls in their family by attempting to get them never to talk loudly or curse, not even when involved in street encounters. As Louise Meriwether explains it in her autobiography, 'Daddy even didn't want me to say darn. He was always telling me: "It's darn today, damn tomorrow, and next week it'll be goddamn. You're going to grow up to be a lady, and ladies don't curse" '(1970: 28). But the problem is more than cursing. Any kind of public talk may not be respectably ladylike. The house is the locus of a woman's sense of respectability, and it is by respectability canons that a woman is judged by her community and especially her peers (Wilson 1969). Communication is regarded as properly restricted there, to the point that silence from children (especially in the presence of Momma) is highly valued.

The major difference between the house and the street worlds, beyond the relative privacy and restriction, lies in the kind of relationships pursued and the varieties of communication used. The house world is populated in the main by members of the family. The home is regarded as the place to keep the family together. Here (and in the church) is therefore where Momma asserts her respectability most fully. In the street world, on the other hand, male friendships are established and kept up, and this is done by maintaining the possibility of *playing* (with all that comes to mean) at all times. This essay deals primarily with the communication events most characteristic of street behaviors, understanding that street includes all areas regarded as public.[1]

Elliot Liebow's study, *Tally's Corner,* describes how one friendship circle operates. His description is characteristic of other such groups.

> On the streetcorner, each man has his own network of . . . personal relationships and each man's network defines for him the members of his personal community. His personal community, then, is not a bounded area but rather a web-like arrangement of man–man and man–woman relationships in which he is selectively attached in a particular way to a definite number of discrete persons . . .
>
> At the edges of this network are those persons with whom his relationship is affectively neutral, such as area residents whom he has 'seen around' but does not know except to nod or say 'hi' to as they pass in the street . . .
>
> In toward the center are those persons he knows and likes best, those with whom he is 'up tight'; his 'walking buddies,' 'good' or 'best' friends, girl friends, and sometimes real or putative kinsmen. These are the people with whom he is in more or less daily, face-to-face contact, and whom he turns to for emergency aid, comfort or support in time of need or crisis. He gives them and receives from them goods and services in the name of friendship, ostensibly keeping no reckoning. Routinely, he seeks them out and is sought out by them. They serve his need to be with others of his kind, and to be recognized as a discrete, distinctive personality, and he in turn serves them the same way. They are both his audience and his fellow actors.
>
> (1967: 161–3)

Liebow's use of the metaphor of performance is appropriate here because friendship is not only defined by whom one may call upon for aid, but more important, with whom one may *play*.

In such a person-centered society a man establishes his reputation. A man with a *big rep* is so judged, in part, by the number of people he is able to call friend and therefore call upon for such goods and services as well as joke with. Both are implied in the word *play*. Because a reputation is so person-centered, it needs to be constantly guarded. As Rap Brown put it: 'Once I established my reputation, cats respected it . . . If I went out

---

[1] I do this recognizing that I am continuing to commit an error of my past studies of Black communication styles, justly pointed out by Valentine (1972), by treating primarily Black male behavior patterns. I have done this because there are more data on this street dimension of Black culture. But I hope to redress this lack in future studies in which the more private and less performance-centered dimensions of talking Black will be discussed. (For preliminary attempts in the United States and the British West Indies, see Abrahams 1970a,b,c.)

of my neighborhood, though, it was another story. I'd be on someone else's turf and would have to make it or take it over there' (H. R. Brown 1969: 15). This is echoed in Piri Thomas' comment, 'In Harlem you always lived on the edge of losing rep. All it takes is a one-time loss of heart' (1967: 58).

This personalistic, reputation-centered approach has been noted by numerous ethnographers. Somewhat complicating the matter, Herbert Gans has noted this feature as a general characteristic of lower-class socialization, which he calls an 'action seeking' style of life; but the manner in which Blacks set up the action and the modes of performance differ from that of any other ethnic enclave. (For an indication that these differences are perceived and maximized on the street level, see Suttles' [1968: 65ff.] description of lower-class Italian-American reactions to Black performance style.)

In such a street world, one must dramatize oneself constantly, and one is therefore always looking for opportunities to do so. Perhaps the most important means one has to do so in the Black world—and especially in the cities—is through verbal performances. In this expressive life style, performance and especially talk become the major means for establishing friendships—a process Rainwater describes as 'a single adaptation in lower-class Negro society, which has as its primary goal the maintenance of reciprocity between members on the basis of a symbolic exchange of selves, *an entertainment of each by the other*' (1970: 378, my italics).

There is ample testimony to the importance of learning to talk well to operate successfully outside the home environment (a move Claude Brown repeatedly calls 'coming out of the house'—'cutting loose from . . . parents' [1966; see esp. pp. 166ff.]). Not only do the ethnographic studies carried out by myself, Kochman, Kernan, Hannerz, Rainwater, the Milners, and others underline this feature of Black life style, but such an in-group commentator as Malcolm X describes how crucial it was to learn to talk right to establish his *rep* wherever he went, especially in Harlem when he was operating as a pimp–waiter (1965). Rap Brown devotes a whole chapter to his street education which emphasizes the relationship between learning to talk well and the development of his reputation:

> I used to hang out in the bars just to hear the old men 'talking shit.' By the time I was nine, I could talk Shine and the Titanic, Signifying Monkey three different ways, and Piss-Pot Peet for two hours without stopping. Sometimes I wonder why I even bothered to go to school. Practically everything I know I learned on the corner . . .
>
> The street is where young bloods get their education. I learned how to talk on the street, not from reading about Dick and Jane going to school and all that simple shit. The teacher would test our vocabulary every week, but we knew the vocabulary we needed. They'd give us arithmetic to exercise our minds. Hell, we exercised our minds by playing the Dozens . . .
>
> There'd be sometimes 40 or 50 dudes standing around and the winner was determined by the way they responded to what was said. If you fell all over each other laughing, then you knew you'd scored. It was a bad scene for a dude that was getting humiliated. I seldom was. That's why they called me Rap, cause I could rap.
> (H. R. Brown 1969: 25–7, 30; for similar accounts see Abrahams 1970a, chapter 2)

It would be easy to conclude from such accounts that this attitude and verbal practice are characteristic only of Black enclaves in the big cities. To do so would be to be misled by the urban terms that Brown uses. In fact, the focus on using (among other techniques) verbal abilities as a means of establishing and maintaining reputation is a widely observed

Afro-American characteristic which extends to Black communities outside the United States (e.g., Wilson 1969; Abrahams & Bauman 1971). But most important for the present argument, verbal *playing* has been reported from a number of non-urban communities (e.g., Ferris 1972; Lewis 1964; Friedland & Nelkin 1971) as part of a complex in which males find meeting places where they can pursue their male expressive behaviors—in spite of it being judged as *bad* by both the respectables and, when pressed to it, themselves.

Although much described in the literature, these behaviors are all too often judged from a Euro-American perspective which sees them as 'idling' or 'killing time' without recognizing the system by which they operate. Street-level terms are *hanging* (Keiser 1969), *hanging out, taking care of business*.[2]

Even those who do not accord much significance to expressive phenomena in their analyses of Black culture acknowledge the importance of a certain range of talking in these interactive settings. For instance, Hylan Lewis in his *Blackways of Kent* reports that in the Piedmont community which he studied there was much 'public idling' which he associated with male behavior. He noted 'specific idling places, informal idling cliques, a range of conventional idling behavior, and certain days and periods when idling is expected' (1964: 68).

The importance of talk in such situations is nowhere so clearly reflected as in the large number of terms describing the varieties of such talk. In fact, these terms are a good index not only to the importance of talk but to the range of speech events whereby such public friend-groups celebrate themselves while getting the action going. The street world is thought of as the public world and therefore one in which playing is appropriate. This does not mean that in verbal interactions on the street only play is found, but rather that it seems to operate as a norm—or at least a constant incipiency—and other events are distinguished from it. This may account for the great number of ground-level distinctions made with regard to verbal *playing* or *signifying*.

Play is a difficult phenomenon to describe in any culture. On the one hand play relies on the distinction between it and the 'real' or the 'serious.' On the other, for such play to operate successfully, there must be a recognizable relationship between it and the real world. One of these vital connections is that for play to operate successfully, there must be a sense of threat arising from the 'real' and 'serious' world of behavior. The threat of incursions from the real world must be constant. That is, in the most successful kinds of play, the most constant message must be the deeply ambivalent one: this is play—this is *not* play. With joking activity (which accounts for most *playing* in the street

---

[2] The term *business* in the sense of personal concerns is a focal term in Afro-American communities. Though this is not the appropriate place to fully explore the semantic field of the Black uses of the term, there are some features which are important to point out. *Business* essentially means 'name' maintenance. Thus, if a woman uses the term, it is liable to be in protection of her sense of respectability, warning others that her doings are 'nobody's business but my own.' On the other hand, when a man says 'I'ma *t.c.b.* [take care of business]' he is generally referring to leaving to see others, to maintain his connections, his friendship (or loveship) networks. *T.c.b.* generally is taken to mean 'I'm going to see a man about something which (I want you to think) is important'; but it also can refer to pursing a sexual conquest or to the sexual act itself. For an important early commentary on the special Afro-American use of the term see F. L. Olmsted, *A Journey in the Seaboard States* (1856: 206).

world) this paradoxical message is very commonly carried out by the use of the same aggressive, hostile formulaic devices found in use in real arguments—i.e., the same curses, boasts, devices of vilification and degradation, etc. This is precisely what one finds in the Black street world—so much so that the passer-by often has a hard time discerning whether joking or a real argument is taking place. Indeed, it becomes an important part of the show on many occasions to keep even the other participants wondering whether one is still playing.

This blurring of the line between play and seriousness is often observable in the terms which are used to describe the communicative event. *Cursing,* for instance, may be either a device of *playing,* or used very seriously, as are *mounting, charging, getting on someone's case,* and many others. The very same words that constitute a *put-down* or a *put-on* in one situation may be used as playful *woofing* or *talking shit* in another. This is why it is important to be at home, on your *own turf,* when you begin to use these devices. One can suddenly find that one has *gone too deep,* and that what one thought to be jokes are being taken very seriously indeed. But it also means that if one wants to test someone on one's own turf, one can use these devices with an outsider without giving clear cues as to whether one is being serious or not. Or in the most extreme circumstances, one can use them to start a real fight. This is why neither the witty, aggressive, traditional devices nor even the generic terms for them can be used as the primary basis of a taxonomy (even though they are the data which originally indicated that a ground-level taxonomy exists).

Only the most extreme forms of play are regarded as appropriate only on the street. The range of joking called (among other things) *talking smart* may occur wherever women and men find themselves in courtship-level conversation—though the smart talk is as often used to fend off a courting move as it is to encourage or continue it. *Talking smart,* however, is primarily regarded as street talk because it involves the kind of display of wit which is most useful and appropriate in public places. Nevertheless, it is a style of talk carried on between the participants without any need for an audience, and is often reported as occurring just between two people who find themselves in some situation of contention. That these *are* reported in anecdotal form, however, indicates the close relationship between such *smart talking* and *talking shit.* A good display of wit is too valuable to waste it only on a two-person conversation. It must be repeated to a larger audience later, one which can admire the witty verbal control.

There are, in this recognition of distinctions within the Black speaking community, three basic kinds of street-talk events: those intended primarily to pass on information, those in which interpersonal manipulation or argumentation involving a display of wit is going on, and those in which play is the primary component of the interaction. This distinction is keyed as much by proxemic and kinesic elements as by verbal means. The more informational, the more private the interaction. The more wit is involved, the more the possibility of onlooker involvement. When men are talking in public and primarily with other men (i.e., *to* them, with messages meant primarily for their ears), the major indication of what range of speaking event is going on is given by how their bodies are stationed. The most casual kind of grouping in which *talking shit* or *woofing* is probably taking place is a group standing or sitting shoulder-to-shoulder, in either a line or semicircle, where the passing action may be observed without disturbing the state of talk. As the discussion gets *deeper* (the more intensively stylized and aggressive or the more personal), the participants get closer to each other, stationing themselves so that you can make eye contact with whoever is talking. The instigators of talk will maintain their mobility, for they will be dramatizing their talk with action. A good talker will somewhat immobilize the others around him. The more one commands attention, the longer his talk is countenanced. He must receive constant verbal and kinesic support from the others. (For interesting pictures, see Keiser 1969: *passim*; Friedland & Nelkin 1971.) This support is indicated in a number of verbal and kinesic ways—one of which is the bending at the waist and knees. The deeper the bending, the greater the supportive intensification, it would seem. In all adult interactions, but especially public ones, participation must be actively indicated constantly. As one commentator noted: 'Unlike a white audience, careful to suppress enthusiasm, the black man and woman were silent [and still] only when they were negative and suspicious' (Keegan 1971: 7).

The older the members of the group talking, the less low-level kinesic activity will go on among the non-talking members. But with adolescents who are just perfecting the style of their *pimp walk* (see Johnson 1971: 19 and Ellis & Newman 1971: 302 for descriptions) there is a need to *style* constantly. As Kenneth R. Johnson describes this grouping technique:

> When talking in a group, the participants (say four or five young Black males) will often adopt a kind of stationary 'pimp strut' . . . while [they] are talking, they stand with their hands halfway in their pockets, and they move in the rhythmic, fluid dance-type way (without actually walking) to punctuate their remarks. The arm that is free will swing, point, turn and gesture as conversation proceeds . . . This kind of behavior always accompanies a light or humorous conversation, or a conversation about masculine exploits. It never accompanies a serious discussion about more general topics (planning something, difficulties with parents, political issues, etc.).
>
> (1971: 19)

If two (or more) people are seen engaging in close talk, facing each other and maintaining eye contact, the assumption is that something *deep* is going on, either one is *running something down* to the other—passing on valid information on which he is supposed to act—or that one is *running a game* on the other, *hyping* or *shucking* him— passing on invalid information. If two are arguing and engaging in talking smart, they will face each other but be farther apart and more mobile than when getting the *run down* on something.

If two (or more) are in a casual state of talk they will signify this by looking outward. This is even true when two friends meet on the street and shake hands. If they are not *hipping* someone to something that is *happening,* they will gaze away even while still shaking or just holding hands. The more other-person-centered the talk becomes (or the 'have you heard about so-and-so' sort concerning mutual friends or acquaintances), the closer the two will come, and the more their bodies will face each other, especially if the news of the other's *business* is concerned with a life-change (moving, any sort of conflict or confinement).

These kinesic and proxemic observations might be used to describe street behaviors of any age. But, as noted above, there are differences in the amount of movement within a group depending on how recently the young men have learned to *walk their walk* and *talk their talk,* to *style* their actions to make themselves appear *cool* (under control through stylistic moves) and *hip* (informed).

Performing by *styling* is thus one of the means of adapting oneself to the street world, of developing a public persona through which one can begin to establish and maintain one's *rep.* Naturally, as a young man learns how to *style,* he is much more self-conscious of how he is coming over to the others, and he therefore constantly looks for openings in which he can demonstrate his styling abilities. At first he does this almost formularistically—by imitation of those whom he has observed and admired. Later, when he has lived with *styling* devices, he will be less self-conscious and more able to take the styling for granted and thus be more message-oriented in his stylized communications.

Though it is in walking and dressing well that such a young man asserts his style most immediately, it is often in learning to *talk shit,* to effectively play with words by *talking that talk,* that his street image will be most firmly established. (This is especially true of the *pimp* or *cat* approach to the streets. The alternative gorilla approach of using one's strength is explored in Abrahams 1970a: 85–96 and in Firestone 1964, and is commented upon in Hannerz 1969: 115 and Milner & Milner 1972: 319–20. For somewhat different taxonomies of available social roles 'on the street,' see Ellis & Newman 1971 and Strong 1940.) This is what Rap Brown seems to have meant when he stressed the origin of his name in his ability to contest effectively with words, and how central this was to his *high rep.*

Because *styling* is so important during this period of life, the Black community tends to view certain performances as being age-specific to adolescence. That is, there are a number of speech events which continue to be played throughout life when men congregate, but because they are more self-consciously stylized during adolescence, their names and the self-conscious dimension of their performance may be rejected. Thus, among the older members of the community, the names for these practices may become pejorative; certainly their practice becomes less habitual, more restricted. But the same patterns of interaction may be observed throughout a man's life as long as he identifies with his peer group and engages in congregations on the street or some other equally public place.

Whenever men get together to engage in talk, this may lead to an increasingly stylized set of behaviors which, as they become more stylized, will be progressively more aggressive, more contest-oriented, and more centered on witty style and delivery. This progression, too, is taken note of in Black terms for self-conscious interactions, being referred to in a number of ways like *going deep, getting heavy, really getting into it,* or *getting to it.* The heavier or deeper the performance, the more attention the interchange will attract, and the more responding movement (a kind of dancing with) and answering verbal response (continuatives of the *right on* variety) will arise.

In this realm there seem to be important age-differentials in what speaking events arise most often in such states of talk. Among the younger adolescents, the devices used are not only more formulaic but also shorter. The older the group, the more time is given the performer to develop his point; thus, jokes, toasts (long narrative often heroic verses), and personal experience narrations emerge more often with older performers.

Hannerz describes such differences in regard to these aggressive verbal practices, focussing on the fuzzy semantic boundaries of the in-group descriptive terms *joning* and *joking.*

> Verbal contests occur among young males as well as among adult counterparts . . . This is the phenomenon which has become most known [in the literature] as 'the dozens,' but it is also known as 'sounding' and under some other local names. The term most often used in Washington, D.C., is *'joning'* . . .
> Joning is an exchange of insults . . . The boundaries of the concept are a little fuzzy; there is some tendency to view joning as any exchange of insults of a more or less jocular type in sociable interaction among children and adolescents. Joning is

definitely associated with joking. For smaller boys it seems to shade imperceptibly into the category of 'cracking jokes,' and when joning occurs in a peer group sociable session it is often preceded and followed by other kinds of jokes. These are also exchanged in a manner resembling a contest, and some of them have a form and content somewhat similar to jones . . .

The exchanges can occur between two boys who are alone, and it is even possible for them to jone on some third absent person, usually one of their peers, but the typical situation involves a group of boys: while a series of exchanges may engage one pair of boys after another, most members of the crowd function as audience, inciters, and judges—laughing, commenting upon the 'scoring,' and urging the participants on . . .

As the boys become men they gradually cease to amuse themselves with joning. Although verbal aggression continues, it becomes less patterned; the insults contain hardly any references to mothers any more, and if a man, often by chance rather than intentionally, should say anything which could be construed as an abuse of another's mother, the latter might simply say, 'I don't play that game no more.'

(1969: 129–30)

Just what the difference is between this and adult joking behaviors is not quite clear from either the literature or my own observations, except that, as noted, the younger men use more formulaic devices, and are therefore less improvisational in their contest techniques than adults. Ferris's (1972) argument with regard to his Mississippi informants suggests that the older one gets, the less fictional and the more personal stories may get.

There is, however, a tendency to identify all such adolescent *playing* with the specific practice of *playing the dozens*. This leads to a use of the same terms for all aggressive play on a more particular level as synonyms for the dozens. But, as Rap Brown pointed out above, these same groups may want to distinguish between different kinds of *playing: cracking* on the other person, on the other person's family, or on yourself. Another important distinction is the use of boasts in the same context.

There are, then, terminological distinctions made by the participants in the public street world of the Black speaking community which suggest the existence of a native taxonomy of ways of speaking. Thus, in my original formulation, I worked out the distinctions on the level of the terms—as they were distinguished by some speakers at some time. But it became clear that these distinctions are acted on even in those Black communities that do not have a contrast-set of terms. Therefore, the taxonomy must be described with regard to the distinctions in speaker-to-speaker relationships and strategies. However, because these terms do provide some sense of the distinction, one ground-level term will be given for each taxonomic slot—and the terms will be surveyed and discussed in an appendix.

I regard this taxonomy as an underlying record of some of the most important distinctions in Black life, felt, acted upon, and judged if not always named by agrarian and post-agrarian Black communities in the United States. Interactions which are named in one community but not in another are nevertheless practiced in both. Further, many of the names for these ways of speaking change constantly from time to time and place to place, but the patterned interactions and the relations between the types of situated speech remain essentially constant (at least as far back as our data will take us).

Fig. 1 presents the relationships between the major ways of speaking on the street, emphasizing the continuities between patterns of interaction and persuasion from casual conversation to stylized playing with words in the aggressive, contest situation characteristic of *playing the dozens* and *woofing*. There are a number of techniques of manip-

Conversation on the streets; ways of speaking between equals					Going deep; talking baad
Informational; content focus. *Running it down*	Aggressive, witty performance talk. *Signifying*				
	Serious, clever conflict talk. 'Me-and-you and no one else' focus. *Talking smart*		Non-serious contest talk. 'Any of us here' focus. *Talking shit*		
	Overly aggressive talk. *Putting down*	Covertly aggressive, manipulative talk. *Putting on*	Non-directive. *Playing*	Directive. *Sounding*	

Conversational (apparently spontaneous)	Arises in conversational context, yet judged in performance (stylistic) terms	Performance interaction, yet built on model of conversational back-and-forth

ulation used in both serious and playful aggressive contexts, like *mounting, bragging,* and others. These will be discussed in the appendix of terms.

The taxonomy is divided in three parts from talk in which information is the focus, to the most stylized, in which more concern is shown for the artful patterning of the utterance than the message. With the former the style is buried in favor of the message; the interaction to be effective must seem relatively spontaneous. With the latter, the message is subordinated or disavowed (since it is all just play) while the intensity and effectiveness of presentation become most important. Between these are interactions in which stylized devices are introduced—and call attention to themselves—but in which message remains as important as style.

The greater the use of wit or special information and energy, the *heavier* the interaction is judged to be, and the more the onlooker is entertained. This is as true of *hipping* or the *put-on* and *put-down* as it is in *woofing,* for such interactions will either draw onlookers or they will become performance pieces in later retellings.

In other words, not only are these distinctions made, but more important, exceptional scenes in which such talking is featured become topics for further talk. And there are numerous ground-level ways in which the effectiveness and usefulness of talk are discussed. Again, the *deeper* the interaction is judged to be the more a recounting is liable to occur. These scenes may be of all three types, those in which *heavy* information is being passed on (*rifting*), where someone is showing his *smarts,* or where a remarkable capping session has occurred.

Less noticed that the aggressive and competitive interactions in Black talk have been those concerned with the discussion and dissemination of information. Only Labov and his associates have analyzed the importance of such talk in street talk, specifically with regard to the concept terms of *rifting* and being *on the square,* local terms for what Dillard has referred to as *fancy talk.*

Rifting is, as Labov *et al.* (1968: 152) describe it, a 'form of display, of both knowledge and verbal style.' The more knowledge one has of a subject the more he is regarded as being *heavy in the head.* Thus, it is not just verbal style which is the mark of the street man-of-words; in certain situations when a potential peer is put *on the square,* expressions of knowledge are equally important. The style of rifting, like that of sermonizing and other formal and oratorical situations involves

> a style of speech—an elevated high flown delivery which incorporates a great many learned Latinate words, spelling out the uncontracted form of function words with characteristic level and sustained intonation pattern that lays extra stress and length on the last stressed word. The occult knowledge which is delivered in this way is described as 'heavy'—it is *heavy knowledge, heavy stuff,* or *heavy shit;* and too heavy for outsiders to understand. Heavy or secret knowledge is learned by rote; adepts are examined in a speech event known as 'putting someone on the square.'
>
> (Labov *et al.* 1968: 136)

Hannerz discusses the place of such *heavy* informational talking in the range of other more playful types.

> All prestige accrued from being a good talker does not have to do with the strictly utilitarian [manipulative] aspect. A man with good stories well told and with a good repartee in arguments is certain to be appreciated for his entertainment value, and those men who can talk about the high and the mighty, people and places, and the state of the world, may stake claims to a reputation of being heavy 'upstairs.'
>
> (1969: 85)

He later discusses two men from the neighborhood in which he worked who were known for this weightiness of knowledge, causing their friends and neighbors to regard them as 'intellectuals' (p. 106).

That this is a Black role-type is noted by many Black writers. For instance, George Cain in his remarkable *Blueschild Baby* observes:

> J.B., the storyteller . . . found in all civilizations, preserver of unwritten histories, keeper of legends and oral tradition. Daily he holds forth, as at an African marketplace. Surrounded by black faces reflecting the moods of his narrations, he translates what is in the white mind and media into the idiom of his audience. Every corner has its J.B., that funny nigger who makes a crowd dance with laughter at themselves and their shortcomings . . .
>
> Many dismiss him as bullshit, unable to see his role or contribution, but like all black people, they're respectful of knowledge so don't protest too vehemently . . . On the absence of truth-telling media James and those like him evolved. Street-corner philosophers with all the technique of gifted actors, they hold the most difficult audience in the world.
>
> (1970: 29–30)

Often this performance of knowledge is commented upon in a metalingual and metacritical way, leading to further routines by the *heavy* talker on his streetcorner training. Typical of such speeches is one reported briefly from a Florida conservative Black politician, Norman E. Jones: 'His education, he once said, consists of "Ph.D.'s" from "the University of Beale Street, the University of Harlem and many other universities throughout the nation—generally called the street where people exist" ' (Hooker 1972: 4; for a longer routine, see Killens 1972: 157).

However, such *heavy* displays are more likely to occur while *playing,* for in the *hanging* situation such *playing* is a constant possibility. It is in this range of situations, also, that there is the greatest number of terms, and they change most frequently. These terms (given in the appendix) sometimes indicate more particularity in distinguishing techniques of wit and argumentation that might have been used to make the taxonomic chart deeper in the realm of playing. For instance, some communities make a distinction between the *clean* and the *dirty dozens.* By this they mean, in the case of the former, that the joke is directly aimed at one of the others in the interacting group, while the latter directs them at some member of the other's family. Further, there are a number of such *clean* techniques, such as *bragging* or *boasting,* in which the main reference is the speaker, or *charging* and *mounting* in which the other is the target; or the general *capping* remark, which may be a witticism which only indirectly downs the other.

Beyond these distinctions, there are terms (and much discussion) which may refer to such intensification of verbal performances—though they may have reference to non-verbal presentational effects. These are terms like *styling, having the flash* (Woodley 1971: 11), *styling out,* or *showing out,* which point out dramatically foregrounded presentational techniques; but more often they are concerned more with clothing and hair style than verbal display.

Similarly, if an interaction is regarded as a dramatic success, comment will occur with regard to how someone really got *on someone's case* or *charged all over him.* (Sale 1971: 90, 104, has the Blackstone Rangers refer to *getting shot through the grease.*) But if such a strategy fails, the instigator is liable to be accused of being *lame, running off at the mouth,* or *talking off the wall shit* (not knowing what he is talking about). Since this arises in comment on the informational content of a person's argument, he also may be accused of wanting to appear to be serious but being interpreted as *playing.* In such a context, any of the terms for *signifying* may be used negatively, like *talking shit* (now with an emphasis on the last word) or *woofing.* Older terms are *spouting* and *muckty muck* (Major 1970) and *boogerbooing* or *beating your gums* (Hurston 1942).

Similarly, terms like *jiving* and *shucking* may be used to call someone at a *lame* use of speech. Or if someone begins to *go deep* in an inappropriate context (not with close enough friends, or using techniques of a younger age-set), he may be called on it with an 'I don't play that shit' kind of remark, or 'I laugh, joke, and smoke, but I don't play' (see Abrahams 1970b). On the other hand, if the thrust of the remarks does hit home but they are regarded as inappropriate—an attempt to start a fight—the response will be the slightly different 'You better not play that shit with *me.*'

In such situations, there are a number of disavowal techniques, reclassifying the remarks into the category of *playing,* like 'Man, I was only bullshitting.' This strategy of trying to get out of an uneasy verbal situation in certain cases is engineered by the other as part of his strategy of a *put-down.* In such a case, the speaker seeking an out will have to do the more extreme act of verbal subjugation termed *copping a plea, gripping* (Kochman 1970; Sale 1971: 43), or the most recently encountered *eating cheese* and *cowdown* (Woodley 1972: 143). This most often occurs when someone (or a group) has really gotten *on your case,* or more extremely if you are suspected of wrongdoing, being put *on the square* (Labov *et al.* 1968).

Perhaps the most important dimension of the discussion on the judgment criteria used with regard to these situated ways of speaking is that one of the best things that can be said of the street talker is that he *comes on baad*. This obvious inversion of the term seems certainly to arise in opposition to the household respectability perspective. It is the expression of this opposition between the two 'worlds' of Black life that presents the largest problem in the description and analysis of an Afro-American world order—the problem of accounting for this high valuation of *baadness*. We know that these values are the opposite of the private respectable world and operate then primarily in the public realm. Furthermore, the recent studies of child rearing and language learning carried on by Young and by Ward indicate that a certain amount of this *baadness* is encouraged among the precocious within the home, with even the baby's first movements being positively interpreted as aggression (Young 1970; Ward 1971). The ramifications of this establishment of the contrarieties between these worlds and the accompanying ambivalent attitude toward public display are only now being noticed and analyzed. But in this area of investigation, I am convinced, lies one of the key dimensions of those role and behavior configurations that will enable us to designate not only the patterns of characteristics of the Black speaking community, but the integrity and uniqueness of Black culture in general.

APPENDIX: THE TERMS

Since the existence of this taxonomy, and the importance of verbal wit in understanding the street world, arose because of the use of terms for ways of speaking in some Black communities, it might be useful to review what these terms are and what speaking strategies and relationships they have been used to name. I will do this in sections, by key terms.

There are certain basic semantic problems involved in such a presentation, however. This is not only because of the number of terms involved, but because the same terms are used in different Black communities at different times to designate different types of speech events. Yet it seems important to present what data are available to demonstrate these problems and to indicate that there is an historical dimension to this taxonomy of ways of speaking.

SIGNIFYING

An example of how semantically confusing such a presentation can become can be seen in Kernan's discussion and review of the scholarship concerning the term *signifying*. In *Deep Down in the Jungle,* reporting on Black folklore in one black neighborhood in Philadelphia, I had heard the term used for a wide variety of verbal techniques united by the single strategy of verbal manipulation through indirection. The examples I reported there, which were quoted by Kerman, were

> [an] ability to talk with great innuendo, to carp, cajole, wheedle and lie . . . in other instances, to talk around a subject . . . [or] making fun of a person or situation. Also it can denote speaking with the hands and eyes . . . Thus it is signifying to stir up a fight between neighbors by telling stories; it is signifying to make fun of the police by parodying his motion behind his back; it is signifying to ask for a piece of cake by saying 'my brother needs a piece of that cake.'
>
> (Abrahams 1970b: 51–2)

Kernan then notes, agreeing that for most of her Oakland informants 'some element of indirection was criterial to *signifying,*' nevertheless 'many would label the parodying of the policeman's motions *marking* and the request for cake *shucking*' (Kernan 1971: 88). It is impossible to judge from her data whether these acts might be both *signifying* (as the general term), and *marking* or *shucking* as kinds of *signifying,* or whether contrast existed among these three terms on the same taxonomic level. For my Philadelphia informants, at least, the former was the case (though the most common term at that time for *shucking* was *jiving,* or, among the older people, *jitterbugging* or *bugging*).

But the labelling problem is even more complicated in Kernan's description of *signifying*; she notes that for Thomas Kochman's Chicago informants, *signifying* and *sounding* are used interchangeably, while most of her Oakland informants 'referred to the direct taunts which Kochman suggests are the formal features of signifying, when its function is to arouse emotions in the absence of directive intent [as in a verbal duelling game] as *sounding* or *woofing*' (1971: 89). But, she goes on, using herself as an informant: 'As a child in the Chicago area, my age group treated *signifying* and *sounding* as contrasting terms . . . *Signifying* . . . was a fairly standard tactic . . . employed in *sounding* (as a verbal insult game). That is, the speech event *sounding* could involve either direct insults *sounds* or *signifying,* indirect insults . . .' (pp. 89–90). However, with my Philadelphia informants, *sounding* and *woofing* were commonly used to refer just to the game of mother-rapping, *playing the dozens.* On the other hand, Rap Brown seems to insist on a basic distinction between *playing the dozens* and *signifying,* in which it is clear that the latter means, for him and his peers, what my Philadelphia informants called *mounting* and what Blacks in many parts of the country last year were calling *charging, cracking,* or *harping.* 'Signifying is more humane [than *playing the dozens*]. Instead of coming down on somebody's mother, you come down on them' (H. R. Brown 1969: 27). He further complicates matters by equating signifying with any kind of intensifying verbal activity (exclusive of the *dozens*), and not just putting someone down, by noting:

> before you can signify you got to be able to rap . . . Signifying allowed you a choice— you could either make a cat feel good or bad. If you had just destroyed someone or if they were down already, signifying was also a way of expressing your own feelings . . . Signifying at its best can be heard when the brothers are exchanging tales.
>
> (pp. 27–30)

Brown here seems to be setting up some kind of range and hierarchy of speaking events running from the most general term, *talking shit,* anyone's talk from the most casual to the most stylized and witty, to *rapping* or semi-public, spontaneously witty talk, to *playing the dozens* and *signifying,* openly competitive, public, witty, hyperbolic, highly stylized talk (including tales). But the place of *signifying* in this speech map would not be validated by Kernan's (1971) or Kochman's (1970) data, nor mine (see also Mezzrow & Wolfe 1969; Anderson 1959; Milner & Milner 1972; Eddington 1967; Hurston 1935 for more specific uses of the term).

These difficulties are more apparent than real, especially to the ethnographer of speaking. Clearly what we have here are terms which are used on more than one level in a taxonomy of ways of speaking, and which are used in different places and times to describe related but different speaking activities. Further, what I hope I have shown in the taxonomy is that with *signifying* we have a term not only for a way of speaking but for a rhetorical strategy that may be characteristic of a number of other designated events.

RAPPING

There are numerous terms to be found for casual talk, such as *beating the gums, gum beating, jawblock* (Mezzrow & Wolfe 1969). But none of these are place-specific to talk in public. With many informants in the last ten years there has been the feeling that the term *rapping* was the appropriate one for this public (street) talking—a perspective seemingly shared by Kochman when he noted that 'Rapping [is] used . . . to mean ordinary conversation' (Kochman 1970: 146; see also Keiser 1969: 72; Milner & Milner 1972: 306; Claerbaut 1972: 77; Woodley 1972: 144). But when asked whether terms like *sounding* or *shucking* were a kind of *rapping,* informants' responses are usually an initial giggle and then an 'I guess so.' I think that the reason my informants laughed when I asked them whether such terms are kinds of *rapping* was that while on the one hand rapping means 'just talking,' on the other hand in its most common uses it refers to interactions somewhat less public than the larger *playing* contest activities. That is, *rapping* in its more pointed uses is something generally carried on in person-to-person exchanges, ones in which the participants don't know each other well; it is often therefore a kind of *out of the house* talking which is primarily manipulative.

Kochman, in his full study of the semantic field of the term *rap,* indicates that he has observed three common uses:

(1) When *running something down,* providing information to someone.
(2) *Rapping* to a woman—'a colorful way of asking for some pussy,' used at the beginning of a relationship only, most used by *pimp-talkers, jivers,* the most fluent and lively men-of-words. This use I have therefore included under the concept term of *running a game* (a placing recognized or accepted by every one of my informants).
(3) As the verbal dimensions of a *con,* when *whupping the game* (Kochman 1970: 147).

TO HIP

Running something *down,* as discussed in the body of the paper, refers to *straight,* valid-information–centered conversations, and may be distinguished from ones in which either *game* is being *run* or *played.* That is, *running it down* commonly means giving advice to someone in a situation in which a decision has to be made, or *hipping* someone to *what's happening,* letting him know of some possible activity or of the doings of others. 'Running it down is the term used by ghetto dwellers when they intend to communicate information, either in the form of an explanation, narrative, giving advice, and the like . . . running it down has simply an informative function, telling somebody something that he doesn't already know' (Kochman 1970: 154–5, with quotations from King 1965, Claude Brown 1966, and Iceberg Slim 1967). 'Run it down: to tell the whole truth of whatever is in question' (Major 1970: 98; see also Killens 1972: 24, 41; Claerbaut 1972: 78; Milner & Milner 1972: 301, *to run down game*). Once one has had it *run down* to him, he is *down, in the know* (cf. Thomas 1967: 210, 243; Milner & Milner 1972: 299).

The earlier term, and one which is still widely in use, is to *hip*—'to inform a person of something he should know; to put [someone] wise' or *to be hipped* (to)—'informed; hep, knowledge; wise to' (Wentworth & Flexner 1960: 258; see also Gold 1960: 146; Milner & Milner 1972: 302; Claerbaut 1972: 68).

The basic distinction here is between the contest-focussed message of *running it down, hipping* someone to something, or *hitting on* a given subject, and the style-focussed message of *signifying,* styling which is foregrounded by the devices of making a point by indirection and wit. This is not to say that *running it down* has no style, or *signifying* has no content, but that their primary focus differs in this regard. Note that *signifying* here is designated only with regard to its street uses (see Kernan 1971: 87ff. for a discussion of sex-specific differences).

TALKING SHIT

Most *signifying* arising in the street world is of a sort in which the participants in the interaction engage in talk to elicit more talk—to get some *action* going. Witty remarks will be made calling for a response in kind. Though such exchanges often sound like arguments to outsiders, there is no rhetorical intent to create a status distinction.

There are many terms which have been employed for this kind of *signifying* play, *talking shit* seeming to be the most common today. Older terms, some of which are still in use, are *woofing* (though in most communities this refers to more particular events like *playing the dozens* or *sounding*), *telling lies, shag-lag,* and *bookooing.* Hurston uses all four terms on this level in her works:

> Woofing is a sort of aimless talking. A man half seriously flirts with a girl, half seriously threatens to fight or brags of his prowess in love, battle or financial matters. The term comes from the purposeless barking of dogs at night.
>
> (Hurston 1935: 305)

She makes it plain, however, in her numerous *woofing* scenes, that 'aimless talking' means an active display of wits.

The term most widely used now is *talking shit,* at least according to students from all over the country. That it is not just a student term is testified by Killens' use of it (Killens 1972: 26, 40), by the Milners (1972: 309), and by Major's reference to the expression and by Friedland and Nelkin's reporting of the term from a migratory labor camp in connection with a man-of-words and his abilities to joke and rhyme on people effectively (Friedland & Nelkin 1971: 152).

On the other hand, there are types of behavior in which the talker does seek to establish dominance or to *signify* to evade a situation in which he is already dominated. A distinction is made between *putting down* or *low-rating* in which witty devices are used to establish dominance, and *copping a plea,* in which an already dominated person attempts to establish equilibrium by admitting his subordinated status. (Kochman 1970 and Rainwater 1970 both report this term, as well as the less extremely deferential *gripping;* see also Major 1970: 41.) Thomas, discussing the strategy, notes: 'Mom was asking us to cop a plea to the white man . . . A—accept, B—behave, C—care.' The term also means *to rat on,* inform on (Thomas 1967: 134, 243). The most recently reported term (from Texas) for this is *eating cheese.* These terms are of recent usage in this sense, but may inhabit the same semantic field as *tomming, jeffing* (cf. Kochman 1970; Eddington 1967) or *playing Uncle Tom*—though in present usage the *tomming* of slaves tends to be regarded as closer to *shucking* in that it uses deference as a means of achieving some sense of dominance, and is therefore one type of *putting on* behavior. In the absence of actual reportings of such behavior labeled as *tomming,* however, I would not so categorize it; it should be noted, however, that the Marster-John stories

(Abrahams 1970a) represent similar accommodative strategies in narrative form to *tomming* (cf. Kochman 1970: 149).

Putting on involves the entire range of strategies for verbal manipulation to establish control. Essentially the term refers to 'play-acting for real,' using any of the devices of playing but in a situation in which eventually a psychological dominance is sought by the speaker, even if the person (or persons) being *put-on* doesn't recognize this. *Putting on* therefore involves a use of any of the strategies in one or another of its manifestations. As *running a game* or *whupping game* (cf. Kochman 1970; Milner & Milner 1972: 301; Claerbaut 1972: 65, 78, 86) it will actively involve all three—deference, dominance, and parity. With other *put-on* styles, the range is not so wide. *Putting on,* in any case, emphasizes the dominance strategy, and would have been regarded as a special kind of *put-down* except that my informants in both Philadelphia and Austin insist that a *put-on* is not a *put-down* but something quite distinct.

The difference is primarily in regard to where the speaker stands in regard to those he wishes to dominate. With a *put-down,* the dominance is already apparently felt, the speaker ratifying the relationship with each *put-down.* With a *put-on,* the dominance is not yet established; thus the speaker needs a less tendentious mode of asserting control, using a wide number of artful talking techniques. That there is a strong relationship between the two is indicated by the recognition by street talkers that some of the techniques of *putting* someone *on* can also be used to *put* them *down.*

PUT DOWN

There seems to be a basic distinction between the *put-down* style that relies on sharpness of perception and verbal focus and one in which the speaker gets louder and louder. This distinction is noted by communities most commonly when *loud-talking* is regarded as an inappropriate way to achieve a put-down. Hurston (1934) defines *loud talk me* in her glossary as 'making your side appear right by making more noise than the others,' but her use of the term in the novel is pejorative (p. 158). On the other hand, Heard gives us a *loud-talking* scene, using the term in which our response is intended to be ambivalent. In this use of the technique by a pimp, he uses a proverb, 'Talk loud and draw a big crowd' (1968: 227; this use of the term differs from its employment in the *put-on*; see below).

Mounting, downing (Abrahams 1970a; Eddington 1967: 198), and *ranking* are the same terms as used in one form of *playing the dozens*; the relationship is hardly fortuitous, for the same verbal devices are used in the *put-down* for serious purposes and in the *dozens* for play. In this serious interpersonal context, when the *mounting* is extended and one person is strongly *put down,* that has been called *getting on his case* or *charging*—though *downing* is not the only technique used in such situations.

PUT-ON

Loud-talking (or *louding*) (in a different meaning than above) and *marking* are two special techniques of achieving a *put-on.* Both involve a performance not overtly directed to the object of the remark. *Louding* is where the speaker is talking to others (or himself) loud enough so that the person referred to can hear—but when that person reacts, the speaker can reply to the effect 'Oh, I wasn't talking to you.' To be pulled off most effectively, the 'overheard' remark must refer to the overhearer in some oblique way. (Kernan 1971 gives an extended description, pp. 129–37, as do Labov *et al.* 1968: *passim,* but esp. pp. 14ff. and 27ff.) Mezzrow & Wolfe (1969) report the practice, perhaps in a more formal game context, as *snagging.* My informants agree that this is a way of *putting* someone *on,* but many argue that it may be a *put-down* as well. Kernan's examples would seem to argue the same way.

Marking, on the other hand, in its largest sense is simply the Black term for dramatic imitation or aping. It is not always used pejoratively. However, when the imitation is addressed to others than the person imitated, and especially when it is done in his presence but without his recognition, this is regarded as a *put-on* device. (*Marking* in the larger sense of imitation can be found in any verbal interaction as an intensifying device, especially in jokes and *getting on* someone's *case.* Kernan surveys the technique and its uses [1971: 137–43]). In the case where *marking* is used as a *put-on* device, it too can turn into a *put-down.*

With *running a game* we are in a domain of street performance in which verbal manipulation is central (see Killens 1972: *passim,* but esp. pp. 22ff.; also Milner & Milner 1972: 301; Claerbaut 1972: 65, 78, 86). Here the speaker uses as many techniques as possible to convince his target audience of the validity of his credentials, so that he may exploit them for sexual favors, money, or simply to enhance his reputation. With professional men of words, the *pimps, jivers, mackmen,* etc., *running* some sort of *game* is a constant preoccupation. Other men share in this to the extent that they have the ability to use their words to assert and maintain their *rep.*

There are many terms for running a game, all more or less synonymous. One term commonly used for this domain is *talking bullshit.* Claude Brown describes his persuasive powers of performance using this term:

> When Dad tried to talk to me, it never work out . . . It was easier for me [to get hit] than trying to listen to all that stupid shit he was telling me with a serious face. Sometimes I would bullshit him by looking serious and saying something that made him think he was saying something real smart. I had a special way of bullshitting everyone I knew, and that was how I bullshitted Dad.
>
> (1966: 45)

Kochman's discussion of *rapping* describes that term as the most casual dimension of the *gaming* complex of terms (see also Suttles 1968: 159; Milner & Milner 1972: 306; Claerbaut 1972: 76). *Jiving* and *shucking* seem to refer to more intensive *rapping,* with an accompanying growth in the amount of purposeful deception involved in such talking. Both of these are complicated terms historically and semantically. *Jive* and *jiving* used to mean simply the argot of the young Blacks on the street (see, e.g., Hurston 1942) and *jive-talk* was still used in this sense until recently. But because of the types who had greatest command over this style of talking, *jive* and *bulljive* came to be used in more and more pejorative contexts, as they are today (Strong 1940; Major 1970; Grange 1968; Rainwater 1970; Gold 1960; Claerbaut 1972; Milner & Milner 1972). The negative features fastened upon are an overstress on *styling* (obviously *styling* which doesn't come off) or too much emphasis on dominance at the expense of the parity strategy implied in *rapping.* Mezzrow and Wolfe make a distinction between *jive* and *high-jive,* the latter involving the use of 'fancy-talk,' a variety more commonly found in the semi-private courtship situation: 'High-jive: intellectual patter, the smoothest and most elaborate line. Highjiver: smooth character with a very fancy and intellectual line of talk' (1969: 306)[3]

Shucking and *jiving* are often used as one term. *Shucking* is also used to refer to any kind of name-establishing *bullshit*, though not so strongly focussed on knowledge of the in-group terms as *jiving* (see Abrahams 1970b, though the etymology for *shucking* there is faulty, as it is in Gold—the base reference of the term almost certainly goes back to a corn-shuck, either in regard to the practice of the corn-shucking performance gathering or to the expression 'lighting a shuck,' i.e., using a burning shuck for light for some peer-grouping activity [cf. Hurston 1934: 206]; Rainwater 1970: 284; Kochman 1970; Cain 1970; Milner & Milner 1972: 307; Claerbaut 1972: 79; Killens 1972: 25, 141).

Shucking, where it is used, refers to the artful means by which one person can get around another by whatever means he can devise. It therefore involves more devious means than *rapping*, especially as Kochman explores the two terms:

> *Shucking, jiving, shucking and jiving* or S-ing and J-ing, when referring to language behavior practiced by blacks when interacting with one another on the peer-group level, is descriptive of the talk and gestures appropriate to 'putting someone on' by creating a false impression, conveying false information, and the like. The terms seem to cover a range from simply telling a lie, to bullshitting, to subtly playing with someone's mind.
>
> (1970: 154)

This use of *shucking and jiving* differs in white–Black interactions only in the actual techniques used, not in the motives or intensity.

More intense and indicating deceit are terms like *hyping* and *conning,* but these are less often used in reference to in-group street-talking activity, and more in commentary on effective talking by some of their members in interactions outside the group (Mezzrow & Wolfe 1969: 306).

HOORAWING

Hoorawing, an active contest of wits in which everyone may join, is the most volatile of all the categories for ways of speaking. It is known by a number of terms even within the same community. *Hoorawing* or *talking hooraw shit* seem to be the oldest terms here according to my older informants in both Philadelphia and Texas. Other names are *signifying* (Kochman 1970; Rainwater 1970), *joning* (Hannerz 1969; Rainwater 1970), *screaming, ranking, cracking, snapping, sounding* (Thomas 1967; Labov *et al.* 1968; Abrahams 1970b), *woofing* (Abrahams 1970b), and *telling lies.* The practice is commonly carried on in trading short formulaic items, but among adults often includes the longer narrative items like *jokes, toasts,* or *stories.* Hurston's books, especially *Mules and Men*

---

[3] Puckett and Dillard discuss the uses of these traditions of eloquence (Puckett 1926: 38 ff; Dillard 1972: 245–59), and I survey the West Indian literature and the possible African backgrounds (Abrahams 1970c). Hannerz discusses the uses of such talk on the streets, as do Mezzrow and Wolfe, though the latters' interpretation seems wong-headed (Hannerz 1969: 85; Mezzrow & Wolfe 1969: 195).

(1935), eloquently describe this practice and with many texts. The importance of this kind of verbal play is discussed throughout the literature (see especially Hannerz 1969; Labov *et al.* 1968; Rainwater 1970; Abrahams 1970a,b; Kochman 1970). The larger term for this kind of *play* is *cutting contest* (see, for instance, Mezzrow & Wolfe 1969: 1971) and, by extension, a friend with whom one can *play*, a *cutting buddy, cutting man,* or *cutty* (Abrahams 1970b).

As Rap Brown pointed out, a distinction is often made between verbal contests involving insults to members of the families of the other contestants and those which aggrandize or deprecate in other ways. Explicitly or implicitly, there are further distinctions made in the playing of the clean dozens: to devices which are *lies* about oneself (whether they are aggrandizing of self doesn't seem to matter—if they are exaggerations they may be termed *bragging,* even if the content is about how poor or hungry or thin you are); to devices which wittily discuss the shortcomings of others, sometimes referred to as *mounting*; and simply witty remarks which build upon the word-play of others, *capping*. (Abrahams 1970d; Eddington 1967:198; Claerbaut 1972:60; Mezzrow & Wolfe 1969:304 define it as 'having the last word, go one better, outdo,' but their use of the term indicates a speaking frame of reference primarily.)

Boasting seems to mean intensive talk about oneself in a contest situation, whether one is emphasizing one's strengths or shortcomings. Thus, there may be exchanges based on how quick one is, how strong, or how hungry, lazy, tired, or whatever. (The same witticisms may be used to discuss someone else, in which case they are noncompetitive devices simply used to flavor conversational discussions.) These self-aggrandizing devices are also called *lies,* though that term is generally used for stories, jokes, and tall tales.

Dick Gregory, in his book *Nigger,* shows how important it was in learning how to cope with the realities of street life (and how he developed his comic sense) to learn a repertoire of these self-degrading *boasts,* by which he could capitalize on an underclassed position, building it into a strength (Gregory 1964:40–2). The technique emerges in many other works by Black authors.

More commonly, such *hoorawing* takes the form of *mounting,* attacking the other(s) by denigrating them. This may be done either by boasting at the same time or just *putting* the other *down*.[4]

REFERENCES

1. Abrahams, R. D. (1970a). *Positively Black.* Englewood Cliffs, N.J.
   (1970b). *Deep down in the jungle . . . ,* revised edition. Chicago.
   (1970c). Traditions of eloquence in the West Indies. *Journal of Inter-American Studies and World Affairs* 12: 505–27.
   (1970d). Rapping and capping: Black talk as art. In J. Szwed (ed.), *Black Americans.* New York, 143–53.

[4] I want to thank John Szwed and Robert Farris Thompson, Tony Terry and Robert Wilson, for talking some of the matters out. To the editors I am even further indebted—and far beyond matters editorial—for they both helped in the conceptualization and rendering of the paper at times when despair had settled in. Beverly Stoeltje's discussion of women *talking smart* clarified my ideas in this area. Marilyn Sandlin, too, bore up under the despair and the frenzy, typing the (too) many drafts. Barbara Babcock-Abrahams not only drew the chart many times, but helped with many other finishing touches.

(1973). *Toward a Black rhetoric: being a survey of Afro-American communication styles and role-relationships*. Texas Working Papers in Sociolinguistics no. 15.

2. Abrahams, R. D. and Bauman, R. (1971). Sense and nonsense in St. Vincent: speech behavior and decorum in a Caribbean community. *American Anthropologist* 73(3): 262–72.

3. Anderson, A. (1959). *Lover man*. New York.

4. Brown, C. (1966). *Manchild in the promised land*. New York.

5. Brown, H. R. (1969). *Die Nigger die!* New York.

6. Cain, G. (1970). *Blueschild baby*. New York.

7. Claerbaut, D. (1972). *Black jargon in White America*. Grand Rapids, Mich.

8. Dillard, J. (1972). *Black English*. New York.

9. Eddington, N. (1967). The urban plantation: the ethnography of oral tradition in a Negro community. Ph.D. dissertation, University of California at Berkeley.

10. Ellis, H. and Newman, S. (1971). 'Gowster,' 'Ivy-Leaguer,' 'Hustler,' 'Conservative,' 'Mack-man,' and 'Continental': a functional analysis of six ghetto roles. In E. G. Leacock (ed.), *The culture of poverty: a critique*. New York. 299–314.

11. Ferris, W. (1972). Black prose narrative in the Mississippi Delta: an overview. *Journal of American Folklore* 85: 140–51.

12. Firestone, H. (1964). Cats, kicks and color. In H. S. Becker (ed.), *The other side*. New York 281–97.

13. Friedland, W. and Nelkin, D. (1971). *Migrant*. New York.

14. Gold, R. (1960). *A jazz lexicon*. New York.

15. Grange, K. (1968). Black slang. *Current Slang* III(2).

16. Gregory, D. with Lipsyte, R. (1964). *Nigger*. New York.

17. Hannerz, U. (1969). *Soulside*. New York.

18. Heard, N. (1968). *Howard street*. New York.

19. Hooker, R. (1972). Florida Black supports Wallace. *Race Relations Reporter* (December): 4.

20. Hurston, Z. (1934). *Jonah's gourd vine*. Philadelphia.
    (1935). *Mules and men*. Philadelphia.
    (1942). Story in Harlem slang. *American Mercury* (July): 84–96.

21. Hymes, D. (1972). Models of the interaction of language and social life. In J. J. Gumperz and D. Hymes (eds.), *Directions in sociolinguistics*. New York. 35–71.

22. Iceberg Slim (1967). *Pimp: the story of my life*. Los Angeles.

23. Johnson, K. R. (1971). Black kinesics—some non-verbal patterns in Black culture. *Florida F/L Reporter* 9: 17–21, 57.

24. Keegan, F. (1971). *Blacktown, U.S.A*. Boston.

25. Keiser, R. (1969). *The vice-lords: warriors of the streets*. New York.

26. Kernan, C. (1971). *Language behavior in a Black urban community*. Berkeley, Calif.

27. Killens, J. (1972). *Cotillion*. New York.

28. King, W., jr (1965). The game. *Liberator* 5:20–5.

29. Kochman, T. (1970). Toward an ethnography of Black American speech behavior. In J. Szwed and N. Whitten (eds.), *Afro-American anthropology: contemporary perspectives*. New York. 145–62.

30. Labov, W., Cohen, P., Robins, C. and Lewis, J. (1968). *A study of the non-standard English of Negro and Puerto Rican speakers in New York City*, vol. II. New York.

31. Lewis, H. (1964). *Blackways of Kent*. New Haven, Conn.

32. Liebow, E. (1967). *Tally's corner*. Boston.

33. Major, C. (1970). *Dictionary of Afro-American slang*. New York.

34. Malcolm X with Haley, A. (1965). *The autobiography of Malcolm X*. New York.

35. Meriwhether, L. (1970). *Daddy was a numbers runner*. New York.

36. Mezzrow, M. and Wolfe, B. (1969). *Really the blues*. New York.

37. Milner, C. and Milner, R. (1972). *Black players*. Boston.

38. Olmsted, F. L. (1856). *A journey in the seaboard states*. New York.

39. Puckett, N. (1926). *Folk beliefs of the Southern Negro*. Chapel Hill, N.C.

40. Rainwater, L. (1970). *Behind ghetto walls*. Chicago.

41. Sale, R. T. (1971). *The Blackstone rangers*. New York.

42. Strong, S. (1940). Social types in the Negro community of Chicago. Ph.D. dissertation, University of Chicago.

43. Suttles, G. (1968). *The social order of the slums*. Chicago.

44. Thomas, P. (1967). *Down these mean streets*. New York.

45. Valentine, C. (1972). *Black studies and anthropology: scholarly and political interests in Afro-American culture*. Reading, Mass.

46. Ward, M. (1971). *Them children: a study in language learning*. New York.

47. Wentworth, H. and Flexner, S. (1960). *Dictionary of American slang*. New York.

48. Whitten, N. and Szwed, J. (1970). *Afro-American anthropology: contemporary perspectives*. New York.

49. Wilson, P. (1969). Reputation and respectability: suggestions for Caribbean ethnology. *Man* 4: 70–84.

50. Woodley, R. (1972). *Dealer: portrait of a cocaine merchant*. New York.

51. Young, V. (1970). Family and childhood in a Southern Negro community. *American Anthropologist* 72: 269–88.

DISCUSSION QUESTIONS

1. To what extent does Black street language rely upon kinesic aids for its effect?

2. Is it likely that, perhaps in lesser degree, such language phenomena observed among Blacks exist also in closely-knit white groups, such as an athletic team or a group of campers? What about a mixed white-Black group?

3. In Abrahams's *Deep Down in the Jungle* or in other items listed in the bibliography, find examples of the varieties of Black speech and comment analytically.

MARY RITCHIE KEY

A graduate of the University of Texas, the author is now professor of linguistics at the University of California, Irvine. She has done research on South American Indian languages and recently has focused upon nonverbal communication. Her publications in these and other linguistic fields are many.

LINGUISTIC BEHAVIOR OF MALE AND FEMALE

INTRODUCTION

This discussion is concerned with the linguistic behavior of male and female and is approached as a linguist would approach any variety of language, holding the basic assumption that there is system in the language and the data gathered can be studied, analyzed, and described.

It is my purpose to outline some areas where preliminary observations have shown distinctions in terms of linguistic structures and social structures. These matters are not new but sufficiently important to merit further thinking and research. In spite of the fact that society seems to operate under the assumption that there are great differences between male and female, relatively few studies have been made on the differences of linguistic behavior.

The material that is available consists of, for the most part, discussions and rediscussions on the male/female distinctions which occur or have occurred in societies other than our own—exotic and aboriginal. Documentation on these goes back to the seventeenth century! Wilhelm Bréton's dictionary of Carib terms, published in 1664, seems to be the first language study which documents non-Western male/female language.

As far as the languages of Western societies are concerned, comments on sex differences have crept into writings and studies on other subjects by authors and scholars such as Mulcaster, 1582, Swift, 1735, Lord Chesterfield, 1754, Greenough and Kittredge, 1901 (Jespersen, 1921).

Around the turn of the century and for a while thereafter interest in 'women's languages' ran high—perhaps triggered by the exotic accounts brought back by travellers who reported this phenomenon in far off places. Today, however, it is a rare thing to find other than sporadic comment on the distinctions between male and female language. Linguists have dealt with other dimensions of language variety, such as child language, socio-economic differences, and literary differences. But the one feature which is universal to all human beings—the sex feature—is rarely discussed. Distinctions are hinted at in linguistic studies, "English words sound differently from male and from female speakers . . ." "Everyone knows that, in the subject of language, women are more conservative than men." In discussions of stylistics there might be bare mention of 'sex styles' and 'word avoidances'. Greenough and Kittredge speak of 'feminine peculiarities'. Systematic studies are needed which will objectively document actual facts about language with regard to male and female, some of which are suggested in this paper.

In examining male/female language I would like to emphasize the importance of taking into account Malinowski's idea of the CONTEXT OF SITUATION, developed from Wegener's "Situationstheorie" of 1885. Every human being participates in many varieties of behavior, depending upon the relationship of the participants, the situation where the interaction takes place, and the whole range of conditions involved. One must acknowledge this great diversity in order to understand how people communicate and why it is that sometimes they do not! Many of the differences which are attributed to male and female behavior are mixed in complex ways with other dimensions of behavior. Differences between the male and female are probably not as great as 'what everyone knows' them to be. What might be conceptualized as a male/female distinction among one substratum of people might be more profitably described along other lines or along WITH other lines of the many dimensional varieties of language. For example, language which might be labelled 'coarse language' (therefore 'unladylike') by one group of people might be acceptably used by women in a higher socio-economic group, or a subculture such as the Hollywood group, or the 'tough' business world.

The role which one is assuming at the moment blurs or highlights male/female differences. The linguistic behavior of men and women in the office or at work might be almost identical, but the same persons will exhibit other linguistic patterns in other situations and in other roles, particularly a sexual role. This statement does not preclude many possibilities of various mixes of language variety. For example, one might have a position in a business office and play a very sexy role, either male or female.

STRUCTURAL FEATURES OF LANGUAGE

The investigation of structural features can follow an outline suggested in linguistic studies: the phonological component, the grammatical component, and the semantic component.

The PHONOLOGICAL COMPONENT includes, roughly, that which is involved in pronunciation, the articulation of sounds, as it were. The GRAMMATICAL COMPONENT includes the analysis of words and how words are strung together, the morphological and syntactic patterns. The SEMANTIC COMPONENT is intricately involved with and perhaps inseparable from grammatical features—a delicate blending that gives meaning to sentences.

Phonological

Pronunciation.   In some languages, in some words, males and females pronounce some sounds with distinct patterns. A few illustrations follow.

Among speakers of Cham in Vietnam (Blood), in women's speech, /r/ becomes /y/ in some circumstances, for example, in initial consonant clusters; /b/ and /d/ are preglottalized; initial /y/ may be glottalized.

Fischer's study among English speaking children which focused on the *-ing* ending of verbs, shows that the *-ing* pronunciation symbolizes female speakers and the *-in* pronunciation symbolizes male speakers. The variations between the pronunciations, however, were not solely sex-differentiated, but were intricately involved with status, personality, mood, formality, and specific verbs. Verbs associated with the *-ing* pronunciation were: *criticizing, correcting, reading, visiting, interesting.* Verbs associated with the *-in* pronunciation were: *punchin, flubbin, swimmin, chewin, hittin.* The semantic categories are obvious; one can further extrapolate on the interest domains permitted boys and girls!

Metcalf, in his study of Mexican-American English in Riverside, California, also found differences in the pronunciation of the *-ing* suffix occurring in male/female speech of adults.

Fasold's study of Detroit speech was concerned with the fronting of the three vowels, /æ, a, ɔ/ among socio-economic classes, but he also found that women outscored men in fronting these vowels.

Phonological features which are sex-differentiated are also corroborated in Shuy's report. The *-in/-ing* distinction above was confirmed; nasalized vowels substituting for final nasal, as in /mæ̃/ 'man' occurred more often in male speech; deletion in final consonant clusters occurred more often in the speech of men; the /θ/ sound in 'tooth' occurred as /f/, /t/, or zero more often in the speech of men.

Significant male/female differences also showed up in the pronunciation or absence of /r/ in Shuy's study and also in Levine and Crockett's earlier study. Both studies conclude that pronunciation features were dominated by young women and further speculate that these features could be indicative of language change.

Suprasegmental Patterns.   A feature of pronunciation is the pattern of SUPRASEG-MENTALS or INTONATION, including the PITCH and STRESS characteristics of speech. No linguistic study has ever indicated basic differences in male/female intonation patterns in English as, for example, one might find in vocabulary differences. It would appear that both men and women use basic patterns without male/female differences, except perhaps quantitatively. It would not be surprising to find individual patterns that could correspond to other idiolectal features already observed in other levels of language. Any student of language recognizes that there are individual characteristics and predilections for certain grammatical constructions and typical vocabulary use. Some persons, for example, use a great many hesitation patterns or uncertainty patterns. Some individuals use a high percentage of patterns that communicate such traits as coyness, bullheadedness, cheerfulness, and sarcasm. It is likely that these linguistic features correlate with personality types. It is also quite likely that women use patterns of uncertainty and indefiniteness more often than men—patterns of PLIGHT.

In a brief exploratory experiment a student of mine listened to children in the 3rd, 4th, and 5th grades retell a story. The girls spoke with very expressive intonation, and the boys toned down the intonational features, even to the point of monotomy, 'playing it cool'.

Lieberman (1968: 45) reports on a study made on infant intonation. A ten-month-old boy and a thirteen-month-old girl were recorded under several different conditions. Quantitative acoustic measurements were made with the infants responding to both parents and while alone. Even at this early age, male and female differences occurred in the infants' babbling with the father and the mother, respectively.

Radio and T.V. broadcasting is a career that is concerned with delivery of speech, particularly the features of pronunciation. Speakers are taught to control the pitch and quality of the voice in order to sound neutral. Henneke and Dumit's handbook for announcers (1959: 19) states that while women were hired by radio stations during World War II, they were not retained after the war because "often the higher-pitched female voices could not hold listeners' attention for any length of time, while the lower-pitched voices were frequently vehicles for an overly polished, ultrasophisticated delivery that sounded phoney." The handbook goes on to say that "Women's delivery . . . is lacking in the authority needed for a convincing newscast . . ." In Germany and in the South, they have not read that handbook, though, because women's voices are heard frequently on the air in both of those areas.

Grammatical

Syntactic Patterns. Patterns in syntax which indicate male/female differences appear to be not as common as features of pronunciation. Females may be inclined to make more use of the intensifiers: *so, such, quite, vastly.* "It was *so* interesting." "I had such fun." Jespersen gives other examples in German, French, Danish, and Russian (1921: 250). Besides these believable examples, Jespersen makes other comments about sentence types and grammatical features that are "the linguistic symptoms of a peculiarity of feminine psychology."

Shuy illustrates other syntactic features which are associated with status types, which he and others observed in the study of Detroit speech: multiple negation, pronominal apposition ("my brother, *he* went to the park"), plurals, possessives, third singular verb inflections. Females are more sensitive to these indicators of lower status, and are less likely to use them, according to the report.

Grammatical Gender. The subject of gender is too familiar to merit taking time to review the systems of gender found in languages of the world. This is not to say that there is sufficient understanding of gender systems in linguistic analysis. For example, more study is needed concerning the relationship of gender to such things as status dimension, animate-inanimate dimensions, categories, and sex divisions.

Semantic

Grammatical Categories. In discussions of structures of languages, semantics comprises an area which is by far the least understood in linguistic theory. Jespersen, in 1924 (pp. 55–57), spoke of NOTIONAL CATEGORIES and extralingual categories. He noted that some of them relate to such facts of the world without—as sex, and others to mental states or to logic. He said, "It will be the grammarian's task in each case to investigate the relation between the notional and the syntactic categories." He then attempted a "systematic review of the chief notional categories in so far as they find grammatical expression, and [an] investigat[ion of] the mutual relation of these two 'worlds' in various languages."

Whorf, in the 1930's, also spoke of categories which marked word classes. He noted certain types of patterning, or linguistic configurations, which he called lexical selection. He believed that MEANING should be stated in terms of the semantic facts linked with the configurations.

Nevertheless, a generation later, there is still not a consensus among linguists whether the role of syntax and the role of semantics should be handled as an integrated system or as separate entities. Therefore, categories such as animate/inanimate, number, status (honorifics) (Prideaux), proximate/distance, dimensional (length, area, volume) (Langendoen, 1965: 40), penetrable (gas, liquid, solid) (Langendoen, 1969: 40), are handled in different ways by modern theorists, and sometimes they are not handled at all. Even though it is yet to be decided whether selectional restrictions are definable in terms of the restraints of syntax alone, or of syntax and semantics in conjunction with one another, it is still possible to make some statements about gender and sex in language and the relationship between grammars and verbal behavior.

Gender and Sex. In this study I am making a sharp distinction between gender and sex. For purposes of distinguishing, I will use the terminology FEMININE and MASCULINE to refer to gender, and MALE and FEMALE to refer to sex. This idea is not new. In Jespersen's *The Philosophy of Grammar*, published in 1924, a chapter is titled "Sex and

Gender''. Royen's study of 1930 also distinguished sex and gender. In this immense work, incidentally, Royen gives the history of all theories concerning grammatical gender in Indo-European.

More recently, Katz and Fodor's (1963: 517) often quoted article on the structure of a semantic theory also differentiates between gender and sex. The SEMANTIC MARKERS, Male and Female, are distinguished from the GRAMMATICAL MARKERS, which, in a given language, would be gender distinctions.

Recent descriptions of language do not always make it clear whether gender is to be considered apart from sex distinctions. Some scholars refer to 'masculine/feminine' and some refer to 'male/female', without making a distinction that one set of terms might apply to gender and another set might apply to sex.

In any case, there seem to be two ways of handling the notion of the division of human beings. Langendoen (1969: 37) represents one way of treating the sex/gender attributes. He uses the binary features with a plus or minus Masculine: [+ Masculine] refers to males and [− Masculine] refers to females. McCawley (1968: 140), in his proposal for the role of semantics in a grammar, uses [+ male] and [− male], though with a different position regarding semantics. He believes that only semantic information plays a role in selection (1968: 134). Postal (1966: 208) includes only the Masculine feature in his analysis of English pronouns.

Another way of treating the semantic distinction of sex is to consider that both of the features, male and female, are a positive condition, and both are given autonomous status and treated as independent wholes. Katz and Fodor (as mentioned) postulate both male and female as semantic markers. Jacobs and Rosenbaum (1968: 63) use two plusses in their feature analysis: ⟨+ masculine⟩ ⟨+ feminine⟩.

Alyeshmerni and Taubr (1968: 184), in their workbook which accompanies Bolinger's recent book, describe *man* and *woman* with a [+ male] and a [+ female] feature, respectively. In explanation of their position, they say that the [+ male] analysis

> . . . defines *woman* as 'an adult human being without maleness,' but it says nothing, for instance, about the fact that a woman has female reproductive organs and not simply an absence of male reproductive organs. We could define '− male' as '+ female', but this would be an ad hoc definition. It would not simplify the grids of such groups as *child, pup, kitten,* and *fawn.* To avoid the ad hoc definition, one must make *female* a feature here, as well as *male.*

Gruber also considers that the condition *female* leads an existence of its own. In this consideration, he also presents a different theoretical approach to selectional features. Gruber suggests "underlying categorial trees" rather than feature matrices in his paper on the "functions of the lexicon in formal descriptive grammars" (1967: 37). He suggests "specificatory categories" vs. "contrastive features", describing lexical items. Gruber makes an important empirical claim, and says further (1967: 24),

> . . . that there should never be a need to call for or specify a word by its lack of some quality (for example, non-human, non-concrete, or non-mass). The existence of one feature does not necessitate the existence of some other feature contrastive to it.
>
> For example, feminine (in the semantic sense) is not the absence of masculine or even the necessary complement of masculine. It is not a linguistic principle that there be two sexes, nor does the existence of one of the sexes necessitate (as a linguistic principle) the existence of the other. We can have them both independently, yet mutually exclusively, generated in the base.

One might conclude that the plus/minus analysis is good Freud, but not necessarily adequate description. It is said (Uhlenbeck) that Royen also criticized Freud for his exaggerated sexualistic doctrines in relation to the science of language.

It is clear that biology is behind certain language structures in unambiguous ways. For example, the person that is pregnant is most certainly female (unless he is a seahorse, my son tells me), and the one who shaves his beard is most certainly male. There are, however, other conceptual categories which reflect male and female images in language. The following examples illustrate these constraints.

> Men bellow; women purr. Men yell; women scream (or squeal).
> . . . vivacious women but not *vivacious men
> Women fret (a recent newspaper headline); men get angry.
> Men have careers; women have jobs (illustration from Eli Ginzberg in *Life Styles of Educated Women*)
> Married women engage in 'homemaking'; single women 'keep house' (also from Eli Ginzberg)

The concept formation that is behind the construction of language expressions such as these is a result of learned categories. Bruner, Goodnow, and Austin in a book called, *A Study of Thinking,* speak of "the invention of categories." They explain (1956: 7) that

> To one raised in Western culture, things that are treated as if they were equivalent seem not like man-made classes but like the products of nature. . . . But there exists a near infinitude of ways of grouping events in terms of discriminable properties, and we avail ourselves of only a few of these.

In an appendix to the same book Roger Brown says (1956: 267),

> I should expect all such semantic categories to be susceptible of functional definition by the method of contextual probabilities. Indeed, I think functional categories are suggested to us by semantic categories.

In my interest and study during the last few years of Boas' and Whorf's "grammatical categories" and more recently the "selectional restrictions" and "groupings" of exponents of transformational theory, I have become intrigued with the groupings in which WOMEN occur. The following illustrations of such groupings were collected at random from a great variety of sources of both written and spoken language. It seems that consideration of these groupings might throw light on the semantic constraints behind such constructions as those previously illustrated in noun-verb and noun-adjective combinations. These notional categories or selectional groupings are powerful forces behind the actual expressions of language and are based on distinctions which are not regarded as trivial by the speakers of the language.

The first examples are from very early times and are quoted in Dinneen's introductory linguistic text (1967: 1952–53). Robert Cawdry published *A Table Alphabeticall* in 1604, saying that he had gathered the words "for the benefit and helpe of Ladies, Gentlewomen, or any other unskilfull persons . . ." Another dictionary of 1623 classed women with "young schollars, clarkes, merchants, as also strangers of any nation". Thomas Blunt intended his *Glossographie* in 1656 for "the more knowing women and less-knowing men".

A more recent scholar was quoted in the *AAUP Bulletin*. This was President Nathan

Pusey of Harvard, who, realizing that the draft was going to reduce the number of men in graduate school, lamented, "We shall be left with the blind, the lame, and the women."

Encyclopaedia Britannica discusses Contract Law and lists the parties who are not legally competent and who enjoy indulgence of the courts. These persons are: minors, the mentally incapacitated, and sometimes special groups such as married women, convicts, and aliens. In earlier times, the state of New York once worded its franchise law to include everyone but women, minors, convicts, and idiots.

Often women have been classed with slaves and children. In Africa secret associations have been formed to keep the woman and children in subjection.

In Mohammedan countries, there are signs on the mosques which instruct, "Women and dogs and other impure animals are not permitted to enter".

In Martin's article on the "Speech Levels in Japan and Korea", he notes linguistic differences in situations of address and terms of politeness in the following situations: women to men, young to old, lower classes to upper classes. Note that the category comprises women, youth, lower classes. In reference to the Bengali language (Chatterji), women are classed with the children and the uneducated. Jespersen (1921: 242) lists the persons who speak Sanskrit: gods, kings, princes, brahmans, ministers, chamberlains, dancing-masters, and other men in superior positions, a very few women of special religious importance. Those who are destined to speak Prakrit are: men of inferior class, like shopkeepers, law officers, aldermen, bathmen, fishermen, policemen, and nearly all women.

Returning to this country and to more recent times, one notes that Women's Liberation has engendered new classifications. A recent newspaper article noted the following group in a news event: Women's Lib people, the Third World people, the Blacks, the Chicanos. An article in *Saturday Review* this year referred to a certain crusader as a "defender of both forms of homosexuality, of Mozart, women's right, and dumb animals". A Fantastic Foster Fenwick cartoon in the Los Angeles Times grouped the following marchers together: "Women's Lib, Teen Age Lib, Pre-Teen Lib, Toddlers' Lib".

In Orange County this year a court scene took place which had to do with Section 415.5 of the Penal Code, which was violated on the University of California at Irvine. The student was charged with using "vulgar, profane or indecent language within the presence or hearing of women or children . . .".

Spiro Agnew added to the collection of groupings which include women, in a speech given on August 26, 1970, Women's Liberation Day. His remarks were something to the effect that it is difficult to tame "oceans, fools, and women".

Pronominal and Nominal Referents.   In English there are times when the grammatical forms of language correspond to the realities of nature. For example, in the sentence, *The boy hurt himself* gender markers and sex coincide. In fact, there are so many examples such as this in English, that we are lulled into the comfortable thinking that all is well and regular. In fact, the pronoun system in English is inadequate to handle the things we want to say, where at times we need ambiguity, or some way to make reference to non-specific persons. The following examples illustrate this lack:

> Someone tried to get in, didn't (he, she, they)?
> Someone owes you money, doesn't (she, he)?
> Someone's knocking, (aren't, isn't) (he, she, they)?
> One of us could go, couldn't (I, you, we)?

Whorf also gave examples of the inconsistent use of pronouns in English:

> (Whorf had two goldfish, Jane and Dick)
> Each goldfish likes its food.
> *Jane likes its food better than Dick.
> *Tom [a dog] came out of its kennel.
> My baby enjoys its food.
> *My baby's name is Helen—see how Helen enjoys its food.
> *My little daughter enjoys its food.
> That's Boston—*I live in it.

The use of the editorial *we* is another example of inconsistency in pronoun referent. Mark Twain commented that "Only presidents, editors, and people with tapeworm have the right to use editorial 'we'."

In addition to the use of pronouns in reference to humans and animals, English may also use pronouns in reference to inanimate things. Grammar books list the rules, for example, Whitehall (1956: 110):

> In this system [of 'hidden gender distinctions'], larger animals are usually "he", while smaller animals, personified countries or states, nature, automobiles, trains, sailboats, and motorboats are usually "she". In short, power represents the masculine, grace the feminine.

In the early 1920's Svartengren did a study of the personal gender for inanimate things. He documents over 200 examples from 175 books. The illustrations are all from men speakers and all of the pronoun referents are the feminine *she/her*. The characters quoted are men "with work-calloused hands and speech uninfluenced by literature"—men from the industries of fur, timber, and mining, as well as cowboys. Svartengren notes the close relation of status of speaker and the use of *she* for inanimate objects. He added that novels dealing with upper and middle classes contributed very little to the collection of examples (1928–39: 51–56). This article brings together a few ideas toward explaining the use of personal gender in referring to inanimate things, such as literary versus colloquial 'homely' style, spoken versus written language, personification of the instrument by the craftsman (the sailor's ship, the soldier's gun, the driver's car), artificial versus natural objects, American versus British dialect, foreign language influence, and emotional characteristics of emphatic expressions (She's a dandy!) (1928–39: 11–14). Svartengren concludes, however, that the explanations are dubious, and after citing several grammarians and their rules, he comments that "usage has broken bonds and widely outstripped the narrow confines of the grammatical rules cited initially" (1928–39: 40).

It is often stated that the pronoun *he* is used in reference to an unspecified, unknown person. In actual usage, however, there is a good deal of inconsistency and confusion. Certain occupational roles are invariably designated with a single gender: doctors, sailors, plumbers, and presidents are "he"; nurses, elementary teachers, and secretaries are "she". In a recent meeting of discussions on books and methodology, the unknown, unspecified English teacher was always referred to as "she". The rule is almost never observed for teachers of lower grades. The rule, however, does seem to be applied to levels above high school. A poem about professors in a recent *AAUP Bulletin* used the masculine referents entirely, along with the nominal referent "a man". A regent of the University of California was quoted in the Irvine student newspaper, when he referred to the faculty as "a distinguished group of men . . .".

A significant reversal of the rule that masculine referents are used for non-specific persons occurred in a term paper turned in to me last year. The antecedent was "a student" and the following referent was "she". Perhaps this student had just heard the joke which is going around the country lately concerning God. When asked to describe God, the informant replies, "Well, to begin with, she's Black!"

One of the most curious examples that I have collected comes from an up-tight etiquette book of the 1930's, which has quaint little chapters on how to behave. Chapter 14 is called "The Sniffler and the Snorter" and refers to the unidentified offender by shifting back and forth between "he" and "she".

> There is no cure. Have pity on HER. Sometimes is it HE who sniffles. It makes no difference. If you beg HER to stop, SHE will continue. If you ask HIM to stop, HE will never call again. (That would be just too bad.)

> Don't tell your friend that HE sniffles, because HE won't believe you. You are the only one who ever accused HIM of such a thing, and while HE's telling you this HE sniffles and doesn't even know it.

> The person who snorts when SHE laughs is also out of order. There is nothing disgusting about this habit but the sound is unpleasant. Watch your laugh and see if you snort.
>
> [Emphasis mine, MK]

This shifting in less deliberate circumstances reflects conceptual structures. In a classroom discussion on cheating, the pronoun *he* was used with reference to students who cheat, and the pronoun *she* was used with reference to students who do not cheat. At times these shifts are status defined. In a planning session for a new project on a University of California campus, there occurred a noticeable shift in the pronoun referents to the hypothetical personnel who were to be employed. When the decision-making personnel were referred to, the pronoun was invariably *he;* when the personnel at the level of secretary were referred to, the pronoun was invariably *she*.

In view of the ability to switch between *he* and *she* among English speakers, in spite of what the rule books say, the next illustration from *The Roberts English Series: A Linguistic Program*, Book 3, is shocking to the point of comedy.

THE SECRET

We have a secret, just we three,
The robin, and I, and the sweet cherry tree;
. . . .

But of course the robin knows it best,
Because HE built the—I shan't tell the rest;
And LAID THE FOUR LITTLE—something in it—
I'm afraid I shall tell it every minute.
. . . .

ANONYMOUS
[Emphasis mine, MK]

It would appear from these anecdotal observations that the grammatical rules often cited for the use of personal gender are a fiction and that actual use does not corroborate the stated rules. There is a need for careful studies on the use of gender to clarify what the real situation is in this uneasy adjustment between language and culture.[1]

ANOMALOUS CONSTRUCTIONS sometimes occur where the pronoun (or noun) referent is not the same gender as the known sex of the precedent. I have recorded eight instances where this takes place. First, non-native speakers have difficulties with the gender system, particularly the covert system, to use Whorf's term. An unusual example was articulated by an Italian woman who spoke English fairly well. In a review of a book which was written by another Italian woman, the speaker consistently referred to the author as ''he''. At the coffee hour later, she explained the discrepancy, ''Well, you just expect a scholar to be a man!''

The second instance is child language. The following examples are from Menyuk's *Sentences Children Use*.

> He's a big train.
> She's a nice daddy.
> It's a good boy.

The third instance occurs in the language of homosexuals. The pronoun *she* is used to designate the female partner. The fourth instance occurs in certain dialects of Black English in such regions as coastal South Carolina, Georgia, and Florida. The illustrations are from Dillard and Steward. See also Svartengren, 1928–39: 48.

> He a nice little girl.
> Here he book.
> Here come he boyfriend.

The fifth instance is a form of baby talk in the Marathi language. ''The use of masculine ending and/or concord for a girl's name, of feminine ending and/or concord for a boy's name, and of neuter ending and/or concord for both . . .'' all show endearment in this variety of language (Kelkar, 1964: 47).

The sixth instance occurs in an expression of insult. Svartengren (1928–38: 49) quotes an example from the *English Dialect Dictionary* from a dialect in England. *She* may be used contemptuously of a man. Kelkar mentions a similar situation in Marathi adult speech where lack of concord denotes contempt (1964: 47).

The seventh instance is a deliberate inconsistency of pronoun referent used for effect by comedians. On a T.V. program heard recently, the audience responded with laughter to the comedian who was telling about a tiger: ''The tiger's name is Sarah. Isn't he nice?''

The last example of nonobservation of selectional restrictions which produces anomalous forms are those utterances which result from fixed gender which does not correspond semantically to the known referent. Whorf's previously cited examples illustrate this nonobservation. Jespersen (1924: 230) speaks of the 'incongruity' in these anomalous constructions and gives examples from other languages.

Martinet gives an example from French, concerning *le docteur,* which may be followed by *elle est dans le salon.* The grammatical gender is masculine, but the pronoun

---

[1] Since this article was in press, I have completed another study which shows significant discrepancies in the uses of pronoun referent: Mary Ritchie Key, ''The Role of Male and Female in Children's Books'', *Wilson Library Bulletin* 46:2 (October, 1971), 167–176.

referent is feminine. Another often quoted example from French concerns the professor (masculine gender) who is pregnant: *Le professeur est enceinte*. Martinet goes on to point out, however, that "in the case of male beings designated by means of feminine nouns, the grammatical concord is preserved: la sentinelle . . . elle . . ." (1962: 15–19).

A summary of the preceding observations on pronominal referents is as follows:

CATEGORY

Inanimate   Gender   {
neuter
feminine
masculine
}

         it: machinery, furniture, [euphemism], linguistics . . .
         they (singular): pants, scissors, clothes . . .
         she: muse, ship, hurricane . . .
         he: ???

Animate   Sex   {
unspecified
female
male
}

    unspecified, singular
        it: baby, child, goldfish, animal . . .
        she: nurse, elementary teacher, small animal . . .
        he: doctor, professor, large animal . . .
        he or *she:* (recent usage shows more occurrences of this alternative)
        we: (editorial)
        they: someone . . .
    female
        she, and *he* for anomalous forms
    male
        he, and *she* for anomalous forms

In conclusion, research shows that there ARE differences in the linguistic behavior of male and female, as well as in references made to male and female though these differences may not occur when speakers are in roles other than the sex role. Some of the grammar-book rules are myths which are not supported by observations on actual usage. Knowledge of the real situation would be enhanced with further research on these matters, some of which have been suggested throughout the paper. Besides these topics, other related matters should be investigated in order to understand the linguistic behavior of male and female. Such possibilities include matters of usage in education, styles of speech, address forms, male and female authors and literature, bilingualism, language and culture, and language change, to name just a few.

REFERENCES

1. Alyeshmerni, Mansoor, and Paul Taubr
   1970 *Working with Aspects of Language* [workbook] (New York, Harcourt, Brace and World).

2. Blood, Doris
   1962 "Women's Speech Characteristics in Cham", *Asian Culture* 3: 3–4, 139–43.
3. Bréton, Wilhelm
   1664 *Dictionnaire Caraibe-Français.*
4. Bruner, Jerome S., Jacqueline J. Goodnow, the late George A. Austin
   1956 *A Study of Thinking* (New York, John Wiley and Sons).
5. Chatterji, Suniti Kumar
   1921 "Bengali Phonetics", *Bulletin of the School of Oriental Studies* 2, Part I, 1–25.
6. Dillard, J. L.
   1967 "Negro Children's Dialect in the Inner City", *Florida Foreign Language Reporter* (Fall), 7–10.
7. Dinneen, Francis P.
   1967 *An Introduction to General Linguistics* (New York, Holt, Rinehart and Winston).
8. Fasold, Ralph W.
   1968 "A Sociolinguistic Study of the Pronunciation of Three Vowels in Detroit Speech" (Washington, D.C., Center for Applied Linguistics), mimeo.
9. Fischer, John L.
   1958 "Social Influences in the Choice of a Linguistic Variant", *Word* 14, 47–56. Reprinted in Dell Hymes, *Language in Culture and Society* (1964), 483–88.
10. Greenough, James Bradstreet, and George Lyman Kittredge
    1901 *Words and Their Ways in English Speech* (New York, Macmillan).
11. Gruber, Jeffrey
    1967 "Functions of the Lexicon in Formal Descriptive Grammar" (Santa Monica, System Development Corporation), (= Technical Memorandum, TM 3770/000/00).
12. Henneke, Ben Graf, and Edward S. Dumit
    1959 *The Announcer's Handbook* (New York, Holt, Rinehart and Winston).
13. Jacobs, Roderick A., and Peter S. Rosenbaum
    1968 *English Transformational Grammar* (Waltham, Mass., Blaisdell Publishing Company).
14. Jespersen, Otto
    1921 *Language: Its Nature, Development and Origin*, Ch. 13: "The Woman", 237–54.
    1924 *The Philosophy of Grammar*, Ch. 17: "Sex and Gender", 226–43.
15. Katz, Jerrold J., and Jerry A. Fodor
    1963 "The Structure of a Semantic Theory", *Language* 39, 170–210. Reprinted in Jerry A. Fodor, and Jerrold J. Katz (eds.), *The Structure of Language: Readings in the Philosophy of Language* (Englewood Cliffs, N.J., Prentice-Hall, 1964), 479–518.
16. Kelkar, Ashok R.
    1964 "Marathi Baby Talk", *Word* 20: 1, 40–54.
17. Langendoen, D. Terence
    1969 *The Study of Syntax: The Generative-Transformational Approach to the Structure of American English* (New York, Holt, Rinehart and Winston).
18. Levine, Lewis, and Harry J. Crockett, Jr.
    1967 "Speech Variation in a Piedmont Community: Postvocalic r", *International Journal of American Linguistics* 33: 4 (Part II), 76–98.
19. Lieberman, Philip
    1968 *Intonation, Perception, and Language* (Cambridge, Mass., MIT Press).
20. McCawley, James D.
    1968 "The Role of Semantics in a Grammar", in Emmon Bach, and Robert T. Harms, *Universals in Linguistic Theory* (New York, Holt, Rinehart and Winston), 124–69.

21. Malinowski, Bronislaw
    1965 [1935] *The Language of Magic and Gardening*, II: *Coral Gardens and Their Magic* (Bloomington, Indiana University Press).

22. Martin, Samuel E.
    1964 "Speech Levels in Japan and Korea", in Dell Hymes, *Language in Culture and Society* (New York, Harper and Row), 407–15.

23. Martinet, André
    1962 *A Functional View of Language* (Oxford).

24. Menyuk, Paula
    1969 *Sentences Children Use* (Cambridge, Mass., MIT Press).

25. Metcalf, Allan A.
    1970 "Characteristics of Mexican-American English", Paper read at the linguistic section, Philological Association of the Pacific Coast, Spokane, Washington.

26. Postal, Paul M.
    1966 "On So-called 'Pronouns' in English", *Monograph on Languages and Linguistics* 19 (Georgetown University Press). Reprinted in David A. Reibel, and Sanford A. Schane (eds.), *Modern Studies in English* (Englewood Cliffs, N.J., Prentice-Hall, 1969), 201–24.

27. Prideaux, Gary Dean
    1970 *The Syntax of Japanese Honorifics* (The Hague, Mouton).

28. Royen, Gerlach
    1930 *Die nominalen Klassifikationssysteme in den Sprachen der Erde: Historischkritische Studie, mit besonderer Berücksichtigung des Indogermanischen* (= *Linguistische Anthropos-Bibliothek* IV) (Vienna).

29. Shuy, Roger W.
    1969 "Sex as a Factor in Sociolinguistic Research" (Washington, D.C., Center for Applied Linguistics), mimeo.

30. Stewart, William A.
    1969 "On the use of Negro Dialect in the Teaching of Reading", in Joan C. Baratz, and Roger W. Shuy, *Teaching Black Children to Read* (Washington, D.C., Center for Applied Linguistics), 156–219.

31. Svartengren, T. Hilding
    1928–1939 "The Use of the Personal Gender for Inanimate Things", *Dialect Notes* 6, 7–56.

32. Uhlenbeck, C. C.
    1932 Review of Gerlach Royen, *Die nominalen Klassifikationssysteme in den Sprachen der Erde, International Journal of American Linguistics* 7: 1–2, 94–96.

33. Whitehall, Harold
    1956 *Structural Essentials of English* (New York, Harcourt, Brace and World).

34. Whorf, Benjamin Lee
    [ca. 1937] "Grammatical Categories", *Language* 21: 1 (1945). Reprinted in John B. Carroll (ed.), *Language, Thought, and Reality: Selected Writings of Benjamin Lee Whorf* (Cambridge, Mass., MIT, and New York, John Wiley and Sons, 1962), 87–101.

DISCUSSION QUESTIONS

1. What linguistic implications do you see in Key's report of two studies finding that young women's pronunciation features are dominant? Do you agree with this position?

2. Try to discover how gender came to be associated with sex in linguistic references. See the *Oxford English Dictionary* under the word *gender*. Distinguish grammatical and natural gender.

3. Find instances of "sexism in language" in your own speech and writing.

4. Would Abrahams's comment about cursing by Black women be at all relevant to white female speech as well?

5. What relevance do you find in Allen's contrasting men's and women's use of Standard English forms in the Upper Midwest?

PART V

LINGUISTICS AND USAGE

If you have ever had your use of English "corrected," or if you anticipate the day when you will feel called upon to "correct" your students' English, you may share in an activity that apparently always has occurred in human society. Variations in language seem always to have led to a search for reasons by which the acceptable could be distinguished from the unacceptable, the right from the wrong. But the reasons have been many and varied.

Anthropologists report that among primitive peoples the speech of the elders carries a prestige powerful enough to check language deviations among the young. Classical grammarians repeated the dictum that *usus* (usage) is the *norma loquendi* (standard of speaking), although the Roman rhetorician Quintilian did not hesitate to observe that it is the usage of the learned, not the vulgar.

The history of attitudes toward English usage reveals a variety of standards of acceptability, often inconsistent and yet usually set forth with a dogmatism worthy of divine inspiration. The articles by Kenneth Wilson, Karl Dykema, and Charles Hartung in Part I show how pervasively the Latin heritage influenced those attitudes, with its effect upon grammar, vocabulary, and pronunciation.

With an early protest against a Latin-based grammar, Joseph Webbe wrote in his *Appeale to Truth,* 1622, that "the way to language" is found in "vse and custome" and that "few of vs, if we consider the Antient Records and Authours of our Nation, can beleeue that a Grammar made in the time of Chaucer, Robert of Gloster, or of Ælfric, can be vsefull now in ours; though doubtless these men wrote in the choisest Dialect the time afforded." In 1658 the grammarian John Wallis also insisted that usage must dictate the choice between language variants. But the voices of these two realists were tiny beside the stentorian clamor that for four centuries denied such recognition of usage, even while sometimes paying lip service to it.

An early basis for rejecting common usage was the belief that only the language of the "Vniuersiti's," that is, Oxford and Cambridge, was really to be approved. Other standards in the eighteenth century enabled chronic criticasters to denounce language forms that did not meet the standard of "logic," or the standard of analogy, or an ill-defined immutable standard of perfection extracted from the Platonic base of neo-classicism. Although toward the end of the century Joseph Priestley, an able grammarian as well as the discoverer of oxygen, pointed out the incongruity of basing rules of English grammar upon Latin grammar, and although the Scottish rhetorician George Campbell nobly defined good usage as "national," "current," and "reputable," the nineteenth century saw the continued dominance of the dogmatic prescriptive stance, with little or no attempt to base that stance upon what people actually said or wrote.

As the twentieth century began, however, Thomas R. Lounsbury, a professor at Yale University, significantly injected more realistic thinking into the controversy about usage by producing *The Standard of Pronunciation in English* (Harper, 1904) and *The Standard of Usage in English* (Harper, 1908), although he, too, postulated a rather narrow focus for that standard. His work was followed several years later by J. Lesslie Hall's *English Usage* (Scott, Foresman, 1917) in which for the first time there appeared the telling evidence that for centuries outstanding writers had blithely ignored the dogmatic rules of the prescriptivists.

The attack on prescriptive dogmatism mounted with the rise of descriptive linguistics in the 1930s, a decade marked by what some have rather grandiloquently termed "the Battle of Usage." Factual evidence began to accumulate. In 1932 Sterling A. Leonard's *Current English Usage,* a monograph of the National Council of Teachers of English, reported the opinions of several groups of judges with respect to a wide range of controversial and noncontroversial language items. He found that their opinions revealed considerable disagreement with the cherished rules of the prescriptivists. Six years later Albert Marckwardt and Fred C. Walcott validated those opinions by such evidence of actual usage as they found in the *Oxford English Dictionary* and the major commercial dictionaries. Their study, *Facts About Current English Usage* (National Council of Teachers of English, 1938), further discredited the prescriptive usage myths of the past. In 1940 Charles C. Fries's *American English Grammar* (NCTE Monograph 10, Appleton-Century, 1940) applied a quantitative measure to the study of the language used in several thousand letters to a government agency and thereby more solidly established a foundation for definitive statements about the relationship of language variants and socioeducational status.

Judgments based upon quantitative researches appeared also in Margaret Bryant's *Current American Usage* (Funk and Wagnalls, 1962). Additional evidence is being made available as linguistic atlas investigation continues, the mammoth computerized corpus of running prose at Brown University is analyzed, and the *Dictionary of American Regional English* nears completion.

Despite such testimony, however, the battle of usage has not ended. Perhaps it never will end, since there always seem to be persons who like to dictate or legislate or otherwise tamper with other people's language. Sometimes their dictates are tempered with a measure of sensitivity for good English, as in Edwin B. Newman's *Strictly Speaking: Will America be the Death of English?* (Bobbs-Merrill, 1974). Sometimes they quite lack any saving grace, as in John Simon's *Paradigms Lost* (Potter, 1980.)

In the meantime, the efforts to categorize and analyze the complexity of usage have continued. The late Porter G. Perrin, who wrote the first textbook to incorporate the descriptive point of view, *Index to English* (Scott, Foresman, 1939), advanced the concept of levels of usage. His concept may have been derived from but was not similar to a breakdown of English variation appearing in the front matter of the first volume of the *Oxford English Dictionary* in 1884. Perrin's concept confused two different categories, as John S. Kenyon then pointed out in an important article, "Cultural Levels and Functional Varieties" (*College English* 10 (1949): 31–36), where for the first time an informal standard was recognized as a functional variety different from a formal standard, and "colloquial" was accepted as a term for a variety of standard.

Besides the several levels posited by Kenyon, J. J. Lamberts suggested the recognition of another level called "hyperstandard," a designation for pretentious and affected speech (*College English* 24 (1962): 141–143), and Martin Joos approached the varieties of style with a classification resembling that in the British recognition of "registers": *The Five Clocks* (Harcourt, Brace, Jovanovich, 1962). Joos's contribution is important to the understanding of the relationship between language forms and the situation of the speaker.

The concept of levels itself was rejected by the senior compiler of this anthology in a paper first read at a meeting of the English Teachers Club of Greater Chicago in 1957 and subsequently modified and expanded in several lectures and articles, as in the article on English usage in the *Encyclopedia of Education* (Macmillan, 1971) and in *Focusing on Language* (eds. H. B. Allen, Enola Borgh, and Verna L. Newsome [T. Y. Crowell, 1975], pp. 158–167). Instead of levels he proposed a continuing dimension of usage. Three dimensions may be visualized in terms of a cube representing the informal–formal range, the speech–writing range, and the standard–nonstandard range. Movement of the cube may then signify two additional dimensions, those of space and time. This concept was modified and amplified by Raven I. McDavid, Jr., with nine not always sharply distinct scales of usage in "Historical, Regional, and Social Variation" (*Journal of English Linguistics* 1 (1967): 25–40). If you are interested in this matter of usage, you will enjoy both the content and the style of J. J. Lamberts's *A Short Introduction to English Usage* (McGraw-Hill, 1972) and Ellsworth Bernard's *English for Everybody* (Dinosaur Press, 1979). If you feel some trepidation at the prospect of teaching usage, you will find help in Robert C. Pooley's *The Teaching of English Usage* (National Council of Teachers of English, 1974).

More recently the lead provided by Joos's insistence upon the significance of occasion and mood has been followed by scholars who might be termed language usage theorists. Their concern is the study of the effect of usage patterns upon the transmission and interpretation of messages. The three articles chosen for this section all examine usage from this perspective. Robin Lakoff first stresses the need to understand the social context in which language is used. In particular, she looks at the social relationship between speaker and listener with regard to its effect upon the politeness of the linguistic interchange. She argues that there is a universal definition of politeness which implies that the speaker acts as though his status is lower than that of the listener. While the precise expression of this relationship differs from language to language, it nevertheless is always present if polite linguistic behavior is to be maintained.

In the next article Dwight Bolinger says that truth is a linguistic question requiring immediate attention. He offers examples and kinds of language usage intended deliberately to confuse and mislead the unwary listener. They significantly disclose the way in which language is employed by business and government propagandists to conceal the truth. His exposé of their methods suggests how you may apply his methods in examining linguistic messages for truth or falsity.

In the final article Sidney Greenbaum examines the effect of verb-intensifier collocations, pointing up the value of listener reaction by comparing the situations in British and American English. The role of what he terms "mutual expectancy" exists, however, in both cultures and helps to produce the effect of allusion. All three articles have useful bibliographies.

ROBIN LAKOFF

A graduate of Radcliffe College and Harvard University, the author taught at the University of Michigan and in 1971–1972 held a fellowship in the Center for Advanced Studies in the Behavioral Sciences before becoming a professor of linguistics at the University of California, Berkeley.

LANGUAGE IN CONTEXT

When studying exotic languages, the speaker of English often runs into odd facts. As if the syntactic, lexical, and morphological peculiarities with which other people's languages are unfortunately replete were not enough to confound the English speaker, he encounters still odder details—things which, as far as he can see, have no analogs in English at all. It is certainly bad enough to encounter case languages, or languages with complex and synthetic tense systems, or absolute constructions, or six words for 'snow'; but at least these are analogous to things that occur in English. But what about certain still stranger phenomena? How does the native speaker ever learn these weird distinctions? How can he ever remember to make them, in the course of ordinary conversation? Doesn't he inevitably (though accidentally) offend everyone he encounters, or incessantly stamp himself as a boob?

The problems I am referring to will of course be immediately recognizable to anyone who has done any reading about almost any language that is not English—that is, I should think, any linguist. I refer to phenomena such as the following:

(i) Particles, like *doch* in German, or *ge* in Classical Greek, or *zo* in Japanese. How do you know when to use them? And how do you know when NOT to? Are they inserted in sentences randomly? Since these particles do not add to the 'information content' conveyed by the sentence, but rather relate this information content to the feelings the speaker has about it, or else suggest the feelings of the speaker toward the situation of the speech act, it is sometimes rather cavalierly stated that they are 'meaningless'. If this were really true, it would of course be impossible to misuse them. But we all know that there is nothing easier for the non-native speaker.

(ii) Honorifics. Asian languages, Japanese in particular, are infamous for containing these. Using them in the wrong situation will, one is assured, result in instantaneous ostracism. But how do you know when the situation is wrong? The non-native speaker apparently never sorts it out. Can the native speaker (who is linguistically naïve) be expected to do any better?

(iii) Many languages have endings on verbs, or special forms related to the verbal system, that are used to suggest that the speaker himself doesn't take responsibility for a reported claim, or that he does—that he is hesitant about a claim he is making or confident of its veracity. How can a speaker keep track of these mysterious concepts? Are speakers of other languages conceivably THAT MUCH smarter than we are? Then why don't THEY have a man on the moon?

The purpose of this paper is to explore these questions. I will not really attempt to answer the question, 'How do they do it?'—we don't know how people do even the simplest and most obvious linguistic operations. But what I will show is that these phenomena also occur in English. It is often not superficially obvious that we are dealing, in English, with phenomena analogous to politeness or hesitance markers in other languages; there are often no special separate readily identifiable morphological devices. Rather, these distinctions are expressed by forms used elsewhere for other purposes. Therefore it is easy to imagine that they are not present at all. But I hope to show that the reverse is true; and further, that if the presence and uses of these forms are recognized, several of the most difficult problems confronting such diverse areas as theoretical linguistics and the teaching of second languages will be solvable. Thus I am in effect making two claims, the first of theoretical, the other of practical, interest:

(a) Contextually-linked linguistic phenomena are probably identifiable, to one extent or another, in all the languages of the world. But one language may have special markers for some or many of these possibilities, while another language may utilize forms it uses elsewhere for other purposes. One language may require that these markers be present, while another may consider them optional, or to be used only in case special classification is desired, or for special stylistic effects. (As we shall see later in this paper, Japanese is apparently a representative of the first class of languages, English of the second. Hence, as many speakers of Japanese have said to me, English sounds 'harsh' or 'impolite' to them; while to the speaker of English, Japanese often gives the effect of being unbelievably subtle, making inordinately many unnecessary distinctions.) But we should ask, not only whether a language is one type or the other or a mixture of both, but also whether this fact about a language is related to any other facts, deep or superficial, about its structure. Since questions of this sort have not been studied in any disciplined way heretofore, nothing is known at present. The answers, if ever found, would be of interest in studies of the lexicon, the forms of logical structure, the identification of linguistically relevant types of presupposition, and many other areas with which linguistic theorists are at present concerned.

(b) If one is to teach second-language use successfully—so that a non-native speaker can use the language he is learning in a way reminiscent of a native speaker, rather than a robot—then the situations in which forms of this type are usable in a given language must be identified. It is obviously useless to try to list or pinpoint the superficial syntactic configurations where they are correctly used; examples will be given later in the paper that illustrate the problem. We must then identify the means by which the second language makes these distinctions, and pair the two, although in terms of superficial syntax, the two languages will appear to have little in common.

We may distinguish certain aspects of context from others. Some have universal linguistic relevance; others may be linguistically relevant under certain conversational situations but not others, or for certain cultures but not others; and still others may never be linguistically relevant as far as we know. So it is normally true in all languages and all situations that one must somehow make clear the type of speech act involved: are you asking a question, making a statement, or giving an order? Ambiguities in this regard are generally not tolerated.[1] Some languages require that you know more about the speech

---

[1] Gordon & Lakoff 1971 discuss a number of interesting cases where, if one looks only at superficial syntactic configurations, apparent ambiguities of this type do in fact exist: e.g., *It's stuffy in here*, most normally a declarative statement, may, under specific, contextually determined conditions, be interpretable as an imperative, equivalent to *Please open the window*. As they show, this does not indicate that such sentences really are ambiguous between the two interpretations: it indicates rather that context must play a role in the interpretation of sentences.

situation than this. English sometimes requires overt notice as to whether the speaker believes a past-time event is relevant to the present, by the use of the perfect tense rather than the preterit. Other languages require that there be overt expression of the identity of speaker and/or addressee: what are their respective social positions? And, related to this, of course, what are their respective ages and sex? English only sometimes requires that these be recognized overtly; other languages, such as Japanese, require it much more often. But it is hard to think of a language that requires one special overt marker if the speaker has blue eyes, and a different one if the speaker has brown eyes. This is contextual information, as real and available to the speakers of a language for the purpose of making distinctions as are differentiation of age and sex; yet only the latter two often occur as linguistically significant contextual information.

In any case, I trust that, by the end of this discussion, it will be perfectly clear that there are areas of linguistic competence that cannot be described in any theory that does not allow an integration of information about the context in which the discourse takes place—sometimes erroneously referred to as 'real-world' as opposed to 'linguistically relevant' situation— and the purely linguistically relevant information the sentence seeks to convey: superficial syntax, choice of lexical items, and semantics aside from contextually-relevant meaning elements.

I shall try to substantiate some of the claims I have been making by looking at examples.

We all know, or at least know of, languages that employ honorifics as essential elements in sentences. Sometimes they occur with personal names, and in these cases it is fairly easy to see what is going on: one usually assumes that the speaker either actually is lower in status than the addressee, or is speaking as if he were. In the latter case, which is perhaps the more usual in conversational situations, it is assumed that this linguistic abasement occurs for reasons of politeness. But an important question is usually glossed over: why is it polite for the speaker to suggest that the addressee surpasses him in status? In some languages we find honorifics related to non-human items, to show that the speaker considers them of importance in one way or another. How is this related to any notion of politeness, which is a concept involving behavior between human beings? Another problem is that many languages apparently have two kinds of honorifics. One is the kind I have just mentioned. But going hand in hand with this is the use of forms that humble or debase the speaker himself, or things connected with him. Translated into English, this often has ludicrous results, e.g. 'Honorable Mr. Snarf have some of my humble apple pie?' This sort of translation is ludicrous for several reasons, but perhaps principally because, by translating the honorific and dis-honorific, if I may use that term, with overt adjectives, the sense of the sentence has been palpably altered. In the original language, the sense of superiority or inferiority conveyed by the honorifics is presupposed, or implicit. The use of adjectives like *honorable* and *humble* makes these concepts explicit. So what had been a tacit suggestion, in effect, is now made overt. The English translations do not, I think, allow the monolingual speaker of English to get any sense of how a speaker of Japanese feels when he is addressed with *-san*. But I believe there are locutions in English whose force comes close to that of the true honorific, because the differentiation in status they establish is implicit rather than overt. These forms are also used for the sake of politeness (as adjectives like *humble* and *honorable* never are).

I said earlier that these contextually-linked forms had not been recognized in English partly because the forms utilized for this purpose had other, more obvious uses. English modals are a case in point. Certain uses of the modal *must* are parallel to the use in other languages of special honorific forms:

    (1) You must have some of this cake.
    (2) You should have some of this cake.
    (3) You may have some of this cake.

Let us assume, for the purpose of analysing these sentences, a special social situation: a party, at which the hostess is offering the guests a cake that she baked herself or at least selected herself, and which she therefore takes responsibility for. In such a social context, 1 is the most polite of these forms, approaching in its range of appropriateness that of a true honorific in languages that have such forms. Further, although in theory 2 should be more 'polite' than 1, in actual use it is not: in the situation established above, the use of 2 would be rude, while 1 would be polite. And 3, which might at first seem the most polite form, actually is the least. Why is this?

    Finding the answer lies partly in determining what constitutes politeness, and of course, its opposite, rudeness. If we can define these notions, then the uses of these modals will be seen to be governed by the same assumptions of politeness as govern the use of honorifics; once the principle is understood, it can be transferred from language to language. What we are dealing with here is something extralinguistic—the way in which individuals relate to one another—that directly affects the use of language. We must understand something about non-linguistic social interaction before we can see the generalization that is in effect regulating the use of sentences like 1–3, along with the use of affixes like -*san* and *o-* in Japanese.

    It is obvious, of course, that what passes for politeness in one culture will appear to a member of another culture as slavishness or boorishness. We are all familiar with examples of this. Then how can we talk about universal conditions governing the use of honorifics and other politeness markers? I think we can assume that there is a universal definition of what constitutes linguistic politeness: part of this involves the speaker's acting as though his status were lower than that of the addressee. What may differ from language to language, or culture to culture—or from subculture to subculture within a language—is the question of WHEN it is polite to be polite, to what extent, and how it is shown in terms of superficial linguistic behavior.[2] Although a speaker may know the universal definition of politeness, he may apply it at the wrong time or in the wrong way if he attempts to transfer the uses of his own language directly into another; hence the ludicrousness that results from taking a polite concept implicit in one language and making it explicit. If, in a given language, one's own possessions are customarily followed by a marker of humility (a situation which perhaps can be symbolized by 4 below), it does not follow that 5, in which what is implicit in the marker in 4 is made explicit, is a reasonable English translation of 4. In fact, as has already been noted, the effect of such bogus translations is generally laughable, and rightly so:

    (4) Have some of this cake-*yecch*.
    (5) Have some of this revolting cake.

---

    [2] So, for example, if an officer in the Army (a subculture with special status-related rules) gives a command to a private, he will not normally preface his command with *please*. Although in most English-speaking groups the use of *please* prefaced to an imperative is a mark of politeness, to use *please* in this situation will be interpretable as sarcastic. Again, in some cultures it is considered polite to refuse an invitation several times before one is conventionally 'prevailed upon' to accept: if a speaker from such a culture finds himself in one where it is considered polite to accept invitations at once with thanks, confusion and worse will inevitably ensue, with each party impressing the other as unbelievably boorish or stupid.

My claim is that a sentence like 1 is a much closer translation of 4 than 5 is, although 5 stays closer to the superficial syntax of the original language. The task of the translator then is compounded: he must translate contextual and societal concepts—contexts that are, strictly speaking, extralinguistic— in addition to merely translating words and ideas and endings.

Let me try to be more specific in identifying 1, but not 2 or 3, as an honorific form in an extended sense of the term. (I will define HONORIFIC as a form used to convey the idea that the speaker is being polite to the hearer.) At first it seems contradictory to say that a sentence containing *must* is more polite than one using *should* or *may*. Going by the ordinary uses of the modals, *must* imposes an obligation, while *should* merely gives advice that may be disregarded, and *may* allows someone to do something he already wanted to do. Surely it should be more polite to give someone advice, or to let someone do as he wishes, than to impose an unavoidable obligation upon him.

Normally this is true, but under special conditions the reverse is the case, and this is the situation in 1–3. If we want to understand why these modals work as they do here, we must ask: under what real-world conditions is it appropriate to use each of these modals? So, for example, if the use of *must* expresses the imposition upon its superficial subject of an obligation (whether by the speaker or by someone else, with the speaker merely reporting the fact), under what conditions in the real world is it necessary to impose an obligation? The answer is simple: it must be the case that the person on whom the obligation rests would not do what he is instructed unless he were obliged to do it. That is, the assumption is that performing the act is distasteful, requiring coercion of the superficial subject.

Now in a normal situation it is not polite to coerce anyone, since, among other things, such action reminds him that you are his superior in power. Thus *must* is normally used for politeness only when it is a second-hand report that an obligation is imposed, on the addressee or on a third person, by someone other than the speaker. In this situation, the speaker is not using *must* as a means of coercion through his greater power or prestige; but he is so doing when *must* reflects the speaker's own imposition of an obligation. In a sentence like 1, the most natural assumption is that the speaker himself is imposing an obligation on the hearer. Then why is 1 a polite offer? Why does one not take umbrage when such a sentence is spoken to one, as a dinner guest, by one's hostess? We seem to be faced with an utterance that is, in a special sense, 'ambiguous'. This is, of course, no normal type of ambiguity, since it cannot be disambiguated by linguistic context or by paraphrase. Rather, the addressee, hearing a sentence like 1, disambiguates it in terms of the social situation in which he is exposed to it.

Let me be more precise. Suppose you overhear the sentence *Visiting relatives can be a nuisance* in isolation. You have no way of knowing whether the speaker is talking about relatives who visit, or the act of visiting one's relatives. But if the hearer has also heard prior discourse, and if, for example, this discourse was concerned with a discussion of the properties of relatives, and when relatives were a nuisance, the hearer is able to disambiguate the sentence by linguistic means.

Now we know that the modal *must* is actually an amalgam of several meanings, all related but differentiable. (I will confine my discussion to the root sense of *must*, for obvious reasons.) As suggested above, these related meanings are:

(a) The speaker is higher in rank than the superficial subject of *must*, in sent. 1 identical with the addressee. As such the former can impose an obligation on the latter.

(b) The thing the addressee is told to do is distasteful to him: he must be compelled to do it against his will.

(c) Something untoward will happen to the addressee if he does not carry out the instruction.[3]

Any of these assumptions might be primary in a given instance. In non-polite situations, normally (a) is paramount in sentences like 6, and (c) in cases like 7; it seems to depend on context.

(6) You must clean the latrine, Private Zotz: this is the Army, and I'm your sergeant.
(7) You must take this medicine, Mr. President, or you will never get over making those awkward gestures.

Theoretically, then, a sentence like 1 should be triply ambiguous, and two of the ambiguities should be rude. In fact, if taken out of context, such a sentence would be just as mysterious to the hearer as *Visiting relatives can be a nuisance*. But just as with the latter, 1 is swiftly disambiguated if one is aware of the context. For 1, it is extralinguistic context: one knows one is being addressed by the hostess proffering her cake, and one accordingly decides on meaning (b). (Of course, if 1 were spoken by a member of the Mafia whose wife had baked the cake, the range of possible choices of meaning might be wider.)

Why are *should* and *may* less polite in this context? In the case of these modals, we are making rather different assumptions about the willingness of the subject to perform the act, and it is here, I think, that the non-politeness lies. With *should,* there is normally no assumption that the action is to be performed against the subject's will: the speaker is making a suggestion to the addressee to do something that might not have occurred to him, but there is no hint that he would be averse to it, or would have to be compelled to do it. In fact, the use of *should* indicates that the speaker is not in a position to use duress to secure compliance: he can suggest but not coerce. In non-polite use, then, *should* is more polite than *must* since the speaker is not suggesting his status is such that he can coerce the addressee. But this implies that he NEED NOT coerce the addressee, and for this reason the 'humbling' force of *must* is absent. But *should* by itself is not really a politeness marker: it does not humble the speaker, but merely makes him the equal of the addressee. So the use of *should* in the dinner party situation is not particularly polite: in fact, it is rather rude, since the hostess is suggesting that it would be better for the addressee if he had some cake—that is, that the cake is too good to miss. From this assumption, the implication follows that the hostess's offering is a good thing—contrary, as we have seen, to the rules of politeness. As a further example of this, consider what happens if the hostess should OVERTLY make the same suggestion. The same sense of impropriety ensues from 8 as from 2:

(8) Have some of this delicious cake.

---

[3] It seems reasonable to believe that, of the three assumptions comprising the meaning of *must* (a) and (c) are first-order presuppositions, and (b) second-order. The reason for making this claim is that (a) and (c) can be questioned, as is typical of first-order presuppositions, while (b) cannot, as the following examples show. In reply, e.g., *You must take out the garbage!*, the respondent might retort, under the appropriate circumstances, with *You can't make me!* or *Who's gonna make me?* (which contradict (a), and are equivalent to 'You don't have the authority'), or with *So what if I don't!* (which contradicts (c), and is equivalent to 'If I don't do it, I won't suffer'). But he cannot reply with* *I want to anyhow!* (which would be a contradiction of (b) and equivalent to 'I am not being made to do it against my will').

But if another guest is offering the cake, both 2 and 8 are perfectly appropriate and usual, since the guest is not praising his own property. This shows that implicit and explicit assumptions—in this case, of the value of one's own possessions—work the same way in determining appropriateness, and both work the same way as honorifics in other languages:

(9) Have some of this '*o*-cake'.[4]

(10) Have some of my friend's '*o*-cake'.

(11) You should have some of her cake.

(12) Have some of her delicious cake.

Finally, it is now easy to see why *may* in 3 is not a polite form: in fact, its use makes two assumptions, both of which are counter to the conventions of politeness: (a) that the person who is able to grant permission (by the use of *may*) is superior to the person seeking it; (b) that the person seeking permission not only is not averse to doing the act indicated, but wishes to do it. Then the further assumption is that, as far as the person receiving permission by sentence 3 is concerned, having the cake is a good thing. As with *should,* this is counter to the usage of politeness.

These examples show several things. First, there are uses of the modals that reflect politeness, in terms of relative status of speaker and hearer, and implicit desirability of the act in question. In this respect these modal uses are parallel to the use of honorifics in other languages. Second, in order to tell how a modal is being used, and whether certain responses to it are (linguistically) appropriate, one must be aware of many extralinguistic, social factors. Just as, in speaking other languages, one must be aware of the social status of the other participants in a conversation in order to carry on the conversation acceptably, so one must at least some of the time in English, a language usually said not to require overt distinctions of this sort.

There are many other examples of politeness conventions explicitly realized in English. One is the use of imperatives, a task fraught with perils for one who does not understand the application of levels of politeness in English. For example, consider the following ways of giving an order. When can each be used appropriately? What happens if the wrong one is used?

(13) Come in, won't you?

(14) Please come in.

(15) Come in.

(16) Come in, will you?

(17) Get the hell in here.

---

[4] According to Tazuko Uyeno, although not every Japanese noun may receive the *o*-honorific prefix, those that can behave as suggested in the text. E.g., the word *taku* 'house' will take the prefix *o*- when it refers to the home of someone other than the speaker and will occur without *o*- when the speaker's own house is being referred to. The same informant points out an interesting difference in polite usage between Japanese and English, also relevant at this point: I have noted above that in English the modal *must,* ordinarily not a polite form, may be interpreted as polite in specific social contexts where one is able to 'ignore' certain aspects of the meaning of *must.* But in Japanese, this is not the case: I cannot use the word-for-word equivalent of 'You must have some cake' as a polite utterance equivalent to its English translation. It would, in fact, be interpreted as rude under the circumstances. One must rather say something like, 'Please have some cake as a favor to me.' Thus it is not necesssarily true that one can 'ignore' the same aspects of meaning in two languages.

It would seem clear that these sentences are ranked in an order of descending politeness. To use 17, your status must be higher than that of the addressee; moreover, you must be in such a situation that you don't even care to maintain the conventional pretense that you are addressing him as an equal. That is, 17 deliberately ASSERTS the superiority of the speaker over the addressee, and as such is rude in a situation in which it is not normal to make this assertion.[5] By contrast, 15 merely implies this assumption of superiority: it assumes compliance, and hence suggests that the speaker has the right to expect this compliance, and that the speaker therefore outranks the addressee; but it does these things much more covertly than 17. But, though not normally a rude form, it is still not really a polite one. Again, however, we must make an exception for one case, analogous to the one made in the first set of cases with modals: if the addressee is at the speaker's door and is a friend, 15 is much more normal than 13–14 as an invitation to enter. The first two, in fact, do not seem polite in this context: they give the impression of forced hospitality. Here again we seem to be depending on a more complex notion of politeness: both 13 and 14, like 2, imply that the addressee has the choice of complying or not—that his status is sufficiently high with respect to the speaker that he can obey or not as he sees fit—while 15, like 1, seems at first to suggest that the addressee has no choice, that his status is so low that he is obliged to obey. Yet both are relatively polite in this sort of social context. The reason in the case of 16 is parallel to that in 1: the speaker is implying here (by convention: he doesn't REALLY make this assumption, of course; it would be bizarre if he did) that the addressee doesn't really want to come in, that he will enter only under duress. Since 13–14 do not allow this assumption, they are less polite. So again the two definitions of politeness—status vs. desirability of the speaker's offering—are at odds, and again the latter seems stronger. When the speaker is not really offering something of his own, the status assumption becomes paramount, and 13–14 become more polite than 15. This is the case in a doctor's office, for example, where the receptionist is more likely to use 13–14. Again, 13–14 are likely to be used for 'forced' politeness—e.g., when inviting an encyclopedia salesman in, under duress. I am not sure why this is so. But it is also true that a superior may address an obvious inferior

---

[5] This claim ignores the 'jovial' use of sentences like 17 as used between close friends, almost invariably male. Other examples are: *Get your ass in here, Harry! The party's started!* and *What makes you think you can go by my house without coming in, you asshole?* It seems that between close male friends in some American subcultures at any rate, the purpose of such otherwise unpardonably rude exclamations is to say, 'We're on such good terms that we don't have to go by the rules.' This linguistic impropriety occurs in relationships of the same degree of closeness as those which allow their members, for example, to invite themselves over to each other's house—otherwise a non-linguistic breach of propriety of similar magnitude. This illustrates again the parallelism of linguistic and non-linguistic concepts of politeness. These examples show, incidentally, that English, like Japanese, makes sex distinctions in the types of sentences possible. While a woman in most American subcultures would never use the above sentences, she might use the following to much the same effect, but lacking the obscenities: *Go ahead, have some more cake, Ethel—you're so fat, who'll notice if you get fatter?* Between very close friends, such a remark might be taken as an acceptable joke, but under any other conditions it is an unpardonable insult. There are other expressions confined to the feminine vocabulary: in particular epithets like 'gracious!' or 'dear, dear'. So English is again not so very unlike Japanese, except that the speaker of English can refrain from these usages altogether, but the speaker of Japanese must make his (or her) sex explicit in most conversations.

(for example, in the army) by 15, with no sense of sarcasm, i.e. no sense that he is being inappropriately polite. But if an officer addresses a private with 13, he is necessarily being sarcastic. There is no possibility of sarcasm, however, in the use of humbling forms of politeness, such as are found in 1 and 15. This is reminiscent of a fact that has been known for some time about presupposition in general: a first-order presupposition may be negated or questioned, under some conditions; a second-order presupposition cannot be. This suggests that the type of politeness involved in a usage like 15 or 1 is more complex in derivation than is the simple status-equalizing case in 13 or 2. In fact, it is probably true that the humbling type allows the status type to be deduced from it (if what I have is no good, one can deduce that I don't outrank you, in this respect anyway), so that the humbling type of politeness is one level deeper than the status type.

There are other assumptions, made in normal conversation, that are not tied to concepts of politeness. These, too, show up in non-obvious ways in the superficial structure. Some types which have been discussed by Grice 1968, as well as by Gordon & Lakoff, are rules of conversation. In a normal conversation, the participants will make the following assumptions, among others, about the discourse:[6]

Rule I. What is being communicated is true.

Rule II. It is necessary to state what is being said: it is not known to other participants, or utterly obvious. Further, everything necessary for the hearer to understand the communication is present.

Rule III. Therefore, in the case of statements, the speaker assumes that the hearer will believe what he says (due to Rule I).

Rule IV. With questions, the speaker assumes that he will get a reply.

Rule V. With orders, he assumes that the command will be obeyed.

All these assume, in addition, that the status of speaker and hearer is appropriate with respect to each other. (Of course, there are special situations in which all these are violated: lies, 'small talk', tall stories, riddles of certain types, and requests as opposed to commands. But in general these conditions define an appropriate conversational situation.)

But sometimes, even in ordinary conversational situations, some of these rules are violated. This is analogous to violating a rule of grammar: normally we should expect

---

[6] These implicit rules show up overtly in certain locutions. Cf. the following:

John is a Communist, and if you don't $\begin{Bmatrix} \text{believe} \\ \text{*obey} \\ \text{*answer} \end{Bmatrix}$ me, ask Fred.

Get out of here, and if you don't $\begin{Bmatrix} \text{*believe} \\ \text{obey} \\ \text{*answer} \end{Bmatrix}$ me, I'll sock you.

I ask you whether John left, and if you don't $\begin{Bmatrix} \text{*believe} \\ \text{*obey} \\ \text{answer} \end{Bmatrix}$ me, I'll be furious.

These examples show that, with each type of speech act—declaring, ordering, and asking—an 'appropriate' type of response is associated, and that this association shows up linguistically in superficial structures.

anomaly, lack of communication etc. When this is done baldly, e.g. by small children or by the insane, we do in fact notice that 'something is missing'; the conversation does not seem right. But in ordinary discourse among normal individuals we can often discern violations of these rules and others, and yet the total effect is not aberrant. One way in which apparent contradictions are reconciled is by the use of particles like *well, why, golly,* and *really.* Although these are often defined in pedagogical grammars as 'meaningless' elements, it seems evident that they have real, specific meanings, and therefore can be inappropriately used. It is therefore within the sphere of linguistics to define their appropriate usage. Moreover, this appropriateness of usage seems at least sometimes to involve the notion of 'violation of a normal rule of conversation'. These particles serve as warnings to participants in the discourse that one or more of these rules is about to be, or has been, violated. When this warning is given, it is apparently legal to violate the rule—that is, of course, only the specific rule for which the warning was given. Otherwise confusion results.

I have shown elsewhere (Lakoff 1970b) that the English particles *well* and *why* function in this way. *Well* serves notice that something is left out of the utterance that the hearer would need in order to understand the sentence—something, normally, that he can supply, or that the speaker promises to supply himself shortly. That is, *well* marks a violation of the second part of Rule II. *Why* indicates that the speaker is surprised at what the addressee has said: it suggests that perhaps the prior speaker has violated Rule I, in the case of a statement, or II, in the case of a question. Other analogous cases in English involve special syntactic configurations rather than particles. Consider sentences like the following:

(18) Leave, won't you?
(19) Leave!
(20) John left, didn't he?
(21) John left.

In the even-numbered examples above, we have tag-forms, one for a command—as discussed earlier—and one for a statement. It is worth asking whether these superficially similar structures have any deeper similarity: whether the reasons for applying tag-formation to imperatives are related to the reasons for applying this rule to declarative statements. It is more or less traditional in transformational literature to suggest that the two types of tags have little in common aside from superficial similarities of formation. But there are reasons for supposing that, in fact, there are real semantic reasons for this apparent superficial coincidence. This is a rather satisfying hypothesis, if it can be substantiated: it would suggest that these two bizarre and highly English-specific formations have a common function, so that two mysteries may be reduced to one.

With reference to Rules III and V above, one way in which a tag-question like 20 is distinguished from an ordinary statement like 21 is that the speaker really is asking less of the hearer. A speaker can demand belief from someone else only on condition that he himself fully believes the claim he is making. But the function of the tag is to suggest that the speaker, rather than demanding agreement or acquiescence from the hearer (as is true in a normal statement), is merely asking for agreement, leaving open the possibility that he won't get it. So a tag-question is really intermediate between a statement and a question: a statement assumes that the addressee will agree, and a question leaves the response of the addressee up to him, but a tag-question implies that, while the speaker expects a certain sort of response, the hearer may not provide it.[7] Hence its statement-plus-question superficial form is quite logical. The effect of the tag, then, is to soften the declaration from an expression of certainty, demanding belief, to an expression of likelihood, merely requesting it—suggesting that Rule III may be ignored.[8]

How do these facts lead to the conclusion that tag-questions and imperatives function in a parallel fashion, and that this function involves the weakening or ignoring of normal rules of conversation? It is clear how 20 operates in this way, as a 'softened' version of 21. We already know that Rule V says that an order normally is given only if the giver can assume it will be followed; and this is true of an order like 19, as well as one like 15. But it is not true of the corresponding tag-imperatives 13 and 18. These sentences allow the addressee the option of obeying or not, as tag-statements like 20 allow the addressee the option of believing (or agreeing) or not. So both tag-types have the same function: to give the addressee an escape from what is normally an ironclad rule. As noted above, the particles *well* and *why,* appended to English sentences, have a similar effect: that of showing that certain of the rules of conversation are about to be violated.

---

[7] As is well known, English has at least two intonation patterns associated with tag-statements (or, as they are more commonly called, tag-questions). One, rising, is closer to a question, as is predictable from the intonation pattern; this expresses less certainty on the speaker's part, and less hope of acquiescence by the addressee. The other, falling, is nearer to a statement, expressing near-certainty, with just the merest possibility left open that the addressee will fail to agree. The second type is often found as a kind of gesture of conventional politeness, meaning something like, 'I have enough information to know I'm right, but I'm just letting you have your say, in order to be polite.' It is interesting that some verbs of thinking, in the 1sg. present, have the same ambiguity resolved by the same difference in intonation pattern, and both types of locutions are used for similar purposes (cf. fn. 8 below). There is a third type of tag-question, used when the speaker definitely knows something is true, based on personal observation, and merely wishes to elicit a response from the addressee. This has the particle *sure* inserted, as in *It sure is cold in Ann Arbor, isn't it?*, vs. *It's cold in Ann Arbor, isn't it?* The latter sentence might be used if the speaker had merely read reports that the average temperature in Ann Arbor was 19°. He could not, under these conditions and if he had never been in Ann Arbor, use the former sentence. In Japanese, according to Uyeno (MS), the particle *ne* expresses both the senses of the second sentence, while its longer form *nee* corresponds to the first sentence.

[8] In fn. 7 I alluded briefly to the uses of verbs of thinking. My point is that verbs such as *guess, suppose, believe,* and sometimes *think,* when used in the 1sg. present, do not describe acts of cogitation: rather, they are means of softening a declarative statement. Consider the following sentences:

(a) I say that Fritz is a Zoroastrian.
(b) Fritz is a Zoroastrian.
(c) I guess Fritz is a Zoroastrian.
(d) Fritz is a Zoroastrian, isn't he?

If sentences like (a) and (b) (cf. Ross 1970) express certainty on the part of the speaker through the (overt or covert) performative verb of declaration, then (c) expresses the speaker's feeling that the event described in the complement of the verb of thinking is a probability rather than a certainty. As (b) corresponds to (a), it is my contention (made for other reasons in Lakoff 1969) that (d) corresponds to (c): in fact, they are closely synonymous in many of their uses, just like (a) and (b). As pointed out in fn. 7, the same disambiguation by intonation exists for both.

Then English has at least two means for indicating this relaxation of rules: the presence of particles, and the use of special transformational rules for this semantic purpose and no other—in this case, of course, tag-formation. It is not known at present whether there are languages that are held to only one option or the other; what is known is that very few languages other than English (actually, none I have ever heard of) utilize such tag-formation rules. Then it should not be strange to find a language expressing analogous functions by the use of particles. A particularly interesting example is Japanese.

As with *well* and *why* in English, the use of any of the numerous particles in Japanese is governed by the extralinguistic context: the status of the participants (involving, among other relevant information, their sexes), the formality of the situation, and so on. Among them is a pair of particles (*ne* and *yo*) whose function apparently is to indicate interference with the normal rules of conversation. In fact, the only way in which one can find a generalization about the uses of these particles is to look at them in this way.[9]

Both *ne* and *yo* may be appended to any of the three sentence-types: declarative, interrogative, and imperative. When analysed superficially, the effect of each seems different for each different sentence-type; but when we bear in mind the issues dealt with above, certain generalizations fall into place. Let us look at some examples: for the convenience of readers who, like myself, are not fluent in Japanese, I have attempted to give symbolic rather than real Japanese examples: I have used English sentences of the appropriate types, with the Japanese particle added in its normal place at the right.

Ne may be appended to declaratives, imperatives, and interrogatives:

(22) John is here *ne*. 'John is here, isn't he?' (a declarative, but without the normal declarative demand for the hearer's belief)

(23) Come here *ne*. 'Come here, won't you?' (an order, but without the normal imperative demand for the addressee's obedience)

(24) Is John here *ne*? 'I wonder if John is here. . . ?' (a question, but without the normal interrogative demand for the addressee's response)

In all three cases, as the interpretations indicate, a normally obligatory rule of conversation is relaxed: the particle *ne* is a signal to the addressee that he may choose to observe the implication (one of Rules III–V) or not, as he decides. The use of *ne* in Japanese (comparable to the use of tag-forms in two of the three English types) allows the ground-rules to be suspended, as it were.

As is true of most particles, the use of *ne* is not completely free. Its use is restricted to informal situations: conversation in small groups, and colloquial writing. (This is true of many English particles as well.) The reason for this seems to be that the use of these particles provides implicit personal information about the speaker—about his sex and status, relative to that of the addressee. On the other hand, part of the idea of 'formality' seems to lie in giving as little personal information as possible, confining the discourse solely to the information one wishes to convey. In formal social situations, for example, the speaker does not inquire about the health of the addressee (unless he is a doctor, in which case it is relevant to the discourse itself), while he typically does in less formal

---

[9] All examples here are from Uyeno, who discusses these cases, with many more examples, as well as other extremely interesting particle uses in Japanese, in her forthcoming dissertation. Kazuhiko Yoshida and Chisato Kitagawa provided enlightening discussion and further examples of these constructions.

dialog. When particles are used in formal prose, they are ones like *indeed*, which give implicit information about the relationship of the various elements in the discourse to one another, and do not involve the speaker's relationship toward the hearer or his feelings toward the information he is conveying.

Aside from this general condition on the use of particles, *ne* is also subject to other conditions, based on the social situation. The speaker must be aware of the relative status of himself and his addressee in order to know whether *ne* is usable in a discourse—i.e., to know whether he can offer his addressee the right to suspend the relevant rule. Again, this can be ascertained by looking at how the particle functions in discourse: roughly, it can be used in situations corresponding to those in which a speaker of English can ask, 'What do YOU think?' Three conditions determine when such locutions are acceptable:

(i) The status of the addressee should be somewhat higher than that of the speaker, since offering a choice is an act of deference. (This may be true even if the participants are in fact social equals, as a 'humbling' gesture of politeness on the part of the speaker.)

(ii) The status of the addressee cannot be very much higher than that of the speaker, since if it is, the speaker doesn't have the right to OFFER a choice.

(iii) The status of the addressee cannot be lower than that of the speaker, since then he would not have the right to MAKE a choice. So we see that both the function and the conditions on the use of *ne* are tied to assumptions made by speaker and hearer about the context—social and linguistic—in which the utterance takes place.

A similar situation can be shown to pertain in the case of *yo*, the other particle mentioned above, which may be appended to declaratives, imperatives, and interrogatives:

(25) John is here *yo*. 'I tell you John is here, (and you'd better believe it).' (a declarative in which the speaker explicitly demands the addressee's observance of Rule III)

(26) Come here *yo*. 'I'm telling you to come here, (and you'd better obey).'[10] (an order in which the speaker explicitly demands the addressee's observance of Rule V)

(27) Is John here *yo*? 'What do you mean, is John here?' 'Are you asking me, "Is John here?" '

This last is possible only as an incredulous echo-question based on a prior question of the addressee's, 'Is John here?' It is therefore a rhetorical question, expecting either a positive or negative answer. The effect is: 'How can you ask such a question, when it's

---

[10] Kazuhiko Yoshida points out that, though this sentence may be used by both men and women, the effect is different. The translation given here is the sense it would have when spoken by a man. If spoken by a woman, it would mean something like, 'I really hope you will come here. Please don't forget.' A strong command has been replaced by an earnest request. The effect of *yo* here in women's speech seems to be something like an attempt to express the idea that the speaker wishes she had the status to insist on the observance of Rule V. The use of *yo* by a speaker of much lower status than the addressee (which, in conventional Japanese society, presumably automatically includes all women) is in a sense contradictory for reasons to be discussed below. The contradiction is resolved by using *yo* to indicate a strong request, rather than a strong injunction that cannot be disobeyed. This is still another example of how non-linguistic context (such as the sex of participants in a discourse) affects the interpretation of sentences, and therefore must be considered part of the linguistic information available to a speaker.

so obvious what the answer must be?' The speaker, in effect, asks why the hearer wants to have Rule IV obeyed.

As is evident from the foregoing, the behavior of *yo* with questions is more complex and much harder to understand, in terms of our tentative generalization, than its use with either of the other two sentence-types. But we may make a start toward analysing it as follows. First, assume that the addressee of 27, A, was the speaker of the immediately preceding discourse—in this case the question, 'Is John here?' Then, of course, A, in asking this normal question, is implicitly making the assumption that the addressee B, the potential speaker of 27, will follow Rule IV. B is of course aware that observance of Rule IV is expected of him, but the question is such that he cannot imagine why A asked the question—i.e., why A expects Rule IV to be followed. So what B is doing in effect, by using sentence 27, is to make Rule IV explicit by calling it into question. Sentence 27, then, means something like, 'I don't see why I have to answer this question, "Is John here?" '; or, perhaps, 'Make it explicit to me why I should be expected to reply.' Where the statement and the command make explicit the fact that they anticipate the ADDRESSEE'S compliance with the rule, the question followed by *yo* comments on the fact that the SPEAKER of the *yo*-question himself has been expected to comply with a rule that he does not, in the present instance, see the reason for. For some speakers, a positive reply is what is obviously anticipated; for others, a negative one. It would not be surprising if some speakers might be able to use 27 in both cases. (Intonation will differ depending on which interpretation is intended.) There are several close parallels in English:

(28) A: Is Agnew a liberal?
     B: *What do you mean,* Is Agnew a liberal?
(29) A: Is Ted smoking a reefer?
     B: *Are you asking me whether* Ted is smoking a reefer?

In both these cases, depending on context, B's response may be construed as being equivalent to 'Of course!' or to 'Of course not!' But, as explained above, this diversity of interpretation is not contradictory, once it can be seen that both replies reflect the speaker's questioning the need for the act of interrogation, or, more precisely, the need for B to follow Rule IV. Then all three cases where the rule of conversation is insisted upon are realized superficially in Japanese by the use of *yo,* and in English by the explicit presence in the superficial structure of the performative verb, normally left implicit (cf. Ross 1970). Thus we see that, to express this notion of insistence on observance, English employs a variation of a transformational rule (i.e., a normally obligatory rule, performative deletion, is in this situation inapplicable), just as it employed a specific transformational rule, tag-question formation, to indicate the relaxation of the observance of the same rule of conversation. For both, Japanese employs particles. And we see again that, although the two languages differ greatly in the grammatical means by which they express this notion, both can express it relatively unambiguously. Further, the languages express the idea in syntactically parallel fashion for the three types of speech acts (though English does not with the equivalent of *ne*-questions). This shows again that we cannot stop our analysis at the point of superficial structure, or at the point of logical structure, in fact: we must ask in every case what the extralinguistic context of a sentence is, what purpose it is used for; only on that basis can we establish whether or not sentences in two languages are parallel. And it should be clear that a theory that does not allow the interrelationship of linguistic and extralinguistic context cannot tell us what is held in common by *yo* and *ne*; by *ne* and tag-questions; by *yo* and the overt presence of the performative; or, finally, by tag-questions and tag-imperatives on the one hand, and explicit declarative, imperative, and interrogative performatives on the other. This is a large chunk of linguistic material for a theory to ignore.

In Japanese, *yo* is apparently much more normal for male than for female speakers, and this is particularly true of *yo* with questions: all my informants, one of them female, agree that a woman would never or rarely use a sentence like 27. Given the conventional status of women in the Japanese culture, it is easy to see why a Japanese woman would never use *yo*. In its non-interrogative use, its purpose is to demand compliance from the addressee. To be able to do so, the speaker must outrank the hearer and must, in addition, be willing to make this relationship obvious. A Japanese woman would not be nearly as likely to do this as would a man. In interrogatives, not only does the speaker do this, but he also questions the right of the addressee (the speaker of the prior question) to expect the rule of conversation to be adhered to, which amounts to a still more overt declaration of higher status on the part of the speaker.

Why should one need to make a demand of this type explicit, when it normally is understood by the addressee anyway? One reason for the use of *yo* or its equivalent occurs when the speaker has some reason to fear that the rule in question may not in fact be obeyed by the addressee. Although one might expect the social situations in which *yo* is usable to be the reverse of those in which *ne* is possible, this is not quite true. We might, for instance, assume that the higher someone is in status, the more appropriate it might be to explicitly demand compliance to the rules. But if one is sufficiently superior, he has no reason at all to fear that his injunctions, explicit or implicit, will be disobeyed. Therefore, *yo* is most apt to be used where the speaker is somewhat superior to the hearer, so that he has the right to make demands, but not so much higher that he has no need to make them. Obviously, *yo* cannot be used by someone of lower social status than the addressee.[11]

Having given evidence that English speakers are capable of making distinctions of the first two types alluded to at the beginning of this paper, let us now examine the third. What about the use of 'dubitatives' and their opposites, as endings on verbs or particles, to express uncertainty or certainty on the speaker's part? I have already given examples of 'dubitatives' in English: the use of *I guess* or of tags, as has been shown, is essentially dubitative in function; it is a sign that the speaker is not altogether prepared to stand by his assertion, in the sense that he does not have complete confidence in what he is

---

[11] An apparent problem for this analysis (or, so far as I can see, any analysis) is the fact that *yo* and *ne* may occur in sentences like this:

    (a) *Kore-wa anata-no hon da wa yo ne.*
    (b) This is your book *yo ne*.

If *yo* demands compliance with the rules of conversation, and *ne* allows relaxation of the rules, is not such a sentence contradictory? As explained by Uyeno, however, the effect of such utterances is to express the speaker's insistence that the addressee acquiesce: i.e., it appears that *yo* modifies *ne*. Thus (a) has as its closest English equivalent a sentence like

    (c) This is your book, isn't it?

This is equivalent to something like, 'I guess this is your book—I certainly hope you'll agree.' Such a sentence might be used in circumstances like this: suppose that the speaker of (c) has previously borrowed the book in question from the addressee. The addressee has,

asserting, since he does not—he cannot, as we have seen—demand the addressee's belief as he ordinarily would. The best he can do is to ask for it. As an example, if I say

(30) John is in Antarctica,

and it later turns out that 30 is not the case, my addressee may later say, 'You were wrong about 30.' If he does, I have no recourse but to agree, providing his evidence is incontestable. But if instead I say

(31) I guess John is in Antarctica

under the same conditions, and later the addressee says, 'You were wrong', then I have the option of replying, 'No, I only said I THOUGHT 30 might be the case.' That is, I can claim I was not really making that assertion. Thus verbs such as *guess* in the 1st person singular, like tags, function as subjunctives do in languages like Latin:

(32) *Marcus Publium interfecit quod*
     uxorem suam corrupisset.   'Marcus killed Publius because he se-
(33) *Marcus Publium interfecit quod*   duced his wife.'
     uxorem suam corrupit.

Here the presence of the subjunctive in 32 indicates that the speaker is not prepared to take responsibility for the claim that the alleged reason is in fact the real reason for an action. With the indicative, as in 33, the speaker implicitly takes responsibility. We have no natural means of expressing this difference in English: we must resort to paraphrase. But we do have analogous devices, illustrated by 31, usable under other grammatical conditions. If we were teaching English to a speaker of Latin, we might want to exemplify this use of *guess* (which I do not believe is found in Latin in this sense) by suggesting parallels with sentences like 32, rather than by resorting to elaborate circumlocutions, which, as we have seen, don't really give the same idea.

English has other devices to express the speaker's acceptance or denial of responsibility for something in an utterance. Like the honorifics discussed earlier, these are not generally recognized as dubitatives or 'certaintives' (if I may coin that term), because they are not characteristically obligatory morphemes, and because they function in only a limited subset of sentence-types. It is not surprising, in view of our earlier findings, to see that modals perform these functions along with many others. With verbs of perception, the modal *can* displays certain semantic properties not derivable from any normal definition

---

throughout the transaction, behaved as though the book were his to lend. But now a third person accosts the speaker of (c), demanding the book back, as if it had always been his. The speaker of (c)—partly because he knows or likes the addressee better than the third person and therefore trusts him more, partly because it is to his advantage for the book to belong to the addressee— still feels fairly confident that the addressee really owns the book. But he is not as sure as formerly, and needs confirmation. His use of (c) is equivalent to saying, first, 'I say this is your book, and I hope you believe it' (i.e., 'This is your book *ne*.') Then he adds, 'I REALLY hope you can go along with this hypothesis; you'd better (for my sake) agree to this'—where *yo* modifies and strengthens the hope of the speaker that the addressee will be able to acquiesce: i.e., 'I'm giving you a chance to relax Rule III, but I hope you don't take it.'

    I am not sure that this is precisely correct; but in any event the effect is not contradictory, and it does seem as though *yo* modifies *ne* rather than the utterance itself, particularly as an utterance like (a) is more apt to be used by women than is a normal *yo*-sentence.

of *can*. As first noted by Boyd & Thorne 1969, under certain conditions sentences containing *can* appear to be synonymous to sentences without it:

(34) I can understand French perfectly.
(35) I understand French perfectly.

But in some contexts where this should be true, particularly when the verb is non-1st-person present, we find that although the denotative content of the sentence pairs remains the same, one member often contains implications that are lacking in the other; e.g.,

(36) That acid-head John hears voices telling him he is Spiro Agnew, so don't play golf with him.
(37) That acid-head John can hear voices telling him he is Spiro Agnew, so don't play golf with him.

In order for 37 to be acceptable, the speaker would have to be making the assumption that the voices were real, rather than hallucinations. Then the effect of *can* in sentences such as these (again, a very restricted subset) is to indicate doubt in the speaker's mind as to the reality of what he is describing—the effect of dubitative morphemes in many languages.

With these two sentences, contrast a situation in which the speaker might normally agree that the phenomena were real which the subject of the sentence was sensing. Then the presence of *can* is at least as normal as its absence:

(38) Mrs. Snickfritz has eyes like a hawk: she can spot dust on your carpet even if you just vacuumed.
(39) Mrs. Snickfritz has eyes like a hawk: she spots dust on your carpet even if you just vacuumed.

There is a distinction in meaning between these two sentences, but it is not the same as the one found in the first pair: in these, in which the first part of the sentence establishes the reality of the dust Mrs. Snickfritz sees, the sentence with *can* seems to be used merely as evidence of her superlative ability, while the sentence without *can* is less an expression of approval or astonishment than a suggestion that Mrs. Snickfritz, because of her punctiliousness, is a pain in the neck.

Elsewhere in the modal system we find a device for expressing the opposite of the dubitative, namely the speaker's certainty that an event will take place. This phenomenon has been referred to as '*will*-deletion', though perhaps, as I have argued elsewhere (Lakoff 1970a), a better name is '*will*-insertion'. In any case, in sentences referring to future events, the absence of *will* indicates that the speaker has reason to be sure that the event will occur, whether because it is scheduled or because he has control over it. (Many things about this phenomenon are still unclear; there are numerous puzzling cases and apparent counter-examples to the generalization just given, but we can assume it is an accurate enough generalization to be used in the present discussion.) In the previous example, the presence of the modal *can* acted as a dubitative marker; here, it is the absence of *will* that acts as a certaintive. Alternatively, we might view the presence of *will* as a dubitative, making the speaker appear less certain about the occurrence of an event in the future than he might be. Whichever way one looks at it, the facts are relatively clear, as in

(40) John dies at dawn.
(41) John will die at dawn.

In 40, the executioner is speaking; he controls John's destiny, and has himself arranged for John's death. In 41, although the executioner could say this sentence, it might also be John's doctor speaking—though he could not say 40, even if he were familiar with the course of John's disease and could be fairly sure when death would occur. He does not (presumably) have a hand in it. However these facts are to be interpreted, I think the use of the modals in sentences 36–41 can be viewed as parallel to that of dubitatives and similar forms in other languages.

Finally, there are still other related facts involving modals and their paraphrases, noted by Larkin 1969. He points out that there is, for many speakers at least, a difference in the appropriate conditions under which these sentences can be used:

> (42) My girl must be home by midnight.
> (43) My girl has to be home by midnight.

By using 42, the speaker takes responsibility for the obligation. But 43 is neutral; he may merely be reporting an obligation he does not necessarily approve of. Compare:

> (44) *My girl must be home by midnight—I think it's idiotic.
> (45)   My girl has to be home by midnight—I think it's idiotic.

In this case, the speaker is not taking or refusing responsibility for the FACTUAL content of the sentence, as he was in the other cases. Here the truth of the modal notion itself is at issue—whether there really is a true 'obligation' involved. I am not sure whether dubitatives in other languages can affect or cast doubt on modality, as these can.

There are examples parallel to Larkin's with other modals; this is not an isolated fact about *must/have to,* as the previous examples were isolated cases with *can* or *will.* This fact suggests a pervasive property throughout the modal system. The existence in English of periphrastic modal forms may not be due wholly to the fact that modals are syntactically defective; there is a real need for the periphrastic forms at a semantic level as well. Compare the following:

> (46) John will shoot the basilisk.
> (47) John is to shoot the basilisk.
> (48) Bill may have a cookie.
> (49) Bill is allowed to have a cookie.

In the first set, *will* is the root sense *will* of command: 'I order that . . .' Thus 46 is a direct order, for which the speaker is assuming responsibility. In 47, he is still transmitting an order, but it may have originated with someone else; it may not be an order he goes along with. For most speakers of American English, 48 expresses the direct giving of permission by the speaker. But 49 may be used to report someone else's giving of permission. Thus, *will/be to* and *may/be allowed to* are parallel to *must/have to.*

I have, then, given examples of phenomena in English and other languages that bear out certain contentions:

(a) Honorifics, particles relating speaker and discourse, and dubitatives (with their relatives) are not confined to those exotic languages that have special exclusive markers for them. They are found in English; but the forms used to indicate their presence are used in other ways in other sentence types, so that they are not readily identifiable. This indicates that languages have many and arcane ways of expressing concepts; we should not assume a language cannot make a distinction just because it has no exclusive form by which to make it.

(b) In order to assign the correct distributions to the forms under discussion, it is essential to take extralinguistic contextual factors into account: respective status of speaker and addressee, the type of social situation in which they find themselves, the real-world knowledge or beliefs a speaker brings to a discourse, his lack of desire to commit himself on a position, etc. We cannot hope to describe or explain large segments of any given language by recourse only to factors which play a role in the superficial syntax: we must take account of other levels of language, which traditional transformational grammar expressly prevents us from doing.[12]

REFERENCES

Boyd, J., and J. Thorne. 1969. The deep grammar of modal verbs. Journal of Linguistics 5.57–74.

Gordon, D., and G. Lakoff. 1971. Conversational postulates. Papers from the 7th Regional Meeting, Chicago Linguistic Society, 63–84.

Grice, H. P. 1968. The logic of conversation. MS, Berkeley, Calif.

Lakoff, R. 1969. Syntactic arguments for negative transportation. Papers from the 5th Regional Meeting, Chicago Linguistic Society, 140–7.

———. 1970a. Tense and its relation to participants. Lg. 46.838–49.

———. 1970b. Questionable answers and answerable questions. To appear in Papers in honor of Henry and Renée Kahane, University of Illinois Press.

Larkin, D. 1969. Some notes on English modals. University of Michigan Phonetics Lab Notes 4.31–6.

Ross, J. R. 1970. On declarative sentences. Readings in English transformational grammar, ed. by R. A. Jacobs and P. S. Rosenbaum, 222–72. Waltham, Mass.: Ginn.

Uyeno, T. MS. A study of Japanese modality: a performative analysis of sentence particles. Doctoral dissertation, University of Michigan.

DISCUSSION QUESTIONS

1. State Lakoff's rule of politeness in your own words. Do you think her formulation of this rule is correct?

2. What is the function of tag-questions in English? What are the extralinguistic considerations?

---

[12] As should be apparent to anyone familiar with other than purely transformational linguistic tradition, the notion that contextual factors, social and otherwise, must be taken into account in determining the acceptability and interpretation of sentences is scarcely new. It has been anticipated by a veritable *Who's who* of linguistics and anthropology: Jespersen, Sapir, Malinowski, Firth, Nida, Pike, Hymes, Friedrich, Tyler, and many others. But the idea has not merely been forgotten by transformational grammar; rather, it has been explicitly rejected. Therefore, to bring up facts such as these within the framework of recent linguistic discussion is to do more than merely restate an old platitude. I hope that by discussing new facts, and expatiating on their theoretical implications, I have shown that contextual factors cannot be avoided by the linguist of any theoretical view, if he is to deal honestly and accurately with the facts of language.

3. Using the methodology developed by Lakoff, work out the proper contexts for the following forms of address: *Mr., Mrs., sir, madam,* and *ma'am.* Do they vary from one section of the country to another?

4. Why are the occupational titles *pastor, doctor,* and *coach* used together with the last name when addressing someone, but not the titles *grocer, housewife,* or *teacher?* What is the approved use of *reverend?*

5. How does the use of linguistic forms of politeness seem to differ between (a) strangers in a formal situation and in an informal situation, and (b) friends in a formal situation and in an intimate situation?

DWIGHT BOLINGER

Bolinger, who describes himself as a "fancy-freelancing linguist" since his retirement from a Harvard University professorship in Spanish, is now a visiting professor of linguistics at Stanford University. During his notable teaching and scholarly career, this paper was delivered as his presidential address to the Linguistic Society of America.

TRUTH IS A LINGUISTIC QUESTION

The drift of this paper can be summed up in an expression that first saw the light of day in 1942. For almost three years, from 1937 to 1939, American volunteers had been part of the army that fought against Hitler and Mussolini in Spain. After the vortex of Hitlerism had finally sucked us in, one would have expected those trained and seasoned young soldiers to be admired for their foresight and sought out for their experience. But nothing of the sort happened. In one of those perverse labelings that propagandists are so good at, they were passed over as 'premature antifascists'. To have admitted their foresight would have been to admit our own lack of it.

Every generation has to rediscover love. So, I suppose, every generation must rediscover jargon. Here is a 1972 definition by L. E. Sissman: 'all of these debased and isolable forms of the mother tongue that attempt to paper over an unpalatable truth and/ or to advance the career of the speaker (or the issue, cause or product he is agent for) by a kind of verbal sleight of hand, a one-upmanship of which the reader or listener is victim.' Stepping back to 1955 we hear James Thurber calling for a psychosemanticist, or for anybody, who could treat us for what he called 'the havoc wrought by verbal artillery on the fortress of reason', by a language 'full of sound and fury, dignifying nothing'. Going back another quarter century to my own college days, there was Sir Arthur Quiller-Couch with his essay 'On jargon' (1916). Running the film in reverse a good 200 years more, Sir Ernest Gowers 1948 quotes an admonition 'delivered to the Supervisor of Pontefract by the Secretary to the Commissioners of Excise'. It reads: 'The Commissioners on perusal of your diary observe that you make use of many affected phrases and incongruous words, such as "illegal procedure," "harmony," etc., all of which you use in a sense that the words do not bear. I am ordered to acquaint you that if you hereafter continue that affected and schoolboy way of writing, and to murder the language in such a manner, you will be discharged as a fool.' It would be a simple matter to round out the history with quotations from Erasmus and Thucydides.

All very interesting, you may admit, but what does it have to do with us? There was a time when it would have been hard to believe that any linguist could admit that it had anything to do at all. Those of us who trekked across the semantic desert of the forties and fifties could hardly have been blamed for feeling that life had lost all meaning, except perhaps differential meaning. Not that there were no respectable scholars interested in how meaning can be abused in language. In 1941 there was a group calling itself the Institute for Propaganda Analysis, numbering among its officers Clyde Beals, W. H. Kilpatrick, and Charles Beard, along with other notables. (I insert at this point, as a sign of the times, the fact that after thirty years of suspended animation the Propaganda

Analysis group began to show signs of life again this fall, and was calling on linguists for coöperation. But the original group had no linguists in it.) Of course there existed at about the same time a flourishing school of General Semanticists, very much involved in such questions. Yet I don't need to remind any of the veterans in LSA how these lower-class people were looked down upon. Leonard Bloomfield regarded their leader, Alfred Korzybski, as a kind of soothsayer, and Korzybski's own jargonesque prose did little to dispel that impression. In any case, linguistic engineering (to use a bit of jargon from our own side) was totally absorbed in establishment activities such as army specialized training, literacy programs, and language policy in emerging nations. This was where the money went and where the action was. The linguist up to very recently has been a more or less useful social sideliner, but not a social critic.

Happily, I think we can say that this aloofness has begun to thaw somewhat. In a sense we are repeating the two phases of the protest movement. First came civil rights. In our terms, this has meant studies of Black English and Harlem Spanish and so-called deficit language in general. Now we are approaching something akin to peace and welfare demonstrations in the form of demands on the 'white standard' for accountability. The National Council of Teachers of English is one step ahead of us. In November they set up a Committee on Public Doublespeak; one of its members, Wayne O'Neil, is also a member of LSA, so we may expect the gospel to be spread any day now. What makes me more certain of this is the fact that the Boston *Globe*, when it carried the account of the Committee on Public Doublespeak, identified Wayne as Rabbi Wayne O'Neil. Robert Hogan, Executive Secretary of NCTE, described the charge of the committee in these terms: "The question is not just whether subjects and verbs agree, but whether statements and facts agree."[1]

Though I suspect that a majority of linguists would still want to reject it, there is also the plea made recently (1972) by Congressman Robert F. Drinan. He was addressing himself to teachers of English, and he had this to say (279): 'In the matter of officially proclaimed marshmallow prose, it does seem to me that you have some professional responsibility.' Whether we deny this or not, we are being pushed toward it by events both in our field and from outside. Take the grammar of the sentence. There aren't many big nuggets left in that gold mine. Right now the prospectors are swarming over presuppositions, higher sentences, and other things whose purpose or effect is exactly to make explicit what writers and speakers get away with in their self-serving prose. Context is in, both linguistic and social. And we have rediscovered the lexicon, including the morass of connotations, euphemisms, and general chicanery. The last refuge left for the weakhearted seems to be phonology. The rest of us are finding it more and more difficult to keep ourselves undefiled.

As for events outside the field, our government—the very government that is the greatest abuser of language—finds itself caught in the embarrasing necessity of enforcing honesty in order to collect its taxes. Only so much money can be squeezed out of a family budget; so, in true gangster fashion, the small-time operators are being liquidated. There are the dealers who for years levied usurious rates of interest and were allowed to get away with it by the neat semantic trick of labeling them 'carrying charges'; also the local rent gougers, and the minor medicine men with their pill-promoting prodigies and their end-product, the drug culture. Government hits back by giving us truth in

---

[1] Boston *Globe*, 22 November 1972, p. 5.

lending, truth in labeling, and truth in advertising. These are narrow gains. If we want the truth that government requires of its own business partners—e.g., which insurers give value for their premiums or which automotive manufacturers build safe transmissions— we still have to go to court to get it. All the same, there is a danger for those bent on concealment. A taste of truth is like a taste of blood. The subject should never have been brought up at all. Now that it has, truth is in the headlines, pushed there by the two-way struggle between governors and governed, each bent on finding out about the other—the governors to sniff out our private feelings, which could pose a threat to our control; the governed to know the decisions that affect them, but of which they may not be the beneficiaries. The medium of all this knowing is language, and linguists are in the line of fire.

If this widespread clamor for truth only embraced the way language is used, it might affect us less intimately. But it is also directed at the way language is. Here the target is not so much government as the whole of society. Julia Stanley 1972a shows us a lexicon replete with terms of barter referring to women, and few or no counterparts referring to men. Robin Lakoff in a similar study (1973) exposes the undertow of condescension and depreciation even in two such innocent-looking terms as *woman* and *lady*. Women are taught their place, along with other lesser breeds, by the implicit lies that language tells about them. Now you can argue that a term is not a proposition; therefore merely having the words does not constitute a lie about anybody. The words may be there, but it takes people to put them together, and so people may be liars but words are not. This argument has a familiar ring. We hear it every time Congress tries to pass legislation restricting the possession of guns. A loaded word is like a loaded gun, sometimes fired deliberately, but almost as often by accident. And even when you feel like firing one on purpose, it has to be in your possession first. Lots of casualties, some crippling ones, result from merely having weapons around.

I'm sure that many linguists will sympathize with these social concerns and agree that they should do something about them—but as citizens, not as linguists. How is truth to be defined so as to involve us professionally? Before I try to answer that, let me at least see if I can show that linguists who already accept some responsibility for language use can't consistently say that truth is irrelevant to linguistics. Here, adopting a suggestion made to me by Julia Stanley, I raise the question of appropriateness in language. Appropriateness is just as pertinent to content as it is to form. If linguists allow themselves a professional interest in how well a dialect or a code fits a place or situation, they cannot logically turn their backs on the fitness of language to facts. Let's hope that this comparison will satisfy at least some of the sociolinguists among us. It will not be quite so easy to convince those who feel that linguists who tangle themselves in anything having to do with messages and contexts thereby cease to be scientific. Still, we can snatch a reminder from what has been happening to us in the last decade or so. We are now fully involved with meaning, and from the meanings of the parts to the meaning of the whole is only one more step in the same direction.

The definition I propose for truth will not make it more precise, but it will establish the right connections. Consider how we use the verbs *inform* and *misinform*. They require either human subjects or message subjects. We say *He misinformed me with his letter* or *His letter misinformed me*, but not *The clouds misinformed me about the coming rainstorm*. Truth is that quality of language by which we inform ourselves. This rules out the logician's analytic truth, which is no more than consistency within language. Literal truth it includes only partially, because literal truth—the kind one swears to tell on the witness stand—permits any amount of evasion. I think it also has to be distinguished from historical truth, because in language that informs there has to be an element of timeliness. We can say of truth what is said of justice: truth delayed is truth denied. But the most insidious of all concepts of truth is that of literalness. Advertising capitalizes on the legal protection that it affords. The California prune-growers tell us that prunes, pound for pound, offer several times more vitamins and minerals than fresh fruit; literally true. The oil industry advertises that no heat costs less than oil heat, which has to be true because no heat costs nothing at all. These cases of verbal thimblerigging depend on an old ethic that winks at the clever and laughs at the gullible. In simpler times they were part of our education; but in today's complex world everyone is an ignoramus about something—about diet, about the workings of our electronic whigmaleeries and arcane bureaucracies, about the flammability of fabrics, the potability of water, or the meaning of Form 1040A. The possibilities of deception have passed the bounds of tolerance. It is no longer innocent fun when the Barnums and Baileys hang up their sign reading 'This Way to the Egress'. The egress has lost her imaginary feathers and shivers out there in the cold with the rest and the best of us.

I have tailored my definition of truth to fit what speakers mean to have understood. Within a social setting, any other definition is a game. Appropriateness is not to be taken between facts and abstract sentences, but between facts and sentences plus their contexts—and contexts include intentions. Not because I can justify it if anyone wants to debate the point, but just to get this kind of truth as pure as I can distill it, I'll go a step farther and say that when two parties are in communication, anything that may be used which clogs the channel, and is not the result of accident, is a lie. I am trying to paint the lie as black as I can by not requiring that it be intentional. There are consciously intentional lies, of course; but there are also lies by habit, and people who believe their own propaganda, and chiefs of state who surely harbor such a concept as that of a little lie being part of a larger truth, on the analogy of War is Peace or what you don't know won't hurt you. So I'd rather make falsehood embrace the hidden and unconscious, as well as the barefaced and deliberate. By contrast, truth would always be prompted by the active willingness to share what we know. There are some people for whom this willingness may be almost habitual. We still try to make it that way with our children, in the small society of the home.

Now I hope I am ready for the linguist who wants to maintain his scientific integrity. I quote from Robin Lakoff again (1972: 907). She writes: 'In order to predict correctly the application of many rules, one must be able to refer to assumptions about the social context of an utterance, as well as to other implicit assumptions made by the participants in a discourse.' The ingredient of the social context that is relevant to truth is the disposition to share what we think or know, and it is reflected in our choice of words and often in our choice of grammar. The very existence of a large part of the lexicon depends on it, and it explains at least part of the survival value of some constructions.

Let me start with some examples from grammar. The easiest to document from current discussions are the ones that involve deletion, so my first example is the case of the missing performative. Parenthetically, if you prefer to believe that a performative is inserted when it is present rather than deleted when it is absent, it makes no difference, since nobody doubts that WHEN they are present, performative verbs are explanatory. Take the case where somebody in authority makes a pronouncement like *America is lagging behind Russia in arms production*. With no indication of the evidence, we have to take the claim on faith. But if the speaker says *I think that America is lagging*, or *My chief of staff informs me* or *I'll just bet America is lagging,* then there is a measure of honesty about how reliable the information is.

Compared with other omitted elements, the missing performative is the least of the deceptions. It is a mere peashooter in the liar's arsenal, because as long as a proposition is straightforward, whether it has an explicit performative or not, most people can muster enough skepticism to ask for proof. It is when other less conspicuous things are deleted that dubious propositions are able to slip past our guard. A number of these have been getting attention of late, especially by Stanley, in studies of what she terms 'syntactic exploitation' (e.g. 1972b).

My first example of these is the old story of the deleted agent of the passive. This is the prime syntactic means for sophisticated gossip. In place of *they say,* where a listener who is on his toes will ask 'Who's *they?*', the speaker removes this temptation by putting the performative verb in the passive and keeping quiet about *they.* In our culture this is a commonplace of newspaper headlines. Shanks and Shaughnessey are having a dispute over a medical bill. Shanks says that Shaughnessey sewed him up with a couple of sponges and a scalpel still inside. Shaughnessey says that's a dirty lie. Depending on how friendly the editor is with one or the other, the headline comes out *Shaughnessey charged with malpractice* or *Shanks charged with slander.* Either way, the reader is invited to fill in the empty slot with more than one agent. The effect is to magnify the guilt of one or the other party.

There are other instances of deleted agents that are more insidious. Stanley (1972c: 17) quotes a paragraph from Dostoevsky in which eight passive constructions without agents succeed one another, creating the impression 'of a faceless society in which the individual has no power, and all activities affecting citizens are carried out by a nameless, impersonal "they" (1972c: 19). To the extent that such a view is accepted, the passive becomes a means of lying on a large scale.

Another of Stanley's examples is the passive adjective. When we use sentences like *In the 5th century the known world was limited to Europe and small parts of Asia and Africa,* what do we mean by *known world?* Known to whom? Since the phrase is a 'syntactic island', it is not open to question, and we are able to get away with ignoring three-fourths of the world's population. As Stanley puts it, 'our attention is focused on the major predication' (1972b: 11), so that we can wonder about the accuracy of the geographical claim, but not about who did the knowing. When Mutual of Omaha proudly announces on its ecology-minded program 'Wild kingdom' (31 December 1972) that *Man protects threatened animals,* it is able to give credit to the well-known human race without at the same time explicitly taking credit away.

Donald Smith 1972 adds a further case of an omitted element and its exploitation, which he terms 'Experiencer deletion'. The most typical sentences are those with the verb *seem*—which, as Smith says (20), 'are favored in certain types of prose and speech such as by bureaucrats, educationalists or anybody who may wish, among other things, to disguise the sources of impressionistic assertions about the world'. One of Smith's examples is this (21), from *Beyond freedom and dignity* by B.F. Skinner: *The need for punishment seems to have the support of history.* Seems to whom? The lack of frankness of this score makes the claim irresponsible.

Not to overstate the case, we should recognize that some inept deletions are not due to attempts at concealment, but to having overlearned a rule of high-school rhetoric: if you're a writer, make your references to yourself as few as possible. The passive with deleted agent is fine for this; it works out well in scientific writing where the emphasis is on processes, not on the people who carry them out. But some writers carry the prescription for self-effacement to the point of passivizing even a performative. So you get successions of more or less normal passives, capped by a sentence like *It is believed that these instructions will prove easy to follow.* This is a fair exchange of modesty for muddleheadedness.

We could go on with more examples from syntax, but it would be tedious because there are probably no two things that can be put together in a sentence that can't be used for some kind of fakery. Linguists make a great thing of the duality that developed between meaningless sub-units and meaningful higher units as defining human language; but long before that, there must have grown up a deadlier kind of duality whereby meanings were divorced from reality. As soon as signs were fully detached from things, it became possible for them to point at something non-existent or at the opposite of what they are supposed to point at. The practical joker who today turns the arrows from right to left on a one-way street surely had his caveman counterpart. This is not to say that bluffing and other forms of disingenuousness are unknown in the animal kingdom; but what distinguishes human mendacity is its capacity for elaboration. By the simple act of negation, any truth we utter can be turned into falsehood. By merely changing the intonation, any doubt can be rendered a certainty.

But the power of the lie carries beyond the realm of elaboration into the realm of invention. We elaborate with syntax. We invent in the lexicon. I suspect that some syntactic lies are beyond our control. When a child is caught red-handed and says *I didn't do it,* it may be an instinctive reaction of self-defense. But the act of coining a new expression is conscious, and any lying there is deliberate. The very act of naming has consequences for our attitudes. Take a sentence like *He responded to her cry of distress:* this uses a syntactic means that is at least neutral as regards sympathy. But in a sentence like *He responded to her distress cry,* you sense an incongruity. *Distress cry* adds something to the lexicon; it sets up a classification, and does it in a clinical way—for observation, not for pity or for hate. Karl Zimmer, in a recent study of nominal compounds (1971: 14), finds that one necessary condition is that they be 'appropriately classificatory' for the speaker—i.e., represent a slice of reality and not a passing event. So by using them we can represent a happening as a thing. Now happenings can be prevented by attacking their causes or their causers, but things have a life of their own. They are independent of us; and if we fail to change them, it is because THEY are capable of resistance. The person who refers to migratory workers as wetbacks or weed-pullers excuses himself from responsibility for illegal entry and bad working conditions. That class of people simply exists.

The act of naming, plus some favorable or unfavorable overtone in the terms selected for it, is the favorite device of the propagandist and the ultimate refinement in the art of lying. Syntax you can penetrate. In a phrase such as *intelligible remark* or *acceptable excuse,* there's a submerged predication, all right; but it's at least represented by a detachable adjective, and if you think of it you can ask 'Intelligible to whom?' But the nominal compound is impervious: the predication is not only buried out of reach but out of sight.

This helplessness, I think, is what has focused the attention of political commentators on the lie of naming. Henry Steele Commager (1972:10) accuses the Nixon administration of replacing the Big Lie with great quantities of lies; but the interesting thing is that all the examples he identifies, as far as language is concerned, are nominal compounds. Here is the paragraph containing them (11): 'Corruption of language is a special form of deception which this Administration, through its Madison Avenue mercenaries, has brought to a high level of perfection. Bombing is "protective reaction", precision bombing is "surgical strikes", concentration camps are "pacification centers" or "refugee camps" . . . Bombs dropped outside the target area are "incontinent ordnance," and those dropped on one of your own villages are excused as "friendly fire"; a bombed house becomes automatically a "military structure" and a lowly sampan sunk on the waterfront a "waterborne logistic craft".' 'How sobering,' he adds, 'that fifteen years before 1984 our own government should invent a doublethink as dishonest as that imagined by Orwell.' Congressman Drinan, after saying that 'Language is not merely the way we express our foreign policy; language is our foreign policy' (279), goes on to add that 'The systematic use of such opaque terms as "protective reaction", and the hollow sentences of war planners, do far more to hide the decision-making process from the people—and from Congress—than any secrecy classification rules' (281). Charles Osgood (1971:4) is equally impressed with the effectiveness of naming; he mentions the title *Camelot* which 'conferred a romantic, even chivalrous, tang to an ill-fated U.S. Army project designed to study the causes of revolutions,' and he says that 'to name an ABM system *Safe-guard* certainly must make its possessors feel more secure. A touch of nobility is added to raw power when intercontinental ballistic missiles are named *Thor*, *Jupiter*, *Atlas*, *Zeus*, and *Polaris*—although I miss the ultimate in semantic deception which would be a missile named *Venus*.'

Again I should pull back an inch or two, so as not to make it appear that I think all the abuses of naming have an ulterior motive. If the habit had not already been there, officialdom could never have made capital of it. Out of its passion for supplying needs and dealing with problems frontally, this society has bred a mania for making everything tangible. It arrests every motion, solidifies every event. The lowly clerk exhibits it when he lets you know that he is *in receipt of* your message—nothing so ordinary as that he has simply received it. The advertiser exhibits it when he offers you, not a product that will make your battery last longer, but one that will give you longer *battery life*. The bureaucrat merely follows suit when, instead of talking about the side that has the most and most powerful planes, he talks about the side that has *air superiority*.

The nominal compound at the service of bureaucracy is only the wholesaling of those embodiments of prejudice that every speech community allows to flourish in its vocabulary, terms in which neutral semantic features are mingled with valuative ones. Most likely everyone here has his own pet collection, from business, government, or daily life. My favorite is this quotation from *The Sonoma County Realtor* of Santa Rosa, California: 'An alert real estate salesman should learn how to express himself well and to use psychology . . . Don't say "down payment"; say "initial investment." Don't ask for a "listing"; ask for an "authorization to sell." Don't say "second mortgage"; say "perhaps we can find additional financing." Don't use the word "contract"; have them sign a "proposal" or "offer" . . . Don't use the word "lot"; call it a "homesite." Don't say "sign here"; say "write your name as you want it to appear on your deed."'[2] Here we see the unremitting struggle to keep concepts free of their associations. A term such as *military conscription* picks up unpleasant connotations along the way, and is replaced with *draft*. *Draft* starts to pick them up in turn and is replaced with *selective service*. Since a nation such as ours no longer wages war but only defends itself, it became

---

[2] Quoted in *Consumer reports*, October 1972, p. 626.

necessary many years ago to change the name of the old War Department to the Department of Defense. In all these examples the exploiters of words are fighting to keep them free of certain semantic features. The other side of the coin is when they cling to features even though the actual conditions are absent, to use the word as a weapon. Calling a person a traitor is like throwing him in prison; both are symbolic acts. *Traitor* is a disgraceful name, prison is a disgraceful place. This works as long as people can be kept from their habit of re-interpreting in the light of the facts, and discovering perhaps that the whole prison concept is a fake. Either way you take it—whether fighting off semantic features from words, or trying, in the teeth of the evidence, to keep them—there is an accelerated rate of semantic change and greater confusion when we try to communicate, and to that extent we can speak of the corruption of language, for it is caused by deliberate and well-financed interference.[3]

I mentioned valuative features. The study of them is one that has gone on sporadically, but has never been central to our discipline. It would be timely to revive it now, especially in the context of paralinguistics, because there is an unmistakable tie with gesture. The more we learn about the concepts of attraction and repulsion, the better we see how pervasive they are in our ways of thinking and in most of our words. Within language, valuative features are transmitted from one part of the lexicon to another by hidden link-ups that doubtless reflect some basic fact about where and how the lexicon is stored in our brains. A few linguists were interested in this a decade or so ago and studied it under the rubric of phonesthemes, a certain type of sound symbolism. Let me give just one example. I was recently struck by the peculiar contrast in a pair of synonyms that, in any literal sense, ought to be about as close in meaning as any two words can get. The Merriam-Webster Third regards them as identical: *baseless* and *groundless*. I was puzzled as to why *baseless* struck me as the stronger of the two; so I put the question to a seminar of three Harvard freshmen I was teaching, and one of them came up with the same explanation that had occurred to me: *baseless* echoes *base*. A baseless accusation, for instance, is one that is not only groundless, but also mean and unworthy. Language is a jungle of associations like this one, where a malevolent guide can lose any simple-minded wayfarer. For us to lead one another without leading one another astray requires a conscious act of will. Truth is not a highway. It is a trail hacked through snake-infested undergrowth.

One form of lying uses all the tricks so far described, but is distinguished from them by sheer quantity. I refer to what we might term obfuscation, more the province of the stylist than the linguist. A piece of obfuscatory prose may contain a message somewhere, but it is lost in the murk of rhetorical self-importance. Stanislav Andreski 1972 cites an example from Talcott Parsons:

> Instead of saying simply that a developed brain, acquired skills, and knowledge are needed for attaining human goals, Parsons writes: 'Skills constitute the manipulative techniques of human goal attainment and control in relation to the physical world, so far as artifacts or machines especially designed as tools do not yet supplement them.

---

[3] As far as advertising is concerned, no further examples are needed, for the mercenary bias is clear. As for government, to quote Drinan again (281), 'the use of empty words by the Defense Department is not the accidental by-product of a metastasized bureaucracy; rather, it is an essential part of a pervasive scheme to keep Defense Department decision-making a secret—unknown and unknowable by any potential critics.'

Truly human skills are guided by organized and codified KNOWLEDGE of both the things to be manipulated and the human capacities that are used to manipulate them. Such knowledge is an aspect of cultural-level symbolic processes, and, like other aspects to be discussed presently, requires the capacities of the human central nervous system, particularly the brain. This organic system is clearly essential to all of the symbolic processes . . .'

Getting back to things of more direct concern to linguists, what if enough of them were to turn their attention to truth and falsehood for it really to make a difference? It is a risky business when scientists start developing tools that are capable of misuse. To bring to light the mechanisms of Machiavellianism may be to provide future Machiavellis with easy access. But I doubt we can teach today's Machiavellis much that they do not already know. This is one game where the con men have less to learn than their victims. Knowing how to lie—brazenly, delicately, urbanely, esoterically—is a question of survival for officials dedicated to fundamentally unpopular causes. For this we can partly blame our own eager acceptance of a cosmetic society. 'America', I once wrote (Bolinger 1962), 'is the first society to achieve a virtual taboo on the unpleasant.' Our advertising has convinced us of it, and our officials are afraid to say otherwise. Language is called upon to do the same thing as psychiatry—in Sissman's words, 'to paper over unpalatable truths'. The most pathetically pertinent example of psychiatric paper-over was aired recently on a Boston radio station. It seems that a psychiatric service has been set up to treat those abnormal people who are afraid of flying. It will not do for a traveling public to harbor any pathological fears about being trapped at thirty thousand feet with no place to go but down. Compare this attitude with that of the maritime regulations, according to which common carriers not only stock up with life preservers and lifeboats, but also conduct regular lifeboat drills among their passengers. Imagine the effect on travel if airline passengers were required to take part in parachute drills; and contrast that with the sweetly offhand voice of the stewardess giving perfunctory safety directions, trusting that her tone and her legs will distract you from her ominous words. This may not be dedication to the utmost in safety, but it is at least dedication to the utmost in playing down the need for it. Forget the parachutes and give us piano bars. When you have government, business, and camp-following psychiatrists teamed up in this fashion to make the normal in OVERT behavior seem abnormal, what can you expect with as pliant a medium as language?

Let's suppose that an aroused public were to begin paying as much attention to linguistic ecology as to environmental ecology. What might some of the reactions to this be—on the part of those who oppose truth—against which we should be forearmed? In business they are already visible as a reaction to the comparatively feeble jabs of the truth-in-this and truth-in-that campaigns (observe, please, that there is as yet no campaign for truth, period). Another possible effect is the heightened reliance on war, especially the selling of war materials. War is popular, among other reasons, because it enables business to get along without customers. There are no finical housewives to complain that the plastic pellets in smart bombs are not penetrating deep enough. Another effect, of more direct concern to us, is the retreat from language. What I outlined in the first part of this talk was the retreat from PROPOSITIONAL language. Things are said, but said in such a way that even professional skeptics have trouble pinning them down. But after all that comes to light; then what? First there's the recourse of not making any claims yourself, but putting them as testimonials. Terence Langendoen 1970, in his critique of the Federal Trade Commission, points out (7–8) that 'all an advertiser needs to do to convert a misleading statement of fact into a misleading statement of opinion (which is hence exempt from sanctions) is to put it in the mouth of a celebrity or ''average consumer.'' ' Of late there has been a further refinement in testimonials, which consists in not making any outright claim, but staging a little dramatization. A pre-Columbian pedant announces that the world is flat, and this proceeds through a series of non-sequiturs to the conclusion that not all aspirins are the same. As a last resort, after the testimonial in its various forms direct and indirect, there remains the recourse of not using language at all, but merely making agreeable noises. We now leave the left hemisphere of the brain and move over to the right. In my personal count of radio and TV ads, I came up with about one in three that uses just language. The rest feature a mixture of language and music or other sound effects. With TV of course there are the dimensions of color and image. It tells us something about the importance of truth to language that the more you insist on truth, the farther those who care little for the truth retreat from language.

Truth is a linguistic question because communication is impossible without it. Unless social interaction is to break down, the lie must always be the exception. Robin Lakoff (1972: 916) sets up five rules which she says 'define an appropriate conversational situation.' Here are the first three:

Rule I. What is being communicated is true.

Rule II. It is necessary to state what is being said: it is not known to other participants, or utterly obvious. Further, everything necessary for the hearer to understand the communication is present.

Rule III. Therefore, in the case of statements, the speaker assumes that the hearer will believe what he says (due to Rule I).

Government and business are making two arrogant assumptions. The first is that it is possible to have one-way monopolistic communication, with the public consuming official verbiage as it consumes the handouts from industry and welfare. The second is that Lakoff's rules are not important, only the illusion of them. Public officials hide behind the images that Madison Avenue creates for them, and lies hide behind the face of truth.

Linguists cannot excuse themselves from these uses of language, though they may find various ways of approaching them. Lloyd Anderson (1970: 1) sees our field 're-opening itself to the study of rhetoric and literature, to communications and psychology, to continuous and fuzzy phenomena of the real world'—including, among its possible contributions, 'new rigorous principles of ''false advertising'' and ''false communicating'' for legal guidelines, for journalistic ethics, to support a new interpretive reporting distinct from propaganda'. It can't come too soon.

REFERENCES

1. Anderson, Lloyd B. 1970. Journalism and linguistics: some mutual interests. Talk at student-faculty seminar, School of Journalism, University of North Carolina, Chapel Hill, October.

2. Andreski, Stanislav. 1972. Social sciences as sorcery. London: Andre Deutsch. (Cited in Time magazine, 25 September 1972, p. 67.)

3. Bolinger, Dwight. 1962. The tragedy must go on. American Liberal, November, p. 26.

4. Commager, Henry Steele. 1972. The defeat of America. New York Review of Books, 5 October, pp. 7–13.

5. Drinan, Robert F. 1972. The rhetoric of peace. College Composition and Communication 23.279–82.

6. Gowers, Sir Ernest. 1948. Plain words. London: His Majesty's Stationery Office. (Cited by Joseph Jones, American Speech 24:121, 1949.)

7. Lakoff, Robin. 1972. Language in context. Lg. 48.907–27.

8. ———. 1973. Language and woman's place. Language in Society 2.45–80.

9. Langendoen, D. T. 1970. A study of the linguistic practices of the Federal Trade Commission. Paper read at LSA, 29 December.

10. Osgood, Charles E. 1971. Conservative words and radical sentences in the semantics of international politics. Social psychology and political behavior: problems and prospects, ed. by Gilbert Abcarian and J. W. Soule, 101–29. Columbus, Ohio: Charles E. Merrill.

11. Quiller-Couch, Sir Arthur. 1916. On the art of writing. Lectures delivered in the University of Cambridge, 1913–14, pp. 83–103. Cambridge: University Press.

12. Sissman, L. E. 1972. Plastic English. Atlantic Monthly, October, p. 32.

13. Smith, Donald. 1972. Experiencer deletion. MS.

14. Stanley, Julia. 1972a. The semantic features of the machismo ethic in English. Paper read at South Atlantic Modern Language Association.

15. ———. 1972b. Syntactic exploitation: passive adjectives in English. Paper read at Southeastern Conference on Linguistics VII, 21 April.

16. ———. 1972c. Passive motivation. MS.

17. Thurber, James. 1955. The psychosemanticist will see you now, Mr. Thurber. New Yorker, 28 May, pp. 28–31.

18. Zimmer, Karl E. 1971. Some general observations about nominal compounds. Working papers in language universals, Stanford University, 5.

DISCUSSION QUESTIONS

1. Why does Bolinger consider truth to be a linguistic question? Do you agree with him? Explain.

2. Find some examples of absent performatives in pronouncements from government and big business. Do they have the effect of a lie?

3. What is the difference in the effect produced by the following statements?
America is lagging behind Russia in arms production.
I think America is lagging behind Russia in arms production.

4. How is the passive used to mislead an audience? Bring into class some examples from a newspaper or magazine.

5. Why is the act of naming such a favorite device of propagandists?

SIDNEY GREENBAUM

A graduate of and former instructor at the University of London, where he worked with Randolph Quirk in the Survey of English Usage, Greenbaum came to the United States in 1968. He taught first at the University of Oregon and then at the University of Wisconsin, Milwaukee, where he is professor of English. He has authored numerous books on grammar and on usage.

SOME VERB-INTENSIFIER COLLOCATIONS IN AMERICAN AND BRITISH ENGLISH

In a recent issue of *American Speech,* Dwight Bolinger made an eloquent plea for the importance of understanding the lexicon, pointing out that linguists have generally been content to leave lexical study to the dictionary-makers.[1] The language models adopted by most American linguists allow little space for the treatment of vocabulary: the relationship between words—in the flow of speech and in paradigmatic sets—is allocated to the two major components, syntax and semantics, and the lexicon is seen as a ragbag of the irregularities and idiosyncracies in language. In a period when most linguists are concerned exclusively with rules it is not surprising that the lexicon is neglected as of little interest.

Many British linguists, on the other hand, have recognized lexis as a separate component or level of analysis of language. In particular, they have drawn attention to one aspect of lexical relationships, the tendency for particular lexical items to cooccur. These relationships are seen as forming lexical patterns syntagmatically and as constituting the basis for lexical sets paradigmatically. So far, most of what has been said has been suggestive and programmatic.[2]

---

[1] D. Bolinger, "Getting the *Words* In," *American Speech* 45 (1970): 78–84. I am grateful to Dwight Bolinger for his comments on an earlier version of this paper. I am also indebted to Douglas Foley for his help in administering and scoring the experiments. The work was supported in part by a grant to the Survey of English Usage by H. M. Department of Education and Science and in part by a grant from the Office of Scientific and Scholarly Research of the University of Oregon.

[2] Discussions of collocation will be found in the following: J. R. Firth, *Papers in Linguistics 1934–1951* (London: Oxford University Press, 1957), pp. 194–214; *Selected Papers of J. R. Firth, 1952–1959,* ed. F. R. Palmer (London: Longmans, 1968) pp. 179–81; M. A. K. Halliday, "Lexis as a Linguistic Level," *In Memory of J. R. Firth,* ed. C. E. Bazell et al. (London: Longmans, 1966) pp. 148–62; T. F. Mitchell, "Some English Phrasal Types," *In Memory of J. R. Firth,* pp. 335–58; J. McH. Sinclair, "Beginning the Study of Lexis," *In Memory of J. R. Firth,* pp. 410–30; A. McIntosh, "Patterns and Ranges," *Patterns of Language,* ed. A. McIntosh and M. A. K. Halliday (London: Longmans, 1966), pp. 183–99; T. F. Mitchell, "Linguistic 'Goings On': Collocations and Other Lexical Matters Arising on the Syntagmatic Record," *Archivum Linguisticum* n.s. 2 (1971): 35–69. Collocational studies going beyond intuitive decisions on the data are to be found in F. Behre, *Studies in Agatha Christie's Writings,* Gothenburg Studies in English 19 (Göteborg: Almqvist and

I want to indicate briefly the lines of interest in lexical cooccurrence referred to in British linguistics as COLLOCATION, before reporting on some research that I have conducted. Unfortunately, the term has been used ambiguously for cooccurrence and (more restrictively) for frequent cooccurrence, usually with reference to specific text material. If we are not concerned with textual analysis it seems more useful to adopt COLLOCABILITY and COLLOCABLE for potential cooccurrence and to reserve COLLOCATION and COLLOCATE for frequent cooccurrence in the language as a whole or (where specified) in a particular variety of the language; COOCCURRENCE and COOCCUR remain available for textual studies. We can therefore say that *turn on* collocates with (among other items) *light, gas, radio,* and *TV*. That is, if we hear or read *turn on,* among the items we might expect to hear or read nearby are *light, gas, radio,* and *TV*. These items and others we might add to them constitute the COLLOCATIONAL RANGE of *turn on.* In this instance there is mutual expectancy: the presence of *light, gas, radio,* or *TV* predicts the presence of *turn on,* though probably less strongly. But the expectancy may be even much stronger in one direction: *rancid* predicts *butter* and *stale* predicts *bread* far more than in the reverse direction. Ultimately, there may be 100 percent prediction from one direction, as in *to and fro, kith and kin,* and *spick and span.*

COLLOCATES—items collocating with each other—need not occur in a particular sequence: *turn on* collocates with *light* in both *Turn on the light* and *The light can now be turned on.* They need not be in the same sentence and can even cross utterances by different speakers: *save* collocates with both *money* and *bank* in *I should be saving more than I do.—Why not put some money into the bank each month?* The obvious question then is how far apart two items can be and still count as collocates of each other. The theory of collocations does not say anything about COLLOCATIONAL SPAN, the distance between collocates. Perhaps this is an empirical problem to be solved with the help of computer studies of vast corpora, but no satisfactory solution has been offered as yet. I shall return to this question later, but we can answer it psycholinguistically by claiming that two items are collocates of each other if they belong to a single remembered set, no matter how far apart they may be in a stretch of language. This claim presupposes that there is an automatic memory in which collocates are stored and from which they can be retrieved. A collocation like *turn on the TV* is then a kind of diffuse lexical item, part of a continuum, where one extreme is words and idioms and the other is the free compatible combination, a collocable string such as *destroy the TV.*

The examples given so far show that the lexical item as collocate is not necessarily identical with the word: *turn on* consists of two words and the collocation of *light* is with *turn- on* rather than with the inflected form *turned on.* Similarly, all the grammatical forms *save, saves, saved, saving* collocate with *bank* and *money* via their common stem. Sometimes the collocation disregards word-class categories, as in the collocations *doggedly insists* and *dogged insistence,* but some collocations are more restricted: though we have both *desperately need* and *desperate need,* we have only *badly need* and not **bad need;* and parallel to *poor pay, poor payment,* and *pay poorly* there is only *pay badly.*

Wiksell, 1967); S. Jones and J. McH. Sinclair, *English Lexical Collocations: A Study in Computational Linguistics* (Birmingham, England: University of Birmingham, Department of English Working Paper, 1973); and a study using the techniques reported on in this paper, S. Greenbaum, *Verb–Intensifier Collocations in English: An Experimental Approach* (The Hague: Mouton, 1970). Comments on collocations appear passim in D. Bolinger, *Degree Words* (The Hague: Mouton, 1972).

J. R. Firth, who introduced the notion of collocation that I am discussing, insisted that meaning in language can be best studied by analyses at different levels. In his view, a statement of total meaning requires separate statements of meaning at various levels of linguistic analysis, including the phonetic, phonological, and syntactic levels. Meaning also includes meaning by collocation. Hence, for Firth, collocational statements contain no reference to syntax or to semantics, as the latter is commonly conceived. The difference between *turn on* in *turn the light on* and *turn me on* emerges on the collocational level from the diverse collocational range going with the two instances of *turn on* which belong to different lexical sets; the lexical difference can be established independently of any other difference. Sometimes distinctions are best made lexically: *He put his students down* ('snubbed') and *He put his suitcases down* are syntactically similar, but collocationally, *put down* is one lexical unit in the first sentence and two in the second. Of course, items in a LEXICAL SET, that is, items having a similar collocational range, often display semantic similarities in the more usual sense of SEMANTIC. But semantic and lexical sets are not necessarily identical. Synonyms may be separated collocationally because of restrictions to a language variety or style. Army *officers* are *cashiered* and *schoolchildren* are *expelled*.[3] As Sinclair points out, *vigorous depression* is a collocation only in meteorology.[4] Synonyms of *vigorous,* such as *energetic* and *forceful,* do not collocate with *depression.* Similarly, items related by inclusion under a superordinate semantic feature do not necessarily have the same collocational range: *blond* collocates with *dumb,* but *brunette* does not; *juvenile* collocates with *delinquency* and *lead* (in the theater), but *youth* and *adolescent* do not. The same applies at the word level. *Half-, semi-, hemi-,* and *demi-* are synonyms with different collocational and collocability ranges, as we can easily see if we try to switch them in such "word collocations" as *half-caste, semi-circle, hemisphere,* and *demigod.* Compare also such pairs as *foretell* and *predict, unwise* and *insane, Nixonian* and *McCarthyite, airtight* and *fireproof.*

Some followers of Firth have required that lexical analysis be isolated from information from other levels of linguistic analysis. Others have sometimes pointed to the need for lexicogrammatical statements that show the interrelationship between collocation and syntactic structure.[5] An example I have used elsewhere illustrates the interaction of collocation and collocability with syntax. The collocation of *much* with *prefer* applies only when *much* is preverb, as in *I much prefer a dry wine,* whereas *much* is not even collocable with *prefer* in postobject position, **I prefer a dry wine much.* On the other hand, *much* collocates with *like* in negative or other nonassertive contexts, *I don't like him much,* but is otherwise not collocable with *like,* **I like him much;* nevertheless, it collocates with *like* in an affirmative sentence if it is premodified, hence *I like him very*

---

[3] Mitchell, 1971, p. 54.
[4] Sinclair, p. 429.
[5] See Halliday, pp. 158–59, and Mitchell, 1971, pp. 47–48, who claims that this is also Firth's view, p. 65. While insisting on separate analyses at the various levels of meaning. Firth also combines information from different levels in his textual analyses. For example, in *Papers in Linguistics 1934–1951* he mentions "collocation with preceding adjectives" and "collocations with or without articles, determinatives, or pronouns" (p. 195), and "the association of synonyms, antonyms, contraries, and complementary couplers in one collocation" (p. 199). But these are ad hoc stylistic comments; he does not point to an interaction between collocation and other levels in the language system.

much. The examples demonstrate that statements of collocation and collocability require syntactic information in at least some instances. The problem of the collocational span, to which I referred earlier, also suggests that collocability should be tied to syntax, though a syntax that caters to connections between sentences. Otherwise, the concept of collocability becomes vacuous, since virtually any two items can cooccur at a given arbitrary distance. And ultimately we must recognize collocable classes that are established semantically and can occur in certain syntactic relationships, as expressed in selectional rules that allow *His sincerity frightens us* and disallow **We frighten his sincerity.* Bolinger has demonstrated, in *Degree Words,* the interaction of collocation with both syntax and semantics; for example, he has shown that premodifying *much* collocates in affirmative sentences with verbs incorporating some feature of comparison: in addition to *prefer,* verbs such as *reduce, exceed,* and *improve* (pp. 194–96).

A collocation in the language is said to be a frequent cooccurrence of two lexical items in the language. But how do we establish that an item is collocated with another item? Well, we can count cooccurrences in a sample of the language or of a particular variety of it—or even examine the works of a specific author, as Behre did for intensifiers in Agatha Christie (see note 2). But collocation is more than a statistical matter: it has a psychological correlate, and I have suggested that earlier by talking about expectancy. We know that items are collocated just as we know that one sequence of items is part of our language and another is not. Both constitute knowledge that speakers have of their language. Of course it would not be surprising if there are instances where people disagree on collocations: they sometimes disagree on whether certain sequences are part of their language. And just as we recognize degrees of acceptability (some sequences seem more obviously all right than others), so we can recognize degrees of collocation (some cooccurrences seem more frequent than others). We can therefore consult our own knowledge of the language, particularly for obvious cases of collocation: *news is released, time is consumed,* and *computer programs run.* But as with questions of acceptability, we can check for biases or failures in introspection by examining samples of actual language or by consulting other people. Elicitation experiments provide access to the cumulative experience of large numbers of speakers.

I have used one method for eliciting data on collocation from informants indirectly. In a series of three experiments conducted at London University and Reading University in 1967, the informants—mostly undergraduate students—were asked to complete sentences of which they were given the opening words, for example *I badly.* They were not told the purpose of the experiments, which was to record the verbs that were triggered by certain preverb intensifiers. The results indicated that there were sometimes strong collocational links between a given intentsifier and a specific verb. The most spectacular example was *entirely* with *agree:* the opening *I entirely* evoked the verb *agree* in 89 informants (82 percent). In addition, for some intensifiers it was possible to group the verbs in a few semantically homogeneous classes and to find some semantic features common to all or most of the verbs. I have discussed the procedures and results of those experiments in my work on verb-intensifier collocations (see end of note 3).

I subsequently repeated several of these completion tests, this time using undergraduates at an American university as informants. I wanted to find out whether similarities existed in American and British English with respect to strong individual collocations and collocational ranges for intensifiers with verbs. It is of course well-known that there are vocabulary differences between the two varieties, with terms that exist in one variety but not in the other or that have a different reference or stylistic flavor in each. It also is probable that there are collocational differences even when the terms seem otherwise to have the same function, and that these differences contribute importantly to the impression that one variety makes on speakers of the other. But these differences are unlikely to be recorded without detailed investigations.

I conducted two experiments that included material previously tested in England. Both were administered at the University of Oregon in 1969. In both experiments the informants were undergraduates (juniors or seniors) at the university and most of them were from Oregon and neighboring states. They were divided about equally between males and females, and majored in a wide range of subjects.

In the course of the first experiment, 86 informants were given completion tests corresponding to those previously given in Britain. Table 1 lists the principal collocates— verbs appearing in at least 10 percent of the responses—for the opening words of sentences in the British and American experiments. Informants were asked to complete the sentences in writing. The table indicates in parentheses the total number of responses for each test.

Table 1   Principal collocates in UK and US tests

I badly	UK (175)	need 113 (65%), want 49 (28%)
	US (84)	need 40 (48 %), want 14 (17%)
Your friend very much	UK (161)	like 46 (29%), want 29 (18%)
	US (80)	like 15 (19%), want 8 (10%)
They all greatly	UK (176)	admire 78 (44%), enjoy 36 (20%)
	US (82)	admire 13 (16%), enjoy 15 (18%), appreciate 20 (24%)
I entirely	UK (108)	agree 89 (82%)
	US (83)	agree 22 (27%), forget 11 (13%)
They all utterly	UK (103)	none
	US (78)	none
I completely	UK (70)	forget 35 (50%)
	US (85)	forget 39 (46%)

There is a remarkable similarity in the list of principal collocates in the two sets of responses. Of the eight in the UK tests, all are also in the US tests.[6] Two additional principal collocates are listed for the US tests: *appreciate* (24 percent) with *greatly*, and *forget* (13 percent) with *entirely;* in the UK tests the frequencies of *appreciate* and *forget* were 3 and 1 percent respectively. A general difference between the two sets is that there appear to be stronger collocational links in the UK results than in the US results.[7]

Most of the collocates for each intensifier can be clustered in ad hoc semantic

---

[6] In the UK test, *hate* is on the borderline as a principal collocate with *utterly*, appearing in just under 10 percent of the valid responses. There is only one instance of *hate* in the US test.

[7] There is evidence from other experimental work to support an explanation for the difference between the UK and US results in two cases; in fact, those where the British informants produced the highest percentages for collocational links: *badly* + *need* and *entirely* + *agree.* It appears that American speakers prefer these intensifiers to be positioned finally in these two collocations. Since the intensifiers were in preverb positions in the experiments, they did not evoke the verbs to the same extent as they might have done if positioned finally. See S. Greenbaum, *Verb-Intensifier Collocations*, p. 64, and S. Greenbaum, "Positional Norms of English Adverbs," *Studies in English Linguistics* 4 (1976), 1–16.

groups of verbs. The groups—each constituting at least 10 percent of the verbs—are listed below for each of the completion tests, with the numbers and percentages for both sets of tests. If a group had at least 10 percent in one set, the total and percentage is given for the other set as well.

I badly	needing and wanting: UK 163 (93%), US 55 (65%)
Your friend very much	liking: UK 50 (31%), US 25 (32%) needing and wanting: UK 49 (30%), US 16 (20%) approbatory attitude (other): UK 42 (26%), US 17 (21%)
They all greatly	approbatory attitude: UK 149 (85%), US 55 (67%) needing and wanting: UK 9 (5%), US 10 (12%)
I entirely	agreeing and disagreeing: UK 99 (92%), US 27 (33%) failure: UK 3 (3%), US 20 (24%)
They all utterly	disliking: UK 23 (22%), US 6 (7%) surprise: UK 0, US 15 (19%) failure: UK 14 (14%), US 20 (26%) exhaustion: UK 10 (10%), US 5 (6%) opposition: UK 17 (17%), US 5 (6%) agreeing and disagreeing: UK 11 (11%), US 1 (1%) disapprobatory attitude (other): UK 17 (17%), US 11 (14%) vocal sound: UK 1 (1%), US 8 (10%)
I completely	failure: UK 44 (63%), US 54 (64%) agreeing and disagreeing: UK 11 (16%), US 8 (9%)

Once again there is considerable agreement between the UK and US results, though perhaps less than for the principal collocates. This similarity is greatest for the collocational groups with *badly, very much, greatly,* and *completely,* and the difference is greatest in the case of *entirely.* The difference is interesting, since a major distinction in the UK results between the collocational range of *entirely* and *completely* is that *entirely* collocates predominantly with verbs of agreeing and disagreeing (mainly the former) whereas *completely* collocates predominantly with verbs of failure to attain a desirable goal or state. The distinction is somewhat blurred in the US results for *entirely:* only a third of the informants selected verbs of agreeing and disagreeing while nearly a quarter selected verbs of failing, among them *forget* (13 percent). The differences between the two results for *They all utterly* are less substantial, since what seems to be the dominant feature common to most verbs is their 'negative' implication.

In the second Oregon experiment there were only 20 informants. Four of the six tests previously discussed were included in a battery of completion tests. But this time the informants were given the same opening five times in succession, thus providing the possibility of 100 responses. Their instructions were so worded as to discourage repetition of the identical sentence but to allow for repetition of at least part of their completion.[8]

---

[8] As with the first experiment, the openings appeared on separate pages of a stapled booklet and the turning of the pages was timed (15 seconds) to encourage immediate reactions. The instructions were read to the informants:

> Every page in front of you will have the beginning or end of a sentence. The sentences are grouped so that you will find five consecutive pages with the same beginning or ending. In each case what you have to do is to complete the sentence. Try to avoid

Table 2   Principal collocates in repeated completion (US tests)

I badly	*total* (97)	want 18 (19%), need 12 (12%)
	weighted (293)	want 56 (19%), need 46 (16%)
Your friend very much	*total* (98)	like 24 (24%), want 14 (14%), be 14 (14%)
	weighted (293)	like 80 (27%), want 43 (15%), be 36 (12%)
I entirely	*total* (99)	agree 10 (11%)
	weighted (298)	agree 37 (12%), forget 42 (14%)
I completely	*total* (99)	forget 17 (17%)
	weighted (299)	forget 68 (23%)

Table 2 lists the principal collocates for the second experiment. The responses have been scored in two ways and the table gives both scores. The first row gives the principal collocates for the total of responses for all five completions, with each completion given equal weight. The possible total if all responses had been valid would be 100. The figures in the second row are calculated on a weighting according to the position of the item in the set of five completions: the first response was weighted as 5, the second 4, the third 3, the fourth 2, and the fifth 1. In the event, there is little difference between the two calculations. With one exception, the principal collocates are the same for both types of scoring and their percentages are similar. The one exception is *forget* with *entirely: forget* is a principal collocate in the weighted scoring only. For the unweighted scoring, it is near the borderline, appearing nine times or in just over 9 percent of the responses.

A comparison of tables 1 and 2 reveals that the two Oregon experiments produced virtually identical lists of principal collocates for the four completion tests. The only exception is the addition of *be* to the collocates for *very much* (see below). There is a tendency for the principal collocates to appear with less frequency in the second experiment, but this is almost certainly an effect of the test design, which is likely to encourage variation. It is therefore all the more satisfying to find such similarities in the two experiments.

I repeat below the semantic groupings for the first experiment, and give the corresponding figures for the second experiment, for unweighted and then for weighted scorings.

I badly	needing and wanting: 1st 55 (65%); 2d 31 (32%), 104 (35%)
Your friend very much	liking: 1st 25 (32%); 2d 23 (23%), 77 (26%)
	needing and wanting: 1st 16 (20%); 2d 18 (18%), 55 (18%)
	approbatory attitude (other): 1st 17 (21%); 2d 11 (11%), 45 (15%)

---

repeating word-for-word a sentence you have already used with the same beginning or ending. For example, if you were given a sentence beginning *Yesterday,* you might complete it by writing down *he had a headache* after the word *Yesterday* on the page. The next page would again have the word *Yesterday,* and you might complete the sentence by writing *I lost my job.* For the third sentence, you could write *I lost my dog.* The only thing to remember is that when I say *Next* you must turn over to the next page, except that you may complete the word you are writing. The first five sentences are intended to give you practice in the task and in the regular intervals of time you will be allowed for the completion of each sentence.

I entirely   agreeing and disagreeing: 1st 27 (33%); 2d 14 (14%), 53 (18%)
                          failure: 1st 20 (24%); 2d 16 (16%), 71 (24%)

I completely   failure: 1st 54 (64%); 2d 41 (41%), 145 (48%)
                          agreeing and disagreeing: 1st 8 (9%); 2d 6 (6%), 24 (8%)

The percentages for the two types of scoring are similar. In general they are close to those for the first experiment. The exceptions are two groups (*badly* and *completely*) that have 65 and 64 percent in the first experiment. Once again, the difference can be ascribed to the effect of test design noted earlier. The test design is probably also responsible for the much larger proportion of verbs that seem to collocate more readily when the adverb is in postverb position.[9] The impulse to vary the sentences could have included the inclusion of verbs like *swim, cry,* and *behave* after *badly,* which imply the interpretation of *badly* as a manner adverb. There probably are at least some instances in the responses of *be* with *very much* where the adverb phrase would more normally appear after *be: Your friend very much is a bore/a graduate/a cheerful person. Very much* seems here a blend of intensifier and modifier of the truth-value of the predication, like *certainly* (compare *Your friend is more a graduate than an instructor*). Since only comparative adjectives are modifiable by *very much,* its truth-emphasizing function is particularly prominent in responses like *Your friend very much is witty.*

We can conclude that, in general, American and British English agree on the most frequent collocates with the six preverb intensifiers that have been investigated. There is also general agreement on the major collocational ranges for most of the intensifiers: expressions of needing and wanting with *badly;* of favorable attitude, particularly liking, with *very much;* of favorable attitude with *greatly;* of negative implication with *utterly;* and of failure with *completely.* One major difference emerged in the case of *entirely.* Whereas for the British informants, *entirely* collocated predominantly with verbs of agreeing and disagreeing, for the American informants it had a greater collocational range, including a sizable proportion of expressions of failure. But even for the American informants such expressions appeared almost twice as often with *completely* as with *entirely.*

The present study implies a dynamic linguistic model that describes the language that real speakers know and use. In such a model, frequency differences are relevant. If we hear that a *student* is *cashiered,* we know the collocation *officer-cashier* and interpret what we hear accordingly, perhaps as suggesting an institution with military discipline. If we hear the expression *senile delinquent,* we are aware of the allusion to the collocation *juvenile delinquent* and understand the behavior indicated. If we say that someone is a *dumb brunette,* we intend to convey a blend with *dumb blond.* And if we say *I utterly agree with you,* the usual negative implication makes what we say more emphatic than

---

[9] There were also a few instances in the first Oregon experiment, somewhat more than in the British experiments. A plausible explanation for this difference is that in the British experiments the opening words were given orally and the informants were then required to write those words down as well as their completions, as a check that they had heard the words correctly. In the Oregon experiments the opening words were given on each page and the informants merely had to complete the sentences. In experiments subsequent to those reported on here, the opening words were given on a slide and the informants were required to write down the full sentence.

if we say *I entirely agree with you* (compare *terribly bright*). Collocability is a creative process, building on collocation. That is the stuff of which poetry is made—and ordinary language.[10]

DISCUSSION QUESTIONS

1. Duplicate Greenbaum's elicitation experiment with some of your friends. Do you get the same results? Explain.

2. Considering that there seems to be a general agreement concerning the collocational range of the most popular verb intensifiers, would you expect propagandists, as described by Dwight Bolinger in the preceding article, to use them to deliberately mislead people? Find some examples in magazines or newspapers to support your point of view.

3. Explain in your own words what Greenbaum means when he refers to the "mutual expectancy" as being important between speaker and hearer in the collocation of verb intensifiers.

4. How does the study of collocation contribute to an understanding of allusions?

---

[10] What I have said has important implications for the way in which words are learned, both in the early years of language acquisition and in the continuing years of vocabulary development. Collocations provide most of the initial lexical units. We eventually break them down into words, but we still retain them as units within our vocabulary store.

PART VI

Although most contemporary linguists—whether descriptive or theoretical—have not been directly concerned with the teaching of English, their influence has led teachers and experimenters in the broad field of applied linguistics and the new kindred fields of sociolinguistics and psycholinguistics to look afresh at old problems and to detect new problems in teaching English. The articles in this section can do no more than offer quick insights into several areas of the English teaching discipline. They have been chosen to help you develop an awareness of the possible applications of your study of the language.

A. SPELLING, GRAMMAR, AND USAGE

Probably to an extent greater than elsewhere in the world, correct spelling has become a social and educational fetish in the United States. Justifiably or not, insistence upon correct spelling has dominated the school since the first of more than 200 editions of Noah Webster's famous blue-backed spelling book appeared in 1783. For many decades—reaching into the childhood of the senior compiler of this book—the weekly list of difficult words with the ritualized Friday test challenged pupils on their progress to a more or less uncertain familiarity with what they were repeatedly told was a most irregular orthography.

But into the jungle of the spelling demons has come the researcher armed with new weapons, data drawn from studies demonstrating the basic regularity of the structures of nearly all English words. The structuralists' concept of the phoneme inevitably led to investigation of the various patterns of correspondence between the phoneme and the grapheme. A mammoth computerized study, not without some linguistic weaknesses, is that of Paul R. and Jean Hanna: *Phoneme-Grapheme Correspondences as Cues to Spelling Improvement* (U.S. Office of Education, 1966). Richard Venezky's *The Structure of English Orthography* (Mouton, 1970) is a most important work. Venezky's article in this section gives a brief introduction to his approach. Then perhaps to be mentioned, although not intended as a guide to spelling, is Noam Chomsky and Morris Halle's momentous *The Sound Pattern of English* (Harper, 1968). A major work dealing with the sounds and stresses of the language, it relates their patterned sequences to those in the spelling.

The teaching of correct usage, determined prescriptively, has likewise been a school fetish since the end of the eighteenth century, and, like the teaching of spelling, it has been affected by the objective attitude of the linguist toward language forms. The height of the controversy over the basis of acceptable usage occurred during the 1930s and 1940s. Since then, textbooks in English have generally adopted the principle that good English is essentially that which is actually used in speech and writing by educated people in positions of influence and prestige. Such grammatical dogmas as the proscription of the split infinitive have largely been replaced by generalizations drawn from observation of the living language. Robert Pooley, who at the University of Wisconsin succeeded the important usage researcher, Sterling Andrus Leonard (*Current English Usage:* NCTE, 1933), here offers advice on what usage matters may best be taught in the elementary and high school years. If you are interested in points of view expressed just after the Battle of Usage, several relevant articles are in the senior compiler's *Readings in Applied English Linguistics* (Appleton, 1958, 1964). An excellent book on attitudes toward usage matters is Randolph Quirk's *The Use of English* (St. Martin, 2nd ed., 1968), with a perspicacious supplement by Jeremy Warburg. Another is by J. J. Lamberts: *A Short Introduction to English Usage* (McGraw-Hill, 1972). The history of such attitudes appears in Richard Foster Jones's *The Triumph of the English Language* (Stanford University Press, 1966) and Susie I. Tucker's *English Examined: Two Centuries of Comment on the Mother Tongue* (Cambridge University Press, 1961).

From the large list of controversial articles about the usefulness of recent grammars in the English classroom we have chosen Elaine Chaika's as both provocative and representative. Forty years ago research reports demonstrated that there was no ascertainable relationship between the teaching of traditional school grammar and language development. Structuralists pointed out that since school grammar was Latin-oriented toward emphasis upon morphology, it could obviously have little relationship to English, which was syntax-based. But before structural grammar could be given a fair trial in school textbooks, its rising sun was eclipsed by transformational-generative grammar, clearly syntax-based. Chaika finds that this grammar, with its focus upon underlying syntax, does have utilitarian value in a composition class.

B. READING

The first major entry by a linguist into the domain of the reading specialists was by the late Charles C. Fries. Fries's *Linguistics and Reading* (Holt, 1962) expanded Leonard Bloomfield's proposal that beginning reading should require rigid one-to-one phoneme-grapheme correspondence in repeated patterns of simple words or even nonsense syllables, such as "Pat the fat cat." Elementary reading textbooks have incorporated some use of this principle without departing from more natural sentences that children might normally use and with the accompanying pictures that Fries decried. Recently, the rapid expansion of the field of psycholinguistics has opened new doors by which to approach reading problems, both on the beginning level and on the remedial level. Kenneth and Yetta Goodman, who have been principal contributors, here offer a somewhat different approach through oral reading, in terms of the oral miscues which they consider as throwing new light upon the reading process itself. Johanna DeStefano then presents a summary statement of the general relevance of psycholinguistic studies to the reading field as a whole. Two very important books are Kenneth Goodman's anthology, *The Psycholinguistic Nature of the Reading Process* (Wayne State University Press, 1968) and Frank Smith's *Understanding Reading: A Psycholinguistic Study of Reading and Learning to Read* (Holt, 1971).

C. SYNTAX AND COMPOSITION

Kellogg Hunt's opening article supports Chaika's argument that transformational grammar has utility in the English classroom. Traditional school grammar, concerned with parsing and taxonomy, well-nigh ignored the problem of forming good English sentences, despite claims for the efficacy of the Reed and Kellogg diagraming devised by Reed in 1868.

What efficacy diagraming has was apparently due to its intuitive grasp of underlying sentence patterns that did not become fully apprehended until the formulation of transformational-generative grammar by Chomsky in 1957.

Hunt's initial approach to the question, "How can we determine sentence maturity?" departed from the older statistical method of counting clauses and sentence length by developing the concept of the T-unit as an easily quantifiable construct that evidenced specific changes during the elementary school years. His study, *Grammatical Sentences Written at Three Grade-Levels* (NCTE Research Report 3, 1965) won the annual NCTE award for distinguished research in English. Hunt thereby opened the door for subsequent milestone studies by John C. Mellon, *Sentence-Combining: A Method for Enhancing the Development of Syntactic Fluency in English Composition* (NCTE, 1969), and Frank O'Hare, *Sentence-Combining: Improving Student Writing Without Formal Grammar Instruction* (NCTE Research Report 15, 1973). In the meantime Hunt pursued his own investigations, the most recent of which he details in the present article.

Joseph Williams, however, detects a certain inadequacy in the sentence-combining approach to sentence improvement and suggests that nonlinguistic factors are too important to be ignored. Donald Freeman next addresses himself to one particular aspect of composition teaching, that of dealing with students whose writing prowess is not commensurate with their age-grade. He strikes a lively note when he argues that through error analysis it is possible to apply what he terms the concept of "agency" as an effective means by which a student can evaluate and improve his own writing.

D. ENGLISH AS A SECOND LANGUAGE AND STANDARD ENGLISH AS A SECOND DIALECT

Because in many English classrooms throughout the country there are some students for whom English is not their native language, the compilers have included the next two articles as aids to the prospective teacher who is unlikely to obtain professional training in teaching English as a second language. Specific further guidance will be found in *Mainstreaming the Non-English-speaking Student,* by Raymond J. Rodrigues and Robert H. White (NCTE, 1981).

Bernard Spolsky weighs critically various approaches to teaching English to speakers of other languages and counsels against wholesale acceptance of any one approach until additional research can be undertaken. Specific consideration of the problems occasioned by the use of "Spanglish" is the thrust of the article by Edna Acosta-Belén. Her essay was chosen because of its relevance to not only Spanish but other mixed-language situations as well.

In the sometimes acrimonious debate over the issue of bidialectalism in the 1960s and early 1970s, some teachers declared that the speakers of Black English should be taught as if they were speakers of a foreign language, with the same methods used in English-as-a-second-language instruction. It soon appeared, however, that the analogy was unsound: Black English is still English, despite its retaining features probably ascribable to an early creole. That recognition, however, did not solve the problem of what to do about it, if anything. Thomas Kochman, with the stance of the psycholinguist, offers his own constructive solution—or partial solution. For a fuller explication of his viewpoint, see his later article—too long for inclusion here—"Standard English Revisited, or Who's Kidding/Cheating Who/Whom?" (*Florida FL Reporter,* Spring/Fall 1974, pp. 31–44, 96).

RICHARD L. VENEZKY

In 1977 Venezky left his post as professor of English and computer science at the University of Wisconsin to become Unidel professor of educational studies at the University of Delaware. He is a consultant to the Oxford English Dictionary Supplement and in 1980 coedited Orthography, Reading, and Dyslexia *(University Park Press). Venezky's doctorate in linguistics is from Stanford University.*

LINGUISTICS AND SPELLING

WHAT LINGUISTICS CAN CONTRIBUTE

The linguist, *qua* linguist, studies language in its various forms, accumulates inventories of phonological and grammatical units, constructs models for bundling these entities together, and speculates on the relationship of his models to nonverbal phenomena. But linguistics, however defined, is not education, nor is it psychology. Therefore, while the linguist can provide reliable data on the pronunciation of a language, the features of its writing system, and the relationship between speech and writing, he cannot, as a linguist, decide how such revelations should be deployed in the teaching of spelling. This latter task involves two major problems that the educator must solve. The first is that the linguist's descriptions are, in some sense, theories or inferences. That is, while he is describing language *habits,* he cannot observe them directly, but must infer them from observations of *behavior.* For example, the linguist observes that English words do not begin with /ŋ/ or /ž/, thus he infers that new words that begin with either of these two sounds would be perceived as non-English-like and would be difficult for English speakers to pronounce. However, the reactions of native English speakers to these sounds is not as predicted by the linguist, as a recent experiment has shown (3). Words beginning with /ž/ apparently are no more difficult to learn than words beginning with /ð/, /š/, or any other sound which occurs initially in English words.

The second problem is that the effectiveness of the methods selected for teaching spelling depends not just upon the linguistic nature of the spelling materials, but also upon the learning abilities of the child, the teaching abilities of the teacher, and the school setting. For example, initial /w/ in many areas has two spellings, as in *wail* and *whale;* the first spelling (*w*) occurs approximately five times more frequently than the second spelling (*wh*). But these facts in no way predetermine how these spellings should be taught. This decision depends upon the age of the children involved, the words which are to be taught, and the relative efficiencies of different basic approaches to spelling. All of these decisions rest primarily with the educator. The most important data which the linguist can provide are those which relate to (*a*) pronunciation, (*b*) the writing system, and (*c*) the relationship between speech and writing. Each of these is discussed in the following pages.

PRONUNCIATION

Dialect Differences

Only a sketch of those features of English pronunciation important for spelling will be discussed here. First among these is dialect differences. American regional speech, primarily of the rural white, has been studied for many years and considerable data are available (9, 10). Recently, studies of urban dialects, particularly of Negroes and Mexican-Americans, have been undertaken (11, 13). The dialect differences brought out in these studies, in relation to spelling, can be divided into four classes: (*a*) regular shifts without merger, (*b*) regular shifts with merger, (*c*) irregular shifts, and (*d*) deletions.[1]

Regular shifts without merger.   These are shifts that generally do not create differences in phonemic systems. For example, the vowel + /r/ sequence in words like *ear* is realized as [ɪr] in Upper Midwestern speech, but generally as [ɪə] in the South.[2] Thus, any pattern derived for Upper Midwestern [ɪr] holds for Southern [ɪə], with the substitution of [ɪə] for [ɪr]. (If [ɪə] occurs elsewhere in Southern speech then the pattern may change.) Such shifts should not, theoretically, cause additional spelling problems.

Regular Shifts with Merger.   In some urban speech, initial /θ/ shifts to /t/.[3] While the shift is regular, that is, all occurrences of /θ/ in one dialect are replaced by /t/ in the other dialect, spelling (but not reading) patterns are affected. For the /θ/ dialect, all occurrences of initial /θ/ are spelled *th*, and all occurrences of initial /t/ are spelled *t*. For the /t/ dialect, initial /θ/ does not exist, and initial /t/ is spelled either *t* or *th*, and nothing in the sounds or meanings of the words will help the speller discriminate the two patterns.

Irregular Shifts.   Sometimes a single sound in one dialect may become two different sounds in another dialect. If this occurs without phonological or semantic conditioning, then new spelling patterns must be written for the second dialect. Such is the situation in the realization of Upper Midwestern /æ/ in Eastern New England. In some words, such as *glass* and *calves*, /a/ is used. In others, such as *hat* and *bag*, /æ/ is used.

Deletions.   A feature common to all urban dialects is the deletion of certain final consonants, especially in clusters like /ld/ and /nt/. Here, of course, fairly predictable spellings become unpredictable since silent letters result from the deletion.

Syllable Division

Syllables are generally not separated by clear pauses in free speech, except where unpronounceable consonant clusters occur, as in *wistful*, where /stf/ must be divided between the /t/ and the /f/. A word like *petal* can be pronounced with the /t/ ending the first syllable, or with it beginning the second, or with it forming a continuous link from

---

[1] These differences are described in relation to Upper Midwestern speech from which shifts or deletions are made. For a description of Upper Midwestern speech, see Allen (1).

[2] This shift holds for both the Upper and Lower South. See Kurath and McDavid (9:18–22).

[3] I am ignoring the situations where the /t/ which replaces /θ/ is phonetically distinct from the /t/ at the beginning of *tin* and *ten*.

one syllable peak to the next, as occurs in most fast speech. To establish spelling rules based upon particular syllable breaks for words like *petal* is to mislead both teachers and students. Unfortunately, what are represented as syllable breaks in a dictionary are not always based upon sound.[4]

ENGLISH ORTHOGRAPHY

The Writing System

A theoretical basis for English orthography has been established through extensive research over the past ten years (14, 15, 16). Most important to this work is the view that English spelling is not simply a defective phonemic system for transcribing speech, but instead a more complex and more regular set of patterns in which both phonemic and morphemic elements share leading roles. The better known morphemic patterns include the noun plural marker -(*e*)*s*, the past tense marker -(*e*)*d*, and the various suffix patterns which cause vowel sound alterations.[5] Note that the noun plural spelling (and the various other morphemes which -(*e*)*s* can represent) stands for three distinct phonemes and all of these have distinct spellings which could have been employed: /s/: *cats*, /z/: *dogs*, /ɪz/: *judges*. Similarly, -(*e*)*d* could be /t/ as *walked*, /d/ as in *canned*, or /ɪd/ as in *mended*.

Basic Units

The letters (graphemes) used to spell English comprise the 26 letters of the Roman alphabet.[6] The units which must be manipulated to relate sound to spelling, however, are not just the letters, but various letter combinations which function as single units, such as *th, ck, tch, oo,* and *ou*; all of these together are called spelling units. The most important spelling units are shown in Table 1.

The need for the classification *spelling unit* is best exemplified by the final *e* rule for single letter vowel spellings. If this rule is stated as follows: "A long vowel sound can be spelled by a single letter vowel, followed by a single consonant letter, and then a silent *e*," words like *axe, bathe,* and *writhe* appear to be exceptions. This pattern, however, is not based upon letters, but upon spelling units. The vowel spelling can be followed by a simple consonant spelling unit plus silent *e*. Complex spelling units—*x, dg, tch, ck*—either stand for two sounds (*x*) or are replacements for doubled consonants (*dg, tch, ck*). Spellings like *th, ch, sh,* and *ph* are simple spelling units since long vowel sounds can be spelled with single vowel letters standing before them (e.g. *bathe, cochineal, kosher, hyphen*); long vowel sounds can never be spelled with single vowel letters before the complex consonant units.

---

[4] "... we especially need to recognize that the hyphenation and syllable-divisions set forth in our dictionaries is very largely arbitrary, and that they therefore do not, in fact cannot, have by the very nature of the situation, any absolute validity" (6: 55).

[5] For a detailed description of these patterns, viewed from the reading standpoint, see Venezky (15).

[6] We might, following Francis (4: 447), include the standard punctuation symbols plus certain suprasegmental features (capitals, etc.) as graphemes.

Table 1   The major spelling units

Consonant Units				Vowel Units		
Simple			Complex	Primary	Compound	
b	k	s	ck	a	ai/ay	oa
c	l	sh	dg	e	au/aw	oe
ch	m	t	tch	i	ea	oi/oy
d	n	th	x	o	ee	oo
f	p	u		u	ei/ey	ou/ow
g	ph	v		y	eu/ew	ue
gh	q	w			ie	ui
h	r	wh				
j	rh	y				
		z				

Relational Units and Markers

Another feature of English orthography which current linguistic research has clarified is the distinction between *relational units* and *markers*. Relational units are those spelling units which relate directly to sound; markers are letters which indicate spelling-sound relationships, or preserve graphemic or morphemic patterns. Final *e* is a marker in *mate* since it indicates the long pronunciation of *a*. It is a dual marker in *rage*, indicating the pronunciations of both *a* and *g* (compare *rag*). In *love*, *e* preserves a pattern which forbids *v* to occur in final position; in *mouse, house,* and *moose* it indicates that the *s* is not a morphemic unit, that is, is not a plural or third singular indicator. In *guide* and *guest*, *u* is a marker, showing the /g/ pronunciation of *g*. All of these patterns relate as much to spelling as to reading; it is the task of the educator to decide if they can aid in the teaching of spelling, and if so, how.

SOUND-SPELLING RELATIONSHIPS

Classification

Sound-to-spelling patterns can best be classed for pedagogical purposes as (*a*) predictable, (*b*) unpredictable but frequent, and (*c*) unpredictable and rare. (The pitfalls inherent in using the terms "regular" and "irregular" to describe these patterns will be discussed shortly.)

Predictable Patterns

Predictable patterns divide into two sub-classes: invariant and variant. Invariant patterns, which are rare in the sound-spelling domain, are those which assign the same spelling to a particular sound (or sound sequence) regardless of its environment. /hw/, for those dialects which have this sequence, is invariably spelled *wh* as in *where* and *when*. When /ð/ and /θ/ occur, they are almost always spelled *th*. (The exceptions are proper names like *Matthew* and a few rare spellings like in *eighth* where /tθ/ is spelled *th*.) Except for *of* and a few double *v* spellings (*navvy, divvy,* etc.), /v/ is invariably spelled *v*. A few other consonant sounds have nearly invariant spellings, but no vowel sounds do.

Many sounds have variant spellings which can be predicted on the basis of either the environment of the sound or the meaning or form class of the word in which it occurs. Final /š/, for example, is almost always spelled *sh* as in *ash*; but initial /š/ can be *sh*, or *s* as in *sure* and *sugar*, or *ch* as in numerous French borrowings like *chalet* and *chef*.[7] (Medial /š/ is considerably less predictable.) Initial /m/ is always spelled *m*; final /m/ can be either *m*, or (in a small group of words) *mn*. This latter spelling can be predicted, however, from the pronunciation of compounds like *autumnal, columnal, damnation,* and *hymnal*. Initial /č/, except for *cello*, is spelled *ch*. Final /č/ is either *ch* or *tch; tch* occurs only after a short vowel sound which is spelled with a single letter, e.g., *batch, etch, itch, blotch, clutch*. *ch* occurs in all other circumstances, including vowel + /r/.[8]

Frequent but Unpredictable Patterns

Many sounds have variant spellings which cannot be predicted, but which occur frequently enough to merit special attention. An example of such a sound is final /o/ which may be *o* as in *go, ow* as in *low*, or *oe* as in *doe*.[9] The frequencies of occurrences of each of these spellings in the 20,000 most common words in English are: *o*: 140; *ow*: 7; *oe*: 12. This class is distinct from the class which follows because new words which are created for English would tend to have one of these spellings if it contained /o/.

Rare and Unpredictable Patterns[10]

Unusual spellings which are limited to a small group of words fit into this class. Some well-known examples are the *f* spelling in *of*, the *au* spelling in *aunt*, and the *ct* spelling in *indict*. These are usually artifacts of isolated sound changes or the inheritances of scribal eccentricity, and while they provide ready offenders for pillorying in spelling-reform diatribes, they represent no serious threat to health and public safety.

The value of this tripart classification is that it separates spelling patterns according to the behaviors which we would expect good spellers to acquire. Predictable patterns, while they may require a concern for environment, are transferable to any word containing the sounds involved. Variant-predictable patterns require attention to such features as position, stress, or following sounds, but can still be transferred once the appropriate features are known. Unpredictable patterns cannot be transferred to new occurrences of the same sounds, but while one anticipates seeing certain frequent, unpredictable patterns in new words, one does not expect to see the rare, unpredictable patterns there. The difference between the two classes is, then, that the first occurs in an open-ended set of words and the second occurs in a closed set.

Regular vs. Irregular

It should be obvious from the preceding discussion that the labels "regular" and "irregular" as applied to spelling patterns are quite misleading. "Regular" is commonly

---

[7] Some rarer spellings are found in *pshaw* and *schist*.

[8] The major exceptions to this pattern are *much, rich, such*, and *which*.

[9] Rarer spellings are *ew* (*sew*), *eau* (*bureau*), and *ough* (*dough*).

[10] Another title for this class is *hapax orthographica*.

defined as the most frequently occurring correspondence,[11] yet this merges predictable patterns like initial and final /č/ with unpredictable patterns like medial /č/. That is, it fails to consider whether the variant spellings are predictable or not. Unfortunately, the term "regular" has become a shibboleth for a method of teaching spelling rather than a description for a rationally derived set of patterns.

Furthermore, the term is quite misleading in that the goal of spelling instruction is to teach correct spelling, not some probabilistic approximation to correct spelling. There are good reasons for teaching sound-spelling relationships, but the percent of regularity of isolated correspondences, no matter how "regular" is defined, is not sufficient. Notice that if a student were taught only the so-called regular spellings for each significant sound in English, he could be expected so spell correctly less than 41 percent of all English words.[12]

SPELLING VS. READING

While spelling patterns have some similarity to reading patterns, the differences are so great that the patterning from spelling to sound seldom mirrors that of sound to spelling. Assumptions about spelling, based upon the writings of linguists who were concerned primarily with reading, must be viewed with caution.[13] Some of the conflicts between reading patterns and spelling patterns are discussed below.

The /w/ Patterns

For those areas of the country which pronounce initial *wh* as /w/, the spelling of initial /w/ is unpredictable, although the reading patterns for initial *wh* and *w* are predictable, in that each is pronounced /w/.[14] The unpredictability of the spellings can be seen from the following examples:

whale	wail	whisk	wisp
wheel	week	whiskey	wisdom
whip	wipe	whistle	wistful

The Medial /t/ Patterns

In reading, *t* between vowel spellings is pronounced /t/ (e.g., *city, satin*), except in certain complex, but patterned environments, where it is /š/ or /č/ as in *nation* and *nature*. Medial

---

[11] In the Hanna studies (7, 8), the most frequent spelling for a sound is classed as the "regular" spelling for that sound, regardless of whether it represents 30 percent, 99 percent, or any other percentage of the spellings for a given sound.

[12] If we begin with the 80 percent regularity figure mentioned above, and assume that there are four sounds in the average English word (and this is a low estimate), then the probability of spelling any word correctly is the product of the probabilities for the individual spellings in the word; $.80 \times .80 \times .80 \times .80$ or .4096 (40.96 percent).

[13] Bloomfield (2) wrote about reading, but never about spelling. Fries (5) proscribed sound-to-spelling concerns from *Linguistics and Reading* (see fn. 13, p. 171). Hall (6) developed his spelling patterns based upon reading, and mentions spelling only in a brief paragraph in the conclusions (p. 59).

[14] The exceptions are the few *wh* words pronounced with initial /h/, e.g., *who, whoop*.

tt is always pronounced /t/. Thus, from a reading standpoint the pronunciations of medial, intervocalic *t* and *tt* are predictable.

From a spelling standpoint, however, the correspondences for intervocalic /t/ cannot be predicted; either *t* or *tt* could occur. Observe, for example, the words shown below:

city	ditty	litany	gluttony
pity	witty	metal	glottal
satin	cotton	motor	latter

The *th* Patterns

For reading, medial *th* spellings are generally unpredictable; they can be /θ/ as in *ether* or /ð/ as in *either*. (Some medial *th* patterns are predictable: *-the* and *-ther*, except for *ether*, are always /ð/.) From a spelling standpoint, as mentioned earlier, /ð/ and /θ/ are almost always spelled *th* (see under heading, "Sound-Spelling Relationships" in this chapter for the exceptions). Some matched pairs are:

apathy	swarthy	nothing	breathing
author	another	pithy	worthy
ether	either	zither	father

CONCLUSIONS

The linguist can provide for educators data on the pronunciation of English, the nature of the writing system, and the relationship between speech and writing. It is the educator's task, however, to determine which of the linguist's offerings can aid in the teaching of spelling, and how they should be used to achieve this end. A rational spelling program, regardless of its pedagogy, must be based upon the speech which the learner uses and not upon an idealized dialect, replete with synthetic syllable breaks and unreduced vowels. If sound-to-spelling relationships are to be used in the program (either overtly or covertly), they must be derived from sound linguistic work which recognizes the units and functions upon which English orthography is based. Rather than the probabilistic relationships inherent in the classes "regular" and "irregular", more pedagogically relevant relationships should be employed for classing sound-spelling patterns. Finally, spelling is not reading. Wholly new patterns must be derived, starting with sound and working towards spelling. This cannot be achieved through a simple reversal of spelling-to-sound patterns, but must come from careful and detailed analysis.

BIBLIOGRAPHY

1. Allen, Harold B. "Aspects of the Linguistic Geography of the Upper Midwest." In *Studies in Language and Linguistics in Honor of Charles C. Fries,* pp. 303–14. Edited by Albert H. Marckwardt. Ann Arbor: English Language Institute, University of Michigan, 1964.

2. Bloomfield, Leonard. *Language.* New York: Holt, Rinehart & Winston, 1933.

3. Brière, E. J.; Campbell, R. N.; and Soemarmo. "A Need for the Syllable in Contrastive Analyses," *Journal of Verbal Learning and Verbal Behavior,* VII (1968), 384–89.

4. Francis, W. Nelson. *The Structure of American English.* New York: Ronald Press, 1958.

5. Fries, Charles C. *Linguistics and Reading.* New York: Holt, Rinehart & Winston, 1962.

6. Hall, Robert A., Jr. *Sound and Spelling in English.* Philadelphia: Chilton Co., 1961.

7. Hanna, Paul R., and Moore, James T., Jr. "Spelling—from Spoken Word to Written Symbol," *Elementary School Journal,* LIII (February, 1953), 329–37.

8. Hanna, Paul R., *et al. Phoneme-Grapheme Correspondences as Cues to Spelling Improvement.* Washington, D.C.: U.S. Department of Health, Education, and Welfare, Office of Education, 1966.

9. Kurath, Hans, and McDavid, Raven I., Jr. *The Pronunciation of English in the Atlantic States.* Ann Arbor: University of Michigan Press, 1961.

10. Kurath, Hans *et al. Linguistic Atlas of New England.* 3 vols. Providence, R. I.: Brown University, 1939–43.

11. Labov, William. "Stages in the Acquisition of Standard English." In *Social Dialects and Language Learning.* Edited by Roger W. Shuy, Champaign, Ill.: National Council of Teachers of English, 1965, 77–103.

12. *Linguistics and English Linguistics.* Compiled by Harold B. Allen. New York: Appleton-Century-Crofts, 1966. [Ed. 2. Arlington Heights, Ill.: AHM, 1977]

13. *Social Dialects and Language Learning.* Edited by Roger W. Shuy. Champaign, Ill.: National Council of Teachers of English, 1965.

14. Venezky, Richard L. *The Structure of English Orthography.* The Hague: Mouton & Co., 1969.

15. ———. "English Orthography: Its Graphical Structure and Its Relation to Sound," *Reading Research Quarterly,* II (Spring, 1967), 75–106.

16. Weir, Ruth H., and Venezky, Richard L. "Rules to Aid in the Teaching of Reading." Final Report, Cooperative Research Project No. 2584 (Stanford University, 1965).

DISCUSSION QUESTIONS

1. Might regional differences in pronunciation, examples of which are given in Allen's article, be relevant to the general teaching of spelling?

2. Search in your dictionary for evidence relevant to Venezky's statement that syllable-division is very largely arbitrary. Compare, for example, *dull-ard* and *dul-ly, fi-nal* and *fin-a-ble, far-thing* and *birth-ing.* Comment also on *ac-cident* and *ax-ing.*

3. Are "markers" synonymous with silent letters? How might your answer relate to the teaching of spelling?

4. Relate the not infrequent student spelling *aditude* with Venezky's remark that *t* between vowel letters is pronounced /t/.

5. In the light of Venezky's article prepare a critique of the treatment of spelling in some elementary language textbook.

ROBERT C. POOLEY

The late Professor Pooley was chairman of the department of integrated and liberal studies at the University of Wisconsin. Long concerned with matters of usage, he wrote books and articles in the field and in 1941 served as president of the National Council of Teachers of English.

THE TEACHING OF ENGLISH USAGE

THE PROBLEM

The successful use of English in adult life rests on a foundation of habits so thoroughly established as to be automatic. For all ordinary purposes of communication, the proficient adult is generally unconscious of language choices; words, idioms, and constructions appropriate to the nature of the communication flow along unimpeded by conscious effort. Only in unusually formal or difficult situations does a person become conscious of the need for closer discrimination in language choices. Even then, experiences gained in observing the speech and writing of others carry him through.

THE ELEMENTARY SCHOOL

However, sensitivity to the varieties of language usage, particularly to certain forms or constructions frowned upon in many social contexts, is not readily gained in the home. Young children learn speech by ear: the words, idioms, and constructions heard in the home and neighborhood are those that characterize the language which they bring to school. Children acquire both standard and variant habits of speech in the most impressionable years of childhood, reinforcing these habits by countless repetitions prior to the influence of school. But the child who employs nonstandard forms or constructions does not use "bad" language; the choices in language use which he has learned to make were and continue to be quite satisfactory and appropriate in the home and neighborhood environment. Thus usage instruction throughout the school years should not be designed to eliminate such preschool language acquisition but to augment it, so that the child is more steadily guided toward greater proficiency in a wider variety of standard forms.

The child who has heard from the cradle onward the patterns of English which lie within the range of nationally accepted usage may have an advantage in the further mastery of a wider variety of socially approved forms. But his mastery of certain standard forms does not thereby exempt him from usage instruction. For children who employ standard forms as well as for those who do not, the fundamental goals of usage instruction are the same: the development of sensitivity to and proficiency in the use of words, idioms, and constructions according to the nature of the communication. The teaching of certain standard forms to students who know only nonstandard forms is necessarily a part of usage instruction designed to instill a sense of social responsibility for language use, but it is only a part. Unfortunately, because of the prevalence of certain nonstandard forms and because of the high priority schools have placed upon their eradication, drill for "correctness," which is after all only a negative kind of instruction, has tended to overshadow and supplant more positive instruction leading to an appreciation of the ways of the English language. The child whose usage has been made reasonably "correct" or standard, but whose sentences are flat, dull, and inexact, has not been taught good English usage. Language free from dialect variation is not necessarily effective language for being more standard. It becomes effective as the child develops a feeling for the bright, sparkling word or phrase, the exact word for his needs, the sentence which says exactly what he wants to say as clearly as possible and in a manner suiting the tone and purpose of the communciation.

This feeling for the fitness of words in their uses is the positive side of usage instruction, and it can be taught well only in situations calling for genuine communication. The goals of language instruction throughout the school years can be achieved only if students become observers of language. Activities which place children in the role of observers are those which establish the attitudes that language is constantly changing and that usage items mastered today may not be the most acceptable ones when they are adults. As observers they will be able to adjust to the culture as it shifts and changes. It is this kind of knowledgeable flexibility which is the ultimate goal of education.

A program of usage instruction will inevitably involve the teaching of speech forms from the standard dialect as substitutions for nonstandard patterns learned in the home and neighborhood environment and reinforced daily out of school. Teachers are thus faced with a very thorny situation. The chief task of language instruction designed to teach certain forms from the standard dialect is to persuade children to substitute new habits for those which they have practiced for many years. But an attack on certain usages of the nonstandard variety may be interpreted as an attack on the child himself and on the culture of his home. From the child's point of view, the language forms he uses are perfectly natural and acceptable. Do not his family and others he holds in esteem use them? The problem is made still more difficult if only a portion of the class regularly employ nonstandard forms. Intensive instruction in standard forms may appear to mean that the teacher favors certain children and not others.

A sound and successful program of teaching usage in the elementary grades can be built upon the understanding and application of four fundamental principles.

1. The teacher must size up the problem of desired usage as it affects the class and plan a campaign to bring about specific results. Every class offers its own challenges which the teacher hopefully will recognize and meet.
2. Children must be aroused to a desire to augment their repertoires to include standard forms in situations requiring them and must be motivated to cooperate actively with the teacher in striving toward the accomplishment of specific results. They must be stimulated to become observers of language, both of their own and of others.
3. Usage instruction must never be divorced from the normal and natural uses of language in the entire school program. This means there should be no language exercise which does not recognize the nature of communication and no use of communication which ignores usage appropriate to the purpose.
4. Students learn standard speech patterns by hearing standard speech patterns. Techniques which provide oral reinforcement are the most effective. Situations which call for the use of oral language, such as storytelling, language games, creative dramatics and role playing, oral reports, etc. are invaluable, but the students must act as observers of the language in order to benefit from the situations.

* * *

THE SENIOR HIGH SCHOOL

In the senior high school the teaching of usage is a twofold responsibility. One part is evaluative, the examination of speech patterns that carry over from earlier years, the choices of usage which arise from increased use of language at a higher level, and the increasing need to attain the standard dialect. The other part is constructive, the teaching of effective patterns of speech for wider needs and the refinement of word-choice to increase the interest and effectiveness of expression. Because the first aspect is the more apparent need and is in nature more concrete, it tends to supplant or overshadow the more important constructive responsibility.

In spite of the limiting influence of dialect variations and the evaluative steps necessary to bring about a broadening of usage, the high school program in language development must not be looked upon as purely corrective. Language instruction in the senior high school must be focused upon the constant expansion of powers to use language effectively for the needs of school and adult life. To this end the major portion of time in the English course should be given to two types of constructive activities:

1. Guided practice in oral language by means of reports, discussions, panels, forums, debates, and extemporary dramatics. These exercises should be conducted so as to provide opportunities for every student to take an active part at frequent intervals and to grow in effectiveness of oral presentation through the guidance of the teacher and the suggestions of fellow students.
2. Constant growth in written language by means of composition exercises at regular and frequent intervals. These written exercises should cover a wide range of subjects, with the time allotment fairly equally divided between two types of writings: (a) factual-expository writing, as in reports, summaries, explanations, arguments, reviews, and editorials; and (b) personal-imaginative writing, as in the relation of personal experiences, essays, narratives, class journals, fantasy, humor, and, in some cases, drama and poetry.

In this constructive program of language development, acceptable usage plays an essential but subordinate part. Every language exercise, oral and written, should have an intrinsic purpose of its own, a purpose recognized by the student and ideally one which challenges him to do his best. Good usage, including a conscious effort to employ appropriate standard dialect forms, should be seen as contributory to the accomplishment of the purpose of the exercise, not as an end in itself. Indeed, the best instruction in language use at the high school level is that which arises naturally from the needs of the students as they strive to accomplish effective expression for a definite purpose. Such instruction makes sense and finds immediate application in the task at hand.

USAGE IN CREATIVE COMMUNICATION

Teaching good usage creatively is inseparable from the art of teaching students to communicate. While the illustrations given here are drawn from written composition, the principles of language development apply with equal force to oral communication. The power to communicate effectively and correctly is advanced as the student makes progress in two areas: (1) an ever-increasing knowledge of his total environment through active living, absorbing experiences, developing new interests, and relating each new specific gain to the total body of his knowledge; (2) an increasing command of words, word groups, and sentence patterns together with increasing sensitivity to usage choices which facilitate the expression and interpretation of his experiences. Teaching the student thus to communicate is the art of composition, and composition is here defined as the personal expression of a person who has something to communicate and has also the desire to make his communication influence others.

Unfortunately, it is possible for students to go through high school and receive good grades in English without learning the difference between exercise writing and communicating. They may write neat and often mechanically perfect papers several pages in length, with paragraphs arranged in proper sequence. But the subject and its treatment are entirely secondhand. The student has absorbed from reading or listening certain facts or ideas which he repeats more or less in his own words with a glib facility. The subject has no real significance to him, nor has it raised any internal response. His product contains nothing which he himself has said. In the process of writing he has been not much more than a kind of automatic relay between the source and the product. That there is a great deal of this so-called composition accepted in the high schools is well known. It is accepted because the concept of communication is not clearly recognized.

The requirements of a good composition are, first, that the subject arise from a genuine need or interest of the student which stimulates him to thought and feeling; second, that he find for himself (with help if needed) the form or plan of the writing to develop it in his own way; and, third, that when finished he has the sense of having made a statement, proclaimed an idea, defended a position, or expressed experiences and feelings in prose or verse which is his own language and in which he can take pride. When these conditions are met in any piece of writing, that writing is truly composition and is genuine communication.

Of equal importance are the evaluations which teachers place on papers. These are not merely grades, or corrections of forms and usages. They should represent appraisal or the measurement of the intrinsic worth of the writing. Such measurement means judgment in three factors: (1) A recognition of what the student set out to do. This will differ for every paper and cannot be taken for granted. Indeed, one of the serious faults in evaluating composition is the confusing of what we think a student ought to do with a subject with what *he* intended to do. So far as in us lies, we must see the project as the author intended. (2) An appreciation of the plan the student adopted to carry out his idea. This means an appraisal of the title and organization of the paper, a recognition of the balance of parts, and a sense of the appropriateness of form and language to the expression of his idea. (3) An evaluation of the success of the communication in terms of what the student set out to do. This judgment comes from a recognition of the clarity of ideas, the sequence of thought, the vividness of illustrations, figures, and conversations, the appropriateness of the usage to these ends, and the sense of completeness of the whole. When the paper has been judged by these three factors, the student is entitled to a statement of appraisal, either orally in a conference or as a written note on the paper.

All these considerations lead to the application of usage standards. There will be questionable usages, of course. The fundamental attitude to take is that the inappropriate forms are not wrong in themselves but are hindrances to the effectiveness of the communication. Every time the reader or listener is confused, irritated, or amused by a detail, the effectiveness of the communciation is weakened to some degree. Appropriate usage permits the reader to gain the full impact of the meaning without any interference by the language used.

Since students are often heedless of expected form and imitative of the language they hear, teachers in the past have devoted time and attention to deviations and undesired patterns of sentence structure, idiom and usage, mechanics of writing, and spelling. The best strategy in approaching such deviations and undesired patterns lies in getting students to see that these deviations have interfered with communication. Therefore, in creative teaching the emphasis will be on the communication and not on the form. When the student has something to say, when he wants to say it as well as he can, and when he appreciates the applause and criticisms of his fellows and of his teacher, the correction of details as impediments to the success of his project makes sense and enlists his personal desire for improvement. On the other hand, decades of experience have proved that the correction of errors as errors, and drill on corrective measures in isolation from the need to communicate, result in discouraging returns from the time and effort expended. It cannot be claimed that attention to communication will eliminate errors. It is possible, however, to staunchly defend the position that emphasis on communication will subordinate the correction of errors to an element of the total success and that this emphasis will provide a genuine motivation toward accuracy and sensitivity to good form, a motivation never aroused by red ink, failing grades, or isolated usage drills.

The plea of this section is that the time given to formal drill and grammatical analysis be transferred to the promotion of good communication. Writing should be frequent and as far as possible voluntary. Much time should be devoted to the hearing and evaluating of writing. Compositions should be read aloud and discussed in groups or circulated in the classroom. And the teaching of usage and correctness should feature creative language situations: How should a certain idea be expressed before a certain audience? What effect do certain phrases have on the intent and tone of communication? How would two people of differing age, social status, or degree of education tell the same story or relate the same event? How would one phrase a story or conversation to show the personality of the speaker? and many similar situations. This positive handling of language will stimulate creative expression, will reveal the relative nature of usage choices and prescriptions, and will provide the ground for the consideration of usage and idiom as they affect communication. Finally, of great importance, the student's attitude will shift from the discouragement of being found always in the wrong to the enthusiasm of experimenting with language, all kinds of language, to discover what he can do with it.

DIALECTS AND THE STANDARD DIALECT

It is a fact of English usage that all speakers of English employ a dialect of English which is the product of a number of factors. Each individual's parents and grandparents, the communities in which he spent his formative years, his schools and his teachers, members of the environment whom he admires and perhaps strives to emulate, the media of public communication—all contribute to the formation of each individual's peculiar dialect. Therefore the term *dialect* may not be used in a pejorative sense, for all persons speak dialects. Children in the schoolroom and youth in high school and college reflect the language variations which have arisen from their social environments.

* * *

Each city, village, and rural region has its own minor language variations, but has also an overall common content which we call American English. In this American English, language scholars identify three major dialect areas: Northeast, Southern, and General American, the latter spoken in all parts of the United States outside the Northeast and the South. Of course there are minor differences distinguishable within these dialects, but that is a matter for scholars to deal with.

A general, common, widely used dialect known as standard English serves as an agreed-upon standard medium of spoken and written communication in all parts of the United States. This dialect incorporates a wide range of functional variety, having sufficient breadth to permit the shades of difference in language use appropriate to specific occasions. The standard dialect is in no way intrinsically superior to any other dialect. Rather, its value lies in its role as a national standard of commonly accepted form. With minor variations, it has international value as well, for its shares in substance the major part of British standard English, Australian standard English, South African standard English, and the standard English of many other parts of the world. To those students who wish to expand the range of alternatives available to them in their professional lives, the value of attaining proficiency in this dialect must be obvious.

It is part of the strategy of modern usage teaching to lead students to recognize this value; the consequent motivation almost insures acquisition of the skills necessary for fluency in standard English. Some children come to school able to speak and write standard English. Many acquire the distinctive features of standard English in the grades and high school. There should be continuous encouragement and open opportunity for every student to learn and use standard English as an essential part of his general education. In the past many teachers attempted to force this dialect upon unready and unwilling students. In the best of modern teaching students are helped to recognize the values of attaining the standard dialect and are given every opportunity to learn and practice it.

Characteristics of the Standard Dialect

In the senior high school, regardless of the previous education of the student, teachers of English have the duty and privilege of presenting the forms of standard English, of helping students to distinguish the variations from their own dialects and to acquire skill and fluency in their use. To accomplish this end, two factors must operate: (1) the teacher must wisely and skillfully present the usage distinctions of standard English; and (2) the student must actively desire to acquire it.

The informal variety of standard English is a broad dialect embracing a large number of minor deviations. The speakers and writers of this dialect are rarely conscious of these minor variations of usage, or else consider them unimportant. But there are specific usages which are not a part of this dialect and become at once noticeable to the users of informal standard English. The student who has been motivated to acquire and employ informal standard English will find that the major part of his own dialect lies within the scope of informal standard English. What he needs to learn, therefore, are which specific items of usage, though natural to him in his own dialect, must be eliminated if he wants to be fully equipped to speak and write the standard dialect.

As an aid to the teacher and student who are working together to achieve fluency in the standard dialect, the following list will be helpful in identifying those usages which lie outside standard English and are therefore to be avoided in the speaking and writing of the standard dialect.

A Guide to a Standard of English Usage for Today

1. The avoidance of strictly local usages, such as "to home," "I'd admire to go," "The cat wants out," "all the farther."
2. The grammatical uses in speech and writing of *I, me, he, him, she, her, they, them.* (Note: "It's me" is fully acceptable; "It's him" and "It's them" are gaining acceptability in informal speech.)
3. The grammatical uses of *is, are, was, were* with respect to number and tense.
4. Use of the historical past forms of common irregular verbs such as *saw, gave, took, brought, bought, stuck.*
5. Use of past participles of the same and similar verbs as in number 4 above after auxiliaries.
6. Avoidance of the double negative: "We don't have no apples," etc.
7. Avoidance of analogical forms: *ain't, hisn, hern, ourn, theirselves,* etc.
8. Correct use of possessive pronouns: *my, mine, his, hers, theirs, ours.*
9. Mastery in writing of the distinctions between *its* and *it's, of* and *'ve,* etc.
10. Placement of *have* or *has* or of their phonetic reductions to *v* or *s* between subject and past participle, in past participle constructions.
11. Avoidance of *them* as a demonstrative pronoun.
12. Avoidance of *this here* and *that there.*
13. Mastery of the use of *a* and *an* as articles before consonants and vowels. (Note: before a pronounced *h* or long *u,* use of *a* is idiomatic in American English.)
14. Grammatical use of personal pronouns in compound constructions: as subject (Mary and *I*), as object of a verb (Mary and *me*), as object of a preposition (to Mary and *me*).
15. The use of *we* before an appositional noun when subject; *us* when object.
16. Correct number agreement with the phrases *there is, there are, there was, there were.* . . .
17. Avoidance of *he don't, she don't, it don't.*
18. Avoidance of *learn* for *teach, leave* for *let.*
19. Avoidance of pleonastic subjects: "my brother he," "my mother she," "that fellow he."
20. Proper agreement in number with antecedent pronouns *one* and *anyone, each, no one, either, neither.* With *everybody, everyone, somebody, someone,* and *none* some tolerance of number has long been acceptable, particularly in informal contexts. . . .
21. The use of *who* and *whom* as referents to persons. (Note: *who* as an objective case interrogative pronoun in initial position is standard.
22. Use of *said* rather than *says* in reporting the words of a speaker in the past.
23. The distinction between *good* as adjective and *well* as adverb.
24. Avoidance of *can't hardly, can't scarcely.*
25. Avoidance of *at* after *where:* "Where is she at?"

The study of any usage list should make the student personally aware of his right to choose some forms and to reject others. His understanding of the consequences of his action will be clear to him as he consults current magazine usage or usage handbook authors. In addition, this approach will provide the more talented students with an opportunity to sharpen their language observations as well as "polish" or "refine" the standard English they have already mastered.

It is suggested that teachers and students consider the fact that the following eight items need no longer be "corrected" in the classroom and that these forms are acceptable to many educated speakers and writers today.

A Guide to Usage Items No Longer Considered Nonstandard English

1. Any distinction between *shall* and *will*.
2. Any reference to the split infinitive.
3. Elimination of *like* as a conjunction.
4. Objection to the phrase "different than."
5. Any objection to "He is one of the boys who *is* . . . ."
6. The objection to "The *reason* . . . is *because* . . . ."
7. The objection to *myself* as a polite substitute for *I*, as in "I understand you will meet Mrs. Jones and myself at the station."
8. Any insistence upon the possessive case standing before a gerund.

By no means does the investigation of usage items need to stop with these eight items. If the need and desire to consider other questions grows out of a study of the first group, the teacher will certainly want to continue the work and foster this kind of interest and spirit of investigation. A number of usage reference books are available today to provide additional controversial items which students may wish to study.

DISCUSSION QUESTIONS

1. Do you accept Pooley's statement that sentences that are "flat, dull, and inexact" do not represent "good English usage"? Is there a necessary dichotomy between correctness and good usage?

2. Does Pooley's program for the elementary school call for what might be called "teacher English"?

3. In discussing style, the nineteenth-century English philosopher Herbert Spencer set forth the principle of economy that would allow in good writing nothing that distracts the reader's attention from the writer's purpose. Relate this to Pooley's own views about usage, and to your own usage.

4. Pooley coalesces the Northern and Midland dialects as minor variations within "General American." Check the data in *The Linguistic Atlas of the Upper Midwest* to see whether these two dialects are justifiably so considered.

5. Compare Pooley's two lists, "A Guide to a Standard of English Usage for Today" and "A Guide to Usage Items No Longer Considered Nonstandard English," with the data in Harold Allen's article in Part IV. Do Pooley's perceptions of good usage agree with the responses of Allen's informants? Comment.

ELAINE CHAIKA

The author's Ph.D. in linguistics is from Brown University. She reports having taught every grade from the fourth through graduate school, and from a one-room country school through an urban inner-city school to her present position as professor of linguistics at Providence College. She is most interested in the language deviations of non-proficient writers and in schizophrenic discourse.

GRAMMARS AND TEACHING

Purely theoretical considerations aside, what difference does it make which grammar the English teacher uses? Why isn't traditional, tried and true as it is, as good for pedagogy as the newer transformational grammar? Each provides a framework for discussing language. For composition classes, especially, one would think that's all that's necessary.

Having taught college composition before and after intensive study in linguistics, I have had much experience in teaching via pre- and post-transformational grammars. Unlike the new math which serves only to explain the old, the "new" grammar, henceforth termed "transformational" or T-G, illuminates the workings of language in ways impossible with the old. The explanatory powers of transformational grammar are not only superior to traditional models, but T-G is simpler. Furthermore, the new grammar provides a potent teaching methodology as a natural outcome of its mode of analysis (see below, and Chaika, 1974). These are not trivial concerns in college classrooms, for recent research (Krashen, 1973) suggests that, after puberty, language learning cannot be effected without overt explanation. As noted in Chaika (1974), learning to write may be akin to language learning.

It is disheartening, therefore, to hear English teachers claim that linguistics has nothing to offer rhetoric, or that, if grammar must be taught at all, it makes no difference which. What is ironical is how often those unimpressed by the revolution in syntax are the very ones who have had a course or two in current theory. Apparently the esoteric polemics of many such graduate courses are of little practical value. Indeed, people in English have been known to become downright hostile to linguistics after such exposure.

Yet, polemics about the intricate details of abstract theories aside, the fundamental insights of current syntactic models offer efficacy for teaching rhetoric superior to traditional grammar. Therefore the polemics in this paper are confined to grammars as they pertain to teaching writing. The following offers what has worked for my composition students as well as for teachers-in-service who have enrolled in my writing workshop.

Briefly, by T-G grammar I mean one that recognizes deep as well as surface structure, with transformations from a basic sentence [NP + VP + (Adverb)][1] accounting for the incredible variety of sentence types and constructions found in English. According to such a view, additional sentences may be embedded wherever noun phrases may occur

---

[1] Noun phrase + verb phrase + optional adverb.

in the deep structure sentence, with subsequent deletions and additions producing surface forms.[2]

Since the same deep structure sentences may be differentially transformed, thereby producing paraphrases or near paraphrases, related sentences in a language must always be considered. Such a grammar has been lately advanced as the basis for sentence combining "grammar-free" writing programs (e.g., O'Hare, 1973). Actually, such methods are grammar free only in their non-use of jargon. Transformations and sentence embeddings can only be effected according to the grammar of a language. In fact, despite all the charges that linguists are "against grammar," T-G methods actually demand a very close attention to the rules of English. It is precisely here, in its superior evocation of those rules, that T-G grammar is so potent a teaching force, for sentence building, as worth-while as it is, is not enough. Explanation of error so that learners get insights into their own productions is equally important, as is teaching neophyte writers how to analyze language for themselves. No one knows how to write who can only mimic textbook examples or teacher correction. The essence of language use, as Noam Chomsky has so often reiterated, is to say what has never been said before, but, I add, to say it in accordance with the rules of the language. If the literature on first language acquisition has any lesson at all for us, it is that humans use language creatively only after ascertaining its rules.

Basically, traditional grammar is concerned with categorizing and labelling, whereas transformational is concerned with processes. Where traditional grammar defines terms, T-G formulates rules. Where traditional grammar looks for differences, T-G looks for "sames." Thus, where traditional grammar sees subordinate clauses, gerunds, participles, and infinitives, T-G sees only sentence embedding. The difference to pedagogy caused by such variation in approach is tremendous. The natural emphasis of T-G is not on parsing, but on the creative process itself; not what a form is, but why it is selected. The entire presentation of transformational grammar thus becomes easily entwined with the teaching of writing. Perhaps even more important, the new grammar demands the recognition of the linguistic genius of every human being, a powerful morale booster to the non-proficient writer. Often the difference between learning and not is one's belief in one's own power.

Since T-G is always concerned with why language operates as it does and how sentences are related to each other, it often uncovers meaninful explanations for what traditional grammars ignore. Once a student of mine wrote, "He succeeded to do it." My correction noted that he had to change it to "He succeeded in doing it." [(*For*) . . . *to*] can't be used after *succeed*. The student complained, "I'll never remember when to use *to* or *-ing*. It's impossible." My response was to explain that [(*for* . . . *to*] typically is used to embed statements which are not necessarily factual, as in:

(1a) Jack tried to get married.
(Jack didn't marry.)
(2a) They reported the storm to have hit the Florida keys.
(The storm may or may not have hit the Florida keys.)
(3a) I'd like to live on the Riviera.

---

[2] Since Chaika (1972, 1974) treats the uses of case grammar, a further modification of T-G as it pertains to rhetoric, it is here ignored.

Conversely, [(possessive) . . . -*ing*] is used for factual embedding, as in:

> (1b) Jack tried getting married.
> (Jack did marry.)
> (2b) They reported the storm's hitting the Florida keys.
> (The storm did hit.)
> (3b) I like living on the Riviera.

Actually, the student himself was able to ascertain the subtle differences in meaning between the (a) and (b) sentences above. This helped convince him, not only that he has knowledge which he can draw upon to become a competent writer, but that he is capable of thinking about language and making judgments about it. It also reinforced classroom lessons on the necessity of paraphrase to yield the precise meaning. Perhaps, most important, a lively discussion of sentence possibilities and syntactic rules ensued from the correction. It is no accident that T-G grammarians, but not traditionalists, noticed the "fact rule." Since T-G advocates are concerned with why and how all sentences of a language are generated, they constantly search for unifying principles and general processes. A theory with deep structure means searching for underlying unity. It is such a search that led syntacticians to note the deep structure similarity of infinitives and gerunds.

After this experience with my student, I asked six excellent conventionally trained English professors how they would justify such a correction. They all characterized the student error as "awkward" or explained "Because I just know what it has to be." Neither response is likely to stimulate the student to think about language. Indeed, such responses make theme correction seem like placation of an idiosyncratic teacher, not a learning experience.

The vagueness engendered by the lack of coherent theory in traditional grammar can actually be a bar to learning. For instance, *The Holt Guide to English,* published in 1972, cites as an example of "awkwardness" in a chapter on style:

> (4) When people cease to tolerate themselves is the time hypocrisy comes about.
> (Irmscher, p. 184)

Irmscher (p. 184) asserts that "the awkwardness results from trying to make a 'when clause' the subject of the sentence." Thus, Irmscher implies that (4) results from a violation of syntactic rules. Whereas it does seem most usual for *when* to embed sentences as adverbs, as in Irmscher's suggested revision,

> (4a) Hypocrisy comes about when people cease to tolerate themselves,

there are allowable instances of *when* embedding subject sentences, as

> (4b) When people cease to tolerate themselves is when they become hypocrites.
> (*suggested by Richard Ohmann*)

In both (4) and (4b) the *when* clause is used as a subject, but the parallelism in the latter makes it more acceptable. Apparently, since "the time" in (4) repeats semantic features of *when*, a stylistic awkwardness results because both clauses in (4) are being used as sentence complements. Neither clause is subordinate to the other, so, stylistically, the repeated elements are best presented by repetition of the same word. Parallelism is stylistically preferable when repeated meanings are grammatically equivalent, but not to employ such parallelism does not create ungrammaticality as Irmscher's second example of awkwardness does:

(5) With physical death does not, nor cannot die the existence of the achievements of man.

This sentence violates an important inviolable rule of English grammar: the subject of a sentence cannot be a prepositional phrase. "With physical death" has been placed in subject position. Furthermore, *die* does not allow the object position in a sentence to be filled, but here "the existence" has been placed there. Nor is (5) one of those sentences which allow inversion of subject and predicate because of a proposed negative or locative adverb, as in

(5a) Never had she run.
(5b) In the corner sat the frog.

Irmscher's example is not a case of mistaken inversion as the auxiliary and verb aren't interrupted by the subject. These are not matters of stylistic preference or awkwardness, but grammatical necessity.[3] By presenting (5) as well as (4) as an example of awkwardness, *The Holt Guide* makes it appear as if the usage of prepositional phrases in subject position may sometimes also be all right when, in fact, it never is. Unfortunately, students often make that error. Irmscher's easy latching onto a label leads him to lose an opportunity to illustrate an important rule of sentence construction. Similarly, his failure to discuss the proscription of complements after *die* means that *The Holt Guide* fails to make an important point about verbs, namely that lexical rules on verbs determine whether object or indirect object positions may be filled (Fillmore, 1968; Chafe, 1970; Chaika, 1972, 1974). Because traditional grammar, unlike T-G, is content to regard each sentence as idiosyncratic and because it is not concerned with discovery of underlying principles of sentence generation, faulty analysis is inherent in it. Because T-G insists that language is comprised of interrelated rules, it allows an explanation to stand only if it provides usable rules applicable to the student's own writing. As a direct outcome of T-G theory, these rules are related to the language as a whole. They are not presented as chaotic, idiosyncratic instances which are ultimately unlearnable. The traditional catchall "awkward" can only lead to confusion. If a stylistic deficiency is presented as a grammatical error, but a student thinks of an instance in which the supposed error is acceptable, the professor's authority is lessened. It seems to the student that English teachers are privy to mysterious, unlearnable knowledge, or that they are addled. Furthermore, the label "awkward" does not tell the student when a given construction may be used, even if the error is accompanied by a sample revision. For the student to be enlightened, several instances of both correct and incorrect usage of a construction must be offered, followed by explication of the principle underlying its use. This explication should follow from

---

[3] This is not to deny that T-G sometimes finds fuzzy borders between grammar and style. Considering dialectal variation and language change, this is not surprising. However, T-G, because of its emphasis on rule formation and "searching" the whole grammar, is less likely to confuse. Furthermore, it keeps an awareness of grammar vs. style before the student at all times because of the insistence on considering all paraphrases.

the examples. The reader familiar with modern grammars will recognize in this suggestion the typical T-G format for explaining a rule.

Harbrace College Handbook, although traditional, does try to be more precise than "awkward," but it, too, fails to distinguish between grammatical and stylistic criteria. For instance, in a chapter entitled "Unity and Logical Thinking," after cautioning students not to allow "excessive subordination" in a sentence (error 23b), it warns against mixing constructions, (error 23c) with

> (6) When Howard plays the hypochondriac taxes his wife's patience.
> [An adverb clause, part of a complex sentence, is here combined with the predicate of a simple sentence]
>
> (Hodges & Whitten, 1972: 262)

Clearly, this error is grammatical. Its correction is not a matter of personal preference or esthetic judgment, but one of necessity. *Harbrace's* explanation seems to be offering the student a general principle, but as noted above, there is no syntactic rule forbidding adverb clauses as subjects of sentences. For instance,

> (6a) *When Howard finds time to go* remains a mystery.

If the *when* clause in (6a) is permissible, then, clearly, (6) is not in error because of mixing constructions. Whether or not a *when* clause can appear as subject depends upon the verb used as predicate. It has long been known that selectional restrictions on verbs determine their subjects (Fillmore, 1968; Chafe, 1970; Chaika, 1972, 1974). The *Harbrace* warning against "mixed constructions" is not only in error, it denies the student a valid and rhetorically important construction: the embedded sentence as subject.

The *Harbrace* correction of (6) compounds the original misanalysis and does so directly because of the lack of a workable definition of a sentence in traditional grammar. *Harbrace* offers as correction to (6) (letters mine):

> (A) When Howard plays the hypochondriac, he taxes his wife's patience. (*complex sentence*) OR
> (B) Howard's playing the hypochondriac taxes his wife's patience. (*simple sentence*)
>
> (Hodges & Whitten, p. 262)

Why is the first correction "complex" and the second "simple" when both convey the same meaning and both contain two predications? "Howard's playing" is equivalent to "When Howard plays—", as the text itself admits by offering these as alternates. Furthermore, if "Howard's playing" is not a transformed deep structure sentence, if it is a simple [possessive + NP] subject, one wonders what Hodges and Whitten would propose to do with the fact that "playing" has an object, "the hypochondriac"? There is no way in any theory of grammar that a noun takes a direct object. With T-G, there is no problem. Both of Hodges' and Whitten's corrections are admissible, but the reason is that "Howard plays the hypochondriac" is a deep sentence. In (A) it has been embedded under Adverb, and Howard himself taxes his wife's patience, as shown in this T-G diagram:[4]

---

[4] Note that this diagram also suffices for the possible paraphrase of (A):

(A1) Howard taxes his wife's patience when he plays the hypochondriac.

(D1)

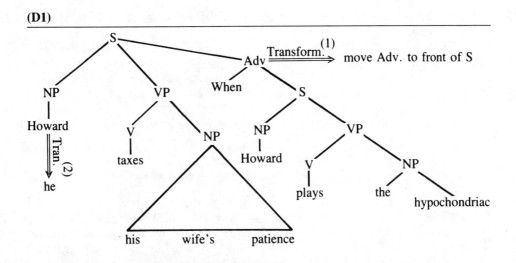

Transformation 2, changing *Howard* to *he* takes place after transformation 1. In (B), the sentence "Howard plays the hypochondriac" undergoes [poss - - *ing*] transformation and fills the subject position, creating not only a stylistic difference, but a connotative one, as shown in diagram (D2). Note that the T-G explanation not only explains in a manner consistent with the rest of the grammar, but also shows why (A) above actually says that Howard is taxing, whereas (B) says his action is, a distinction Hodges & Whitten don't make. Given the ad hoc, imprecise analyses that their lack of coherent theory leads to, traditionalists often don't seem to have a principled basis to justify such distinctions. Ultimately, traditional terminology like "mixed construction" and "awkwardness" leads to needless complications in the grammar. Because such terms are undefined, if not undefinable, they lack explanatory power. T-G is simpler and more effective not only

(D2)

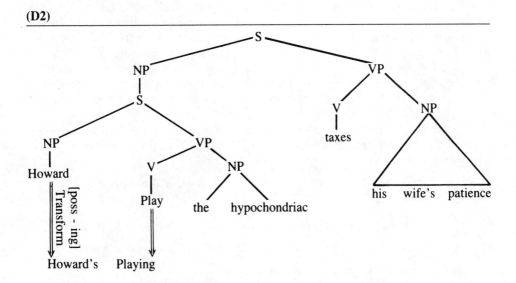

because of its coherence, but because it always explains in terms of the basic sentence and a few embedding and deletion rules.

Another example of the needless proliferation of terms in traditional grammar is afforded by *Harbrace's* conventional treatment of "misplaced parts, dangling modifiers" (Hodges and Whitten, 1972:273–281). Transformational grammar treats these, predictably, as one error. All are caused by improper deletion, as explained below. In contrast, *Harbrace College Handbook* carefully delineates dangling participial, gerund, and infinitive phrases and dangling elliptical clauses. The term *dangling* is defined as

> a construction that hangs loosely within a sentence; the term *dangling* is applied primarily to incoherent verbal phrases and elliptical clauses. A dangling modifier is one that does not refer clearly and logically to some word in the sentence.
>
> (p. 277)

"Hangs loosely" is, if anything, vaguer than "awkward" to the non-proficient writer. "Incoherent" is precise enough. However, not one example given of dangling anything is incoherent. Each is not only interpretable, but quite usual in ordinary conversation. There's the rub for dangling constructions. Because ordinary speech is so ephemeral, and must be coded so quickly, there seems to be a general rule for understanding: "Interpret on the basis of the nearest thing it could mean given the context." This is why we can understand babies and foreigners. In speech, application of language rules needn't be exact, only exact enough so an interpretation can be made. Furthermore, speech is aided by gesture, tone of voice, and facial expression, all decoding aids denied in writing. Students often carry over speech habits to their writing. They have to be apprised of the difference in convention between the two modes of communicating. An unacceptable construction may be perfectly coherent, yet because it defies literary syntax, mark its writer as uneducated. Thus, the *Harbrace* example

> Taking our seats, the game started.
>
> (p.278)

apparently means *we* took our seats. However, the canons of the written dialect demand that the subject of the embedded sentence be identical to the subject of the main, so that this should mean: "The game took our seats." Our knowledge of the world tells us this is impossible, so that the correct meaning of "we took our seats" is forced. The fact that something can be understood is no guarantee that it is syntactically correct. Native speakers often reject as ungrammatical perfectly comprehensible and coherent structures; for example: "John disappeared the cake." Thus, equating ungrammatical items with incoherence, as *Harbrace College Handbook* does, vitiates the concept of correctness in syntax, so vital to the rhetoric class.

Since all of the dangling phrase-types presented in *Harbrace College Handbook* admit of the same explanation, as noted above, all will be considered together, one from each of the categories that the book presents:

> (7) The evening passed very pleasantly, eating candy and playing the radio.
>
> (p. 278)

> (8) By mowing the grass high and infrequently, your lawn can be beautiful.
>
> (p. 279)

> (9) To write well, good books must be read.
>
> (p. 279)

Students used to the concept of transformed sentences have no difficulty retrieving the deeper structures. They readily supply:

(7a) The evening passed pleasantly. We ate candy. We played the radio.
(8a) Your lawn can be beautiful. (by) You mow the grass high and infrequently.
(9a) Good books must be ready by anyone (in order to, for) (Anyone, People) write (s) well.

Hodges and Whitten do ask, after (8), "Who is to do the mowing?" (p.279). Actually, no native speaker has any difficulty understanding that the mowing is done by *you,* even in the dangling construction. Furthermore, Hodges and Whitten's correction

By *mowing the grass* . . . you can have a beautiful lawn

doesn't have a surface subject on *mowing* either. Yet, no explanation is offered for this correction's not being dangling. That is, Hodges & Whitten never say why "By mowing" in one instance doesn't inform us who is doing it, but in the second, does. Using the concept of deep structure and embedded sentences, the students see graphically that the subjects of embedded and main sentences aren't identical in (7–9) above, respectively. Therefore, no subject can be deleted in any of these as they stand. The students learn one simple rule: if a subject of an embedded sentence is deleted, it must be identical to the surface subject of the main sentence. By contrast, teaching students what infinitives, gerunds, and participles are, much less explaining when they "hang loosely," involves needless hours of class time. Then, too, with no notion of deep structure and transformations, no rationale can be offered for when we rightly can or can't supply a particular subject if it hasn't been overtly stated as in (7–9) above.

For instance, *Harbrace* offers as a correction for (7):

(7b) We passed the evening pleasantly, eating candy and playing the radio.
(Hodges and Whitten, 1972: 278)

Lacking a theory of deep structure and transformations, they offer no rationale for changing the subject of *pass.* The T-G approach demands that reasons be given for all corrections. As just noted, there is a general rule in writing "It can't be deleted unless it's repeated." The subjects of *eating* and *playing* have been deleted, but the only surface subject is *evening.* An *evening* can't eat or play; hence a subject must be provided which can. This subject must be animate and probably human, as humans play radios. *Eat* and *play,* must, of course, share the same deleted subject as they are joined by *and.* Only if the subject is identical may it be deleted and the verbs so joined. Fortunately, *pass* may also have a human subject if the time passed is made an object.[5] Since there is no context provided, any human subject may be selected; hence, the given correction of "The evening passed . . ." to "We passed the evening . . ." This may seem to be nit-picking. Indeed, for such a simple correction it would be, except that much of what actually occurs in themes is not so obvious. By always insisting upon principled explanations the professor ensures that students become used to analyzing language, paying close attention to sentence structure.

T-G sometimes explains to students why they are prone to certain errors. Thus, one reason for the creation of dangling constructions as in (7) is that the writer is aware of

---

[5] For details of case grammar see Fillmore, 1968. For its application to rhetoric, see Chaika, 1972, 1974.

the deep structure noun. Therefore, he embeds sentences with the deep noun in mind, forgetting that, in writing at least, only surface subjects count for deletion.

The correction of (8) also proceeds by supplying a subject for the embedded sentence:

(8b) If you mow the grass high and infrequently, your lawn can be beautiful.

OR

(8c) By mowing the grass . . . you can have a beautiful lawn.

Again, this last is offered by *Harbrace* and involves rewriting the main sentence. When this text does such rewriting, it offers no explanation, unlike the T-G corrections which proceed directly from the deep structures of the given sentences.

Finally, (9) can be corrected to:

(9b) To write well, anyone must read good books.

Harbrace corrects (9) to:

(9c) To write well, a student must read good books.

However, there is a general rule of deletion that says that *anyone* or its equivalent can be deleted. This operates throughout the language, as in "To know her is to love her" which means "For anyone to know her is for anyone to love her." The problem in (9) is actually that "good books must be read" is a passive sentence with its agent deleted. It must have an active counterpart. "Anyone must read good books." In the passive, the [*by + anyone*] can be omitted by regular rule of agent deletion. *Harbrace's* making *student* the subject of *read* is unmotivated, as there is no rule of "*student* deletion" in the absence of that noun elsewhere in the grammar. Furthermore, patently (9) must refer to all people not just students. Finally, *Harbrace* never explains that (9) dangles only because the main sentence has been passivized, so that the agent no longer appears as subject; thus, their correction simply reinstates that agent subject by conversion back to the active. A paraphrase utilizing the passive transformation might also be discussed for its stylistic effects:

(9d) For anyone to write well, good books must be read.

T-G encourages paraphrasing as traditional grammars do not. It keeps before the student always that there are many ways to express one idea but that each must conform to the rules of the language.

The dangling elliptical clause as presented by *Harbrace* can be troublesome to students, especially since the given definition is circular: "An elliptical clause—that is, a clause with an implied subject and verb . . ." (p. 280). Structural cues are more helpful. Question words: *who, what, which, when, while, where,* all double as sentence embedders. The NP following them must represent a complete deep structure sentence. Thus, when we see the *Harbrace Handbook* example

(10) When only a small boy, Father took me with him to Denver.

(p. 280)

we know this must mean "When I was a small boy," but that the "I was" was erroneously deleted. *Harbrace Handbook* does supply the "I was," but gives no rationale for so doing. This makes correction a matter of mind reading.

T-G grammar automatically considers other possibilities by virtue of its rules. The verb BE and its subject frequently can be deleted in embedded sentences. Here it can't be, only because the surface structure subject of the embedded and main sentences are not identical. If the main sentence is transformed so that "I" becomes its surface subject, the "ellipsis" can remain. That is "I was" can be deleted:

(10a) When only a small boy, I was taken to Denver by my father.

Harbrace doesn't even consider this quite ordinary alternative, perhaps because it confounds the category of "elliptical clause."

The tree diagrams of T-G grammar are exceptionally useful for two knotty composition problems: comma splices and fragments. It is very easy for students to map their theme sentences on the basic tree. If every position under S is filled and a new S must be started, the student sees where a conjunction or embedder is required. For instance, the following comma splice gets mapped in (D3).

(11) Oscar's car broke down last week, it's a clunker.

(D3)

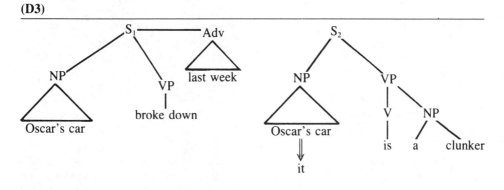

There is no place to fit "it's a clunker" under S1. As there is no conjunction or embedder preceding "it's," there is no way to attach it to any part of that sentence. The student readily sees that this must be punctuated as a separate sentence. Alternatively, an embedder like *because* could be employed to heighten the causal relationship between the event and the explanation. Then, too, since "Oscar's car" is mentioned in both sentences, the second could be embedded by *which*, as:

(11a) Oscar's car, which is a clunker, broke down last week.

For some reason, the act of tree diagraming leads to the cessation of comma splices. There seems to be psychological validity to such an approach to "sentence sense." Peter Blackwell, Headmaster of the Rhode Island School for the Deaf, reports (personal communication) that drawing trees is a potent method of teaching the deaf what a sentence is. He has elementary school children making syntactic trees. Teachers in my workshops found that tree diagraming of their own sentences was an easy task for fourth graders.

Fragments are equally amenable to visual explication. The idea of sentence must be defined in structural terms, for it is structure, not thought, complete or otherwise, that signals an independent sentence. For instance, native speakers have no difficulty distinguishing nonsense sequences as sentences or fragments, despite the fact that no "thought" can be distinguished. Note,

(12) The glorbey dale gyred a biffle.

This is a sentence, whereas the following is not:

(13) Glinking a darby biffle

The structural cues in (12) show us that a [NP + VP] has been completed, whereas those of (13) show us that the subject NP and *BE* are omitted, as *-ing* on a verb signals an independent predication only if an auxiliary *BE* precedes it, as in *is going, can be going, has been going*. The *-ing* on a verb with no auxiliary always denotes an embedded sentence. Here, there is no sentence into which (13) is inserted; hence, it is a fragment. In order to display such fragments, we must *add* aux (auxiliary) to our VP, as in (D4):

(D4)

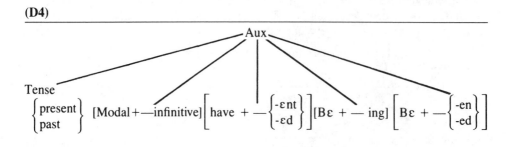

Note: Where—indicates, verb or next auxiliary is inserted. *Examples:* will go; will have gone; is going; is gone; shall be going; can have been going; must have been being paid.

If an *-ing* has been utilized as a full verb without its requisite auxiliary, this fact leaps up at the student as [one] who is inserting a fragment into the tree. Similarly, if the vital subject NP is missing, its lack is instantly seen, more quickly than from a long-winded verbal explanation. A common fragment type serves as example:

(14) Twitching his tail impatiently.

(D5)

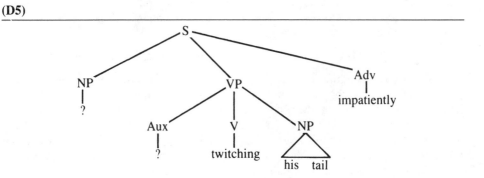

That the subject NP and requisite auxiliary, *BE,* are missing is self-evident.

Fragments, actually, often are another instance of improper deletion. In conversation, it is usual not to repeat parts of a sentence already uttered. Instead, only the new constructions are supplied with the understanding that they be mentally tacked onto the original. This habit not only speeds communication, but reinforces the unity of discourse. The propensity toward fragments in writing is but a carryover of this phenomenon. Indeed, students readily see that deliberate use of fragments is one way to simulate a casual, conversational style.

A complete comparison of traditional and transformational grammars in terms of efficacy for pedagogy would require a fair-sized tome. The foregoing attempts to show that T-G, because of its coherence and simplicity, provides a rational basis for correction of errors and discussion of style. Moreover, because equivalent sentences, paraphrases, are an integral part of T-G syntax, as are the consequences of applying different transformations, students are automatically taught sentence creation in the grammar lessons. Because T-G is so discoverable, whether because it conforms to the speaker's own intuitions, or its simplicity, or both, students can easily supply paraphrases and analyses on their own. This, in turn creates an interest in discussing language which is vital to rhetoric. Using a T-G model, the professor assures students that by virtue of their humanity, they already know a great deal about language. This is reinforced when students see that they can create transformations and judge grammaticality often as accurately as the professor when syntax is discussed. It isn't that the teacher's superior familiarity with written dialect is questioned. It's just that students see they already possess a tremendous body of language knowledge upon which they can build. This is not true of complex, often counterintuitive, traditional models of grammar. Nor does traditional grammar provide a natural basis for exercises in sentence creation. T-G, with its theory of sentence embedding which emphasizes deep structure complete sentences underlying surface fragments, provides a natural model for combining and separating sentences for different effects. Hence, which grammar is chosen for the rhetoric classroom may have a profound effect on what is learned in that class. Transformational grammar, if understood by the teacher, can create a good learning environment.

The question naturally arises whether one must be a full-fledged linguist to use T-G grammar. Teachers in my writing workshop have learned enough in eight weeks to utilize T-G both for devising exciting lessons and for correcting student compositions. They report to me that their sutdents, many very low achievers, not only responded with surprising enthusiasm to grammar discussions, but afterwards produced writing far beyond what anyone had thought possible.[6]

The texts for this workshop were Rosenbaum and Jacobs, *Transformations, Style and Meaning;* Jacobs & Jacobs, *College Writer's Handbook;* and Elgin's *Pouring Down Words*. There are several new and old explications of modern syntax available, but since each has its merits and shortcomings, no titles can be recommended without a review, preferably comparative. For structural definitions of the parts of speech, so much more learnable than the traditional semantic ones, Francis (1958) still stands.

---

[6] Notions of deep structure and transformations were typically introduced by having students break long sentences into their several kernels; then, where possible, retransforming kernels into paraphrases of the original. It was found that even fourth graders could do this with ease. Furthermore, mapping sentences on trees was not at all difficult, even for the "lowest" high school groups. That they could do it, moreover, spurred these adolescents in subsequent writing assignments. I am especially indebted to Mr. Vincent Ciunci of Pawtucket East High School, RI, and Ms. Bonnie Olchowski of Central High School, Providence, RI, for showing me what such high school students could learn from a T-G methodology. Neither of these teachers had any T-G training beyond my workshop.

The unwary must be cautioned. Some texts, such as *The Holt Guide,* may actually contain sections describing T-G (pp. 496–500), apparently knowledgeably; yet in no way are they modern grammars. The section is window dressing. Most of the analyses of error are traditional; none, or virtually none, of the insights of T-G are actually applied. Irmscher, for instance, consistently fails to treat the passive as a transformation from an active (pp. 445, 453, 454), just as the bulk of his explanations are wholly pre-T-G. The mere inclusion of trees and terms like "kernel sentence" does not make a transformational grammar. Rather, look to see if the rules are presented only in the context of sentences showing when to and when not to use a construction. Note if several possible paraphrases are offered, with some discussion of when each is most appropriate. Look for discussions of presupposition as a governing factor in choice of transformation. Check whether the text consistently presents sentence types as transformations from kernel(s). Even if the text passes "the T-G test," however, don't be afraid to question any sentence analysis that doesn't accord with your native speaker intuition. Any grammarian occasionally falls into the trap of a glib analysis that doesn't cover enough instances. Besides, improving on some other scholar's rule is delicious.

BIBLIOGRAPHY

Bach, Emmon & Robert Harms, eds. *Universals in Linguistic Theory.* New York: Holt, Rinehart & Winston, 1968.

Chafe, Wallace. *Meaning and the Structure of Language.* Chicago: University of Chicago Press, 1970.

Chaika, Elaine. *Models of Grammar and the Pedagogical Problem.* Diss. Brown University, 1972.

———. "Who Can Be Taught?" *College English,* 35 (Feb. 1974), 575–583.

Elgin, Suzette. *Pouring Down Words.* Englewood Cliffs, NJ: Prentice-Hall, 1975.

Fillmore, Charles. "The Case for Case," in Bach & Harms, eds. *Universals in Linguistic Theory.* New York: Holt, Rinehart & Winston, 1968.

Francis, W. Nelson. *The Structure of American English.* New York: The Ronald Press, 1958.

Hodges, John & Mary Whitten, eds. *Harbrace College Handbook, Seventh Edition.* New York: Harcourt, Brace, Jovanovich, 1972.

Irmscher, William. *The Holt Guide to English.* New York: Holt, Rinehart & Winston, 1972.

Jacobs, Roderick & Peter Rosenbaum. *Transformations, Style, and Meaning.* Waltham, MA: Xerox College Publishing, 1971.

Jacobs, Suzanne & Roderick Jacobs. *The College Writer's Handbook, Second Edition.* New York: John Wiley & Sons, 1976.

Krashen, Stephen. "Two Studies in Adult Second Language Learning." Paper delivered at Linguistic Society of America, annual meeting 1973, San Diego, CA.

O'Hare, Frank. *Sentence Combining.* NCTE Research Report #15. Urbana, IL, 1973.

DISCUSSION QUESTIONS

1. How might Chaika modify her article after reading Chomsky's lecture with its revision of the concept of surface structure?

2. How and to what extent has knowledge of traditional school grammar been relevant to your own writing?

3. Does Chaika's semantic distinction between, for example, *tried to get married* and *tried getting married* accord with your own language experience?

4. Do Chaika's examples of T-G applications offer specific implications for understanding and eliminating any problems in your own writing?

5. On what basis can the inclusion of a T-G unit in a composition text fairly be considered "window-dressing"?

6. How much work in T-G grammar do you think a writing teacher should have had?

KENNETH S. GOODMAN
YETTA M. GOODMAN

The Goodmans, both professors of education at the University of Arizona, are a distinguished team of teachers and research scholars in the field of reading. Yetta Goodman was president of the National Council of Teachers of English in 1979, and Kenneth Goodman received its distinguished research award in 1975. Both have published books and articles in the field.

LEARNING ABOUT PSYCHOLINGUISTIC PROCESSES BY ANALYZING ORAL READING

Over the past dozen years we have studied the reading process by analyzing the miscues (or unexpected responses) of subjects reading written texts. We prefer to use the word *miscue* because the term *error* has a negative connotation and history in education. Our analysis of oral reading miscues began with the foundational assumption that reading is a language process. Everything we have observed among readers from beginners to those with great proficiency supports the validity of this assumption. This analysis of miscues has been in turn the base for our development of a theory and model of the reading process.

In this paper we will argue that the anlysis of oral reading offers unique opportunities for the study of linguistic and psycholinguistic processes and phenomena. We will support this contention by citing some concepts and principles that have grown out of our research.

We believe that reading is as much a language process as listening is. In a literate society there are four language processes: two are oral (speaking and listening), and two are written (writing and reading). Two are productive and two receptive. In the study and observation of productive language, we may analyze what subjects say or write; however, except for an occasional slip of the tongue, typographical error, or regression to rephrase, speech and writing offer no direct insight into the underlying process of what the speaker or writer intended to say. The study of receptive language—listening and reading—is even more difficult. Either we analyze postlistening or postreading performance, or we contrive controlled-language tasks to elicit reactions for analysis.

Reading aloud, on the other hand, involves the oral response of the reader, which can be compared to the written text. Oral readers are engaged in comprehending written language while they produce oral responses. Because an oral response is generated while meaning is being constructed, it not only is a form of linguistic performance but also provides a powerful means of examining process and underlying competence.

Consider how Peggy, a nine-year-old from Toronto, reads aloud. Peggy was chosen by her teacher as an example of a pupil reading substantially below grade level. The story she read was considered to be beyond her current instructional level. Peggy read the story hesitantly, although in places she read with appropriate expression. Below are the first fourteen sentences (S1–S14) from "The Man Who Kept House" (1964, pp. 282–283).

In this and other excerpts from the story the printed text is on the left; on the right is the transcript of Peggy's oral reading.

text	transcript
(S1a) Once upon a time there was a wood-man who thought that no one worked as hard as he did.	(S1b) Once upon a time there was a wood-man. He threw . . . who thought that no one worked as hard as he did.
(S2a) One evening when he came home from work, he said to his wife, "What do you do all day while I am away cutting wood?"	(S2b) One evening when he . . . when he came home from work, he said to his wife, "I want you do all day . . . what do you do all day when I am always cutting wood?"
(S3a) "I keep house," replied the wife, "and keeping house is hard work."	(S3b) "I keep . . . I keep house," replied the wife, "and keeping . . . and keeping . . . and keeping house is and work."
(S4a) "Hard work!" said the husband.	(S4b) "Hard work!" said the husband.
(S5a) "You don't know what hard work is!	(S5b) "You don't know what hard work is!
(S6a) You should try cutting wood!"	(S6b) You should try cutting wood!"
(S7a) "I'd be glad to," said the wife.	(S7b) "I'll be glad to," said the wife.
(S8a) "Why don't you do my work some day?	(S8b) "Why don't you . . . Why don't you do my work so . . . some day?
(S9a) I'll stay home and keep house," said the woodman.	(S9b) "I'll start house and keeping house," said the woodman.
(S10a) "If you stay home to do my work, you'll have to make butter, carry water from the well, wash the clothes, clean the house, and look after the baby," said the wife.	(S10b) "If you start house . . . If you start home to do my work, well you'll have to make bread, carry . . . carry water from the well, wash the clothes, clean the house, and look after the baby," said the wife.
(S11a) "I can do all that," replied the husband.	(S11b) "I can do that . . . I can do all that," replied the husband.
(12a) "We'll do it tomorrow!"	(S12b) "Well you do it tomorrow!"
(S13a) So the next morning the wife went off to the forest.	(S13b) So the next day the wife went off to the forest.
(14a) The husband stayed home and began to do his wife's work.	(S14b) The husband stayed home and began to do his wife's job.

Peggy's performance allows us to see a language user as a functional psycholinguist. Peggy's example is not unusual; what she does is also done by other readers. She processes graphic information: many of her miscues show a graphic relationship between the expected and observed response. She processes syntactic information: she substitutes noun for noun, verb for verb, noun phrase for noun phrase, verb phrase for verb phrase. She transforms: she omits an intensifier, changes a dependent clause to an independent clause, shifts a "wh-" question sentence to a declarative sentence. She draws on her conceptual background and struggles toward meaning, repeating, correcting, and repro-cessing as necessary. She predicts grammar and meaning and monitors her own success.

She builds and uses psycholinguistic strategies as she reads. In short, her miscues are far from random.

From such data one can build and test theories of syntax, semantics, cognition, comprehension, memory, language development, linguistic competence, and linguistic performance. In oral reading all the phenomena of other language processes are present or have their counterparts, but in oral reading they are accessible. The data are not controlled and clean in the experimental sense. Even young readers are not always very considerate. They do complex things for which we may be unprepared; and, not having studied the latest theories, they do not always produce confirming evidence. But they are language users in action.

MISCUES AND COMPREHENSION

If we understand that the brain is the organ of human information processing, that the brain is not a prisoner of the senses but that it controls the senory organs and selectively uses their input, then we should not be surprised that what the mouth reports in oral reading is not what the eye has seen but what the brain has generated for the mouth to report. The text is what the brain responds to; the oral output reflects the underlying competence and the psycholinguistic processes that have generated it. When expected and observed responses match, we get little insight into this process. When they do not match and a miscue results, the researcher has a window on the reading process.

Just as psycholinguists have been able to learn about the development of oral-language competence by observing the errors of young children, so we can gain insights into the development of reading competence and the control of the underlying psycho-linguistic processes by studying reading miscues. We assume that both expected and unexpected oral responses to printed texts are produced through the same process. Thus, just as a three-year-old reveals the use of a rule for generating past tense by producing "throwed" for "threw" (Brown, 1973), so Peggy reveals her control of the reading process through her miscues.

We use two measures of readers' proficiency: *comprehending,* which shows the readers' concern for meaning as expressed through their miscues, and *retelling,* which shows the readers' retention of meaning. Proficient readers can usually retell a great deal of a story, and they produce miscues that do not interfere with gaining meaning. Except for S3, S8, and S9, all of Peggy's miscues produced fully acceptable sentences or were self-corrected. This suggests that Peggy's usual concern was to make sense as she read. In contrast, many nonproficient readers produce miscues that interfere with getting meaning from the story. In a real sense, then, a goal of reading instruction is not to eliminate miscues but to help readers produce the kind of miscues that characterize proficient reading.

Miscues reflect the degree to which a reader is understanding and seeking meaning. Insight can be gained into the reader's development of meaning and the reading process as a whole if miscues are examined and researchers ask: "Why did the reader make this miscue and to what extent is it like the language of the author?"

Miscue analysis requires several conditions. The written material must be new to the readers and complete with a beginning, middle, and end. The text needs to be long and difficult enough to produce a sufficient number of miscues. In addition, readers must receive no help, probe, or intrusion from the researcher. At most, if readers hesitate for more than thirty seconds, they are urged to guess, and only if hesitation continues are they told to keep reading even if it means skipping a word or phrase. Miscue analysis, in short, requires as natural a reading situation as possible.

Depending on the purpose of the research, subjects often have been provided with more than one reading task. Various fiction and nonfiction reading materials have been used, including stories and articles from basal readers, textbooks, trade books, and magazines. Subjects have been drawn from various levels in elementary, secondary, and adult populations and from a wide range of racial, linguistic, and national backgrounds. Studies have been concluded in languages other than English: Yiddish (Hodes, 1976), Polish (Romatowski, 1972), and American Sign Language (Ewoldt, 1977). Studies in German and Spanish are in progress.

The open-ended retellings used in miscue analysis are an index of comprehension. They also provide an opportunity for the researcher or teacher to gain insight into how concepts and language are actively used and developed in reading. Rather than asking direct questions that would give cues to the reader about what is significant in the story, we ask for unaided retelling. Information on the readers' understanding of the text emerges from the organization they use in retelling the story, from whether they use the author's language or their own, and from the conceptions or misconceptions they reveal. Here is the first segment of Peggy's retelling:

> um . . . it about this woodman and um . . . when he . . . he thought that he um . . . he had harder work to do than his wife. So he went home and he told his wife, "What have you been doing all day." And then his wife told him. And then, um . . . and then, he thought that it was easy work. And so . . . so . . . so his wife, so his wife, so she um . . . so the wife said, "well so you have to keep," no . . . the husband says that you have to go to the woods and cut . . . and have to go out in the forest and cut wood and I'll stay home. And the next day they did that.

By comparing the story with Peggy's retelling and her miscues, researchers may interpret how much learning occurs as Peggy and the author interact. For example, although the story frequently uses "woodman" and "to cut wood," the noun used to refer to setting, "forest," is used just twice. Not only did Peggy provide evidence in her retelling that she knew that "woods" and "forest" are synonymous, but she also indicated that she knew the author's choice was "forest." The maze she worked through until she came to the author's term suggests that she was searching for the author's language. Although in much of the work on oral-language analysis mazes are not analyzed, their careful study may provide insight into oral self-correction and the speaker's intention.

There is more evidence of Peggy's awareness of the author's language. In the story the woodman is referred to as "woodman" and "husband" eight times each and as "man" four times; the wife is referred to only as "wife." Otherwise pronouns are used to refer to the husband and wife. In the retelling Peggy used "husband" and "woodman" six times and "man" only once; she called the wife only "wife." Peggy always used appropriate pronouns in referring to the husband and wife. However, when cow was the antecedent, she substituted "he" for "she" twice. (What does Peggy know about the sex of cattle?)

Comparing Peggy's miscues with her retelling gives us more information about her language processes. In reading, Peggy indicated twice that "said" suggested to her that a declarative statement should follow: One such miscue was presented above (see S2); the other occurred at the end of the story and is recorded below.

text	*transcript*
(S66a) Never again did the woodman say to his wife, "What did you do all day?"	(S66b) Never again did the woodman say to his wife, "That he . . . what did you do all day?"

In both instances she corrected the miscues. In the retelling she indicated that after "said" she could produce a question: "And then, from then on, the husband did . . . did the cutting and he never said, 'What have you been doing all day?' " Even though she had difficulty with the "wh-" question structure in her reading, she was able to develop the language knowledge necessary to produce such a structure in her retelling.

It has puzzled teachers for a long time how a reader can know something in one context but not know it in another context. Such confusion comes from the belief that reading is word recognition; on the contrary, words in different syntactic and semantic contexts become different entities for readers, and Peggy's response to "keep house" suggests this. In S3, where the clauses "I keep house" and later "and keeping house" occur for the first time, Peggy produced the appropriate responses but repeated each several times. In S9 she produced "stay home and keep house" as "start house and keeping house," and she read the first phrase in S10 as "If you start home to do my work." The phrase "keep house" is a complex one. First, to a nine-year-old "keep" is a verb that means being able to hold on to or take care of something small. Although "keeping pets" is still used to mean taking care of, "keeping house" is no longer a common idiom in American or Canadian English. When "stay home" is added to the phrase "keep house," additional complexities arise. Used with different verbs and different function words, "home" and "house" are sometimes synonyms and sometimes not. The transitive and intransitive nature of the verbs as well as the infinitive structure, which is not in the surface of a sentence, add to the complexity of the verb phrases.

Peggy, in her search for meaning and her interaction with the print, continued to develop strategies to handle these complex problems. In S14 she produced "stayed home"; however, in S35 she encountered difficulty with "keeping house" once again and read: "perhaps keeping house . . . home and . . . is . . . hard work." She was still not happy with "keeping house." She read the phrase as written and then abandoned her correct response. Throughout the story "home" appears seven times and "house" appears ten times. Peggy read them correctly in every context except in the patterns "staying home" and "keeping house." Yet she continued to work on these phrases through her interaction with the text until she could finally handle the structure and could either self-correct successfully or produce a semantically acceptable sentence. Thus Peggy's miscues and retelling reveal the dynamic interaction between a reader and written language.

ORAL AND WRITTEN LANGUAGE

The differences between oral and written language result from differences of function rather than from any differences in intrinsic characteristics. While any meaning that can be expressed in speech can also be expressed in writing and vice versa, we tend to use oral language for face-to-face communication and written language to communicate over time and space. Oral language is likely to be strongly supported by the context in which it is used; written language is more likely to be abstracted from the situations with which it deals. Written language must include more referents and create its own context minimally supplemented by illustrations. Written language can be polished and perfected before it is read; therefore, it tends to be more formal, deliberate, and constrained than oral language.

For most people, oral-language competence develops earlier than written-language competence because it is needed sooner. But children growing up in literate societies begin to respond to print as language almost as early as they begin to talk. Traffic signs and commercial logos, the most functional and situationally embedded written language in the environment, are learned easily and early (Goodman & Goodman, 1979). Despite their differences and history of acquisition, oral- and written-language processes become parallel for those who become literate; language users can choose the process that better suits their purposes. Readers may go from print to meaning in a manner parallel to the way they go from speech to meaning.

Since the deep structure and rules for generating the surface structure are the same for both language modes, people learning to read may draw on their control of the rules and syntax of oral language to facilitate developing proficiency in written language. This is not a matter of translating or recoding print to sound and then treating it as a listening task. Rather, it is a matter of readers using their knowledge of language and their conceptualizations to get meaning from print, to develop the sampling, predicting, confirming, and correcting strategies parallel to those they use in listening. Gibson and Levin (1975) seem to agree with us that recoding print to sound is not necessary for adults, and Rader (1975) finds that it is not even necessary for children.

We are convinced that oral and written language differ much more in how they are taught than in how they are learned. Although most oral-language development is expected to take place outside of school, the expectation is that literacy development will take place in school programs under teachers' control. Attempts to teach oral language in school are not noted for being as successful as what children achieve outside school. Similarly, literacy instruction is not totally successful. Furthermore, capable readers and writers demonstrate the use and integration of strategies not included in the structured literacy curriculum. Although this paper is primarily concerned with the study of the reading process and not with reading instruction, we are convinced that a major error in many instructional programs has been to ignore or underestimate the linguistic competence and language-learning capabilities of children learning to read.

READING AND LISTENING:
ACTIVE RECEPTIVE PROCESSES

A producer of language can influence the success of communication by making it as complete and unambiguous as possible. The productive process must carry through from thought to underlying structures to graphic or oral production. Written production, particularly, is often revised and edited to correct significant miscues and even to modify the meaning. The receptive process, however, has a very different set of constraints. Listeners and readers must go through the reverse sequence from aural or graphic representation to underlying structure to meaning. Receptive language users are, above all, intent on comprehending—constructing meaning.

Readers and listeners are *effective* when they succeed in constructing meaning and are *efficient* when they use the minimal effort necessary. Thus, through strategies of predicting, sampling, and confirming, receptive language users can leap toward meaning with partial processing of input, partial creation of surface and deep structures, and continuous monitoring of subsequent input and meaning for confirmation and consistency.

Many miscues reflect readers' abilities to liberate themselves from detailed attention to print as they leap toward meaning. Consequently, they reverse, substitute, insert, omit, rearrange, paraphrase, and transform. They do this not just with letters and single words, but with two-word sequences, phrases, clauses, and sentences. Their own experiences, values, conceptual structures, expectations, dialects, and life styles are integral to the process. The meanings they construct can never simply reconstruct the author's conceptual structures. That every written text contains a precise meaning, which readers passively receive, is a common misconception detrimental to research on comprehension.

We have argued above that reading is an active, receptive process parallel to listening. Oral-reading miscues also have direct parallels in listening. Although listening miscues are less accessible, since listeners can only report those they are aware of, still these must be quite similar to reading miscues. Anyone who has ever tried to leave an oral message knows that listening miscues are surely not uncommon. In both reading and listening, prediction is at least as important as perception. What we think we have heard or read is only partly the result of sensory data; it is more the result of our expectations.

A major difference between reading and listening is that the reader normally can regress visually and reprocess when a miscue has led to a loss of meaning or structure. The listener, on the other hand, must reprocess mentally, await clarification, or ask a speaker to explain. Furthermore, the speaker may continue speaking, unaware of the listener's problem. Readers are in control of the text they process; listeners are dependent upon the speaker.

The receptive activity during the reading process is especially evident in two different types of miscues—those that are semantically acceptable with regard to the whole text and those that are semantically acceptable only with the prior portion of the text. A miscue may change the author's meaning; but, if it fits the story line, it can be considered semantically acceptable. For example, in S2 of the story Peggy read "when I am always cutting wood?" for "while I am away cutting wood?" These two miscues produced a sentence that fitted in with the meaning of the rest of the story. The more proficient a reader is, the greater the proportion of semantically acceptable miscues. The proportion and variety of high-quality miscues suggest that good readers constantly integrate their backgrounds with that of the author as if they are putting the author's ideas into their own language. This ability is often seen in oral language as a mark of understanding. "Tell me in your own words" is a common request from teachers to discover whether a student has understood something.

Semantically acceptable miscues may be more complex than word-for-word sub-stitutions. Many readers produce reversals in phrase structures such as "said Mother" for "Mother said" or other types of restructuring like the one Peggy produced in S12: "Well, you do it tomorrow" instead of "We'll do it tomorrow." Although it seems that Peggy merely substituted "well" for "we'll" and inserted "you," the miscue is more complex at phrase and clause levels. Peggy inserted an interjection prior to the subject "you" to substitute for the noun phrase. There was also a substitution of the verb phrase because the verb marker "will," indicated by the contraction of "we'll," was omitted, and the verb "do" has been substituted for "will do." In addition, Peggy shifted intonation so that the wife rather than the husband says the sentence. Apparently Peggy thought the wife was going to speak, and her shifted intonation reflected changes in the grammatical pattern and meaning, although the sentence retained its acceptability within the story.

A reader's predicting strategies are also evident in those miscues that are acceptable with the prior portion of the text but that do not produce fully acceptable sentences. Such miscues often occur at pivotal points in sentences such as junctures between clauses or phrases. At such points the author may select from a variety of linguistic structures; the reader may have the same options but choose a different structure. Consider these examples from Peggy's reading:

text	*transcript*
(S38a) ''I'll light a fire in the fireplace and the porridge will be ready in a few minutes.''	*(S38b) ''I'll light a fire in the fireplace and I'll . . . and the porridge will be ready in a flash . . . a few minutes.''*
(S48a) Then he was afraid that she would fall off.	*(S48b) Then he was afraid that the . . . that she would fall off.*

Peggy's use of ''I'll'' for ''the'' in the second clause of the first example is highly predictable. Since ''and'' generally connects two parallel items, it is logical that the second clause would begin with the subject of the first clause. The substitution of ''the'' for ''she'' in the second example occurs frequently in young readers' miscues. Whenever an author uses a pronoun to refer to a previously stated noun phrase, a reader may revert to the original noun phrase. The reverse phenomenon also occurs. When the author chooses a noun phrase for which the referent has been established earlier, the reader may use that pronoun. In the second example, Peggy was probably predicting ''the cow'' which ''she'' refers to. These miscues clearly show that Peggy is an active language user as she reads.

Readers' monitoring of their predictions is observed through their self-correction strategies. Clay's (1967) research and our own (Goodman & Burke, 1973) support the idea that a miscue semantically acceptable to the story line is less likely to be corrected than one that is not acceptable or is acceptable only with the immediately preceding text. For example, of the ten semantically acceptable miscues that Peggy produced in the first excerpt, she only corrected one (''all'' in S11). However, of the six miscues that were acceptable only with the prior portion of the text, she corrected four. Such correction strategies tend to occur when the readers believe they are most needed: when a prediction has been disconfirmed by subsequent languages cues.

Sentences that are fully unacceptable are corrected less than sentences with miscues acceptable with the prior portion of the sentence. Perhaps it is harder for readers to assign underlying structure to sentences in which fully unacceptable miscues occur. Without such a structure, they have difficulty unpacking the grammatical or conceptual complexity of a sentence and so are less able to self-correct. We believe that the two most important factors that make reading difficult are hard-to-predict grammatical structures and high conceptual load (Smith & Lindberg, 1973). What any particular reader finds hard to predict and difficult depends on the reader's background and experience.

The linguistic and conceptual background a reader brings to reading not only shows in miscues but is implicit in the developing concepts or misconceptions revealed through the reader's retelling. Peggy added to her conceptual base and built her control of language as she read this story, but her ability to do both was limited by what she brought to the task. In the story, the husband has to make butter in a churn. Peggy made miscues whenever buttermaking was mentioned. For example, in S10 she substituted ''bread'' for ''butter.'' The next time ''butter'' appears, in S15, she read it as expected. However, in S18, ''Soon the cream will turn into butter,'' Peggy read ''buttermilk'' for ''butter.''

Other references to buttermaking include the words "churn" or "cream." Peggy read "cream" correctly each time it appears in the text but had trouble reading "churn." She paused about ten seconds before the first appearance of "churn" and finally said it. However, the next two times churn appears, Peggy read "cream."

text	*transcript*
(S25a) . . . he saw a big pig inside, with its nose in the churn.	(S25b) . . . he saw a big pig inside, with its nose in the cream.
(S28a) It bumped into the churn, knocking it over.	(S28b) It jumped . . . it bumped into the cream, knocking it over.
(S29a) The cream splashed all over the room.	(S29b) The cream shado . . . splashed all over the room.

In the retelling Peggy provided evidence that her miscues were conceptually based and not mere confusions:

> And the husband was sitting down and he poured some buttermilk and um . . . in a jar. And, and, he was making buttermilk, and then, he um . . . heard the baby crying. So, he looked all around in the room and um, . . . And then he saw a big, a big, um . . . pig. Um . . . He saw a big pig inside the house. So, he told him to get out and he, the pig, started racing around and um . . . he di . . . he um . . . bumped into the buttermilk and then the buttermilk fell down and then the pig, um . . . went out.

Peggy, who is growing up in a metropolis, knows little about how butter is made in churns. Although she knows that there is a relationship between cream and butter, she does not know the details of that relationship. According to her teacher, she has also taken part in a traditional primary-school activity in which sweet cream is poured into a jar, closed up tightly, and shaken until butter and buttermilk are produced. Although Peggy's miscues and retelling suggest that she had little knowledge about buttermaking, the concept is peripheral to comprehending the story. All that she needed to know was that buttermaking is one of the wife's many chores that can cause the woodman trouble.

Reading is not simply knowing sounds, words, sentences, and the abstract parts of language that can be studied by linguists. Reading, like listening, consists of processing language and constructing meanings. The reader brings a great deal of information to this complex and active process. Whenever readers are asked to read something for which they do not have enough relevant experience they have difficulty. That is why even proficient adult readers use such excuses as "It's too technical" and "He just writes for those inside the group." For this reason, proficient readers go to pharmacists or lawyers, for example, to read certain texts for them.

ORAL AND SILENT READING

The basic mode of reading is silent. Oral reading is special since it requires production of an oral representation concurrently with comprehending. The functions of oral reading are limited. It has become a kind of performing art used chiefly by teachers and television and radio announcers. We have already explained why we use oral reading in miscue analysis. But a basic question remains: are oral and silent reading similar enough to justify generalizing from studies of oral-reading miscues to theories and models of silent reading?

In our view a single process underlies all reading. The cycles, phases, and strategies of oral and silent reading are essentially the same. The miscues we find in oral reading occur in silent reading as well. Current unpublished studies of nonidentical fillers of cloze blanks (responses that do not match the deleted words) show remarkable correspondence to oral-reading miscues and indicate that the processes of oral and silent reading are much the same (Lindberg, 1977; Rousch).[1]

Still, there are some dissimilarities between oral and silent reading that produce at least superficial differences in process. First, oral reading is limited to the speed at which speech can be produced. It need not, therefore, be as efficient as rapid silent reading. Next, superficial misarticulations such as "cimmanon" for "cinnamon" occur in oral reading but are not part of silent reading. Also, oral readers, conscious of their audience, may read passages differently than if they read them silently. Examples are production of nonword substitutions, persistence with several attempts at problem spots, overt regression to correct miscues already mentally corrected, and deliberate adjustments in ensuing text to cover miscues so that listeners will not notice them. Furthermore, oral readers may take fewer risks than silent readers. This can be seen in the deliberate omission of unfamiliar words, reluctance to attempt correction even though meaning is disrupted, and avoidance of overtly making corrections that have taken place silently to avoid calling attention to miscues. Finally, relatively proficient readers, particularly adults, may become so concerned with superficial fluency that they short-circuit the basic concern for meaning. Professional oral readers, newscasters for example, seem to suffer from this malady.

THE READER: AN INTUITIVE GRAMMARIAN

Recently, linguists have equated or blurred the distinction between deep structure and meaning. We, however, find this distinction useful to explain a common phenomenon in our subjects' reading. Moderately proficient readers are able to cope with texts that they do not understand by manipulating language down to a deep structure level. Their miscues demonstrate this. Readers may also correctly answer a question they do not understand by transforming it into a statement and then finding the sentence in the text with the appropriate structure. Thus, when confronted by an article entitled, "Downhole Heave Compensator" (Kirk, 1974), most readers claim little comprehension. But they can answer the question, "What were the two things destroying the underreamers?" by finding the statement in the text that reads, "We were trying to keep drillships and semi-submersibles from wiping out our underreamers" (p. 88). Thus it is dangerous for researchers and teachers to equate comprehension with correct answers obtained by manipulating and transforming grammatical structures. Our research may not prove the psycholinguistic reality of the deep structure construct as distinct from meaning, but it demonstrates its utility. In our research we judge syntactic acceptability of sentences separately from semantic acceptability, since readers often produce sentences that are syntactically, but not semantically, acceptable. In S10 Peggy read "If you stay home to do my work" as a sentence which she finally resolved as "If you start home to do my

---

[1] Rousch, P. *Miscues of special groups of Australian readers*. Paper presented at the meeting of the International Reading Association, Miami, May 1977.

work." This is syntactically acceptable in the story but unacceptable semantically since it is important to the story line that the woodman "stay home."

The first evidence used to separate syntactic from semantic acceptability came from research on the phenomenon of nonwords. Such nonsense words help give us insight into readers' grammatical awareness because sentences with nonwords often retain the grammatical features of English although they lose English meaning. Use of appropriate intonation frequently provides evidence for the grammatical similarity between the nonword and the text word. Nonwords most often retain similarities not only in number of syllables, word length, and spelling but also in bound morphemes—the smallest units that carry meaning or grammatical information within a word but cannot stand alone, for example, the *ed* in carri*ed*. The following responses by second, fourth, and sixth graders represent nonwords that retain the grammatical function of the text (Goodman & Burke, 1973). A different subject produced each response. Notice that "surprise" and "circus" are singular nouns and that, in producing the nonwords, the subjects did not produce *s* or *z* sounds at the ends of the words as they would with plural nouns.

expected response	*nonword substitutions*
Second graders:	
The *surprise* is in my box.	*supra, suppa*
Then they will know the *circus* is coming.	*ception, chavit*
"Penny, why are you so *excited?*" she asked.	*excedled, encited*
Fourth graders:	
He saw a little *fawn.*	*frawn, foon, faunt*
What queer *experiment* was it?	*espressment, explerm, explainment*
Sixth graders:	
Clearly and *distinctly* Andrew said "philosophical."	*distikily, distintly, definely*
A *distinct* quiver in his voice	*dristic, distinc, distet*

There is other evidence in miscues of readers' strong awareness of bound morphemic rules. Our data on readers' word-for-word substitutions, whether nonwords or real words, show that, on the average, 80 percent of the observed responses retain the morphemic markings of the text. For example, if the text word is a non-inflected form of a verb, the reader will tend to substitute that form. If the word has a prefix, the reader's substitution will tend to include a prefix. Derivational suffixes will be replaced by derivational suffixes, contractional suffixes by contractional suffixes.

Miscue analysis provides additional data regarding the phenomenon of grammatical-function similarity. Every one of Peggy's substitution miscues in the portion of the text provided earlier had the same grammatical function as the text word. Table 1 (Goodman & Burke, 1973) indicates the percentage of miscues made by a sample of fourth and sixth graders that had the same grammatical function. These substitutions were coded prior to any attempt to correct the miscues.

Our research suggests that nouns, noun modifiers, and function words are substituted for each other to a much greater degree than they are for verbs. Out of 301 substitution

Table 1   Percent of miscues with grammatical function similarity

Identical Grammatical Function	4th Graders	6th Graders
Nouns	76%	74%
Verbs	76%	73%
Noun modifiers	61%	57%
Function Words	67%	67%

Source: K. S. Goodman and C. L. Burke, *Theoretically based studies of patterns of miscues in oral reading performance, final report.* Detroit: Wayne State University, 1973 (ERIC Document Reproduction Service No. ED 079 708), p. 136.

miscues produced by fourth graders, only three times was a noun substituted for a noun modifier, and sixth graders made such a substitution only once out of 424 miscues.

Evidence from miscues occurring at the beginning of sentences also adds insight into readers' awareness of the grammatical constraints of language. Generally, in prose for children, few sentences begin with prepositions, intensifiers, adjectives, or singular common nouns without a preceding determiner. When readers produced miscues on the beginning words of sentences that did not retain the grammatical function of the text, we could not find one miscue that represented any of these unexpected grammatical forms. (One day we will do an article called "Miscues Readers Don't Make." Some of the strongest evidence comes from all the things readers could do that they do not.)

Readers' miscues that cross sentence boundaries also provide insight into the readers' grammatical sophistication. It is not uncommon to hear teachers complain that readers often read past periods. Closer examination of this phenomenon suggest that when readers do this they are usually making a logical prediction that is based on a linguistic alternative. Peggy did this with the sentence (S35): "Perhaps keeping house is harder than I thought." As previously noted, Peggy had problems with the "keeping house" structure. She resolved the beginning of this sentence after a number of different attempts by finally reading "perhaps keeping home is hard work." Since she has rendered that clause as an independent unit, she has nothing to which she can attach "than I thought." She transformed this phrase into an independent clause and read it as "Then I thought."

Another example of crossing sentence boundaries occurs frequently in part of a story (Moore, 1965) we have used with fourth graders: "He still thought it more fun to pretend to be a great scientist, mixing the strange and the unknown" (p. 62). Many readers predict that "strange" and "unknown" are adjectives and intone the sentence accordingly. This means that when they come to "unknown" their voice is left anticipating a noun. More proficient readers tend to regress at this point and correct the stress patterns.

PARTS AND WHOLES

We believe that too much research on language and language learning has dealt with isolated sounds, letters, word parts, and even sentences. Such fragmentation, although it simplifies research design and the complexity of the phenomena under study, seriously distorts processes, tasks, cue values, interactions, and realities. Fortunately, there is now a strong trend toward use of full, natural linguistic text in psycholinguistic research. Kintsch (1974) notes:

> Psycholinguistics is changing its character. . . . The 1950's were still dominated by the nonsense syllables . . . the 1960's were characterized by the use of words lists, while the present decade is witnessing a shift to even more complex learning materials. At present, we have reached the point where lists of sentences are being substituted for word lists in studies of recall recognition. Hopefully, this will not be the end-point of this development, and we shall soon see psychologists handle effectively the problems posed by the analysis of connected texts. (p. 2)

Through miscue analysis we have learned an important lesson: other things being equal, short language sequences are harder to comprehend than long ones. Sentences are easier than words, paragraphs easier than sentences, pages easier than paragraphs, and stories easier than pages. We see two reasons for this. First, it takes some familiarity with the style and general semantic thrust of a text's language for the reader to make successful predictions. Style is largely a matter of an author's syntactic preferences; the semantic context develops over the entire text. Short texts provide limited cues for readers to build a sense of either style or meaning. Second, the disruptive effect of particular miscues on meaning is much greater in short texts. Longer texts offer redundant opportunities to recover and self-correct. This suggests why findings from studies of words, sentences, and short passages produce different results from those that involve whole texts. It also raises a major issue about research using standardized tests, which utilize words, phrases, sentences, and very short texts to assess reading proficiency.

We believe that reading involves the interrelationship of all the language systems. All readers use graphic information to various degrees. Our research demonstrates that low readers in the sixth, eighth, and tenth grades use graphic information more than high readers. Readers also produce substitution miscues similar to the phonemic patterns of text words. Although such phonemic miscues occur less frequently than graphic miscues, they show a similar pattern. This suggests that readers call on their knowledge of the graphophonic systems (symbol-sound relationships). Yet the use of these systems cannot explain why Peggy would produce a substitution such as "day" for "morning" or "job" for "work" (S13). She is clearly showing her use of the syntactic system and her ability to retain the grammatical function and morphemic constraints of the expected response. But the graphophonic and syntactic systems alone cannot explain why Peggy could seemingly understand words such as "house," "home," "ground," and "cream" in certain contexts in her reading but in other settings seemed to have difficulty. To understand these aspects of reading, one must examine the semantic system.

Miscue analysis shows that readers like Peggy use the interrelationships among the grammatical, graphophonic, and semantic systems. All three systems are used in an integrated fashion in order for reading to take place. Miscue analysis provides evidence that readers integrate cue systems from the earlier stages of reading. Readers sample and make judgments about which cues from each system will provide the most useful information in making predictions that will get them to meaning. S2 in Peggy's excerpt provides insight into this phenomenon. Peggy read the sentence as follows: "One evening when h . . . he came home from work he said to his wife I want you [two second pause] do . . . all day [twelve second pause]." After the second pause, Peggy regressed to the beginning of the direct quote and read, "What do you do all day when I am always cutting wood?'' Peggy's pauses and regression indicate that she was saying to herself: "This doesn't sound like language" (syntactically unacceptable); "this doesn't make sense" (semantically unacceptable). She continued slowly and hesitatingly, finally stopping altogether. She was disconfirming her prediction and rejecting it. Since it did not make sense, she decided that she must regress and pick up new cues from which to make new predictions.

In producing the unacceptable language segment "I want you do all day," Peggy was using graphic cues from "what" to predict "want." She was picking up the syntactic cues from "he said," which suggested that the woodman would use a declarative statement to start his conversation. From the situational context and her awareness of role relationships, she might have believed that, since the husband was returning home from working hard all day, he would be initially demanding to his wife. When this segment did not make sense to Peggy, she corrected herself. She read the last part of the sentence, "when I am always cutting wood," confidently and without hesitation. She was probably unaware that "when" and "always" are her own encodings of the meaning. She had made use of all three of the cue systems; her words fit well into the developing meaning of the story; therefore, she did not need to correct her miscues. We believe that both children and adults are constantly involved in this process during their silent reading but are unaware that it is taking place.

There are many times when the developing meaning of a story is so strong that it is inefficient to focus on the distinctive graphic cues of each letter or each word. As long as the phrase and clause structure are kept intact and meaning is being constructed, the reader has little reason to be overly concerned with graphic cues. Peggy read "day" for "morning" in S13 and "job" for "work" in S14. These miscues have a highly synonymous relationship to the text sentence, but they are based on minimal or no graphic cues. In S38 Peggy indicated to an even greater extent her ability to use minimal graphic cues. Her prediction was strong enough; and she was developing such a clear meaning of the situation that "in a flash" was an acceptable alternative to "in a few minutes," although she caught her miscue and corrected it.

Another phenomenon that exemplifies the interrelationship among the cueing systems is the associations readers develop between pairs of words. Any reader, regardless of age or ability, may substitute "the" for "a." Many readers also substitute "then" for "when," "that" for "what," and "was" for "saw" in certain contexts. What causes these associations is not simply the words' look-alike quality. Most of these miscues occur with words of similar grammatical function in positions where the resulting sentence is syntactically acceptable. Differences in proficiency are reflected in the ways readers react to these miscues: the more proficient reader corrects when necessary; the less proficient reader, being less concerned with making sense or less able to do so, allows an unacceptable sentence to go uncorrected. This process can only be understood if researchers focus on how readers employ all the cues available to them. For too long the research emphasis on discrete parts of language has kept us from appreciating how readers interrelate all aspects of language as they read.

Sooner or later all attempts to understand language—its development and its function as the medium of human communication—must confront linguistic reality. Theories, models, grammars, and research paradigms must predict and explain what people do when they use language and what makes it possible for them to do so. Researchers have contrived ingenious ways to make a small bit of linguistic or psycholinguistic reality available for examination. But then what they see is often out of focus, distorted by the design. Our approach makes fully available the reality of the miscues readers produce as they orally read whole, natural, and meaningful texts.

Huey (1908/1968) once said:

> And so to completely analyze what we do when we read would almost be the acme of a psychologist's achievements, for it would be to describe very many of the most intricate workings of the human mind, as well as to unravel the tangled story of the most remarkable specific performance that civilization has learned in all its history.
>
> (p. 6)

To this we add: oral reading miscues are the windows on the reading process at work.

REFERENCES

1. Clay, M. M. The reading behaviour of five year old children: A research report. *New Zealand Journal of Educational Studies*, 1967, **2**, 11–31.

2. Ewoldt, C. *Psycholinguistic research in the reading of deaf children*. Unpublished doctoral dissertation, Wayne State University, 1977.

3. Gibson, E., & Levin, H. *The psychology of reading*. Cambridge, Mass.: M.I.T. Press, 1975.

4. Goodman, K. S., & Burke, C. L. *Theoretically based studies of patterns of miscues in oral reading performance, Final Report*. Detroit: Wayne State University, 1973. (ERIC Document Reproduction Service No. ED 079 708)

5. Goodman, K. S., & Goodman, Y. Learning to read is natural. In L. B. Resnick & P. Weaver (Eds.), *Theory and practice of early reading* (Vol. 1). Hillsdale, N.J.: Erlbaum Associates, 1979.

6. Hodes, P. *A psycholinguistic study of reading miscues of Yiddish-English bilingual children*. Unpublished doctoral dissertation, Wayne State University, 1976.

7. Huey, E. B. *The psychology and pedagogy of reading*. Cambridge, Mass.: M.I.T. Press, 1968. (Originally published, 1908.)

8. Kintsch, W. *The representation of meaning in memory*. Hillsdale, N.J.: Erlbaum Associates, 1974.

9. Kirk, S. Downhole heave compensator: A tool designed by hindsight. *Drilling-DCW*, June 1974.

10. Lindberg, M. A. *A description of the relationship between selected pre-linguistic, linguistic, and psycholinguistic measures of readability*. Unpublished doctoral dissertation, Wayne State University, 1977.

11. The man who kept house. In J. McInnes, M. Gerrard, & J. Ryckman (Eds.), *Magic and make believe*. Don Mills, Ontario: Thomas Nelson, 1964.

12. Moore, L. Freddie Miller: Scientist. In E. A. Betts & C. M. Welch (Eds.), *Adventures here and there* (Book V-3). New York: American Book Co., 1965.

13. Rader, N. L. *From written words to meaning: A developmental study*. Unpublished doctoral dissertation, Cornell University, 1975.

14. Romatowski, J. *A psycholinguistic description of miscues generated by selected bilingual subjects during the oral reading of instructional reading material as presented in Polish readers and in English basal readers*. Unpublished doctoral dissertation, Wayne State University, 1972.

15. Smith, L. A., & Lindberg, M. A. Building instructional materials. In K. S. Goodman (Ed.), *Miscue analysis: Application to reading instruction*. Urbana, Ill.: ERIC Clearinghouse on Reading and Comprehension Skills and National Council of Teachers of English, 1973.

DISCUSSION QUESTIONS

1. How can "miscues" reveal a person's linguistic competence? Compare the Goodmans' opinion with that of DeStefano.

2. Would you conjecture that the proportion of miscues correlates most closely with age, variety of experience, intelligence, or linguistic sophistication?

3. In an impromptu oral reading by a class member, note and analyze the miscues—if any.

4. Does a miscue that is syntactically but not semantically appropriate suggest why some students find it hard to answer comprehension questions?

5. How might the insights offered by the Goodmans be used in improving the reading prowess of students?

JOHANNA S. DeSTEFANO

The author, a professor of childhood education and co-director of the Program on Language and Social Policy at The Ohio State University, is a well-known writer of books and articles in the field. She is also an associate editor of the forthcoming Dictionary of Reading and Related Terms *and has served as a member of the NCTE Commission on the English Language.*

There are cultures, not all of which are literate; but there is also a world-wide culture of which writing [and reading] is a part. Literacy, for better or for worse, will have to be taught, for all of the foreseeable future.

Dwight Bolinger, 1975, 497

LANGUAGE AND READING

One of the major extensions of communicative competence in our society is literacy. Learning to read is a major achievement in a student's language development, and the ability to read plays a major role in many people's lives, since the written word has a central function in our society as a primary transmitter of the culture. In fact, the place of reading instruction is probably questioned less than almost any other aspect of the school curriculum. Parents, teachers, national leaders—almost everyone—express concern about students learning to read. Gibson and Levin (1975) note that "reading has received more attention than any other aspect of education. The ability to read *well* (my emphasis) is the basis for success in school and later, so there is small wonder that instruction in the early grades is organized around learning to read" (1975, p. 3).

Moira McKenzie, speaking of reading in Great Britain—but applicable here in the United States as well, asserts rightly, I think, that "there is no controversy about the fundamental importance of becoming literate. The argument wages around the most effective and long lasting way in which this can happen" (*Contact,* 1976). This question of how to teach reading most effectively has engendered a variety of reading methods and materials, research studies and countless articles and books on the topic. It is also a crucial question for us as teachers that remains a sometimes puzzling one to answer, despite all of the time spent on it, in the face of certain students' difficulties in learning to read—at all curricular levels. And in the face of certain other students who know how to read when they come to school—the "early reader" group.

However, we do know the answer—or answers—is one that encompasses a variety of factors including fitting a learner with appropriate materials and learning strategies. We include learner-specific factors such as previous exposure to reading (and degree thereof), motivation to learn to read and interest in reading, and possible cultural differences and attitudes toward reading. We also include the reading process—what does one do when one reads? What is highly skilled reading? And what does one do when one learns to read well? How do we mesh this process with instructional strategies and materials for successful reading? What strategies, techniques, and materials are useful for which individual students?

And we will ask, of course, what contributions can linguistically based studies make to our answers to the question of how to teach reading—of expanding communicative competence in one of the most crucial ways in a person's life? First, answers to how to teach reading must include information on the nature of the learner. Much current research is being done on the reading process—what one does when one reads. Also, we now know much more about possible cultural influences on learning to read and on the motivation to learn to read—another aspect of the learner.

To elaborate, linguistic and psycholinguistic studies in particular have begun to give us insight into the reading process, both in the sense of decoding (being able to recognize the words on the printed page) as reading and in the sense of comprehension as reading. Much emphasis has been placed on comprehension or getting meaning from the written language, because we recognize that decoding simply doesn't go far enough. We don't want our students to "bark at print," as it's sometimes rather graphically put. (I get an image of trained seals lined up in rows balancing flash cards on their noses.) How many of us have heard students read orally, sometimes fluently, and then not be able to answer comprehension questions? What has broken down in the reading process, in the development of literacy, so that a student can't understand what he or she has read? (And this does not refer to a fifth-grader decoding a college physics text; it refers to conceptually "appropriate" material.) We are now beginning to be able to answer some of these questions.

Also the teacher's behavior in this process of learning to read and of reading itself is a major factor. Some studies have shown, in fact, that teacher behavior may be one of the most crucial factors in reading success. If this is the case, linguistic findings—to be useful—will have to influence that behavior in some way. We will explore some possibilities for teacher behavior here.

Discussed below in some detail is the sociocultural environment of both the learner and the teacher with attendant influences on the learning and teaching of reading. In recent years, an awareness of the importance of these factors in success in reading has been growing among teachers and educators. This awareness is partly because of a broader understanding of the concept of cultural clash as it enters into the area of reading. We know we need to understand where, geographically and socially, the students come from if we're to maximize communicative competence, including competence in literacy.

Answers must also provide information on methods and materials, even if they are negative instances of what materials aren't too useful or what strategies aren't particularly productive. And sometimes it is not that the information provided by linguists is not perhaps helpful, but that the specific applications made by the linguists are not useful. For example, because of linguistics, we know quite a bit about how the phonemes of American English correspond to patterns in the written language that must be "deciphered" in reading. But materials based on very high regularity between phonemes and letters of the alphabet—"A fat cat sat on a mat"—have been found to be less effective in teaching reading than was hoped. This whole area of linguistic contributions to methods and materials will be dealt with in detail later in this chapter.

THE READING PROCESS

What does one do when reading? A good question, as it is not something we can see or hear unless the reading is being done aloud. We can ask questions about the material. But we can only infer what the reader *does* when reading silently. This is where we need a theory to propose the outlines of the process and to explain the observable behavior.

The theory must also take into account the printed page, which becomes the input instead of speech. In reading we've moved to another language mode—that of writing rather than speaking. The theory, then, must take into account the learner, the task—reading, and the medium—the written language. From these specifications—who the learner is, what goes on during reading, and what the characteristics of the printed page are—a teacher can form hypotheses about reasonable instructional procedures and materials. These hypotheses, in turn, may be linguistically based in a broad sense. The teacher can then test the hypotheses with students, see the results, and either modify or have the theory confirmed in some aspects.

This is the prime importance of any theory—to serve as a system of "explanations" for observable behavior, which serves as a basis for making hypotheses and as a coder of events. It serves as an organizer of experience and provides a set of "suggestions" for further organization of experience. . . . In a rule-governed way they modify their sets of language rules more and more toward the adult set, but in their own way. It is postulated that they make hypotheses about what these rules are (unconsciously, of course) and modify them according to input from the environment sifted through their developmental patterns.

Teachers can also be characterized as hypothesizers. They, too, must look at the environment—the students in the room—and check their hypotheses against the students' behavior. A more efficient hypothesizer has an articulated theory or set of theories about, for example, students' reading behavior. This is the importance of theory: to provide as sound a base as possible for hypothesizing about what well help students learn to read—that is, to acquire the mature process of reading—and then to provide an interpretive framework for the data collected or observed about the students' reading. Theory should not justify practice, as it has all too often been used to do in the classroom, but it should perform the two above functions at least in the light of observation. The problem of theory being used to justify practice is mentioned because linguistic theory has sometimes been used in just this way in education. And when any theory that has not been translated thoughtfully into practical applications is applied directly, the results are often less than educative. What generally happens is that the content of the theory is directly taught to students who may see few implications in it for them. What should have remained teacher knowledge was made student knowledge as well. And the actual lessons were justified by the assertion that they reflected the latest theory.

THEORIES ABOUT THE READING PROCESS

With that preamble about the role of theory in teaching reading, what sorts of theories are there about the process of reading? As you can well imagine, there are many—too many to be covered in a book of this type and size. But there are parts of several that seem to have quite a bit of hypothesizing power as well as explanatory power for teachers of reading.

To begin with, reading can be characterized as a "conceptual process, a tool for thinking and learning that can take the place of first-hand experience" (Gibson, 1972, p. 3). Gibson and Levin also define reading as ". . . extracting information from text" and further, ". . . as an actual process, self-directed by the reader in many ways and for many purposes" (1975, p. 5). The perceptual part of the process or processes is thus put in perspective vis-à-vis the meaning aspect. This is important because some definitions of reading largely rest on "code-cracking," in which certain perceptual aspects are primarily stressed. In other words, some scholars would maintain that when a student has learned to decipher words and letters from the printed page, the ability to read has largely been acquired. But in the above definitions, meaning is heavily stressed as a part of the reading process.

In reading, as with speech, meaning is carried by means of language. However, the eye is the major receptor rather than the ear, especially with accomplished readers. And the graphemic system (letters and their combinations) is primary in the written language instead of the phonemic system (sounds and their combinations) as in speech. These differences have implications for learning to read, that is, for the acquisition of the reading process. However, the basic process is part of our language system as a whole, and many of these strategies employed by children learning to speak are probably employed by those same children learning to read.

Reading Strategies

What are some of these strategies used by the learner? Certainly we can again place the student in the role of hypothesizer as we did for language acquisition. Information comes to the student about those marks on the printed page. This information comes on a variety of levels—semantic, syntactic, graphophonic (meaning the phoneme-grapheme, sound-symbol correspondence), perceptual, and simply mechanical in the sense of learning to move your eyes from left to right when reading English. Ultimately the student learns to coordinate all these levels, connecting the various processes to ". . . extract a sequence of cues from printed texts and relate these, one to another, so that he understands the precise message of the text'' (Clay, 1972, p. 8). Probably this is done by the student's formulating hypotheses and then testing them through experience with reading. And again, we assume that the student moves through a series of hypotheses, constantly moving toward an adult set for reading.

Remember, of course, that the beginning reader may make use of radically different hypotheses from those of a mature reader. You have probably noticed students who move their lips when they are reading silently. This is evidently a residue from making overt phoneme-grapheme correspondences in the early reading stages. This is when the child would say ''cat'' when c-a-t was presented. Children spend a great deal of time *saying* what they see rather than *nonverbally* recognizing it. This is not ''acceptable'' adult reading behavior. These stages will be examined in more detail later in this chapter.

Hypothesizing is a process of seeking patterns, a very general human activity. Any theory of the reading process should ''plug into'' some of the most general processes of human cognition and behavior.

But a theory also must give explanatory power to actual reading behavior, which is observed by you as the teacher. In order to do this, we need more specific concepts within the theory. One concept you are already familiar with is that of distinctive features. . . . There are many different types of distinctive features, based upon the various linguistic, psychological, and physiological systems in the reading process. One set is perceptual features in letters and printed words. For example, there are feature contrasts in letters such as straight versus curve (*l* vs. *c*), horizontal or vertical versus diagonality within straight as a category (— vs. /, as in Z), and open versus closed within curve as a category (*c* vs. *o*). Gibson also includes redundancy as in *W*, where one half the letter is like the other half versus discontinuity as in *L* (Gibson and Levin, 1975).

Often with beginning readers, you can see the general language process of progressive differentiation among features taking place. First a student may confuse *b* and *d,* not taking into account the *direction* of the round part of the letter in relation to the straight part. Later that is sorted out with little difficulty by most students. (A few may have perceptual problems, which make those discriminations difficult.) So at first the similarity between *b* and *d* is noticed, then the difference that makes the difference. Progressive differentiation may also operate on letter positions in a word. It is not at all unusual for beginning readers to confuse *saw* with *was*. It's as though as long as all the letters are there, the specific arrangement doesn't matter. Later it does, as the student comes to know that *saw* and *was* are letter sequences that signal two different words with very different meanings. There are distinctive differences in the positions of the *s* and *w*. Another example is the pair *mane* and *mean,* although Fries would also add *man* to that set (1962, p. 201). The difference between *man* and *mane* is one letter; the difference between *mane* and *mean* is one of letter placement differences being distinctive.

The skilled reader actively searches for distinctive differences, with knowledge of the rules supplying information on where to look for them. But remember that a skilled reader's rule set is different from a beginning reader's. The former probably doesn't perceive single letters but, instead, clumps of them, which are distinctive in English orthography, such as *th* and *ch*. This perceptual information is then skillfully organized into higher-order units, which ultimately yield meaning. Gibson (1973) notes that beginning readers often have trouble grasping the meaning of what they're reading. It's as though the perceptual tasks are almost too much for them, and they haven't learned to process the features that will yield the meaning. Certainly this is not surprising; it's a type of "not seeing the forest for the trees." Again, *saw* and *was* are similar perceptually but not semantically. And phonologically no one would confuse the two. Yet those two systems may be ignored in face of the perceptual similarity—the student reading *was* as *saw* or vice versa. But rule systems are built to handle the entire reading process, and it's not surprising that many beginning readers start with a piece of the system. A very real burden is on the beginning reader, who has these hierarchies of distinctive features to learn and sort out.

FEATURE-ANALYTIC THEORY OF READING

Probably one of the most direct applications of the concept of features to the reading process is Frank Smith's feature-analytic theory of reading (1971 and 1975), which postulates feature lists for virtually all the aspects of reading from decoding through meaning. The semantic feature lists . . . consist of a bundle of features, some distinctive and some not, that specify the meaning of the lexical item or *word,* this latter term being more common in discussions of reading. There are also the feature lists identifying a phoneme and the lists identifying a letter in the alphabet and, presumably, sets of letters. Such a model takes the place of the more traditional explanations of reading and gives a more unified explanation to the phoneme-grapheme correspondences than does the traditional phonics approach.

It is proposed that the skilled reader bypasses the acoustic cues or features and uses the visual set to determine the meaning of a word or phrase or sentence. As I have noted elsewhere, "Sound is evidently bypassed for a direct use of the visual system." (DeStefano, 1977) In other words, there is little or no "inner speech" while the person is reading and *no* lip movement. The individual instead has another set of cues that are *not* sound cues. Certainly that would help to explain the speed a skilled reader can achieve without sacrificing meaning. But there are other sets of features that enter into "reading for meaning." Syntactic features also enter into extracting meaning from the printed page. In other words, we use knowledge of how words pattern in English to predict the next group of words. If you were to read, "She ate———and butter," you'd probably fill *bread* in that slot. Part of your choice would rest on syntactic restrictions specifying a noun in that position, and part would be semantic. If you were to read, "She ate bread———butter," you'd undoubtedly put in *and*. If you read, "She———bread and butter," you'd be likely to add *ate* rather than *made,* but this position has perhaps fewer restrictions on it than the others above. A less mature reader may not make the same predictions with the same ease, presumably because the feature sets are not fully acquired. Data from the above procedure and sentence repetition tasks do in fact seem to indicate that young children's feature sets are not complete; therefore, they cannot predict as well as older children or adults lexical items that fit the already begun pattern. . . .

Obviously we need to know much more about features of various types—semantic, syntactic, visual, acoustic, and more—before we can delve into detail about the ways in which a beginning reader's lists are incomplete. However, the concept of features as presented by various psycholinguists is a unifying one, with far more explanatory power about the reading process than many of the more traditional views. Sound-letter (phoneme-grapheme) correspondences don't explain enough, especially in a mature reader. Perhaps this oral-visual schema explains virtually nothing about what a fluent reader normally does. Gibson and Levin contend that ". . . the reader processes the largest structural unit that he is capable of perceiving and that is adaptive (has utility) for the task he is engaged in" (1975, p. 23). Smith asserts that "Fluent reading requires the constant making of hypotheses about meaning in advance that are tested with a minimum of visual information . . ." (1974, p. 238). Notice he doesn't even allude to sound-symbol correspondence, but only allows visual information from the printed or written symbols.

Another psycholinguistic (and psychological) concept with explanatory power for the reading process is the notion of *redundancy,* which allows in another powerful notion—prediction. A mature and fluent reader makes predictions (or hypotheses) about the printed page—meaning predictions. And redundancy helps reduce uncertainty and narrow the field of possible predictions, thus speeding up reading. Redundancy occurs when we get the same information from more than one source. "General consensus" is redundant because "consensus" already carries in its meaning "general." Repetition of words and phrases is obvious redundancy and can be very effective as in poems, children's stories, and the like. We have old saws like "Practice (repetition) makes perfect." In natural language, we also have a great deal of redundancy of various types. In speech we have acoustic, syntactic, and semantic redundancy. In the written language we have visual, orthographic (spelling system), syntactic, and semantic redundancy (Smith, 1971). Let's look closer at redundancy within the written language:

The student didn't know the an———.

Visually, if that came at the end of the page you could simply turn it and find the last letters. Orthographically, you "know" the *an* won't be followed by certain letters such as *f, h, p, a, r,* or *z* because those combinations don't occur often or at all in English spelling patterns. Syntactically, we would expect the word to be a noun or adjective, since it follows an article *the* and is in a common English noun or adjective position. We wouldn't expect another verb or adverb there. Semantically, we know something about what happens to students in classrooms. They are asked questions and expected to give *answers.* It could be *anagram* possibly, but not *antibody,* which you don't *know* but may *know about.* All this information is redundant; the skilled reader doesn't need four different sets of cues as to what the rest of the word is. Smith, who explains this process very clearly (1971, pp. 20–1), suggests that the skilled reader needs much less visual information than the beginning reader. The former's three systems—orthographic, syntactic, and semantic—are more complete than the latter's. Thus the beginning reader may need much more redundancy—from a variety of systems—in order to extract meaning from the reading material—or may rely heavily on one type of redundancy, which is not optimal for reading, but over which he or she has some control.

There are two other types of redundancy commonly discussed. One is distributional redundancy, which has to do with the probability of a certain event or item appearing. For example, in the English orthographic system, not every letter has the same chance of occurrence in words. Some letters are far more common than others. That is part of the reason for the keys of a typewriter being arranged as they are with the *z* and *q* in extreme corners. Commonly occurring letters are the vowel letters *a, e, i,* and *o* and the consonant letters *n, s,* and *t.* According to Smith (1971, p. 22), *e* occurs 40 times more often than *z,* the least frequently used letter of the alphabet. As mature readers, we probably have a good sense of what we expect to see on the printed page based at least somewhat on distributional redundancy not only of letters but also of words. That is, given a certain topic, certain words will appear far more frequently than others. And in general writing, function or "empty" words such as *is, the, a, and,* and *so* will appear far more frequently than "content" words.

Sequential redundancy is the type of redundancy having to do with the predictability of events or items in sequence, as the term would imply. The examples:

> She ate bread and————.
> She————bread and butter.
> She ate————and butter.
> She ate bread————butter.

would all be sequential redundancy. It also occurs within words, as in g–rl. No skilled reader of American English would have trouble reading that word. In fact, sequential redundancy is recognized in Hebrew and other Semitic language writing systems to the extent that the vowel sounds are not indicated in writing, only the consonants. In English as well, consonant letters and groups probably carry a far higher information load than the vowel letters. Compare g—rl to–i– or c–ll to–e—or–a–. In c–ll, you can reduce the uncertainty at least to *cell* or *call* or *cull* (if you know that word), and context would certainly reduce even those uncertainties to one choice. Given the sentences:

> She will————me on the telephone.

and

> She studied a————under the microscope.

and

> She————ed walnuts by hand.

you can assign *call, cell,* and *cull* accurately. But a beginning reader whose language systems are not as developed could have more trouble making the assignments as the sequential redundancies could not be exploited—they haven't yet been recognized as redundancies.

A skilled reader can be far more economical in reading than a beginning reader because he or she can employ the various types of redundancy to increase reading speed. Smith states:

> . . . the more redundancy there is, the less visual information the skilled reader requires. In passages of continuous text, provided the content is not too difficult, every other letter can be eliminated from most words, or about one word in five omitted altogether, without making the passage too difficult for a reader to comprehend— provided that he has learned the rules related to letter and word occurrence and co-occurrence[1]

(Smith, 1971, p. 23).

It would seem then, that as teachers of beginning readers, we can help them discover the redundancies in the printed language and help them learn to exploit them. What can they use? According to Smith (1971), first graders can use sequential redundancy in the sense of being able to more easily identify single letters appearing in three-letter words than in isolation. By fourth grade, students could equal adults in the use of sequential redundancy of identifying letters in words. But there are other redundancies in the language that may not develop as quickly but could be exploited by students. Hopefully research will begin to reveal more specifics about these redundancies.

DIAGNOSIS OF READING

We have described only briefly some characteristics of the reading processes of the skilled reader that have been revealed in psycholinguistically oriented research and theory. As teachers you must know what a mature reader does before you can effectively help a beginning reader become fluent. And you also need to know about strategies students use to learn to read and to help them make the match with more mature strategies. What are some things they do? How can we diagnose their level of development of the ability to read? Kenneth and Yetta Goodman and Carolyn Burke have done a great deal of work on what they call the *miscue,* which they feel reveals the "psycholinguistic guessing game"—that is, the process of learning to read. In other words, students when they read *orally* attend to certain features on the printed page in correspondence with their own language systems—the phonological, syntactic, and semantic. They "guess" in trying to make all these sets match so they can derive meaning from the written material. Sometimes, since the "guesses" are not quite accurate or adequate, the student reads something that isn't actually on the page. That is called a *miscue* in the sense of *miss-cue-ing* from the material and from the student's own language and experiential systems. For example, Yetta Goodman and Burke (1974) cite the following:

> *Text: To get her poor dog a wig.*
> *Child reading: To get her poor dog play hair.*

This is obviously a high-level response, but indicative of some feature sets that don't

---

[1] *Occurrence* and *co-occurrence* are used in the sense that when a certain letter or word appears, we expect another particular one, or one from a particular set of others. So, in English, nouns or adjectives follow an article such as *the,* but not verbs or prepositions.

quite match those of more fluent readers. It wasn't that the child didn't know *wig,* but her *play hair* indicates a different concept of what a *wig* is.

Generally, the miscues made by students reading orally are patterned, and the patterns of miscues change with the skill of the reader. Less skilled readers tend to make miscues that are syntactically at variance with the text they are reading, while more skillful readers will tend to stay within a given syntactic pattern, even if it requires correction on their part of their initial reading. For example, a second grader read "Then Tiny played firmly pushing Shiny . . ." while the text read "Then Tiny playfully pushed Shiny . . ." The syntax in the oral reading definitely does not fit the syntax of the text. A fourth grader read "Tame birds may be given gravel . . ." while the text was "Tame birds *must* be given gravel . . ." Even though the meaning was changed, the syntax of the original was adhered to.

. . . [A] child's grammatical system continues to develop during school age. Knowledge of what follows what syntactically or which elements pattern with which other elements becomes refined, and patterns are probably much more apparent to a more syntactically mature student. This knowledge is revealed in the reading process through certain types of miscues.

Another developmental aspect shown in the type of miscues made is that of the semantic system. The more proficient a reader, the fewer changes he or she will make in the meaning of the text in oral reading. For example, the same second grader read "things Fox" for "Shiny Fox" with no attempt at correction. At another point he read "tribe" for "tardy" in "We are going to be tardy." (It is unlikely that he meant *tribe*— he was probably miscueing somewhat on the grapheme-phoneme relationship.) He corrected *tribe* to *tried,* again not a happy semantic choice. On the other hand, the fourth grader read "Birds have to eat gravel" while the text was "Birds have to eat *the* gravel." Looking at the whole text, the omission of *the* did nothing significant to change the meaning.

The correction of a miscue can also help to reveal stages in the acquisition of reading. A student miscueing without correcting, especially the semantic ones, may not be reading for meaning. If a student miscues but corrects to either the text or something close to the text, then some comprehension probably can be assumed. In other words, the student has gone beyond simply decoding. The corrections of the more proficient readers are in that direction—correction for meaning. Also, the more skilled readers tend to produce more complex miscues that ". . . involve more integration of the meaning, the grammatical and sound systems of the language with the graphic input and the experience and background of the child" (Goodman and Burke, 1974). Many of these miscues tend to point out strengths in a student's acquisition of reading because the tendency of mature readers to miscue to preserve the meaning of the text indicates their ability to derive meaning from the printed page. Also, staying within the same syntactic category on a miscue indicates the reader's ability to exploit at least some of the redundancies and feature sets of the syntactic system of the language.

However, I must point out that oral reading—reading aloud—is different from silent reading. There is another skill set overlay in oral reading that doesn't exist for silent reading. Thus miscues may illuminate certain aspects of the reading process, but cannot be taken to be totally revealing. They are, in my estimation though, useful as a diagnostic tool at the early stages of learning to read.

As you can see, the areas and branches of linguistics offer preliminary work on the reading process and a student's acquisition of that process. These bits and pieces have strength because of their origins in a more general linguistic theory. Obviously a great deal of research is needed—which in turn may change the existing theories substantially. But such modifications are not problematic in and of themselves. They are merely part of the entire process. However, both data collected from students who read and theory are needed, since the field of reading needs them both to pull itself out of the methods-materials quagmire onto more solid diagnostic ground where instructional behavior is motivated by a well-founded theory instead of a series of alinguistic or nonlinguistic assumptions about what it is to read.

CULTURAL INFLUENCES ON LEARNING AND TEACHING READING

As teachers wishing to maximize communicative competence through reading, we need to be aware of what cultures both we and the learner come from. The phenomenon of cultural clash . . . all too often influences behavior in the classroom to the point of blocking learning. This clash situation can and does exist for literacy learning far more than is commonly anticipated. Why, we ask. Doesn't everybody want to learn to read? Isn't this a national goal? Yes, this is a national goal; but the motivation to learn to read is a complex one, often modified by a variety of cultural and developmental factors. As a national goal, reading has been introduced to certain groups whose cultures are either not literate or, if literate, see reading in English as destructive to their culture.

Let's look at oral cultures first. There are several in the United States, which have long oral traditions: black culture, various American Indian cultures, and some aspects of Chicano culture. . . . [C]ultural information is passed largely by word of mouth and by doing—children working alongside their parents or other adults. Oral culture also contains many traditional oral forms. The toasts, or epic poems, of black culture are one example. In Finland, the national epic, the *Kalevala,* was until the late 1800s a collection of oral poems in a distinct metric pattern. These oral tales were told by people called *kanteles* (meaning, literally, singers) who would travel from village to village chanting the tales, accompanying themselves on a zitherlike instrument. The story lines of the tales were all memorized; the actual wording and use of stock phrases to finish the metric pattern of a line was up to the individual kantele. The better turn of a phrase, the more witty the kantele, the more famous he or she was. Elias Lonnröt, the man who first collected most of the oral tales and wrote them down, found one woman who knew *several hundred* with all the twists and turns of plot. With the coming of literacy to Finland, which is now about 99% literate, the kanteles are no longer to be found, since the tales are written down for all to read—and all can read them. The Finns accepted literacy in Finnish, which was, until relatively recently for Europe, an oral language, not a written one. With the coming of literacy most of the oral traditions are disappearing.[2]

In the United States many oral traditions have also disappeared with widespread literacy. But several cultures still hold to theirs, such as the toasts and other verbal forms

---

[2] The documentation for this comes from a variety of conversations I had with various Finns when visiting Finland. The *Kalevala* holds a central place in the national identity, and all school children learn large amounts of the epic by heart. We have nothing really comparable to it in our culture.

in black culture. These remaining oral forms have an ancient history, so ancient as to antedate by far the *Iliad* and the *Odyssey,* originally oral poems themselves, which were written only later. Such venerable beginnings indicate that oral traditions are not inferior to literary ones; they are simply older and different.

In an orally based culture, reading has little place or may be seen as peripheral to the cultural reward system. In other words, you get no special status by being able to read or to read well. Status accrues instead to the proficient ''rappers'' and toasters, those verbally facile who can turn a good phrase. (Remember how H. Rap Brown got his name—[see discussion of rapping in the article by Abrahams.]) Or other cultures may value the faultless recitation from memory of long sagas and rituals. There may even be taboos against writing any rituals down, much like the ban on being photographed laid down by some members of the Amish religious sect here in the United States. However, some materials are being produced that are written versions of toasts, oral poetry, and so on. Conceivably, if this trend continues, the oral cultures in this country will become literary as well—as happened in Finland. But this is only a supposition on my part, and no one knows how long it would take. However, oral cultures in the United States are surrounded by a literary culture—as Finland was too.

The dominant culture in the United States has a literary tradition; black culture and Indian cultures are oral. What does this mean for the motivation to learn to read for a child from one of these cultures? It may mean that there is relatively little, since reading is a largely unrewarded activity in his or her culture or in the subculture. Many black parents want their children to learn to read. They have adopted many of the ''mainstream'' values, including reading. But in the subculture of the child, there are other signals that essentially communicate a lack of value for reading. Labov and Robins (1973) found among black male adolescents in Harlem an almost total lack of interest in reading, particularly among those who were well integrated into the peer group, street subculture. Upon questioning it was found that members of a certain street group didn't have any idea how well each other read. Generally their reading ability was at least several years below grade level, and not one in that group was able to read above the fifth-grade level.Thus eighth graders were reading at no more than a fifth-grade level. Within the group, status and position were assigned totally independently of reading ability. As a matter of fact, any *school* success was irrelevant to the street subculture and its set of values.

What does this mean for teachers of students whose peer subculture or even adult culture is either hostile or oblivious to reading? It means that motivation certainly cannot be stirred merely by saying it's wonderful to learn to read. What satisfaction will these students get out of it *now*? How can you motivate a six-year-old by talking about the importance of reading in creating job opportunities when he or she is 18? And another problem: reading is seen within the matrix of the school subculture, toward which there may be great hostility on the part of the students and possibly the parents. It is often seen as alien to and alienating from the parents' culture. William Labov and Clarence Robins' Harlem street groups saw school as hostile and irrelevant to their lives. They tended to associate reading with feminity, as the teachers are mostly female, and girls often are able to read better than the boys. Thus if they read well, they would appear unmasculine. The boys in these groups value intelligence, but do not see any connection between intelligence and reading ability. They also value language ability, but that is oral rather than written. Motivation for reading? ''Teachers in the city schools have little ability to reward or punish members of the street culture, or to motivate learning by any means'' (Labov and Robins, 1973, p. 319).

It is highly unfortunate that when these boys grow older, they begin to subscribe to the adult values, which do hold more with the "mainstream" value set. But they lack necessary reading skills at least partly because of the cultural clash during the developmental reading years. So cultural clash can be extremely damaging and can contribute materially to failure as an adult when value sets shift.

How do we cope with such a clash? Labov and Robins suggest a cultural intermediary in the school, someone the boys can identify with and who also values reading—for example, a literate black man from their area who was once in a gang. What else could be done by the teacher individually? Certainly a realization of the clash is extremely important: the students are not "lazy" or "bad." Instead they are subscribing to a set of values that is much more important to them at that time. Also, school can be made to be a less hostile environment for these children. Cultural differences can be taken into account, and behavior appropriately evaluated. Perhaps with less hostility there can be more acceptance of the value of reading or at least a tolerance for it. Also, materials could be generated from the students' culture. The oral tales ("toasts") could be written down—along with song lyrics and other oral forms—and used as basic reading materials. In that way, one form the students know and understand could help make a bridge to literacy instruction; their culture would appear in the school. Obviously, cultural clash is a very real and difficult problem, but it is one we can deal with in order to maximize communicative competence for all students.

But what of cultures in which the adults are also hostile to literacy in English? In these cultures the problem is compounded. In black culture many of the parents are sympathetic if not extremely positive about literacy, and they speak English as their first language. On the other hand, in the Cherokee culture in Oklahoma, the adults are sympathetic to literacy in Cherokee but not in English. Among the Cherokees (Walker, undated), there has long been a literary tradition begun by Sequoya, an individual who created a syllabary for the Cherokee language evidently between 1809 and 1821 (Bolinger, 1975). A syllabary is a system of symbols in which a symbol stands for a syllable in a language rather than a single sound (phoneme). The Cherokee syllabary consists of 85 symbols, one representing the phoneme /s/, and the rest representing either vowel syllables or syllables consisting of consonant plus vowel sounds such as *sa, do,* and *lu* (Bolinger, 1975, p. 487).

It has been found to be common for an adult Cherokee to teach himself or herself to read. And the children quickly become literate. According to Willard Walker, who has researched Cherokee literacy, the Cherokees were estimated to be 90% literate in their own language *by the 1830s*. By the 1880s, it is also estimated that the Western Cherokee had a higher English literacy level than the white population of either Texas or Arkansas.

Walker states:

> Since the federal government took over the Cherokee school system in 1898, Cherokees have viewed the school as a white man's institution which Cherokee children are bound by law to attend, but over which their parents have no control. . . . Most Cherokee speakers drop out of school as soon as this is legally possible. While in school, they learn relatively little due to the language barrier and also due to this unfortunate, but accurate, definition of the school as a white man's institution. As a further complication Cherokee parents are well aware that educated children tend to leave the community, either geographically or socially. To them the school threatens the break-up of the family and division of the community, precisely those consequences which no genuinely tribal society can tolerate. . . . (undated, p. 6).

It seems clear that the startling decline during the past sixty years of both English and Cherokee literacy in the Cherokee tribe is chiefly a result of the recent scarcity of reading materials in Cherokee, and of the fact that learning to read has become associated with coercive instruction, particularly in the context of an alien and threatening school presided over by English-speaking teachers and controlled by English-speaking superintendents and PTA's which conceive of Cherokee as a 'dying' language and Cherokee school children as 'culturally improvised' candidates for rapid and 'inevitable' social assimilation. Indians and whites alike are constantly equating competence in the school with assimilations into the white middle class. . . . For the Cherokee community to become literate once again, Cherokees must be convinced that literacy does not imply the death of their society, that education is not a clever device to wean children away from the tribe. This is not a uniquely Cherokee situation. Identical attitudes toward education and the school no doubt can be found in Appalachia, in urban slums, in Afro-Asia, and, indeed, in all societies where the recruitment of individuals into the dominant society threatens the extinction of a functioning social group[3] (undated, p. 10).

We have already discussed the hostility toward school in the urban slums. School, then, is often seen as an enculturating tool of the dominant society. Since reading and literacy are a major part of "mainstream" culture, they are seen as part of that enculturation. But all too often reading failure and difficulties are blamed on physiological or psychological problems, and the cultural input is largely, if not entirely ignored. (Ethnocentrism again?) How can we talk about decoding problems if the child comes to school perhaps overtly hostile to the idea of learning to read or learning to read English? Where is the initial motivation to learn to read? And if the school is hostile to a student's culture, as all too many are, where is that motivation going to come from in school? If the teacher is also hostile, the classroom situation itself will not provide the motivation either.

What can we as teachers do? First, we can realize that the cultural hostility is only partly manifested in the school situation: cultural clash occurs 24 hours a day and not just in the school building. Generally the schools reflect the values of the dominant culture, which does negatively assess many other cultures. As teachers, you can be alert to the possibility of such clash in your classroom and in the school as a whole and examine in depth your own feelings and attitudes toward the students who come from cultures other than your own. Reading is learned in a cultural setting of which you and your students are a part. This cannot be overlooked if we are to be successful in helping more students maximize their communicative competence.

LANGUAGE VARIATION AND READING: DIALECT AND SOCIOLECT CONSIDERATIONS

Since students speak a variety of American English as their native language, what input might their sociolect or dialect forms have into the learning of reading? This is an extremely complex question, fraught with much controversy and having available relatively little research to help settle it. Kenneth Johnson and Herbert Simons (1973) have recently

---

[3] Willard Walker, "An Experiment in Programmed Cross-Cultural Education: The Import of the Cherokee Primer for the Cherokee Community and for the Behavioral Sciences," undated mimeo. Reprinted by permission of the author.

done research into black vernacular-speaking students' ability to read materials written in so-called standard English and in black vernacular to try to discover the consequences of that sociolect's forms in the reading process. Their preliminary findings indicate the children read no better in the vernacular materials than they did in the so-called standard material. They suggest one factor contributing to this lack of difference might be the fact that the students had already learned to read the so-called standard, being in the second and third grades in Oakland, California, schools. Therefore, they were already acquainted with "standard" forms in certain material and had little or no trouble comprehending them. Johnson and Simons propose that a group of students should be taught from the beginning with vernacular readers and then compared with those reading "standard" texts from the beginning. These are only some of the complexities and controversies emerging from the question about the influence of sociolect on reading.

There are reading researchers as well as teachers who feel that materials written in a vernacular variety—whether it be dialect or sociolect—are not necessary. To begin with, these varieties are oral; generally, they have no written form. So when they have to be written down, there are difficulties in deciding how to spell certain forms as well as in deciding how often to put in forms such as multiple negatives. First, the spelling problem: it seems simple, but how should /ɪŋ/, a frequent ending set of phonemes, be written—as *swimmin'* or *swimmin?* (The apostrophe is sometimes used to indicate something is "left out." But some linguists feel nothing is in fact left out. The /n/ is simply an alternate form of final /ŋ/. Hence the controversy.) Or how does one write *will,* which is often pronounced something like /wɪw/? Do you write *wiw* or *wi* or *will?* And does the student recognize *wiw* any better than *will* as being what he or she says? A study by May (1976) indicated that children who spoke Black English experienced no interference from their variety in identifying words spelled in traditional orthography. So *wiw* may be no clearer than *will.* And do we do this for so-called standard-speaking students who also say /wɪw/ in certain sound environments? No, we don't. So what forms of a variety are important in reading? We don't know. And how do we spell them? How close a phoneme-grapheme correspondence is useful? A study by Gillooly (1975) may shed some light on these questions. Initially, close correspondences such as those found in i.t.a. . . . had some advantages over traditional spelling; word recognition skills were better as was spelling, but *not* paragraph-meaning scores. But by fourth grade, students read traditional orthography better than any system of closer phoneme-grapheme correspondences.

A second point is the frequency of certain forms. Remember that there is inherent variation in speakers' speech. No one uses multiple negatives all the time; the incidence of use of the form depends to a great extent on the social situation the speaker is in. Therefore, how often should multiple negatives appear in the written materials? And this question applies to other forms in a given oral variety. What is the frequency of appearance that will seem realistic to a vernacular-speaking student? We have no answer to that question at this time.

These problems, added to a variety of other factors, have led to serious questioning of vernacular reading materials. Other factors have to do with the reading process itself. Students learn to make sound-symbol correspondences. Is there any reason to think that a so-called closer correspondence would make learning to read easier? Many researchers feel there is not, that the connection between letters and sounds is arbitrary enough to begin with for all students, so that a variety of strategies is necessary and *useful.* Richard Rystrom (1973, p. 4) has found indications that beginning first-graders have very little idea of the adult connections between sounds and letters. Furthermore, these first-graders he studied were both vernacular and nonvernacular-speaking children. They seem to start at the same point, and many end up at the same point—being able to read "regular" reading materials.

There is another very practical problem arising from teacher reaction to the sociolect. It has been noted that students when reading aloud will often put in certain forms from their sociolect. For example, I've heard black vernacular-speaking students read, "I axed Susie could she go wif me" for "I asked Susie if she could go with me." That sentence is a sociolect rendition of the second; they mean the same thing. So is it a mistake? Should it be corrected by the teacher and pointed out to the student that he or she did not read what was on the page? I suggest not. First of all, it is not a mistake. The student is obviously reading with meaning, since the sentence is being reproduced, although in the student's own variety. That means some sort of processing has taken place. In fact, these variety renditions can be looked at very positively as a sign that the student is in fact comprehending at least something he or she is reading. Strict adherence to the forms on the printed page means relatively little in the reading process, therefore, it need not be stressed that much. This means that you as a teacher need to be very aware of the various forms in sociolect and dialect renditions in oral reading in order to assess an individual student's progress in the acquisition of the reading process. Information on these forms is available in a variety of sources, one of which is DeStefano, 1973 (see Bibliography).

REGISTER SWITCHING AND READING

Register switching is another type of social variation in language. What is its place in the learning and teaching of reading? First, in English we have registers in both the written and spoken modes with attendant differences. These differences are learned by students who must deal with these forms not found or found only infrequently in the spoken language. And we as teachers should be as aware as possible of the differences in the forms found in the written language.

In a very real sense, all students, no matter what sociolect or dialect they speak, are a certain "distance" from the forms they must learn to read, particularly in more advanced reading in the upper grades. For example, passives are not used frequently in any spoken variety of American English. Nor are poetic inversions, such as "came the dawn," found to any great extent in speech. Long appositive phrases such as "my uncle, the one who now lives in Paris when he isn't touring the world in his yacht . . ." are also more common in writing. These are only some of the syntactic differences between speech and writing that must be dealt with by students reading the written language. Contrastive comparisons between forms in the spoken and written modes would be helpful to all students learning to read. In fact, Carol Chomsky (1972) has proposed that children's exposure to the written forms of the language by their own reading as well as by adults reading to them positively influences their language development between the ages of 5 to 10. Evidently students do take advantage of the variety and complexity of the written language as they read it or as it is read to them. No matter what level I taught at, I read aloud to my students almost daily, bringing to their ears usually more difficult material than they could comfortably read at first (in high school, it was Shakespeare).

Second, learning to read can be put in a register acquisition framework. A student learning to read more and more difficult material will learn to read descriptive prose, poetry, scientific writing, newspapers, and so forth. Little, if any, of this may be *produced* by the student, but the receptive competence can be there. The acquisition framework can also be useful for students with different varieties of American English. You can see them expanding their repertoire of registers, which calls for a higher use of certain socially unmarked forms, and they can see themselves doing this, too. There is really no need to put a maximum emphasis on language differences, but all students need competence in various facets of their native language.

Sociolinguistic research and perspective have a great deal to offer that is important in the area of reading. Language use is a social act that takes place in a social context. Reading is part of that social act in a social context. If the factors contributed by a social situation with all of its cultural constraints are forgotten, a great deal of reading is also forgotten. We have already mentioned that unfavorable social conditions may make it almost impossible for reading to be learned. As teachers we cannot forget the social setting and its influence on teaching and learning to read. We cannot forget the Cherokee students' response to reading in English (Walker) and the Harlem black adolescents' response to reading (Labov and Robins, 1973). What influences may we have operating in our own classroom?

BIBLIOGRAPHY

1. Bloomfield, Leonard, and Clarence L. Barnhart. *Let's Read*. Detroit: Wayne State University Press, 1961.

2. Bolinger, Dwight. *Aspects of Language*. Second Edition. New York: Harcourt, Brace, Jovanovich, 1975.

3. Burke, Carolyn. Audio tape of children reading selected passages for miscue analysis, including a selection entitled "Smart Birds." No date.

4. Butler, L.G. "A Psycholinguistic Analysis of the Oral Reading Behavior of Selected Impulsive and Reflective Second Grade Boys," Unpublished doctoral dissertation, The Ohio State University, 1972.

5. Chomsky, Carol, "Reading, Writing and Phonology," *Harvard Educational Review, 40* (1970), 278–309.

6. ———, "Stages in Language Development and Reading Exposure," *Harvard Educational Review, 42* (1972), 1–33.

7. Clay, Marie M. *Reading, The Patterning of Complex Behavior*. Aukland, N.Z.: Heineman Educational Books, 1972.

8. Dale, Philip S. *Language Development*. Second Edition. New York: Holt, Rinehart, and Winston, 1976.

9. DeStefano, Johanna S., "Oral Language Development and Learning to Read and Spell," lecture given at the University of Victoria, British Columbia, March 1, 1977.

10. Downing, John, "The Reading Instruction Register," *Language Arts, 53*, No. 7 (October 1976), 762–766.

11. Fries, Charles C. *Linguistics and Reading*. New York: Holt, Rinehart and Winston, 1963.

12. Gibson, Eleanor J., "Reading for Some Purpose: Keynote Address," in *Language by Ear and by Eye*, edited by James F. Kavanagh and Ignatius G. Mattingly. Cambridge, Mass.: The M.I.T. Press, 1972, pp. 3–19.

13. Gibson, Eleanor J., and Harry Levin. *The Psychology of Reading*. Cambridge, Mass.: The M.I.T. Press, 1975.

14. Gillooly, W.B., "The Influence of Writing-System Characteristics on Learning to Read," *Reading Research Quarterly, 8* (1975), 167–199.

15. Goodman, Yetta, and Carolyn L. Burke, "Do They Read What They Speak" in *Language and the Language Arts,* edited by Johanna S. DeStefano and Sharon E. Fox. Boston: Little, Brown and Co., 1974.

16. Johnson, Kenneth R., and Herbert D. Simons, "Black Children's Reading of Standard and Dialect Texts," *Reading News, 2,* No. 3 (August 1973), 2.

17. Labov, William, and Clarence Robins, "A Note on the Relation of Reading Failure to Peer-Group Status in Urban Ghettos," in *Language, Society and Education: A Profile of Black English,* by Johanna S. DeStefano. Worthington, Ohio: Charles A. Jones Publishing Company, 1973, pp. 312–323.

18. May, L., "Black Second Graders' Perception of Their Dialect Speech and Their Ability to Recognize Traditional Orthography," paper presented at the annual meeting of the International Reading Association, May, 1976.

19. McKenzie, Moira, "Learning and Literacy," *Contact, 29,* 1976.

20. Papandropoulou, Ioanna, and Hermine Sinclair, "What's in a word?", *Human Development, 17* (1974), 241–258.

21. Rystrom, Richard, "Perception of Vowel Letter-Sound Relationships by First Grade Children," *Reading Research Quarterly.* Vol. IX, No. 2 (1973–1974), 170–185.

22. Sakamoto, Takahiko, and Kiyoshi Makita, "Japan," in *Comparative Reading, Cross-National Studies of Behavior and Processes in Reading and Writing,* by John Downing. New York: The Macmillan Co., 1973, pp. 440–465.

23. Savin, Harris B., "What a Child Knows About Speech When He Starts to Learn to Read," in *Language by Ear and by Eye,* edited by James F. Kavanagh and Ignatius G. Mattingly. Cambridge, Mass.: The M.I.T. Press, 1972, pp. 319–326.

24. Smith, Frank. *Understanding Reading.* New York: Holt, Rinehart and Winston, 1971.

25. ———. "Reading," in *Language and the Language Arts,* edited by Johanna S. DeStefano and Sharon E. Fox. Boston: Little, Brown and Co., 1974.

26. ———. *Comprehension and Learning.* New York: Holt, Rinehart and Winston, 1975.

27. Walker, Willard, "An Experiment in Programmed Cross-Cultural Education: The Import of the Cherokee Primer for the Behavioral Sciences." Mimeo, No Date.

DISCUSSION QUESTIONS

1. Say these aloud: "everyone must dree his own weird"; "Someone faxed the clarms"; "We scrambled six eggs." When you said each one, were you reading? Relate your response to the perceptual aspects vis-à-vis the meaning aspects.

2. If Chomsky is right about the built-in mechanism for syntactic growth, why in your opinion do children differ so widely in their ability to learn to read?

3. Indicate at least four kinds of variation possibly represented by this visual symbol series without loss of comprehension: "I asked Susie if she could go with me."

4. If the key to reading improvement is motivation, is sociolinguistics relevant to the problem?

5. Compare DeStefano's views with those of Anthony Kroch, Robbins Burling, and Roger Abrahams in Part IV.

KELLOGG W. HUNT

An Iowan (University of Iowa Ph.D., 1942) who sought a balmier clime, Hunt retired in 1973 as emeritus professor of English at Florida State University. His prolific and influential studies in the development of language skills won him the National Council of Teachers of English award for distinguished research in 1964.

EARLY BLOOMING AND LATE BLOOMING SYNTACTIC STRUCTURES

For a dozen years now I have been interested in describing the syntactic structure of the sentences produced by schoolchildren as they pass from the early grades to maturity. The children and their sentences obviously do mature, and the more we know about the process, the more we can hope to help them in their writing, and perhaps also in their speaking and reading and thinking. If the description of such a process is comprehensive enough, that description becomes a scientific theory, a model. It can then be tested in unanticipated ways, and thus be either confirmed or disconfirmed by the data obtained with the new procedure. In this chapter I will present certain new data that bear upon an earlier theory, confirming it at certain points and refining it at still other points.

My first studies (Hunt 1964, 1965, 1967), like other studies of the sixties and before, worked on a large body of writing, one thousand words from each student. For a fourth grader to write a thousand words sometimes took a whole school year. This writing was on whatever topic the children happened to be concerned with in the normal course of their schoolwork. The writing was free of any control from me, the investigator, including subject matter and style. I will refer to such writing hereafter as *free writing*.

Since completing those studies in the 1960s, I have conducted two other studies (Hunt 1970, and 1974 unpublished) using a carefully controlled method for eliciting writing from students of different ages. I call this kind of writing *rewriting*, in contrast to *free writing*. Obviously it is a special kind of what we ordinarily think of as rewriting. A student is given a passage written in extremely short sentences and is asked to rewrite it in a better way. Once this is accomplished, the researcher can study what changes are made by students at different grade levels.

There are several advantages to this procedure. For one thing, since all students rewrite the same passage, all students end up saying the same thing—or almost the same thing. What differs is how they say it. Their outputs are strictly comparable. The differences are unmistakable, so a smaller corpus of writings can be used. A second advantage of the rewriting technique is that students can be confronted with specific syntactic problems which the investigator wants them to handle. To discover their method of handling an unusual problem in their free writing, the investigator might have to wade tediously through a vast corpus. A third advantage is that a student's syntactic maturity can be tested with a rewriting instrument in less than a class period, but to get a representative sample of a fourth grader's free writing would take many hours.

There is, of course, a danger in generalizing from a single rewriting instrument. The results obtained will depend to some extent on the problems set. Insofar as the investigator sets an abnormal task he or she will get an abnormal result. These results need to be checked against free writing. For instance, in one of the rewriting studies, not one of the 250 students participating, some of them twelfth graders of superior IQ, produced a single noun clause. But in another rewriting study, covering comparable age groups, noun clauses were produced with an average frequency of about one per student. There is nothing mysterious here. The difference in the outputs was determined by the difference in inputs. One instrument provided abundant opportunity for the production of noun clauses; the other provided none. We predicted that difference when we designed the two instruments.

In order to review two of the claims I made in the sixties about syntactic maturation, I must first introduce the term "T-unit." The easiest way to explain what I mean by this term is to use examples. My favorite example is the following passage written by a fourth grader. As you will see, this fourth grader wrote intelligibly enough—even forcefully— but he didn't punctuate at all. He wrote all this as a single sentence.

> I like the movie we saw about Moby Dick the white whale the captain said if you can kill the white whale Moby Dick I will give this gold to the one that can do it and it is worth sixteen dollars they tried and tried but while they were trying they killed a whale and used the oil for the lamps they almost caught the white whale.

Now let me cut this passage into its T-units. I will define a T-unit as a single main clause[1] (or independent clause, if you prefer) plus whatever other subordinate clauses or nonclauses are attached to, or embedded within, that one main clause. Put more briefly, a T-unit is a single main clause plus whatever else goes with it. Here is the passage reprinted, with each T-unit numbered and beginning a new line:

1   I like the movie we saw about Moby Dick the white whale.
2   the captain said if you can kill the white whale Moby Dick I will give this gold to the one that can do it
3   and it is worth sixteen dollars
4   they tried and tried
5   but while they were trying they killed a whale and used the oil for the lamps
6   they almost caught the white whale.

As you read those T-units, you may have noticed that each one is a grammatically complete sentence, regardless of the fact that one begins with *and* and another with *but*. (Of course they are grammatically complete; each contains a main clause.) You may also have noticed that they are the shortest stretches of wordage that the passage can be cut into without creating some fragment. (Of course they cannot be reduced further; each contains only one main clause.) For example, if we cut the first of these into two pieces, one of the pieces would be a fragment.

> I like the movie (grammatically a sentence)
> we saw about Moby Dick, the white whale (grammatically a fragment)

---

[1] A clause is defined here as a subject (or coordinated subjects) with a finite verb (or coordinated finite verbs).

Perhaps it would be safe for us to think of T-units as the shortest grammatically complete sentences that a passage can be cut into without creating fragments—but it is safe to do so only so long as we remember that two main clauses must be counted as two T-units. The T in T-unit stands for "terminable." Grammatically, a T-unit can be terminated with a period or other terminal mark.

The reason for defining a T-unit, as distinguished from a sentence, is simply that the T-unit turns out, empirically, to be a useful concept in describing some of the changes that occur in the syntax of the sentences produced by schoolchildren as they grow older. When we know what a T-unit is, we can understand certain measures of maturity that we could not understand without it.

On the basis of my studies of free writing in the sixties, I made two broad claims. One was that as schoolchildren get older, the T-units they write tend to get longer, measuring length as the mean number of words per T-unit. This claim might be called the T-unit length hypothesis. To get the mean T-unit length of the passage already analyzed, one simply counts the total number of words (in this case 68) and divides it by the number of T-units (in this case 6, giving a score of 11.3). The score for any other passage would be arrived at in the same way.

The T-unit length hypothesis is easy enough to prove true or false. All one has to do is get a representative sample from a school population of one age and another from a comparable population of another age and compute the scores for the two samples. If the score for the older group is larger, then that evidence tends to confirm the claim; if not, then that evidence tends to disconfirm the claim. So many researchers have found that their evidence tended to confirm the claim, that I suppose it is now accepted by all persons who know about such matters.[2]

A second broad claim which came from my study of free writing in the sixties is that as schoolchildren get older they tend to consolidate into their T-units a larger and larger number of what transformational grammarians call S-constituents. An S-constituent is something abstract, not something concretely and tangibly observable like a word. Roughly speaking, an S-constituent is the abstract structure that underlies the simplest of sentences—what used to be called kernel sentences. Several S-constituents may underlie a single sentence of ordinary complexity. For instance, in *Aspects of the Theory of Syntax* (1965), Chomsky indicated that three S-constituents underlie the sentence "The man who persuaded John to be examined by a specialist was fired." One S-constituent would be the abstract structure underlying "Someone fired the man." A second would underlie "The man persuaded John." A third would underlie "A specialist examined John." My claim was that as schoolchildren grow older, they consolidate a larger and larger number of such S-constituents into their actual T-units. We might call this the "number of consolidations" hypothesis.

Since S-constituents are abstract and theoretical, it is not possible to prove or disprove this hypothesis easily and directly like the other one. Nonetheless, it is an

---

[2] Various extensions and refinements to the claim have been made. One of the first (Hunt 1967) was that T-unit length tends to vary with mental age, not just chronological age. Another (O'Donnell, Griffin, and Norris 1967) was that T-unit length in speech as well as writing tends to increase with age. Another (Pope 1974) is that T-unit length for fourth graders varies somewhat with the mode of discourse.

interesting experiment to study how schoolchildren consolidate, not abstract S-constituents which underlie extremely simple sentences, but extremely simple sentences themselves.

This is what a rewriting instrument can show. And now we will look, in some detail, at the changes made by schoolchilden on the first six sentences of the "Aluminum" passage. Here are those six.[3]

1 Aluminum is a metal.
2 It is abundant.
3 It has many uses.
4 It comes from bauxite.
5 Bauxite is an ore.
6 Bauxite looks like clay.

How would students of different grade levels rewrite this passage?

A typical output of a fourth grader is printed in the right-hand column below. The input is reprinted in the left-hand column.

1 Aluminum is a metal.
2 It is abundant.
3 It has many uses.
4 It comes from bauxite.
5 Bauxite is an ore.
6 Bauxite looks like clay.

Aluminum is a metal and it is abundant. It has many uses and it comes from bauxite. Bauxite is an ore and looks like clay.

What syntactic changes has the fourth grader made? In the last T-unit he has deleted the subject, coordinating the two predicates. In addition he has put *and*'s between two pairs of T-units. In summary, then, he has coordinated two pairs of T-units and one pair of predicates. That is all.

How would a typical student rewrite these same six input sentences four years later, that is, as a typical eighth grader? His output is printed in the right-hand column below.

1 Aluminum is a metal.
2 It is abundant.
3 It has many uses.
4 It comes from bauxite.
5 Bauxite is an ore.
6 Bauxite looks like clay.

Aluminum is an abundant metal, has many uses, and comes from bauxite. Bauxite is an ore that looks like clay.

The eighth grader takes the predicate adjective of the second input and makes it a prenominal adjective, *abundant metal*. He coordinates three predicates, inputs 1, 3, and 4. He transforms input 6 into a relative or adjective clause. He does not coordinate any full T-units.

To avoid tedium, I will not show how a typical tenth grader or even twelfth grader would rewrite this. Instead, see how a typical skilled adult, someone whose articles appeared in *Harper's* and *Atlantic,* would rewrite it.

---

[3] The "Aluminum" passage can be found in its entirety at the end of this chapter.

1   Aluminum is a metal.

2   It is abundant.

3   It has many uses.

4   It comes from bauxite.

5   Bauxite is an ore.

6   Bauxite looks like clay.

Aluminum, an abundant metal with many uses, comes from bauxite, a clay-like ore.

This typical skilled adult transforms the predicate adjective of input 2 into a prenominal adjective, *abundant metal,* as did the eighth grader. He reduces input 1 to an appositive, *Aluminum, an abundant metal.* He changes the verb *has* from input 3 to the preposition *with.* He changes the predicate *looks like clay* into the modifier *clay-like.* He transforms input 5 into a second appositive, *bauxite, a clay-like ore.*

Looking back at these three sample rewritings, let us see whether they tend to confirm or disconfirm the two claims made earlier. You will recall that one of the claims made on the basis of free writing was that the number of words per T-unit increased with the age of the writer, at least through twelfth grade, and the number was still greater for skilled adults. Even in our tiny sample of three rewritings we can see this tendency manifest. Our fourth grader produced twenty-five words in his five T-units, for an average of five words per T-unit. The eighth grader produced twenty words in two T-units, for an average of ten words per T-unit. The skilled adult produced thirteen words in one T-unit. So our increase has been from five to ten to thirteen.

This increase is not far off the means in the full experiment, where fifty students out of several hundred from each grade were chosen so that their scores on standardized tests would represent a normal distribution of scores from high to low. The grades chosen were 4, 6, 8, 10, 12, a total of 250 schoolchildren. In addition, out of a number of authors who recently had published articles in *Harper's* or *Atlantic,* twenty-five rewrote the passage. They are here called skilled adults. Furthermore, twenty-five of Tallahassee's firemen who had graduated from high school but had not attended college rewrote the passage too. They will be called average adults.

For this larger population of 300 writers in the ''Aluminum'' study, the words per T-unit increased at every two-year interval, the difference being significant at the .01 level. Here are the figures for G4, G6, G8, G10, G12, average adults, and skilled adults: 5.4, 6.8, 9.8, 10.4, 11.3, 11.9, 14.8. Notice that average adults are only a little above twelfth graders, but skilled adults are far above both groups.

So there is no doubt that the rewriting study tends to confirm the claim about T-unit length. How about the other claim—the one about the number of S-constituents or simple input sentences? Our fourth grader consolidated the six input sentences into five main clauses, five T-units. Put the other way around, we could say that his five T-units are derived from six input sentences, six S-constituents. The average for his five T-units, then, is six divided by five, or one and one-fifth (1.2) input sentences per output T-unit. The eighth grader consolidated the same six input sentences into a mere two T-units, so we could say that the average for him is six divided by two, or three input sentences per output T-unit. Where the fourth grade score is about one, the eighth grade score is about three. The skilled adult consolidated all six inputs into one output T-unit. So we would score him six input sentences per output T-unit.

To review, then, the fourth grader's score is about one; the eighth grader's score is three; the skilled adult's score is six. These scores increase with age, so the samples, which are fairly typical of the rewritings from a large number of carefully selected subjects in the full experiment, provide data that tend to confirm one claim of the theory.

For these 300 writers, a tabulation of their 10,000 input-output structures indicated that the number of input sentences per output increases at every age level, just as the theory would predict. Here are the scores for G4, G6, G8, G10, G12, and skilled adults: 1.1, 1.6, 2.4, 2.8, 3.2, 5.1. Notice that skilled adults are almost as far above twelfth graders as twelfth graders are above fourth graders.

When studying free writing, a researcher sees only the output. The input lies hidden in the writer's head. Its presence is conjectural and can only be inferred. But in rewriting, one sees both input and output equally well. Neither is conjectural. So the results of the rewriting instruments are critical to the theory, and, as we see, they support both of the claims.

So far in this chapter I have supported the claim that successively older students can consolidate a successively larger number of simple sentences into a single T-unit. Usually when writers consolidate, they employ some sentence-combining transformation. They reduce one of the sentences to something less than a sentence, perhaps to a phrase or a single word. Now we will look at certain of these syntactic changes to see which ones are used commonly even by the youngest writers, which are used commonly only by middle grade writers, and which are used commonly only by the oldest writers. Thus we can separate the early blooming syntactic structures from the later blooming and even the latest blooming structures.

At the outset we noticed that our fourth grader joined two pairs of his T-units with *and's*. He did so with grammatical correctness. He put his *and's* in the right place, at the boundaries between the T-units. He knows where those boundaries come. But hereafter he will learn to do this less often. Young children do it correctly but profusely. Older writers do it correctly but parsimoniously. In the "Aluminum" passage a typical fourth grader coordinates 20 pairs of T-units; a typical sixth grader about half as many, 9; a typical eighth grader, 6; a tenth grader about 3; a twelfth grader maybe 2; and a skilled adult 1 or 2 for an average of 1.6. So we see that T-unit coordination blooms early, immediately starts to die, but lingers on for years, being gradually smothered by its relatives.

Coordination between predicates blooms early too, but it fades very little thereafter. Our fourth grader coordinated two of them, our sixth grader coordinated three, but our skilled adult knew too many better things to do . Typically, the number of coordinated predicates increases a little from G4 to G6 and then drops off slightly. For the large sample the actual frequency is 1.9, 2.2, 2.2, 2.0, 2.0; for average adults 1.9; for skilled adults 1.6. The number of opportunities to coordinate predicates is 26, but no one took more than about a tenth of these opportunities.

Can we say anything more about growth in coordination with *and?* Perhaps a little. Consider what we might expect to be a slightly more difficult problem. Here are two adjoining input sentences:

23   It contains aluminum.
24   It contains oxygen.

Here both subjects are the same, so we might delete one of them and get a coordinated predicate.

It contains aluminum and contains oxygen.

But both verbs are the same too, so we might delete both a subject and verb and get coordinated objects:

> It contains aluminum and oxygen.

This is the more mature construction.

Almost all of the writers in grade six and older used this more mature construction, deleting both the subject and verb. But among the youngest group, the fourth graders, almost half deleted nothing at all, and of the remaining half more chose the less mature construction. So even within coordination using *and,* there are grades of maturity: least mature is to delete nothing; more mature is to delete the subject; most mature is to delete both subject and verb.

Another fairly early bloomer grows out of inputs like one and four:

> 1   Aluminum is a metal.
> 4   It comes from bauxite.

Our skilled adult consolidated these two by deleting *is* from the first sentence and making it an appositive:

> Aluminum, a metal, comes from bauxite.

He also made an appositive out of another pair.

> 4   It comes from bauxite.
> 5   Bauxite is an ore.

This became

> . . . comes from bauxite, an ore.

The "Aluminum" passage provided two more pairs of sentences that invited appositives to be formed. Ability to write appositives was in full bloom by grade eight, but not by six or four. Here is the number of appositives produced by successively older grades: 1, 8, 36, 30, 34.

But not all transformations are in full bloom as early as coordination and the appositive. For instance, look at these two inputs:

> 1   Aluminum is a metal.
> 2   It is abundant.

Our eighth grader moved the adjective *abundant* out of its predicate position in the second sentence and put it in front of the noun *metal* in the first sentence.

> Aluminum is an abundant metal.

Thus two T-units become one larger T-unit.

The "Aluminum" passage provided six pairs of sentences like this, inviting a predicate adjective to become a prenominal adjective in some adjoining input sentence. The fourth graders performed this transformation 13 times, sixth graders 66 times, eighth graders 140 times, tenth graders 212 times, and twelfth graders 223 times. Here we have the strongest kind of evidence of a steady increase in transformational facility. This transformation blooms more and more profusely with age.

Our skilled adult did something else that the younger writers did not do. Consider the second of these two sentences.

> 5 Bauxite is an ore.
> 6 Bauxite looks like clay.

Half the skilled adults changed the predicate *looks like clay* into an adjective, *claylike ore*. The younger students did not do so nearly as frequently. In fact, the number of occurrences from youngest grade to oldest was: 1, 2, 3, 10, 14. This change begins to bloom only as late as the tenth grade, where the frequency suddenly triples. But even as late as the tenth grade only a fifth of the writers make the change, whereas among skilled adults half do. So this is a late blooming accomplishment. (It probably is not actually a transformation.) What in effect has happened in this change is that the skilled adult has shifted the grammatical category from verb phrase to adjective.

Older students make other syntactic category shifts more readily. For instance, our skilled adult changed the predicate or verb phrase *has many uses* into a prepositional phrase, *with many uses*. Still other older writers changed that verb phrase to an adjective, *useful*. Three-fourths of the skilled adults did one or the other. But only *half* the twelfth graders did; a *fourth* of the tenth graders; a *fifth* of the eighth graders; and only a *twelfth* of the sixth graders. No fourth grader did. So here again we have a highly discriminating measure of maturity, and a relatively late bloomer.

Francis Christensen, in his study of rhetoric, has singled out certain constructions as being particularly indicative of adulthood. One of those appears three times in this sentence which he cites from E. B. White. I have italicized the key words.

> We caught two bass, *hauling* them in briskly as though they were mackerel,
>   *pulling* them over the side of the boat in a businesslike manner without
>   any landing net, and *stunning* them with a blow on the back of the head.

Here we have four verbs with the same subject, all describing the same event. The input sentences, reduced to their skeletons, would be these:

> We caught two bass.
> We hauled them in briskly.
> We pulled them over the side.
> We stunned them.

These four sentences can be reduced to a single T-unit if we get rid of the repetition of subjects and add *-ing* to the verbs:

> We caught two bass, hauling them in briskly, pulling them over the side, and
>   stunning them.

Of the 300 persons who rewrote "Aluminum," not one of them produced this construction. Out of 10 fourth graders who rewrote "The Chicken,"[4] not even one produced it. By 10 eighth graders who rewrote it, it was produced once:

> She slept all the time, laying no eggs.

---

[4] Mean T-unit length for "The Chicken" is G4, 6.7; G6, 8.3; G8, 10.2; G10, 10.9; G12, 12.0; University, 13.0. The passage can be found in its entirety at the end of this chapter.

By 10 twelfth graders this construction was produced twice. Here are both examples.

> The chicken cackled. waking the man.
> Blaming the chicken, he killed her and ate her for breakfast.

But the university students produced 14 examples. In fact, 9 out of 10 university students studied produced at least one example, whereas only 1 out of 10 twelfth graders had done so. In the little time between high school and the university, this construction suddenly burst into bloom. Here are some examples from those 14 occurrences.

> He caught the chicken, *planning* to eat it the next morning, and placed it in a pen located below his window.
>
> The old man caught the chicken and put her in a pen under his window *planning* to eat the chicken for breakfast the next monring. Early the next morning a sound woke the man, and *looking* out the window, he saw the chicken and an egg.
>
> *Living* alone in his farmhouse, and without any neighbors, there was no one for him to talk to, so he passed his days working in his garden, growing vegetables and grain. . . . *Thinking* what a delicious breakfast the chicken would make, he caught her and put her in a pen outside his window.

For our purposes here, this is a long enough list to demonstrate that some syntactic structures bloom early and some late.

It seems likely that this theory of syntactic maturity applies to languages other than English, perhaps even to all human languages. The "Aluminum" study has been replicated in the Netherlands by Reesink et al. (1971). Reporting their findings in *Psychological Abstracts* they conclude, "The similarity between Dutch and American children in syntactic development is outstanding."

Furthermore, an investigation into Pacific Island languages and some Asian languages has begun at the East-West Center in Honolulu (Hunt 1974, unpublished). The rewriting instrument already referred to as "The Chicken," after being found to discriminate significantly between grades 4, 6, 8, 10, and 12 in English, was translated into a number of Pacific Island languages and some Asian languages. Those translated versions were then rewritten by children aged about 9, 13, and 17, who were, for most languages, native speakers of the language tested. So far, papers in Fijian, Indonesian, Korean, Laotian, and Marshallese have been scored for words per T-unit. For each of those languages the scores for the oldest group are distinctly higher than the scores for the youngest. The scores for the middle group lie in between. The papers in Japanese have been scored, not for words per T-unit, but for number of S-constituents per T-unit, and the results for Japanese are almost exactly the same as for English, supporting the theory.

There seems to be no doubt that syntactic maturity, as measured here, can be enhanced by a sentence-combining curriculum. This seems to be definitely established for grade four (Miller and Ney 1968; Hunt and O'Donnell 1970) and for grade seven (Mellon 1969; O'Hare 1973). For grade four, Hunt's curriculum covered seventeen sentence-combining transformations and included many multi-sentence embeddings. Students responded both orally and in writing. They not only combined sentences, as is done, at least hypothetically, in writing and speaking, but they also broke them back down, as is done, again at least hypothetically, in reading and listening. At the end of the year, 335 students in the experimental and control sections were tested in several ways. On the "Aluminum" passage test, the number of input sentences consolidated per T-unit was, for control students, 2.6; for experimental students, 8.3. Such a difference is unquestionably significant, and would have taken about two years more to accomplish had there not been this instruction.

In their free writing, experimental students wrote significantly longer T-units, indicating greater maturity. They also wrote themes about twenty-five percent longer than those written by students in the control group. These same students were tested to see whether this curriculum affected their reading comprehension. It might be expected that the decomposing of complicated sentences into their underlying component sentences would make students more conscious of the syntactic problems in reading comprehension. The results of the posttesting were far from conclusive and far from complete, but at least the findings were encouraging rather than discouraging. On what Stedman calls a Reading Structure test, the experimental students scored significantly higher than the control students at the end of the year.

The elementary grades would seem to be an especially appropriate place to use a sentence-combining curriculum; the use of many middle-bloomer transformations increases rapidly at this age. Surely it is possible to test whether a transformation can be taught at a certain age by a certain amount of repetition, or cannot be taught at all until later. Burruel, Gomez, and Ney (1974) have already begun to experiment on how to measure the teachability of a certain structure by a certain method at a certain age. Thus they report, for example "the *who/which* embedding was performed with a 40% error rate on the first day. By the third day, the students had improved, showing a mere 4% error rate. Some exercises, such as the embedding of conjoined adjectives, proved highly resistant to improvement, manifesting a 50% error rate over four succeeding lessons (p. 219)." The kind of information given previously as to which structures bloom early and which bloom late would be preliminary to actual measures of teachability at a given level.

In the mid-seventies, then, the English teaching profession has a theory of syntactic development that covers a broad range of structures. It also has more than one way of measuring progress toward the goal of skilled adulthood. There is also evidence that curricula already known can enhance syntactic maturity and perhaps assist reading comprehension. One might reasonably hope that a period of rich and varied curricular experimentation would now commence. There are not many areas in the language arts where the goals are as clear and as measurable as in this area, and yet where so little experimentation has occurred.

To the present time, the teaching of language has been guided almost exclusively by the rhetorician's intuition. But the theory of syntactic development reviewed here does not rest upon intuition alone; it rests on a solid body of experimental data. Linguistics will be of vastly greater help to language teaching as it begins to be able to make such statements as: "This structure has this meaning in this environment for this reason." Up until now, only rhetoricians have made such statements, but their intuitive perceptions have often been vague. Linguists now are beginning to devote a great deal of attention to the meaning of surface structure differences, to such matters as presupposition and entailment. As they begin to study the relation between syntax and semantics, they are approaching the rhetoric of the sentence. As they do so, they may be able to say less vaguely some of the things rhetoricians have already said. And if they can say them less vaguely, they can say them more teachably. When that happens, we English teachers can be grateful.

The two passages from which some of the exercises in this chapter were drawn follow.

ALUMINUM

Directions: Read the passage all the way through. You will notice that the sentences are short and choppy. Study the passage and then rewrite it in a better way. You may combine sentences, change the order of words, and omit words that are repeated too many times. But try not to leave out any of the information.

Aluminum is a metal. It is abundant. It has many uses. It comes from bauxite. Bauxite is an ore. Bauxite looks like clay. Bauxite contains aluminum. It contains several other substances. Workmen extract these other substances from the bauxite. They grind the bauxite. They put it in tanks. Pressure is in the tanks. The other substances form a mass. They remove the mass. They use filters. A liquid remains. They put it through several other processes. It finally yields a chemical. The chemical is powdery. It is white. The chemical is alumina. It is a mixture. It contains aluminum. It contains oxygen. Workmen separate the aluminum from the oxygen. They use electricity. They finally produce a metal. The metal is light. It has a luster. The luster is bright. The luster is silvery. This metal comes in many forms.

THE CHICKEN

Directions, Read the story all the way through. You will see that it is not very well written. Study the story, and then write it over again in a better way. You will want to change many of the sentences, but try not to leave out any important parts of the story.

A man lived in a farmhouse. He was old. He lived alone. The house was small. The house was on a mountain. The mountain was high. The house was on the top. He grew vegetables. He grew grain. He ate the vegetables. He ate the grain. One day he was pulling weeds. He saw something. A chicken was eating his grain. The grain was new. He caught the chicken. He put her in a pen. The pen was under his window. He planned something. He would eat the chicken for breakfast. The next morning came. It was early. A sound woke the man. He looked out the window. He saw the chicken. He saw an egg. The chicken cackled. The man thought something. He would eat the egg for breakfast. He fed the chicken a cup of his grain. The chicken talked to him. He talked to the chicken. Time passed. He thought something. He could feed the chicken more. He could feed her two cups of grain. He could feed her in the morning. He could feed her at night. Maybe she would lay two eggs every morning. He fed the chicken more grain. She got fat. She got lazy. She slept all the time. She laid no eggs. The man got angry. He blamed the chicken. He killed her. He ate her for breakfast. He had no chicken. He had no eggs. He talked to no one. No one talked to him.

BIBLIOGRAPHY

1. Burruel, Jose M.; Gomez, Julie; and Ney, James W. "Transformational Sentence-Combining in a Barrio School." In *On TESOL 74*, edited by Ruth Crymes and William Norris, pp. 219–30. Washington, D.C.: Teachers of English to Speakers of Other Languages, 1974.

2. Christensen, Francis. *Notes Toward a New Rhetoric.* New York: Harper and Row, 1967.

3. Hunt, Kellogg W. *Differences in Grammatical Structures Written at Three Grade Levels.* Cooperative Research Project, no. 1998. Washington, D.C.: U.S. Office of Education, 1964.

4. ———. *Grammatical Structures Written at Three Grade Levels.* NCTE Research Report, no. 3. Urbana, Ill.: National Council of Teachers of English, 1965. ERIC Accession no. ED 113 735

5. ———. *Sentence Structures Used by Superior Students in Grades Four and Twelve and by Superior Adults.* Cooperative Research Project, no. 5-0313. Washington, D.C.: U.S. Office of Education, 1967.

6. ———. "Syntactic Maturity in Schoolchildren and Adults." *Monographs of the Society for Research in Child Development* 35 (February 1970).

7. Hunt, Kellogg W., and O'Donnell, Roy. *An Elementary School Curriculum to Develop Better Writing Skills.* Tallahassee: Florida State University. U.S. Office of Education Grant no. 4-9-08-903-0042-010, 1970. ERIC Accession no. ED 050 108.

8. Mellon, John C. *Transformational Sentence-Combining: A Method for Enhancing the Development of Syntactic Fluency in English Composition.* NCTE Research Report, no. 10. Urbana, Ill.: National Council of Teachers of English, 1969.

9. Miller, Barbara, and Ney, James. "The Effect of Systematic Oral Exercises on the Writing of Fourth-Grade Students." *Research in the Teaching of English* 2 (1968): 44–61.

10. O'Donnell, Roy C.; Griffin, William J.; and Norris, Raymond C. *Syntax of Kindergarten and Elementary School Children: A Transformational Analysis.* NCTE Research Report, no. 8. Urbana, Ill.: National Council of Teachers of English, 1967.

11. O'Hare, Frank. *Sentence Combining: Improving Student Writing without Formal Grammar Instruction.* NCTE Research Report, no. 15. Urbana, Ill.: National Council of Teachers of English, 1973.

12. Pope, Mike. "The Syntax of Fourth Graders' Narrative and Explanatory Speech." *Research in the Teaching of English* 8 (1974): 219–27.

13. Reesink, G.P.; Holleman-van der Sleen, S.B.; Stevens, K.; and Kohnstumm, G.A. "Development of Syntax among School Children and Adults: A Replication-Investigation." *Psychological Abstracts* 47: 10536.

DISCUSSION QUESTIONS

1. How carefully was Hunt's experiment controlled?

2. How have his findings been validated?

3. In what way has current linguistic theory been relevant to this experiment?

4. Analyze a piece of your own writing in order to determine your own syntactic maturity.

5. Develop your own sentence-combining exercise.

JOSEPH M. WILLIAMS

The author is professor of English and linguistics at the University of Chicago and also the Peter Ritsma professor in The College. Among his many publications is Origins of the English Language: Social and Linguistic History *(Free Press, 1975).*

NON-LINGUISTIC LINGUISTICS AND THE TEACHING OF STYLE

Not too many years ago, a seminar at the MLA set as its topic why linguistics in the service of literary criticism had been such a failure. That seminar could have asked why it had also failed in composition, for at that time, those attempting to exploit linguistics in teaching writing could have pointed to little that was promising and to less that had been delivered, particularly on any of those occasionally extravagant predictions made in '50's and '60's. It's certainly not too late for such a seminar, because in the few years since then, not many of even the more modest promises have been realized.

Labov, Fasold, Wolfram, Shuy, and Stewart[1] have provided us with sophisticated descriptions of social dialects. And others, Pike and D'Angelo,[2] have associated contemporary grammatical theory to the traditional arts of discovery and arrangement. And then there is sentence combining, perhaps the most promising development in the last several years.

Ironically, of course, systematic sentence combining, intellectually legitimized by transformational grammar, might never even have been conceived had Chomsky not made a theoretical error in *Syntactic Structures,*[3] had he realized then, as he did later in *Aspects,*[4] that a grammar generating sentences recursively would not need sentence-embedding transformations. And had there been no sentence-embedding transformations in 1957, then Bateman and Zidonis in the early 1960's and later Mellon and O'Hare[5] might never have recognized how transformational grammars could be used in teaching composition.

Regardless of its legitimacy, of course, if sentence combining fulfills its most modest promise, students will develop a maturity of style earlier than they otherwise

---

[1] The bibliography is very large. The following are themselves significant studies and contain extensive bibliographies. William Labov, *Language in the Inner City: Studies in the Black English Vernacular* (Philadelphia, 1972); Walt Wolfram and Ralph Fasold, *The Study of Social Dialects in American English* (Englewood Cliffs, N.J., 1974).

[2] Richard E. Young, Alton Becker, and Kenneth Pike, *Rhetoric: Discovery and Change* (New York, 1970); Frank D'Angelo, *A Conceptual Theory of Rhetoric* (Cambridge, 1975).

[3] Noam Chomsky, *Syntactic Structures* (The Hague, 1967).

[4] *Aspects of the Theory of Syntax* (Cambridge, Mass., 1965).

[5] Donald Bateman and Frank Zidonis, *The Effect of a Study of Transformational Grammar on the Writing of 9th and 10th Graders* (Champaign, Ill., 1966); John Mellon, *Transformational Sentence Combining* (Champaign, Ill., 1969); Frank O'Hare, *Sentence Combining* (Champaign, Ill., 1973).

might have. And if it even partly fulfills its more dazzling promises, it will help students think, organize, and argue beyond their grade level.

Now certainly, our least task in teaching composition is to develop in our students a level of minimal syntactic competence, however we define that competence. But minimal competence is surely not our only task, nor even our most important one. We don't judge carpenters by how accurately they cut their wood; accuracy is a prerequisite for becoming a carpenter. In the same way, minimal linguistic competence, defined as control over the grammar of standard written English and the ability to write sentences at an appropriate level of syntactic maturity, is only a prerequisite for learning how to become a writer able to meet the demands of a literate adult life.

And it is this question that I want to address here: why contemporary linguistics has offered so little that takes us beyond describing the grammar of standard written English and beyond providing some of the theory for setting a level of syntactic maturity at 1.74 clauses per T-unit and 11.5 words per clause.[6]

Some of the reasons for this failure are easy enough to propose. H. L. Mencken, not half in jest, I think, offered one:

> With precious few exceptions, all the books on style in English are by writers quite unable to write. The subject, indeed, seems to exercise a special and dreadful fascination over schoolma'ams, bucolic college professors, and other such pseudo-literates. One never hears of treatises on it by George Moore or James Branch Cabell, but the pedagogues, male and female, are at it all the time. In a thousand texts they set forth their depressing ideas about it and millions of suffering high-school pupils have to study what they say. Their central aim, of course, is to reduce the whole thing to a series of simple rules—the overmastering passion of their melancholy order, at all times and everywhere.[7]

I can't recall which of my graduate-school teachers it was, but what he said about discovering the structure of the language we were working in, Kikuyu I think, seems relevant to this problem of discovering and describing the structure of not just minimally competent but rhetorically appropriate language. He said that if we wanted a really sound analysis of Kikuyu, it would probably be easier to teach linguistics to a Kikuyu than for a linguist to learn Kikuyu. It would be a little unfair, I think, to claim that in the same way it is probably easier to teach linguistics to a native speaker of clear and graceful prose than to teach clear and graceful prose to a linguist, for of course there are many able writers among linguists—Jim Sledd, Raven McDavid, Dwight Bolinger, and, certainly, many others.

But I think the general force of the analogy holds. English-speaking linguists are competent to deal with the grammar of English. But I am less certain that those who have tried to use linguistics in teaching writing have demonstrated any special sensitivity in describing what invests prose with more than mere grammatical or quantitative acceptability. In fact, I think a case could be made that even those concerned with developmental quantitative syntactic maturity may be so basically mistaken about what constitutes it that, if they are not teaching the wrong thing, then they may not be teaching at least one very important right thing. But more of that later.

---

[6] O'Hare, p. 22.

[7] H. L. Mencken, *Prejudices,* Fifth Series (New York, 1966), pp. 196–7.

However mistaken many editors and writers may be about the folklore of grammatical usage, they usually write well, or at least they recognize good writing when they see it. They may not be able to explain in the most fashionable grammatical terminology why a piece of writing is good or bad, but their sensitivity to clear writing parallels that sense of grammaticality which we attribute to native speakers of a language and by which we test our grammatical descriptions.

Now these are, admittedly, comments ad hominem. But I think we have to distinguish between defining syntactic maturity on the one hand by quantifying grammatical features of writing and on the other defining syntactic maturity on the basis of informed judgments about a passage, and then manipulating the passage in search of grammatical features relevant to our sense of stylistic acceptability, much the same way as we manipulate the grammatical structure of sentences in search of grammatical acceptability. It is a distinction that goes to the heart of the way in which linguistic stylistics has been practiced for the last half century, particularly, but not exclusively, in regard to the teaching of writing.

When we teach writing, what we teach about style depends on what we think we can verify and publicly demonstrate. And what we are able to verify and demonstrate usually depends on the categories and processes and relationships in our theory. If our theory includes the category "word," and we can agree on how to apply the definition, then we count words. If the system includes the category "clause," we count clauses. If it includes "transformation," we count transformations.

When a theory becomes so intrinsic a part of our intellectual baggage that, as with the dialects we speak, we eventually become unaware that we are speaking through the vocabulary of a particular theory, then we may also become unaware that we are not likely to look for anything except those features toward which our theory directs us, much less what other features there might be, not defined by our theory.

This problem is particularly acute when the theory we use in an investigation of one area was originally devised to answer not the questions we have posed about that area, but rather some other set of questions. This is the case with all current theories of syntax pressed into the service of style and composition.

Before 1957 (the date is symbolic) descriptivists were most concerned with gathering reliable data from observed linguistic behavior and with formulating empirically verifiable discovery procedures that would systematically process the data into a constituent-structure grammar, a grammar usually organized from the bottom up, from phoneme through morpheme and syntagmeme.

After 1957, public behavior as a source of data gave way to introspection; formalizable discovery procedures gave way to informal heuristic methods based on paraphrase, ambiguity, anomaly, and so on; and a concern with constituent structure alone gave way to a concern with relating surface and increasingly remote structures. Generative grammars are rhetorically organized not from the bottom up but from the top down, with sentence in the initial statement and statements subsequent to it moving through semantics and syntax to statements about acoustic features.

At first glance, one would think that generative grammars would have revolutionized the study of style, emphasizing as they do the intuitive sense of linguistic appropriateness, and explanatory rather than descriptive statements.

But descriptive and generative grammars share two features that for our purposes are I think fatal to their uncritical use in stylistic analysis. First, neither directly addresses how the structure of a sentence is experienced, either from the point of view of the speaker/writer or reader/listener. Both are, to this degree, text-centered. And yet if style is a component of rhetoric, as it must be in the teaching of composition, and rhetoric is the art of moving audiences, such text-centered theories must in some critical respects, miss the point.

This pre-occupation with text-defined structures has been particularly reinforced for those of us trained in graduate schools of English where for so many years the New (now old) Criticism dominated critical thinking. Like linguistics, the New Criticism is an enterprise that centers on the text, excluding on principle any critical consideration of the intention of the writer or the experience of the reader. But even if we set aside the question of whether the affective and intentional fallacies are indeed fallacies in literary criticism, I cannot conceive that they should determine how we think about style and composition.

The second flaw is that both descriptive and generative grammars either initially or eventually make the sentence the highest hierarchical structure in the system. Although there has been a good deal of work recently into the functional analysis of sentences and into text grammars,[8] just about all of those investigations *begin* with terms drawn from a theory of sentences in isolation. Our ignorance about the structure of discourse has prevented us from formulating a theory of sentences whose categories and relationships would intersect with, or at least impinge on the categories and relationships constituting that theory of discourse. One principle in constructing theories of systems composed of hierarchically interlocking sub-systems is that boundary conditions are set from without rather than from within, and that to some degree parts take their character from the whole they constitute. In the case of sentences, they are constituent parts of and therefore shaped by a larger whole, the discourse they occur in.

It is the difference between A. A. Hill struggling in his *Introduction to Linguistic Structures,*[9] to move from phoneme to morpheme, from lower to higher, and Chomsky and Halle in *The Sound Pattern of English*[10] demonstrating that a syntactic description, the higher hierarchical system, is a prerequisite to a phonological description, the lower hierarchical system. If sentences are shaped by the discourses they appear in, quantitative analyses cannot capture that shape, particularly when only those features relevant to the structure of sentences constitute the terms of the theory.

A particularly relevant example of the problems raised by these points is the research into sentence maturity, based largely on the T-unit, and its ratio to words and clauses. Let me say at the outset that I think the work of Hunt, O'Donnell and others[11] on syntactic structures at various levels is an invaluable resource. Without it, we would be much the poorer. But it is an entirely text-centered study that does not make clear whether 1.74 clauses per T-unit and 11.5 words per clause have any affective reality. We have no idea at what point a text composed of T-units increasingly below those figures would be perceived as "immature." Or what happens when the clause ratio goes down and the

---

[8] The growing literature on text grammars requires a bibliography of its own. One of the more useful recent publications, particularly in regard to its extensive bibliography on the subject is M. A. K. Halliday and Ruqaiya Hasan, *Cohesion in English* (London, 1976).

[9] A. A. Hill, *Introduction to Linguistic Structures* (New York, 1958).

[10] Noam Chomsky and Morris Halle, *The Sound Pattern of English* (New York, 1968).

[11] Kellogg Hunt. "Syntactic Maturity in Schoolchildren and Adults," *Monographs for the Society of Researchers in Child Development,* No. 134, Vol. 35, No. 1 (February, 1970). Roy C. O'Donnell, "A Critique of Some Indices of Syntactic Maturity." *Research in the Teaching of English,* Vol. 2, No. 1 (Spring, 1977), pp. 49–53.

word ratio goes up. Or vice versa. Or whether there is such a thing as too much maturity. And if there were, how we would know.

Hunt and O'Donnel left a gap in their counts, I think. They provide data on several grade levels through the 12th, and for superior adults, presumably those writing for publication. What we do not find are data gathered from the prose of non-superior adults, those who write for the everyday purposes of commerce and industry, who write hasty and unedited but surely, in some sense, mature prose. In order to fill this gap, Professor Rosemary Hake of Chicago State University and I collected samples of prose written for internal use at a large manufacturing concern in the Chicago area. We asked the supervisors providing the samples to judge them as well or badly written by whatever intuitive judgment they wanted. The documents judged badly written had a clause to T-unit ratio of about 1.5, roughly equivalent to the prose of a ninth grader. The documents judged as well written, on the other hand, had a clause to T-unit ratio about 1.3, equivalent to the prose of a seventh grader.

Now clearly something is wrong here. None of these documents could we mistake for the work of a seventh grader, or even a ninth grader. Whatever syntactic maturity infuses these texts, clause to T-unit ratios seem not to be affectively salient, at least in the way we might predict, and certainly not independently of other features.

I would like to discuss one syntactic feature which I will simply claim is more affectively salient than almost any other syntactic feature that invests a passage with the *appearance* of maturity. And that is the abstract normalization, the noun formed from the cognate verb. I have elsewhere reported on some of the work that Professor Hake and I have been doing in this area, so I will summarize it here only briefly.[12] We have found that an essay written in a nominal style not only tends to be graded higher than precisely the same essay written in a verbal style, but also tends to be perceived as better organized, better supported, and better argued than the corresponding verbal paper. Here is an example:

> My *preference* is for *life* in a large city because there I would have a *freedom* to do things that can't be done in a small town. In a small town, a person's *life* has to be like his neighbor's. There is a *need* for his *conformity* to their *beliefs* in regard to proper *behavior*.

> I *prefer* to *live* in a large city because there I would be *free* to do things that can't be done in a small town. In a small town, a person has to *live* the way his neighbors do. He *needs* to *conform* to what they *believe* is the proper way to *behave*.

Although the frequent use of these abstract and deadly nouns rather than those concrete and lively verbs contradicts everything we tell our students about good writing, a great many teachers of English, perhaps most, apparently take a nominal style as evidence of thoughtful, mature writing. Nominalizations reduce the proportion of clauses to T-units because clauses become noun phrases, thereby increasing, of course, the words-per-clause ratio:

| When we *discussed* | why he *failed* | it *influenced* | what we *decided*. |
| Our *discussion* | of his *failure* | *influenced* | our *decision*. |

---

[12] . . . The preliminary report is available on request.

In our experimental verbal papers, for example, the clause-per-T-unit ratio was about 2.4, considerably above the superior adult's 1.74. Our nominal papers had a clause to T-unit ratio of about 1.6, about on a par with an eleventh grader. Yet it was these latter papers, the nominal papers, that usually received the higher grade. This supports the observation that longer clauses characterize more mature writing, but contradicts the corollary observation that, as writing matures, the ratio of clauses to T-units increases.

So among a text-centered T-unit analysis, a reader-centered affective analysis, and a textbook-centered rhetorical analysis, we have a contradiction. At least insofar as nominalizations are concerned, if we urge our students to write in that concise and verbal style we all say we support, then they will write like high school students in the length of their clauses, and like superior adults in the number of their clauses, but in the process perhaps elicit from their teachers the unfavorable judgements that seem to be associated with a verbal style. On the other hand, if we train them to increase the number of words per clause, they must correspondingly decrease the number of clauses, and if they associate nominalizations with more complex writing, as almost all writers do, they will write in a style that we all say we condemn for its lack of grace and vigor, but which seems to get better grades. That ghostly chortle belongs to H. L. Mencken.

We might be able to resolve part of this contradiction if we simply modified what we say to match how we actually respond, or at least how most of our evaluators responded, much as we have been asked to modify our attitudes about standard English. But that won't do because, unlike dialects, a heavily nominal style is not only rhetorically mendacious but cognitively difficult. Several experiments done in the early '60's by E. B. Coleman[13] provide some evidence that in comparison to a verbal style, a nominal style is more difficult to process. Professor Hake and I recently developed some additional evidence. We gave two passages differing only in their nominal and verbal style to over 70 typists at different levels of ability and education. On a words-per-minute basis, they typed the verbal style about 15% faster than the nominal, and made about 20% fewer errors. So we can choose between these styles not simply on the basis of taste but, if pushed to the wall, on a cost-accounting basis as well.

Now if a nominal style is so affectively and cognitively salient, why is it that studies of syntactic maturity have devoted so little attention to it? In the first place, despite some references to transformational grammar, these analyses use a syntactic theory derived for the most part from traditional and descriptive grammars. The theory simply has no well-defined and prominent category that accommodates nominalizations, that demands that nominalizations be one of the first categories attended to. In the rhetoric of traditional grammar, the most prominently displayed categories are called *noun, verb, adjective,* and *adverb; declarative, interrogative,* and *imperative; simple, compound, complex,* and *compound complex; active* and *passive.* But we have no reason to believe that those categories are the most salient to the experience of a sentence.

Hunt devoted a few words to the subject of verbal nouns and, under a different heading, a few more to gerunds.[14] But he did not discuss them together, because gerunds with their empirically observable *-ing's* are objectively different from abstract nominalizations of the *discover/discovery, translate/translation, report/report types.* So his theory

[13] E. B. Coleman, "The Comprehensibility of Several Grammatical Transformations," *Journal of Psychology,* Vol. 48, No. 3 (Sept. 1964), pp. 186–190.
[14] Hunt, op cit.

distinguished that which, from the point of view of the **text grammar,** was structurally different, but which from the point of view of the **text experience** may be identical.

But even if his theory had provided a clearly defined category of verbal nouns in general, it would not have singled out nominalizations as any more or less affectively salient than any other category. No statistic based on text-centered analytical categories has any prima facie relevance to what is rhetorically salient, or by extension, to what we should be teaching.

No, in fact, I think the problem is even more complicated than I have just described, because affective salience is not a simple function of particular syntactic features but of features foregrounded in a context that is both linguistic and non-linguistic. I overgeneralized a bit when I said that our evaluators generally seemed to prefer a nominal style. Some of the pairs of papers they read were intrinsically well-organized, well-supported, well-argued; others were disorganized, weakly supported, illogically argued, and so on. The high school teachers in the group generally preferred the nominal papers regardless of their intrinsic quality. But the college teachers were more selective. They generally preferred the nominal version of the good papers, but among the bad papers either failed to prefer one over the other, or preferred the verbal.

In other words, in different non-linguistic contexts, the same linguistic features were perceived in different ways. We think that a reader reading a nominal style in an intrinsically good paper sensed a match between an abstract, i.e., educated or mature, style and clear thinking; a competent reader reading nominal style in an intrinsically bad paper responded to the abstract style as an attempt to cover up with turgid language an absence of careful thought.

If this is so, then it leads to an important though certainly not new principle of stylistic analysis. Any conception of a whole must come from a sequential perception of its parts; but it is equally true that the sequential perception of the parts depends on a developing conception of a whole. How we understand the general stylistic demands of the genre is an obvious example. Our understanding of the specific relationship between speaker/writer, reader/audience, subject matter, and situation in light of the informing intention of a passage is a much more complex event. The beginning of Lincoln's Second Inaugural Address is in a relatively nominal and passive style:

> At this second *appearing* to take the oath of the presidential office, there is less occasion for an extended *address* than there was at the first. Then a *statement,* somewhat in detail, of a course to be pursued, seemed fitting and proper. Now, at the *expiration* of four years, during which public *declarations* have been constantly called forth on every point and phase of the great *contest* which still absorbs the *attention,* and engrosses the energies of the nation, little that is new could be presented.

He could have written more directly

> As I appear here for the second time to take the oath of presidential office, I have less occasion to address you at length than I did at the first. Then it seemed fitting and proper for me to state in detail the course I would pursue. Now after four years have expired, during which I have been constantly called on to declare publicly on every point and phase of the great contest which still absorbs the *attention,* and engrosses the energies of the nation, I could present little that is new.

Because we know Lincoln was a serious man speaking on a serious occasion, we respond to the indirect style of the original version by directing our attention away from Lincoln and toward the serious occasion.

None of this should surprise us since that idea has for a long time been the staple of gestalt psychology. But it does have some important consequences in the analysis and teaching of style, not the least of which is, first, the importance of perceived intention as an informing principle that shapes the developing perception of a whole and, second, the potential meaninglessness of statistics. It certainly suggests that a reader who senses a specific and clear-cut intention reads and integrates all the details of the text to that intention. And that is the mirror image of what many teachers of composition have observed, that if a writer has a sense of his intention and direction, he will make fewer errors of all kinds, from organization to grammar to spelling.

If this is the case, then there are some special questions we should ask about sentence combining and other teaching methods that concentrate on sentence style.

Professor Hake and I have been conducting another research project, this one comparing the effects of sentence combining with sentence imitation. One group of high school students, over a hundred, are combining sentences; the others are imitating the same sentence structures that are the goal of the combiners. One difference between what we are doing and what most other sentence-combining projects that I have heard about are doing is that in every case, the students are working with sequences of three sentences constituting a short discourse. Another difference is that we have avoided narrative and descriptive sentences and are working almost entirely with expository forms. For example, this is what the combiners end up with, and the imitators begin with:

> This country should ratify the ERA because women must have rights equal to their responsibilities. Our society needs a law which would guarantee that everyone is equally protected from discrimination. Such protection will come, though, only when we all recognize what we lose in an unjust world.

We have no comparative results yet; however, the teachers teaching the units have reported that when students combining sentences are not familiar with the content of the kernel sentences (which was often the case because I had no idea how little most tenth graders know about anything—what the CIA is, what interest on a bank account is, what the Viet Nam war was), they have a difficult time doing the combining exercises. But the sentence imitators, who are given familiar topics to use in their imitations, seem to have little trouble. We believe this happens for the following reason: when a student has a clear conception of the content he is working with and is, in effect, provided with an intention that infuses that content, he can manipulate the grammatical structures and their logical relationships with relatively little difficulty. But when the content makes little or no sense to him, then the logical relationships are very unclear, and when the logical relationships are unclear, then the syntactic relations will also be unclear. The imitators, on the other hand, are provided with subjects that they know something about, and so are able to formulate a reasonably clear intention that lets them match their own ideas and intentions to our syntactic patterns.

Now what does this imply? It may be that sentence-combining exercises allow students to make readier use of their store of ideas and information because more complex sentences let them integrate more ideas more easily. If the experiments conducted so far have emphasized narrative and descriptive writing, as do most of the exercises I have seen, then we might explain the success of sentence combining, as others have, as the students' increased ability to express what they already know in larger structures—

structures that—if they are narratives—are in effect pre-shaped by the recollection of the event—by what must be virtually an inherent sense of storyhood.

But expository writing sets different demands. The subject matter is usually not as immediately available as the matter of a recollected narrative. The shape of the discursive essay does not present itself as readily as the shape of a story or the description of a scene. Successful expository writing depends on a control of syntactic structures, but more so than narrative writing on seeking out an informing intention and on generating ideas other than those that are merely ready to be released by complex syntactic structures.

So it may be that practice in the traditional arts of invention and of formulating a clear intention, in shaping a discourse on the one hand, and practice in sentence structure on the other will have mutually beneficial effects. As one is strengthened, so is the other. Whether combining or imitation is the more effective in developing more effective sentence structures remains to be seen.

I have one final reservation about the research into syntactic maturity based on contemporary syntactic theory, about defining maturity on the basis of feature counts and creating exercises designed to raise those counts to appropriate levels. I suggested it when I wondered whether it were possible to be too mature. The major problems of contemporary prose written by adults, both in our edited public discourse and in our unedited private memos and reports, are not the problems of immature, undeveloped sentences, but of sentences that are too indirect, too long, too verbose, too complex, too abstract, to be easily understood. If anything, it is this post-remedial problem of tangled and turgid writing that a theory of style should address, the kind of writing we find in sentences such as

> There is now no effective mechanism for introducing into the initiation and development
> stages of reporting requirements information on existing reporting and guidance on
> how to minimize burden associations with new requirements.

The clause to T-unit complexity of that passage is 2.0, and the words per clause average is 16, very mature indeed. In this light, the premium placed on quantitative linguistic complexity without the qualification of a linguistic definition of clarity should make us pause.

We need a theory of sentences in which clarity would be a concept that we could not escape addressing, and that would ineluctably lead to exercises that would concentrate on clarity along with complexity. The fact that we are a long way from such a theory does not mean that we do not know what we must know in order to formulate one.

For one thing, we require a much fuller and more careful analysis than we have of topicalization, both how it occurs in a sentence and the rhetorical functions it can serve. We need, as odd as it sounds, a good description of the way sentences end. The categories of rheme or comment that match theme and topic are too crude to account for the problems of stress and emphasis. Incidentally, in addition to their familiar topicalizing function, nominalizations have another rhetorical use, to end sentences with an emphatic thump.

We shall certainly need a category in the analysis that we might call **metadiscourse:** all the elements in a sentence that refer to the process of discoursing, as opposed to the specific reference of the discourse. I have in mind what goes on in a sentence such as

> I believe that in regard to the American pharmaceutical industry, we can say that there
> seems to be excessive federal government regulation.

On its most ordinary interpretation, the sentence is not about me as a believer or about us as sayers, but about the American pharmaceutical industry. That is the topic of the sentence, that for which the rest of the sentence exists. The comment, the statement about the topic, is *excessive regulation by the federal government*. Everything else: *I believe that in regard to* and *we can say that there seems to be* is metadiscourse, discourse about discourse, elements referring not to the referents external to the discourse but to the act of discoursing, to how we should take the truth value or probability of the propositions about those external referents.

We also have to distinguish very clearly how semantic concepts such as agency, action, and patient intersect with these rhetorical functions. For example, *American pharmaceutical industry* is the topic but the patient of the action underlying the climax of the comment: *regulation/regulate*. The agency is at the end of the comment: *federal government*. The order is not agent-action-patient but patient-action-agent. Were there a perfect intersection between topic and comment and agent and action/patient, the sentence would have read

> I believe that in regard to the federal government, we can say that there seems to be excessive regulation of the American pharmaceutical industry.

But that would have changed the perspective of the sentence, requiring a different perspective in any discourse in which such a sentence appeared, and that would in turn require a different intention infusing the perspective of the discourse infusing the perspective of the sentence.

Note that to describe these aspects of rhetorical structure we have not yet needed any grammatical terminology. Eventually, of course, we would. The topic is not expressed in the subject of the main clause but as the object of a compound preposition *in regard to*; the comment is the complement of the metadiscourse verb *be*. The agency is the object of the preposition *by* in a noun phrase; the action is the noun in the predicate noun phrase; and the patient is the object of the compound preposition. Had there been a perfect correlation among these three levels of discourse, among the rhetorical, grammatical, and semantic structures, the sentence might have read

> The federal goverment is *excessively* regulating the American pharmaceutical industry.

semantic structure	agent	action	patient
grammatical structure	subject	verb	object
rhetorical structure	topic	comment	
	The federal government	is excessively regulating	the American pharmaceutical industry.

There is a fourth level of analysis that intersects with the semantic structure expressed by the particular words: the structure of real-world events. Contract these three sentences:

(1)   The forest   provided me with   everything I needed.
(2)   I   found   everything I needed in the forest.
(3)   Everything I needed lay waiting for me   in the forest.

In the real world, forests and things cannot act; I can. But the *forest* is a seeming agent in (1), a literal locative in (2) and (3). *Everything* is a seeming agent in (3), an object in (1) and (2). *I* am the agent in (2), a dative object in (1) and (3). We can see the difficulties raised by introducing this level of analysis in these two sentences:

> A great idea suddenly came to me.
> I suddenly got a great idea.

What is most important in all of this, I think, is that the grammar of the sentence need not be the **first** level of analysis. When we begin with grammar, with subjects, verbs, and objects, those categories become the presiding terms of our analysis and all other terms and levels of analyses flow from them. But if we begin where the experience of the sentence is, with the rhetorical and semantic structure and *then* integrate a necessary grammatical description with those levels, we have the beginnings of a theory which would allow us to deal with the experience of a discourse rather than the solipsistic terms of a theory of sentences.[15]

Several years ago, when I first became interested in stylistics, in graduate school, I asked a visiting fireman from MIT about the rules (that overwhelming passion of our melancholy order) that might explain good and bad writing. He shriveled me with a glance and announced that that was not linguistics. I was too chagrined to ask him what it was (fearing he would answer "remedial composition," perhaps), and I labored along on and off for several years, doing that thing that had no name. In fact, I think now I was doing linguistics all along. I — like most of us interested in style and both composition and literature — had simply been asking questions that required theories different from those we were using on Kikuyu.

Now I prefer to think of it all as non-linguistics. The secret to using the term is to pronounce the initial *linguistics* in a slightly condescending tone. I would like to think that the second linguistics, the kind I have been discussing here, would at some point include a good deal of what the first linguistics is all about. But it doesn't start there.

DISCUSSION QUESTIONS

1. Does Hunt's later study (the preceding article) meet Williams's criticism of the limitations of sentence-combining research?

2. If nominalizations are recognized as ultimate transforms of T-units, might Hunt's results be acceptable to Williams? Would Freeman's "agency" proposal be relevant?

3. What nonlinguistic factors does Williams find significant in estimating maturity of style?

4. If in Williams's research the sentence-combiners and the sentence-imitators had been given the same essential content, might the results have been different?

5. What role would Williams assign to linguistics in stylistic analysis?

---

[15] A fuller version of this description appears in "Literary Style: A Personal Voice," in *Style and Variables in English,* ed. Timothy Shopen and Joseph M. Williams (Cambridge, Mass.: Winthrop, 1980).

DONALD C. FREEMAN

Now professor of English and coordinator of research for the writing program at Temple University, Freeman previously taught at the University of Massachusetts and the University of California, Santa Barbara. He has written and edited widely in literature and composition.

LINGUISTICS AND ERROR ANALYSIS: ON AGENCY

When you come to remedial composition as late in life as I did, you realize very quickly that the world is a much less orderly place than you had thought. Yet the problems in the prose of students in the remedial situation are a never-ending source of fascination to me; equally, I confess, attempts at their solution often are a source of the most exquisite kind of frustration. As a linguist, I realize that my discipline has been greatly oversold as a panacea for the ills of written expression; at the same time, I persist in the illusion that linguistics can make a contribution to the teaching of composition. What follows is an attempt at beginning such a contribution.

There are many areas of teaching composition in which linguistics can be of little or no assistance. I doubt that linguistics can do much to help us with such questions as logic, organization, connotation, or diction. I think it *can* help on the question of simply getting students to *write grammatical sentences*. Partly for this reason, the following discussion is based solely on sentence-level analysis. This position may seem to be a restriction of the potential contributions of linguistics, but this skill—simply writing grammatical sentences—is, in the experience of every composition teacher I know, the hardest single thing to teach the student in a remedial composition course.

The way linguistics can help get students to write grammatical sentences is in the construction of a new system of error analysis, and, through that analysis, construction of a pedagogical grammar: a handbook organized in structure and sequence for the classroom situation, and based as far as possible on modern linguistic insights.[1] Developing a system of error analysis can be done, in my view, only by extensive analysis of problem essays from the real world. I recognize that error analysis is only half, and perhaps not even that much, of the task which faces us. But I believe that remedial strategies for improving student writing can arise only from an empirically grounded system of error analysis; they cannot be constructed *a priori*. In this respect, I favor the inductive method of Mina Shaughnessy over the deductive method of E. D. Hirsch, Jr.[2] I am going to

---

[1] Insights, that is, somewhat deeper than the following, gleaned from a handbook proposal that I reviewed for a publisher not a month ago: "A sentence is a complete thought."

[2] See Mina Shaughnessy, *Errors and Expectations* (New York: Oxford University Press, 1977), and E.D. Hirsch, Jr., *The Philosophy of Composition* (Chicago: University of Chicago Press, 1978). I have outlined my reasons for preferring Shaughnessy's approach to Hirsch's in a review of *The Philosophy of Composition*, "Toward Relative Readability," *Chronicle of Higher Education*, April 3, 1978, p. 18.

sketch out briefly here one little corner of what such a system might look like, using the sentence as the basic unit; plainly, the insights of recent work in text grammars, speech acts, and related areas will play an important role in any elaboration of a system of this kind. The theoretical basis of this discussion is a deliberately simplified version of the so-called standard theory of transformational-generative grammar.[3]

How can this version of modern linguistics help us to construct a system of error analysis? I believe that the set of analytical pigeonholes that we now use to classify the range of problems in composition is constructed wrongly. Much of current error analysis, as that analysis is reflected in the organization of most existing handbooks, consists of putting square pegs in round holes. Subject-verb agreement, for example, is a host of errors, not one: a graduate student in Temple University's internship course for teachers of composition analyzed a large sample of real-world sentences and concluded that there are at least eight different kinds, most of which have very little to do with another. Other studies arising from this course have yielded comparable results for such categories as faulty parallelism and diction. Similarly, as will be suggested in what follows, a group of what have been thought to be heterogeneous and unrelated errors can, under this kind of analysis, be considered under a single rubric.

Modern linguistics has changed the size, shape, and number of many analytical pigeonholes in the theory of language. For example, generative phonologists have shown that the change from hard *g* to soft *g* in the pair *regal* and *regicide,* and from hard *c* to soft *c* in *medical* and *medicine* are the product of one linguistic rule,[4] not two; transformational syntacticians have shown that the sentences *colorless green ideas sleep furiously* and *lazy over the jumped fox quick dog brown* are ungrammatical in two ways, not just one.

Modern linguistics also has fostered a view of the overall structure of human language strongly compatible with what we do in the remedial situation: that language has not only a surface structure, the organization of the sentence as we hear it or see it on the page, but an underlying structure roughly corresponding (and how roughly is by no means agreed upon) to its propositional content. To use classical examples, again, the sentence *Invisible God created the visible world* contains, in its underlying structure, three propositions: *God created the world, God is invisible,* and *the world is visible.*[5]

Propositional analysis of this kind is analogous in important ways to what we do when we analyze tangled syntax in problem essays: we conduct a rough-and-ready analysis of the underlying structure of offending sentences, and then try to figure out how and where they went off the rails. I am proposing as a basis for a new system of error analysis, a slightly, but only slightly, formalized version of this procedure, and I am going to develop it from a real student essay.

* * *

---

[3] That is, the theoretical position put forward in Noam Chomsky, *Aspects of the Theory of Syntax* (Cambridge, Mass.: The MIT Press, 1965), which I have adapted to my purposes here.

[4] The rule is called Velar Softening in Noam Chomsky and Morris Halle, *The Sound Pattern of English* (New York: Harper & Row, 1968).

[5] See Chomsky, *Cartesian Linguistics* (New York: Harper & Row, 1966), p. 33.

CAN I TAKE YOU TO THE MOVIES?

I prefer movies to plays for a number of reasons. First, movies have a wide variety of technical advantages that plays just can't compete against. Casting of movies is varied, whereas in a play the actors have to be limited to a certain number due to the size of the stage. Advantages in terms of make-up and costume design also make a movie more enjoyable as well as a worthwhile visual experience in comparison to a play.

Editing, cutting, and being able to alter the finished product are only a few examples of the technical superiority that a movie has over a play. The finished movie with all its corrections and adjustments help to make the movie as perfect as possible. A play, however, since they are performed live leave mistakes, even in the case of professional actors, to present a real problem that a movie has already been able to take care of. Since a movie has no restrictions in terms of scenery the advantages and different places a movie can be shot at also make for a major advantage. A movie can take place all over the world, and special effects such as earthquakes cause for more excitement and in turn a superior product.

Casting, which in theory is unlimited in movies is severly [sic] limited in plays which, once again, proves to be an advantage for movies. The availability of famous actors for even a cameo role can make a movie worthwhile; plays on the other hand can't afford to pay a stars salary for only a moments work. The number of actors, itself is a factor in this comparison to [sic]. A play being restricted to a limited number of scenes and major roles doesn't have the access to the amount of stars that a movie does.

Costumes and make-up play a more visual role in movies than they do in most plays. With the natural limitations that plays carry with them, they don't have the advantages of camera angles and other filming techniques that a director can use in a movie. The camera can fool the human eye, and in conjunction with make-up and costuming makes for a much more enjoyable performance.

In closing, I hope I have accurately shown that movies have many advantages over plays, and, overall, presents a more diverse and entertaining medium than that of a play. For the reasons stated above, I hope to have explained why movies appeal to me more than plays do.

* * *

This essay is a typical product of a middle-level remedial composition course. It has many of the subjective, impressionistic features we attribute to what we call the ''remedial'' essay: its syntax is clotted; it is wordy and vague; it has a kind of lameness to it. There is here, typically for the remedial essay, no sense of someone *acting* in the world, an intuition to which I should like to return.

We can also observe a number of objective features in this prose which correspond at many points to the subjective ones: excessive use of the passive voice, faulty number agreement in pronoun reference, subject-verb agreement errors, vague pronoun reference, faulty parallelism, periphrastic constructions like ''in terms of,'' ''in comparison to,'' and ''make for,'' and faulty personifications: ''plays can't afford to pay a stars salary. . . .'' The essay certainly provides us with ample justification for the requisite number of red marks, and enough *topoi* for the divinely ordained twenty-minute conference.

But somehow these features fail to capture the essence of the problem in this essay; moreover, I believe it is wrong to treat them as unconnected to one another, as existing grammar books do. There is a thread connecting the seemingly diverse problems in five sentences which to me typify this essay's difficulties. That thread is what I would like to call *agency,* and whatever remedial exercises one designs on the basis of analysis should direct the student toward increasing the sense of *agency*—of someone acting on someone or something in a world. In what follows I do propose some revisions, but I am more concerned at this point with restructuring the system of error analysis that must precede these proposals for revision than with the revisions or the remedial exercises themselves. Here is the first of these sentences:

> Editing, cutting, and being able to alter the finished product are only a few examples of the technical superiority that a movie has over a play.

This sentence seems to be falling apart because of the gerunds. The standard transformational analysis of gerunds is that underlying them are predications with subjects: X edits, X cuts, X is able to alter, etc. But, in the context of this essay, *Who* edits, cuts, etc? A film director. And there is a cause-effect relationship between these actions (which have an agent) and the technical superiority that this student is claiming for movies over plays. If the student revises toward greater overt agency, the vagueness of this sentence can be greatly reduced:

> Because a film director can edit, cut, and alter the finished product, a movie is technically superior to a play.[6]

Sentence 2 seems to me to run afoul of a second class of verb-related nouns: *-ion* and *-ment* nominals.[7]

> The finished movie with all its corrections and adjustments help to make the movie as perfect as possible.

Who corrects and adjusts? Again, our old and hard-working friend, the film director. In using these verb-related nouns the student has created what has been aptly termed a "wall-eyed sentence." The nouns are grammatically subordinate to "the finished movie," but are also, by virtue of proximity, candidates for the subject of "help," which magically becomes plural as the finished movie helps make the movie perfect. When the student revises toward greater agency, this redundancy, along with the opportunity these nouns create for subject-verb agreement error, disappears:

> As the director corrects and adjusts in finishing the movie, he can make the final product as perfect as possible.

Sentence 3 presents somewhat more complex problems:

> A play, however, since they are performed live leave mistakes, even in the case of professional actors, to present a real problem that a movie has already been able to take care of.

---

[6] I hold no brief for the elegance of these revisions, only for their slight superiority to the originals.

[7] In later developments of the theoretical position of Chomsky's *Aspects*, *-ion* nominals like *correction* were shown to be present in the lexicon, not derived by transformation. But that refinement does not affect the points at issue here.

Here the agents, the professional actors, are grammatically subordinated into some kind of sentence adverb, and further effaced by the periphrastic "even in the case of." *Who* makes mistakes? Plays don't; they don't even leave mistakes (rather, mistakes remain in them—another agency problem). Professional actors make mistakes. And if the student is encouraged to elevate this agent-action nexus to the main subject-verb nexus of the sentence, much of the muddy verbosity disappears. And, because this revision necessarily simplifies the sentence's clausal structure, the opportunities for subject-verb agreement errors[8] diminish:

> Even professional actors make mistakes, which in movies can be edited out, but in live plays cannot.

The same problem—too deep a subordination of the only possible agent-action nexus in the sentence—afflicts Sentence 4:

> With the natural limitations that plays carry with them, they don't have the advantages of camera angles and other filming techniques that a director can use in a movie.

The only possible agent, the director, is subordinated in a *that*-clause which modifes a compound noun phrase which is in turn subordinated to the direct object of the sentence. If, in revising, the student can be persuaded to construct the sentence around this crucial agent-action nexus, the result is much less vague:

> The director of a movie can use the advantages of camera angles and other filming techniques that the director of a play, with its natural limitations, cannot.

Finally, Sentence 5:

> The camera can fool the human eye, and in conjunction with make-up and costuming makes for a much more enjoyable performance.

Here the subject of "makes" is grammatically "the camera," but conceptually it is three things: the fact that the camera can fool the eye, makeup, and costuming. I think, however, that the real culprit here is not so much faulty parallelism, but yet another word derived from a verb—here, the adjective *enjoyable*. *Who* enjoys? The audience enjoys, or we enjoy. *What* do we enjoy? We enjoy movies more than we do plays. Again, a revision by the student in the direction of greater agency clarifies an otherwise loose and unwieldy sentence:

> We enjoy movies more than we do plays because of the greater visual effects of makeup, costuming, and camera techniques, which can fool the human eye.

I have some observations to make about this exercise as a whole. If I have selected the right sentences as illustrations, their problems suggest that nouns and adjectives derived from verbs create difficulty. Verbs and words derived from verbs have more obligations than other words do; they require subjects, expressed or implied, or at least an awareness on the part of the writer that the subject of a verb-derived word is empty. Transformational analysis of these words and the difficulties they entail makes this

---

[8] At Temple, we call these opportunities "garden paths."

property of verb-derived words more explicit, and should guide the design of remedial strategies and exercises.

A second observation is that agency problems often are signalled by high incidence of abstractions, often complex ones, in subject position. Of the eighteen sentences in this essay, seven have abstractions as subjects: "casting of movies," "advantages in terms of makeup," "editing, cutting, and being able to alter the finished product," "the advantages and different places a movie can be shot at," "casting," "availability," and "number." Abstractions have far fewer, if any, opportunities to be agents. Only three human subjects appear—all of them first person singular, in the obligatory and familiar opening and closing formulae—and human beings are the best agents of all.

These proposed revisions are far from perfect: on the one hand, they probably are better than we could reasonably expect from remedial students; on the other, they certainly can be improved upon (one difficulty in proposing revisions is keeping intended meaning more or less constant). The revisions are in any case in isolation from their contexts, and it is precisely in this area of supra-sentence revision that text linguistics and discourse analysis may have more to tell us. The remedial procedures—a set of suggestions for revision—are very much subsequent to the construction of a system of error analysis of which this paper is a very small and highly tentative part.

What I am suggesting, basically, is that linguistics can be of the greatest help to the teaching of composition not in presenting a bundle of rules to be taught directly to students—that approach, in the sixties, was an unqualified disaster—but as a tool that can provide a set of heuristic devices for the construction of a pedagogical grammar in which it might be better, instead of sections on, say, subject-verb agreement, pronoun reference, and parallelism, to have a section on agency, where the particular kinds of these errors illustrated here would be discussed in one place, and other kinds lumped together in other sections as yet unlabeled and unknown (for example, morphology, or word-formation, a reasonably unified topic treated in a unified way in no pedagogical grammar book I know). A forthcoming study[9] of linguistics and the teaching of grammar shows that linguistic theory of a rather sophisticated sort can provide arguments for ordering, in a pedagogical grammar, topics like subject-verb agreement, for which there is a mechanical procedure for determining whether the rule is applied correctly, before topics like pronoun reference, where there isn't always such a procedure. Analytical insights of modern linguistics, in short, even the very crude versions of them I have shown here, can help construct a new system of error analysis with differently shaped clusters of persistent student problems related to one another in ways not hitherto—or even yet—perceived. And these insights also can provide a well motivated and non-ad-hoc basis for sequence in the composition curriculum.

Three general objections frequently are made to proposals of this sort. Linguists argue, on the one hand, that this particular kind of language in use is much too complex and unsystematizable for the analytical procedures of formal linguistics, and, on the other, that the linguistic system used is much too simple-minded. These objections seem to me to be opposite sides of the same coin: the goodness of fit—or lack thereof—between the formal elegance of modern linguistics and the manifest inelegance of the remedial situation. It appears, for example, that I would adjure students always to place agents

---

[9] Justine T. Stillings and Muffy E.A. Siegel, "Teaching Grammar: Some Linguistic Predictions," Temple University Department of English unpublished ms.

in subject position with as little subordination as possible, and to avoid verb-derived adjectives and nominals, when in fact both the passive voice and the gerund, to name but two of the troublesome constructions discussed here, have their uses. Throughout this essay I have used the term "agency" in an extremely loose sense, without the formal rigor of the case grammarians, and I have based discussion on a model of tranformational-generative grammar now very considerably altered from its original version in significant details.

To these objections I rejoin that there is a very considerable distinction between a scholarly grammar and a pedagogical grammar. In the present state of our knowledge we cannot hope to systematize all of the problems in the teaching of remedial composition. In this programmatic statement I have sought to use what I believe to be one of the greatest strengths of modern linguistics—its analytical powers—to describe one small part of those problems: a part not hitherto thought to be a coherent entity. From this description should follow a set of remedial strategies such as exercises and revision procedures, which would have as their aim not essays comprised of monotonous sequences of agent-action-goal sentences, but an awareness in the student of (in the present case) agency as an important and identifiable component of writing, just as, say, parallelism and punctuation are important and identifiable components of writing. Future work along these lines should seek to isolate and describe other parts, and fit these parts into a structure, a pedagogical grammar, which will look quite different from existing peda-gogical grammars and from scholarly grammars.[10]

For this effort to have any reasonable chance of success, questions internal to linguistic theory will have to be disentangled, to the extent that they can be, from questions internal to remedial composition. I have, therefore, based this discussion on a model of grammatical theory which at least has the advantage of a reasonable degree of currency. Like any field of serious inquiry, linguistics is in a state of constant ferment and change. But I think linguists cannot—must not—delay making significant contributions to the analysis and remedy of writing problems until the structure of English is fully described and agreed upon. The entire history of modern linguistics strongly suggests that this consensus will never be attained. Like the teaching of English composition itself, the contributions of linguistics to that enterprise will be messy and piecemeal for the foreseeable future.

A third and more serious objection to what is proposed here is raised by composition teachers: that analysis of this sort is within the reach of any good, experienced composition teacher's intuitions. Composition teachers have always known, for example, that there is an implied subject for the verb-derived noun *adjustment;* it is a common remedy to suggest that students revise muddy sentences so that the agent is in subject position instead of in some subordinate clause. In response to this objection, I would argue that linguists have made few if any discoveries about the structure of English (as opposed to the structure of linguistic theory) that composition teachers have not already known as independent facts. But there is a difference between a fact and a systematized fact. It is a fact that if you sit under an apple tree in late September, an apple is likely to fall

---

[10] The only reasonably full transformationally based scholarly grammar of English is Robert P. Stockwell, Paul Schachter, and Barbara Hall Partee, *The Major Syntactic Structures of English* (New York: Holt, Rinehart, and Winston, 1973).

nearby; and it is a fact that the sun rises and sets at predictable times. But these facts look very different when embedded in a theory of gravity, inertia, mass, and acceleration.

Similarly, it is a fact that the so-called "misrelated modifier" occurs when a participial clause does not modify the subject of the sentence in which it occurs; it is a fact that vagueness occurs when a student uses gerund subjects, verb-derived nouns, in such a way that the subjects of the verbs from which the gerunds are derived cannot be clearly identified. But these facts look very different when they are seen as part of a theory in which both clauses and derived nouns are related to full predications whose structure can provide a principled basis for analysis and remediation.

Pedagogical grammar has been apple-dropping, in my judgment, for quite a long time. Much of it always will be, probably; but after a quarter-century of intensive research in the structure of English, linguistics should be able to systematize some aspects of pedagogical grammar for the teaching of composition. The most promising locus for this sort of enterprise, I contend, is in the development of an empirically based system of error analysis. This essay is a small step in that direction.

DISCUSSION QUESTIONS

1. What two kinds of ungrammaticality are illustrated by Freeman's five examples?

2. What relationship is there between propositional analysis and Kellogg Hunt's concept of sentence maturity?

3. Have you had writing problems that could not have been solved by Freeman's "agency" approach?

4. How has Freeman's error analysis drawn upon recent linguistic theory?

DENNIS E. BARON

The author is an assistant professor of English and linguistics at the University of Illinois. He reports that he is preparing a book on eighteenth- and nineteenth-century attempts to "plan the American language." Previously he taught at Eastern Illinois University, at City College of the City University of New York, and, in France, at L'Université de Poitiers.

NON-STANDARD ENGLISH, COMPOSITION, AND THE ACADEMIC ESTABLISHMENT

The teaching of language in the schools has traditionally been an attempt, sometimes subtle, sometimes overt, at social engineering: getting a group of people to adopt an arbitrarily prescribed elite dialect. There are three basic approaches to the problem of non-standard speech: eradication, bi-dialectalism, and non-directivism. Those who would eradicate non-standard speech and writing operate under the delusion of a white man's burden of absolute cultural supremacy. "Proper" usage is seen as the outward sign of deep-structural grace, while nonstandard usage is regarded as evidence of physical and moral decay. As Ben Jonson put it, language must be freed "from the opinion of Rudeness, and Barbarisme, wherewith it is mistaken to be diseas'd."[1] The eradication approach to Black English and other non-elite dialects has so far proven to be an obvious linguistic, not to mention social, failure.

The bi-dialectal, or white-man-speak-with-forked-tongue, approach has problems too. While it ostensibly encourages pride in non-standard dialects, it also generates antagonism and linguistic insecurity. It stresses the socially limited role that non-elite dialect can play in white middle class society, and implies that the use of non-standard English anywhere but in the home or on the street is utterly without redeeming social value.

The non-directive approach is based on the premise that language systems always tend to be maximally efficient over their range of contexts; they respond to, rather than dictate, what needs to be said within a particular speech community. People within the speech community are inherently multidialectal.[2] They can style switch, accommodating their language to the speech situations within the realm of their social experience. The only way to master a dialect (and to learn a new language) is total immersion in the natural social milieu where that dialect is spoken (i.e., not in school), where social intercourse between the "learner" and the "natives" is unimpeded and relatively without stress. For example, the only way for non-standard English speakers to become adequate

---

[1] Ben Jonson, "The English Grammar," in *Ben Jonson: The Prose Works*, ed. C. H. Herford, Percy Simpson, & Evelyn Simpson (Oxford: University Press, 1947, rpt. 1965), vol. VIII, p. 465.

[2] Uriel Weinreich, William Labov, & Marvin I. Herzog, "Empirical Foundations for a Theory of Language Change," in *Directions for Historical Linguistics*, ed. W. P. Lehmann & Y. Malkiel (Austin: University of Texas Press, 1968), pp. 95–188.

users of standard English is to modify the social system so that they become accepted by the white middle class power structure. However, once this happens, the laws that affect linguistic equilibrium will operate on both elite and non-elite dialects and a new "standard" will arise.

This brings us to the most pressing problem to be considered in this paper. Since the social upheaval and consequent social mobility that are necessary for the leveling of American English dialects do not seem to be imminent, it is necessary to deal with the practical problems that non-standard speakers and writers face in college. Are we, for example, to tell users of Black English and other non-elite dialects that the only way to succeed in what they already know to be elitist institutions is to turn middle class and white? Can we reaffirm an elitist theory of English composition that is contrary to what we know about the nature of language? To deal with these questions we must consider the relationship between written codes and non-standard language.

Spoken language relies heavily on non-verbal factors to convey meaning. Gesture, tone of voice, facial expression, eye contact, all available as support systems in the spoken code, cannot be reproduced in writing; part of the overall message is sacrificed for the added permanence that writing provides. Much material in certain spoken codes (particularly conversation) is left unsaid, "understood" by speaker and audience. In written codes it is more difficult to do this; ambiguity and confusion can result, particularly when the audience is not personally known to the writer. Written codes develop a set of emphasis structures which replace some of what has been lost by the encoding process, e.g., the use of italics to replace spoken emphasis, the punctuation system, various types of shorthand such as the symbols of mathematics. Still other structures, e.g., the tropes of rhetoric or the metrical patterns of poetry, tend to occur primarily in the written code, although they are by no means restricted to it (since literature was originally an oral art, many of its structures derive from the spoken code). Differences in the role structure constraints on speech and writing account for many of the differences between the two codes.

The minimal role structure for a spoken communication consists of speaker, message, and audience. The message is an interface between speaker and audience, revealing the speaker's meaning and attitude. The intelligibility of the communication depends on the satisfaction of a number of "happiness" conditions of performance as well as content, e.g., the speaker must be audible, speech must be reasonably unimpaired by fatigue or the introduction of certain chemicals into the blood, the audience must pay attention, the message must have a decodable meaning. But except for instances where role-switching between audience and speaker is inhibited or not permitted, e.g., formal lectures, military commands, spelling bees, a certain amount of latitude is permitted in satisfying these conditions. The spoken code is generally more informal about constraints on content than is the written code; we expect less of a speaker than of a writer. It is much easier to dismiss an incorrect answer when it is spoken than when it is written on an exam; it is easier to shrug off a dull lecture than a dull article.

When role-switching occurs, the audience becomes the speaker, adding to, commenting on, ignoring, or questioning the message of the previous speaker. If part of the initial message was not clear, the audience may call for explanation or repetition. Role-switching in written communications is generally more difficult to accomplish. The writer may be dead or otherwise unavailable for questioning. At best, there is a considerable delay between the encoding of the message and the audience response: books must be typeset, proofed, printed, and distributed before they can be reviewed; letters must suffer the vagaries of the postal service; interoffice memos must brave the dangers of the shredder; compositions and exams must be graded long after they are of any importance to their authors.

Although it is possible to achieve instant role-switching in the written code when dealing with a computer, for example, in making hotel or plane reservations, this type of communication is still fairly limited in its applications (in view of the questionable efficiency of reservations computers it may be that role-switching does not occur at all). Other writing situations involving instant role-switching, e.g., games such as Scrabble or tic-tac-toe, and computer teaching machines such as Plato IV, are highly formalized and also of limited application. The writer must therefore assume an additional burden of self-consciousness: he must be able to calculate, without the feedback from a normal speech event, the effect of his message on the audience. For example, in some speech situations a certain amount of informality with regard to pronoun reference is permitted, since the audience may ask "Who's on first?" if things get confusing. Greater care in the use of pronouns is required in written communications to avoid ambiguity and insure intelligibility. Similarly, writers employ schemes of organization and development in order to formalize the communication and minimize interference in comprehension. Such schemes are used in speech as well, but it is permissible to stray from the organizing principle, for example, of a lesson plan, filling in omitted material at the end of the hour by saying, "Oh, I forgot to mention that . . ." or by answering audience questions.

A linguistically based rhetoric, of the sort hinted at by Van Dijk[3] and other text grammarians, can distinguish the organizing structures of a text, the global constraints which operate across sentences to control pronominalization, phonological and syntactic patterning, and the general semantic structure of a discourse. Such a rhetoric would show that one of the primary distinctions between the spoken and written codes is the greater amount of interference with global constraints permitted in the spoken code without loss of intelligibility; even in a highly formal lecture or performance situation, the audience is permitted to interfere with the communication by yelling "Louder!" "Encore!" or "Boo!", interrupting the organization of speech, possibly causing the speaker to repeat, revise, or terminate the communication.

Language is an efficient system, and communication will take place in a speech event (i.e. the conditions of intelligibility will be satisfied) if the participants are able to reach a linguistic equilibrium. In writing situations the equilibrium must be prejudged by the writer. When this judgment is inaccurate, because of carelessness or insensitivity to the requirements of the writing code, writing becomes inefficient. The problem is compounded in non-standard English writing because a written code must be created for users of what has been primarily a non-literate dialect. This is not to say that speakers of non-standard English do not write. Rather, they have not generally been encouraged to use their native speech in writing the sorts of extended compositions (factual or fictional) required in school, and to a more limited extent, in real life. They have, instead, been forced to use standard English for these purposes. In such situations, Labov's comment on speech is even more appropriate for writing: "Whenever a speaker of nonstandard dialect is in a subordinate position to a speaker of a standard dialect, the rules of his grammar will shift in an unpredictable manner toward the standard."[4] The result is a spoken or written act that partly follows the non-standard rules, and partly

---

[3] T. A. Van Dijk, *Some Aspects of Text Grammar* (The Hague: Mouton, 1972).

[4] William Labov, "The Study of Nonstandard English," in *Language,* ed. V. P. Clark, P. A. Eschholz, & A. F. Rosa (New York: St. Martin's Press, 1972), p. 394.

accommodates itself to the standard or to what the speaker thinks the standard rules are (in which case hypercorrection is likely to occur).

The non-standard dialect that has received most attention lately is Black English. There has been some discussion as to whether Black English is actually distinguishable from Southern White English. While both forms share many phonological and syntactic features, it is clear that the semantic component of Black English is different from White English, and that some elements of black American society have chosen Black English as a focus for social cohesion and ethnic pride. In addition, Black English is used by some writers as a legitimate vehicle for non-ethnic poetry and prose fiction and for scholarly writing, as well as for intra-group communication. Southern White English is used in writing only to evoke dialect and give regional color. Whether he affirms or rejects Black English, a native Black English speaker must translate his own speech into a written code which does not match his language. Consequently it is more difficult for such a speaker to prejudge the effect of communication in either standard or non-standard writing.

Non-standard dialects have been shown, by Labov, to be logical, rule-governed language systems.[5] They are not restricted codes (in Basil Bernstein's sense),[6] nor are they in any way inferior to the standard language of the white middle class. Social, political, or intellectual power does not guarantee the effective or sensitive use of language, nor does it automatically confer any sort of aesthetic sensibility.

Language is maximally efficient, able to communicate exactly what the culture using it needs to communicate; dialect works the same way. Speakers whose dialect is labeled non-standard are capable of communicating the same sorts of information as those using the standard language, although in many instances their social position prohibits them from making such communications, or their efforts are ignored or disparaged by elite dialect speakers. There is no linguistic need to abandon one's native dialect in favor of the standard, although there is often great social pressure to do so.

Written codes tend to become independent of the spoken language from which they derive. Literary language furnishes the most obvious example, but the phenomenon is found to an even greater degree in academic English. At the extreme, the written code becomes prescriptive, offering itself as a model for speech, rather than a representation of it. The code is held up to students for emulation, and it is expected that they will utilize it both during their academic careers, and later on, in the world of business. But the model remains, despite the great number of "relevant" freshman texts that have appeared each year since Donatus, undefined and erratically enforced. Students often complain that they are required to perform in standard language, but that the standard changes so from one teacher to another that they find themselves off balance most of the time. They see that students using non-standard dialects are required to change their language or drop out, while the writing of their teachers does not appear to them to be distinguished by clarity or aesthetic value.

Despite their training, many students are unable to identify standard writing. In a recent study[7] I found many students classifying as standard passages containing syntactic

---

[5] William Labov, "The Logic of Nonstandard English," in *Linguistics and the Teaching of Standard English to Speakers of Other Languages or Dialects*, ed. James E. Alatis (Washington, D.C.: Georgetown University Press, 1969).

[6] Basil Bernstein, *Class, Codes, and Control* (London: Routledge & Kegan Paul, 1971).

[7] Dennis E. Baron, "Reactions to Written Non-Standard English: Toward a Formal Description of the Written Code of Non-Standard English," a paper presented at the American Dialect Society (Northeast) meeting at Pennsylvania State University, April, 1974.

and dictional complexity (qualities that they have noticed in writing presented to them as a model) which were in fact quite deviant. Furthermore, many passages that were rated by the students as standard in terms of conventional categories (clarity, grammaticality) were downrated when it came to emotional response. Students recognized standard language, or attempts at it, but did not necessarily approve of it.

Another effect of prescriptive language teaching in the schools is the passivization of students. Their language is continually under review by the teacher. Every recitation, every question, every excuse note, no matter how tangential to the educational process, presents a test of language. Spelling, as they say, always counts. It is common, then, for students to try to evade responsibility for their statements, lest they be incorrectly formulated. Their sentences undergo *ego reduction* transformations: a response to a question often begins, "This is probably wrong, but . . ." and a student-initiated question takes the form, "This is a dumb question, but. . . ." There is a marked tendency for students to use the passive voice and the indirect question in dealing with instructors. Those who cannot defend themselves from linguistic attack by means of indirect statement make no statements at all, retreating from the menace, or make any statement whatever, hoping that some relief may follow the inevitable confrontation.

Louis Kampf and Paul Lauter comment on the tendency for schools to reinforce the linguistic insecurity of non-elite speakers by conditioning them to failure: "The process of maneuvering students to internalize failure . . . becomes one of the functions 'culture' courses serve in the academy. For such reasons, freshman composition has long been the major 'flunk-out' course in big, 'open-admissions' public universities. The people flunked, or put into 'special skills programs' from which they never emerge, are those who lack the veneer of middle-class language and culture."[8]

If prescriptive grammar is linguistically unsound for speech, it is unsound for writing. But the non-directive approach to composition does not require that students be abandoned to the non-linguistically oriented academic wolves, nor does it insure the production of anarchic, impressionistic prose. Rather, it requires far greater attention to the structure of language than does the blind imitation of a prescribed standard. Students must be made aware of the capabilities and limitations of language situations rather than of their own capabilities and limitations vis à vis a standard language which may be, at least in its written form, a foreign language as well. It is not reasonable to expect a non-standard speaker to write in standard dialect if in fact that speaker cannot use the standard speech code confidently; that would be like expecting a French major to write like a member of the French Academy.

Most people, whether they consider themselves speakers of standard English or not (despite their linguistic insecurity, most people consider their speech relatively standard), do not write according to even the most general prescriptions of the prescriptivists. The tendency to write as one speaks is overwhelming, and is reinforced by assertions of literature and creative writing teachers that the best literary dialogue is that which approximates ordinary speech most closely. Once the constraint of the schoolroom disappears, this tendency will prevail. Forms like *should of, alright,* and *tho,* which reflect speech patterns rather than prescriptive grammatical logic, are appearing more frequently in legitimate print media.

---

[8] Louis Kampf and Paul Lauter, eds., *The Politics of Literature* (New York: Random House, 1973), p. 23.

The differences between standard and non-standard writing codes can be characterized formally. The standard writing code has become independent of the spoken code in that it is conventionalized and therefore largely unresponsive to variations in speech. For example, although many, if not most, speakers do not pronounce the first *r* in February, the conservative spelling system retains it in the written code. The written code can standardize spelling, but it can only delay, not prevent, phonological change. As a result, it is very difficult, in fact, to portray ordinary speech or dialogue accurately, and it is almost impossible to portray dialect in writing.

The non-standard code, not having an established literary tradition to constrain it (e.g., many black authors adopted the standard code), is more responsive to the spoken code. Thus, for example, the phonological suppression of features such as final unstressed syllables is incorporated into the written code producing, among other things, uninflected past tense forms of verbs. One of the problems that can arise in the non-standard code is interference with intelligibility that results not from non-standard dialect forms, but from insufficient attention to the requirements of writing as a process distinct from speaking. Inhibition of role-switching requires a kind of linguistic clarity of the written communication that is not required of the spoken one.

As Labov demonstrated the logic of non-standard spoken English, so Bailey and Robinson demonstrate the logic of its written counterpart.[9] Bailey finds that many composition "errors" are the result of "rule governed phonological differences between elite and non-elite dialects. . . . Once examined in the light of the facts of language variation in America, the apparently unsystematic 'mistakes' in the essay prove to be the consequence of a consistently applied interpretation of the spoken language" (Bailey, p. 407). What most teachers have regarded as accidents of performance or the ineptitude of students is shown, in fact, to be rule-governed behavior keyed to the deep or intermediate structure differences between dialects. That such behavior is legitimate cannot be questioned. What to do about it is another problem. Prescriptivists (and liberal elitists in general) fear a breakdown in communication if non-standard dialects are allowed to proliferate. They fear a lowering of standards in the academy and the consequent decay of western society as we know it.

Breakdowns in communication can only occur as the result of interference in the communication system. The existence of a widespread network of instantaneous electronic communications media generally available to the public will tend to prevent the geographical isolationism that can foster the development of dialect. And the same system minimizes sociological isolation by insuring passive knowledge of a common form of English for those who watch television or listen to the radio. Interference in the writing system must be regarded as interference with intelligibility rather than the offending of sensibilities. Nonstandard writing, when it reflects spoken non-standard dialect, should not present much interference to those familiar with the dialect. Furthermore, it should not present that much interference for those with little or no knowledge of the dialect, since the dialect differences between elite and non-elite forms are fairly low-level ones. There are, it would seem, very few cases of true linguistic ambiguity; context generally

---

[9] Richard W. Bailey, "Write Off vs. Write On: Dialects and the Teaching of Composition," & Jay L. Robinson, "The Wall of Babel; or, Up Against the Language Barrier," in *Varieties of Present-Day English,* ed. R. W. Bailey & Jay L. Robinson (New York: Macmillan, 1973), pp. 384–408 and 413–448, respectively.

points the interpretation. Language, even written language, does not follow the dictates of formal logic unless forced to do so. How many times do we read student papers, knowing perfectly well what the student intended to say, and quarrel with the usage? If we know what the student meant, then communication has occurred. It is not fair to confuse formal logic with intelligibility, nor is it really fair to externalize the situation by arguing that someone else might not understand what was said. Logic does not necessarily suffer when verbs (in speech or writing) lose tense marking. If tense is significant in the utterance, it will be marked contextually. This is, of course, nothing new, as we know from the historical development of the future tense in English.

The function of the composition teacher, then, should be to focus the student's attention on the intelligibility requirements of the written code, rather than to attack the student's use of language. The arbitrary standards of correctness must be ignored, the relative means of effectiveness must be stressed, the student must develop a self-confident attitude toward his language.

Errors, in writing, are only those elements which interfere with intelligibility, i.e., which function as disruptive communications noise. As such, they are contingent on the role structure of discourse, in the sense that some audiences are less bothered by some kinds of noise than by others. (Student audiences are less bothered by certain types of noise than are teacher audiences.) The non-standard code permits greater interference with global constraints than does the standard. Noise potential is higher because prescriptive grammatical and stylistic rules may be applied haphazardly by both writer and reader, but noise tolerance is also higher than in the standard code. It would be best, then, to start with an audience that is most receptive to the speech of the student (this may or may not be other members of the class) and proceed from there. It may be possible for the student to write relatively audience-independent compositions, but it is not necessarily desirable to do so. It is more important to develop in the student a sense of the conative function of communication so that he may be able to direct his writing as he pleases, rather than to encourage him to be as innocuous as possible.

The student should be led to look at a composition in terms of its global structure, or principle of organization. This is more than just an outline; it includes all of the forces influencing the writer in the writing situation, and therefore can serve as an aid in the interpretation of more particular structure. I am not advocating that we grudgingly accept imprecise thinking—but imprecise writing does not necessarily indicate imprecise thinking. I am merely suggesting that we assume the student has some control over what he is doing.

The time allotted to composition courses is too short (and teachers are generally too unwilling) to allow for the teaching of linguistics as well as writing. In fact it is probably unwise to try to teach writing as linguistics. But it is possible to gear a course toward the exploration of some of the practical functions of language, and to try to develop a sense of self-confidence in the students. Once they achieve this, they will be able to absorb the finer points of standard and non-standard writing on their own, if they want to.

Of course, language systems naturally develop prestige dialects, generally reflecting the language of the political and socioeconomic power structure. They are also subject to change, despite the activities of that power structure, and all language change must be, initially, non-standard (hence non-prestigious). Not all teachers can be expected to have the linguistic sensitivity to realize the arbitrary nature of prestige standards and the function of non-elite dialect in the linguistic system; many who do are unwilling to act on this knowledge, preferring not to interfere with the academic establishment. Composition courses are expected to be service courses for all departments of the university. But teachers of composition should not be expected to teach what is essentially language etiquette when it conflicts with sound lingustic principles. Students know the social realities of linguistic prejudice; they have strong prejudices of their own. They also know when they are being asked to sell out. They, not their teachers, must judge when a linguistic compromise is called for. The teacher can try to explain some of the functions of language; the student must decide what to do with it.

DISCUSSION QUESTIONS

1. Do you think that an "elite" dialect is an inevitable feature of any human society? (Your answer will affect your response to Baron's argument.)

2. Do you agree that it is unreasonable to expect a nonstandard speaker to write in standard dialect if in fact that speaker cannot use the standard speech code with confidence?

3. If you as a teacher should receive a student composition containing most of the Black English language features (see the articles by Michael Linn in Part II, Robbins Burling in Part IV, and Thomas Kochman at the end of Part VI), what specific action would Baron's advice lead you to take?

4. Compare Baron's and Robert Pooley's attitudes toward teaching standard usage. Which do you think would have greater benefit for the student?

RICARDO L. GARCIA

Formerly at the University of Oklahoma, the author is now associate professor of education and director of multicultural education at the University of Utah. He has recently written a textbook, Teaching in a Pluralistic Society, to be published by Harper & Row.

A LINGUISTIC FRAME OF REFERENCE FOR CRITIQUING CHICANO COMPOSITIONS

When an English teacher critiques a composition written by a Chicano, strange expressions may appear, such as "on the forest" instead of "in the forest"; many of these expressions are superficial variations of English that the Chicano brings to the language that should not count against the Chicano's grade for the composition. Yet, because English teachers are generally unaware of the linguistic process of interference, they tend to rate such expressions as improper English. What follows is an attempt to explain the linguistic process of interference as it applies to the Mexican American student when he composes an essay. The term "Chicano" is used to define Mexican American, Spanish American, or Hispano students who are to some degree Spanish-English bilinguals.

LINGUISTIC INTERFERENCE AND THE CHICANO

When the Chicano is producing speech in one of his languages, Spanish or English, phonemes and morphemes from the second language may intrude on the speech of the first, a natural mixing of linguistic components that occurs when languages come into contact with each other. Weinreich, one of the early scholars who attempted to describe the semantic systems of bilinguals, proposed that interference occurred in three areas: the phonic, the lexical, and the grammatical.[1] To a large extent, Weinreich's description of interference as it applies to the Chicano is accurate. While speaking his *caló,* or dialect of English, the Chicano thinks little of borrowing and mixing of Spanish and English phonic, lexical, and grammatical elements. For example, a Chicano will write the expression, "yeah, no?" meaning "this is true, isn't it?" which is a literal translation from the Spanish "Si, no?" The Spanish expression is natural; the English seems contradictory.

Linguistic interference is a natural phenomenon that occurs whenever two languages come into contact. Unfortunately, English teachers have treated the *caló* as serious defects in English, especially as the *caló* appears in compositions, an error that the teacher makes due to ignorance, bias, or linguistic insecurity.

---

[1] Uriel Weinreich, *Languages in Contact* (New York: Linguistic Circles of New York, 1953), chapter 1.

PHONOLOGICAL INTERFERENCE

Studies on the Chicano's English phonology have reported that the Chicano experiences phonic interferences with English phonemes that either do not exist in Spanish or are pronounced differently. As early as 1917, the Chicano's English phonology was described as a variant of his Spanish phonological system.[2] Espinosa attributed this to speech mixture in the Southwestern United States that occurred when the Chicano's Spanish and the Anglo's English phonetic systems came into contact. More recent studies have reported that the Chicano experiences interferences with vocalic, consonantal, and suprasegmental phonemes when he speaks English.[3] The Chicano's phonemic system filters the phonemes of English to the nearest equivalent phonemes in Spanish, which is to say that the Chicano substitutes Spanish phonemes for the English so that it is not uncommon to hear consonantal substitutions such as "hands" /hændz/ when "hangs" /hæŋz/ is meant, or vocalic substitutions such as "heat" /hit/ when "hit" is meant. Suprasegmental substitutions refer to the sing-songy rhythm attributed to the Chicano's English contour patterns.

Note the phonological interferences in an excerpt from a theme written by a Chicano:

> *This* pictures show Indians riding through the mountains. One Indian seems to be the leader. *Hes hans* are held up high, telling the others to follow.

The three italicized words are examples of phonological interference. "This" is pronounced as though it were "these" by the Chicano so that the Chicano is not committing a number error; he is spelling the word phonetically according to his *caló*. Again, the English "his" is pronounced as "he's" by the Chicano so that "hes" is a phonetic rendering. In both the "this" and "hes" pronunciations, the Chicano is using the Spanish sound /i/ or "long e" in place of the English /ɪ/, because the /ɪ/ sound does not exist in his Spanish phonetic system. In neither vocalic variation is the Chicano making a grammatical error; he knows that "pictures" is plural and requires "these," and he knows that "he's" is a contraction of "he is," and indeed when he spells "hes" he is making a distinction between "he's" and "his." Consonantal substitutions occur when the Chicano writes "hans" for "hands," a substitution referred to earlier in this essay.

Essentially, phonic interferences are aural/oral discrimination difficulties which occur during the filtering process. They are quite easy to understand when one considers that there are only five Spanish vocalic phonemes, for example, as opposed to eleven English vocalic phonemes. The Chicano must learn the distinctions /iɪ/ /eɛæ/, /ʊu/, /aɑ/, and ɔo/ on the basis of the five Spanish vocalic phonemes /i/, /e/, /a/, /u/, and /o/. Unless he is trained to hear and make the English distinctions, he will tend to substitute the Spanish phonemes.

---

[2] A. M. Espinosa, "Speech Mixture in New Mexico: The Influence of English on New Mexico Spanish," *The Pacific Ocean in History,* ed. H. M. Stephens (New York: Macmillan, 1917), pp. 408–428.

[3] Gloria Jameson, *The Development of Phonemic Analysis Oral English Proficiency Tests for Spanish-Speaking School Beginners* (Austin: University of Texas Press, 1967), pp. 61–141. See also, Stanley Tsuzaki, *English Influence on Mexican Spanish in Detroit* (The Hague: Mouton, 1970); and Lurline Coltharp, *The Tongue of the Tirilones* (University City: University of Alabama Press, 1965), pp. 75–91.

MORPHOLOGICAL INTERFERENCE

Studies on the Chicano's morphology report that the Mexican American experiences lexical interference while speaking Spanish or English, thus tending to speak a portion of both languages simultaneously.[4] Essentially, the Chicano borrows words from both Spanish and English, regardless of which language he is speaking. He tends to anglicize Spanish words and hispanicize English words, as in the expression: *"Vamos pa la dance,"* or "Your mother is planching." In the former expression, the English word "dance" has been hispanicized to conform to the Spanish; in the latter the word for "ironing," *"planchado,"* has been anglicized to "planching" to conform to the English.

What occurs is a blending of two languages; hispanicized English words are altered to conform to the Spanish pattern of word structure, as the inflected ending of *"ganga"* for the English "gang." The Chicano is aware of such blendings and labels them *Anglicismos,* i.e., Anglicisms, and does not consider them unusual. Spanish words such as *mesa, plaza,* and *rodeo,* along with many other terms associated with ranching activities, have been mixed into standard English. English neologisms have been formed from the Spanish such as the popular "mustang" from the Spanish *mesteño* or "pinto" from the Spanish *pinto.* But even though this type of mixing is not unusual, the Mexican American's language mixing in the southwest is held in disrepute, being described by such pejoratives as "Tex-Mex" or "Poncho."[5]

Note the morphological interference that appears in the writing of a Chicano:

> This pictures show Indians riding through the mountains. One Indian seems to be the leader. Hes hans are held up high, telling the others to follow him. That's some *ganga,* this Indians. Probably, they will ride *on* those trees to the town where they will paint it *colorado.* They will drink a lot of *birria* and sing a lot of *songas,* but no one will give a care that they do this things.

"Ganga," "birria," and "songa" are hispanicized versions of "gang," "beer," and "songs." "Colorado" is a direct borrowing from the Spanish word meaning "red." "On those trees" means "in those trees" and is meant so by the Chicano. Because the preposition "en" in Spanish can be used either as "in" or "on," the Chicano uses only "on" in English, although he knows the difference between "in" and "on" as expressed in English. Other idiomatic interferences can occur, depending upon the Chicano's knowledge of Spanish.

The Chicano's morphology exhibits lexical interference in both Spanish and English. The Chicano borrows words and expressions from English or Spanish when he does not know or cannot immediately recall the equivalent in the language he is speaking. Generally, the Chicano's Spanish lacks the vocabulary refinement necessary to manage English neologisms. Isolated from the Latin cultures, and in many cases from the general American culture, the Chicano finds it necessary to hispanicize and anglicize neologisms that do not already exist in his lexicon. The purpose of the borrowing process is to extend the Chicano's vocabulary so that he can express himself in either the Spanish or English communities.

---

[4] George C. Barker, *Pachuco: An American-Spanish Argot* (Tucson: University of Arizona Press, 1948), pp. 12–18. See also, Coltharp, *Tongue of the Tirilones,* pp. 75–91.

[5] Thomas P. Carter, *Mexican Americans in Schools: A History of Educational Neglect* (New York: College Entrance Press, 1970), pp. 112–118.

Interference and the language variations it causes are important only to the extent that they cause the Chicano negative language attitudinal problems. If latinized phonemes and anglicized morphemes do little to hamper the Chicano's cognitive activities in the school, then there is little need for concern. But, if teachers take the attitude that there is a single correct enunciation of particular phonemes and that any neologisms are an adulteration of the English language, then the significance of the Chicano's alterations is most serious. And to a large extent this has in fact been the attitude of educators who teach Chicano youth. Chicano English and Spanish have been described by teachers as "inferior" or "improper."[6] It is significant to note that rarely is the Chicano taught in his own dialect of English or Spanish as is the middle class, monolingual student taught English. Only five and a half percent of all Chicano students receive some form of English as a Second Language (ESL) instruction. Less than two percent of all teachers of Chicanos are assigned to ESL programs, and most of these teachers have as little as six semester hours of training in ESL.[7]

INTERFERENCE AND CHICANO COMPOSITION

Given interference on the phonological and morphological levels of structural analysis, one would suspect that interference would occur on the syntactic level; one would suspect that the Chicano would mix the syntactic patterns of Spanish and English. Yet, it is almost inconceivable that a Chicano would mix the syntactic patterns of the two languages if he is to speak coherently in either language. Spanish—a synthetic, highly inflected language—and English—an analytic, highly uninflected language—are almost opposite in syntactic structure. Research is not available to indicate that the Chicano inflects English as though it were Spanish, or that he excludes inflections from Spanish as though it were English. On the contrary, Peña's research indicates that Chicano first graders are capable of using basic syntactic patterns of both Spanish and English and that they have little difficulty handling fundamental transformations in either language.[8]

The writer conducted a comparative study on the syntactic patterns utilized by lower and middle class Chicanos and found that all of the Chicanos utilized the syntactic patterns that are basic to American English; they did not experience syntactic interference even though they were Spanish-English bilinguals.[9]

Understand that the Chicano exhibits a wide range of bilingualism; he may be bilingual only to the degree that he understands Spanish when it is spoken to him; obversely, he may be completely literate in Spanish and English, being able to speak, read and write in both languages. Given this wide range of bilingualism in the Chicano student population, the English teacher should not assume that all Chicanos will experience interference when composing themes. Much depends upon the Chicano's linguistic

---

[6] Carter, *Mexican Americans in Schools*, pp. 97–106.

[7] U.S. Commission on Civil Rights, *The Excluded Student* (Washington: U.S. Government Printing Office, May 1972), pp. 21–49.

[8] Albar Peña, *A Comparative Study of Selected Syntactical Structures of Oral Language Status in Spanish and English First Grade Spanish-Speaking Children* (Austin: University of Texas Press, 1967).

[9] Ricardo Garcia, "Identification and Comparison of Oral English Syntactic Patterns of Spanish-English Speaking Adolescent Hispanos," Diss. University of Denver 1973, pp. 86–100.

community, where he may or may not hear and speak both Spanish and English. More importantly, the English teacher should consider phonological and morphological variations in Chicano compositions as natural manifestations of the language of the community. English teachers might best identify the variations and then utilize them in creative writing activities. Just as John Steinbeck had an ear for the *calós* of migrant Anglo peoples, and just as this talent is desirable in creative writing, the English teacher might do well to encourage the Chicano to develop an ear for the richness of his *caló*. Several Chicano poets, for example, are now experimenting with the Chicano *caló* as a viable medium for images that portray the Chicano experience in the United States.[10]

Also understand that this essay is not the final word on Chicano English as it appears in compositions. But hopefully it will provide the English teacher a frame of reference by which the Chicano's composition can be more equitably critiqued.

DISCUSSION QUESTIONS

1. How would you define Garcia's "linguistic frame of reference"?

2. Compare Garcia's position with that of Baron.

3. Would the appearance of, say, "I no like popcorn" in a Chicano student's composition be relevant to Garcia's opinion that Spanish and English syntactic patterns would not be mixed? If you should receive this sentence from a Chicano student, how would you seek to help the student—or would you simply ignore it?

---

[10] Victor Ochoa, *Nationchild Plumaroja* (San Diego: Toltecas en Aztlan Centro Cultural de la Raza, 1972).

BERNARD SPOLSKY

A native New Zealander, Spolsky has led a full and active career of teaching, with positions at McGill University and Indiana University before going to the University of New Mexico to become professor of linguistics, anthropology, and elementary education, and, in 1972, dean of graduate studies. In 1980 he left to become professor of English in Bar-Ilan University in Israel. The present article was originally read at the Fifth International Congress of Applied Linguistics in Montreal in 1978.

CONTRASTIVE ANALYSIS, ERROR ANALYSIS, INTERLANGUAGE, AND OTHER USEFUL FADS

The notion of progress in science, the idea that one's work is adding to the sum of human knowledge, is as important a motivation for endeavor in language pedagogy as in other fields. However, when we read theories of the sociology of knowledge such as the work of Thomas Kuhn, or when we look at a history of our own field such as that by Louis G. Kelly, we wonder whether this view is not a delusion. As Kelly put it:

> Nobody really knows what is new or what is old in present-day language teaching procedure. . . . much that is being claimed as revolutionary in this century is merely a rethinking and renaming of early ideas and procedures . . . (Kelly, 1968, p. ix).

In a slightly different analysis of the history of language teaching, Karl C. Diller argues that the last 100 years has seen a back-and-forth struggle between two main theories:

> . . . the history of foreign language teaching did not have a linear development.
> . . . The great theoretical division between linguists—the empiricists versus the rationalists—also divides the language teaching methodologies (Diller, 1971, p. 5).

The question of whether or not we are making progress becomes more serious, as Diller points out, because of the obvious discrepancy between, on the one hand, the successful second language acquisition demonstrated by huge numbers of proficient bilinguals and, on the other, the regular failure of second language teaching in so many school language programs. This not only makes the debate more bitter, but leads, he points out, to the fact that "the 'new' methods for language teaching which are continually being invented are advertised as if they were patent medicines for some heretofore incurable ailment" (Diller, p. 2).

If one is to remain optimistic about the possibility of progress, and to deal with the charge that all we have is a collection of fads, whether methods aimed at financial success or theories intended to improve the academic standing of the proponents, it is first necessary that we distinguish between the various panaceas proposed to the language teaching problem, and the gradual development of a body of practices and principles firmly anchored in sound theory and based on empirical practical experience.

We have, alas, too many cases of the former. My own favorite, for its enthusiastic account of a discovery of the way to teach languages, is the delightful book published by Francois Gouin in 1880 under the full title: *Essai sur une reforme des méthodes d'enseignement: Exposé d'une nouvelle méthode linguistique: l'art d'enseigner et d'étudier les langues*. Gouin describes first his own attempts to learn German. He started, as one trained in Greek and Latin would automatically do, with the only method he knew, "le procédé classique." "Apprendre des mots d'abord, puis des règles pour grouper ces mots et en faire des phrases, me semblait résumer tout l'art, tout le secret, toute la philosophie du langage" (p. 15). His second attempt, equally unsuccessful in making him able to carry on a conversation or follow a lecture, was to memorize 800 roots listed in alphabetical order; next he tried translation; then the famous Ollendorf method, which he thought would be effective for the book was already in its 54th edition—"Le monde entier étudiait donc dans ce livre!" (p. 27). Forty-five lessons and four weeks later, it was clear that he was nowhere nearer his goal. For a week or so, Gouin next tried total immersion, sitting patiently (like so many of our students) in a classroom to see if the words of the professor would finally start to make sense. His final effort was to memorize a dictionary, but even this failed to teach him German. He went home to France, exhausted and disappointed. But there was a happy ending, for Gouin at least, for while he was on holiday, his observations of the play and conversation of children led him to the discovery of his own method, the panacea long sought, the system of the verb. It is Diller who shows that Gouin did make a real contribution to the field: the notion of the series provides meaningful practice and leads to quick and easy memorization. His weakness, typical in the field, was assuming that this single insight was a sufficient basis for language teaching.

We have, as you are all aware, our own contemporary methodological break-throughs, ranging from the dullness of mim-mem to the fantasy of suggestopedia. It is beyond the scope of my paper to deal with these fads; rather I want to concentrate on the equally faddish theoretical labels that mark the jargon of our field. Three of the buzz-words that have been liberally sprinkled throughout writing on the theory of second language pedagogy over the past three decades are *contrastive analysis,* which dominated the field from 1945 until 1965 but has shown remarkable stamina under fire, *error analysis,* which has fought for higher or equal billing since 1965, and *interlanguage,* which has been in vogue for the last five years or so. As is pointed out in an excellent review article by Sridhar (1976) which the author was kind enough to bring to my attention, these may be "looked upon as three evolutionary phases in the attempt to understand and explain the nature of the FL [foreign language] learner's performance" (pp. 278–79). They are also, as Sridhar shows, more than this, for each involves a set of major assumptions about language acquisition and implies specific methodological practices for language teaching. Sridhar argues well that they are complementary rather than competing approaches to the realization that second language learners make mistakes.

Contrastive analysis was originally developed by Charles Fries (1945), expanded and clarified by Robert Lado (1957), and demonstrated by innumerable dissertations and, at its best, in a still widely used series of studies under the editorship of Charles Ferguson. *Contrastive analysis* assumed that many of the mistakes made by learners are caused by differences between the native and target languages, and led to a large number of extremely valuable language descriptions and pedagogical grammars. *Error analysis,* deriving essentially in its recent importance from the seminal paper by Corder (1967), showed how systematic errors are interpretable as giving evidence of the learning process and so brought research in second language acquisition into theoretical connection with work in first language acquisition. *Interlanguage,* a term coined by Selinker (1972), that seems to make somewhat stronger claims than implied by Corder (1971) with "idiosyncratic dialect'' or Nemser (1971) in a more Skinnerian framework with ''approximative system,'' makes even clearer the similarity to first language acquisition studies by focussing attention on the learner's knowledge of the target language as a whole, and provides room, through the notion of fossilization, for an ultimate connection with various sociolinguistic studies of language variation.

As Sridhar shows, each of these approaches is an attempt to deal with evidence provided by a language learner's performance that might tell us about the nature of the learning process and help us alter the teaching techniques we provide to improve this performance. They also represent, I believe, a reaction to current theories and practices in linguistics, and so demonstrate the special relationships that underlie the field of applied linguistics especially as it is involved with the field of language teaching.

At an earlier Congress (Spolsky 1974) and elsewhere (Spolsky 1969, 1974, 1978), I have attempted to analyze and demonstrate the nature of the relation between a practical problem such as language teaching and the theoretical fields such as linguistics that have implications for it. In the model that I now favor, the field of second language pedagogy (a subfield of educational linguistics which itself is concerned with all aspects of the interaction of education and language) must derive its theoretical base from three distinct (but related) areas of linguistics.

> The theory of language developed within linguistics is either a part of, or at least must be fully consistent with, the theory of learning that is the concern of psychology. From these two theories there develops a theory of language learning, the study of which is the function of psycholinguistics. The theory of language learning must itself be consistent with a theory of language use, the concern of sociolinguistics. The language description must be based on a theory of language. Second language pedagogy, one of the fields of educational linguistics, has direct relationships with the three fields of general linguistics, psycholinguistics, and sociolinguistics.
>
> From general linguistics, language pedagogy requires what is best called a pedagogical grammar, a grammar that may readily be adapted to the varying demands of the teaching situation. A pedagogical grammar is classified as a practical grammar and should be judged by the criterion of usefulness rather than the theories of adequacy or simplicity postulated for pure grammars. From psycholinguistics, and so indirectly from psychology, language pedagogy needs explanations or testable hypotheses of the way language learning, whether of a first or subsequent language, takes place. And from sociolinguistics, language pedagogy will learn more about the conditions in which language use is developed, the attitudes and motivations of language learners, and the development of communicative competence (Spolsky 1978, pp. 5–6).

It is instructive to look at the way the three approaches fit into the above model. Each has a different emphasis: contrastive analysis is most concerned with language description (general or autonomous linguistics), error analysis with language acquisition and learning (psycholinguistics), and interlanguage with communicative competence (sociolinguistics); and the claims that each makes are weakest outside its chosen area. Contrastive analysis was most useful in providing a framework for the development of useful pedagogical grammars. Its practical orientation enabled applied linguists to overcome the metatheoretical view preceding Chomsky (1957) that required every language to be described in its own terms, without reference to other languages or to putative universals. It provided justification also for theoretical descriptions of those aspects of a language that were believed to be most useful to language teachers, and a framework for continued practical and eclectic descriptions through the days of bitter controversy that followed the development of transformational grammar, and in the continuing uncertainties of the absence of an accepted single paradigm for language description. Sridhar summarizes well the controversies over approaches to contrastive analysis, shows how strong was emphasis on phonology and syntax and what large gaps have been left, and recognizes the difficulties in agreeing on a theoretical base for contrastive analysis. The problem is simply posed: ideally, a contrastive analysis is a simple mechanical drawing together of two complete grammars written in similar terms. For structural linguists, such grammars were theoretically incompatible: contrastive analysis therefore lacked theoretical justification. Transformational grammars on the other hand assume universals, so that a complete transformational grammar is (again quite theoretically) already a contrastive analysis with all other languages. In fact, as has long been accepted in practice, a contrastive analysis is concerned with covering "approximately the same ground that the language teacher is called on to deal with explicitly in the classroom" (Langacker 1968). This is essentially what the useful contrastive analyses (such as Moulton and Stockwell and Bowen) do, which is why they remain standard texts in the training of language teachers. Their practical usefulness outweighs qualms about their theoretical strength.

Looked at then as a method of providing classroom teachers and textbook writers with pedagogical grammars without having to be overmuch bothered by the rigorous arguments of those doing autonomous linguistics, contrastive analysis has been of fundamental use to second language pedagogy. Its use in the psycholinguistic area, in providing some notion of the nature of language acquisition and teaching, has been considerably less. Since Brière (1968) showed the inadequacy of contrastive analysis as a method of predicting hierarchy of difficulty, there has been little evidence put forward in support of the strong form of contrastive analysis or of particular claims for its pedagogical value. I think it is safest to sum things up by saying that there is good reason to believe that a contrastive analysis is a useful (some would say necessary) preliminary to the development of good teaching materials, but none for suggesting that it is in any way a sufficient condition or a complete basis for a theory of language learning. This pragmatic approach is well illustrated by one of the latest contrastive analyses to be published, *An Introductory English-Polish Contrastive Grammar,* by Jacek Fisiak, Maria Lipinska-Grzegorek, and Tadeusz Zabrocki, which is clearly labeled a theoretical contrastive study:

> The present *Grammar* is not a PEDAGOGICAL (i.e., applied) CONTRASTIVE GRAMMAR. It is not interested in setting up hierarchies of difficulty or explicitly defining areas of potential interference. It does not interpret linguistic facts in pedagogical terms. It is entirely neutral towards any type of application (p. 7).

Nonetheless, the authors rightfully assume that it will be useful to teachers, students, and linguists. Even though contrastive analysis has not lived up to its promise of explaining the nature of the language learning process and of making it possible to develop error-free learning, it has played a useful role in encouraging the kind of language descriptions that are needed by language teachers and learners.

Error analysis was another attempt to fill the gap. Its development and popularity derived from a number of trends in the work of linguists in the late sixties. At the same time that transformational grammar was dealing with the notion of universals and so removing one of the underpinnings of earlier contrastive analysis, it added a new problem in its methodological reliance on the intuition of native speakers as normal data. This is particularly inconvenient in the case of studies of children acquiring their own first language and persons acquiring a second language. Corder (1967), influenced no doubt by work in the study of second language acquisition (e.g., McNeill 1966), solved this methodological problem by arguing for the study of systematic errors in the performance of second language learners. One of the most important results of this emphasis has been to stimulate a great deal of research on the nature of second language learning that parallels similar work in first language studies. This work has largely been concerned with varying theories of the nature of language acquisition and with debate over the relative importance of external and internal processes. An excellent general survey of error analysis is provided in the papers collected by Schumann and Stenson (1974); they include articles that point out the theoretical failure of contrastive analysis and with the potential practical and theoretical values of the new field.

In recent years, there has appeared a large number of papers that deal with differences or similarities in the order of second language learner's acquisition of specific features. Dulay and Burt (1974a) report on a number of studies of the errors made by children learning English as a second language and consider that they are similar to those made by children learning English natively. The greatest number (87 percent) they considered to be "developmental," that is, like those that a native language learner makes, rather than a result of interference. They believe therefore that "the account of language acquisition offered by first language research has proved to be a most productive predicter of children's errors in second language acquisition" (p. 134). Similar results are reported in other studies such as Milan (1974) and Gillis and Weber (1976). When, however, one looks more carefully at the actual order of acquisition, certain doubts seem to arise. A second paper by Dulay and Burt (1974b) finds a number of differences that leads them to conclude that "we can no longer hypothesize similarity between second language and first language acquisition" (p. 255). Similarly, Bailey, Madden, and Krashen (1974) report results similar to Dulay and Burt's, showing some similarity in order of acquisition between adults and children learning English as a second language that is still different from the order in first language acquisition.

These seeming contradictions are perhaps to be explained by the somewhat limited scope of the research that has been done to date. Dealing with the wider question of the applicability of second language acquisition research, Tarone, Swain, and Fathman (1976) point out that a great deal of the work in second language acquisition has in fact looked at product rather than process. Working with a comparatively limited number of morphemes, there is found evidence of the linguistic knowledge of second language learners at a given stage rather than evidence of the underlying process. The strategies and processes have not yet been fully studied; the individual variables (age, sex, etc.) have not been taken into account; the environmental variables have not been fully investigated, and the basic methodology of data collection remains underdeveloped and the validity of instruments unclear. The methodology of the studies and the statistics they use have also been questioned by Rosansky (1976). In spite of these problems, and in spite of the fact that errors related to overgeneralization, too, have been shown to be only a partial explanation of a language learner's performance, and so only of limited use in establishing a useful theory of second language acquisition and related model of second language pedagogy, the field of error analysis provided a very useful bridge to studies of first language acquisition, and helped maintain an excitement and seeming respectability that has attracted a good number of bright young researchers into the field.

The concentration of students of second language acquisition on product rather than process is perhaps best exemplified by the great attention they choose to pay to something that a number of them label *interlanguage*. The first clear exposition of the notion was in a paper by Corder (1967). In that paper, Corder proposed that a study of what he called the second language learner's "transitional competence" would reveal systematic errors arising not from interference from the native language so much as giving evidence of the nature of the learner's "approximative system." Within a few years, clearly under the impact of studies of first language acquisition as much as following Corder's lead, error analysis replaced contrastive analysis as a principal activity of those concerned with research in the area of language learning. A clear change of approach and goal was also evident: those who had worked in the field of contrastive analysis clearly considered themselves applied linguists, their assumption being that the contrastive analysis would make it possible to prepare more efficient materials. Those working in error analysis, on the other hand, consider themselves much more students of psycholinguistics whose studies might lead to some understanding of the nature of second language acquisition and not necessarily to some immediate way to improve second language teaching.

It is perhaps because of this distinction in approach that the notion of interlanguage has become comparatively popular. Interlanguage, first used by Selinker (1972), is generally defined as a "system" that is "distinct from both the native language and the target language" (Selinker, Swain, and Dumas, 1975). A good deal of work in second language acquisition has been to attempt to establish the existence and nature of these interlanguages. There is an interesting change of perspective. Whereas to traditional language teachers (and probably to most students) a learner's control of a language at a given stage is assumed to be transitional, with both teacher and learner concerned to move it closer to the target, the student of interlanguage appears to be much more satisfied to accept it in its own right as an object for synchronic study. Serious problems, of course, arise from the fact that these learner's transitional systems do not turn out to be either stable or widespread. The degree of variation that is found causes concern. For example, Cancino, Rosansky, and Schumann (1975) found evidence of considerable variability in the order of acquisition. Looking at Arab students learning English, Scott and Tucker (1974) looked very hard to find some degree of regularity in their errors. Their conclusions suggest some confusion. They "found errors that were sufficiently frequent and regular, as well as instances of correct usage apparently following standard English rules, for us to assume that we were dealing with a rule-generated language system . . ." On the basis of their studies at two periods of time, they thought it reasonable to claim that they were dealing with "two approximate systems: although, recognizing all the differences that did occur, they recognized that they were dealing with "twenty-two idiosyncratic dialects."

In the study of speakers of four languages (Arabic, Spanish, Persian, and Japanese), Diane E. Larsen Freeman (1975) found a high level of agreement in the kinds of errors made, but still a great deal of evidence of apparent individual and language group variation. To deal with some of these contradictory results, Lonna J. Dickerson (1975) proposes that interlanguages, like real languages, should be seen as having variable rules: "Like native speakers, second language learners use a language system consisting of variable rules. Their achievement of the target language comes about through gradual change by using, over time, greater proportions of more target-like variance in an ordered set of phonetic environments" (p. 407). These arguments have been extended by Wayne B. Dickerson (1976) who demonstrated that the observations of five Japanese speakers learning English One over a year provide data showing the kind of patterned variation and wave change postulated by Labov to explain language change. On the basis of this analysis, he argues that we are dealing with variable rules working in a native grammar (Japanese-English), which might be referred to as interlanguage provided interlanguage is defined to include variable rules. He proposes variability analysis rather than error analysis, and suggests that the failure of contrastive analysis has resulted from its refusal to accept variable rules.

As may be apparent from some of the references earlier, a good deal of the difficulty of this area arises out of first assuming an interlanguage, a presumably complete grammar that has been internalized by the learner, but attempting to establish its existence by using fairly limited tests of errors made with certain morphological elements. As a result of this sketchy sampling of a learner's knowledge, the picture that emerges remains as confused as some of the statements made about second language acquisition.

Perhaps one of the greatest weaknesses of studies of second language acquisition is that they still are concerned with too simple a view of the process. As Tarone, Swain, and Fathman point out, they seldom go beyond syntactic questions, and are often limited to analysis of the order of acquisition of specific morphemes. In this, they are like many of the earlier studies of first language acquisition, with attempts to write simple grammars for learners. One can certainly sympathize with Adjemian (1976) who calls for "painstakingly designed studies repeated at various intervals, yielding both longitudinal and setting-specific data" (p. 319). Those studying first language acquisition have found it necessary to move to much more complex approaches: to attempt semantic, cognitive, and pragmatic explanations of the process, and to argue that each type of explanation may be important at the various stages of development. Studying second language learners in action could, as Ervin-Tripp pointed out, be a very valuable way of learning more about the whole process of language acquisition; and recognizing the more complex models needed in first language studies will be a vital step in clarifying some of the confusions of present second language acquisition research.

In some ways, interlanguage can be considered no more than a relabeling of part of the process, an attempt to add respectability to the study of errors. It is certainly a simpler name than the successive approximations of programmed instruction, or Nemser's approximative system, or even Corder's idiosyncratic dialect. As a theoretical construct, it seems to ignore the Saussurean distinction between *langue* and *parole* or the general distinction between language and idiolect. What is most intriguing about its use, however, is the potential it gives for relating studies of second language pedagogy to sociolinguistics. This possibility is noted by Sridhar who points out how it relates language teaching to the study of nonstandard dialects. There has long been debate in the teaching of English over the status of the various local standards, equivalent in some ways to a fossilized interlanguage. The term is quite useful in this context, for it suggests a pragmatic acceptance of a local variety of the target language, or better, a realizable target variety. A recent meeting dealing with the various (understandably but regrettably named) Englishes shows the potential value of this approach. The notion, and the term, then, has use in the sociolinguistic domain. It is much less useful in either general or psycholinguistic areas: while it is clearly useful to describe a generally accepted variety of language, there is much less use in an extensive description of an individual learner's transitional competence. Similarly, the static concept of an interlanguage is of limited value for understanding a dynamic and ongoing process.

At the same time, working more or less within the interlanguage paradigm, scholars such as Schumann (e.g., 1974) and Krashen (e.g., 1976) are starting to develop more complex models that take into account contrastive analysis, error analysis, and interlanguage theories. I believe, then, that we can conclude that while these theoretical notions were fads, unable (like the various new teaching methods) to solve alone all the problems of language teaching, each contributed to our understanding of the nature of the language acquisition process, so that we can still assume that there is progress in our field.

REFERENCES

1. Christian Adjemian, 1976. "On the nature of interlanguage systems." *Language Learning*, 26: 297–320.

2. Nathalie Bailey, Carolyn Madden, and Stephen D. Krashen, 1974. "Is there a natural sequence in adult second language learning?" *Language Learning*, 24: 235–243.

3. Eugène John Brière, 1968. *A Psycholinguistic Study of Phonological Interference*. The Hague: Mouton.

4. Herlindo Cancino, Ellen Rosansky, and John Schumann, 1975. "The acquisition of the English auxiliary by native Spanish speakers." *TESOL Quarterly*, 9: 421–430.

5. Noam Chomsky, 1957. *Syntactic Structures*. The Hague: Mouton.

6. S. Pit Corder, 1967. "The significance of learners' errors." *International Review of Applied Linguistics*, 5: 161–170.

7. S. Pit Corder, 1971. "Idiosyncratic dialects and error analysis." *International Review of Applied Linguistics*, 9: 147–159.

8. Lonna J. Dickerson, 1975: "The learner's interlanguage as a system of variable rules." *TESOL Quarterly*, 9: 401–407.

9. Wayne B. Dickerson, 1976. "The psycholinguistic unity of language learning and language change." *Language Learning*, 26: 215–231.

10. Karl Conrad Diller, 1971. *Generative Grammar, Structrual Linguistics, and Language Teaching*. Rowley, Massachusetts: Newbury House Publishers.

11. Heidi C. Dulay and Marina K. Burt, 1974a. "Errors and strategies in child second language acquisition." *TESOL Quarterly*, 8: 129–136.

12. Heidi C. Dulay and Marina K. Burt, 1974b. "A new perspective on the creative construction process in child second language acquisition." *Language Learning*, 24: 253–278.

13. Jacek Fisiak, Maria Lipinska-Grzegorek, and Tadeusz Zabrocki, 1978. *An Introductory English-Polish Contrastive Grammar*. Panstwowe Wydawnictwo Naukowe.

14. Charles C. Fries, 1945. *Teaching and Learning English as a Foreign Language*. Ann Arbor: University of Michigan Press.

15. Mary Gillis and Rose-Marie Weber, 1976. "The emergence of sentence modalities in the English of Japanese speaking children." *Language Learning*, 26: 77–94.

16. Francois Gouin, 1880. *Essai sur une reforme des méthodes d'enseignement: Exposé d'une nouvelle méthode linguistique: l'art d'enseigner et d'étudier les langues*. Paris: Fischbacker.

17. Louis G. Kelly, 1969. *25 Centuries of Language Teaching*. Rowley, Massachusetts: Newbury House Publishers.

18. Stephen D. Krashen, to appear in Dingwall, W. (editor). "Second Language Acquisition." *Survey of Linguistic Science*.

19. Robert Lado, 1957. *Linguistics Across Cultures*. Ann Arbor: University of Michigan Press.

20. Ronald W. Langacker, 1968. Review of Stockwell and Bowen. *The Sounds of English and Spanish*. *Foundations of Language*, 4: 211–218.

21. Diane E. Larsen-Freeman, 1975. "The acquisition of grammatical morphemes by adult ESL students." *TESOL Quarterly*, 9: 409–419.

22. David McNeill, 1966. Developmental psycholinguistics. In F. Smith and G. A. Miller (editors). *The Genesis of Language: A Psycholinguistic Approach.* Cambridge, Massachusetts: Massachusetts Institute of Technology Press, 15–84.

23. John P. Milan, 1974. "The development of negation in English by a second language learner." *TESOL Quarterly,* 8: 137–143.

24. W. Nemser, 1971. Approximative systems of foreign language learners. *International Review of Applied Linguistics,* Vol. 9, No. 2, pp. 115–123.

25. Ellen J. Rosansky, 1976. "Methods and morphemes in second language acquisition research." *Language Learning,* 26: 409–425.

26. John Schumann, 1974. "Implications of Pidginization and Creolization for the Study of Adult Second Language Acquisition." *New Frontiers in Second Language Learning,* Schumann, John and Stenson, Nancy, editors, Rowley, Massachusetts: Newbury House Publishers.

27. Margaret Sue Scott and G. Richard Tucker, 1974. "Error analysis and English language strategies of Arab students." *Language Learning,* 24: 69–97.

28. Larry Selinker, 1972. "Interlanguage," *International Review of Applied Linguistics,* 10: 209–231.

29. Larry Selinker, Merrill Swain, and Guy Dumas, 1975. "The interlanguage hypothesis extended to children." *Language Learning,* 25: 139–152.

30. S. N. Sridhar, 1976. "Contrastive Analysis, Error Analysis and Interlanguage, Three Phases of One Goal?" *Indian Linguistics,* 37: 258–281.

31. Bernard Spolsky, 1969. "Linguistics and Language Pedagogy—Applications or Implications?" pp. 143–155 in *Monograph Series on Languages and Linguistics,* 20th Annual Round Table, edited by James E. Alatis, Georgetown University Press.

32. ———, 1974a. "The Navajo Reading Study: An Illustration of the Scope and Nature of Educational Linguistics." *Volume III, Proceedings of the Third Congress, Association International de Linguistique Applique, Copenhagen 1972.* Applied Linguistics, Problems and Solutions, edited by J. Ovistgaard, H. Schwarz, and H. Spong-Hanssen. Heidelberg: Julius Groos Verlag, pp. 553–565.

33. ———, 1974b. "Linguistics and Education: An Overview." Pages 201–206 in *Current Trends in Linguistics, Volume 12: Linguistics and Adjacent Arts and Sciences.* The Hague: Mouton.

34. ———, 1978. *Educational Linguistics: An Introduction.* Rowley, Massachusetts: Newbury House Publishers.

35. Elaine Tarone, Merrill Swain, and Ann Fathman, 1976. "Some limitations to the classroom applications of current second language acquisition research." *TESOL Quarterly,* 10: 19–32.

DISCUSSION QUESTIONS

1. How can Spolsky's use of the term "fads" be justified?

2. What correlation can be found between linguistics per se and the several approaches to the study of second-language acquisition?

3. Does it seem likely to you that a speaker of German, a speaker of Chinese, and a speaker of Spanish would attain control of English morphemes in the same order?

4. Should research in language acquisition include concern with reading comprehension skill as an isolable skill? Relate your response to the concern with Black English.

5. Does second-language acquisition seem to be identical with first-language acquisition? See the articles by Roger Brown and Breyne Moskowitz in Part III. Are second-dialect learning and second-language learning the same?

EDNA ACOSTA-BELÉN

The author, an assistant professor of Hispanic studies at the State University of New York in Albany, has published in the areas of Spanish literature, linguistics, and bilingual education. She is a Columbia University Ph.D.

"SPANGLISH": A CASE OF LANGUAGES IN CONTACT[1]

There are virtually no studies that define the parameters of "Spanglish," a so-called dialect that is generally described as a particular mixture of Spanish and English and which is presumably used by Spanish-speaking communities in the United States. In recent years the use of "Spanglish" has become a major controversial issue in education at all levels—from the primary grades through college. There is a widespread negative attitude towards its use, which creates feelings of inferiority and alienation for those who allegedly use it. Speakers of a non-defined mixture of Spanish and English are judged as "deficient" or "sloppy" speakers of Spanish and/or English, and are often labelled "verbally deprived," "alingual" or "deficient bilinguals" because supposedly, they do not have the ability to speak either Spanish or English well.

Much of the controversy over Spanglish arises out of the lack of understanding of the nature of this process. No research studies have described the linguistic features that define Spanglish: is it merely a matter of incorporating English words into Spanish, or is it also the borrowing of phonological and grammatical structures from English? Given an adequate description of Spanglish, one can ask: do users of Spanglish speak only Spanglish, or do they also speak English or Spanish in other situations? Is Spanglish used by all generations of Spanish-speaking immigrants in the U.S., and if it is, are there qualitative differences among generations?

Despite the lack of systematic data required to answer the above questions and to put Spanglish in its proper sociolinguistic perspective, undocumented statements emphasizing the negative values placed on Spanglish—and therefore on its speakers—are often made. One of the strongest statements has been made by Carlos Varo (1971: 109).

> El "Spanglish" es . . . una enfermedad crónica, como puede serlo el sentimiento de dependencia y la frustración que busca un escape por la droga, el alcohol o la violencia física o sexual.[2]

In this paper we would like to take the first step towards a general description of Spanglish, consider some of its sociological and educational implications, and provide insight into a language issue which does not pertain exclusively to Puerto Ricans or other

---

[1] This is a revised and updated version of the article "On the Nature of Spanglish," *The Rican: Journal of Contemporary Puerto Rican Thought 2*, 2, 7–13.

[2] "Spanglish" . . . is a chronic illness just like the feelings of dependency and frustration which seek escape by means of drugs, alcohol or physical or sexual violence." (Author's translation)

Spanish-speaking groups in the U.S., but which arises every time groups speaking different languages come into contact.

The various groups of immigrants who came to the U.S. for the first time were compelled by sheer necessity to acquire some knowledge of the English language in order to function in their new environment. The establishment of ethnic communities within this country created a situation of cultural contact and hence of language contact. As part of the adaptation to the new setting the immigrant began to undergo a process of deculturation (loss of his/her own culture), and of acculturation (adoption of the dominant culture of the society).

It is well known that the ethnocentric foundations of American society have always encouraged the "melting pot" ideology. Making the immigrant conform to the standard cultural values of the society has been "the most prevalent ideology of assimilation in America throughout the nation's history" (Gordon 1964: 89). Immigrants have perceived the adoption of the dominant society's cultural and linguistic behaviors as a ladder to social mobility, which also brought the accompanying loss of important aspects of their native cultures. In many instances, linguistic acculturation, in this case mastery of English to the detriment of the native language, became a major part of the immigrant's accommodation to a new and different way of life.

Researchers have examined the linguistic process of language contact by studying the language behavior of immigrant groups in the U.S. Among them, Einar Haugen (1969), in his study *The Norwegian Language in America,* describes how the Norwegian immigrant created an instrument of communication which expressed the new aspects of American society in all those fields in which the Norwegian participated. Haugen also documents the influence on the Norwegian language of the social pressures the immigrant felt—Norwegians were ashamed to display their native speech in front of "Yankees." Thus, as Norwegians learned English words, these were incorporated into their native language replacing Norwegian words, and in other instances new words were created in spite of having adequate Norwegian equivalents. Haugen illustrates this when he colorfully describes the coming of the Norwegian to America:

> In order to 'maeka ei levving' they had to scratch about for a 'jabb' which often meant that they had to join a 'kru' (crew) of some kind and work under a 'bas' . . . Many Norwegians found work in the 'lomberkemper' which were located in the 'peinri' (pineries) . . . As soon as they could, they acquired a 'farm' which it never occurred to them to call 'gard' as they had done in Norway. With the word came all its derivatives 'farma' (to farm), 'farmar' and 'farming'. If they could not afford to buy a farm they might 'renta' and live as 'rentarar' (renters), which entirely replaced the Norwegian 'leiga' and 'leilending'. (76–77)

These examples illustrate the linguistic mechanisms generally used in the "Americanization" of immigrant languages. That is, the grammatical rules of the native language are applied to "borrowed" English words. From his research Uriel Weinreich (1968) reaches a similar conclusion: "the vocabulary of a language . . . is beyond question the domain of borrowing par excellence" (56). In summary, "it is the language of the learner that is influenced, not the language he learns. English is hardly influenced at all by the immigrant languages, but these are all influenced by English" (Haugen 1969: 370). Table 1 clearly illustrates this phenomenon for Norwegian, Dutch, Polish, Finnish, Italian, and Spanish. All of these immigrant groups (as well as many others) "made up" their own words by incorporating English words into the phonological and morphological systems of their respective languages.

Table 1

English	Norwegian-American		English	American-Dutch
anyway	eunivei		trouble	troebel
fixes	fiksar		to move	moeven
factory	fektri		stores	storen
makes	mekar		to drive	drivuen

English	American-Polish		English	Finglish
truck	trok		store	stoori
street car	strytkara		teacher	titseri
job	dziab		baby	peipi
payday	pedja		to clear	kliinaan

English	Italo-American		English	Spanglish
furniture	fornitura		furniture	furnitura
nurse	nursa		nurse	norsa
to fix	fixare		to fix	fixear
trouble	trobolo		trouble	trobol

The dynamics involved in the contact of two language groups suggest in a general sense that the language of any given group of immigrants within the American society is going to be affected or influenced by English; that is, in this specific social context, the language of the minority will be affected by the language of the majority.

Further evidence of this process is provided by one of the most recent immigrant groups to the United States, the Puerto Ricans. When the first generation of Puerto Rican immigrants came to the U.S., their native Spanish came into contact with English. As part of the process of adaptation to the new environment, there were objects, functions, and new experiences that could not be expressed in the immigrant's language or that were better expressed in English. As new cultural patterns had to be learned, consequently, a linguistic means for expressing new objects and new ways had to be found. Spanish-speakers began to borrow certain lexical items from English and to incorporate them into their own speech by applying Spanish phonological and morphological rules to them. This is how words and phrases like : ''la factoría'' (the factory), ''la grocería'' (the grocery store), ''el rufo'' (the roof), ''la jira'' (the heater), ''rapear'' (to rap), ''vacunear la carpeta'' (to vacuum the carpet), and many others came into existence.

As was the case for Norwegians in the U. S., the Puerto Ricans also felt social pressures to speak English: speaking English was a sign of mobility. Thus, in many cases, newly learned English words began to replace Spanish words in everyday speech. Little by little, new words were formed which created an atrophy of forms or words in the native tongue that were no longer needed or used. As a result, words that were previously expressed in Spanish are now often expressed in ''Spanglish.'' Other examples of this process are: ''lonche'' (lunch), ''lonchar'' (to lunch), ''furnir'' (to furnish), ''furnitura'' (furniture), ''guachear'' (to watch), ''guachiman'' (watchman), etc. Spanglish, therefore, reflects a linguistic adaptation of immigrants to the new environment, produced by the social pressures felt towards learning the English language. Salvador Tió (1954), a well known Puerto Rican writer, tells a humorous story in one of his essays, which illustrates our previous points, about an old Puerto Rican woman who would say the rosary at the wake every time someone in the community died. In Puerto Rico the litany went: 'que Dios lo saque de penas y lo lleve a descansar.'' (May God grant him eternal rest.) After she had moved to "El Barrio" in New York the prayer underwent some changes and ended up as "que Dios lo saque de 'trobol' y lo lleve a un sitio 'naiz' " (245).

Although the issue of Spanglish might look superficially similar to the imposition and influence of English on the Spanish spoken in Puerto Rico, the situation of the Puerto Ricans in the U. S. is qualitatively different. The linguistic process that we have described has taken place with *all* immigrant groups that have come to America in spite of the fact that the situation in their mother countries was completely different from that of the Puerto Ricans. Ricardo Cornejo (1973) mentions a process undergone by Mexican-American children in the Southwest that is similar to the one we have described; therefore, no direct relationship can necessarily be drawn between the influence of English on the Spanish spoken in Puerto Rico and the issue of "Spanglish" in the U. S.

The children of first generation immigrants tend to be dominant in the language of the dominant society, in this case English. Since children born in the U. S. of Puerto Rican parents no longer have the same opportunity to learn Spanish (although bilingual education is beginning to change this situation), their vocabulary is less extensive and they learn the words that the previous generation borrowed or adapted from English, sometimes without knowing that they are not Spanish words. They also continue to borrow lexical items from their dominant language and incorporate them into Spanish when attempting to speak it. These children would not recognize many words as English, for they have been adopted and given a form which do not markedly distinguish them from Spanish words. After years of using such borrowed words, they are often perceived as part of the Spanish lexical stock by Puerto Ricans who were born or raised in the U. S.

To study the pervasiveness of the use of Spanglish one may ask several related questions: Given a Spanglish word, is it perceived as acceptable Spanish? Does the speaker use it himself? If the word is not acceptable Spanish, does the speaker know the "correct" Spanish equivalent? These questions were the focus of a pilot study conducted this past year with twenty Puerto Rican college students at the State University of New York at Albany, most of whom considered themselves bilingual in English and Spanish.

Each student was given a list of 50 Spanglish vocabulary words commonly used in his/her community. After each word, the students were asked to indicate whether they knew the "proper" Spanish word, if there was one. The data collected indicated that 67% of the Spanglish words were considered acceptable Spanish by the students and 72% of the words were commonly used by them. Students were able to provide only 35% of the "correct" Spanish equivalents. In other words, in most cases the students reported that the "Spanglish" words they often use are considered by them as acceptable Spanish.

The results of this pilot study suggest either of two possibilities: that children of first generation Puerto Rican parents are slowly but surely losing command of their Spanish as it is spoken in Puerto Rico; or, they never acquired it in the first place, and instead they acquired the language spoken in their own community which includes a great number of Spanglish words or phrases. It is an unchangeable reality that Spanglish words are constantly used and created within the Spanish-speaking communities, and as it has been shown, this is a process of languages in contact that cannot be eliminated. This of course in no way implies that Puerto Ricans in the U. S. are incapable of speaking the so called "standard" Spanish.

Often confused with the borrowing of English lexical items into the Spanish language, is another pervasive linguistic process common to bilinguals; namely, the switching from one language to another during a conversation. This process, known as code-switching, has been erroneously labelled Spanglish. Numerous research studies have shown that bilinguals tend to switch from one language to the other depending on the situation. A bilingual does *not* switch when the other speaker is monolingual, but only when both are bilinguals (Haugen, 1969). Thus, switching is an option available to bilinguals, and is not a "deficiency" as commonly claimed. Gumperz and Hernandez (1971) have pointed out that "in spite of the fact that (such) extreme code switching is held in disrepute, it is persistent wherever minority language groups come in close contact with majority language groups under conditions of rapid social change" (316). They also explain how this alternation between the two language systems carries meaning and "serves definite and clearly understandable communicative ends" (327).

These observations about the nature of "Spanglish" suggest a more rigorous linguistic study to determine the extent of the influence of English in different Spanish-speaking communities in the U. S., and the directions that Spanglish is taking. Up to the present, nothing we have observed contradicts the thesis that so far, Spanglish has basically maintained its Spanish structure. Expressions like "está en el beisman" (he is in the basement), "el rufo esta liqueando" (the roof is leaking), "tengo un apartamento furnido" (I have a furnished apartment), "hay que vacunear la carpeta" (the carpet has to be vacuumed) illustrate that Spanish syntactic structures will prevail.

Like any other group of immigrants that came to America, the Puerto Ricans tried to follow the path leading to the "melting pot." Those groups that were considered "white" in terms of this society's racial definitions were successful. Those who were considered "non-white" discovered that in spite of their efforts to "Americanize," they were rejected and stigmatized (Seda Bonilla 1971). This attitude created in them feelings of inferiority, identity crisis, and even shame at displaying their native culture and language to members of the dominant society. They soon discovered that acceptance into American society was not after all guaranteed by Anglo-conformity, that is, by the adoption of the American culture and the English language. They were still considered inferior and pushed into a position of marginality within this society. Naturally, this has resulted in the internalization of a negative self-image.

Cultural pluralism, the preservation of the culture and of immigrant groups within the U. S., has become a goal, for many, for alleviating the deplorable condition of racially differentiated minorities. Ethnic Studies and Bilingual Education programs have become the instruments for change: they are designed to help minority group members function positively within the society by making them aware of their own cultural values and assets.

Even within these programs, however, Spanglish continues to be a delicate issue. Many educators and other observers frequently show amusement or indignation when they hear Spanglish being used. Even those who use it are very defensive about the issue when it is brought to their attention. Spanglish is perceived to be a corruption of the Spanish language or even worse, to be an expression of scorn or rejection on the part of the immigrant towards his mother tongue. Such indignation stems largely from the application of rigid and somewhat antiquated standards of linguistic purity. There is also a failure to understand that speech mixture among immigrant groups is something universal that has occurred whenever language groups come into contact.

The issue of Spanglish, however, does entail serious complications and therefore is a subject that should be discussed, since most teachers in bilingual education programs will have, at some point, to make decisions about how to deal with it in the classroom. First of all, it creates a barrier between Puerto Ricans who were born in the U. S. and those in Puerto Rico. Language is a factor that divides both groups. After all, the language of the Puerto Ricans is Spanish, and to accept anything else could be detrimental to

Puerto Rican culture. Historically, the first generation of Puerto Ricans that came to the U. S. spoke Spanish with all regional differences characteristic of Puerto Rican Spanish. Their children, however, who are born or raised in the U. S. usually speak English as their native language. Thus, when these children later go to Puerto Rico they feel like outsiders because they do not speak Spanish like a native. On other occasions, when they try to speak Spanish, they may feel ashamed because they are constantly told by Latin Americans and even Anglos who know Spanish that their Spanish is not "correct."

As if this were not enough, Spanglish has been used by the dominant society to support the idea that minorities are "linguistically deficient" and/or "verbally deprived." From both sides, then, there is a rejection of the immigrant's language. Obviously this has a serious impact on the individual's self-concept.

In 1970, when the New School of Social Research offered a course in Spanglish, supposedly to help American professionals understand the "jargon" of the Puerto Ricans, the School was in fact reinforcing the stereotype of a Puerto Rican dialect which is different from and inferior to the so called "standard" Spanish. At the same time, they were also reinforcing the negative image of the immigrant who cannot speak either English or Spanish well. These educators failed to understand both the nature of Spanglish and the fact that even those who use Spanglish in certain situations may be dominant in either Spanish or English, depending on which generation of immigrants they belong to.

If follows from this discussion that certain educational decisions must be made—bilingual education programs have become a national priority. To accomplish the major objective of bilingual education programs—which is to start "where the child is" and also to make the children feel free to express themselves in the language they know—an understanding of the nature of Spanglish as well as other nonstandard dialects is essential for both teachers and educators in general. This does not mean that the child should not be given the opportunity to know all the available options, like learning the so-called "standard" Spanish. After all, these children will also have to function in other social contexts outside of their own community, so they should be provided with the opportunity to also learn the kind of language that will help them communicate effectively in other environments.

Teachers must be aware that criticizing children because they do not "know how to talk" brings only feelings of inferiority that may cause irreparable damage to the child's self-esteem. Therefore, the teacher should be prepared to clearly understand language differences in order to establish more productive communication with the child.

DISCUSSION QUESTIONS

1. Does "Spanglish" fit Spolsky's definition of interlanguage?

2. Compare the viewpoint expressed here with that held by Ricardo Garcia.

3. Explain code-switching and its function among "Spanglish" speakers.

4. The author asserts that nonwhite Puerto Ricans are more disadvantaged than white Puerto Ricans. If this implies that color is more significant than language conformity in gaining social and economic opportunity in the United States, does Puerto Rican society itself hint at a solution?

5. Do you accept the author's view of the teacher's responsibility in the education of Spanish-speaking students?

THOMAS KOCHMAN

A graduate of New York University, the author, after teaching at Northeastern Illinois State College, became professor of communication at the University of Illinois, Chicago Circle, with writing and research interest in Black speech behavior, cross-cultural communication, and language policy in the schools.

SOCIAL FACTORS IN THE CONSIDERATION OF TEACHING STANDARD ENGLISH

The purpose of this paper is two-fold: one, to weigh the educational value of an oral language program which attempts to teach standard dialect to speakers of a nonstandard dialect, and two, to consider the probable success of such a program, given present social trends.

My first quarrel with such a program is that it does not develop the ability of a person to use language which I would further define as performance capability in a variety of social contexts on a variety of subject matter. Instead, we utilize valuable time to set up drill exercises which are designed to get the individual to replace socially stigmatized forms with socially preferred ones. I cannot endorse as valid a program that sacrifices individual language growth in exchange for some nebulous and highly problematic "social security." The child comes to us with some ability to play the horn and no ability to play the piano. This type of program presumes that a mediocre ability to play the piano is to be preferred to a better than average ability to play the horn. I cannot accept this thesis.

Underlying this approach seems to be a misapplication of Basil Bernstein's terms which falsely equate *restrictive code* and *elaborated code* with, respectively, nonstandard dialect and standard dialect.

It ought to be noted, as Bernstein uses the term, *code* is not to be equated with *langue*, but *parole*, not with *competence* but *performance*. What is restrictive or elaborated is not in fact the *code* as sociolinguists use the term, but the message.

This false equation is further reinforced by the observation made by some that speakers of standard dialect possess more elaborate uses of language than speakers of nonstandard dialect. This coincidence is erroneously interpreted to be causal, *viz*, that speakers of standard dialect are more capable *because* they speak standard dialect. You hear remarks such as "there are things you can't say in nonstandard dialect." These people overlook the fact that standard dialect speakers are so designated by their educational level which often includes being better educated in the *use* of language. What limitations there are exist in the abilities of the speakers.

I might add that many elaborate users of language perform in the nonstandard dialect of the Black Urban Communities and the Kentucky mountains. People who make observations such as the one cited in the paragraph above generally know little of the high degree of prestige associated with verbal ability and consequent high degree of verbal performance in the above named sub-cultures and my guess is that they care to know even less.

The point here is that you can and do have elaborate performance in nonstandard dialect as well as standard and restrictive performances in standard dialect as well as nonstandard.

My second quarrel with such a program deals with what can be called its efficiency quotient. How much time and drill are required to acquire the new set of language habits necessary to produce even a mediocre and restrictive performance in standard dialect? Speech teachers tell me that with maximum cooperation it takes several months of drill to get a person to say *ask* who formerly said *aks*. My own observation tells me that the input in time and effort is prodigious and the results negligible. Tying in this remark with those made earlier, how might this time be spent in a fashion more beneficial to the language growth and development of the learner?

My third quarrel deals with the exaggerated importance English and Speech teachers attach to being able to perform in a prestige dialect, far beyond its net social worth. How important is it really to getting or keeping a job, to getting the greatest amount of cooperation from your audience, or even to being necessary to the aesthetic of a speech event.

As regards getting a job there are any number of factors that take precedence over ability to perform in standard English such as labor supply and demand, race, membership in the dominant group, educational level, and presently, ability to threaten the establishment. Some factors influencing social and economic success are social background: race, dominant group membership; ability to manipulate people and situations; skill in exploiting others' abilities to personal advantage; acquiring political and social contacts; ability to project personality; ability to demonstrate skills of intelligence, aggressiveness, shrewdness, guile and judgment; and most important, the ability to bluff, i.e. deceive others about one's *actual* knowledge, intelligence, etc. Add to that, being a member of a group that constitutes a present threat to the establishment.

As regards the thesis that standard dialect is necessary to get the greatest cooperation from the audience, I have witnessed too many speech events where the audience accommodated the speaker on *his* terms and others where an accent actually added to the *authoritativeness* of the speaker. Also, it seems to me that speaking a *regional standard* that is different from the audience's might involve the same social handicap as speaking a nonstandard dialect. Educated South Midlanders experience much the same difficulty as uneducated ones in getting housing in Chicago. People from Chicago, New York and elsewhere seem to have different social attitudes towards regional standards and rank them differently on a social scale; yet we don't advocate that regional standard speakers accommodate the audience by modifying their speech. The point is if we are attempting to educate people that one regional standard is as good as another, why not educate them that all dialects are equally good.

The final point here is that the aesthetic of a speech event involves a great deal more than the simple use of standard dialect speech forms. I have in mind such qualities as the ability to project personality, style, self-assurance, authoritativeness, native coloring, in a fluent manner, regardless of dialect.

I just read where the BBC in London is permitting the reporting of news events in dialects other than the Received Standard. They have found that news broadcasted on the *scene* by reporters in local dialect added a touch of "realism" to the presentation.

The second part of this paper proposes to deal with the probable success of such a program, given present social trends. The audience might well wonder why I am pursuing this aspect after I have just apparently concluded that such a program is not educationally fruitful. You ask, "If it is not educationally sound, why is it necessary to consider whether it is possible?" Your logic is flawless but unhappily it is based on the illusory assumption that what is done in the *classroom* is done only after it is decided that it is worth doing. My observations at English, Speech and TESOL conventions and in school classrooms in the past persuade me that teachers and supervisors are concerned almost exclusively with methodology—"how to teach it"—and are gratuitously deaf to the logically antecedent question of "whether to teach it at all." This portion of the paper is especially aimed at them.

What are the teaching problems facing the teacher who attempts to teach the prestige form of a dialect to, let us suppose, Black children, against whom the focus of such a program is generally directed? The two teaching problems he will have to face are social in origin. They are the problems of motivation and reinforcement. Let us consider motivation first.

There are basically two reasons for wanting to learn a second language or dialect: cultural identification and/or functional need. With respect to the first reason we must take into account the alienation Black people feel; with regard to the second reason we must consider the credibility gap that has been created because of the failure of Blacks who had skills to get meaningful jobs. How has language teaching contributed to the alienation and credibility gap we now face? How have both contributed to the failure and frustration of students, producing a drop-out rate of 1000 students a month in our Chicago schools?

In the past and generally up to the present time children have encountered in the English and Speech classrooms the prescriptive approach. This approach advanced the superiority of the standard dialect and through the process of exclusion, negation and derogation the inferiority of the nonstandard dialect, and by direct implication the inferiority of the speakers who speak it and the inferiority of their culture which produces it. You who are unwilling to accept this implication, ask yourselves why English spoken with a French accent is socially acceptable, even "charming," while English spoken with a Black accent is not. The inescapable social truth of the matter is that people's attitudes towards other people's speech are merely an extension of people's attitudes towards their culture and the people of that culture. This point is not missed by the culturally different when they enter the middle class establishment of the schoolroom.

What was the underlying perspective behind this approach? Assimilationist! What was the justification? At worst, it was arrogant ethnocentrism; at best, it recognized that the society is prejudiced and the way to escape discrimination was by losing your group identification. Your perspective and attitude said: obliterate what is culturally different, or if you can't, conceal it; relegate it to the inside of your homes. The penalty for non-assimilation was a social ostracism, so the groups that could assimilate did, but often with much bitterness and resentment, and then only partially.

The groups that couldn't assimilate or chose not to, like American Indians, Blacks and Mexican-Americans, were and are relegated respectively to the societal oblivion of the reservation and the ghetto. They have been the invisible people of our society.

The assimilationist approach made people resentful, resistant to learning. Now it has made them angry enough to demand, through petition and boycott, an end to this kind of attitude and teaching.

It is to the credit of the linguistic approach that it has at least recognized that the speaker's native dialect has cultural value for him and is not to be tampered with. It advances the teaching of standard English as a second dialect. It is a step in the right direction but it hardly goes far enough. The problem is in its supposedly "realistic" approach. It says, "People make social judgments all the time. We live in a socially stratified and deterministic society. Recognize it! Conform to the existing social order and its rules." Unfortunately, the linguistic approach accepts as social determinant the same obnoxious and racist standards as the prescriptive-assimilationist approach and in so doing merely perpetuates the alienation begun with its predecessor.

If a child does not wish to identify with the larger society, emphasize the *functional* value of performing in standard dialect; "He'll need it to get a better job," or "Teach it to him so that he will be able to decide later on whether he wants to use it or not." This "functional need" motivation falls on unbelieving ears. The Black child knows that he pays the social price for being Black, not because he does or does not speak standard dialect. He asks, "Why do I have to speak better than the white man to get the same job?" Do you need to be able to perform in standard dialect to be a carpenter, plumber, brick layer, construction worker, or printer, or to be any trade or non-trade union employee? How many white collar jobs require the ability to perform in standard dialect? Are Blacks going to believe that they are being discriminated against in all of these jobs because they don't speak standard dialect? In 1963 for those Blacks who attended college, their median income was only 60% of that of whites with comparable education. In 1966 Blacks with an eighth grade education earned 80% of what whites earned with comparable education. If educational level, which is a far more significant employment factor than ability to perform in standard dialect, has not been effective in reducing the disparity between Black and white income why should Blacks believe performing in the prestige dialect will. According to a 1967 report[1] entitled *Chicago's Widening Color Gap,* "Negro college graduates in Chicago earn less than white high school drop-outs" (pp. 80–81). It is to be noted also that the higher the educational level, the greater the disparity between Black and white income.

With regard to the problem of reinforcement, where is the child going to use, outside of the classroom, the dialect the teacher is attempting to teach him inside? And if he can't find a place to use it, how is he going to acquire a "new set of language habits." The area in which he lives reinforces his native dialect, not the standard. In Chicago, it is not unusual for a Black child to have attended 100% Black schools up to and through high school. Clearly, the linguistic approach presumes that *integration* will take place; either that Black families will move into white areas or that Black children will be bussed into white areas where reinforcement of standard dialect can take place. Demographic statistics show a contrary trend, viz., Black communities are becoming "blacker" and white communities "whiter." Even in communities such as Maywood, Joliet and Wheaton with which I am partly familiar, with a majority white population, the Blacks invariably live in segregated housing, and socialization in the high school is almost invariably *intra*-group with very little chance of reinforcing prestige dialect patterns assuming even that white high school students speak them.

Finally, the linguistic approach is based on a social fallacy, viz., that the social order is immutably stratified, that the social judgments that people are making today are the same judgments that they will be making fifteen or even five years from now. I find this assumption challenged by present social trends. The walls of racism are even today starting to crumble and those teachers using the linguistic-integrationist approach will find themselves accused of having made a pact with the same devil as those using the prescriptive-assimilationist approach.

I see our society experiencing the throes of social reform this very minute. Our

---

[1] By Pierre de Vise, Dept. of Sociology, De Paul University, December 1967, Inter-University Social Research Committee, Report No. 2.

cherished prejudices and practices are being assaulted at every turn, besieged with long hair and "bad manners" on the one hand and Black Power and creative disorder on the other. What if Blacks succeed in changing the social order so that they and their culture will no longer be regarded as inferior by the larger society? What if, in twenty years, you will regard a Black accent comparably to the way you regard today the accent of a German professor, French singer, or British actor? Does it really matter how people of status speak? You say, what if the social order is not changed? Then I ask you, What have you accomplished in your program: the ability to avoid some stigmatized forms which are so stigmatized because the people who speak them are?

Will speaking better remove the stigma attached to that person? At the Democratic convention Julian Bond probably spoke "better" than most people there. Will speaking better make Bond president? I doubt it, but Black Power might.

It ought to be clear by this time that what is emerging in our society today is a resurgence of ethnic pride as well as attempts by ethnic communities to establish control over their own destiny. Not only are the culturally different resisting or rejecting the assimilationist pressure of the present establishment, they are also no longer relegating or subordinating their own culture to the inside of their homes. Ultimately, the choice of what is to be taught and how it is to be taught is the learner's, and educators, like everyone else in our society, will have to respond to the challenge of being "relevant" in both our goals and our methods or be faced with empty classrooms and "student schools."

My conclusion is apparent. The present efforts to teach a prestige form of speech to nonstandard speakers are educationally wasteful and the effective realization is socially improbable, unless the express desire and cooperation of those learning it are forthcoming. That decision will be neither yours nor mine to make!

You who will persist in your efforts despite the resistance of your students, their parents and communities, do so at your own peril.

DISCUSSION QUESTIONS

1. Does the high degree of verbal performance alluded to here and described by Roger Abrahams in Part IV necessarily call for the use of Black English features?

2. How valid do you consider Kochman's analogy with regional dialects, remembering that Black English itself is essentially a Southern dialect spoken in the North?

3. Do you think that Kochman's linguistic diversity is educationally or socially feasible without a fundamental shift in social patterns in the United States?

4. How does Kochman's attitude toward drills correspond with Courtney Cazden's findings—reported by Breyne Moskowitz in Part III—that language interaction is more productive than constant correction in helping children acquire language?

PART VII

LINGUISTICS AND THE DICTIONARY

The dictionary that you, as a freshman, were expected to have and use was the product of a long history and a long tradition—history, because dictionary making had its origin in the glossaries of the Middle Ages, and tradition, because for nearly 250 years a dictionary has popularly been considered "the last word," the ultimate authority.

The first real English dictionaries, in the seventeenth century, were essentially collections of "hard words," words not ordinarily known or used and hence requiring dictionary definitions of some kind. Even the dictionary of Nathan Bailey in 1730, with its attempt to list all the words of the language, kept to the simple purpose of defining meaning. But in 1755 Samuel Johnson's *Dictionary of the English Language* changed the picture. Though ostensibly acknowledging that language constantly changes, Johnson in practice considered his great work as an authority, and its users, lacking such a recourse as the French had in their Academy, so considered it as well. Johnson was the first dictionary maker to indicate extensively his personal judgment about the use of words, indeed to such an extent that of the 41,443 entires in his two-volume work, no fewer than 1,150 bear such judgmental labels as "low," "improper," "ludicrous," and "burlesque."

The extraordinary prestige enjoyed by Johnson and his 1755 dictionary not only led to several successful later editions but also induced succeeding lexicographers to assume the same prescriptive role, a role that in the schools came to be recognized as the normal responsibility of a dictionary maker.

The contrary style of dictionary, with completely objective and descriptive entries, was that of the monumental, scholarly *New English Dictionary on Historical Principles,* the first fascicles of which began to appear in 1884 and were followed by others until its completion in 1928. It was renamed the *Oxford English Dictionary* upon its second printing in 1931. This approach strongly influenced the editors of the *Century Dictionary,* published in the United States in 1889, but the successful dictionaries of the day in this country were those of Noah Webster and Joseph Worcester, both of which gave the public what it apparently wanted—to be told what was "right" and what was "wrong." But Webster's dictionaries, which survived the battle between these two competitors, gradually moved closer to the descriptive point of view. When the second edition of *Webster's New International Dictionary* was published in 1934 it could frankly disclaim any privilege of dictatorship and declare that its authority was only as reliable as it faithfully reflected actual usage. Since, however, it retained such familiar usage labels as "colloquial" and since few persons read the fine-print policy declaration in the front matter, no particular furor was raised by this shift in policy.

Yet, as one commentator bluntly put it, "All hell broke loose" when in 1961 the third edition, with no real change in policy or principle, contained a misinterpreted note on *ain't,* dropped the usually misunderstood usage label "colloquial," and, for a reason never quite thoroughly disclosed, included proper nouns without initial capital letters. Quite ignoring the manifold intrinsic value of this great dictionary and, indeed, usually without even looking at it, scores of critics seized upon a few unfortunate statements in advertising blurbs, rose with hue and cry, and leaped to the attack upon the surprised and bewildered editors. Literary critics, newspaper editorialists, pious commentators of all sorts denounced the third edition in strident tones as contributing to the degradation and downfall of the English language. It was two or three years before an effective counterattack appeared in the reviews of competent critics. A documented case history of this peculiar series of events is that by James H. Sledd and Wilma R. Ebbitt, *Dictionaries and* That *Dictionary* (Scott, Foresman, 1962).

Although subsequently the superb quality of the *Webster Third*, as it is often called, was recognized by both the general public and the schools and colleges, one of its features, the use of citations from popular writers to illustrate word use, had so infuriated some authors and critics that they proposed and ultimately espoused the preparation of a dictionary in the authoritarian tradition of Samuel Johnson, one in which their opinions as usage judges could be deliberately set forth. That dictionary is *The American Heritage Dictionary of the English Language* (Houghton Mifflin, 1969).

The attention to lexicography aroused by this second "battle of the dictionaries" has been only one of a number of factors leading to a greatly heightened scholarly interest in the art and science of dictionary making. In 1972 a group of distinguished linguists and editors from several countries met in New York for the first major conference in the field. Its proceedings appeared as *Lexicography in English,* edited by Raven I. McDavid, Jr., and Audrey Duckert (New York Academy of Sciences, 1973). In the preceding year a bequest had given Indiana State University, Terre Haute, a great collection of English dictionaries, an act that led to that institution's granting the first graduate program with a degree in lexicography and to the founding of the Dictionary Society of North America.

Because the prescriptive tradition in the schools has often obscured the full resources of a good dictionary, we have taken from the second edition of *Readings in Applied English Linguistics* the still important article by Mitford Mathews, who outlines a number of values to be found in referring to a desk dictionary. Also from that edition we have retained the dispassionate critical comment on the *Webster Third* by the late Albert Marckwardt. His article may well be compared with that by Robert L. Chapman, "A Working Lexicographer Appraises *Webster's Third New International Dictionary*" (*American Speech* 46[1967]: 202–210).

The next article, by R. W. Burchfield, is relevant to the persistent eighteenth- and nineteenth-century attitude of deference to the presumed superiority of the English of England. Although Noah Webster had believed that the differences between British English and American English would eventually lead to their becoming two different languages, there was still a strong feeling, particularly in the eastern states, that somehow the English of England was better—a feeling that even now surfaces in the occasional appearance of the spelling *theatre* and of *-our* endings and of the pronunciation of *either* as /ayðɚ/. H. L. Mencken, in the first three editions of his *The American Language* (Knopf, 1919, 1921, 1923), countered this belief with his own attitude much like that of Webster. But the leveling effect of transoceanic travel and communication led Mencken to reverse himself with this statement in the preface to the fourth edition (1937): "The Englishman, of late, has yielded so much to American example, in vocabulary, in idiom, in spelling and even in pronunciation, that what he speaks promises to become, on some not too remote tomorrow, a kind of dialect of American, just as the language spoken by the American was once a dialect of English."

Marckwardt and Randolph Quirk similarly expressed this belief in their joint BBC and Voice of America broadcasts. See *A Common Language* (Voice of America, 1964; distributed by NCTE). Now Burchfield, from his vantagepoint as editor of the Oxford English dictionaries, disagrees with his fellow-countryman Quirk by arguing that the evidence points to an ultimate language split such as that foreseen by Webster and the early Mencken. He offers a new perspective with which to understand the American reception of the *Webster Third*.

That the intentions of the editors of the *American Heritage Dictionary* were commendable is conceded by Archibald Hill, whose ultimate negative reaction is based upon the choice and function of the usage panel whose judgments appear with respect to the use of controversial words.

Thomas Creswell, in the final article, draws upon his own major study to document the subjectivity and inconsistency of commercial dictionaries with respect to their decisions about usage. His specific data are well worth close study. Particularly does Creswell show how the *American Heritage Dictionary* panel members were often strikingly at odds with one another and how collectively they often disagreed with the usage decisions of the nine other dictionaries investigated for the study. Creswell adds a constructive note with his description of a procedure the use of which could yield greater objectivity.

You will find additional information about lexicography in the following:

Aarsleff, Hans. ''The Early History of the OED.'' *Bulletin of the New York Public Library* 66(1962): 427–439.

Creswell, Thomas L. *Usage in Dictionaries and Dictionaries of Usage*. Publication of the American Dialect Society, nos. 63–66. University of Alabama Press, 1975. Reviewed by Thomas L. Clark, ''The Usageasters,'' *American Speech* 55(1980): 131–136.

Friend, Joseph H. *The Development of American Lexicography, 1798–1894*. The Hague: Mouton, 1967.

Hulbert, James R. *Dictionaries: British and American*. Rev. ed. New York: Philosophical Library, 1968.

Mathews, Mitford M. *A Survey of English Dictionaries*. London: Humphrey Milford, 1933.

Starnes, Dewitt, and Gertrude E. Noyes. *The English Dictionary from Cawdrey to Johnson, 1604–1755*. University of North Carolina Press, 1946.

MITFORD M. MATHEWS

Now retired from a position as lecturer in linguistics at the University of Chicago, Mathews gained distinction as the editor of the Dictionary of Americanisms on Historical Principles *(University of Chicago Press, 1951).*

THE FRESHMAN AND HIS DICTIONARY

When I was a small boy a carpenter once said in my presence that few workmen, even among master mechanics, knew more than a fraction of the uses of an ordinary steel square. The remark amazed me, as at that early age I thought a carpenter's square was a very simple tool. It certainly appeared so to me,—nothing more than two flat pieces of metal forming a right angle, and useful in marking a plank that one wished to saw in two in something like a workmanlike manner. True, the instrument has numerous markings and numbers on it, but I had never seen anyone making the slightest use of these, so I had concluded they might be ignored.

When I became older and found that large books have been written on the uses of the steel square, I changed my mind about the simplicity of the tool and the limited range of its usefulness. For many years as I have observed the use made of dictionaries by even good students, I have been reminded of that remark by the carpenter about steel squares.

Dictionaries are tools, and they are much more complicated, and capable of many more uses than students suspect. All of us know students need encouragement and guidance in the use of dictionaries, and perhaps there are few teachers of freshman composition but that devote a part of their program to an effort to help students form the habit of consulting dictionaries. Composition books for freshmen point out the need for instruction of this kind.

Despite what is being done, however, the fact is easily observable that few students are able to use their dictionaries with anything like efficiency. Certainly there must be very few of those who come up through the grades these days who are not familiar with the details of looking up words in dictionaries, but it is one thing to find a word in a dictionary and quite another to understand fully the information there given about it. It seems to me that college freshmen are fully prepared for and could profit by a well-planned introduction to the larger of the English dictionaries, and an acquaintance with what they contain. Such a program might well include material of the following kinds.

1. Students should know something about the large, unabridged dictionaries to which they have ready access in college. They might well be given brief sketches of the *Oxford English Dictionary,* the *English Dialect Dictionary,* by Joseph Wright, the old *Century Dictionary* (12 volumes), and the modern unabridged *Webster.* These may be called the "Big Four" in the dictionary field, and while it is certainly not anticipated that the freshman will ever provide himself with all of them, it is a cultural experience for him to become acquainted with the circumstances under which each of them was produced, and with the special excellencies each exhibits.

An acquaintance with these larger works will not only make the student aware of what kind of information about words is available in them, but it will leave him much better prepared to make efficient use of the desk-size dictionary with which he has some familiarity.

Many years ago a graduate student inconvenienced himself greatly to come a long distance to see me to ask if I could help him secure some information about the term "poll tax." He was preparing a doctor's thesis, he told me, and needed to know how long this term had been in the language, what its basic meaning was, and what other meanings it may have had in the course of its use in English. He was most surprised when I opened the *OED* to the appropriate place and showed him that all he needed to know about this term had been available within a few feet of his desk in the school where he was studying. It is not at all likely that any but the exceptional student will ever need all the information about words that the larger dictionaries afford, but it is well worth the while of every student to become acquainted with the fact that such information is available for those who at any time need to make use of it.

It is to be hoped that in such general instruction as may be given about the different dictionaries, some emphasis will be placed on the fact that modern dictionaries do their utmost to *record* usage, not to *prescribe* it. The tendency to regard the lexicographer as a linguistic legislator is so deep-seated that it will probably never be entirely overcome. The habit of thought that is back of such expressions as "the dictionary now permits us to pronounce it thus," has been with us for a long time, and will continue. But every student should have the wholesome experience of being taught that dictionaries attempt to give commonly accepted usage, and that correctness in the use of language varies sometimes according to time and place.

2. Along with some information about the origin and scope of the large dictionaries mentioned, there should be given some elementary information about the history of the English language and the place it occupies with reference to the others of the Indo-European group. I am certainly not foolish enough to suggest that all teachers of freshman composition become instructors in Germanic philology. What I have in mind is nothing more detailed than could be easily covered in one, or at most two, class sessions, the over-all relationships of the languages being presented briefly, with a few well chosen examples to indicate the relationship of a few of them.

The desirability of this elementary acquaintance with the linguistic position occupied by English is brought out quite clearly by Professor Pei in his *Story of Language:*

> Many years ago, I was requested to tutor in French a young girl who had to take College Entrance Examinations. Knowing that she had had four years of Latin as well as three years of French, I spared no occasion in the course of the tutoring to remind her that certain French words which she had difficulty in remembering came from Latin words which she knew. For a time she took it patiently, though with a somewhat bewildered air. But one day she finally blurted out: "Do you mean to tell me that there is a *connection* between Latin and French?" In the course of four years of one language and three of the other, it had never occurred to any of her Latin teachers to inform her that Latin had descendants, or to her French teacher to tell her that French had a progenitor!

3. The attention usually devoted to instruction in the use of the dictionary apparently stresses spellings, meanings, and pronunciations somewhat in the order here given. Certainly these are conspicuous features of any dictionary, and it is altogether desirable for students to be encouraged to turn to these works when they are confronted with a problem of the kind indicated.

The impression, however, inevitably conveyed by instruction restricted altogether to employing the dictionary as a problem-solver, is that such a book is of no particular use unless there is a problem requiring immediate attention. Students are sorely tempted to so manipulate things as to avoid encountering problems that drive them to a dictionary. It is to be feared that, for many of them, the dictionary is a form of medicine to be resorted to only in time of unavoidable need. They associate it perhaps with castor oil or some other undesirable, dynamic type of cathartic. It is a most helpful thing for the student to learn that dictionaries are filled with interesting information from which one can derive much pleasure and instruction, even though he may not be confronted with an urgent problem of any kind.

Students should be encouraged to develop a wholesome curiosity about words that present no particular problem in spelling, pronunciation, or meaning. As a rule, the words we know well do not rise to the surface of our consciousness. It is only rarely that some common, everyday term forces itself upon our attention so urgently that for the first time we turn to the dictionary to see what lies back of it.

This use of the dictionary when there is no immediate, pressing need to do so, this giving attention to words we have known for a long time but have never grown curious about, is most rewarding. This kind of use of the dictionary we may think of as the labor of free men; the forced use is more properly likened to that of slaves.

On every hand there are words of fascinating backgrounds about which the dictionary has much to teach us. Certainly the name *Jesus*, that of the founder of Christianity, is well known to all those with whom you and I come in contact. Perhaps few of us have ever felt impelled to look the word up in a dictionary, or even realized that dictionaries contain it. As examination of the dictionary, however, reveals that the name his parents gave the Saviour was Joshua, and it was by this thoroughly Jewish name that He was known by those He lived among.

The first accounts of His life were written in Greek, and in these writings *Joshua* was transliterated into *Jesus*, a name that is certainly not Jewish in its present dress and at the same time appears odd as a Greek name.

Not even a grade-school pupil is likely to be baffled by *ostrich*, but one who is allergic to words may well become curious about it. Allow it to become the focus of your attention for a moment and see how odd the word appears. Make a guess as to where you think it might have come from, and then check up on yourself by turning to the dictionary. You may be surprised, as I was, to find the word is made up of two, one from Latin and one from Greek, which have so blended as to obscure altogether the fact that the expression signifies "bird-bird" or "bird-sparrow." It is a good term to bear in mind and use upon those of our brethren who insist that only "pure English" should be used, and profess to be pained by such obvious hybrids as *cablegram* and *electrocute*.

There may be few teachers who have discovered how rewarding it is to look curiously at the scientific terms used in dictionaries in the definitions of plants and animals. These expressions are usually hurried over by most of us as being the exclusive property of scientists and of very little interest for others.

It is surprisingly interesting to linger over such terms. It is a gratifying experience to discover one that yields its significance somewhat readily. Our common mocking bird, for instance, is *Mimus polyglottos*. The ingenuity needed for deciphering this expression is possessed by all of us. *Mimic* and *polyglot* are all we need to see that our expression means "the many-tongued mimic," a fitting description of the bird in question.

In the spring when the snow has melted, and the earth is warming up from its long cold sleep, the cheerful piping notes of a very small frog begin to be heard in the woods and marshes. People call this little creature a *spring peeper* because of the season when his little peeping notes are first heard, but scientists dub him *Hyla crucifer*. As we puzzle over this name we are likely to give up on *Hyla* for there is no other word in the English language with which we can, perhaps, associate it profitably. It has descendants among us, but we are not likely to be acquainted with them.

Crucifer though is easier. Even if we do not know that a *crucifer* is one who carries a cross, especially in a church procession, we can reason out the two elements in the word and see that it must have the meaning of one who carries a cross. Our ability to reason out this much of the scientific expression may increase our curiosity about the first element *Hyla*. Here is a helpful hint. As we all know, these scientific genus names are often from Greek. So we are reasoning sensibly when we suppose *Hyla* is Greek.

The fact is elementary that when we are confronted with a Greek word which begins with an *h*, i.e. with a rough breathing, it behooves us as cautious scouts to cast about in our minds for a possible Latin cognate beginning with an *s*. Substituting an *s* in *hyla* we come up with *syla*. Let us study *syla* a bit. It is almost a word. If we might be so bold as to insert a -v- and make it *sylva* we have a word that is in our dictionary, and one we met in a slightly different form, *silva*, when we studied first-year Latin.

The little detail of why this -v- is necessary need not bother us in the slightest at this point, because we are just having fun with no idea of becoming linguisticians. And this is it. *Hyla* and *sylva* go together and they both mean wood or forest. Now we can interpret this *Hyla crucifer* "the (little) fellow who lives in the woods and carries a cross," and when we find that this spring peeper has a dark marking on his back shaped like a cross, we are indeed gratified that now light is shining where previously all was darkness.

A teacher who is fortunate enough to have an assiduously cultivated curiosity about words will over and over again bring to a class gleanings of unexpected sorts from dictionaries. Such sharing of treasures will do more than anything else to bring home to students the fact that dictionaries are not dull, enlarged spelling books. They are filled with such a number of things that we can never exhaust their treasures but we can all be as happy as kings as we come time after time upon interesting nuggets of the kind just mentioned.

DISCUSSION QUESTIONS

1. What advantages do you see in having a dictionary that is descriptive rather than prescriptive?

2. Compare your desk dictionary's definition of *wit* with that in the *Oxford English Dictionary*. How do they differ?

3. Using your own dictionary, ascertain the location of the following colleges: Allan Hancock College, Cottey College, and Yuba College. Which are coeducational?

4. Look up five words you have not previously had any curiosity about. Report what interesting information you discover.

5. What do these names mean: *Alphonso, Daniel, Edward, Elizabeth, Chiquita,* and *Molly?*

6. Does your dictionary tell you the approximate location of the homeland of the original Indo-Europeans? What is it?

ALBERT H. MARCKWARDT

After a long teaching career at his alma mater, the University of Michigan, Marckwardt went to Princeton University as professor of English and then, after retirement, returned to teach at Michigan for one year and spent another year as visiting professor at the East-West Center in Honolulu. Outstanding scholar in English linguistics, he served as president of the Linguistic Society and of the National Council of Teachers of English, directed the Linguistic Atlas of the North Central States, and served briefly as director of the English Language Institute at Michigan and of the Center for Applied Linguistics in Washington. He died in 1975.

THE NEW WEBSTER DICTIONARY:
A CRITICAL APPRAISAL

A complete revision of our largest commercially produced dictionary of the English language has become a regularly recurring event in American life. Upon occasion the time table has varied a bit, but the following listing reveals an astonishing degree of regularity over the past century:

An American Dictionary of the English Language (Royal Quarto Edition, Unabridged)	1864
Webster's International Dictionary	1890
Webster's New International Dictionary	1909
Webster's New International Dictionary (Second edition)	1934
Webster's Third New International Dictionary	1961

Of the five Webster editions listed above, probably none has called forth such extremes of critical comment as the recent Webster Third. It has been characterized as "a very great calamity." Its general tone has been described as "a dismaying assortment of the questionable, the perverse, the unworthy, the downright outrageous." At the same time, other reviewers speak of the work as "an intellectual achievement of the very highest order," and "a reference work which worthily carries on a tradition of great reference works."

These extremes of praise and blame are reminiscent of the reception of the 1828 edition of *An American Dictionary of the English Language,* compiled by Webster himself and the real parent of the long line of dictionaries which bear his name. At that time a reviewer in *The Southern Literary Messenger* denounced the treatment of pronunciation as horrible and the orthography as abominable. The English *Quarterly Review* judged it "a decided failure, conducted on perverse and erroneous principles," and, in much the same vein as some of the critics of the Webster Third, complained that "we do not recollect ever to have witnessed in the same compass a greater number of crudities and errors, or more pains taken to so little purpose." But Webster's 1828 work had its admirers as well, particularly among the Germans, who praised the profound learning that it reflected.

The disparate comments on Webster's early work are of interest today only as a historical phenomenon, but those which have been applied to the Webster Third have given rise to considerable confusion. It is scarcely possible for both the critics and the admirers to be right in all that they say, and one may reasonably ask what a more dispassionate evaluation might be.

In approaching such an appraisal, we must understand first of all that the American lexicographer in his concern with current English faces something of a dilemma. He is the inheritor of two traditions clearly in conflict, both of which have their roots in England.

The earlier tradition is that of Samuel Johnson, the compiler of the 1755 *Dictionary of the English Language,* who lent the first touch of sheer genius to English lexicography. In the preface of this great work, he pointed out that "every language has its improprieties and absurdities, which it is the duty of the lexicographer to correct or proscribe." According to him, the function of a dictionary was one, "by which the pronunciation of our language may be fixed and its attainment facilitated; by which its purity may be preserved, its use ascertained, and its duration lengthened." That Johnson was expressing the spirit of his age is shown by comments such as that of Lord Chesterfield, who wrote, "We must have resource to the old Roman expedient in times of confusion and choose a Dictator. Upon this principle I give my vote for Mr. Johnson to fill that great and arduous post."

This concept of the lexicographer as linguistic legislator or arbiter, if not absolute dictator, is still strong in the United States. It is frequently reflected, and indeed encouraged, by the slogans which dictionary publishers—not the editors, let me hasten to say—choose to advertise their wares. The very phrase, "Supreme Authority," which the G. and C. Merriam Company used to employ, supported this view of the dictionary; whether intentionally or not is open to conjecture.

The slightly later and opposed tradition is that of the lexicographer as the objective recorder of the language. For the English-speaking nations this concept was first realized on a substantial scale in what is now known as *The Oxford English Dictionary* but originally entitled *A New English Dictionary on Historical Principles*. Here the purpose is stated as follows:

> The aim of this dictionary is to present in alphabetical series the words which have formed the English vocabulary from the time of the earliest records down to the present day, with all the relevant facts concerning their form, sense-history, pronunciation, and etymology. It embraces not only the standard language of literature and conversation, whether current at the moment or obsolete, or archaic, but also the main technical vocabulary, and a large measure of dialetical usage and slang.

Note that this statement contains not one word about fixing the language, about proscription or prescription of any kind. Operating on this basis, the lexicographer contents himself with setting down the record, leaving its interpretation to the reader. Needless to say, the prestige of the *Oxford English Dictionary* is enormous; it is generally conceded to be superior to the corresponding major dictionaries for the other western European languages. The principles on which it is based were formulated as early as 1859.

The conflict of principle which has been pointed out need not necessarily be troublesome. If the language involved is confined as to number of speakers and is the vehicle of a static and stabilized society, there is virtually no problem. But this is not the case with English, which is spoken natively by some two hundred and seventy millions, spread over five continents of the globe. In the United States, at least, the language is that of a highly mobile society, both geographically and up and down the social scale.

Under such circumstances, the linguistic reporter and the legislator are more likely to seem to be working at cross purposes.

Nevertheless, it is clearly evident that as the various editions of Webster march down the century, the statements of principle which are to be found in them move steadily away from the Johnsonian or prescriptive concept toward the descriptive position of the Oxford editors. The following excerpt from the front matter of the 1934 edition (p. xxvi) refers specifically to pronunciation, but it is a fair representation of the attitude of its editors toward all language matters:

> The function of a pronouncing dictionary is to record as far as possible the pronunciations prevailing in the best present usage, rather than to attempt to dictate what that usage should be. In so far as a dictionary may be known and acknowledged as a faithful recorder and interpreter of such usage, so far and no farther may it be appealed to as an authority.
>
> In the case of diverse usages of extensive prevalence, the dictionary must recognize each of them.

A somewhat broader treatment of the editorial function is to be found in the Introduction (p. xi) to the 1934 Webster:

> Both Samuel Johnson and Noah Webster conceived it to be a duty of the dictionary editor to maintain the purity of the standard language. However, with the growth in literacy of the past century, and the increase in fiction and drama, in radio and motion picture, of the use of dialect, slang, and colloquial speech, it has become necessary for a general dictionary to record and interpret the vocabularies of geographical and occupational dialects, and of the livelier levels of the speech of the educated.

It would be difficult to imagine a more cogent or forthright exposition of the descriptive function of the dictionary than these two statements of editorial policy. The first of them apparently satisfied the editors of the Webster Third, for they repeat it in their Introduction (p. 6a) with only one minor expansion: "best present usage" of the earlier edition now reads, "general cultivated conversational usage, both formal and informal." This offers additional support for the conclusion that with respect to the conflict between opposing lexicographical concepts, the descriptive had been accepted, the prescriptive rejected, as early as 1934. Whatever differences there may be between the 1934 and 1962 editions, they are not matters of policy or principle. They are instead differences in the way in which a principle common to both dictionaries has been realized.

Lexicographical policy is not ordinarily a matter of absorbing interest, but it has been necessary to deal with it at some length because the Webster Third has been criticized on occasion for repudiating, even sabotaging the principles of the second edition. Such charges serve only to reveal a total lack of awareness on the part of the critic as to what these principles were, as well as an inability to distinguish between principle and practice.

The extremes of public reaction to the new Webster must therefore be understood in terms of editorial decisions on a practical rather than a theoretical level. Such an understanding may best be attained by considering certain of the practical questions which confronted the editors, what the decisions on them were, and what the reasons for them may have been.

At the very outset of their preparations, the editors apparently felt an obligation to increase considerably the amount of evidence upon which the new dictionary was to be based. Dictionary evidence normally exists in the form of citation slips, the products of an extensive reading program. The citations are filed under their appropriate headwords, and in the editing process they constitute the raw material for the definitions and in fact for most of the word treatment.

At the time of the compilation of the second edition, the files in the Springfield offices held some 1,615,000 citation slips. In the years intervening between the two editions, as the result of what must have been a tremendous effort, this figure was nearly quadrupled. Just under 4,500,000 citations were added, resulting in a total of 6,000,000, a number approximately equalling the collection for the *Oxford English Dictionary,* but far more heavily concentrated on the language of the present day. In addition, the *Dictionary of American English* and the *Dictionary of Americanisms* had both been completed in the years 1944 and 1951 respectively, constituting a further increase in the size of the corpus available to the editors of the Webster Third. As a result, they found themselves with approximately 50,000 new words, that is, words not entered in the Webster Second, and 50,000 new meanings for words already entered.

At this point physical and financial factors enter into consideration. For a number of reasons, undoubtedly based upon a century of business experience, the publishers are firmly committed to a single-volume dictionary. They had made the Webster Second as large, that is to say thick, as any one volume could possibly get and still assure a back that might withstand the rigors of long and constant use, particularly in schools and libraries. Thus it was manifestly impossible to increase the number of pages by the ten or fifteen percent necessary to accommodate the new entries. If these were to be included, something had to come out. The kind of material that was removed forms the basis of some of the criticisms of the present edition.

The first excision consisted of the materials which, in earlier editions, had been placed below the horizontal line running across the page. These included archaisms, dialect forms, variant spellings, and proper names. To quote the editors, ''Many obsolete and comparatively useless or obscure words have been omitted. These include, in general, words that had become obsolete before 1755 unless found in well-known major works of a few major writers.'' Incidentally, the significance of the date 1755 can scarcely escape one's attention. In the first place it was the publication year of Dr. Johnson's dictionary. Moreover, as a deadline for obsolescence, it marks an advance of two centuries and a half over the corresponding date of 1500 for the Webster Second. Thus, in word selection as well as in other matters, the emphasis is clearly placed upon the current state of the language.

Getting rid of the obsolete and the obscure did not in itself solve the space problem. Still other things had to go, and these taken together constitute the parts essential to a peripheral function of the dictionary long cherished by Americans—the encyclopedic function. In the process of elimination, the editors removed among other things:

1. The gazeteer section.
2. The biological section.
3. Titles of written works and works of art.
4. Names of characters in fiction, folklore, and mythology.
5. Names of battles, wars, organizations, cities, and states.
6. Mottoes and other familiar sayings.

There have been further excisions as well. Color plates and illustrations are reduced in a proportion somewhere between one-fourth and one-third. Even the number of pages has gone down from 3210 to 2720.

This elimination of encyclopedic material has caused anguish. "Think, if you can," complains Wilson Follett, "of an unabridged dictionary from which you cannot learn who Mark Twain was, or what were the names of the apostles, or that the Virgin was Mary, the mother of Jesus of Nazareth, or what and where the District of Columbia is." Actually, this is not at all difficult. The great Oxford comes immediately to mind, as does Henry Cecil Wyld's *Universal Dictionary of the English Language,* or any of the great academy dictionaries of such languages as French or Spanish.

Nevertheless, Follett's reaction will be shared by many Americans. In the past, dictionaries published in this country have cheerfully served an encyclopedic as well as a lexicographic function, and ironically enough it was Noah Webster himself who was primarily responsible. His first dictionary, published in 1806, included tables of the moneys of most of the commercial nations in the world, tables of weights and measures, ancient and modern, the divisions of time among the Jews, Greeks, and Romans, and an official list of the post-offices in the United States, to mention only a few of the extra features. Although the editors of the current volume have broken with their progenitor in cutting out these impedimenta, they have not at all departed from the essential principles of lexicography in so doing.

Undoubtedly they felt that the considerable increase in the number of illustrative citations would readily compensate for the loss of the peripheral material. Such citations do constitute the core of the reportorial dictionary. For instance, there were no citations for the adjective *oratorical* in the second edition; the Third has three. The second edition gave three identified citations for *chase,* verb. In the Third, there are four identified and seven unidentified citations.

According to the Preface of the current edition, "More than 14,000 different authors are quoted for their use of words or for the structural pattern of their words . . ." Many of these are contemporary. The reader is also informed that the verbal illustrations (citations apparently unidentified as to author) are "mostly from the twentieth century."

This innovation has met with something less than universal approval, a reaction not so much attributable to the editorial policy itself as to some of the advertising antics of the business office. The original brochure, announcing this edition as "one of the most remarkable literary achievements of all time," included among the list of authors cited such names as Billy Rose, Fulton Lewis, Jr., Art Linkletter, Dinah Shore, Ted Williams, and Ethel Merman. In addition there were Harry Truman, Dwight D. Eisenhower, John F. Kennedy, and Richard Nixon, whose names were undoubtedly signed to reams of material which they did not compose. To the sympathetic this signalled a conscious attempt to include a wide range of current authors. To the critical it betokened a lack of discrimination and responsibility. Actually, the citations from such sources are few in number and small in proportion.

A point which must be taken into account here is that which was made at the very outset of this essay, namely that the life of a Webster edition is roughly calculated at twenty-five years. Thus, the overriding concern of the dictionary is quite appropriately the language in its current state. It is on these grounds that the editors may logically justify the preponderance of citations from current authors, irrespective of lasting literary merit. It may be assumed that in the 1986 edition many of them will be discarded, to be replaced by others from the 1970's and early 1980's. In this respect the Webster practice will differ sharply from that of the *Oxford English Dictionary,* for which no new edition was contemplated, although certainly only a small proportion of the authors cited in that work are literary giants of lasting reputation.

Another departure in the Webster Third from the practice of earlier editions, which has given rise to considerable criticism, is the treatment of what are called *status labels*. Here again some of the disapproval has its source in misunderstanding. Basically, the editors have developed a terminology which is at once semantically neutral and more precise than that which has been employed in the past. The label *illiterate* has been discontinued. It has become a term of censure rather than a dispassionate indication of the inability to read and write. The current replacements, *substandard* and *nonstandard* are matter-of-fact rather than pejorative and permit a gradation of acceptability, the latter indicating a wider range of occurrence than the former, although it is applied to a smaller number of words and expressions. American dialect ascriptions represent a great advance in precision over those of the second edition in that they reflect an adaptation of the terminology for the various dialect areas developed by Professor Hans Kurath, editor of the Linguistic Atlas and the most eminent linguistic geographer in the country. It was unfortunate, however, that the editors chose not to indicate those words current in all regions of the United States but not in England or other parts of the English-speaking world.

Another innovation in the Webster Third is the elimination of the label *colloquial*. There are two conceivable reasons for this: In the first place the term is ambivalent, signifying informality on the one hand and the spoken rather than the written medium on the other. It is customary now among students of the language to be somewhat more precise, recognizing not only *colloquial* but *casual* and *intimate* as further gradations of the spoken variety of the language, any of which not only may be but are regularly employed by speakers of unquestioned cultivation.

An even greater objection to the label *colloquial* is the persistence with which an unfavorable connotation has adhered to it. Dictionary users never interpreted the term in the way in which dictionary editors intended. It was not meant as a condemnation either in the Webster Second or in the various abridged dictionaries based upon it. The editors took great pains to say so, both in the prefatory material and in the definition of the word itself, but this went quite unheeded. So for the present edition the staff was faced with the alternative of finding an acceptable substitute less liable to misinterpretation, or of eliminating the label altogether. It chose the latter, partly perhaps because of the unsatisfactory experience of other dictionaries which had experimented with a substitute.

In general the changes in the choice and ascription of labels reflect an endeavor to achieve greater precision and objectivity. The attempt at precision undoubtedly finds some adherents, although there will be disagreements over the application of the labels in specific instances. The attempt at objectivity has, understandably enough, resulted in the disappearance of the censorious tone which, for many, seemed to be part of the proper function of the labels *colloquial* and *illiterate*. To such persons, the lack of censure will be understood as a lowering of standards.

In dealing with pronunciation, the editors of the Webster Third had to contend with two factors which had not faced their predecessors. One was a new electronic development, namely voice amplification. The other was a new concept in the analysis of language, that of the phoneme or meaningful unit of sound.

Voice amplification affected the kind of pronunciation which the dictionary undertook to record. In preloud-speaker days, the second edition of Webster recorded what it called "formal platform speech," the speech of cultivated users of English, speaking formally with a view to being completely understood by their hearers. That there were other types of pronunciation wholly appropriate to less formal situations was readily conceded by the editors, but they evidently felt that their editorial responsibility could be discharged with the greatest amount of effectiveness and least confusion by indicating just the one.

The microphone has changed all this. Certain devices of articulation necessary for clarity when the speaker was forced to depend on lung power to make himself audible to the last row of a large auditorium are no longer necessary. Nor are they often employed today. They have gone, along with the orotund periods of the old-time spellbinder.

This change led the Webster editors into a complete revision of the manner in which evidence on pronunciation was collected. Where Webster Second had attempted a sampling, by means of written questionnaires, of the pronunciation of persons who did a considerable amount of public speaking, the Webster Third staff turned its attention directly to the language itself rather than to opinion about it. They listened to radio, television, and recordings; to speech in all parts of the country and in all types of situations. Again, as with the citations for word occurrences, forms and meanings, the body of evidence was tremendously increased in range and scope, but certainly less skewed toward a single type of pronunciation.

In any English dictionary, and particularly one designed for use in the United States, a decision upon the particular system, or respelling, to indicate pronunciation always poses a problem. For a number of reasons, the American public has been unwilling to accept the International Phonetic Alphabet; nor is this a particularly economical device when a number of variants must be shown. The Webster Second continued with few changes the system of its predecessors, which was cumbersome in that a single sound was indicated by more than one transcription, and confusing in that a single character sometimes covered far more latitude than the user was likely to realize.

The editors of the current edition have attempted to take advantage of a concept basic to present-day linguistic science, that of the phoneme. A cogent discussion of this concept and its impact upon the way in which pronunciations are indicated may be found under the rubric *phonemicity* in the Webster Third *Guide to Pronunciation*. The general result has been the disappearance of a rash of diacritics which made the earlier dictionaries difficult to read and to interpret. Some useful characters have been taken over from the phonetic alphabet, notably the elongated *n* to indicate the usual sound of *ng*, and most important, the inverted *e* or schwa for the neutral vowel used in weakly stressed syllables. The latter, it must be confessed, is an innovation in which Webster followed some of its competitors. At all events, the public will no longer be misled into believing that the final vowel of *caucus* is somehow different from that of *fracas*.

Unfortunately the necessity of economizing on space has led to the excision of the authoritative treatments of the individual sounds of English which lent scholarly distinction to the second edition though perhaps read by only a few. Also, certain innovations of the Webster Third will cause annoyance until the public becomes accustomed to them. One of these may well be the indication of stress by a mark preceding rather than following the syllable. The removal of the pronunciation key from the bottom of the page is another. The use of a modified *d* character to indicate what the editors call, "the usual American pronunciation of *latter*," will seem to the critical like countenancing the slipshod, and it is possible that a *t* with a diacritic might have served quite as well without outraging quite so many sensibilities.

With pronunciation as with countless other features of the dictionary, the editors have attempted to present the facts of the language as they saw them. It is an honest presentation, maintaining the principles and the concept of the dictionary characteristic of previous editions, but carrying them out with greater consistency and basing them upon far more evidence. There have been errors of judgment, more often perhaps with respect to manner of presentation than in the interpretation of the facts which are reported, but this is inevitable in an undertaking of such magnitude.

My comments so far should have suggested, to a degree at least, the reasons for some of the changes which are to be found in the Webster Third. They have not yet given an answer to the question which was initially posed: why the extremes of praise and blame. The encomiums are easy to account for. They represent the approval of those who accept the descriptive principle and find in the current product a generally conscientious and more thorough implementation of it than is otherwise available.

The chorus of protest is somewhat more complex in origin. It is in part the expression of a desire for linguistic authoritarianism, an attitude which can be explained only in terms of a number of complex and interrelated factors in American cultural history. Added to this is the mistaken notion that the Webster Third represents a change in lexicographical principle, an error which is fostered by the more complete coverage and greater accuracy of the edition. The excision of certain kinds of non-essential material represented a sudden departure from a time-honored practice. Finally, there is, as always, a tendency toward careless reading and inept comparison. Upon occasion a judgment objected to in the third edition was already present in the second, and there is the amusing instance of the critic, writing in a semi-sophisticated weekly, who was outraged by what seemed to him to be undue permissiveness. But some of the matters about which he complained were already present in the 1909 edition.

In the light of all this, one can only say that by a more literal acceptance of its declared function, and by running counter more obviously to what people want or think they want in a dictionary and to what they think they have been getting, the Webster Third represents a calculated risk of $3,500,000. Depending on one's point of view, it is either a courageous or a foolhardy venture into the latter half of the twentieth century. For the staff, who in the face of the public clamor must wonder if it has been at all worthwhile, there is only the dubious comfort in Macaulay's words, "The best lexicographer may well be content if his productions are received by the world in cold esteem."

DISCUSSION QUESTIONS

1. In your own words describe the two traditions of lexicography in the United States.

2. To what does Marckwardt attribute the negative reaction to the *Webster Third* by popular reviewers? Which side of the conflict would you take?

3. How important do you consider status labels for lexical entries? If you were an editor, would you use the same as in the *Webster Third?*

4. Select from one of the lists in Harold Allen's article in Part IV five words showing a status contrast between Type I and Type III informants and compare their labels in the *Webster Third* and those in the *American Heritage Dictionary*. Do you find any correlation between the labeling and social class usage?

R. W. BURCHFIELD

Born in Australia in 1923, Burchfield now resides in England, where as chief editor of the Oxford English dictionaries he has been responsible for editing the various parts of the OED Supplement, beginning in 1972.

ON THAT OTHER GREAT DICTIONARY . . . AND THE AMERICAN LANGUAGE

"I have a cursed hankering after certain musty old values", says Lord Peter Wimsey in Dorothy Sayers' *Gaudy Night*.

And so, it seems, have a great many people when they pause to think about the language we use, particularly when they encounter a newly invented word or phrase. How many of us would react neutrally, or even possibly in a friendly way, to a word I came across recently in a leaflet about pets? An American magazine, it said, is in process of publishing a list of cat horoscopes. A Leo cat, born between 24 July and 23 August, is described as super-arrogant, and should be owned only by people born under certain favourable signs, Taurus, Scorpio, and one or two others. On the other hand, Cancer cats are moody and should be owned only by Cancer people. "Astromogology [it declared] should be a fascinating new science."

Such a word, grotesquely misformed but in use commercially, points the way to one of the major problems facing lexicographers in the present century. "Put it in the dictionary", cries one, "it's in use." "Over my dead body", cries another, "it's a horrible word."

Let me focus a little more closely on the problem of "words in use" and their inclusion in dictionaries. The oldest contributor to the *Oxford English Dictionary* recently submitted what he called "the last gathering of a very old tree"—he said that he is "now touching 96" and can no longer go on with the work. The quotations he sent consisted of fifty or so neatly copied-out examples from his usual range of slightly recondite literary and religious sources, and in his covering note he added:

> "I cannot sufficiently deplore the inclusion of obscene words and senses in the O.E.D. 'Climate of opinion' cannot excuse the horrors of great apostasy now evident and for the moment triumphant. I hope that I will be pardoned for saying this but I must deliver my soul. Also I deplore the great space given to American and Australasian slang or colloquial, while Newman's excellent word *groundstead* and the like are overlooked or omitted."

Here is a commanding and a respected voice— the man in question was born in the 1880s just as the *O.E.D.* was beginning to appear, and he knew Sir James Murray well. Obscenities, Americanisms, Australianisms, these should be excluded; and excellent words like *groundstead*, formed, it will be noticed, from two words of Anglo-Saxon origin, should be placed in the lexicon. He wrote to me in 1976 but his views are those of most scholars who were young at the beginning of the century.

Now let me quote another opinion from the less distant past, a writer in the *Times Literary Supplement* (2 September 1926) just half a century ago:

"America is not likely to develop a new language until its civilisation becomes more complicated and more refined than that of Britain; and there are no indications that this will ever happen. Meanwhile, America will continue to provide a small number of new words which can usefully be digested by the parent language."

Who would you think wrote that? T. S. Eliot, no less, with uncharacteristic complacency. The target is in part the same, the American language, transatlantic yeast seen by him from a distance to be slowly but harmlessly fermenting.

At the turn of the century and soon afterward several new dictionaries appeared, some of them in the Johnson tradition, some simpler like the *Concise Oxford* in 1911, and some more complicated like the *Century Dictionary*, the Funk & Wagnalls dictionary, and the incomparable *O.E.D.* itself. The loyal subjects of Queen Victoria, of Edward VII, and of George V, and their analogues in America and in the old colonies, in general felt that the language was in good hands—what could go wrong with Webster's editors, Murray, and the Fowlers as custodians of the language? Just one small cloud stood on the horizon. What if these great dictionaries omitted items that should have been included?

In 1888 one Mrs Anna Randall-Diehl, American despite her hyphenated name, wrote a book called *Two Thousand Words and their Definitions: Not in Webster's Dictionary*. Some were very obvious words, like *astrakhan, asymmetrically*, and *bacteriology*; others were of less validity, like *bibliosponge*, "one who gets the reading of books without buying them, a book borrower." Almost as soon as the *O.E.D.* was finished another pointer-out of omissions, G. G. Loane, issued a list of a thousand words that the author claimed should have been included. And so the target became "omissions", thousands and thousands of them. A dictionary without, for example, *catharism* ("pretended perfection") and *grigger* ("name of a shrub in Africa") simply wouldn't do. Even the largest dictionaries came to be thought by some scholars as Crown Jewels with the sceptre missing and a bauble or two besides.

By the early 1930s, however, Britain could sit back and admire the completed *O.E.D.*, and America had its splendid second edition of Webster's New International, the English one in thirteen volumes and the American in either one or two depending how it was bound up. The lexicographers were given their knighthoods—some of them anyway—and the Prime Minister, Stanley Baldwin, gave a memorable speech in the Goldsmiths' Hall in London. In Oxford the dictionary-makers dispersed, and the books and unused quotation slips were put away in old tea-chests. The language kept ticking away but no one was there in the cuckoo-echoing, towery city to collect the new words. The Old Ashmolean, where the *O.E.D.* had been prepared, became the Museum of the History of Science; and the dictionary people went off to write *The Hobbit*, articles for encyclopaedias and *Festschriften*, and, some of them, to prepare dictionaries of the English of specialised regions or of much older periods.

But in Springfield (Massachusetts), Webster's staff went on collecting examples of current American English use. The world learned about nudism, jazz, existentialism, pesticides, plastics, and all the rest, and the Merriam-Webster citation files became more and more extensive. Newspapers, scholarly and literary works, works about every aspect of American life—some by competent writers and some by dunces—all yielded up their vocabulary to the Webster files. The compilers of the dictionary braced themselves for the preparation of a new edition, to be called the Third New International, and by 1961 it was ready to be published. Everything seemed to be in order. The language belt needed to be adjusted here and there to make room for the new words: so they decided to leave out most of the proper names and also literary words that had passed into oblivion by 1755 when Dr Johnson's dictionary was published. This done, they could let the belt out a notch or two to admit all the new words, and the result, they hoped, would be an excellent dictionary.

But something happened that nobody had counted on. A decade-and-a-half later we are all accustomed to public scandals of the larger order (Watergate, Lockheed, and so on), and to the iniquity of individuals. Disloyalty, sabotage, wanton destruction, all these are familiar enough to us all. But who could have predicted that a *dictionary* could be regarded as an instrument of sabotage, and its editor guilty of some sinister conspiracy to let the ogre of permissiveness loose upon the lawn? It is instructive to recall what kind of reception Webster's Third received.

> The anxiously awaited work that was to have crowned cisatlantic linguistic scholarship with a particular glory turns out to be a scandal and a disaster. . . .
>
> Webster III, behind its front of passionless objectivity, is in truth a fighting document. And the enemy it is out to destroy is every obstinate vestige of linguistic punctilio, every surviving influence that makes for the upholding of standards, every criterion for distinguishing between better usages and worse. . . .
>
> Webster's has, it is apparent, surrendered to the permissive school that has been busily extending its beachhead on English instruction in the schools. . . .
>
> We suggest to the Webster editors that they do not throw out the printing plates of the Second Edition. There is likely to be a continuing demand for it.
>
> The editors of this wondrous stew do not feel they have any duty toward their own language.

In 1963 Rex Stout's novel called *Gambit* opens with his main character Nero Wolfe depicted as burning a copy of a book:

> There's a fireplace in the front room. . . . He's seated in front of it . . . tearing sheets out of a book and burning them. The book is the . . . third edition of Webster's New International Dictionary. . . . He considers it subversive because it threatens the integrity of the English language.

Why should this massive scholarly work have been so cruelly received? I do not think that the explanations hitherto put forward are entirely satisfactory.

The completion of the *O.E.D.* in the 1930s marked the end of an era in lexicography—the end of the period of the recording of the central core of English. Murray's celebrated chart in the Introduction to the *O.E.D.* had indicated the limits of this central core by means of an elliptical diagram. Outside the acceptable and recordable band lay the unwanted areas of dialect, technological language, foreign words that were only partially naturalised, and many kinds of ephemerality.

The spoken and written language of the educated middle and upper classes was certainly acceptable: indeed most of the sources cited in the *O.E.D.* were from the works of such people. The vocabulary of the colonies—and most of them were still colonies while the separate parts of the dictionary were being published—was also acceptable because it was distant and exotic and represented no threat to the continuity and to the dominance of the English used in Britain. Working-class speech in this country had been set down in literary works by writers from higher levels of society. If it was plain or colourful or vulgar or ungrammatical at times it was because the speech of the lower orders was thought to display all these qualities in turn or simultaneously. Demotic English was quotable in the dictionary in so far as it showed a non-conquering of the Received Language. The modern sub-cultures, with their tiresome jargon, had not appeared. The working classes had not discovered the dreadful drill of union solidarity, Butlins, package holidays in Spain, the family car, the TV set, Ian Fleming, bionic woman, and all the rest.

American dictionaries, including Webster's second edition of 1934, remained somewhat obsequiously unaware of the distinctive way in which the American language was developing. That relatively small segment of the English language that had been traditionally placed in the main English dictionaries was considered to be representative enough for this second edition of Webster. It was published and the minstrels in the mead-halls sang in praise of it all. But outside the mead-halls, as in *Beowulf,* lay fens and bogs and dark forests of language not at that stage considered to have a place in dictionaries. And a new theory of "language in use", of descriptivism as opposed to prescriptivism, was making itself felt.

Baseball players and popular entertainers were writing books, as was Mickey Spillane, and others for whom verbal infelicity hardly mattered. Mystical religions and drug-taking were studied and mildly experienced by mescaline-taking Aldous Huxley. And then hordes of young people took over from him on the trail of hallucinatory experiences, and wrote books and magazine articles notable for their frankness but rarely for their command of the English language.

Webster's staff went on reading such works, and by the end of the 1950s had an unparalleled collection of vocabulary from areas of language not hitherto recorded on any scale in dictionaries: the new unbeautiful language of the technologists, of Madison Avenue, the Pentagon, and Hollywood, of dissident groups, and of the racial minorities of the United States, Yiddish speakers, Blacks, Chicanos, Puerto Ricans, Polish, Pennsylvanian Dutch, and so on.

Chutzpah joined the language, and *dunk,* and *hopefully* in its now deplored use. Repugnant acronymic formations proliferated as if to underline the linguistic impoverishment and superficial ingenuity of the modern period. None of this mattered to begin with as the hospitable English language had absorbed many such individual items and other word-forming techniques in the past. But by 1961 the spring had become a flood, and the flood a torrent. By a "words in use" doctrine, insisted upon by linguistic theorists, nearly everything noticed by the scanning eye of the dictionary readers needed to be included. The central approved band of vocabulary had been invaded by numberless items from the peripheral classes of vocabulary that up till then had been excluded.

The editor of Webster's Third, Dr Philip Gove, no compromiser he, accepted that his duty lay in setting down the language as he found it in his files. If some people with university degrees were using *disinterested* and *infer* in ways which had hitherto been frowned upon, he recorded them as acceptable new uses. He seemed to be on the side of the disreputables, and to be thumbing a nose at those who valued discrimination in the use of words.

He also maintained the American tradition of defining words in an encyclopaedic manner. For example, the word *hotel* was defined as follows:

A building of many rooms chiefly for overnight accommodation of transients and several floors served by elevators, usu. with a large open street-level lobby containing easy chairs, with a variety of compartments for eating, drinking, dancing, exhibitions, and group meetings (as of salesmen or convention attendants), with shops having both inside and street-side entrances and offering for sale items (as clothes, gifts, candy, theater tickets, travel tickets) of particular interest to a traveler, or providing personal services (as hairdressing, shoe shining), and with telephone booths, writing tables, and washrooms freely available.

Now what happens, one might ask, if the hotel you slept in last week lacks some of these features? Is it therefore not a hotel? The British tradition of defining is much simpler: in the *Shorter Oxford,* for example, the word *hotel* is defined simply as "an inn, esp. one of a superior kind."

In the unprecedented conditions of the 30-year period since the early 1930s, the American language had moved on from a kind of late Mayflower period to a much more strident stage, marked by brash innovation of vocabulary at various levels of society, by an abandonment in many quarters of any concept of well-formedness for words and sentences, by an invasion of the central area of traditional American English by the language of the technologists, by the syrupy double-talk of politicians and strategists, and by the unacceptable or nonstandard grammar of the speech of certain ethnic minorities.

And when this was all set down with deadly accuracy in Webster's Third, the American language was no longer to be regarded as an acceptable model to the outside world. The lexicographers' "sabotage" lay in not concealing what had happened to American English, which now, it had to be admitted, was being used, and recorded as being used, by large and powerful groups of people who did not speak the admired and approved form of English that had been handed down from generation to generation since the arrival of English settlers in North America. Meanwhile in Britain—Oxford, York, Manchester, and elsewhere—the traditional patterns of language that had existed in these islands for centuries remained essentially undisturbed. The regional forms of English used in our great cities and in rural areas retained their strength and continuity. The children of the new minorities (for example, the migrant Pakistanis in Bradford and elsewhere) were acquiring regional English modes of speech, and were forming their sentences in an English way. British lexicographers, under constant surveillance from journalists and other linguistically conservative groups and individuals, benefited from the traditional slowness of their trade, but much more from the power of English society to absorb its minorities.

Some aspects of Webster's Third seem to me somewhat less than admirable, particularly the encyclopaedic nature of the definitions, and the cumbersome way in which varieties of pronunciation are indicated, and in which capitalisation is presented. It is a shame, though, that this other great dictionary, with all its meticulous scholarship, should have had to withstand such a furious onslaught, and that the late Dr Gove should have been arraigned, as it were, for un-American activities, when the proper target should have been meretricious tendencies in American English itself.

I do not know how a language can be put into reverse, or modified, except by the consent of the whole linguistic community. But so long as it stays on its present course it seems to me that American English will become an increasingly unappealing model for people at a distance, as it is already for those sections of American opinion that retain their belief in Lord Peter Wimsey's "musty old values."

DISCUSSION QUESTIONS

1. To what does Burchfield attribute the negative reception of the *Webster Third*? Is his position the same as that of Marckwardt?

2. As a dictionary user, do you concur with Burchfield's criticism of the *Webster Third*? Explain.

3. Be ready to discuss your reaction to Burchfield's statement: "so long as it stays on its present course . . . American English will become an increasingly unappealing model for people at a distance. . . ."

4. In 1948 the Webster publisher, the G. and C. Merriam Company, invited a number of linguists to a meeting for a discussion of proposed innovations in the projected third edition. At that meeting Charles C. Fries suggested that the new dictionary should assume that the normal usage is colloquial and that noncolloquial forms therefore be labeled "literary." What would Burchfield's reaction have been?

ARCHIBALD A. HILL

After receiving his doctorate at Yale, the author taught at the universities of Michigan and Virginia before joining the faculty at the University of Texas, where he retired in 1972 as professor of English and linguistics. His distinguished career was marked by service as secretary-treasurer of the Linguistic Society from 1952 until 1958 and as its president in 1969. His Introduction to Linguistic Structures is the last major work in structural linguistics (Harcourt, 1958). He has focused attention upon the relationship between linguistics and literature.

LAYMEN, LEXICOGRAPHERS, AND LINGUISTS

The task of giving a Presidential Address for the Linguistic Society of America has never been one to take lightly, and as our science advances, the task has grown more difficult. Once our membership would have listened patiently to details of Indo-European phonology, even though few of us were experts in that field. And once we listened with equal patience to an enumeration of all the discoverable meanings of a single word. But nowadays, even in linguistics, the demand is for relevance, so that a President cannot address himself solely to his own group of specialists; and if he chooses the area of theory which is now so fashionable, he runs the opposite peril from boredom—that of controversy. If he can avoid both boredom and controversy he is doubly fortunate, but most of us must be content with avoiding just one at a time. I have tried, in selecting a topic, to steer clear of abstract theory, to find a subject where we, as linguists, might reach at least a modicum of convergence, and where we might have some hope of affecting, for the better, one of the established and institutionalized activities of our culture. The area I have chosen is dictionary making—more particularly the making of dictionaries meant for the general educated public, not lexicons for professional linguists and scholars.

The most compelling reason for this choice of subject is that, for the general public, dictionaries are the most important books that can be written about language. For better or worse, our culture defines words as the basic units of language, and is left merely puzzled by the mention of morphemes, sememes, formatives, or distinctive features. As for ordered rules, the public would be pretty sure to suppose that they meant such things as the distinctions between *shall* and *will*. While concern with words and wordbooks is important to the users of the language, there is a more immediate reason for my choice. We have recently had a little flurry of dictionary making—*Webster's Third* in 1961, *The Random House Dictionary* in 1966, and *The American Heritage Dictionary* in 1969. And, indeed, the last two of the three are attempts to produce a dictionary more in accord with what the public wants than was *Webster's Third*. We all remember the foofaraw over *Webster's* and the unpleasant role that 'structural linguists' were cast in—as the villains who were responsible for destroying standards of correctness, of beauty, and of clarity. It was not particularly relevant that the 'structural linguists' described by Dwight Macdonald bore no very close resemblance to any group that linguists would call by that name; it is equally irrelevant that linguists, structural or other, do not hold the doctrine of 'anything goes' with which we are so regularly taunted. The public chooses to blame us for destroying the basis of standards merely because we think of standards as culturally controlled—not based on immutable law. The public will not change, and we will continue to suffer from the odium philologicum unless we can find a way of establishing more friendly communication.

There is much to criticize in these latest dictionaries, but the most recent of them has devised a technique which at least suggests a way to establish better communication with the public. The *Heritage Dictionary* referred questions of disputed usage to a 'Usage panel' of 104 members. The establishment of such a panel seems hopeful to me because it is a device very similar to the 'naïve expert speakers' used as the authorities on 'rightness' by anthropological linguists, and elaborated into jury groups on occasion, as by Ilse Lehiste in her investigation of juncture. The Usage panel is described as consisting of 'novelists, essayists, poets, journalists, writers on science and sports, public officials, professors'. They are praised for having in common 'a recognized ability to speak and write good English'. Such statements, amply backed up by their names and credentials, surely describe them as expert users of the language. Are they also naïve experts? I should say they are. The best example of naïveté is quoted by Morris Bishop in his introductory essay to the dictionary, giving Dwight Macdonald's reaction to *enthuse*: 'By God, let's hold the line on this one!' And of the general attitude of the panel, Bishop observes that 'they tend to feel that the English language is going to hell if "we" don't do something to stop it . . .' It would seem to me, therefore, that the Usage panel comes pretty close to being the jury of naïve expert users of English which a linguist might have chosen.

There are criticisms of how the panel was chosen, however, which may be worth making. First of all, three of the panel are professional linguists, and it seems to me that all professional linguists should have been excluded on the ground that they are of questionable naïveté. Similarly, two of the panel have been publicly identified with rather extreme anti-linguistic statements. People of such views should also have been excluded on the ground that they are quite as atypical as linguists. I do not know how these panelists were actually chosen, but there is no discussion which suggests that they were a random sampling of a larger population, which is the method of choice that would have seemed preferable to me.

Other criticisms of the usage panel have to do with how it was used. Most importantly, it was not used enough. For instance, in the entry for the relative pronoun *that*, there is a usage note of fifty lines, which goes quite fully into the use of *that* with various kinds of clauses. The only citation of a panel verdict occurs under one of the examples. The example is 'a law that is not supported by the public . . .' It is said that 54 percent of the panel found *which* acceptable here, 'though many of that number specify *that* as the preferable choice.' In other uses, there is sometimes no use of the panel at all. For instance, the only note on *burgle* is that it is a back formation; *aggravate* in the sense 'make angry' is merely labeled 'informal', and *complected*, in 'dark-complected', is called regional. Examples of quite proper use of the panel are the statements under *transpire* in the sense of *happen*, 'not acceptable to 62 percent of the Usage panel', and *none*, which must always take a singular verb according to 28 percent of the panel. In short, had I been compiling the dictionary I would have given the actual votes on every disputed usage, and confined my discussion largely to these ballots. The percentages give a pretty accurate picture of the social attitudes toward given usages. They are more accurate than such statements as this: 'Because the distinction between restrictive and non-restrictive clauses is not always easy to make, the choice between relative pronouns often rests on personal interpretation.' The statement is true enough, but not very helpful. Even more importantly, the writers of usage notes should have followed the first rule of field investigation when questioning an informant. The investigator must faithfully accept the informant's statements about what is right and wrong in grammar, syntax, and vocabulary, but must pay no attention to the informant's rationalizations. A typical rationalization which should have been excluded is one under 'aren't I' quoted from Louis Kronenberger: 'A genteelism, and much worse than *ain't I.*' The comment is interesting and there is a good deal of truth in it; but citing a panelist by name lends the comment prestige, and thus suggests that the construction is being ruled out on the basis of the authority of an expert—not simply because of the value judgment of a 'naïve expert user', something which is far different from an expert authority. Further, since *aren't I* is explainable as the simple extension of the uninflected base form, as in *needn't he,* and is also the natural form in England, Kronenberger's comment is certainly not all of the truth.

I feel that the *Heritage* Usage panel, in short, is no more than a suggestion of what can be done. Surely balloting could have been extended to matters of pronunciation, as with *nuclear,* where *Webster's Third* alone records the pronunciation /núwkyələr/, and then with the comment 'chiefly in substandard speech'. One can be permitted to wonder whether the avoidance of pronunciation rulings was not more nearly a matter of timidity than space. At least, *Webster's,* so regularly condemned for being permissive, has here condemned the usual pronunciation of a beloved late President.

As I have said, in employing a Usage panel there should be a determined effort to confine rulings on usage to the results of balloting alone. Balloting, of course, is related to the whole vexed question of grammaticality, now firmly stated to be measured by every language-user's internal monitor, and to be gradient in the sense that each individual speaker could arrange a series of questionable forms on a scale from totally acceptable to totally unacceptable. Ballot results, however, give only the statement that a certain number out of a total accept such and such a construction. It is by no means certain that vote-gradience agrees at all with the results of scale-gradience. Scale-gradience is, however, quite beyond the reach of any kind of jury operation practicable for the making of a dictionary, and is probably not helpful in reaching all-or-none decisions on individual forms. The best study of grammaticality that I know of, Quirk & Svartvik 1966, presents, as a part of the experiment, a ballot from a randomly chosen jury of educated speakers, giving their emotionally based reactions to individual forms. The Quirk & Svartvik experiment completely avoids reliance on confused and confusing notions of authority, of etymological logicality, of beauty or ugliness of sounds or forms, or, above all, protection of the language. To say it again, in the hope of being even clearer, Quirk & Svartvik ask the language-user a thoroughly legitimate question: do you like this form, or don't you?

The *Heritage* invites the kind of criticism a newspaper reviewer directed against it, when she said: 'To me, this intrusion [the balloting on usage] is irrelevant, obnoxious, and presumptuous. Ten years from now, we may have a hard time remembering [who] many of the panelists were, and as a group they do represent, after all, a subjective choice' (Petoski 1969). It is obvious that the reviewer has a point, since the dictionary has indeed mixed reliance on authority with balloting. On the other hand, I believe quite firmly that dictionary users have a real right to know what language attitudes are. If, in giving a formal talk, I say /núwkyələr/ and get blackballed for it, I have a perfect right to know what I did wrong. And I also have a right to know that when I use 'fulsome praise' to mean great and sincere praise, many will construe it as an insult.

To bring the matter back from laymen to linguists, it is true that linguists can and should be useful in supervising the choice of jurymen, and in devising the alternatives that the jurymen are given for classifying their responses: acceptable in talking to the members of one's family, acceptable in formal writing, acceptable in formal speech such as a lecture, and so on. The jury decision is a tool that has been available for a long time, and I think that linguists have been, and still are, to blame for not making enough use of it. Unfortunately, linguistic literature is full of statements that some pair of utterances are different, or are not different, where the decision is based on nothing more than introspection. And as for matters of acceptability and usage, it is notorious that we all follow the advice of Sir Philip Sidney's Muse: 'Fool . . . look into thy heart, and write!' I believe that the long tradition of using our own Sprachgefühl for matters of usage may have introduced too much subjectivity in our investigation of the basic same-different relationship in language. In fact, I believe very strongly that we should increase our use of jury-testing a hundredfold, and that doing so would give a firmness to many statements that are now all too flabby.

I have talked about jury testing and balloting at this length because I believe that such tests can also be applied to other dictionary tasks, which are not always performed to perfection. One main task for any dictionary is to isolate the words which it describes. The task is not easy, and we linguists have not helped very much with it—shying away from meaning, as is well known, because we believed it to be an indivisible continuum. As a result, practical lexicographers have relied on spelling and etymology, I think sometimes unwisely. *Course* and *coarse* are thought of as different words because they are spelled differently. *Compound* in *compound noun* and in *marched across the compound* are differentiated on the ground of etymology. But to rely on spelling to differentiate *coarse* and *course,* where the pronunciation is the same, leaves one wondering what is done when two suspected forms are spelled alike but pronounced differently, or are pronounced differently and also have differing meaning or reference. An extreme case is the placename *Cairo,* made to sound like *care* in Illinois, and like *fire* in Egypt. Both *Random House* and *Heritage* give these forms as sub-entries of the same word instead of as separate main entries.

Before we try to thread our way through these various distinctions, a little theory is necessary. Consider forms which are different in sound. If the pair are different, or may be different, only in a non-significant way, as by the presence or absence of final release in a word like *cap,* a dictionary should certainly disregard this difference. If the difference is significant, as in *mats / gnats,* obviously it should be taken account of. But what of the difference in the final sound of the stem in *house* singular vs. *houses* plural? Here the guiding principle is apparent: the difference is systematic and can be stated by a rule of sufficiently great generality so that it applies to a considerable number of similar forms. Dictionaries are fully justified in assuming that *house* and *houses* contain the same stem form. The decisions, however, are less than fully consistent. Thus *Webster's* (p. 16a) speaks of homographs, forms spelled alike though sounding different, as with '1 *are* (in *the boys ARE in here*)' and '2 *are* (in *one ARE equals 100 square meters.*)' *Arc* noun and verb, which are spelled alike, pronounced alike, and etymologically related, are treated as separate words by *Webster* since they are different parts of speech. But in *Random House* and *Heritage,* the two *arcs* are treated only as subentries, not as separate words. For real confusion, however, one can consult the several entries of *flee* and *fly.* All three of our dictionaries treat these as different words; but since they are at least related etymologically, one wonders what the basis of distinction has been, especially since one of the ways in which some uses of *fly* is defined is to substitute *flee.* The various entries of etyma are sufficiently variant so that, even with the best will in the world, a reader would be unsure as to whether the forms were, or were not, identical in etymology. If identical in etymology, why are they separate words, where the two *Cairos* are mere subentries? Our lexicographers do not tell us.

I think the basic principle should be that differences in sound are significant if they correlate with differences in words or word-elements. Differences in words and word-elements are significant if they correlate with differences in sentences. Thus one's notion of significant difference ultimately and always rests on differences in sentences, and I know of no final authority of such same-different questions except the jury of native speakers. As a simple example, /ay/ and /iy/ are significantly different sounds because they identify the different words *sweep* and *swipe,* which identify the sentences 'She's always sweeping something' and 'She's always swiping something'. They are still significantly different sounds in /íyðər/ and /áyðər/; but since a jury will tell us that 'I'll take /íyðər/' is the same sentence as 'I'll take /áyðər/', we must conclude that /íyðər/ and /áyðər/ are forms of the same word. We can apply these principles with fairly clear results and without much difficulty. *Fly* and *flee* are different words, because a jury will readily decide that 'Our troops will fly home' and 'Our troops will flee home' are different sentences. We do not need to concern ourselves with the fact that in one sentence there is a clear reference to air transport, where there is no such reference in the second sentence, because the same-different decision is enough. Another instance, slightly different since it involves a difference in ending, rather than a difference in the stem, is *flew* and *flied*. All three of our dictionaries record the form *flied,* but give it only as a sub-entry under *fly*. Yet, once again, any randomly selected jury would say immediately that 'He flied into right field' and 'He flew into right field' are different sentences. The result is that *flied* and *flew* are differing words, and should have separate entries. It also follows that, when the sentence is 'He will fly into right field', we can have either one word or the other, depending on whether the speaker would use the first or second past-tense form when the sentence is varied in time.

The examples thus far given are simple, even obvious. The next are not quite so easy. Suppose we deal with *fly* in 'Birds FLY', and *fly* in 'Boys FLY kites'. We cannot call on difference in morphology to settle the question of unity or diversity for us, since the past tense is *flew* in both sentences. The question cannot, I think, be solved without reference to other examples which show some of the same characteristics. The basic problem is whether or not a word can pass freely between classes, in this instance intransitive verb to verb with complement, without changing identity. It is pretty clear that there are instances in which verbs do move from intransitive to transitive, as in 'John likes TO EAT' and 'John likes to EAT CANDY', where no one in his senses would say that we are dealing with anything but identical forms. There are others where it seems at least reasonably clear that verbs do indeed change identity when moving from the intransitive to the transitive class. An instance is from *Webster's,* though there the somewhat surprising transitive use is entered simply as a sub-classification under the normally intransitive verb. The form is *vanish,* for which *Webster* quotes the sentence 'You can vanish the coin completely'. It seems to me quite counter-intuitive to call this the same word as the *vanish* of 'His courage vanished'. My decision that the two occurrences of *vanish* represent different entities needs a little discussion, however, since it would seem to run counter to what I take to be normal decisions about identity with some other verbs, such as *die* or *laugh*. That is, it is usual to call these verbs pure intransitives; yet they occur with complements in sentences like 'He died a hero's death' and 'He laughed a loud laugh'.

I do not believe that many analysts would describe 'He died' and 'He died a hero's death' as containing different verbs. Why, then, the differing decision with *vanish*? The difference is that we can set up a rule that some pure intransitives have the ability to occur with complements, if the complement is cognate in form and meaning with the verb. *Die* and *death*, *laugh* noun and verb, are such cognate pairs. But there is no cognate noun for *vanish*, so that 'He vanished the coin' does not fall under the exceptions which are explainable, such as 'He laughed a loud laugh'. We must therefore decide that the two occurrences of *vanish* are different words.

Thus we can clearly make use of a principle which I would formulate as follows: we separate words when to do so preserves a rule of syntax which proves useful elsewhere in description of structure. The rule seems simple thus stated, but it is not altogether easy to apply it to sentences like 'Birds FLY' and 'Boys FLY kites'. If we look at the first sentence, we can find only a limited group of possible complements, which can be broadly described as either cognate, as in 'Geese fly long flights', or limited to nouns of distance, as in 'Birds fly many miles'. With the second sentence, the conditions are different. Jespersen (1914: 331–3) set up a class of verbs called the 'move-change class', the characteristics of which were that there could be an animate subject with an inanimate complement, as in 'John moved a chair'; but if the animate subject was absent, the complement could become the new subject, as in 'The chair moved'. Genuinely intransitive verbs did not fall into this group, since one could have either 'John trembled' or 'The chair trembled', but one could not have 'John trembled the chair'. Consequently for *tremble* there is no switching of actor and complement. Many genuinely transitive verbs do not fall into this class, since one can have 'John ate the pie', but this does not become 'The pie ate'. To apply this kind of reasoning to the two *fly* sentences, I think we can justify separating the two occurrences. 'Boys fly kites' is a move-change verb, since we can easily change it into 'Kites fly'. In 'Birds fly', on the other hand, we do not have a move-change verb, but a genuinely intransitive verb which can have either an animate or inanimate subject, as in 'Birds fly' and 'Bullets fly'. The peculiar alternation of subject and complement is absent. In these several instances we should still make use of a jury, but use it in a different fashion. That is, having hypothesized the existence of a rule, we should test it to see whether or not its application to an identified form produces a grammatical result.

To consider the question of identity further, notice *shovel* in this pair of utterances: 'a long-handled shovel' and 'He'll shovel it up'. I am reasonably sure that any jury would say they are the same words. But why? It is true that there are no significant differences in spelling or pronunciation, and none in etymology. I do not believe that any of these similarities are the deciding factors. The two are noun and verb, and consequently occur in such typical sentences as 'That is a good shovel' and 'He shoveled it'. That is, in nearly all instances other words, word order, or grammatical endings will serve to identify the sentences as different, so that the mere verbness and nounness is redundant. The rule holds, I think, even with forms which have some difference of pronunciation, as with *separate* verb vs. *separate* adjective. Since in all normal instances we can expect the other words, endings, or order positions to distinguish the sentences, the part-of-speech difference does not justify our separating the words. The conclusion that separation was justified in 'Birds FLY' in contrast to 'Boys FLY kites', however, would seem to be a contradiction. There is, indeed, at least one sentence type, with no redundancy, where the class membership of *fly* determines which sentence is occurring. The sentences are the two familiar versions of 'Flying planes can be dangerous'.

These sentences, however, merely prove that the two types for all 'move-change' verbs are different, as in 'Changing money can be troublesome'. The conclusion with *fly*, on the other hand, is not based on meaning but on grammaticality. That is, 'Flying planes can be dangerous' permits of expansion to 'Drunken pilots flying planes can be dangerous', since, in this sentence, *fly* is a move-change verb. In 'Flying bullets can be dangerous' no such expansion is possible, and 'Drunken soldiers flying bullets can be dangerous' is ungrammatical. So far as my limited testing goes, a jury can be relied on to show convergence in rejecting such sentences. The rule is, then: if a given operation is applied to two apparently identical sentence types, with different results, then the sentence types are different, even though no minimally different sentences can be found for the test.

Our last example brings me to the most important kind of decision a lexicographer has to make in identifying words. Again, I can approach it only by giving a little theory first. I believe that most of us would agree that a word has several components: the sounds which occur in it (including the pattern of intonation), the co-occurrence permissions and prohibitions which characterize it, and its meaning. Here I am thinking of the kind of meaning which I have called correspondence meaning—the correspondence between the occurrence of a linguistic item and a non-linguistic object, action, event, or the like. Not all words have correspondence meaning, of course. When it occurs, however, it is always the most important part of language, and is ultimately the reason for the existence of language. The difficulty is that of circularity. If meaning is the ultimate goal of speech, how can we use it also as the tool by which we reach that goal? That is, if we reach the meaning of a form by knowing its identity, how can we also use its meaning to establish its identity? Put this way, the problem I am raising is seen to be the reason that linguists were timid for so long in reaching semantic decisions. Yet it is also clear that laymen have never been thus timid. A layman would never have the slightest doubt in saying that 'Flying planes can be dangerous' is one sentence if it contains *flying* number one, and another sentence if it contains *flying* number two. We have learned of late to respect the layman and his judgment, and condemn many learned pronouncements as 'counter-intuitive'. In short, I think we must accept the layman's position. The two *flyings* are indeed different, and are differentiated by their meanings; and if the position is circular, the world has been circulating for a very long time without noticeable damage. There must be a way of quieting the doubts which linguists held for so long.

I believe the proper way is once again through the jury test, and that it is made possible by one of the stranger qualities of language. Meaning is never given by an item which is totally unpredictable. It only occurs when an item is one of a set of possibilities already defined by the context. In fact, this characteristic of meaning has led me on occasion to define meaning as partial predictability. That is, if I have a sentence with a blank at the end of it, I know a great deal about what must occur in that blank. I can use a Chomskyan sentence as my example: 'Look at the cross-eyed . . .' The blank can be filled only by a noun, an animate noun (or its representative in art), and a noun indicating a being with the characteristic called platyrrhine. If I put in *girl, man,* or *monkey,* the sentence is meaningful. If I put in *pork-chop* or *live-oak,* the result is at least near-meaningless. The dependence of meaning on context is not only well known, it is so all-pervasive that it has often enough led linguists to say that meaning IS context. The statement seems to me to be true enough, but also one that can lead to misunderstandings. It is probably a truism to say that the meaning of any term would be completely defined if all the utterances were known. Yet it is even more of a truism to say that such complete presentation is a manifest impossibility. The impossibility of completeness led many linguists, at least in the thirties and forties, to try to rely on descriptions of broad classes of contexts, concluding that if the classes of contexts were essentially different, the terms being investigated were different identities. This conclusion seems to me false, or at best confused.

An example has been quite recently furnished, and is one I am grateful for. In a witty passage from a penetrating analytic paper given last November at Austin, Charles Fillmore remarked that there was a time when a typical classroom demonstration consisted, or might have consisted, of comparison of the terms 'maternity dress' or 'paternity suit'. The first part of the demonstration would have consisted of the phonological and combinatory patterns of compounding. I would add a parenthetical note to the effect that this part of the demonstration would also have relied on supra-segmental phonology to demonstrate that the two terms were indeed compounds, separate from a nonce-construction of modifying noun and head, as in 'paper tube'. This particular part of the demonstration still seems to me basically sound, though in this context probably irrelevant. Whatever the two terms are, the patterns by which they are constructed are the same. Then, said Fillmore, the second part of the demonstration described the very different kinds of contexts in which each term was appropriate, and the conclusion that the two terms were after all different was then triumphantly reached. I presume that contemporary linguists would dismiss the conclusion based on summary of contexts primarily because it is impractical, and would rely instead on speaker-intuition. I agree, of course, that the two terms are different, but would reject not only the reliance on difference of context, but also the reliance on speaker-intuition, unless intuition can be checked.

To continue with Fillmore's example, we can first say that one part of it is a little hasty. The two terms are obviously different because *maternity* and *paternity* are different words. I hope I am not doing Fillmore an injustice in saying so, since my quotation is necessarily from memory. At any rate, the underlying and more important question is whether *suit* is parallel to *dress* in that both belong to the class of articles of clothing, or whether it is something different. I, as a member of the group of neo-Bloomfieldians, was uncomfortable in the face of the necessity of saying that the items which I shall call $suit_1$ and $suit_2$ were, as everyone knows, different. I certainly in the past must have relied on difference of context, as we all did in the days before the great transformation. Yet even then I was uncomfortable with such a decision, and would now say flatly that the decision was erroneous. Difference in context or environment does not prove difference of identity in meaningful forms. If anything, it would prove that they were variants of the same entity. That is, in dealing with sounds we use not DIFFERENCE in environment to decide on difference in identity, but contrariwise, IDENTITY of environment. We decide that the sounds /p/ and /b/ are different because they occur in such identical environments as / . . . æt/. Since they occur in this environment, they distinguish the words *pat* and *bat,* and the words, in turn, distinguish the sentence 'I gave it a pat' from 'I gave it a bat'. Again in sounds, we use DIFFERENCE in environment to decide that two sounds are identical. The vowel of *man* occurs with nasal consonants, while the vowel of *bat* occurs with oral consonants. We decide that the difference between nasal and oral vowels does not distinguish words or sentences, and that nasal and oral vowels are variants of identical sounds. Yet when we describe words, we take a different and quite contrary position. We say that $suit_1$ occurs only in environments which mention articles of clothing, and $suit_2$ only in environments mentioning law courts. If we decided on the identity of words in the same way that we decide on the identity of sounds, we would have to say that $suit_1$

and *suit₂* were in complementary distribution—and, to use a bit of the jargon once so fashionable, that they were allologs of the same lexeme.

I think that it is possible to establish the two kinds of distribution—that is, complementary and contrastive—for meaningful forms such as *suit₁* and *suit₂* where nothing in phonology or morphology can be relied on. We can set up a jury test for the utterance 'He brought a suit'. We do this by devising two differing contexts for the utterance. One might be: 'He came in shorts, but that didn't matter. *He brought a suit.*' The second could be: 'He had been threatening for years to do something about the damages he had experienced at the hands of that company, and he finally did something about it. *He brought a suit.*' In giving the test, it must be made clear that the only part of the relatively long utterances being tested are the two instances of 'He brought a suit'. I have tried just this test on three graduate classes, none sophisticated in linguistics, and am therefore sure of the result. All sixty students responded that *He brought a suit₁* is a different sentence from *He brought a suit₂*. That is, *suit₁* is a three-part entity consisting of vowels and consonants, supra-segmental accompaniment, and syntactico-semantic identity, and since it occurs in the same linguistic environment as *suit₂*, which is also a three-part entity, the two entities distinguish the two sentences just as *bat* and *pat* distinguish sentences.

Setting up such a test may be an ultimate reliance on meaning, but I do not believe that the reliance on meaning here is in any way unsound. I would agree with a statement once made to me by Noam Chomsky, that the only kind of reliance on meaning which is certain to fail is the attempt to define the meaning by pointing to objects and classes of objects in the outside world. It is to be noted that the jurors are not asked about the meaning of terms, or to explain why they say that the two sentences are different. They are asked only to discriminate between identity and difference, the same discrimination jurors are asked to make with *pat* and *bat*. I think all of us are agreed that if we ask jurors WHY forms are different, instead of simply 'same or different', we will get rationalizations which are not useful, but merely confusing. Furthermore, I think it is useful to study language as if there were a sharp boundary between what occurs within sentence borders and what reaches beyond. My two test-utterances of 'He brought a suit' are quite indistinguishable if pronounced alone, but easily separated if the sentences are placed in a larger context. If we then recognize that there is a difference between context within sentences and contexts reaching beyond sentences, many of our problems are resolved. In believing that the search for larger contexts to determine identity is justified, my reason is the truism that context does indeed give meaning, and that no hearer can understand the meaning of a sentence unless he knows the context in which it occurred. Every hearer assumes that sentences are to be interpreted in accord with maximum congruence with their environment, not minimum. This is the essence of the formulation which I have called the Joos Law, and have used for a good many years—the formulation that of possible meanings for an unknown term, in situations where the meaning of the context is known, that meaning is best which contributes least to, or changes least, the total context. The formulation was given in a paper before this Society in 1953 by Martin Joos (cf. also Joos 1958a: 286). A kind of corollary of the Joos Law can be formulated thus: in cases of homonymy, where the homonyms can be put into identical sentences, juries will supply the semantic content of the homonyms in accord with the larger context in which the phonologically identical sentences are placed.

The fact that identification of *suit₁* and *suit₂* is of some importance in practical lexicography is shown by the fact that all three of the dictionaries enter the two forms as differing meanings of the same word, not as separate words. In this the dictionaries are doubtless influenced by etymology, which is the same for both forms at least in the sense that they go back to the same etymon, though it is also true that they have differing histories of derivation. Acceptance of the idea that *suit*₁ and *suit*₂ are different words would have made the lexicographer's task of describing meanings distinctly easier.

It is possible, however, that some linguists harbor an objection to my test sentence, *He brought a suit*. The test sentence makes it reasonably clear that the original *maternity dress* and *paternity suit* are separate entities, but it is still possible to object that it is not alone the difference between *suit*₁ (which belongs to the class of clothing, and so is like the *dress* of *maternity dress*) and *suit*₂ (which belongs to the class of legal actions) which distinguishes the particular sentences I chose. There is also a difference in meaning of the two instances of *brought*. In one the verb means roughly to transport something towards the speaker, the person spoken to, or the person spoken of—a verb which is then structurally opposed to *take*. In the second instance the verb means (again roughly) to initiate a legal action. Neither transporting nor motion hitherward are present in the second verb. Would a lexicographer, or a linguist for that matter, be therefore justified in saying that *brought*₁ and *brought*₂ are separate words? None of our three dictionaries regard them as separate words, though they all recognize the separate meanings. Also, so far as my rather desultory questioning of laymen goes, the normal intuitive response is that these two forms are variants of the same word; but with the two *suits*, the intuitive response is that they are separate. I do not wish to rely very heavily on such responses, since they are difficult to check, and in general I would rather keep my use of juries to queries involving contrast alone. I could, of course, set up sentences like 'He brought it', and then invent differing contexts for two utterances of them, thus concluding that the two occurrences of *brought* are, after all, different words. The demonstration would be, I think, fallacious, since in each sentence *it* is a substitute for avoidance of repetition, and in differing contexts it would be substituting for quite different forms. That is, I believe that the two meanings of *brought* do indeed occur only in differing contexts, which can be easily defined, and which are narrow enough so that they occur in single sentences. To mean 'instigated,' *brought* must have a complement consisting of some such words as *suit, legal action* or the like. Under such circumstances, the semantic components found in *brought* when it occurs before a physical, transportable object are cancelled—much as, in the instance of the much belabored *bachelor*, the component of 'maleness' is cancelled in *bachelor girl*. That *brought* [*a*] *suit* meaning 'instigated a legal action' is a rather special sort of unity is, of course, further shown by the fact that it can occur in the form *brought suit*, unpredictably without an article, even though *suit* in this sense is countable, singular, and not previously mentioned.

It should now be clear that I chose my sentence—or rather my homonymous pair of sentences—deliberately. 'He brought a suit' contains homonyms of different types, although dictionaries commonly treat both *brought* and *suit* alike, relying on their etymologies. In these days when we can follow John Firth in saying that linguistics is no longer solely, or even mainly, a historical discipline, there is no reason for such reliance on etymology. One form, *brought*, represents a special variant—an alloseme in Bloomfieldian terms; the other represents a separate sememe. I think these statements bear out the native speaker's intuition about identity and difference of forms.

A principle can now be formulated, for acceptance or rejection. Context within the borders of a sentence cannot be used to establish difference of suspected homonyms. That is, if one of the homonyms always occurs in sentences which are otherwise different, the distribution is non-contrastive. Context CAN be used to establish difference of suspected homonyms if they occur in homonymous sentences which are then shown to be different by differing sentence-contexts.

There remains another situation in which it is possible to criticize dictionary practice. There is a passage in a recent article by William Morris, the Editor-in-Chief of the *Heritage Dictionary,* in which he says (1969: 202–3):

> We have [abandoned] both alleged historical fact and alleged statistical fact [and arranged] the meanings of a word in a natural flow. This consists of finding a central sense and arranging the others from it. Such a method . . . represents the 'shape' or pattern of the word in the mind of the native speaker, regardless of how the pattern came about.
>
> When we described the plan at the first meeting of our linguistic panel, Morris Halle of MIT, one of the leading modern linguists, became quite excited and felt we were getting on to some of the most exciting new work in linguistics, dealing with semantic intuition.

It is true that Morris does indeed open the door to a dictionary description which makes use of speaker-intuition. But the notion that a dictionary completed in 1969 has actually mapped the patterns of words in the minds of native speakers is one that I find faintly amusing. Our English dictionaries do better, certainly, than at least one bilingual dictionary I had to use for purposes of practical communication in a language I do not speak. This dictionary seemed at first not to have an entry for *toilet*—astonishing enough for any dictionary having any pretensions at all to practicality. The word was there, however, tucked away as a sub-entry under *toil*. While we do not go that far in distorting native speaker intuition of the pattern of words, it seems to me that to treat *suit of clothes* and *suit at law* as sub-entries of the same word also distorts native speaker intuition, and does it for reasons of history which have been supposedly abandoned.

How far we are from mapping meaning in a natural flow can be shown by a linguistic statement familiar to all of us. In their influential article of 1963, Katz & Fodor (pp. 185–90) present four meanings for *bachelor,* drawn from a pair of dictionaries, the *Shorter Oxford dictionary* and *Webster's new collegiate dictionary*. The meanings, moving across their tree diagram from left to right, are: (1) human male who has never married; (2) human male who is young, and is a knight serving under the standard of another knight; (3) young human who has the lowest academic degree; and (4) young male fur-seal who is without a mate during the breeding season. I am certainly not alone in feeling that meanings arranged so as to put the unmated human being and the unmated seal at opposite extremes seem strange. As far as this particular native speaker's intuition is concerned, the arrangement is counter-intuitive. I would certainly agree that if we are dealing with some such word as *rabbit*, the native speaker begins by mapping the syntactico-semantic classes to which the word belongs, moving in an orderly flow from larger to smaller successively. Thus *rabbit* is a noun, of the count class, animate, mammalian, edible and either domestic or wild. There is no difficulty in arriving at a class sufficiently circumscribed so that we have indeed mapped the native speaker's semantic intuition. But with *bachelor* there is serious difficulty. We can start our mapping without trouble: *bachelor* is a noun, countable, animate, mammalian, all without disagreement. For two of the meanings we add human, possibly also male and young, and arrive at the two meanings 'holder of the lowest academic degree' and 'Knight serving under the banner of another'. There is no separation until we get to the last stage, that of the particular type of hierarchy to which the individual belongs. But if we start out to map so as to get to 'unmarried man' and 'unmated seal', we have to abandon the large class HUMAN, and rely on making MALE our largest class after mammalian. There is no way in which this can be satisfactorily represented on a binarily branching tree: the contradiction is the same as that which faces bibliographers who draw up manuscript trees, showing that manuscripts *a* and *b* are descended from *X*, and *d* and *e* from *Y*, though *d* sometimes contradictorily takes its readings from *X*. Or, closer to home, this is the classic dilemma of historical linguists faced with drawing a tree for the Indo-European languages, where Slavic and Germanic belong to satem and centum branches respectively, but share such other characteristics as the case ending of the dative plural and large numbers of etymologies. In linguistics, we all know that the solution which has been generally acceptable is the wave diagram of overlapping circles. For the native speaker's intuitive semantic descriptions, I think the necessary answer is that there is a *bachelor*$_1$ and a *bachelor*$_2$, the first with HUMAN as a main classifier, and the second with MALE. The fact that components are thus shared in a contradictory way is due to the obvious fact that words are associated, even when they can be shown to be distinct. Otherwise punning would be impossible. For *bachelor*$_1$ and *bachelor*$_2$, the circular arrangement of meanings proposed by Martin Joos (1958b: 60–1) in his description of CODE seems to me a reasonable supplement to the binarily branching tree, though obviously not of great help to the practicing lexicographer, who must somehow arrange his entries serially. For such a worker, the native speaker intuition tested by a randomly selected jury is the indicated resort. Ask a dozen randomly selected native speakers of English the meaning of the word *bachelor,* giving no context. I should be astonished if the response was not always 'unmarried man'. This then is the form which should be given first, with 'unmated fur seal' as a sub-entry immediately following. The meaning 'holder of the lowest academic degree' should be a separate entry, with the meaning 'knight serving under the standard of another' as its sub-entry. Here the heraldic meaning is the sub-entry because it is now surely unlikely to occur before 'holder of the lowest academic degree' in any intuitive mapping of meanings.

I have at last come to the end of my suggestions for dictionary makers, and I can only hope that most linguists will agree with some of them, and that some will agree with all of them, to distort President Lincoln. Yet surely there is a reservation that must occur to many. Dictionaries are made by publishers and professional communicators, not by linguists. So how can we make our criticisms felt, presuming that we have them? The answer lies in the fact that very many of us are frequently engaged in the making of little dictionaries—for instance, the vocabulary of medieval German poetry that led Martin Joos to the formulation of the law which I cited earlier. Or we are called on to produce bilingual dictionaries of various sizes; or we make studies of usage, that is, of speaker-writer attitudes towards words. If these specialized works are made coruscating examples of improved methods, we can be sure that eventually, perhaps with glacial slowness, but also with glacial inevitability, the dictionary makers will follow.

REFERENCES

1. Jespersen, Otto. 1914. A Modern English grammar on historical principles, vol. 3. London: Allen & Unwin. (Reprinted, 1954.)
2. Joos, Martin. 1953. Towards a first theorem in semantics. Paper presented at the Annual Meeting, Linguistic Society of America, 29 December.

3. ———. 1958a. Review of A glossary of American technical linguistic usage, by Eric Hamp. *Language* 34.279–88.

4. ———. 1958b. Semology, a linguistic theory of meaning. Studies in Linguistics 13.53–70.

5. Katz, Jerrold J., and Jerry A. Fodor. 1963. The structure of a semantic theory. *Language* 39.170–210.

6. Morris, William. 1969. The making of a dictionary—1969. *College Composition and Communication* 20.198–203.

7. Petoski, Catherine. 1969. New dictionary has its ups and downs. *Austin American-Statesman*, 5 October, T28, col. 5.

8. Quirk, Randolph, and Jan Svartvik. 1966. Investigating linguistic acceptability. (Janua linguarum, series minor, 54.) The Hague: Mouton.

DISCUSSION QUESTIONS

1. Do you agree with Hill upon the desirability of a usage panel of some kind? How about his opinion that such a panel should be composed of naïve speakers rather than trained linguists?

2. Why does Hill think that a usage panel should be restricted to balloting and refrain from editorial comment?

3. Produce additional examples of words with puzzling identities to illustrate the points Hill makes with *Cairo, house, fly,* and *vanish,* and be ready to discuss them.

THOMAS J. CRESWELL

The author, professor of English at Chicago State University, has written and published in the field of usage, notably his monograph Usage in Dictionaries and in Dictionaries of Usage *published in 1975 by the American Dialect Society (Publication of the American Dialect Society, nos. 63–64).*

USAGE IN CONTEMPORARY AMERICAN DICTIONARIES[1]

A study of mid-twentieth century American practice in the treatment of problems of usage in general-purpose dictionaries reveals little real change from the authoritarian and idiosyncratic practice characteristic of Samuel Johnson's 1755 *English Dictionary*. More than two centuries of linguistic and lexicographic scholarship have altered somewhat the tone of statements about usage in dictionaries, but have had little apparent effect upon the objectivity of judgments. When the user of a modern dictionary finds that a locution is censured or assigned a restrictive label, all that he can really be certain of is that the compiler believes the implied judgment to be accurate.

This unfavorable characterization of modern practice in the identification and analysis of "problem" locutions is based upon a detailed analysis of the treatment accorded 318 specific locutions in ten dictionaries.[2] The items selected for study are those on which the editors of *The American Heritage Dictionary* (AHD) reported votes by the AHD Usage Panel, which consists of 105 distinguished writers, editors, and belletrists. A list identifying the items by entry word in the AHD is attached. As the present report is concerned only with broad characterization of objectivity and reliability in assessments of usage rather than with the details of the treatment of specific individual locutions, the usage problems dealt with in the entries are, for the most part, not further specified here. The usage notes occur in 226 entries in AHD, deal with 247 "kinds" of problems—137 diction, 52 grammar, 30 idiom, 26 word formation, and 2 spelling problems—and report Usage Panel votes on 318 specific locutions.

All of the items voted on by the AHD Usage Panel were deemed by the editors of AHD to represent problems in usage or items of controversy in usage. Usage Panel votes on the 318 items range from 0 percent to 99 percent acceptance or approval of the questioned locution, with about 150 of the items being approved by more than 50 percent of the Panel. It is difficult to evaluate the meaning of the percentage votes reported in AHD. If the votes are interpreted in the manner devised by Sterling Andrus Leonard, who also reported votes by a panel of experts in his pioneering *Current English Usage* (1932),[3] the AHD Panel is found to have rated 16.6 percent of the usages *Established,*

---

[1] This paper was originally presented at the Seminar on Bilingual and Monolingual Lexicography held at the Annual Meeting of the Modern Language Association, New York, December 27, 1974.

[2] A list of the dictionaries, including abbreviations by which they are referred to here, is included in the bibliography.

[3] Approval by 75 percent of those consulted classifies a usage as *Established,* by less than 25 percent *Illiterate,* by from 26 to 75 percent *Disputable.*

55.1 percent *Disputable,* and 28.3 percent *Illiterate.* Evidence of the conservatism of the AHD Usage Panel is found by analysis of their votes on 7 locutions which were rated *Established* in the Leonard study, in Albert H. Marckwardt and Fred Walcott's *Facts About Current English Usage* (1938) and in Raymond D. Crisp's 1971 dissertation, *"Changes in Attitude Toward English Usage."* Both the Leonard and the Crisp studies report judgments by a panel of "experts"; Marckwardt and Walcott base their ratings on evidence from OED citations and similar sources. Of 7 locutions rated *Established* in all three of those studies, the AHD Usage Panel rates only 1 as *Established;* 3 are rated *Disputable* and 3 as *Illiterate.* Of 36 items rated *Established* in the most recent of these studies, Raymond Crisp's 1971 survey, only 5 are rated *Established* by the AHD Panel; 21 are rated *Disputable* and 13 *Illiterate.*[4]

The conflict of opinion between the AHD panel and the panels of Leonard and Crisp plus the citation evidence of Marckwardt and Walcott is merely the tip of the iceberg. Analysis of the treatment of the 318 locutions in nine additional modern American dictionaries reveals even more complicated variation in assessment.

On only two of the 318 locutions considered here are all ten of the dictionaries in agreement that their use should be restricted. The two locutions are, not surprisingly, "Ain't I?" and "It ain't (raining)". Even this "agreement", however, finds highly diverse forms of expression in the various dictionaries. On the first of the two, "Ain't I?", the AHD Usage Panel casts a resounding vote of disapproval, 99 percent disapproving its use in writing, 84 percent its use in speech. W2 labels "Ain't I?" *Dial. or Illit.;* W3, and WC7, and WC8, in usage notes, limit its use to informal speech; RHD and RHCD label it *Nonstand. U.S., Informal Brit.,* and warn against its use in a note; NWD1 and NWD2 label it *Colloq.* and, in a note, indicate that it is criticized by some and defended by others, taking no stand on the issue themselves; SCD labels it *Illit. and Dial.* and characterizes it in a note as nonstandard. Much the same kind of variation in treatment of "It ain't (raining)" is found in the ten dictionaries. Treatment of these two usages represents the nearest approach to agreement or unanimity which can be found in the dictionaries studied.

The comparison of the treatment of usage in a number of dictionaries is made difficult by the wide variation in practice in the application of labels and in the use of notes on usage in the various dictionaries. They indicate restrictions on the use of a locution in at least four ways: through application of a restrictive label, through a usage note, through discrimination in a synonymy, and through verbal illustration or citation. So that meaningful comparisons among the dictionaries can be made, in the following discussion and tabulations treatment of an item is described in one of the following ways: the item is either *Not Treated* (N), *Accepted* (A), or *Restricted* (R). *Not Treated* means that the locution is not entered, defined, listed, or referred to in the dictionary in question; the item may occur as an entry word, but the specific usage problem or use of the item discussed in the AHD note is not treated in that entry or elsewhere. *Accepted* means that the item is entered with no indication of restriction or possible restriction on its use, or it is discussed in the entry or in a separate note or synonymy and pronounced acceptable for use in all styles and at all levels, without restriction. *Restricted* means that the item

---

[4] The AHD Panel ratings total 39 rather than 36 because for 3 locutions—*anxious, can* (b), and *me*—separate votes are reported on use in writing and in speech; for all three the votes classify the item as *Illiterate* in writing, *Disputable* in speech.

is either assigned a restrictive label or it is discussed in a note or synonymy with indication of general disapproval of its use or of some limitation on its use; all instances of status, stylistic, and geographic labeling are placed in this classification.

A given locution can be placed in one of seven categories on the basis of its treatment in the nine dictionaries other than AHD: (1) items *Not Treated* in any of the nine dictionaries; (2) items *Accepted* in all; (3) items *Restricted* in all; (4) items either *Accepted* or *Not Treated* (*Accepted* by all dictionaries which treat them, but not all dictionaries treat them); (5) items either *Restricted* or *Not Treated* (again, *Restricted* by all which treat them, but not all treat them); (6) items either *Accepted* or *Restricted* (treated in all nine dictionaries, but opinion as to acceptability is divided); and finally (7) items which fall into all three classifications—*Not Treated, Accepted, Restricted* (at least one of the nine dictionaries treats the item in question in each way). Table 1 shows the number of items which fall into each of these seven groups in the nine dictionaries other than AHD.

Table 1   318 AHD usage items classified as to treatment in nine other dictionaries

Classification	Number of Items	Percentage of Total
Not Treated (N)	21	7
Accepted (A)	29	9
Restricted (R)	2	0.5
Either Not Treated or Accepted (N/A)	68	21
Either Not Treated or Restricted (N/R)	19	6
Either Accepted or Restricted (A/R)	77	24
Either Not Treated, Accepted, or Restricted (N/A/R)	102	32
Total	318	

The obvious conclusion to be drawn from the data in Table 1 is that there is a very low level of unanimity among the dictionaries. Only 16.5 percent of the 318 items receive the same treatment (either *Not Treated, Accepted,* or *Restricted*) in all nine dictionaries. At the other end of the scale, just about double that number, 32 percent, receive all three treatments in the nine dictionaries. The remainder, slightly over 50 percent, receive some combination of two treatments (*Not Treated/Accepted, Not Treated/Restricted, Accepted/Restricted*); nearly one-quarter of the items, 24 percent, are in the *Accepted/Restricted* category, indicating that the dictionaries disagree flatly with each other.

No correlation can be found between the votes by AHD Usage Panel members and the judgments of the other nine dictionaries: (1) the 21 items *Not Treated* by any of the nine other dictionaries received votes of approval by from 0 percent to 87 percent of the AHD Usage Panel; (2) the 29 *Accepted* items received votes of from 10 to 90 percent approving; (3) the two *Restricted* items have been discussed above; in the "combination" categories (4), (5) and (6), AHD Usage Panel approval votes ranged, respectively, from 3 to 96 percent, and from 1 to 92 percent; in (7), the category of items receiving all three kinds of treatment in the nine dictionaries, the range is from 0 to 99 percent approval.

If treatment of the 318 items is analyzed on a dictionary-by-dictionary basis, the extent of disparity and disagreement among the dictionaries becomes even more obvious. Table 2 shows the wide range among the nine dictionaries other than AHD in reaction

Table 2   Treatment by nine dictionaries of 318 usages on which an AHD Usage
Panel vote is reported

Dictionary	Not Treated	Accepted	Restrictive Label Only Applied	Note Agrees With AHD Majority	Note Disagrees With AHD Majority	Total
W2	108	59	89(6)ᵃ	49	13	318
W3	55	244	7	5	7	318
WC7	130	177	1	6	4	318
WC8	104	203	0	7	4	318
RHD	87	137	25(14)	57	12	318
RHCD	85	144	28(16)	52	9	318
NWD1	128	96	66(4)	18	10	318
NWD2	81	149	49(5)	31	8	318
SCD	94	92	52(12)	60	20	318
Total	872	1301	317(57)	285	87	2862

ᵃ Figures in parentheses represent instances in which both a label and a note appear. The figures
outside parentheses in the "label" column do *not* include those within parentheses.

to the 318 items. The ranges of performance demonstrate the sweeping nature of difference
both in habitual practice and in "permissiveness" among the nine dictionaries.

The number of items *Not Treated* by the nine dictionaries ranges from a low of 55
in W3 to a high of 130 in its first abridgement, WC7. In the *Accepted* column, the number
of items ranges from 59 in W2 to 244 in W3. It must be remembered in evaluating this
last figure that no attempt has been made in this study to weigh the citations or verbal
illustrations offered by W3 or to use them to classify items. If an item is defined and/or
illustrated in W3, and if no restrictive label or other indication of limitation is found in
the entry, the item is classified as *Accepted*.

The third column in Table 2 shows the relative extent of exclusive dependence
upon usage labels as indicators of status in the nine dictionaries. Figures in parentheses
following the amounts in column 3 show the number of additional labels applied along
with a note by each dictionary. The practices revealed by these figures are, obviously,
erratic. It appears to be accidental rather than planned when a dictionary uses both a label
and a note to indicate restriction. Columns 4 and 5 show the relative amounts of agreement
and disagreement with the AHD Panel majority expressed in notes in the nine dictionaries.
Range is, as usual, quite wide: in number of notes agreeing with the AHD Panel majority,
the low is 5 in W3 and the high 60 in SCD; in notes disagreeing, the range is from 4 in
WC7 to 20 in SCD.

A different kind of insight into the treatment of the 318 usages in the nine dictionaries
is furnished by combining the figures in Table 2 into two broad categories.

Combined as they are in Table 3, the figures provide a simple index of the extent
to which each of the dictionaries and all of the dictionaries combined acknowledge as
problems in usage the 318 items voted upon by the AHD Panel. Column 1 in Table 3
combines the amounts in columns 1 and 2 in Table 2; column 2 totals the remaining
columns. The range in acknowledgment of the existence of problems in the items
concerned is from 11 out of 318 in WC7 to 151 out of 318 in W2. If the three recent
Merriam-Webster dictionaries are removed from consideration, on the grounds that they

avoid making judgments on most items, the range narrows to from 88 in NWD2 to 151 in W2.

The totals in Table 3 show that in 689 of 2,862 possible cases the dictionaries studied acknowledge the existence of a problem; in 2,173 cases they do not. The ratio is almost exactly 1:3. If the three recent Merriam-Webster dictionaries are removed from the calculation, the figures become 648 *Acknowledged* and 1,260 *Not Acknowledged,* a ratio of almost 1:2. This means that, even making the best possible case for the items singled out for study by AHD by eliminating from consideration three avowedly non-judgmental dictionaries, in only one of every three possible cases does another dictionary consider or treat the item in question as a problem. This consideration or treatment does not mean, it must be remembered, that the dictionaries doing so agree with AHD judgments on the items, but simply that they in some way raise a usage issue about those items. As has been made clear earlier, agreement with AHD Usage Panel votes is far lower than the ratio 1:2 suggests.

The data presented here place in serious question the claims to objectivity and descriptive accuracy in matters of usage made by modern dictionary editors. AHD takes an unabashedly *ipse dixit* position, saying that the best authorities on usage are "professional writers and speakers" and furnishing as a guide to good usage percentage votes from an assemblage of 105 individuals who meet AHD criteria for membership in that group. W2 asserts that it has determined the truth about usage through "the carefully checked judgment of the editorial staff". RHD and RHCD judgments are "based on extensive research and thoughtful consideration", filtered through "experts", and then reviewed by "a group of editors and teachers". NWD2 says that it specifies "the status of any usage, as determined by trained lexicographers after a careful study of current writings and speech and disregarding the crotchets and prejudices of individuals". The other dictionaries make similar assertions, all claiming descriptive accuracy and objectivity. When, however, actual performance is evaluated across all the dictionaries studied, it becomes clear that the descriptive objectivity is that of the blind men examining the elephant. Each dictionary comes up with a different image of sociolinguistic reality. Each

Table 3 Acknowledgment as usage problems by nine dictionaries of 318 usages on which an AHD Usage Panel vote is reported

Dictionary	Existence of Problem Not Acknowledged	Existence of Problem Acknowledged	Total
W2	167	151	318
W3	299	19	318
WC7	307	11	318
WC8	307	11	318
RHD	224	94	318
RHCD	229	89	318
NWD1	224	94	318
NWD2	230	88	318
SCD	186	132	318
Total	2173	689	2862
Total Without W3, WC7, WC8	1260	648	1908

dictionary practices an objectivity unique to itself. If an item is unanimously or almost unanimously condemned by the AHD Usage Panel, there is no way of predicting whether other dictionaries will even acknowledge that the item presents a problem in usage, let alone whether they will accept or restrict it.

The search for consistency in the treatment of usage among the dictionaries considered in this study must be acknowledged a failure. Every analysis presented in the preceding pages shows that, in dealing with the 318 items under study, the ten modern dictionaries are far, far more often in disagreement than they are in agreement. The dictionaries' claims of objectivity and authoritativeness in the treatment of usage must be rejected. If they were either objective or accurate, they could hardly disagree as often as they do.

The reason for the observed inconsistency is obviously the dependence of the dictionaries on opinion rather than on observation of actual usage as a guide. The results of such dependence are manifested, unintentionally, I am sure, in a usage note from AHD.

> *Flaunt* in the sense of *flout* (to show contempt or conspicuous disregard for) is rejected by 91 percent of the Usage Panel. A dissenting member of the Panel observes that it is "in too general use to be ignored." However, although its appearance in print since the 1930's (especially in the United States) is widely attested, *flaunt* in this sense remains a malapropism in the judgment of most writers and editors.

The conviction underlying this pronouncement, put in the baldest terms, runs something like the following: "Use of a locution by numbers of writers in well-edited publications renders it suitable for use by others, except when, because we dislike it, we 'writers and editors' wish to condemn it. If we condemn it, it is unsuitable." It is a fact, of course, that such condemnations, if voiced frequently and vigorously, carry great weight among certain of those aspiring to recognition as members of a well-educated, highly literate elite. Nevertheless, that small group does not, in the final analysis, control the direction of change in the language.

Even Dr. Johnson recognized the futility of his efforts and the inadequacy of opinion, no matter how "logical" or "well-informed" or "dedicated to preserving the beauty and purity of the language", as a shaper of language. I think it is time that modern lexicography catch up with Dr. Johnson. Elsewhere, I have proposed a method for deriving usage labels and discussions of usage from the examination of available bodies of language material such as the Brown University *Standard Corpus of Present-Day Edited American English*.[5] Present-day practice in the development of definitions is based firmly on the practice of collecting citations in which context helps define sense. There is no deterrent that I know of to following the same practice in the making of judgments about the status and stylistic implications of locutions. It is time that lexicography abandoned the self-gratifying luxury of serving up idiosyncratic snippets from among the whims and crotchets of editors or compilers or "experts" as information about modern American usage.

---

5 Thomas J. Creswell: *Usage in Dictionaries and in Dictionaries of Usage*. Publication of the American Dialect Society, Nos. 63–64, April–November 1975. University of Alabama Press.

APPENDIX

226 ENTRIES IN THE *AMERICAN HERITAGE DICTIONARY* CONTAINING USAGE NOTES
IN WHICH VOTES BY THE *AHD* USAGE PANEL ARE REPORTED ON 318 LOCUTIONS

Numbers following entry words indicate the number of specific locutions upon which a Usage
Panel vote is reported in the note at that entry. Where no number appears, a vote is reported on
only one locution.

about	dilemma	lack	shakedown 2
above 2	discomfit	latter	shall
advise	disinterested	leave 2	shambles
agenda 2	dive	like 2	should 2
ain't 3	done	likely	sick 2
alibi 2	dope 2	loan	simultaneous
all	double negative	materialize	so 2
alternative	doubt 2	me	some
anticipate	dropout	medium 2	someplace
anxious	drunk	mighty	sometime
any	due	most 2	someway
anyone	each 2	mutual 2	sound
appreciate	each other 2	myself 2	spark
as	either	nauseous	spell
author	enormity	negotiate	spiral
back 2	enthuse 2	nicely	split infinitive 4
bad 3	epithet	none	spoof 2
badly	equal 2	normalcy	stall 2
balance	erratum 2	noun 4	stomp
balding	escalate	oblivious 2	straddle 2
behalf	escape	O.K. 4	suffer
better	ever	one 2	sustain
between 2	farther 3	only 2	tend
bid	fault	outside	that
bimonthly	few 3	over	this
bit	finalize	overly	though
blame	first 2	participle 3	through
boast	flammable	personality	thusly
bug	flaunt	practically 2	too
burgeon	follow	predicate	transpire
bus 2	foremost	premiere	trek
but 2	fortuitous	presently 2	tribute
buy	gambit	proportion	trigger
can 4	gauntlet	prove	truculent
cannot	gift	provided	try 2
careen	good 2	quick	tycoon
celebrant	graduate 2	quite 4	type 2
center	groom	quiz 2	unexceptional
certain	hang 2	quote	unique
claim	head	raise 3	upcoming
cohort	headquarter	rambunctious	upward
commentate	hectic	rarely	various
compare 3	help	rate 2	very 4
compensate	hopefully	rattle	viewpoint
complete	host	regard	were 4

comprise 2	human	rendition	whence
condition	identify 2	renege	which
consensus	idle	replica	while 3
consequential	ilk	responsible	who 3
contact 2	important	reverend 2	whose
cope	individual 3	rile	why
data	infer	ring	win
debut	insignia 2	saving	-wise
definite	internecine	scan	wish
deprecate	interpretative	seem	Xmas
develop	intrigue	senior citizen	zoom 2
different 3	kind 3		

BIBLIOGRAPHY

Dictionaries

1. The American Heritage Dictionary of the English Language. New York: American Heritage Publishing Company and Houghton Mifflin Company, 1971 (AHD)

2. Funk and Wagnall's Standard College Dictionary: Text Edition. New York: Harcourt, Brace and World, Inc., 1963 (SCD)

3. The Random House College Dictionary. New York: Random House, Inc., 1972. (RHCD)

4. The Random House Dictionary of the English Language: The Unabridged Edition. New York: Random House, Inc., 1971 (RHD)

5. Webster's New Collegiate Dictionary. 8th ed. Springfield, Mass.: G. & C. Merriam Co., 1973. (WC8)

6. Webster's New International Dictionary of the English Language: Second Edition. Unabridged. Springfield, Mass.: G. & C. Merriam Co., 1959. (W2)

7. Webster's New World Dictionary of the American Language: College Edition. Cleveland and New York: The World Publishing Co., 1959. (NWD1)

8. Webster's New World Dictionary of the American Language: Second College Edition. Cleveland and New York: The World Publishing Co., 1972. (NWD2)

9. Webster's Seventh New Collegiate Dictionary. Springfield, Mass.: G. & C. Merriam Co., 1963. (WC7)

10. Webster's Third New International Dictionary of the English Language: Unabridged. Springfield, Mass.: G. & C. Merriam Co., 1966. (W3)

Usage Studies

1. Crisp, Raymond D. "Changes in Attitude Toward English Usage." Ph.D. dissertation, University of Illinois. 1971.

2. Leonard, Sterling Andrus. Current English Usage. English Monograph No. 1, National Council of Teachers of English. Chicago: National Council of Teachers of English, 1932.

3. Marckwardt, Albert H. and Fred Walcott. Facts About Current English Usage. English Monograph No. 7, National Council of Teachers of English. New York: D. Appleton-Century Co., Inc., 1938.

DISCUSSION QUESTIONS

1. Compare Creswell's views of the usage panel with those of Archibald Hill. Would Hill's kind of panel be likely to yield more reliable results?

2. Why do dictionaries differ so greatly? Do the differences reflect respective attitudes toward informal speech? What would have been the attitude of the usage panel of the *American Heritage Dictionary* toward informal speech?

3. Why in your opinion was there unanimous disapproval of *ain't* among panel members and also among dictionary editors? Remember that *ain't* is the normal phonetic development of *amn't* and of *haven't*. What is your own attitude? Do you use it?

4. How does Creswell's view of a dictionary's function differ from that of Albert Marckwardt and of R. W. Burchfield?

PART VIII

LINGUISTICS AND NAME STUDY

Research in the study of names, technically known as onomastics, has long engrossed the attention of European scholars, but only recently on this side of the Atlantic has it been raised above the status of dilettantism. Its general level was that of the newspaper filler reporting that an Ohio village is named Pratts Fork or that a governor of Texas had named a daughter Ima as a sentence opener to go with the family name, Hogg. True, several good place-name studies of the state names appeared in the first half of the century, but it was not until George R. Stewart devoted a scholar's attention in his semi-popular but significant works that the status of onomastics rose appreciably. See especially his *Names on the Land* (Houghton Mifflin, 1945, 1960, 1967) and *American Place-Names* (Oxford University Press, 1970).

The founding of the American Name Society in 1951 and of its scholarly journal *Names* in 1952 finally created a focus and a home for serious researchers. Scholarly articles and annual national and regional meetings have so greatly stimulated the study of both personal names and place-names that onomastics seems now to have won a secure standing among the scholarly disciplines. But because the European interest in etymology was much less relevant in American name study, linguists still shied away from it. Among the first to rank names as worthy of academic attention was the late Francis Utley, whose major article on the subject is here reprinted in part. A much more searching analysis, necessary after the brilliant but inadequate monographs by Gardiner and Pulgram alluded to in the article, is that by John Algeo, who with some penetration delves into the troublesome question "What is a proper name?"

More recent concern with personal names has been shown by psycholinguists investigating the psychological process of name-giving, the reactions of individuals to their own names, and the psychological effect of giving up a family name. Such studies, on a small scale, have proved of great interest to students, most of whom have an easily aroused curiosity about their own names and nicknames, the names of people they know, and the names and nicknames of places in their locality. Such interest has been encouraged in several special programs during conventions of the National Council of Teachers of English, where a number of classroom research projects have been reported. The inclusion of these two articles by Utley and Algeo is designed to meet that growing interest.

FRANCIS LEE UTLEY

Teacher and outstanding scholar in several fields—medieval literature, folklore, linguistics, onomastics—Utley was a professor of English at The Ohio State University.

THE LINGUISTIC COMPONENT OF ONOMASTICS

Onomastics has many components; the question at issue is whether certain of these, like history, logic and etymology, have tended to obscure and overwhelm the potential linguistic component. If the answer is yes, the responsibility for correction lies not only on the historian, logician and etymologist, but also on the modern linguist, structural or transformational, who has been slow to plow in onomastic pastures. Before turning to the narrower range of linguistics, let us glance at some of the uses to which onomastics has been put by the other disciplines.

I

In Europe there has been no lack of rigor in the conduct of the study of proper names. One need merely cite the work of Ekwall, Mawer and Stenton, Adolf Bach and Dauzat to underline the point. They all have demonstrated how place-name study can supplement archaeology in writing the prehistory of Europe. Mawer and Stenton, by meticulous work with Celtic, Scandinavian, Norman and Anglo-Saxon elements in English place-names, have provided valuable information not only about migrations but also about the settlements and feudal law which followed them.[1] Jean Adigard des Gautries has particularized the Viking settlement of Normandy by describing the extent and nature of Scandinavian names.[2] Dauzat, through a study of the names associated with bodies of water, has shown the relationship of Gaul to Roman,[3] and Ekwall has similarly revealed the important Celtic element in the conservative river-names of England.[4] Through place-names Bach sheds light on the early neighbors of continental Germania,[5] and various Italian scholars make them yield data for the substratum question.[6] The predominantly Brythonic character of Celtic place-names in England argues against the older theory that Goidelic Celts were prior in that region.[7]

---

[1] See the publications of the English Place-Name Society and Sir Frank Stenton, *Anglo-Saxon Britain*, 2nd edition (Oxford: Clarendon Press, 1947).

[2] *Les noms de personnes scandinaves en Normandie de 911 à 1066 (Nomina Germanica* 11, Lund, 1954).

[3] Albert Dauzat, *La toponymie française* (Paris, 1946), pp. 103–141.

[4] Eilert Ekwall, *English River Names* (Oxford, 1928).

[5] Adolf Bach, *Deutsche Namenkunde*, 3 Bände in 5 (Heidelberg: Carl Winter, 1952–1956), I. 2, 1–88; see Anton Scherer, "Der Stand der Indo-germanischen Sprachwissenschaft," *Trends in European and American Linguistics, 1930–1960* (Utrecht: Spectrum, 1961), pp. 228–229.

[6] Carlo Battisti, "Orientamenti generali della lingistica in Italia," *Trends,* p. 246.

[7] P. H. Reaney, *The Origin of English Place-Names* (London, 1961), p. 97.

Indeed, the plotting of place-names on maps for historical purposes is physically similar to the plotting of dialect features, including place-names like the *caster-chester* group, and it is not surprising to find that place-name study has close ties with the respectable field of linguistic geography. Such a map and its attendant discussion by Dauzat inform us that in Beauce place-names in *-ville* date back to the Merovingian epoch, those in *-villiers* to the later clearings, and those in *Ville-* (Villeprévost) to the areas which resisted clearing and thus were named after the eleventh century.[8] Reaney (pp. 44–48) has testified to the value of the derivatives of OE *hyll*: Yorkshire Hoyland, Kentish Helsted, North Riding Hilton, Staffordshire Hulton, in establishing Old and Middle English dialect regions. Place-names help to clear up the error of assuming that West Saxon æ and *ea* join to become Southwestern *a*, an error of Marjorie Daunt, Robert Stockwell and C. W. Barritt.[9] Providing as they do firm locations, place-names are of great value in supplementing the tentative localizations of charters and manuscripts, made doubtful by scribal admixture and complex provenance.[10] The river-name technique is equally useful for establishing the linguistic geography of Celtic Britain,[11] Gallo-Roman France,[12] and the Slavic-German east.[13]

Onomastics has likewise contributed to the study of literature both in its historical and its aesthetic dimensions. Ekwall's comments on an OE *Godleofu* have obvious significance for the name of Harry Bailly's shrewish wife in the *Canterbury Tales*.[14] Loomis makes place-names central to the discussion of Arthurian origins: Melrose and Mons Dolorosus; Edinburgh, Danebroc and "le Castiel as Puceles"; Glastonbury and the Isle of Glass (Isle de Voirre or Land of Goirre); Camelot and Avalon; Scaudone, Sinadon, Stirling and Snowdon.[15] Ekwall, unable to identify the last element of the magical name Tintagel, believes the first element to be a blend of the prosaic words *dun* "hill" and *tin*.[16] Documenting the aesthetic implications of names is not difficult; one need cite only the practices of John Milton, Stephen Vincent Benet, Archibald MacLeish and Marcel Proust—above all the last, who makes of place-names and their etymology a clue to the reconstruction of the past as evocative as the *madeleine* itself. When James Tait ascribes

---

[8] Dauzat, pp. 49–51.

[9] Sherman Kuhn and Randolph Quirk, *Language* 29 (1953), 150; they cite diphthongal *ya, ia, ye, ie* from these sources.

[10] Samuel Moore, Sanford B. Meech, and Harold Whitehall, "Middle English Dialect Characteristics and Dialect Boundaries," *University of Michigan Publications, Language and Literature* XIII (Ann Arbor, 1935), pp. 1–60. See the review by O. Arngart, *Studier i Modern Sprakvetenskap* 17 (1949), 17–29, which stresses the value of the use of place-names.

[11] Reaney, pp. 78–79, 88–89.

[12] Dauzat, pp. 103–141.

[13] Bach, 2.2, 15.

[14] Eilert Ekwall, *Early London Personal Names* (Lund, 1947), pp. 39–40; on Chaucer see John M. Manly, *Some New Light on Chaucer* (New York, 1926), pp. 80 to 81.

[15] Roger S. Loomis, *Arthurian Tradition & Chrétien de Troyes* (New York: Columbia University Press, 1949), pp. 110–117, 219, 480, 482, 490. See also J. S. P. Tatlock, *The Legendary History of Britain* (University of California Press, 1950); Reaney, *Origins*, pp. 69, 187 (Castle Hewin from Ywain?; Tarn Wadling from "the tarn of Gwyddelen, the little Irishman"), 79 (the god Lugus, whom Loomis equates with Lancelot).

[16] Eilert Ekwall, *The Concise Oxford Dictionary of English Place-Names*, 2nd edition (Oxford, 1940), p. 453.

English Belvoir, Beaulieu, Beaurepaire, Beaumont and the like to a kind of pastoral enthusiasm of sensitive Norman aristocrats he is perhaps not too far from a reasonable generalization;[17] perhaps these rough lords were themselves not too far in spirit from a group of twenty or so schoolgirls who accompanied a friend of mine on his first trip down the Grand Canal in Venice, and who made the vaporetto resound at every turn and every view with "Che beya, che beya!" The magic of the city has been lost on him ever since. But linguists, somewhat wary of ethnocentric views of "beauty in language," will think Tait somewhat impressionistic when he applies the name "ugly" to the reduction of Stoke Courcy and Stoke Gomer to Stogursey and Stogumber.[18] Perhaps he is reflecting Shaw's characterization of the John Bullish chaplain de Stogumber in *St. Joan,* which appeared in the same year as the first volume of the English Place-Name Society's *Introduction.* William A. Read shows more linguistic sophistication when he comments that Tickfaw, harsh as it may sound, is the designation of a beautiful little river which flows through the piny region of Louisiana; the name, in the Choctaw tongue *tiakfoha,* probably signifies "pine rest," or more freely, "rest among the pines."[19] According to George Stewart the basic meaning of Minnesota, "muddy river," was transformed by the local pride of romantically inclined native sons to "cloudy river," "sky-blue river" and then to "sky-blue water,"[20] a phrase which agonized sopranoes in the first quarter of this century. As always the strict linguist is likely to be something of a spoilsport.

* * *

Folk-etymology is a branch of folklore and a legitimate subject for study, though its use in onomastics proper should be largely iconoclastic. It is probably *arrière-pensée* which led some Indians to explain Manhattan as "where we all got drunk"; the hundred or so Lover's Leaps are well-known varieties of local legends spontaneously generated; Ticklenaked, 'Scape-Whore and Longacoming represent innocent Indian names now misunderstood.[21] Newport News really reflects the name of the Brothers Newce.[22] Barking is naturally brought into association with the Isle of Dogs, Barnwell is interpreted by the semi-learned as "children's springs," and a Cornish Marchas dyow leads to Market Jew.[23] Even more perilous are the ways of bilingualism, which must convert unfamiliar clusters to something both phonemically and semantically more familiar: Chemin Couvert to Smackover, L'Eau Froide to Low Freight, Purgatoire to Picketwire, Ypres to Wipers, and Route de Roi to Rotten Row. Only the phonemic conversion is obvious in *Ni Bthaska*

---

[17] A. Mawer and F. M. Stenton, edd., *Introduction to the Survey of English Place-Names,* Part I (Cambridge, 1924), pp. 115–116; confirmed by Reaney, p. 193.

[18] Reaney, p. 120.

[19] *Florida Place-Names of Indian Origin and Seminole Personal Names* (Louisiana State University Press, 1934), p. 78.

[20] *Names on the Land* (New York, 1945), pp. 278–279.

[21] Stewart, pp. 69, 109, 129. The Maine Lover's Leap is clearly of white manufacture; see Fannie H. Eckstorm, *Indian Place-Names of the Penobscot Valley and the Maine Coast* (Orono, Maine, 1941), p. 16. For treatments of folk etymology see Eckstorm, pp. xvi–xvii; Robert L. Ramsay, A. W. Read and E. G. Leach, *Introduction to a Survey of Missouri Place-Names* (University of Missouri studies 9, 1, 1934), pp. 17–18, 24–25, 35; Reaney, pp. 14–16, 26; Bach 1.1, 38–39.

[22] Stewart, p. 58.

[23] Reaney, pp. 1–2, 15.

ke, which is said to mean to the Omaha Indian "water flowing through a plain," a proper enough name for the region which contains the Platte River.[24] This explanation seems prosaic enough to take seriously. One may explain the present form of Nebraska simply as a reduction in English of the unlikely cluster [bθ] to the more common [br], though one could counter with some such nonce construct as *Rob Thackeray* if one wished to be skeptical. It may well be that the resonant [r] in Omaha has some affinity with a slightly retracted and more fortis fricative [θ], and that the sound could therefore be heard by an English speaker in two ways, much like Japanese [R], which we hear both as [r] and as [l]. No demonstration of folk etymology can ever improve on the strange career of York: from a Celtic Eburos "yew tree" as base for Eburacon, to an Old English Eoforwic "wild-boar place," to a Danish Yorvik "bay, inlet," and thence to the modern forms, with the New World New York, an heritage from James II, once Duke of York.[25]

Etymology has not surprisingly been called an inexact science, when York can go through such transformations and when Churchill, a common enough name, can be referred either to a British *crūc* "hill" or an OE *cirice* "church."[26] One simple axiom might be that in place-name etymology we should not only suspect all names of being homonyms in their various occurrences, but that we should suspect any proper noun of *not* being a homonym of the common noun it looks like, as will Orchard < OE Archat < Welsh argoed "shelter of wood,"[27] as opposed to orchard < OE ortegeard < hortus + ʒeard (*NED*). Mere "metathesis" or phonemic alternation to fit the normal English phonemic pattern is all that is needed to explain the change of L Rutupia to OE Repta, since the [tp] cluster is unlikely in English.[28]

The inconsistency, of course, is in the phenomena and not in the scientist; to demonstrate the alternate possibilities and to fix some of them in certain cases on the basis of a lengthy list of attested variant citations is what the etymological scientist is called upon to do. His "laws" may follow from that; and prediction is not impossible within probability limits. Only a list of well-documented variant spellings can give us the assurance we have in deriving Jay Wick in Essex from an original Claccinga-wic "the dairy-farm of the people of Clacc," via forms like Clacken-gewick and Clacton Jaewyke, with clipping of the first element and continued confusion of the morphemes or combining-forms.[29]

It is easy to see why the linguist does not find place-names paradigmatic, and refers them hastily to that harmless drudge the lexicographer. The assurances of the linguist that *his* methods are foolproof, when followed with rigor and theoretical consistency, are slightly shaken in this field, where certain linguistic purists have been often shown to be in need of a little external history. Hamsey (Sussex), for instance, was explained by a linguist as OE *hammes ēa* "stream bordering the enclosures" or *hammes ēg* "island or marshy land in the bed of a river," a thoroughly reasonable use of predictable etymological morphemic probabilities. Seven years later another linguist, who was also a historian,

---

[24] J. T. Link, *The Origin of the Place-Names of Nebraska* (Nebraska Geological Survey, University of Nebraska Bulletin 7, Second Series, 1933), p. 38.

[25] Stewart, pp. 78–81; Reaney, p. 24; Ekwall, *Concise Oxford Dictionary of English Place-Names*, pp. 519–520.

[26] Mawer and Stenton, *Introduction*, I, 28.

[27] Reaney, pp. 125–126.

[28] Mawer and Stenton, I, 17.

[29] Reaney, p. 114.

showed that the 1321 Hammes Say was a proper enough division, reflecting the Norman owner, Geoffrey de Say. To the linguistic purist Linshields (Northumberland) could mean either "lime-tree shiels (hut or shed)" or "shield by the lynn or pool"; to the geographer who has been there and seen the lynn and felt the climate, which could not possibly foster a lime tree, there is only one alternative.[30] Child as a surname is pretty surely OE *cild* "a child," but the psychological reasons for such namegiving are none too clear.[31] Something more than linguistics was needed to reveal that many medieval London apprentices gave up their own surnames in favor of their master's name,[32] a status-seeking gesture akin to the immigrant's change of name in America and the Negro slave's adoption of the White surname he knew best.[33] The study of linguistics, in search for its own scientific status, could stand a little humility and interdisciplinary courtesy; it may stumble badly as it shrugs off non-linguistic evidence and raises its eyebrows.

II

Such contrition in the presence of ancillary disciplines is highly desirable as we proceed to assert that American onomastics needs much more linguistic rigor than it has yet acquired. Only the most invidious linguist will cavil, except in details, at the onomastic work of H. L. Mencken and George Stewart, both of whom have brought lively style and wit to their popular books on the subject. Stewart, indeed, has shown us recently a model of depth study in his argument that OE *leah*, which has been generally held to mean "a woods" as well as "a clearing in a woods," can only mean the woods after it has been cleared.[34] But Mencken always disclaimed knowledge of such linguistic fundamentals as phonology, and Stewart's *Names on the Land* is primarily an account of how the land was named, instead of how names fit into a grammar or how they evolve linguistically. For better or worse these excellent stylists are our models; and hence there is in this country a tendency to make name study a matter largely of entertainment (Mencken's Positive Wasserman Johnson)[35] or of regional pride, as when Stewart confronts the British carpers at American violations of onomastic good taste with a sarcastic list from England including Maidenhead, Great Snoring, Shitlington, and Ashby de la

---

[30] Reaney, pp. 18–19.

[31] Ekwall, *Early London Personal Names*, pp. 144–145; P. H. Reaney, *A Dictionary of British Surnames* (London, 1958), p. 67.

[32] Eilert Ekwall, *Variation in Surnames in Medieval London* (Lund, 1945).

[33] H. L. Mencken, *The American Language: Supplement II* (New York, 1948), p. 420, 447.

[34] "*Leah, Woods* and Deforestation as an Influence on Place-Names," *Names* 10 (1962), 11–20. In 1962 Kelsie Harder and Meredith Burrill had an interesting discussion of rigor within onomastics itself; Professor Harder has kindly let me see the notes. The concern was not with linguistic and theoretical rigor so much as with accurate reporting, which has its own special rules. It is interesting to note that the Board of Geographic Names with Burrill, and the Stockholm Commission for the Naming of Streets with Gösta Langenfelt, have done yeoman service in converting onomastics from casual impressionism to a serious methodology; in this case the applied science has preceded the theoretical. [At the second Annual Names Institute, May 11, 1963, Professors J. B. Rudnyćkyj, Alfred Senn, and C. L. Wrenn held a panel discussion on "Onomastic Rigor."]

[35] Stewart, p. 15; H. L. Mencken, *The American Language*, 4th edition (New York, 1938), p. 525.

Zouche.[36] Of the fifty states only about twenty have book-length studies corresponding to the thorough examination which the English Place-Name Society is systematically giving to the British counties, or to Adolf's theoretical and exhaustive German grammar of place-names, or to Dauzat's ingenuity and skilful use of maps for France. There is little consistency of plan among them, and the laudable work of Edward C. Ehrensperger, Hamill Kenny, William A. and Allen W. Read, J. T. Link, Fannie Eckstorm and a few others is belied by the casual work of the majority.[37]

Perhaps it is not surprising that American onomastics has had, in Prince Hal's words, but a pennyworth of linguistic bread to balance an intolerable deal of non-linguistic sack. Most of a state dictionary's entries consist of an endless account of secondary borrowing of names of place and person from England or elsewhere in Europe. We might, except for regional pride, better exclude all secondary borrowings from abroad except where, as with Worcester, Massachusetts and Wooster, Ohio, a significant linguistic change is involved. Perhaps we are justified in awaiting the last volume on the British Isles before proceeding to a planned national project for the whole United States—a much to be desired goal. But we should then remember to our shame that in systematic dialect studies our Linguistic Atlas was the pioneer, and the English and Scots projects the followers. The British have, indeed, heeded our stimulus in dialect studies before our project was anywhere near completed. There would be no harm, then, in planning a stateside project now, before the missiles destroy both the Treasury and ourselves.

There can be no question that serious linguists have been discouraged by the non-linguistic components of onomastics. As Malkiel says:

> The main idiosyncrasy of etymology stems from the fact that, unlike most cognate disciplines, it operates consistently with fragmentary evidence, with dotted evolutionary lines. Every etymologist protests that he would prefer to rely, in his reconstructions, on a vastly increased stock of recorded forms; few would be candid enough to admit that truly complete records would deprive the etymologist's endeavors of their real charm, even of their *raison d'être*. The sparseness or even unavailability of critically needed material has fascinated some workers (moulding, in the process, their personalities) and has, with equal power, repelled others.[38]

Where attested documentary materials exist throughout the century for place and personal names, the puzzle element is not so great as it is with the residues of the etymologist of common words, yet it is always there. In America William A. Read and Robert L. Ramsay have been model workers in their careful segregation from the total corpus of dubious problems and puzzles;[39] thus they have been both a caution and a spur to other students.

Their work and that of their colleagues make it clear that the greatest challenge to

---

[36] Stewart, p. 35; compare his own warning, pp. 278–279. The rhapsodic element appears on pp. 3–4, a natural place for it in a trade-book. Such a tone is notably absent from Reaney's popular *Origin of English Place-Names*. Reaney, on the other hand, could do with some of Stewart's style.

[37] See the reviews of Fitzpatrick's *Nebraska* (T. M. Pearce), Barnes and Granger's *Arizona*, and Gudde's *California* (William Bright) in *Journal of American Folklore* 75 (1962), 76–82; for linguistic matters the Bright reviews are especially pointed.

[38] *Word* 18 (1962), 200–201.

[39] Read, *Florida Place-Names*, pp. 43–55; Ramsey, pp. 26–38.

American onomasticians lies in the sphere of Indian names. These present many methodological difficulties: the lack of good printed grammars and dictionaries of the many Indian languages, the obsolete nature of many of the manuscript materials found in the Smithsonian Institution and elsewhere, the time-depth problem, since many of the names may go back to a period three hundred years or more before lexical and grammatical material was collected, and so forth. Long ago Lewis Morgan showed us how chaotic was the spelling of Iroquois names in various MSS.[40] We are not even sure what language to call upon, since nomads cannot be tied to place.[41] Yet it is possible to do systematic work. Fannie Eckstorm, taking advantage of the early collections for the Eastern Woodlands area, has canvassed part of Maine for us.[42] Most of the Southeast has been covered by William A. Read with similarly well-disciplined studies.[43] Hamill Kenny has turned his talents to Maryland.[44] George Stewart has noted that Indian names are not merely good or poor phonetic records of Indian sounds, but that we must also reckon with folk etymology and loan translations;[45] he reminds us that J. Hammond Trumbull did pioneer work along these lines in 1870.[46] What we probably need more than anything else is a basic dictionary of combining-forms from a wide assortment of Indian place-names, to parallel the work of Mawer and of Smith in England, and the work on non-Indian topographical names by McMullen and McJimsey in the United States.[47] River-name techniques, so useful in Europe, pay dividends in American Indian names as well. In Eckstorm's Maine a whole group of localities stem from a form *Mata-* with a basic meaning "at the end of," but specifically meaning "at a river mouth."[48] In Florida and Alabama, as W. A. Read has shown, a Creek *wi-* and a Seminole *wiwa*, both meaning

---

[40] *League of the Ho-De-No Sau-Nee or Iroquois* (New Haven: Human Relations Area Files, 1954), 1.47 (first edition 1901).

[41] Read, *Florida Place-Names*, pp. 56–66. Both Indians and whites were borrowers; Catawba was borrowed from South Carolina by Indians; Kalamazoo and Manhattan were borrowed by whites from Indians. As Stewart, pp. 8–10, remarks, whites were more accustomed to definite names than Indians, and hence they may have been the stimulus to much late Indian naming. Whites also misunderstood many ephemeral Indian names as permanent; see Nils M. Holmes, *Indian Place Names in North America* (Uppsala, 1948).

[42] *Indian Place-Names* as cited in note 21.

[43] *Florida Place-Names* as cited note 20; see also his *Louisiana Place-Names of Indian Origin* (University Bulletin 19, Louisiana State University, 1894); *Indian Place-Names in Alabama* (Louisiana State University Press, 1937).

[44] *The Origin and Meaning of the Indian Place-Names of Maryland* (Baltimore, 1961). Another study, not as systematic as one would like, but addressing itself to the proper task, is William M. Beachamp, *Aboriginal Place-Names of New York* (Bulletin 108, Archaeology 12, New York State Museum, Albany, 1907).

[45] Stewart, pp. 108–110.

[46] Stewart, p. 333.

[47] E. Wallace McMullen, Jr., *English Topographical Names in Florida, 1563–1874* (Gainesville, Fla., 1953); George D. McJimsey, *Topographic Terms in Virginia* (Columbia University Press, 1940). Ehrensperger's classificatory system in *South Dakota Place-Names* provides similar evidence. See also Ramsay, pp. 22–23; 116 to 120; Link, p. 19; George P. Krapp, *The English Language in America*, 2 vols. (New York, 1925), 1.19–89, 134–135, 161. Krapp's formal discussion of "Proper Names," 1.169–224 should be more often consulted by students than it apparently is.

[48] Eckstrom, pp. 58–63.

"water," create a whole set of reflexes, such as Wetumpka "sounding water," Whitewater Bay (a calque), Willochochee "little big river," Weekiwachee "little spring," Wauchula "stale water," and Weelawnee "yellow water."[49] In Alabama *Oak-* or its equivalent creates a multiple series of creeks.[50]

But American place-names are not all a matter of puzzles. George Stewart's book, with its salutary emphasis on process, provides us with a decade of characteristics of American naming, as valid for science as those characteristics of Germanic, Old High German, and Old English which we have learned in our graduate seminars. His list, compiled from the whole book, includes:

(1) map consciousness in naming (Long Island, which would never appear long to the naked eye; "branch" for many streams in the Eastern United States; and perhaps Oregon from a misreading of "Ouisconsin" on a map[51]

(2) extensive use of borrowed names[52]

(3) many new combining forms: creek (in a new meaning), swamp, pond

(4) many successive names for the same topographical feature (the Hudson River was successively called Mauritius, North, Manhattans, River of the Mountains, Groote)[53]

(5) many strata (Dutch, Spanish, French, English, all borrowing from the Indian aborigines and from each other)

(6) systematic naming (as on the Lewis and Clark Expedition)

(7) emphasis on meaningful names (the transparency of Wolf Meadow as against British Woolley)[54]

(8) new geographical features used as combining forms (prairie, arroyo, canyon)

(9) names linked with men and events (the many Lincolns, Columbuses, etc.)

(10) variety and lack of conservatism (Hell's Gulch, Oshkosh, Beaumont).

Of these only the third, the fifth and the eighth allow much scope for truly linguistic activity. Hence it is not merely the nature of the American scholar, but also the nature of the naming-process and our closeness to it in time, which has kept us from more rigorous use of linguistics in onomastics.

But the American linguist is not confined to the place-names of his own country, which are somewhat defeating to his axiom that all linguistic processes are unconscious. Should he deny diachronic approaches completely, including etymology and the rigorous methods inaugurated by British scholars, he would cut down the scope of onomastics severely. I hardly think that we need to limit the field; it is becoming apparent that the refusal to apply categorical and theoretical techniques to the older forms of a language

---

[49] *Florida Place-Names*, pp. 38–41, 54–55, 69; *Indian Place-Names in Alabama*, pp. 76–77.

[50] *Indian Place-Names in Alabama*, pp. 46–49.

[51] Stewart, pp. 153–155. I cite this specific reference because the Oregon etymology still shocks many hearers, and is therefore by no means proven.

[52] A few American names went to England, such as Quebec, New York, New England, Virginia, California; see Reaney, p. 220.

[53] Stewart, p. 69.

[54] Stewart, p. 115. Perhaps this is why an American linguist finds a theory like that of Gardiner so difficult to accept. It would rule out the bulk of American place-names. Contrast Reaney, pp. 17, 50, 116–123.

is not consistently the heuristic device that some enthusiasts have claimed, and that the lack of progress in these fields may be due to negligence on the part of modern linguists as well as that of old-line philologists. Happily there are evidences, in Martinet, Lehmann, and a host of others, to indicate that historical linguistics (and its relative onomastics) are about to have the attention they deserve.

III

We have said enough about the diachronic, and it may be useful now to approach onomastics with some of our favored modern and synchronic procedures. The narrowest form of linguistic component, which would include phonemic, graphemic, morphemic and syntactic approaches, is largely undeveloped. Andre de Vincenz, in a paper offered to this Congress but not delivered, argues that the contrastive techniques of modern structuralism can be used to isolate morphemic, syntactic and semantic features in proper names as opposed to common nouns.[55] He finds little phonological contrast.

On the whole I agree about phonology, so long as we confine ourselves to purely synchronic techniques. But etymologies in general and place-names in particular, we have seen, provide a most exceptional area for the discussion of the "exceptions" in the fine print of historical grammars,[56] and a whole new grammar of sound-change can develop from the close study of names and their startling variants. In this discussion it is hard to divorce graphemics from phonemics, since one of the characteristics of place-names is that they are often pronounced in a way wholly unpredictable from the spelling. True, this is characteristic of English words in general (compare the *ghoti* = *fish* gambit), but Worcester (English [wustər] Massachusetts [wərsestər] or [wəsestə] with its Ohio derivative Wooster [wuwstər]),[57] Cholmondeley, Ruthwell Cross (said now to be often pronounced in accordance with the spelling, instead of the traditional [rivəl]), Los Angeles, Gallipolis, Wilkes Barre, Chicago, Sevenoaks, and Beauchamps all suggest the need of a special graphemics for proper names. Misreadings of old letters, like *t* for *c* as in OE *þēot-denu* > *þetdene* read as *þecdene*, or OE *w* as *p* (Thunoreslowe–Thunoreslope) are factors in name development.[58] Hence the vigorously supported axiom that American researchers working in the field use the utmost care in recording the authoritative local pronunciation, even when it seems an obvious inference from the letters.[59] In another aspect of graphemics, it is apparent that capitals are not an absolute indication of a proper name[60] (French *jeudi* and *janvier*, English *the sun*, German *das Wasser, die Schweiz*, English *Big Man on Campus*). Yet one should not be so awed by absolutes that one

---

[55] *Preprints of Papers for the Ninth International Congress of Linguists* (Cambridge, Mass., 1962), p. 21.

[56] Malkiel, *Word* 18 (1962), 211–212.

[57] Krapp, *English Language in America*, 1.59.

[58] Reaney, pp. 22, 120.

[59] Ramsay, pp. 16, 23. One recalls the story of the group of betters in a bar who were debating about the pronunciations for Hawaii [həwa+i] and [həva+i]. They agreed to accept the first newcomer as authority, and did so, but their assurance was somewhat dampened when one of them said "Thank you" and he answered [yuwr + velkəm].

[60] Gardiner, *The Theory of Proper Names: A Controversial Essay*, 2nd edition (London: Oxford University Press, 1957), p. 53.

ignores the value of capitals; the process of *a flat rock*'s becoming *Flat Rock* (Michigan) is of significance despite all the cautions about capitalization one must utter.

Special phonologies have been written for proper names,[61] and there would be value in compiling some of these, comparing them with the other patterns of the language, and seeking some system for them. Folk etymologies of the Smackover-Chemin Couvert variety would play a large part in such a compilation. One potential line of investigation is the possible importance of suprasegmentals. The proper name often stands alone as train-call, citation form, or response sentence; more so, one assumes, than other words. Possibly the 3–1 pitch pattern, with its attendant stresses and terminals, creates certain special features in proper names. When he remarked on the special distinctiveness of the sound of proper names, Gardiner may have been more cautious than he needed when he said, "It is of course not meant that proper names are pronounced more loudly or emphatically than other words."[62] True enough in ordinary contexts, perhaps. But the special distortions of the train call, and the patterns which surround the child's name as pronounced by the irate, seeking mother, do provide special contexts. And even in ordinary contexts the 3–1 pattern may have created a contour which dominates the proper name. *Spain* is basically a monosyllable, but its pronunciation as citation form surely suggests a disyllable to conform to the falling pitch. Robert Lees has noticed an interesting and unexplained contrast between Mádison Strèet and Màdison Ávenue. But neither Hill in his review, nor Lees's,[63] note that it can be Màdĭsŏn Strĕĕt as well, an important contrast to distinguish the Street from the better-known Avenue. The inimitable local pronunciation of New Orleans may be a similar result of conformation to pitch pattern. The shortening of *La Villa Real de la Santa Fé de San Francisco* to *Santa Fe* and of *El Pueblo de la Reína de los Angeles de la Porciúncula* to *Los Angeles* would be predictable either according to the obsolescent ease theory or to what we know of American lack of pride in leisure, but the contour of the remnants left after the clipping may owe as much to suprasegmental pattern as to religious piety. The frequently cited contrast between ³*Whíte Hoùse*¹ and ²*whîte*³'*house*¹ may be further evidence of such contextual contour. With all these names we appear to be safely in a synchronic closed system, though if we were to transgress into diachrony we might well call upon another contributory factor, the Germanic fixing of the accent on the first syllable.[64] To avoid infinite regression of causes, we should end our brief phonological discussion here.

We have said enough about combining-forms and phonemic clusters to indicate the importance of morphemics in historical onomastics. But if *partisan, citizen,* and *denizen*[65]

---

[61] Hamill Kenny, *West Virginia Place Names* (Piedmont, West Virginia, 1945), pp. 48–56; Bach, 1.1, 38–43; Ekwall, *Early London Personal Names,* pp. 179–198; Reaney, pp. 198–202.

[62] *Theory of Proper Names,* p. 40.

[63] *The Grammar of English Nominalizations* (Indiana University, 1960), p. 120; reviewed by Archibald Hill in *Language* 38 (1962), 440.

[64] For Germanic fronting of accent in borrowed words see Bach, 1.1, 31–32.

[65] The question is the meaning of the morpheme (—zən) which has a clear formative meaning in the first two words but not in the third. Harold Whitehall, as a synchronic linguist who recognizes his etymological responsibilities, once told this anecdote to a group of English students in the relatively new *Denney* Hall at Ohio State University. A clear voice from the audience explained that in this locality there was no problem about the third word's two morphemes, or about the general meaning of the suffix.

present a problem to the synchronic morphemicist, surely the -*ing* names present an even greater one. It is a long time since such names were thought to be confined to a tribal or a family cognomen, and very likely few structural linguists have bothered much with the type. Again I would make the charge that this is lack of courage; a grammar which does not include proper names is no grammar at all. The assertion that proper names are rare and therefore not paradigmatic is specious; we live among them every day and use them incessantly. Yet I know of no synchronic technique which could make the brilliant series of analyses which culminates in Smith's long entry, which distinguishes four varieties of -*ing* (1234) along with three extended forms: (1) a common noun-forming suffix (Fleming); (2) a singular place-name and river-name forming suffix (Deeping); a true patronymic (Æthelwulfing); (4) a connective particle (Wolverley, which hides an original -*ing*); (5) an -*ingaham* for group-names (Aldringham); (6) an -*ingas* for folk and group-names (Hastings); and an -*ingtun* = -ing^4 + tun (Teddington).[66] Smith's elaborate dissection of the -*by* derivatives[67] is a similar challenge which modern morphemicists would probably prefer not to take up, unless they fell back on a broad and unsatisfying rubric like "bound form used as a suffix in a place-name." A similar systematization of high value which can be attained by no synchronic technique is Bach's masterly account of the clipped forms of personal names.[68] The merged forms behind modern bound forms, originally free forms, like -*grave, -grove, -greave; head* and *Howden,*[69] continue the morphemic paradox. An unusual affix, which the paradigmatic linguist is apt to disregard, is the pot of gold for the fortune-seeking etymologist.[70]

One does not find in English the easy contrast between appellative and family name which de Vincenz finds in Russian;[71] functional shift is here as usual obscured in English words. But perhaps we could contrast William and Williams, John and Jones; baker and Baxter; oak, Sevenoaks, and Snooks. The trouble would be that the loss of meaning, usually posited of proper names, destroys a simple differential contrast which might be called common noun vs. proper name. The blurring between the combining form and the bound form, the common noun and its derivative proper noun, is excellently shown in Rune Forsberg's study of Old English place-names.[72] Hockett remarks that Big Chief Rain-in-the-Face, though no doubt invented, reflects the Indian composition of personal names from other syntactic groups than mere nominalizations; [awa·nohape·w], for instance, means "he sits in fog."[73] The modern problem of the submorphemic categories of which Dwight Bolinger and Morton Bloomfield have apprised us[74] is curiously paralleled by Danish and Old English alliterating dynastic names: Healfdene, Heorogar, Heoroweard,

---

[66] A. H. Smith, *English Place-Name Elements,* 2 vols. (English Place-Name Society 26, Cambridge University Press, 1956), 1.282–303; see also Bach, 2.2, 458–464; Reaney, pp. 99–116.

[67] Smith, 1.66–72; Reaney, pp. 171–172.

[68] 1.1, 97–138.

[69] Smith, 1.207, 236; for further "convergers" and "divergers" see Reaney, p. 42.

[70] Malkiel, *Word* 18 (1962), 214–215.

[71] *Preprints,* p. 21.

[72] *A Contribution to a Dictionary of Old English Place-Names* (Nomina Germanica 9, Uppsala, 1950).

[73] Charles F. Hockett, *A Course in Modern Linguistics* (New York, 1958), p. 311.

[74] Bolinger, "Rime, Assonance and Morpheme Analysis," *Word* 6 (1950), 117–136; Bloomfield, "Final Root-Forming Morphemes," *American Speech* 27 (1953), 158–164.

Hroðgar, Hreðic, Hroðmund, and Hroðulf.[75] In later Old English times there is a more factitious use of full combining-forms like Wulf- and Æðel-.[76] Morphemics and morphophonemics are the stepsisters of the structural hierarchy;[77] they provide scarcely so many triumphs as phonemics and, of late, syntactics. There is still, despite these cautions, ample value in the contrastive techniques of modern morphemics. But we must ask ourselves whether any synchronic method besides morphemics, applied rigorously, would lead to such an analysis of Oxshott as "where the ox was shot," which Reaney (p. vii) cites as a special horror. The true analysis, "Ocga's scēat, the projecting piece or corner of land belonging to Ocga," demands all the resources of historian, geographer, and linguist-philologist.[78]

IV

Finally, there is syntax. On the simple etymological level this merges with morphology, since combining-forms, lost to sight in modern zero variations because of inflectional reduction and the rise of word order as signal, must be reconstructed by a look at their old full combinations. Hence the careful student of word-composition must concern himself with lost inflections. We have fossilized reflexes from OE dative plurals like *Inhrypun > Ripon, wudu-hūsum > Woodsome;* genitive plurals like *bulena hyrst > Bolneherst > Bolnburst, calfra-tūn > Calverton;* adjectival inflections like dative singular *nīwan-hām > Newnham.*[79] Larger syntactical patterns are sometimes preserved, as in Thurleigh from *æt þære lēaʒe* "at the glade or wood," Nash from *æt þæm æscum* "at the ash tree," Ray, Rea, Rhee and Rye from *æt þær ēa* "at the river" or *æt þær ēg* "at the water." Other prepositional formations with the noun, leading to a proper name, are Bythorn (*bī-, bē*), Teyning (*betwēonan*), Underhill and the like.[80] Personal names as well as place-names preserve ancient syntax, as with Roger Agodeshalf 1222 "in God's name, for God's sake."[81] Thus English, like Hockett's Menominee, allows syntactical structures not originally nominal in nature to become proper nouns. The genitives need not, any more than in Modern English, all be inanimate; compare Maplesden "maple tree's woodland pasture."[82] Celtic, Latin and French word order survives in such words as Bryn Mawr (wood big), Stokes Regis, and Marylebone, the last pronounced [márləbòwñ] with a typical accent and pitch contour. German personal names show an alternation between appositions (adjunctive) and genitival compounding: Gottfried Eberhard and Gottfried Alt, Gottfried Eberhards Sohn, Gottfried des Schneiders Sohn. Bach is able to write a fairly complete grammar of such compounding.[83]

Sooner or later when grammarians discuss the syntax of proper names they generally

---

[75] Fr. Klaeber, ed., *Beowulf and the Fight at Finnsburg,* 3rd edition (New York, 1941), pp. xxx–xlv.

[76] Reaney, pp. 50–51.

[77] See, for instance, Henning Spang-Hannssen, "Glossematics," in *Trends,* p. 145.

[78] Ekwall, *Concise Oxford Dictionary of English Place-Names,* p. 339; Smith, *English Place-Name Elements,* 2.102–103.

[79] Reaney, pp. 38–40.

[80] Reaney, pp. 30–32, 37–38; Smith, pp. 13–14.

[81] Ekwall, *Early London Personal Names,* pp. 135, 198.

[82] Reaney, p. 53.

[83] Bach, 1.1, 61–66.

agree that proper names differ in some fashion from common nouns in their use of the articles *a* and *the* and in their use with adjectives and as adjectives. Jespersen gives us the fullest grammar, and it may be noted that he makes a fairly sharp division between personal and place-names, a division which lends some support to my argument that *proper name* is a much harder thing to define than *personal name* and *place-name*. Inductive lists like Jespersen's are convincing enough, taken in themselves; the real trouble arises when we attempt to identify proper names in discourse. Jespersen says that personal names like John, applied to one definite person, generally take the zero article, whereas place-names sometimes take the definite article and sometimes not. River-names are originally without the article, but probably through ellipsis of "River" forms like The Thames are common enough. (Gardiner denies the ellipsis.)[84] Oceans and seas generally have *the*; lakes have zero; countries, islands, mountains, towns, parks, streets, except where plural, have zero. For buildings the common form is zero plus determinative word and building-name, as in Westminster Abbey, New Scotland Yard; but contrast The Tower, The Empire State Building.[85]

This is enough to show that our grammar of proper names is likely to prove complex. German is generally said to possess the article in names of nations, as in *die Schweiz*, but *Russland* is a common enough type.[86] *Le Havre* remains transitional in French; Dauzat illustrates it, without premeditation, when he cites in another connection "Le Havre *de Grâce* (ancien nom du Havre)."[87] *Je vais au Havre* is the regular idiom, not **Je vais à Le Havre*. Personal names are slightly different. My colleague Mme. Monicque Léon tells me that a name like Le Corbusier is fairly constant, as in *Je parle à le Corbusier*, but that in Besançon (the Auvergne) *Je parle au Corbusier* is a frequent variant. If one looks at the names beginning with *La* and *Le* in Dauzat's dictionary one will find almost the whole section a mass of cross-references to the simplex, a sure sign of the impermanency of the article.[88] It is clear that no simple contrast is available for zero article and *La/Le* in French personal or place-names.

A. H. Smith, who is usually almost the final authority in such matters, has an entry under *þe* which is anything but lucid: "Its use implies that the name was still significant and probably often an appellative rather than a formal p.n." He then cites *Even Swindon* from a ME *Theveneswyndon* "the level swine hill," *Thurleigh* from OE *æt þære leaʒe*, and some wrong divisions, like *Ede Way* from *þeod weg* and *Ramacre* from *þréom aecere*, "at the three acres."[89] Here we have the placid assumption that a name becomes a proper name only when it loses its descriptive significance (Mont Blanc is no proper name, but Popocatepetl is one). That Smith does feel a faint hesitation is evidenced by his less than precise qualifications: "probably often an appellative." The false divisions enforce the idea of lost signification, but what about the fossilized preservation of *the* in Thurleigh? Does this not "signify" long life for the determiner, much as in plurals like The Dalles and The United States and in a singular like The Empire State Building?

The indefinite determiner likewise plays a part in such development. We recall that

---

[84] *Theory of Proper Names*, p. 21.
[85] Otto Jespersen, *A Modern English Grammar*, 7 vols. (Copenhagen, 1909–1949), 7.544–579.
[86] Bach, 2.2, 67, 115–120.
[87] Dauzat, p. 12.
[88] *Dictionnaire étymologique des noms de famille et prénoms de France* (Paris, 1951).
[89] Smith, 2.202, 213.

a proper noun may evolve into a common noun, and in more subtle ways, we should remark, than in MacAdam, Quisling, and Watt. George Stewart has sought to explain the British-American divergence of "a woods" and "a wood," the second to prescriptionists a somewhat illogical expression. In cleared England "a wood" would be a commonly encountered small grove. American settlers, however, were originally confronted with "the Woods," an extensive forest, to all appearance continent-wide. Then, as clearings emerged and "the woods" became small tracts of forest once more, "a woods" became the unspecific form.[90] This demonstration is certainly a victory for the combination of synchronic and diachronic linguistic techniques, unless its semantic underpinning rules it out of court.

Pulgram rightly considers the article no final indicator of proper or common noun; in support of his relative scale from the extensive meaning of common noun and intensive meaning of proper noun he cites the king of England vs. "The King!"[91] Here one falls back on capitals, which if they have linguistic meaning at all, must involve some kind of suprasegmental increment. There is a similar contrast between titles like "the president of Kappa Sigma," "the president of Harvard University," and "the President of the United States." I cite the last with a capital, which I believe is fairly common, but it is not absolutely necessary, and might depend on rhetorical emphasis as well as convention. In the 1930's there was at Harvard considerable dispute on the subject. Hitherto "the President" without specification always meant the president of the university. For the first time then, with Franklin Delano Roosevelt, enthusiastic converts were using it to mean the President of the United States. Thus we had a serious clash of semantic ambiguities, unrelieved by grammatical sign.

A mental set leading to such a clash is especially well illustrated in England. Call it provincialism or local pride as you will, the phenomenon, though well outside the realm of linguistics, depends on linguistic signals. The Folklore Society in London means the British Folklore Society; we must say the American Folklore Society. Similarly with the Philological Society and the Linguistic Society of America. British titles, indeed, move slowly into the anonymous, or perhaps we should call it the allegorical. King Edward VIII becomes the Duke of Windsor. We have the Lord Chancellor, the Prime Minister, the Speaker, the Lord Mayor—much more commonly, I should think, than in even official circles in Washington, though no doubt imitative protocol does sometimes create the Secretary of the Treasury or the Chief Justice instead of Secretary Rusk and Chief Justice Warren. I well remember my own experience when an old friend lost his identity and was absorbed into the Commonwealth. It was when I received a Christmas card for the first time from "the Consul of Canada and Mrs. Newton."

At an American college or university today "the Dean" would mean very little; deans like professors are a dime a dozen. But in a summer cottage one may become the Dean or the Professor again. We once had a department chairman called the Boss; he is still called that today, though he has been successively a dean and a private citizen. Closely related as transition forms are such words as "the City" and "the Island." Any group of English speakers with a few exceptions would, when asked what the City is, be likely to answer the center of London or of Paris. But a son at Cornell University has

---

[90] *Names* 10 (1962), 18–20.

[91] Ernst Pulgram, *Theory of Names* (Berkeley, 1954), pp. 46–49; for the complexities of titles see Jespersen, *Modern English Grammar*, 7.562–69.

informed me that there it means one thing and one thing only—New York City. Perhaps this is merely a specificity created to contrast with the State of New York. But "the Island" has no such contrast-pattern; it is simply Long Island. Does it become that to avoid the dialect perils of [làhŋgáylən]? A regionalism of semantics, in short, to replace a regionalism of pronunciation? Probably any suburbanite, even in Kalamazoo, would speak of going to "the city"; whether he would capitalize it in emphasis or in writing is unpredictable.

We may agree, then, that the absence of articles in plurals of place and personal names, and their presence in singulars, is a general tendency in English, but we clearly cannot assert the contrast as an absolute. We must have, as in Jespersen, a number of subclasses, and allow for the special changes in Pulgram's intensity of meaning spectrum in various localities, where the attitude towards the name in question may vary. Some of these could perhaps be called dialectical, and cause no harm to the generalization about the *langue* as against the *parole*.

Another common generalization about proper names is that they, like pronouns, are unlikely to be preceded by adjectives. No doubt this is the source of Hockett's designation (p. 312) of proper names as similar to anaphoric substitutes, as well as the justification for the constituent structure rule in generative grammar which reads:

Name → Name
            prop
    Name
            pron

The rule assumes a logical similarity in proper name and pronoun signalled by grammatical similarity, which includes both absence of preposed adjectives and absence or presence of articles. Yet surely we commonly speak of "beautiful Ohio," "the Beautiful Ohio," "this free and independent United States," "a free and independent United States." "A beautiful *she*," on the other hand, sounds boldly Shakespearean, and might in most grammars be described as a pronoun which has shifted to noun function. Though it is probably substandard to say "I believe in United States," I have found the usage in many student papers. Hence the generative rule is at most a statistical statement of preponderance rather than an absolute, since the equivalence of proper name and pronoun is merely approximate.

Closely allied is the problem of the use of proper names as adjuncts or adjectives. Some would argue that we never say "a United States flag," since we have a corresponding adjective, "an American flag"; but the difference is probably one of rhetorical levels rather than of linguistics. Surely there is nothing wrong with "United States Government"; "American government" is ambiguous, in view of the other governments in this hemisphere. *China* and *Chinese* offer a set of derivative contrasts parallel to German *die Schweiz* and *schweizer(isch)*, but though we speak of Chinese communism, Chinese art, and Chinese girls, we always did speak of the China trade when there was one. Adjectives, by the way, are not proper nouns; then why do they take to capitalization? In English, that is; French and German in their respective ways keep a contrast. The difficulties are demonstrated by Hill's attempt to deal with "the fact that unmodified proper names also appear as group 1 modifiers, as in *the good old Smith hóuse*." We cannot, he says, transpose to "This good old house *is Smith" as we can to "This good old house is stone.'' Instead we must say "This good old house is Smith's.''[92] Hill has uncovered a genuine feature about the use of the adjunct, but he misses an obvious ambiguity in the transformed nominalization "the good old Smith house." It *may* go back to a kernel sentence "This good old house is Smith's," but it also may go back to other kernel sentences, the first of them the most likely of these three: "This good old house is the Smith family's," or "This good old house once belonged to a man named Smith." There is an apparent lack of specification in the adjectival-adjunct use which is like that in "the American government," though the latter is semantic, and the former syntactic.

Obviously our grammar of proper names needs much fuller exploration than is possible in this paper. I pose one final possibility, which may help sketch a few geographical features on the map of darkest Onomastica. Could we, seeking to find a formal signal to clarify the spectrum of intensive and extensive meaning identified by Pulgram, say that proper names are names which do not take restrictive WH-clauses in English? I offer this tentatively, since I do not recall its suggestion before. The experiment should prove useful. Contrast:

> Basingstoke, which is a large town, is dull to live in.
> The Basingstoke which is a large town is dull to live in.

Compare:

> The Rome which is in Italy is larger than the Rome which is in New York.

Perhaps we can extend this to personal names as well (we should recall that our grammar generally has to keep these two subclasses well apart).

> You are not the John Brown I know.
> You are not *the* John Brown, I know.
> You are not John Brown.
> You are not John Brown, who has grey hair.

I think we may have something here. One will admit to some difficulty with distinguishing between restrictive and non-restrictive modifiers themselves, with equating linguistic and graphemic signals. Yet surely there are formal distinctions which work fairly well. "The man who came to dinner" and "The John Brown I know" are alike in being a one-stress, one-pitch nexus, as opposed to "The man, who came to dinner," and "*The* John Brown, who has grey hair." And even elusive features like plus vs. single bar juncture or single vs. double bar juncture may correlate with the stress and pitch, and show up as commas in written English.

Perhaps there is a spectrum of relativity and free variation here, but if so it may correspond in some measure to the relativity of Pulgram's intensive vs. extensive meaning. The point is that, if more than one Rome or John Brown is involved, we are moving towards a class noun and away from a proper noun. The restrictive modifier is a signal of this larger class. Narrow the horizon, and there can be only one Rome or one John Brown; then no restrictive modifier is needed, though one may always give additional specifications about these more proper nouns, if one wishes. One will indeed be likely

---

[92] Archibald A. Hill, *Introduction to Linguistic Structures* (New York, 1958), p. 232.

to use a non-restrictive clause or a modifier following the noun, because in English it is generally less likely (though not impossible) that such a modifier will be preposed:

> Rome, which is in Italy, is magnificent.
> Rome, full of Americans, is magnificent.
> Rome, running with fountains, is magnificent.
> Rome, of all places, is magnificent.

But notice that these non-clausal modifiers could equally be "restrictive," that is, pronounced without the intonational features we associate with non-restriction. The single dominant stress would move, in sentences two, three and four, to *Americans, fountains* and *all.*

> Rome full of Americans is magnificent.
> Rome running with fountains is magnificent.
> Rome of all places is magnificent.

But not

> *Rome which is in Italy is magnificent.

We cannot develop all the possibilities here. But consider another set:

> I like a girl.
> *I like a sky (*The sky,* though uncapitalized, is unique, and hence like *the sun,* often called a proper name).
> *I like a United States
> I like a United States which is free and independent.
> I like a free and independent United States.
> I like a blue sky.
> I like a sky which is blue.
> I like the United States.
> I like Rome.
> *I like a Rome.

Such sets are enough to say that a special grammar of proper names is desirable and possible, though not exactly what that grammar is.

Of all those we have read we have found Pulgram most valuable for theory and Jespersen for English examples. We may therefore close with a paraphrase of Pulgram's statement that proper names are a category as universal as phonemes, morphemes and sentences—a category more universal than "nounlike and verb-like form-classes, categories of number, person, case, and tense, or grammatical positions of actor, verbal goal, and possessor."[93] Pulgram himself is quoting Leonard Bloomfield. It might be well to modify the much-debated term *universal* with a very valid term, not enough used by linguistics, "semi-universal," since the realm here involved is that of a positive one, and there is always the possibility that a tribe might turn up in the Amazon country or on the moon to destroy the universality. Clearly from what we have said we may see that, though the category "proper noun" is universal or semi-universal, its syntactic and other linguistic signals may differ greatly from one nation, language or dialect to another.

---

[93] Pulgram, p. 49.

If we were willing to work on a priori grounds, as we have not done in this paper, we would have to go back to my statement that to the first man the first woman was a proper noun, as well as a helpmate. Perhaps many things are proper nouns in speech which are not in language. As our experience grows wider, departing from the idiolect, many proper nouns are bound to become common nouns. "Last night there were four Maries." Yet we also create new proper nouns all the time: Levittown, Telestar, the Kennedy Administration. So the universality, a priori or inductive, is not merely tribal; it includes civilizations as well.

DISCUSSION QUESTIONS

1. What place-names in your locality reflect settlement history?

2. To what extent might etymology be important in the study of place-names in your own state?

3. What can you learn from the pronunciation of Pierre (South Dakota), the Thames River (Connecticut), Joliet and Cairo (Illinois) and Los Angeles? Compare also Dells of the Wisconsin River and The Dalles in Oregon; the pronunciations Détroit and Detróit.

4. Does Utley's test for a proper name seem generally workable?

JOHN ALGEO

Algeo, professor of English at the University of Georgia, is a member of the editorial advisory board of Names and the director of the NCTE's Commission on the English Language.

SEMANTIC NAMES: THE KIND OF MEANING

If the amount of meaning a name has, whether none or infinite or some unspecified intermediate quantity, is not an adequate characterization of the class, the kind of meaning may be distinctive. It will be helpful, therefore, to look at some of the ways a name can be used to see whether there is a clue in them to a more adequate definition of the term. In each of the following sentences, *Thomas* is used in a different sense:

1. His name is Thomas.
2. Here are Catherine and Thomas.
3. She was a Thomas before she married.
4. I remember a younger Thomas.
5. He is trying to be another Thomas.
6. Looking in the mirror, he saw a Thomas looking back.
7. The dress she bought is a genuine Thomas.

In the first sentence, *Thomas* is really a citation form and might more properly have been written in italics: "His name is *Thomas*." The sentence in which it occurs is a metalinguistic one, being language about language. Such uses must be set apart, because in them the referent of the word is the linguistic form of which the token is an exponent. The name in the other sentences might be glossed as follows:

2. '(the) person (I intended and expect you to identify) called *Thomas*'
3. 'member of the Thomas family (i.e., family called *Thomas*)'
4. 'particular aspect of Thomas (i.e., person called *Thomas*)'
5. 'person with some characteristics of a particular Thomas (i.e., person called *Thomas*)'
6. 'image of Thomas (i.e., person called *Thomas*)'
7. 'product of Thomas (i.e., person called *Thomas*)'

What all the glosses have in common is that they include either the word *Thomas* as a citation form or a term that must itself be so glossed. The examples therefore suggest that a proper name may be defined as a word whose definition includes a citation of the word itself. In the gloss for sentence (2), the citation form occurs as an element in a differentiating clause that directly modifies the genus, whereas in sentences (3) through (7) the citation form is an element in a clause that glosses some modifier of the genus. Names of the former kind can be called primary proper names, and those of the latter kind secondary proper names. Between these two sorts of names there are a number of differences in addition to the form of their glosses.

The bestowal of a primary proper name on a referent is ad hoc, in that there is no way to predict what primary name may be given to any particular referent. Consequently there is no way to know the correct use of primary names apart from observing instances of their use. Secondary names are bestowed according to rule and consequently their correct use does not depend on such observation. A speaker can know that a person is named *Catherine* only if he has heard or seen the name used in connection with her, and the initial decision to call her *Catherine* was an act of name-giving. On the other hand, if a speaker knows the name of the family to which an individual belongs, he will know what last name the individual bears without ever having heard or seen it used of the individual, and the initial application of the family name to the individual was not an act of name-giving at all because it follows automatically from general rules in our society. A family name is shared by the members of a family group and is regularly changed only by legal procedure, such as adoption or the marriage of females, as a concomitant of change of family membership. A family name is therefore primarily the name of the family group and only secondarily the name of an individual member.

Many secondary names have a tendency to pass easily into appellatives, so that whether a given use is proper or appellative may not be immediately clear. If we say, "Edinburgh was the Athens of Scotland," *Athens* is used as a secondary proper name meaning 'place with certain characteristics of Athens'; it will generally be understood as metaphorical, intended to call the original Athens to mind. However, if we say, "He is attending an academy," a metaphor is unlikely; the connection with the proper name *Academy* has faded, leaving the word as a pure appellative. Words continually move from the status of proper names, via secondary use, to the status of appellatives (see Partridge 1950 for examples). There may be doubt about the standing of a word that is in the process, for example *Casanova, Mata Hari,* or *Valentino,* and it is quite possible that from some speakers *Bluebeard* is a secondary proper name, derived from the Perrault character, while for others it is a simple appellative meaning 'uxoricide.'

The distinction between primary and secondary names is as "delicate" (in Halliday's sense) as it seems advisable to make. It would be easily possible to recognize more remote derivations. Thus *Israel* 'country called *Israel*' is a primary name; *Israeli* 'citizen of Israel (i.e., country called *Israel*)' is a secondary name; and *sabra* 'native-born Israeli (i.e., citizen of Israel [i.e., country called *Israel*])' would then be a tertiary name. Nothing prevents names being quarternary, quinary, and so on; however, the distinctions cease to have any practical significance. In common usage, primary and usually also secondary names are felt to be proper; tertiary (and higher degree derivations) are not. For practical purposes, a proper name can be said to be a word like *Thomas,* whose meaning is 'person called *Thomas,*' or like *Chicagoan,* whose meaning is 'inhabitant of the place called *Chicago.*' More generally, a proper name is primarily any word *X* whose meaning can be expressed as 'entity called *X*' and secondarily any whose immediate definientia include a term with such a meaning.

It may be objected that this schema for defining names is circular or involves infinite regression, on the grounds that the definition includes the term being defined (Brøndal 1948: 60; Searle 1969: 139). But the grounds are illusory and the objection invalid. The illusion of circularity is created by the appearance of the citation form *X*—whatever it may be, *Thomas,* for example—both as the definiendum and as part of the definiens. An examination of what is meant by "citation form" is therefore in order, followed by a more careful restatement of the definition schema for names.

Citation forms are used in a variety of ways. For example, we can say either "*Cat* is spelled with three letters" or "*Cat* has three letters," using the two statements interchangeably. However convenient it is to vary one's expression in this way, the two statements are not equivalent, strictly speaking, because the citation form *cat* stands for different things in the two uses. The first statement might be paraphrased as "{cat} is spelled with three letters," that is, the lexical formative or morpheme is represented by a three-letter spelling; the second statement as "⟨cat⟩ has three letters," that is, the orthographic sequence is composed of three letters. The subjects are not interchangeable: "{cat} has three letters" is nonsense because morphemes are not composed of letters. We can also say things like "*Cat* is pronounced /kæt/," "*Cat* is a noun," "*Cat* means 'domestic feline,'" or "*Cat* is the genus 'feline' delimited by the differentia 'domestic,'" or any combination of such statements. By making all these statements about the same citation form *cat,* we seem to be saying that they are all true of the same entity. They are not. The citation form *cat* is a covering label, a fudge form, that can stand for any of several entities existing on different linguistic strata. To speak more precisely, we would have to make statements like the following:

> ⟨cat⟩, which is the spelling for the morpheme {cat} and represents the pronunciation /kæt/, has three letters.
>
> /kæt/, which is the pronunciation of the morpheme {cat} and can be spelled ⟨cat⟩, consists of three phonemes.
>
> {cat} is a noun, is pronounced /kæt/, is spelled ⟨cat⟩, and means 'domestic feline.'
>
> 'cat' is a shorthand way of expressing the genus 'feline' and the differentia 'domestic,' which is the meaning of {cat}.

Normally, there is no harm in using the citation form *cat* as a cover term for any of ⟨cat⟩, /kæt/, {cat}, or 'cat.' It is convenient typographically and lets us be looser with our wording than we would have to be if we were expressing ideas with greater exactness. If, however, we are misled by this loose practice to hypostatize a single entity behind the cover term, mischief may result. One possible bit of mischief is that the definition schema proposed above may be thought of as circular. If, however, we replace the citation form in that schema with more precise expressions, we have the following:

> The definition of any proper-name morpheme (sequence) {X} is 'entity (with such other differentiae as are appropriate) referred to in speech as /Y/ and in writing as ⟨Z⟩.'

A specific example of the schema is the following:

> {Thomas} means 'person referred to in speech as /táməs/ and in writing as ⟨Thomas⟩.'

When the ambiguity represented by the citation form is eliminated from the definition, the vicious circularity disappears too.

It may also be objected that this approach to defining the proper name does not distinguish it from a common appellative (Ullmann 1952; Sørensen 1963: 23). That is, if *Bill* means 'entity called *Bill,*' it is proposed that *boy* similarly means 'entity called *boy.*' But there is an important difference between the two sorts of words, and their meanings are not parallel. Suppose a strange animal wanders into my garden from the wilderness and I call out to my wife in the house, "There is a beast in our garden." Then she might ask, "Well, is it a cat, or an elephant, or a unicorn?" and I could reply, "It's a cat" or "None of those—it's an alligator." Though I had never seen the particular beast before, I would know whether it is or is not a cat. However, if my wife should ask instead, "Well, is it Macavity, or Pyewacket, or Caligula?" I would have to answer something like, "How should I know—we haven't been introduced yet." To know that a creature is appropriately referred to by the word *cat*, it is not necessary to observe anyone calling it "cat." But to know that the same creature is appropriately called *Pyewacket*, it is necessary to observe some instance of the use of that name with reference to the creature.

It is necessary to distinguish between the bestowal of a name and its subsequent use, a distinction that is not the same as that between the invention of an appellative neologism and its subsequent use. The invention (which can be taken here as including borrowing) of a new common word like *googol* or *sputnik* is parallel to the invention (or borrowing) of a new name like *Mauvenia* or *Rukmini*. The use of the appellative *sputnik* to refer appropriately to a particular object (an artificial satellite) is parallel to the use of *Rukmini* to refer appropriately to a particular person (a woman named *Rukmini*). But with names there is an event other than invention or use, an event that is not paralleled by anything connected with appellatives. Names are bestowed on particular individuals, and for a name to be associated with an individual, it is necessary that an act of bestowal should have taken place (Hockett 1958: 311). Appellatives are invented and used; names are invented, bestowed, and used. The bestowal of a name may be deliberate, though informal, as when parents consider what name to give a new child; it may involve elaborate and extensive study, as when a public relations company gives a new name to a movie star; it may be off-hand, as when a child casually names a pet turtle. But in every case there is a specific act by which the name is first assigned to the bearer. There is no such act for appellatives. Appellatives are used but not bestowed; use of a name presupposes an act of bestowal. Thus the definition of a proper name X as 'entity called X' specifies not only a sufficient, but also a necessary condition for the correct application of the name. If the creature in my garden is a domestic feline, I will know that it is appropriately referred to by the word *cat* even though no one has ever before so referred to it. I cannot under similar circumstances know that it is to be called *Pyewacket*.

It is presumably this characteristic of the application of names that led Mill to conclude they are connotatively meaningless. However, Mill's conclusion goes too far by unnecessarily restricting what is to be accounted meaningful. What we are to understand by the term *meaning* is a vexed question. Gilbert Ryle (1957: 128) has observed that "preoccupation with the theory of meaning could be described as the occupational disease of twentieth-century Anglo-Saxon and Austrian philosophy." It would be hubristic here to suggest any cure for the disease. But if we say that a word's meaning is a statement of the conditions necessary for its appropriate use, or as Ryle (1957: 143) puts it, "to know what an expression means . . is to know the rules of the employment of that expression," then no word can be meaningless. Just as part of one meaning of *cat* is that any possible referent be a domestic feline, so part of the meaning of *Pyewacket* is that any possible referent be in fact called *Pyewacket*. To be a cat it is not required that a creature ever in fact be so called; to be a Pyewacket, it is. Thus names and appellatives alike are meaningful words in the vocabulary, although their kinds of meaning differ.

The significant contrast between names and appellatives is not to be overlooked. In addition to the differences in the content of their definitions, names, unlike appellatives, are freely and imaginatively created de novo, as the colorful examples of personal names collected by Thomas Pyles (1947, 1959) attest. Moreover, the bestowal of names, whether traditional or innovative, is a prerogative of every speaker blessed with the possession of children, pets, boats, or other such nameables. It is hard for anyone to invent a new appellative and get his application of it accepted by others; but when it comes to names, every citizen is the equal of the primordial Name-giver of Plato's *Cratylus*. Also unlike the process of associating an appellative with a thing, the giving of names often involves a formal ceremony, a ritual or legal imposition, as in christenings, registrations, and launchings, which regularly include a performative utterance by which the name is made official: "Name this child. William Henry." Indeed appellatives are not "given" at all; they belong to a thing automatically by virtue of other characteristics it possesses. Names, however, are bestowed by someone, and only after that initial use in the act of bestowal do they become a characteristic of the subject to be observed by others and thus imitated.

It is also possible that names are governed by laws, synchronic and diachronic, that are different from those applying to appellatives (Mańczak 1968a, 1968b). Moreover, the name-stock of any language includes potentially the names of all other languages. Whereas appellatives are only exceptionally borrowed, the reverse is true for names. Names translated either as calques like *Red Square* and *Arch of Triumph* or as established native equivalents like *Leo* for *Lev* (Nikolaevich Tolstoi) are comparative rarities, the normal procedure being to accept the foreign name as a loan with whatever phonological, orthographical, and grammatical adaptations the borrowing language requires. So English has *The Hague* not *The Port*, *Vladivostok* not *Lordeast*, and *Juan Carlos* not *John Charles* for the Spanish royal person.

The grammar of names and appellatives is not altogether the same. The morphology of names need not follow that typical of nouns. In syntax, also, names have special characteristics. Thus, they alone occur in various naming constructions: *a man named*, *Ishmael by name*, *of the name Ishmael*, and so forth. The earlier history of such constructions in Indo-European has been treated by Hahn (1969); something like them may be presumed to occur in all languages. They were studied at least as early as the fourteenth century, when Thomas of Erfurt recognized a class of expressions with a *verbum vocativum* in his modistic grammar (Bursill-Hall 1966: 141). Some constructions of the type seem to admit either proper names or appellatives: "They called him Ishmael"; "They called him a rascal"; "They called him a sailor." However, the superficially similar constructions have quite different interpretations when a proper name and when an appellative is used in them. Thus it is a fact that the referent is Ishmael because he is so called; but it would be wrong to say (barring an extreme nominalist stance) that he is a rascal or a sailor because he is so called. In such constructions, names are used as citation forms and might be italicized or put in quotation marks, but appellatives do not normally have that interpretation; that is, in "Call me Ishmael," the word *Ishmael* is "mentioned," but in "Call me irresponsible," the word *irresponsible* is "used." Similarly, a sentence like "This is Golda" is ambiguous between two meanings: on the one hand, it may be an identification, with the sense 'This is the person Golda (whom I presume you know about)'; on the other, it may be an introduction, with the sense 'This person (whom I do not presume you to have any prior knowledge of) is called *Golda*.' With the first sense *Golda* is being used; with the second, mentioned. Appellatives occur with "introduction" meanings only in very restricted contexts, chiefly pedagogical, as when in a foreign language class, an instructor says, "This is a *kulero*, and this is a *telero*."

Such striking peculiarities mark names as a special kind of lexical item, but hardly exclude them from the realm of linguistic fact. Indeed, it may be said that there are three main kinds of vocables in the lexicon: those words that form closed systems in the grammar, such as the articles, pronouns, auxiliaries, and some prepositions and conjunctions; second, appellative nouns and those verbs, adjectives, and so forth that form open sets and constitute the bulk of words listed in general dictionaries; and last, names, which are often excluded from dictionaries on either theoretical or practical grounds. It is the contention of this study that there is no valid theoretical basis for excluding names from a dictionary, although their vast numbers and the small amount of linguistic information appropriate to each offer ample practical justification for leaving them out of general dictionaries. When dictionaries do include names, they tend to give encyclopedic rather than linguistic information about them, that is, they tend to discuss prominent persons or places named rather than the names themselves. There are exceptions, such as the "Pronouncing Vocabulary of Common English Given Names" appendix in the Merriam *New Collegiate* dictionaries. Fuller examples of appropriate lexicographical treatment of names are specialized works like Withycombe (1950) and Smith (1956); an early example is Walker (1818). On the other hand, a work like *Webster's Dictionary of Proper Names* (Payton 1970) is actually an encyclopedia of proper names, as are most works treating place names.

Names, whether considered lexically or referentially, are of many kinds, of which names of persons are the most central. Alone among nameable objects, persons are always assumed to have names. Whereas places, astronomical bodies, and events may be nameless, if we encounter an anonymous person, we ask about his name and if it is inaccessible, like Robinson Crusoe in his discovery of Friday, we supply the lack. Some entities, like animals and supernatural beings, will be expected to have names just in case they are treated as persons in other ways, such as requiring the relative *who* rather than *which*. Personal names are central in another way also. Although systems differ from culture to culture, it is common for a person to bear both primary and secondary names as part of a unified naming system. Other kinds of nameable objects seldom have names of both kinds.

Personal names are of two main sorts: legal names and bynames. Their kinds vary according to the naming system, some of whose manifold variations are noted by Lévi-Strauss (1966: 172–216), but include given names (*Pollyana, Timothy*), which are primary proper names, and secondary proper names such as patronymics (*Thorkelsdóttir, Ivanovich*) and family or clan names (*Jones, MacIntosh*). Some naming systems distinguish between an autonym, which is most like a given personal name in the English system, a teknonym, meaning 'father or mother of so-and-so,' and a necronym, which defines the individual's kinship to some deceased relative, for example, *Elder-brother-dead;* one person may have several such names that he bears serially according to the changing events of his life (Lévi-Strauss 1966: 191–96). Bynames include hypocorisms (*Will, Bill, Jeannie*—although such apparent pet names can also occur as legal names), epithets used in addition to another name (*Stonewall Jackson, Jack the Ripper, Ethelred the Unready*) or in place of it (*Hotspur, Old Baldy*), code names (*M, 007*), noms de guerre (*Leclerc*—as for the general Vicomte de Hautecloque of the North African campaign), pen names (*George Sand*), stage names (*Engelbert Humperdinck*), aliases adopted for concealment (*John Smith*), and other pseudonyms (*Atticus*—as for Addison). Although they are grammatically common, descriptive phrases like *the Iron Duke, the Blessed Virgin, the Little Corporal, the White Queen,* and *the Lone Ranger* may be conventionalized in a way that makes them epithetic names. Bynames seem always to be primary proper names, even when they are based on secondary names. Thus the use of a hypocoristic form of a family name, such as *Jonesy,* is not predictable in the way the family name itself is and accordingly must be defined as a primary name.

A term for members of a group, organization, or community is a secondary proper name because the definition of the term will include reference to the name of the group. Thus names of nationalities like *Spaniard* can be defined as 'native or citizen of Spain (i.e., the country called *Spain*),' *Angle* as 'one of the Germanic tribe of Angles (i.e., the group called *Angles*),' *DeMolay* as 'member of the Order of DeMolay for Boys (i.e., the organization called *Order of DeMolay*),' and *mafioso* as 'member of the Mafia (i.e., the organization called *Mafia*).'

Titles, as well as some kinship and occupational terms, are regularly used with personal names, but are not themselves names since they can be defined without reference to their signaling value. Even when used alone as grammatically proper nouns, as in ''Dad is in the closet where Momma hung him,'' ''Doctor will see you now,'' or ''Mister, you're next,'' such words are appellatives, not names. To know that a woman can be called *Madam*, it is not necessary to hear her so called.

The nonce use of expressions like *sleepyhead, big spender,* or *smartaleck* as proper nouns, for example in ''See whether you can get sleepyhead to bed,'' does not imply that they are names, since an appellative definition will adequately account for the pseudo-name use. Personifications, as in Bunyan's ''Wherefore *Mercy* began thus to reply to her Neighbor *Timorous*,'' are problematical. They function grammatically in every way like proper nouns, but they are probably best accounted appellatives rather than names, since the personification has the designation it does not merely because it is so called but because it is characterized by the quality signified by that designation.

A noteworthy item is *Joe Doakes,* which has two uses (apart from any occurrence as a genuine personal name, not under consideration here). First, it is used in the sense 'average, common man,' as in ''Joe Doakes pays the taxes and fights the wars.'' Second, it is used with the sense 'person' of one whose name is unknown, as in ''The next Joe Doakes who cuts in front is going to get a surprise.'' What is noteworthy about *Joe Doakes* is that it has all the associated characteristics of a name: it is capitalized, is syntactically a proper noun, and has the appearance of a hypocoristic given name plus a family name. However, in neither of the uses noted above is it a name. In both it is simply an appellative, as the glosses show. Indeed, *Joe Doakes* is the very antithesis of a name, for we can be reasonably confident that anyone of whom the term is used is not in fact called *Joe Doakes*. Moreover, users do not need to have observed an instance of its application to a person before knowing that it can be applied to him; rather *Joe Doakes* is used of a particular individual precisely when the speaker has not observed any use of his name, or it is used of a type, for which a name, in the strict sense, is not possible. *John Doe, Richard Roe, John Stiles,* and *Richard Miles* similarly are antinames, though with the added complication that they are used in the legal register in the general sense 'unnamed party to legal proceedings' and are further differentiated as the first, second, third, and fourth such parties. In effect, these terms constitute a special third-person pronoun system for the category ''proximity.'' Like *Joe Doakes,* they are not names.

Names for nonpersons are less interesting onomastically because there is little variety in the kind of name, however much variety there may be in the things named. Names are given to places: eschatological realms (*Eden, Lotus Land*), astronomical bodies (*Aldebaran, Big Dipper, Venus*), topographical features of many kinds (*Fujiyama, Mississippi, Old Faithful, Sahara, Golden Horn, Heartbreak Ridge, Garden of the Gods, Gulf Stream, Micronesia, Okefenokee*), and political divisions (*Nepal, Danelaw, Ulster, Mohenjodaro, Cherokee Strip, Covent Garden, Portobello Road, Loop*).

Although the difference between proper names and appellatives is a discrete one, it is sometimes hard to decide whether a particular item is a name or not. Thus *Polaris* is an appellative if it is defined as the 'star most nearly aligned with the earth's axis over the north pole,' in which case, 12,000 years from now, as a result of the earth's precession, the star called Vega will be Polaris. On the other hand, *Polaris* is a name if, like *Regulus* or *Vega*, it is simply what a point of light is called. In the latter case, the fact that it was the polar star at the time it was named is a historical fact rather than a rule of usage.

Names are also given to historical events, whether their duration is brief or lasting: *Hegira, Children's Crusade, Glorious Revolution, Fifth Republic, Age of Reason*, and *Cenozoic Era*, for example. Place names are often used for events: *Vatican II*, before *Munich*, since *Kent State*. Many names of events are specialized uses of appellative phrases. Thus, *civil war*, as a common appellative, applies to any military conflict between sections or parties of the same nation; but the phrase can become conventionalized as the name for one or more particular historical events, such as the English Civil War of the 1640s or the American Civil War of the 1860s. The descriptive accuracy of the phrase is then no longer apposite. Indeed, in the case of the American conflict, the question of whether the war was a civil one or one between sovereign states was the immediate issue over which the war was fought. Despite the existence of alternative names of various descriptive implications, such as Horace Greeley's *Great Rebellion*, the United Daughters of the Confederacy's *War Between the States*, and a score of others recorded by McDavid and McDavid (1969), the appellative meaning of such expressions is largely irrelevant to their use as names. As witness to that irrelevance, there is a reference of the *New Orleans Times-Picayune* to the ''Spanish War Between the States,'' cited by the McDavids as an amusing example of linguistic hyperdelicacy.

Whether *Monday* and other similar terms for recurring periods in the calendar are proper names has been the subject of much debate. Gardiner (1954: 53–54), in a spirit of compromise, called them ''common proper names,'' but the implications of such a *coincidentia oppositorum* are not altogether clear. If a definition like 'second day of the week' is appropriate for *Monday*, it is an appellative, as are the names of holidays, months, and seasons.

Many other things receive names: institutions and organizations (*Royal Academy, Republican Party, General Motors, NAACP, Yale, Dodgers*), beliefs and practices (*Islam, McCarthyism*), animals (*Checkers, Moby Dick*), plants (*Yggdrasil, Bo Tree, General Sherman Tree*), and gems (*Koh-i-noor, Cullinan*). Generic terms, whether English or Latin, popular or learned, are appellatives (*bald cypress, Taxodiaceae*). Artifacts are named: ships (*Pinafore*), trains (*Twentieth Century Limited*), aircraft (*Spirit of St. Louis*), spacecraft (*Odyssey*), weapons (*Hrunting*), buildings (*Alhambra, Madison Square Garden, Kremlin*), and various objects (*Holy Grail, Big Ben, Liberty Bell*).

Works of art customarily have titles as a special kind of name: books (*War and Peace*), periodicals (*Time*), comic strips (*Peanuts*), musical pieces (*Gaudeamus Igitur*), documents (*Tanaka Memorial*), plays (*The Tempest*), poems (*The Seasons*), paintings (*American Gothic*), prayers (*Angelus*), statuary (*Wingless Victory*), films (*The Great Dictator*), television programs (*All in the Family*), speeches (*Gettysburg Address*), and— although they are perhaps not works of art—laws, treaties, and the like (*Mann Act, Atlantic Pact*).

Names that are in fact used of only one referent, for example *Popocatepetl*, offer a problem in the form of their definition. As a name, the definition of *Popocatepetl* must be of the form 'entity (or perhaps more specifically, volcano) called *Popocatepetl*'; but because the word has unique reference, there is a possibility of defining it extensionally as 'volcano near Mexico City, 17,887 feet in height' or, more precisely, to include within the definition a location by the coordinates of longitude and latitude. There are practical difficulties in doing so. As Landau (1967: 13) has observed, "no present grid system, or locating technique, can tell us precisely enough where most places on earth really are." Although we might conclude that language is imprecise enough to use imprecise coordinates, there are also theoretical objections to a definition that implies the volcano has the name *Popocatepetl* because of its location.

Similarly it might be supposed that the name of a particular person could be defined as referring to the individual begotten of such-and-such parents, at such-and-such a time, as Tristram Shandy was of Mr. and Mrs. Shandy in the ill-starred night between the first Sunday and the first Monday in the month of March, in the year of our Lord 1718. But the supposition is wrong, not merely because the same name can be given to more than one individual or because of practical difficulties in ascertaining the time and agents of begetting, but because so to define a name would imply that an individual has the name he does by virtue of the circumstances of his begetting. On the contrary, as is well-known, Tristram was so named because he was so called by the Reverend Mr. Yorick, in the face of the best parental intentions.

Extensional definitions, it has already been argued, are categorically wrong for linguistic purposes. They deal not with language, but with things. They are appropriate not for a grammar or dictionary, but for an encyclopedia. Language is used to talk about particulars; but within a language system, all terms are general terms.

An important, but still unanswered, question is what constitutes nameability, what properties a subject must possess in order to be eligible for a name. The requirement most often suggested is that the thing must be one that holds a special interest for speakers (Christophersen 1939: 63; Russell 1948: 89; Gardiner 1954: 45; Pulgram 1954: 32; Sørensen 1963: 105; Waismann 1965: 198; Zabeeh 1968: 67). Chomsky (1971: 14) suggests that nameability depends on the "function of an object in a space of human action," which is perhaps only another way of talking about "interest." It is clearly right that to be named, a thing must be something in which speakers might be interested, but that is a necessary rather than a sufficient condition. There are many things in which speakers have a reasonably strong degree of interest, such as a lawn that needs weekly mowing, a beefsteak on one's plate, or an antique firescreen. Yet outside fantasy, where all is possible, it would be exceedingly odd to call a lawn *Filbert*, a steak *Hank*, or a firescreen *Zoe*. The problem is not that the particular names are incompatible with their referents; it is rather that such referents do not get named, no matter how much interest we may have in them.

Another obviously necessary (but also insufficient) requirement is that the thing to be named must be recognizable as a gestalt. "Thing-ness" does not, however, require spatiotemporal continuity. As Chomsky (1971: 14) points out, certain works of art, such as mobiles, are nameable although they lack spatial continuity; and the science-fictional James Kirk, transported from his spaceship to the surface of an alien planet, remains James Kirk although continuity is broken (the counterfactual nature of the example is irrelevant since the fiction is put forth not as fantasy, but as a reasonable possibility and is accepted as such by the audience).

A number of other criteria have been proposed: that names are given to entities so similar to one another that the differences between them are difficult to recognize or describe; that names are useful for entities that can serve as reference points for identifying other entities; that names, being economical means of referring, are given to objects for which such economy is desirable; and that names are given to things not susceptible to systematic ordering or for which standardized order seems inappropriate (Gardiner 1954: 45; Shwayder 1963: 57). None of the foregoing are quite satisfactory criteria; and, indeed, it would be possible to argue for the exact opposites of the first and last.

There are also two sufficient, although not necessary, conditions for nameability: personhood and prominence. All persons are expected to have names; indeed an individual's name is bound up with his personhood, a nameless creature being thereby depersonalized. Nonhumans that are personalized are also usually named, for example, pets and supernatural powers. God's name may be ineffable, but he has one; the absolute which is unnamed is also impersonal.

Things that are prominent of their kind by virtue of intensity, size, duration, complexity, or whatnot are likewise nameable. Thus rivers have names, though the small creek flowing by my door has none. The clock at Westminster is *Big Ben,* but that in the local courthouse is anonymous. The *Star of India* is named, but not the stone in my wife's ring. Hurricanes are *Agnes, Beulah,* and the like, whereas tornados and summer storms are nameless. This criterion does not fully explain why some things are named and others not. Thus the event of 1666 when half the capital of England burned down is called the *Great Fire of London.* The event of 1945 when much of the city of Hiroshima was destroyed has no distinctive English name, although it can be described by various appellative phrases. How prominent a thing must be before it is named is subjective and partly a matter of chance.

Although the decision of whether to name or not to name is sometimes arbitrary or conventional, any subject that is either a person or exceptionally prominent of its kind is regularly given a name. And all named things may be presumed to be the objects of human interest and to have a gestalt-like cohesiveness. Beyond these criteria the requirements for nameability are not clear, although they are matters of some interest and may reasonably be supposed to be universals of human behavior.

The kind of definition that has been proposed here for proper names is not wholly new. It is implicit in Mill's (1843: 1.2.5) observation that "when we predicate of anything its proper name, when we say, pointing to a man, this is Brown or Smith, or pointing to a city, that is York, we do not, merely by so doing, convey to the hearer any information about them, except that those are their names." Although Mill did not draw it, the obvious conclusion would seem to be that the information conveyed by a word is its meaning and therefore the meaning of a name is that the referent is so called. Marty (1908: 438, 509) and Funke (1925: 79) also noted this implication of the use of names, but it was Gardiner (1954) who recognized and most insistently called attention to the central role played by the "distinctive sound" of a name in its use. Gardiner's *Theory of Proper Names* is distorted by his almost exclusive attention to "embodied" proper names, that is, names with a definite referent in an act of parole—an ironic distortion in view of the fact that Gardiner was one of the chief proponents of Saussure's langue/parole distinction in England in the face of resistance to such dichotomizing by his contemporary J. R. Firth, who thought of it as "a quite unnecessary nuisance" (1957: 144, 179, 227; Langendoen 1968: 47). If we apply Gardiner's general theory to a consideration of "disembodied" names as units in the system of langue, a definition of the kind presented here follows naturally. With respect to ordinary language, Gardiner's work on names is the most important theoretical statement in recent times.

Another implicit recognition of the kind of meaning proposed here for names can be seen in Strawson (1950: 188): "What is . . . implied . . . by my now referring to someone by name is simply the existence of someone, *now being referred to,* who is *conventionally referred to* by that name'' (Strawson's italics). Although it is not true that the use of a name implies the existence of the referent (in the ordinary sense of *existence*), since fictional *Mrs. Miniver* is as good a name as historical *Mrs. Bracegirdle,* Strawson is certainly right that the referent may be assumed to be conventionally referred to by the name; it is this fact that the definition schema formalizes. Although Church (1956: 5) did not himself limit the term so, he observed that ''*proper name* is often restricted to names . . . which have as part of their meaning that the denotation is so called or is or was entitled to be so called.'' And according to Ryle (1931: 27), when we understand a proper name, ''we know that someone in particular is called by that name by certain persons.'' Zink (1963: 491) similarly combines a so-und-so-genanntsein view of the meaning of names with an interpretation requiring them to have unique reference, when he proposes that ''the meaning of a particular proper name 'P.N.' would be the meaning of the expression 'the person truly named ''P.N.'' who is or was at the time T at place P.' '' Although he puts most emphasis on the means by which a name is bestowed (as by christening or the inheritance of a patronym), Shwayder (1964: 453) argues the use of a name ''always implies that the speaker believes that the indicated denotatum has been given that name.''

Finally, Bach (1968: 92) wants ''to postulate that all nouns (at least common nouns) are derived in one way, namely from structures of roughly the form

$$Det + one + S$$

where S is further developed into a sentence of the form

$$Det + one + Aux + be + Predicate\ nominal''$$

and subsequently he notes that ''within the framework suggested here, names could be treated in two ways: They could be allowed to occur as alternatives to variables within sentences, or they could be derived from embedded sentences involving the predicate 'is called ———' or the like. If the latter course is followed, one could deal with the semantic content of names in a way parallel to that of other 'nouns' '' (121). The first alternative follows the tradition of assuming that names have unique referents. . . . The second, however, is the treatment that is advanced in this [article] as the most accurate statement of a name's meaning, in the sense of a rule that governs its use. It is also in keeping with the logical tradition of Russell (1905) and Quine (1950: 220) that proposes to treat all singular terms as descriptions and to reanalyze descriptions as predications; in this tradition, too, all terms are general terms. Such a convergence of disciplines in their view of language is a welcome sign of the general usefulness of the analysis. Ordinary language and the predicate calculus may have a resemblance on the semantic level.

The approach to defining proper names in this chapter has several advantages that have not always been recognized:

1. It maintains that in respect to having meaning, proper names are normal words in the lexicon rather than peculiar ''meaningless'' words or extralinguistic phenomena. It normalizes proper names in this way because it regards their referents as belonging to intensional classes, like those of common nouns. In effect it says that Thomases are individuals who can be recognized by the fact that people apply the name *Thomas* to them, thus treating an individual's name like any other attribute by which he can be recognized and defined.

2. The form of the definition allows other attributes to be incorporated into it. If "A Boy Named Sue" is incongruous, the incongruity can be explained by a definition of the name *Sue* as a 'female person named *Sue*.' To the extent that names have connotations (in Mill's sense) those connotations can be included in their definitions, thereby also providing a partial explanation for the belief that proper and common names differ by degree. The necessary and sufficient condition for a proper name is that its definition be of the form 'entity called *X*'; if other information is included, for instance 'human' or 'female' or 'canine,' the name, while remaining categorically proper, becomes more common-like in its effect.

3. The distinction between primary and secondary proper names also formalizes the belief that proper and common names differ by degree rather than categorically. The formal difference between the meanings of primary names, like *Delilah* 'person called *Delilah*' or *Chicago* 'place called *Chicago*,' and those of secondary names, like a *Delilah* 'person with characteristics of a particular Delilah' or *Chicagoan* 'inhabitant of Chicago,' explains why there has been disagreement about whether items of the second kind are proper names, appellatives, or some sort of semiproper name.

4. On the other hand, the apparent circularity of the definition explains why Mill and others have thought names to be meaningless. If we are told we are to see a whale, we can confidently infer some things about the creature—that it is aquatic, warm-blooded, and probably big. But if we are told we are to see Shome, all we can be sure of is that the entity can be called *Shome*. That is the meaning of the name, but it does not add much to our knowledge of the name-bearer. And consequently it is easy to conclude that names have no meaning.

5. It has often been observed that users of a name must be supposed to know some facts about the named object that could be taken as the meaning of the name. But . . . if we take the sort of facts that are usually suggested as illustrations—that Aristotle was the student of Plato, or was the teacher of Alexander, or was born at Stagira—we have to conclude either that the meaning of a name is infinite, if we take the sum of those facts, or that it is indeterminate, if we take any part of them. There is, however, one fact about any referent that every namer of the referent must surely be assumed to know: that the referent is called by the name used in making reference; and it is this generally known fact that the definition specifies. Thus the position taken by those, like Frege, who believe a name to have some sense is also justified, but the definition makes that sense definite and describable, whereas otherwise it is not.

6. The definition treats names as an autonomous and purely intralanguage semantic category. On the one hand, it escapes the problems that come from trying to base a definition on extralinguistic reference; and on the other hand, it does not assume that the semantic class of names must be isomorphic with any grammatical, phonological, or orthographic classes. English has capitalized versus lowercase words in its orthography, proper versus common nouns in its grammar, and names versus appellatives in its semantics, but the various classes, though partly correlate, are independent of one another. In general, names are proper nouns and are capitalized, but exceptions are easy to find. In respect to naming, language would seem to be a multileveled and polysystemic phenomenon.

7. Finally, the definition has, it would seem, a fair chance of being a universal of language. It is highly probable that all languages have words for which a necessary defining characteristic is that such a word can be applied to an entity just in case the entity is actually called by the word. Efforts to define a name orthographically, phon-

ologically, or grammatically will end in language-specific phenomena that are of limited interest to the general theory of onomastics; the name as a universal is a semantic category.

A name is therefore a word people use to call someone or something by. So we may conclude that Hermogenes was right after all, and Cratylus wrong. If people called him *Hermogenes,* that was his name, because what a man is called is, after all, what a name *is.*

REFERENCES

1. Bach, Emmon. 1968. "Nouns and Noun Phrases." In *Universals in Linguistic Theory,* eds. Emmon Bach and Robert T. Harms, pp. 90–122. New York: Holt.

2. Brøndal, Viggo. 1948. *Les Parties du discours: études sur les catégories linguistiques.* Traduction française par Pierre Naert. Copenhagen: Einar Munksgaard.

3. Bursill-Hall, Geoffrey. 1966. "Aspects of Modistic Grammar." In *Report of the Seventeenth Annual Round Table of Linguistics and Language Studies,* ed. Francis P. Dineen, pp. 133–48. Monograph Series on Languages and Linguistics, no. 19. Washington: Georgetown University Press.

4. Chomsky, Noam. 1971. *Problems of Knowledge and Freedom.* New York: Random House.

5. Christopherson, Paul. 1939. *The Articles: A Study of Their Use in English.* Copenhagen: Einar Munksgaard.

6. Church, Alonzo. 1956. *Introduction to Mathematical Logic.* Princeton: Princeton University Press.

7. Firth, J. R. 1957. *Papers in Linguistics, 1934–1951.* London: Oxford University Press.

8. Funke, O. "Zum Definition des Begriffes 'Eigenname.' " In *Probleme der englischen Sprache and Kultur,* Festschrift für Johannes Hoops. Germanische Bibliothek, Abt. 2, Bd. 20.

9. Gardiner, Alan. 1954. *The Theory of Proper Names.* 2nd ed. London: Oxford University Press. First printed in 1940.

10. Hahn, E. Adelaide. 1969. *Naming-Constructions in Some Indo-European Languages.* Cleveland: Case Western Reserve University Press.

11. Halliday, M. A. K. 1961. "Categories of the Theory of Grammar." *Word* 17: 241–292.

12. ———. 1967–1968. "Notes on Transitivity and Theme in English." *Journal of Linguistics* 3: 37–81, 199–294; 4: 179–215.

13. Hockett, Charles F. 1958. *A Course in Modern Linguistics.* New York: Harcourt.

14. Landau, Robert M. (357–03–6623). 1967. "Name or Number—Which Shall It Be?" *Names* 15: 12–20.

15. Langendoen, D. Terence. 1968. *The London School of Linguistics: A Study of the Linguistic Theories of B. Malinowski and J. R. Firth.* Research Monograph, no. 46. Cambridge: MIT Press.

16. Lévi-Strauss, Claude. 1966. *The Savage Mind.* Chicago: University of Chicago Press.

17. Mańczak, Witold. 1968a. "Le Nom propre et le nom commun." *Revue Internationale d'Onomastique* 20: 205–18.

18. ———. 1968b. "Onomastik und Struckturalismus." *Beiträge zur Namenforschung* 3: 52–60.

19. Marty, Anton. 1908. *Untersuchungen zur Grundlegung der allgemeinen Grammatik und Sprachphilosophie.* Vol. 1. Halle: Max Niemeyer.

20. Mill, John Stuart. 1843. *A System of Logic.* Reprint. New York: Harper, 1846.

21. Partridge, Eric. 1950. *Name into Word: Proper Names that Have Become Common Property.* New York: Macmillan.

22. Payton, Geoffrey. 1970. *Webster's Dictionary of Proper Names.* Springfield, Mass.: Merriam.

23. Pulgram, Ernst. 1954. *Theory of Names*. Berkeley: American Name Society. Reprint from *Beiträge zur Namenforschung*, vol. 5, no. 2.

24. Pyles, Thomas. 1947. "Onomastic Individualism in Oklahoma." *American Speech* 22: 257–64.

25. ——. 1959. "Bible Belt Onomastics; or, some Curiosities of Anti-Pedobaptist Nomenclature." *Names* 7: 84–100.

26. Quine, Willard Van Orman. 1950. *Methods of Logic*. New York: Holt.

27. Russell, Bertrand. 1905. "On Denoting." *Mind* 14: 479–93.

28. ——. 1948. *Human Knowledge: Its Scope and Limits*. New York: Simon and Schuster.

29. Ryle, Gilbert. 1931. "Systematically Misleading Expressions." In *Logic and Language*, ed. Antony Flew, pp. 13–40. Garden City, N.Y.: Doubleday, 1965.

30. ——. 1957. "The Theory of Meaning." In *Philosophy and Ordinary Language*, ed. Charles E. Caton, pp. 128–53. Urbana: University of Illinois Press, 1963.

31. Searle, John R. 1958. "Proper Names." *Mind* 67: 166–73.

32. ——. 1969. "The Problem of Proper Names." In *Semantics—An Interdisciplinary Reader in Philosophy, Linguistics, and Psychology*, eds. Danny D. Steinberg and Leon A. Jakobovits, pp. 134–41. Cambridge: At the University Press, 1971.

33. Shwayder, D. S. 1963. *Modes of Referring and the Problem of Universals: An Essay in Metaphysics*. University of California publications in Philosophy, no. 35. Berkeley: University of California Press.

34. Smith, Elsdon C. 1956. *Dictionary of American Family Names*. New York: Harper.

35. Sørensen, Holger Steen. 1963. *The Meaning of Proper Names*. Copenhagen: Gad.

36. Strawson, P. F. 1950. "On Referring." In *Philosophy and Ordinary Language*, ed. Charles E. Caton, pp. 162–93. Urbana: University of Illinois Press.

37. Ullman, S. 1952. Review of *Theory of Proper Names*, by Alan Gardiner. *Archivum Linguisticum* 4: 66–67.

38. Waismann, F. 1965. *The Principles of Linguistic Philosophy*, ed. R. Harré. New York: St. Martin.

39. Walker, John. 1818. *A Key to the Classical Pronunciation of Greek, Latin, and Scriptural Proper Names*. New York: Collins and Hannay.

40. Withycombe, E. G. 1950. *The Oxford Dictionary of English Christian Names*. Oxford: Clarendon.

41. Zabeeh, Farhang. 1968. *What is in a Name? An Inquiry into the Semantics and Pragmatics of Proper Names*. The Hague: Nijhoff.

42. Zink, Sidney. 1963. "The Meaning of Proper Names." *Mind* 72: 481–99.

DISCUSSION QUESTIONS

1. How is a citation form different from an appellative? When and how do you use citation forms in your own communication?

2. How does your dictionary treat proper names?

3. Would you agree that personal names are more interesting than place names? Do you know family names that bear an overtone of appellative meaning no longer applicable?

4. What kinds of meaning are conveyed by the names of rock bands, athletic teams, and military units such as the Green Berets and the Black Watch?

5. Discuss the possibility of a human society without proper names.

PART IX

LINGUISTICS AND LITERATURE

Although the application of linguistics to the study of literature may seem a recent development, actually the relationship is old and honorable. Because language is the vehicle by which literature is transmitted and because most of the older forms of language are preserved chiefly in literary texts, the same scholars studied both the language and the text. Their discipline was known as philology. Classical philologists studied the languages and literature of ancient Greece and Rome. Romance philologists studied the older literature and languages of France and Italy. English philologists studied the language and literature of the Anglo-Saxons and of Wyclif and Chaucer.

Two developments gradually weakened that close relationship. One was the introduction of modern and, later, even contemporary literature into universities as a legitimate field of study; the other was the development of concern with and research in synchronic linguistics dealing with lesser known and exotic languages as well as, somewhat later, the familiar European lanuages. Particularly did the growth of structuralism provide an academic direction in departments of English that somehow seemed almost alien to the interests and values sustained by teachers of literature.

Yet during the structural period from the 1920s to the 1960s there were linguists who sought to maintain and even strengthen the tie between literature and linguistics, between literary study and language study. Foremost among these linguists has been Archibald Hill, who with Harold Whitehall held an important language and literature seminar at Indiana University in 1953. Indeed, except for his climactic *Introduction to Linguistic Structures: From Sound to Sentence in English* (Harcourt, 1958), nearly all of Hill's scholarly publications have been devoted to demonstrating the relevance of linguistics to the study and interpretation of literature.

The rise of transformational-generative grammar in the 1960s opened a new and wider door through which to approach literary materials. Although Chomsky himself did not engage in literary criticism or analysis, he provided a dynamic theory that his followers have significantly applied in the analysis of metrics by means of generative phonology, in the analysis of meaning through tracing surface structure to deep structure, and in the analysis of imagery by examining levels of grammaticality.

The three selections in this anthology illustrate two linguistic approaches to literature. In the first, Hill describes the general position of the structuralist when he looks at a literary document. Like certain literary critics, he holds that to appreciate a poem one must have at least some knowledge of the culture in which it was written. He demonstrates as well how the structuralist studies analogy in order to enhance enjoyment of a poem.

The next two articles draw upon the theory of generative grammar. Paul Kiparsky speculates that many of the traditional and arbitrary conventions of literature are anchored in grammatical form and are the result of how language itself is structured. He says that the linguistic "sames" that are relevant to poetry are also the ones that are significant in grammar. Then Richard Ohmann depicts the examination of the relationship between deep structure and surface structure, a relationship that clarifies the distinction between form and content.

Some additional references are as follows:

Chatman, Seymour, and Samuel Levin. *Essays on the Language of Literature*. New York: Houghton Mifflin, 1967.

Freeman, Donald C. *Linguistics and Literary Style*. New York: Holt, Rinehart and Winston, 1970.

Jakobson, Roman. "Linguistics and Poetics." In *Selected Writings of Roman Jakobson*, Vol. V. The Hague: Mouton, 1971.

Love, Glen A., and Michael Payne. *Contemporary Essays on Style: Rhetoric, Linguistics, and Criticism*. Glenview, Ill.: Scott, Foresman, 1969.

Traugott, Elizabeth Closs, and Mary Louise Pratt. *Linguistics for Students of Literature*. New York: Harcourt Brace Jovanovich, 1980.

ARCHIBALD A. HILL

See the headnote on p. 490.

POETRY AND STYLISTICS

All the world knows that poetry is to be enjoyed and that enjoyment is its sole reason for being. When no one enjoys a poem, it is promptly forgotten. I have no wish to disagree with such a set of self-evident truisms. I wish instead to point out that, true as such statements may be, they are not the whole truth about poetry and that to assume that they are the whole truth not only makes us misunderstand the nature and function of poetry but also blinds us to much of the beauty of poetry and dulls us to its enjoyment.

For one thing, if all that matters about poetry is the enjoyment and if enjoyment is its only measure, we are immediately faced with a question—whose enjoyment? We live now in a splintered kind of society in which each one of us must choose between a myriad of competing groups—we can be Republicans or Democrats; Episcopalians, Baptists, Catholics, or Mormons; scientists, businessmen, soldiers, or technicians. It is less and less possible for any one man to embrace the experience of more than a few of these competing groups. The result is that the broad base of shared experience—the property of the whole community—which was the foundation of truly national poetry like the Homeric epics, is no longer characteristic of our society. Poetry speaks, not to the whole community, but to this or that splinter of it at a time. We have western poets, eastern poets, English poets, American poets, religious poets, antireligious poets, intellectual poets, and antiintellectual poets. We even have groups who are antipoetic and believe that all poets and all who enjoy poetry belong to a splinter group. We have no poets and no poetry that can speak clearly and without necessary interpretation to all speakers of English as Homer spoke to all the Hellenes.

If poetry is thus no longer an art with the wide and unquestioned appeal it had in the days of scops and troubadours, the critic and the teacher of literature find themselves in an uncomfortable position. Neither can any longer say without fear of contradiction that every speaker of English enjoys this poem deeply and that, therefore, it is great. Nor can they measure a poem by the permanence of its appeal since many readers reject older literature as hard to understand. The differentiation that has splintered our contemporary literature has cut literature off from the past as well. We cannot, certainly, assume that young people are automatically equipped to read the poetry of Wyatt and Surrey. To read the poetry of Wyatt and Surrey it is as necessary to study it as it is to study any poetry from a community different from our own—it is always necessary to know the code before we can get the message. Those who have faced the task of teaching poetry in contemporary America sooner or later begin to ask themselves embarrassing questions about who enjoys the various kinds of poetry they teach. T. S. Eliot appeals to sophisticates; Joyce Kilmer, to Babbitts. Perhaps there is an easy answer for those who know which group is more valuable to our society and which group should, therefore, be the arbiter of taste. Yet many teachers will admit that we cannot judge between groups in any high-handed and authoritarian fashion and that we cannot even take the judgments handed down to us from a time when our society was less complex and the poetically excellent was simply defined as what an English gentleman would like.

It would seem that, if we who study poetry are to be able to talk about it to others than the members of our various tiny groups, we should find some other approach than pure enjoyment. We should find, or create, an approach that takes as its aim a secure and demonstrable increase of understanding. Some say that such an approach is impossible without sacrifice of the enjoyment that all agree is the basis of poetry, as it is of all art. To say so is to give a counsel of despair. A more hopeful belief is that understanding is a good in itself and that understanding need not be in conflict with other things that are good. It is not an unreasonable position to say that all things in the world of man and nature can be studied by the human intelligence. True, we shall never reach complete understanding of anything in the world of man and nature. If we should say that it is therefore useless to strive for comprehension, we would abdicate our heritage. Or if we should say that poetry belongs in a world that transcends intelligence and, so, is something that we cannot know, we are confusing the world of man—since poets are men—with the world beyond the world of men, which, indeed, we cannot know.

In this essay I shall once more try to give an approach that is based on understanding and that studies the poem itself, not what kind of readers should enjoy it or how much. I hope, moreover, that such an approach not only may not reduce enjoyment but even increase it and enrich it. Also, as I have often said, what I shall say is in the nature of a hypothesis, delivered with the reservation that, when more is known, what I say now may seem naïve or positively wrong.

I shall begin with a mapping of the field of literary study in relation to a similar map for the field of linguistic study. I have in two of the essays (the analyses of *Pippa's Song* and *The Windhover*) referred briefly to these maps, but it is my intention now to give them in full detail. In mapping the area of linguistics, structural linguists often use the figure of three levels;[1] the lowest and the highest are outside language proper, but each has connections with it. The middle area is that of language per se, within which falls all that we know of its structure. The lowest level is that of the material from which talk is made, that is, sounds and articulations. On this level, sounds are without language function and are mere noises. To use an example described by Edward Sapir a generation ago, we may make nearly the same noise in blowing out a candle as in giving the initial sound of the word *when*.[2] A student of the lowest level of communication, like a sound spectrograph, could describe exactly the physical properties of the sound, but, like the sound spectrograph, he would not know whether the sound was used in the word or in blowing out the candle.

At the highest level, on the other hand, is the nonlinguistic world of objects, actions, states, and relationships. When we establish a correspondence between items of language and something in the real world, we have established meaning—the kind of meaning we can call correspondence meaning. This kind of meaning is what we are most conscious of and which is most important to us.

The area of language proper, which is a sort of island between sounds and articulations on the one hand and meanings on the other, has four sublevels. The first three are fairly obvious. They are, first, the level of patterned and functioning sounds,

---

[1] The formulation given here is based on George L. Trager's paper "The Field of Linguistics." *Studies in Linguistics*. Occasional Paper 1 (1949).
[2] Edward Sapir, "Sound Patterns in Language." *Language* 1 (1925): 37–38.

or phonology; second, the level of patterned and functioning word-elements, or morphology, the product of which is the word as it appears in isolation; and, third, the level of syntax, the patterning and functioning of words in relation to each other, the product of which is the sentence, again as it appears in isolation. In describing the fourth and last of the sublevels, however, I am departing at least slightly from earlier formulations. The fourth level is that of sentences in relation to each other, the product of which is the structure of discourse. It is characteristic of this level that the structures which comprise it spread, much of the time, over more than one sentence, though it is also true that they may, on occasion, appear within a single sentence.

I have said that the most important kind of meaning is that which I have called correspondence meaning. Another kind of meaning, however, appears on all the levels of the area of language proper and underlies the area of correspondence meaning. This is the kind of meaning that can be described as the quality of partial predictability. That is, if I should use a nonsense word, it would be meaningless because it is outside the system of my language. Being outside the system, it would be impossible for a hearer to predict that I was going to use it. On the other hand, if I should always clear my throat at the end of every sentence, my hearers would soon know exactly when I was going to clear my throat, since they would know, without listening for the throat clearing, that a sentence was ending. In such circumstances, the throat clearing would be totally predictable and, once again, meaningless. Whatever occurs with total and predictable regularity can be disregarded since it can carry no new information.

As for the partial predictability of language items, I can illustrate hurriedly by pointing out that no English word or sentence begins with the sound which is final in *sing*. If we happen to turn on a radio in the middle of a sentence and happen to hear the final sound of *sing* without anything preceding it, we automatically guess that something is ending, not that something is beginning. On the level of words, if we hear the definite article *the*, we again guess, this time that the next word may be a noun or adjective but is not going to be a verb or pronoun. And, finally, on the level of sentence relationships, if we hear "The book is in English," we guess that this particular book has been mentioned in a previous sentence. As for partial predictability in relation to correspondence meaning, note that, if we hear "There's a rabbit in the garden," we expect to be able to check the statement by finding the creature, though we recognize that the statement might be mistaken. If, on the other hand, we hear "There's a hippogriff in the garden," our attempts at checking will be in vain. The act of prediction, being based on an only partial quality, has failed us.

I can now bring this to bear on poetry at last. First, poetic structure is like language structure in being something that can be mapped in terms of levels. Many critics have said that literature may be like language but is somehow more than language and different from it. I believe that such statements are explainable in terms of the diagram that I am describing. As for the likeness, literature can also be described as having three levels. The lower level is not literature but is the material out of which literature is made, as language is made of sounds. Literature has a middle area, which is the area of literary structure and all that we know about it, and it has an upper area, in which the items and, even more, the structures of literature correspond with something on the outside, thus setting up once more the phenomenon of correspondence meaning.

The way in which this map of literary structure differs from the map of language is that the two are not perfectly parallel. What goes into the nonliterary lower level is most of the area of language structure. That is, the material of which literature is made is the sum total of phonology, morphology, and syntax. And it is extremely important to state emphatically that these things are not literature in themselves. The area of the level immediately below language, on the other hand, it totally irrelevant to literature. As the critic W. K. Wimsatt once remarked, the number of vibrations per second in the vowel /æ/ has nothing to do with the way in which *gentleman* is made meaningful in John Ball's couplet

> When Adam delved and Eve span
> Who was then a gentleman?[3]

One of the reasons linguists have suffered justified attacks in the past is that we have often assumed that vowel and consonant counting is the way to show that linguistics is relevant to literature.

I have said that the area of language and its structure is the lowest level for the literary student. In general, the statement is obvious. We all know that it is well to understand the grammar and vocabulary of a poem before we begin to dogmatize about it. We have all had students, for instance, who did not know that in Shakespeare's song about *Fancie,* the word means the first stage of love rather than an image in the mind, or the like.[4] Similarly we have all corrected students who suppose that Portia is personifying the candle by her use of *his* in the line "How farre that little candell throwes his beames,"[5] since the pronoun is no more than the Elizabethan equivalent of *its*. Unfortunately, however, critics are often less knowledgeable about the way in which pitch and stress have a bearing on meaning. Still sticking to Shakespeare, I remember correcting a student who was reading aloud from *Othello,* and who read the messenger's line in the first act, "The *Ottamites,* Reueren'd, and Gracious,"[6] without the proper comma intonation, making it mean "The Ottamites [who are] Reueren'd and Gracious," instead of the vocative form addressed to the Duke.

The central area of literary structure falls on the uppermost area of language—the area of sentences and their relations to each other—within the totality of the poem or discourse. A convenient name for this area is style, meaning by that the area of sentence-syntax. I am aware of the many other definitions of style, and I do not wish to quarrel with them. Style and the study of it, stylistics, are convenient designations for an important area, and I shall continue to use them, as I have said. The content of this stylistic area is clearly the area in which many, if not all, literary devices fall. For instance, rhyme and meter extend over the whole of a poem, no matter how many sentences it may contain. Also, it is a truism that much of style consists in congruent selection of vocabulary, as when Henry James is supposed to have said, "If the handle is depressed, egress will be facilitated." The sentence is isolated, it is true, but it is nearly certain that any other sentences in the same discourse would have had vocabulary congruent with what is here.

---

[3] W. K. Wimsatt was refuting a book which maintained that the explanation of rhyme was essentially acoustic ("One Relation of Rhyme to Reason," in *The Verbal Icon* [Lexington: University of Kentucky Press, 1954], p. 166). The fact that I do not agree with Wimsatt's own explanation of rhyme does not detract from the fact that the remark quoted is most acute.

[4] See "Toward a Literary Analysis," chap. 2, where the song is analyzed in detail.

[5] *The Merchant of Venice*, act 5, sc. 1, line 90.

[6] *Othello,* act 1, sc. 3, line 33.

Note how very different the quoted sentence is from another that contains the same information but a very different vocabulary: "Shove the handle down to get out."

I shall not divide the area of literary structure with extreme minuteness, since this is a familiar field. However, it certainly contains at least three major sublevels, one being a phonological area more important to poetry than to prose but by no means lacking in prose. Here belong the structures of rhyme, meter, alliteration, assonance, and the like. The second sublevel is that of congruence in vocabulary, as in the supposed Jamesian sentence quoted above. The third area is a statable total pattern most clearly seen in poetry but also found in prose. By this I mean the kind of patterning that may be analogical or even allegorical or merely a pattern that has recognizable symmetry, as when Edgar Allan Poe in the poem *To Helen* says Helen calls the wanderer, first, to ancient Greece, then to ancient Rome, and that these taken together make "Holy Land."[7]

When we pass to the uppermost level, literature characteristically shows more sublevels than does ordinary language. There we find the simple correspondence level of information, real or fictitious. Thus the statement that Kubla Khan built a palace has simple correspondence meaning. There is also a second level, that of correspondence between the total structure of the poem and the outside nonliterary world. *Kubla Khan* has a correspondence of the total structure with the dream world that Coleridge conjured up. The song *Tell me where is fancie bred* has a total structural meaning corresponding to the philosophical structure of Elizabethan love lore. And, of course, allegorical works like *Pilgrim's Progress* or *In the Penal Colony* show this total structural correspondence meaning minutely elaborated. The final level of meaning is that which is most peculiarly proper to literature and the presentation of which is the most important purpose of literary art. This is the level of correspondence with cultural values.

It should not be thought that these levels are necessarily absent in ordinary uses of language, though it is clear that, in a simple sentence like "It's going to rain today," only simple correspondence meaning is present. Also, the level of style is essentially absent in such a sentence, which characteristically is apt to be isolated and not a part of a unified discourse. In a set of directions for using a mechanical tool, however, clear stylistic structures are apt to be found, and, certainly, in a culture like our own, which is strongly mechanical in orientation, a good portion of cultural values are found as well. Yet, characteristically, the several levels of meaning are central to literature and therefore strongly elaborated. In ordinary language they may be absent or rudimentary. The levels of language and literature can now be mapped as shown in table 1.

This long description of the relation of literature and language can be concluded by pointing out that the kind of meaning that consists of partial predictability of occurrence also occurs in the various levels of literature just as it does in language. Thus the phonological structures of poetry show recurrence and are thus partially predictable. The occurrence of "June" in the tenth syllable, to give a hackneyed example, predicts that the twentieth syllable will be "moon," or the like—at any rate that the sound sequence /-uwn/ will recur. But I should wish to be emphatic in stating that the phonological

---

[7] In a previous article I gave a brief analysis of the last verse of this poem. There I pointed to the lines "Ah, Psyche, from the regions which/are Holy Land!" So far from being unskillful because the rhyme falls on a word which is ordinarily unstressed, the penultimate line seems to me the climax of the poem. The pattern of full stress on the relative, followed by pause, is one used in speech for emphasis and is so eminently proper for the keystone of Poe's tripartite arch of Greece, Rome, and the Holy Land.

Table 1 Levels of language and literature

Level	Language	Literature	Level
Uppermost nonlanguage	Correspondence meaning	Cultural values Structural and analogical meaning Correspondence meaning	Uppermost most nonliterary
Language proper	Structure and function of sentences, discourse structure or style	Content structures of literature Phonological structures of literature (rhyme, meter, etc.)	Literature proper
	Structure and function of words, syntax Structure and function of meaningful elements, morphology Structure and function of sounds, phonology	Language as material of literature	Lowest nonliterary
Lowest nonlanguage	Articulations and sounds	Irrelevant	

structures do not have imitative value except very briefly and relatively unimportantly and are thus devoid of any kind of correspondence meaning.[8]

For the content structures of literature, note that congruity of vocabulary occurs over the whole of the discourse and strongly influences the occurrence of individual words. Similarly, the occurrence of a type of construction, such as the balanced sentences of Edward Gibbon, influences the type of sentence structure just as congruity of vocabulary influences the occurrence of words.

Poetry, more than any other kind of literature, heightens and exploits stylistic structures and devices. Rhyme and meter are phonological devices and structures spreading over the whole of the poem. Poetic diction is a special stylistic type of lexicon, and the figures and images of poetry are stylistic devices of content, in which we rightly feel that the real heart of the poem often lies. This stylistic heightening makes possible an aim that the poet almost always holds—he tries to transcend the linguistic meanings by giving stylistic structures which change them and add to them so that the whole of the poem has meaning, which would escape us if we considered only its parts.

One of the ways in which modern poetry—that kind where *modern* might almost be in quotation marks—differs from traditional poetry is that the poet often says something that would be quite ungrammatical on the linguistic level, hoping that it will become meaningful on the stylistic level. Thus, E. E. Cummings wrote "anyone lived in a pretty how town."[9] As ordinary English, the line does not make sense. Yet, as we read the

---

[8] I have elsewhere fully expressed my skepticism on onomatopoeia; see "Sound Symbolism in Lexicon and Literature," in *Studies in Linguistics in Honor of George L. Trager*, ed. M. Estellie Smith (The Hague: Mouton, 1973), pp. 142–147.

[9] For further discussion, see "Some Points in the Analysis of Keats's *Ode on a Grecian Urn*," chap. 10.

poem as a whole, the general stylistic structure enables us to translate it approximately as "an ordinary man lived in an ordinary, pretty kind of town." Cummings has played a sort of game of linguistics against stylistics; yet the game is not so different from the ordinary procedure of the poet; its strangeness consists only in that he adopts the linguistically unpredictable deliberately.

In bringing this fairly extensive discussion of theory to bear on two individual poems, I shall confine myself to the use that the poems make of a single stylistic device. The device is analogy. Nothing is new in saying that poets make use of analogies; the familiar terms *metaphor* and *simile* describe two main types of them. What I shall try to show is that development of analogy is the device by which the poet gives stylistic unity to his poem and makes it meaningful in ways beyond the meaning of sober everyday sentences. We shall see that the device is characteristic of poetry and that it may lead to stylistic meanings almost as much in conflict with linguistic ones as were the stylistic and linguistic meanings in the line from Cummings.

Our first poem is this from Carl Sandburg:

Desolate and lone
All night long on the lake
Where fog trails and mist creeps,
The whistle of a boat
Calls and cries unendingly,
Like some lost child
In tears and trouble
Hunting the harbour's breast
And the harbour's eyes.[10]

The poem obviously offers no very great difficulty in understanding. The whistle of a boat reminds the poet of a lost child crying, and that seems clear enough. The analogy is overt, since the poet tells us flatly "like some lost child." Yet the simple overall structure is not quite all that is here since the separate parts of the two halves of the analogy are brought into a more detailed relationship with each other. The whistle is to the boat on the lake as sobs are to the child away from its mother. The phrase "the harbour's breast" gives us a compressed subanalogy—breast is to mother as X is to harbor. Note that we are left to supply the identity of the missing X—one of the two places in the poem where we meet such an implicit analogy. The X is not hard to supply; in this case it is the mooring at which the boat comes to rest. The second X, of course, is in the compressed phrase "harbour's eyes," where eyes are to mother as X is to the harbor—evidently the harbor's lights.[11]

Sandburg's little poem is obviously a simple one. If it has interest, it must somehow be in the analogies around which it is built. We can point to a number of ways in which these analogies are interesting. The first one is of no great literary importance, though

---

[10] Carl Sandburg, "Chicago Poems," in *Selected Poems of Carl Sandburg*, ed. Rebecca West (New York: Harcourt, Brace & Co., 1926), p. 31, no. 2.

[11] The analogy in "harbour's eyes" is not perfectly successful. The infant may search for the mother's breast, arms, or lap but scarcely for the mother's eyes. These are the instruments of the mother's search, rather than the goal of the infant's desire. I have not mentioned this defect in the body of the essay, since it seems irrelevant to a discussion of the manner in which analogies contribute to the total meaning of the poem.

of interest to us in this kind of study. By throwing together items that belong to the two halves of his analogy—*eyes*, which belongs with the child-mother half, and *harbour*, which belongs with the boat-harbor half—Sandburg gives us a phrase that is compressed— "harbour's eyes"—and leaves one term in his proportional analogy as an unsolved *X*, which the reader must supply. The reader can be relied on to solve it since the structure of the analogy forces the solution. This sort of unsolved *X* is one of the principal ways in which an analogy is made to say something that is there stylistically but linguistically not present at all.

Second, the poem starts with a simple comparison. Probably none of us has failed to respond to the loneliness of a train or boat whistle at night. The ascription of human emotional value to such a sound is a commonplace and might be considered one of the tritest comparisons a poet could make. It is the points of correspondence, as the single general analogy is worked out in a series of linked subanalogies, that give the poem structure, unity, and some sense of originality. Further, as by now we might expect of a poetic structure, it suggests correspondence with the nonliterary world of cultural values—we can extrapolate from literary structure to a structure of meanings. For me, at least, the lost boat, compared to a child who has lost the security of his mother's breast, suggests an identification with the society we live in. We, too, are lost and long to return to a simpler society in the childhood of the world. The Sandburg poem is simple, indeed, but the stylistic structure is certainly more meaningful than would be the linguistic statement—that boat sounds like a lost child.

The second poem is different from the first because it has been so institutionalized that we accept it, without thinking about it or really reading it, as merely a part of our traditions. Also, it can be read and valued highly without working out the analogies it contains; it can give, indeed, the impression of being completely understood with no analysis at all. The analogies must therefore, if study of them is to be justified, modify or increase the understanding of the poem enough to make their exposition worth the effort and must not spoil our appreciation of the poem.

COMPOSED UPON WESTMINSTER BRIDGE, SEPTEMBER 3, 1802

Earth has not anything to show more fair;
Dull would he be of soul who could pass by
A sight so touching in its majesty:
This City now doth, like a garment, wear
The beauty of the morning; silent, bare,
Ships, towers, domes, theatres, and temples lie
Open unto the fields, and to the sky;
All bright and glittering in the smokeless air.
Never did sun more beautifully steep
In his first splendour, valley, rock, or hill;
Ne'er saw I, never felt, a calm so deep!
The river glideth at his own sweet will:
Dear God! the very houses seem asleep;
And all that mighty heart is lying still![12]

---

[12] William Wordsworth. *The Complete Poetical Works of William Wordsworth*, ed. John Morley (London: Macmillan & Co., 1898), p. 178.

I do not need to comment on the surface meaning of the poem. All of us recognize that Wordsworth saw the city in unwonted beauty and was moved by it with a religious emotion. All of us can share the emotion. Let us see how study changes our emotion and whether study enriches it.

We can pass over the first three lines as not relevant to our purposes; they contain no important analogies. The first analogy is in the fourth and fifth lines

> This City now doth, like a garment, wear
> The beauty of the morning;

That is, beauty of the morning is to the city as garment is to X. Only human beings—normally, at least—wear garments. The city is, then, like a human being. The garments are next described:

> . . . silent, bare,
> Ships, towers, domes, theatres, and temples lie
> Open unto the fields, and to the sky;

The garment is not like a suit of clothes or an overcoat. It is such as to reveal the city and its structures. We can express all this by an analogy that builds on the first one: The city wears a garment that reveals its structures as a human being of X type wears a garment that reveals its body. The garment that thus reveals beauty is not the sort of garment we talk about as worn by men or children. It is like the garment of a beautiful woman, and the city is not merely like a human being but like a woman.

The city-woman, further, lies in a calm and beautiful morning sleep. As well as the city and its parts, another set of entities can be found in the poem. The entities are fields, sky, and river. They can easily be grouped as belonging to the non-man-made nature, opposed in principle to the man-made city. A very common attitude in our literature is the idea that God made the country, but man made the town—true or not, we all know the attitude. Yet the relation given here of these representatives of nature is not one of conflict with the city. The city-woman and its structures "lie/Open unto the fields, and to the sky;" and below, "The river glideth at his own sweet will." The analogy can be constructed thus: Nature is to city as X is to woman. I submit, therefore, that language and situation in this poem lead to the conclusion that the final missing X is lover and that nature and city are compared to man and woman in the sleep of lovers.

I am aware enough that these analogies, thus made overt, might be thought of as shocking. Yet, they need not be and should not be. A further statement in the poem throws light on how we are to view the comparison ". . . sun . . . / In his first splendour." One way of reading this phrase would be to take it as a reference merely to the first light of this particular September 3. But throughout the poem we find hints that the scene is touched by a lost beauty—the air is smokeless, for instance, though presumably Wordsworth's negative statement implies that it was not often so. Wordsworth uses *temples* instead of the more prosaic and realistic *churches* as if he were suggesting a past more beautiful than the usual present.[13] For these reasons, I believe that "first splendour" refers

---

[13] Professor Yalden Thompson of the University of Virginia pointed out to me—when this paper was read there—that I might well be wrong in interpreting "temples" as churches, since the Inner and Middle Temples of law are visible from Westminster Bridge. I am uncertain about the matter, but the general context still suggests to me an ancient rather than a contemporary interpretation. The point, of course, is not crucial to the total interpretation.

to the dawn of the world rather than to the dawn of September 3. City and nature are as lovers but lovers with an innocence and beauty lost since Eden.[14]

I do not think I need to carry the central city-woman analogy much further into the realm of correspondences and cultural values. It is enough to say that man and nature are reconciled, released, and united as a man and woman are in love. Wordsworth did not often talk so of the works of man, and I think we can agree that he is a greater poet for the vision of a reconciliation, which he grasped that morning on the bridge. The analogies are, I believe, the central structure of the poem—they are the way in which the larger unity of style is made to transcend the limitations of the linguistic statements. Wordsworth's success could not be achieved without them, I feel sure. His success, in turn, is a revealing example of the way in which poetry is language, yet more than language and different from it.

DISCUSSION QUESTIONS

1. Do you agree with the two premises that poetry is to be enjoyed and that we can enjoy it more fully if we study it?

2. Explain what Hill means by correspondence meaning. How does it differ in literature, particularly poetry, from its use in everyday language?

3. Why is partial predictability of interpretation so important to the realm of meaning?

4. How does each of the two poems that Hill analyzes demonstrate that stylistic structure is more meaningful than linguistic structure? Why is analogy significant for stylistic structure?

---

[14] The interpretation of the sonnet here given was worked out without attention to the biographical background of composition. I have been reminded by my friend and colleague of many years' standing, Martin Joos, that Wordsworth has told us that the poem was written as he was at the beginning of a happy journey to the Continent, and we know that it was written rather shortly before his marriage. The exhilaration of the journey and the impending marriage account for the exalted mood of the poem, in which Wordsworth reveals a great deal of his feelings, perhaps more than he knew or would have wished.

PAUL KIPARSKY

A *Helsinki native, Kiparsky acquired a background in European historical linguistics before completing his graduate work at the University of Minnesota and the Massachusetts Institute of Technology. He has remained at M.I.T. as professor of linguistics. His specialties have been phonology, historical linguistics, and the relationship between linguistics and literature. He has been a fellow at the Centre for Advanced Study in Sanskrit, University of Poona, India.*

THE ROLE OF LINGUISTICS IN A THEORY OF POETRY

Of all art forms, literature, and especially poetry, has the greatest continuity of form in the Western tradition.[1] Since classical antiquity, the visual arts and music have been changed profoundly through the introduction of entirely new forms of expression and organization. Consider, for example, how painting was changed in the Renaissance by the discovery of perspective, or how music was changed by the development of chordal harmony. It is impossible, however, to point to any such spectacular enrichments of technique in poetry. Styles and conventions have shifted, but no truly new forms have emerged. Both of the fundamental stylistic elements of poetry—figurative expression, using, for example, metaphor and metonymy, and schemes of formal organization such as those of parallelism, meter, rhyme, and alliteration—have existed from the beginning.

It is true that their relative importance changes all the time. In particular, the rules governing what must, may, and cannot be obligatory in a piece of verse vary from one age to the next. For example, alliteration was obligatory in Old English poetry a thousand years ago, but cannot be obligatory today, and rhyme, which was never an obligatory formal element in Old English, can and in certain forms of verse must be used now. Many such seemingly radical changes in poetic form are actually more or less automatic responses to linguistic change. Alliteration, for example, seems to be found as an obligatory formal element only in languages where the stress regularly falls on the same syllable in the word, which then must be the alliterating syllable. Old English was such a language, for the stress fell predictably on the root syllable. In modern English, on the other hand, words with the same root can be stressed in many different places (take, for example, *ób li gate, ob líg a tor y,* and *ob li gá tion*). When this kind of stress system was established in English, verse forms with fixed alliteration were abandoned. The rhymed verse forms which took their place were made possible, or at least more natural, by the evolution of English, specifically by the fact that English lost most of its inflectional endings. Most richly inflected languages do not use rhyme, and those that do, like Russian, tend to avoid rhymes that depend on grammatical endings.

When a particular element ceases to be obligatory, it remains as an optional element in the poetic repertoire of a language. In fact, optional elements of form in a poem are

---

[1] This work was supported in part by grants from the National Institutes of Health (5 TO1 HD00111) and the National Institute of Mental Health (2 PO1 MH13390).

more significant than obligatory elements, precisely because the poet has chosen to use them. In plain rhymed verse, a pair of rhyming words may or may not be related in meaning.[2] Where rhyme is not obligatory, on the other hand, those words which do rhyme are almost always significantly related, as they are, for example, in the internal rhyme in Hopkins' line.

And all is seared with trade; bleared, smeared with toil. . . .

Similarly, compare the obligatory and therefore only potentially meaningful repetition of lines in refrains or blues verses, with the free and therefore necessarily significant repetition of the line, in Frost's "Stopping by Woods,"

And miles to go before I sleep.

In obligatory formulaic parallelism, like that found in the Finnish *Kalevala,* the parallel lines may contrast with or complement each other, but they may also be little more than paraphrases. But where parallelism is used as a free feature, it is always essential to the meaning, as in George Starbuck's "Of Late."

"Stephen Smith, University of Iowa sophomore, burned what he said
    was his draft card"
and Norman Morrison, Quaker, of Baltimore Maryland, burned what
    he said was himself.
You, Robert McNamara, burned what you said was a concentration
of the Enemy Aggressor.
No news medium troubled to put it in quotes.

As a further example, consider Starbuck's use of rhythm. Because he has not tied himself down to a fixed meter, he can use rhythmic variation to reinforce his meaning. The slow regular dactylic rhythm of the second line breaks down completely when McNamara's lies are cited in the third and fourth lines. The changed rhythm also contributes to the sense by directing an accusing stress onto the second "you" in the line,

You, Robert McNamara, burned what you said was a concentration
of the Enemy Aggressor.

In such ways, "free verse" actually frees verse schemas for significant use; hence it can be a more difficult and a more expressive poetic form than regulated verse.

Perhaps our first impulse is to attribute the fact that the forms of poetic expression have not changed much to the sheer weight of the Western literary tradition. However, there are several reasons for believing that we must attribute it, at least in part, to the intrinsic nature of verbal art. In the first place, from the available information it appears that all literary traditions, including those of primitive societies in many of which oral poetry plays an important role, utilize the same elements of form as Western poetry, and no exotically different ones. In fact it is not clear that there is any such thing as "primitive literature." Furthermore, many of the changes in poetic form, at least in the last 200 years, have been conscious innovations made by poets deliberately breaking with tradition. Yet even this conscious search for new forms has left the basic elements of expression

---

[2] On the potential semantic function of rhyme, see W. K. Wimsatt, *The Verbal Icon* (Lexington, Ky.: Kentucky University Press, 1954).

essentially unchanged. Certain schemas have gone from obligatory to free or vice versa, and the grammar of poetic language has changed, for example, in its treatment of inversions. The reason, as I will try to show here, is that a good number of what we think of as traditional and arbitrary conventions are anchored in grammatical form, and seem to be, at bottom, a consequence of how language itself is structured.

The *theory of literature* usually concerns itself with classifying, analyzing, and comparing forms of verbal art which do, in fact, exist. But one could ask what characterizes existing forms of verbal art that differentiates them from forms which have never actually come into existence. Could we develop, in other words, a counterpart in the theory of literature to universal grammar in linguistics?[3] Although certain limits are implicit in traditional esthetics and rhetoric, neither poets nor students of literature have thought much about the intrinsic limits of poetry, any more than football players or spectators think much about gravity. The limits of poetic form are simply psychological givens, just as gravity is a physical given. In trying to define them we will have to make the effort, required wherever man studies his own nature, of not taking the "natural" for granted.

Our starting point will be the observation that various aspects of form all involve some kind of recurrence of equivalent linguistic elements.[4] They differ only in what linguistic element is repeated. Recurrence of *syntactic* elements is called *parallelism;* recurrence of *stress* and *quantity* (and, in some languages, *tone*), is called *meter;* and various kinds of recurrence of *vocalic* and *consonantal* sounds are called *rhyme, alliteration, assonance,* or *consonance.*

We can therefore conceive of poetic form in terms of certain *patterns,* such as *aa, aab, abab,* which are filled by *linguistic* (syntactic and phonological) *elements.* A pattern which is filled in a particular way may be termed a *schema.* A given pattern therefore underlies many potential schemas. For example, *abab* is a *rhyme schema* if *a* and *b* are units which are phonological sames of the kind we commonly called rhyme. If they are units of stress or quantity it is a *metrical schema.* For example, if *a* is an unstressed syllable, and *b* is a stressed syllable, the pattern *abab* represents iambic dimeter.[5] The same pattern, *abab,* can also be a *schema of syntactic parallelism,* such as that found in the first verse of Shelley's "Song to the Men of England."

> Men of England, wherefore plow
> For the lords who lay ye low?
> Wherefore weave with toil and care
> The rich robes your tyrants wear?

---

[3] An initial attempt, modeled on linguistic theory, is Manfred Bierwisch, "Poetics and Linguistics," *Linguistics and Literary Style,* ed. D. Freeman (New York: Holt, Rinehart & Winston, 1968).

[4] This is expressed in Roman Jakobson's famous statement: "The poetic function projects the principle of equivalence from the axis of selection into the axis of combination." "Linguistics and Poetics," *Style in Language,* ed. T. Sebeok (Cambridge, Mass.: M.I.T. Press, 1960).

Note the caesurae (obligatory clause boundaries at a certain point of the line) could be considered either as patterned recurrence of sentence boundaries, or perhaps better as a form of parallelism at the level of sentences. Enjambment may be considered simply as absence of "caesura" at the end of a line.

[5] The distinction between the abstract pattern and its linguistic implementation in the domain of meter has been drawn particularly clearly by Morris Halle and S. J. Keyser, "Chaucer and the Study of Prosody," *Linguistics and Literary Style.*

Understanding this distinction between the abstract pattern and the linguistic sames that are used to fill it will help us to approach in a more precise way the question of the intrinsic limits of poetic form.

The range of patterns in actual poetic use is small. Surprisingly enough, certain patterns of considerable formal simplicity are never utilized in the construction of verse. For example, one rarely encounters patterns which call for repeating sequences of more than three elements. The pattern *abcdabcd*, for example, is rarely used either as a rhyme schema, or as a pattern of parallelism. The choice of pattern, of course, depends in some measure on what sort of linguistic element is to fill it. For example, the pattern *abcabc* is common in short-term, line-internal recurrence, such as meter, but not so common in cross-line recurrence such as parallelism and rhyme, evidently because it is psychologically easier to keep track of as many as three elements if they recur fairly quickly. However, the fact remains that overriding constraints prevent the use of some potential patterns, regardless of the linguistic elements which might be used to fill them.

The range of linguistic *sames* actually in poetic use is likewise limited. One can easily dream up great numbers of plausible-looking principles of organization which no poet ever uses, and, more importantly, which even the most experimental poet would intuitively recognize as irrelevant were he introduced to a piece of work based on them. (Of course, if he were challenged to do so, he might detect them, by much the same process that a code is cracked.) For example, no one thinks of filling in a stanzaic pattern on the principle that the last words of certain lines must contain the same number of sounds. Nor do we find a type of rhyme in which the last sound or the last *n* sounds must be the same. (We will return to this question in the discussion of slant rhyme below.) Naturally not, we might say. But a visiting Martian might find these nonexistent conventions no more peculiar than, for example, the Earthlings' custom of *rhyming*, whereby the last stressed vowel and anything that follows it must be the same.

To answer our Martian's objection would require a theory of poetic form that included a precise answer to the following two questions:

> What patterns are relevant in poetry?
> What linguistic sames are relevant in poetry?

Such a theory does not exist, although we do have certain useful bits and pieces. In what follows I should like to sketch out a partial answer to the second of these questions, in which I will argue that linguistics has a key role to play.

An initial tentative answer is this: *the linguistic sames which are potentially relevant in poetry are just those which are potentially relevant in grammar*. Since one part of the theory of generative grammar is a precise characterization of what sames are relevant in grammar, we can test this hypothesis very specifically. In fact, the hypothesis is so rich that its implications can hardly be grasped yet, let alone fully tested. All we can do here is to explore its consequences in particular areas. By doing so, we can clarify some long-standing questions of poetics as well as some that have thus far gone unasked.

Transformational grammar defines "grammatically relevant sameness" in terms of syntax by analyzing the constituent structure of sentences. First of all sentences are analyzed according to tree diagrams like (A) on the opposite page. Such a tree structure shows how a sentence can be analyzed on various different levels. For example, depending on which level of the tree one looks at, the sentence in diagram (A) is described as made

(A)

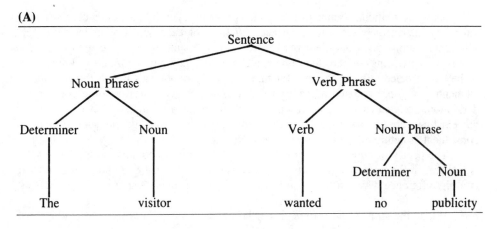

up of

$$\text{Determiner} + \text{Noun} + \text{Verb} + \text{Determiner} + \text{Noun}$$

or of

$$\text{Noun Phrase} + \text{Verb} + \text{Noun Phrase}$$

or of

$$\text{Noun Phrase} + \text{Verb Phrase}.$$

Such trees can be turned into other trees according to *transformational rules*. The tree above is a surface structure and has undergone a number of transformations; it derives directly, for instance, from another tree, shown in the next illustration, which is one step closer to the original, or *deep structure,* a tree in which the negation marker stands at the beginning of the sentence. The transformational rule moves the negation marker "not" into the determiner "any" of tree (B), and the resulting "not any" becomes "no" in the phrase "no publicity" of sentence (A). In this transformation, "any publicity" is changed at the Determiner + Noun level of the tree. Other transformations, such as the passive transformation, would treat it at the Noun Phrase level.

(B)

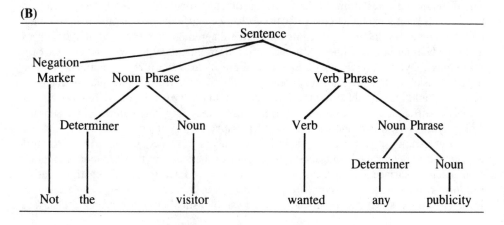

A transformational syntax of a language provides a derivation from a deep structure via many intermediate trees to a surface structure for each sentence in the language. These derivations say what elements can and cannot count as the same with respect to syntax: two elements count as the same at a given stage in the transformational derivation if they are labeled alike in the tree for that stage. My hypothesis is that those syntactic elements which are counted as parallel for purposes of verse are, at some point in the derivation, counted as sames according to transformational grammar. Let me now map out existing varieties of syntactic parallelism in poetry, using the syntactic notions of constituent structure and transformational rules.

The poetry of both Walt Whitman and Dylan Thomas abounds in parallelism; this is one reason for the driving, incantatory quality which they have in common. But there is a big difference between the parallelism of the poets, as is clear from these excerpts.

> Where the striped and starred flag is borne at the
>   head of the regiments;
> Approaching Manhattan, up by the long-stretching
>   island,
> Under Niagara, the cataract falling like a veil
>   over my countenance;
> Upon a door-step . . . . upon the horse-block of hard
>   wood outside,
> Upon the race-course, or enjoying pic-nics or
>   jigs or a good game of base-ball, . . .
>   Whitman, *Leaves of Grass*

> A process in the weather of the heart
> Turns damp to dry; the golden shot
> Storms in the freezing tomb.
> A weather in the quarter of the veins
> Turns night to day; blood in their suns
> Lights up the living worm.
>   Thomas, "A Process in the Weather of the Heart"

The difference derives from the level of constituent structure for which the parallelism holds. Walt Whitman characteristically uses what we may call *loose* parallelism, in which only the highest syntactic constituents of the tree diagram are the same; although he uses a place adverbial in every line, each one differs from the others in form and complexity. In contrast, Dylan Thomas uses a *strict* parallelism, in which even constituents on the lower levels of the tree diagram are parallel. In other words, Whitman uses larger syntactic blocks to build his parallel structure. Now all form in poetry is potentially functional: this syntactic difference, for example, corresponds directly to the contrast between the "metonymic" Whitman and the typically "metaphoric" Thomas.

But parallelism can vary stylistically not only with respect to the level in the tree at which it is determined, but also with respect to the stage in the syntactic derivation from deep to surface structure for which it holds. Aside from actual repetition (as in refrains or blues verses) no syntactic parallelism is ever required to be complete on the level of surface structure. Even the strictest parallelism allows divergence of surface structure according to certain types of transformational rules that delete and reorder constituents. Thus, Dylan Thomas'

> The force that through the green fuse drives the flower
> Drives my green age,

is strictly parallel to

> The force that drives the water through the rocks
> Drives my red blood,

in spite of the fact that the constituents are crossed. Even in the obligatory strict parallelism of Finnish folk poetry, word order may vary freely.

Similar observations may be made about syntactic deletion. In Finnish folk poetry a verb is frequently "missing" in the second line. In nearly all such cases, the second line is derived from a structural parallel to that of the first by a transformational process (the *Gapping* rule) which calls for the deletion of a repeated verb in the second of two parallel sentences.

So far, we have discussed three variables pertinent to the analysis of poetic form:

1. The choice of abstract pattern: How is the recurrence of linguistic elements organized? For example, do we have symmetry (*abab, aabb*), antisymmetry (*abba*), or closure (*aab, ababcc*)? Is the structure hierarchical (stanzas) or linear (stichic verse)?

   The other two variables have to do with how the abstract pattern is matched with linguistic elements.

2. The choice of linguistic elements: What are the syntactic or phonological building blocks which are subject to patterned recurrence? For example, do we have strict parallelism, where identity is maintained down to the smaller constituents of the tree, or loose parallelism, involving only the major constituents?

3. The choice of the derivational stage: Where in the transformational or phonological derivation do we make the match between linguistic elements and abstract patterns? For example, do we define parallel structure before or after the passive transformation has been applied—that is, is an active sentence regarded as parallel in structure to a corresponding passive one?

These three variables are, in principle, independent of each other. Theoretically, either strict or loose parallelism in terms of linguistic elements could hold either at a point in the transformational derivation near the deep structure or close to surface structure. However, there is in fact a close relationship among the three. The tighter the constraints on the abstract pattern, the stricter the parallelism tends to be, and the closer it holds to surface structure.

There is still a fourth variable, namely the grammar itself. Poetic language differs grammatically from regular speech. Poetry may use stylistic inversions not allowed in prose, as in "The force that through the green fuse drives . . . ." Such inversions are not imitations of Latin, as is sometimes claimed. Rather they are applications of transformational rules that have only limited existence in standard English prose. The extent to which special rules for poetic language have been acceptable is an important stylistic variable in English poetry. From Gray to Wordsworth, poets sought a more "natural" poetic diction and a major aspect of their effort was the conscious elimination of inversions. A hundred and fifty years later, however, inversions were brought back with a vengeance by E. E. Cummings, in whose hands they once again became an integral structural device.[6]

Poetic language differs, however, from Standard English in far more than word-order transformations. Perhaps the most striking characteristic of modern poetry is the stretching of grammar. This has led, in recent discussions of poetic language in the framework of generative grammar, to what has at times been a somewhat simplistic reliance on the concept of *ungrammaticality* or *deviance*. Metaphor, in particular, is frequently linked with a certain type of semantic deviance. However, it is clear that nondeviant sentences can have metaphorical interpretations: take, for example, "He came out smelling like a rose." In fact, the processes by which we give metaphorical interpretations to deviant sentences are the same as those by which we understand latent meaning in nondeviant sentences. Semantic deviance does not cause metaphorical meaning, but rather brings out what is already latent by blocking out a literal meaning, just as an eclipse of the sun does not "cause" the moon to shine, but makes its light perceptible by blocking out the sun. In general, then, deviance is a device of *foregrounding*. However, not all grammatical foregrounding involves changing the rules of grammar. Existing rules can also be utilized in new ways. For example, in Starbuck's poem, cited above, the striking phrase "burned what he said was himself" is not ungrammatical, but it is an unusual construction which may never have been used before.

We turn now from the syntactic to the phonological side of the language, where an examination of patterns has some rather surprising consequences, especially with regard to our habit of thinking of rhyme and alliteration as the simple repetition of sounds. We will find that the same four variables we distinguish in syntax also hold in phonology.

In addition to a set of transformational rules by which the syntax of sentences derives from a deep structure, grammar contains a set of phonological rules[7] by which the phonetic forms of words are derived from more basic underlying forms. The word "publicity," for example, which could be transcribed phonetically as /pəblísətī/, is derived, by a series of steps, from the more basic form /publik + iti/. The k as the basic form (which we can hear in the related words "public" and "publication") is converted to an s sound (indicated in the spelling by c) before front vowels such as i. Other rules place the stress on the third syllable from the end, and weaken all unstressed vowels except the last, which gets lengthened. Thus the *phonological derivation* of "publicity" is as follows:

/publik + iti/	basic form
publis + iti	change of k to s
publís + iti	placement of stress
publís + itī	lengthening of final i
pəblís + ətī	weakening of unstressed vowels

---

[6] In her unpublished Harvard dissertation, Irene Fairley shows that Cummings employs several syntactic systems, one of which is quite traditional in the form of its inversion rules.

[7] A detailed analysis of the rules of English phonology is given in Noam Chomsky and M. Halle, *Sound Pattern of English* (New York: Harper & Row, 1968).

Investigation of the way such rules work has become the primary concern of phonologists in recent years, replacing their earlier preoccupation with problems of determining and classifying the phonemes of a language. This research is beginning to make clear that a surprising amount of the system of phonological rules of a language, which one might have thought was a rather arbitrary and unstructured part of its grammar, is actually determined by general principles. Phonological rules ring changes on a fixed repertoire of rules which, though very large in absolute terms, is still only a tiny portion of the huge total which could be imagined. Hence my hypothesis, that the linguistic elements which can count as sames in verse are just those which can count as sames in grammar, can be tested in phonology as well as in syntax. A comparison of the repertoire of phonological rules with the repertoire of metrical and rhyme schemas used in verse does indeed reveal a number of striking homologies.

Consider first this simple example. We know that "having the same number of sounds" is of no relevance whatever in versification, whereas "having the same number of syllables" is of fundamental importance. There is no explanation for this fact in the theory of prosody. But the fact has an exact counterpart in phonology. There are no known phonological rules which differentiate among words on the basis of how many sounds they have. The class of words containing exactly three phonemes (for example, "end," "shock," "Anna") is a linguistically irrelevant pseudoclass which plays no role in grammar. But there are, of course, rules which count syllables: in many languages stress falls on the *n*th syllable from the beginning or end of a word, monosyllabic words have special phonological properties, and so on. Therefore, it seems that rules of versification are based on facts which are at bottom linguistic, and that systems of metrics must be explained by phonology.

Consider rhyme and alliteration, which are often defined as involving "repetition of sounds." This definition is, in fact, inaccurate. It fails to cover, for example, the type of rhyme known as *slant rhyme*, which is widely used by Dylan Thomas and Sylvia Plath. In slant rhyme, consonants after the last vowel must be the same, but words ending in vowels are considered to rhyme regardless of what the vowels are.

In Sylvia Plath's *Medallion*, which uses terza rima with slant rhyme throughout, we find rhymes like

> wood/dead/crooked/
> him/flame/time
> light/that/trout
> ocher/fire/there

but we also find

> jaw/arrow/eye

where the requirement is satisfied without any "repetition of sounds."

Alliteration of consonants, as found, for example, in the old Germanic languages including Old English, is a mirror image of slant rhyme. In Old English, words alliterate if their stressed syllables begin with the same consonant (with the special proviso that *sp, st,* and *sk* behave as if they were single consonants). But words whose stressed syllables begin with vowels alliterate freely with each other (*Atol ȳda geswing,* "terrible swirl of waves"). Thus the rule for alliteration (and its inverse, slant rhyme) is *not* that syllables must begin (or end) with the same sound, but rather that *if* the syllables begin (or end) with a consonant, then the consonants must be the same. If they begin (or end) with a vowel, they need not repeat the same sound.

How is it possible that certain words rhyme and alliterate without having any sounds in common? This question again has no answer in the theory of prosody. The fact that all vowels alliterate with each other has in fact provoked many ingenious but unsuccessful attempts to conjure up word-initial ghost consonants of some kind to "carry" the alliteration (which would imply similar ghost consonants at the ends of words to "carry" slant rhyme). But the problem is not merely that some rhyme and alliteration does not fit the traditional definitions of these concepts, but more importantly, that when the sound in question is a vowel the pattern which one would expect to be normal, that in which the first or last sounds are identical, does not seem to occur at all.

Let us turn to a grammatical analogue of rhyme and alliteration to see if corresponding phenomena are found there. Consider phonological processes of *reduplication,* which copy part of a word for grammatical purposes. It is interesting that we never find among them rules of the form "reduplicate the first (or last) sound of a word," just as we found no such rules for rhyme and alliteration. Rather, the typical form of reduplication is that of Gothic, where some verbs make their past tense by doubling their initial stem consonant, *if any,* and adding *ai* (pronounce like *e* in *get*):

saltan	"salt"	*sai-salt*	"salted"
haitan	"call"	*hai-hait*	"called"
slepan	"sleep"	*sai-slep*	"slept"
aukan	"increase"	*ai-auk*	"increased"
aikan	"renounce"	*ai-aik*	"renounced"
(ga) staldan	"obtain"	*(ga) stai-stald*	"obtained"

Note that this is very reminiscent of old Germanic alliteration, and even parallels the special treatment of *sk, sp,* and *st* as single units. Thus, the reduplication rules of phonology serve as well to circumscribe the kinds of rhyme and alliteration used in poetry.

Again, we have seen how a fact about the structure of verse derives from a fact about the structure of language. The question of how all initial vowels can alliterate with each other is a parallel question to that of how the *ai-* of *ai-auk* can be considered a reduplication of *auk.* Our answer is that language allows certain ways of organizing sounds, and that poetic form must draw on this organization.

More generally, consider how a word can be broken down into parts relevant to verse patterns. We can represent these patterns (or "analyses") by means of the standard notations used in phonology. For example, letting C stand for *consonant,* V for *vowel,* and # for *word boundary* (indicating whether the sound is an initial or a final sound), we can form the following notations:

#C	"a word-initial consonant"
#CV	"a word-initial consonant followed by a vowel"
V#	"a word-final vowel"
C_0	"any number of consonants"

Each of these expressions defines a class which might be referred to in a phonological rule.

The word "flash," for example, could pattern, for purposes of rhyme and alliteration, in the following ways:

$$\left.\begin{array}{ll} \#C & \text{f.} \\ \#C_0 & \text{fl.} \\ \#C_0V & \text{fla.} \end{array}\right\} \text{alliteration}$$

$$\begin{array}{lll} VC_0\# & \text{.ash} & \text{rhyme} \\ V & \text{.a.} & \text{assonance} \\ C_0\# \text{ or } C\# & \text{.sh} & \text{slant rhyme} \end{array}$$

$$\left.\begin{array}{ll} \#C_0 \ldots C_0\# & \text{fl.sh} \\ \#C \ldots C_0\# & \text{f.sh} \end{array}\right\} \text{pararhyme (as in Wilfred Owen's poetry)}$$

Now each of these patterns is potentially a pattern in a linguistic rule as well as a rule of versification. The first three represent types of *reduplication* which occur in various languages of the world. The others are found in English in sound symbolism (*phonesthemes*).[8] Thus, an example of a sound symbolism pattern of the form $C\#$ is "fuzz," "buzz," "fizz," "razz" "jazz." An example of $VC_0\#$ is "smash," "crash," "bash," "dash." And $\#C \ldots C_0\#$ is illustrated by "pitter," "patter," "putter," or "tick," "tack," "tock."

We have seen that elements are considered to be syntactically parallel even after certain syntactic transformations have reordered or deleted constituents. In other words, to match them exactly we would have to imagine them as they were before they were so transformed. This phenomenon has a counterpart in phonology. It sometimes happens that phonological schemes such as meter and rhyme must be matched to linguistic forms *before* certain phonological rules have been applied to them.

We already made this assumption implicitly in speaking of the slant rhyme of vowel-final words like "arrow" and "eye." While it is true that these words end in a vowel in their basic phonological form, this vowel gets a consonantal glide sound inserted after it by a rule of English phonology, so that "arrow," as it is actually pronounced, ends with a *w* sound and "eye" ends with a *y* sound. For purposes of versification, however, we treat these words as if they really ended in vowel sounds—that is, we apply the rhyme schemes to them before the glide insertion rule is applied.

Examples in which poetic form "looks back" at phonological forms which are not phonetic, can be cited from many languages. In German, most poets rhyme *Mund* "mouth" and *bunt* "colorful" (both pronounced with *t*, but different in basic form, since when you add an ending, such as *e, Munde* is pronounced with a *d*). Some poets, however, like Stefan George, who strove to achieve unusually pure poetic language, consistently avoid such rhymes. In other words, Stefan George's poetry rhymes according to forms more basic than that in which final stops are unvoiced.

There are cases where a whole block of phonological rules must be peeled away in this fashion before the schema which underlies a given meter is revealed. This is true of the Finnish *Kalevala* as recited by the bards of Ingermanland, and of the *Rigveda* of ancient India. The complexity in these traditions of the interaction between phonological

---

[8] R. Wellek and A. Warren, *Theory of Literature* (New York: Harvest Books, Harcourt, Brace & World, 1961), p. 148.

and metrical structure makes them a kind of laser beam with which we can probe into the way language is structured in the mind, via the way it is structured in poetry.[9]

Thus phonological identity in poetry is not a matter of phonetics alone, any more than syntactic identity is a matter of surface structure. In fact, we have arrived at the somewhat surprising conclusion that identity of sound is neither a necessary nor a sufficient condition for rhyme and alliteration.

These observations suggest that at least some constants of poetic form are dependent on the structure of language itself. The intrinsic structure of language, the raw material of poetry, is carried over into poetry. By virtue of the nature of the patterns that are relevant in poetry, the structures involved are primarily those which are universal rather than those which apply only to a particular language. Hence the homologies between grammar and poetry account, at least in part, for the universality of poetic form.

To be sure, that summary of my thesis is rather more sweeping than is justified by the concrete examples analyzed here. I have, after all, dealt only with external form, and hardly touched on such deeper questions as figurative language. Although I believe that it is in these areas that linguistics will make its greatest contribution to literary studies, I have here chosen more tangible aspects of poetic form since the linguistic approach can be more clearly illustrated with them. Furthermore, the linguistic semantics needed to tackle problems such as metaphor is only now beginning to exist. The current work which is being done in this area is highly encouraging, as are many other applications of linguistics to literary problems: Ohmann's syntactically based studies of prose style, for example, and the approach to the structure of narrative initiated in V. Propp's classic work on folktales.[10]

---

[9] P. Kiparsky, "Metrics and Morphophonemics in the Kalevala," *Linguistics and Literary Style*, "Metrics and Morphophonemics in the Rigveda," *Contributions to Generative Phonology*, ed. M. Brame (Austin: University of Texas Press, 1972); Howard Lasnik, "Metrics and Morphophonemics in Old English Verse," *Linguistic Inquiry*, forthcoming; Stephen Anderson, "U-Umlaut and Skaldic Verse," *Festschrift for Morris Halle*, eds. S. Anderson and P. Kiparsky (New York: Holt, Rinehart and Winston).

[10] R. Ohmann, "Generative Grammars and the Concept of Literary Style," *Word*, XX (1964), 423–439; V. Propp, *Morphology of the Folktale* (Austin: University of Texas Press, 1968). For a new linguistic approach to the question of modes of narrative, such as "narrated monolog," see S. Y. Kuroda, "Where Epistemology, Style and Grammar Meet," *Festschrift for Morris Halle*.

DISCUSSION QUESTIONS

1. What evidence is there that the changes in the Western literary tradition largely result from the intrinsic nature of verbal art? How would Chomsky's view of human language support this point of view?

2. In what ways does poetic language differ from Standard English? Discuss both syntactic and phonological differences.

3. Why does no poetic theory examine these two questions: (a) What patterns are relevant in poetry? (b) What linguistic sames are relevant in poetry? Discuss the roles that phonological and syntactic parallelisms play in answering the second question.

4. In what ways can free verse "be a more difficult and a more expressive poetic form than regulated verse"?

RICHARD OHMANN

Ohmann, a professor of English at Wesleyan University, has recently completed his editorship of College English. *He has long been interested in the relation of linguistics to literary study.*

LITERATURE AS SENTENCES

Critics permit themselves, for this or that purpose, to identify literature with great books, with imaginative writing, with expressiveness in writing, with the non-referential and non-pragmatic, with beauty in language, with order, with myth, with structured and formed discourse—the list of definitions is nearly endless—with verbal play, with uses of language that stress the medium itself, with the expression of an age, with dogma, with the *cri de coeur*, with neurosis. Now of course literature is itself and not another thing, to paraphrase Bishop Butler; yet analogies and classifications have merit. For a short space let us think of literature as sentences.

To do so will not tax the imagination, because the work of literature indubitably *is* composed of sentences, most of them well-ordered, many of them deviant (no pejorative meant), some of them incomplete. But since much of the same holds for dust-jacket copy, the Congressional Record, and transcripts of board meetings, the small effort required to think of literature as sentences may be repaid by a correspondingly small insight into literature as such. Although I do not believe this to be so, for the moment I shall hold the question in abeyance, and stay mainly within the territory held in common by all forms of discourse. In other words, I am not asking what is special about the sentences *of literature*, but what is special about *sentences* that they should interest the student of literature. Although I employ the framework of generative grammar and scraps of its terminology,[1] what I have to say should not ring in the traditionally educated grammatical ear with outlandish discord.

First, then, the sentence is the primary unit of understanding. Linguists have so trenchantly discredited the old definition—"a sentence is a complete thought"—that the truth therein has fallen into neglect. To be sure, we delimit the class of sentences by formal criteria, but each of the structures that qualifies will express a semantic unity not characteristic of greater or lesser structures. The meanings borne by morphemes, phrases, and clauses hook together to express a meaning that can stand more or less by itself. This point, far from denying the structuralist's definition of a sentence as a single free utterance, or *form,* seems the inevitable corollary of such definitions: forms carry meanings, and it is natural that an independent form should carry an independent meaning. Or, to come at the thing another way, consider that one task of a grammar is to supply structural descriptions, and that the sentence is the unit so described. A structural description specifies the way each part of a sentence is tied to each other part, and the semantic rules

---

[1] I draw especially on Noam Chomsky, *Aspects of the Theory of Syntax* (Cambridge, Mass., 1965) and Jerrold J. Katz and Paul Postal, *An Integrated Theory of Linguistic Descriptions* (Cambridge, Mass., 1964).

of a grammar use the structural descriptions as starting point in interpreting the whole. A reader or hearer does something analogous when he resolves the structure and meanings of sentences and thereby understands them. Still another way to approach the primacy of a sentence is to notice that the initial symbol for all derivations in a generative grammar is "S" for sentence: the sentence is the domain of grammatical structure—rather like the equation in algebra—and hence the domain of meaning.

These remarks, which will seem truisms to some and heresy to others, cannot be elaborated here. Instead, I want to register an obvious comment on their relevance to literary theory and literary criticism. Criticism, whatever else it does, must interpret works of literature. Theory concerns itself in part with the question, "what things legitimately bear on critical interpretation?" But beyond a doubt, interpretation begins with sentences. Whatever complex apprehension the critic develops of the whole work, that understanding arrives mundanely, sentence by sentence. For this reason, and because the form of a sentence dictates a rudimentary mode of understanding, sentences have a good deal to do with the subliminal meaning (and form) of a literary work. They prepare and direct the reader's attention in particular ways.

My second point about sentences should dispel some of the abstractness of the first. Most sentences directly and obliquely put more linguistic apparatus into operation than is readily apparent, and call on more of the reader's linguistic competence. Typically, a surface structure overlays a deep structure which it may resemble but little, and which determines the "content" of the sentence. For concreteness, take this rather ordinary example, an independent clause from Joyce's "Araby": "Gazing up into the darkness I saw myself as a creature driven and derided by vanity." The surface structure may be represented as follows, using the convention of labeled brackets:[2]

$$^S[^{Adv}[V + Part \ ^{PP}[P \ ^{NP}[D + N]]]$$
$$^{Nuc}[N \ ^{VP}[V + N \ ^{PP}[P \ ^{NP}[D + N \ ^{Adj}[V + and + V \ ^{PP}[P + N]]]]]]]]$$

The nucleus has a transitive verb with a direct object. In the deep structure, by contrast, the matrix sentence is of the form $^S[NP \ ^{VP}[V + Complement + NP]]$: "I + saw + as a creature + me." It has embedded in it one sentence with an intransitive verb and an adverb of location—"I gazed up into the darkness"—and two additional sentences with transitive verbs and direct objects—"Vanity drove the creature," and "Vanity derided the creature." Since "darkness" and "vanity" are derived nouns, the embedded sentences must in turn contain embeddings, of, say "(Something) is dark" and "(Someone) is vain." Thus the word "vanity," object of a preposition in the surface structure, is subject of two verbs in the deep, and its root is a predicate adjective. The word "creature," object of a preposition in the surface structure, also has a triple function in the deep structure: verbal complement, direct object of "drive," and direct object of "deride." Several transformations (including the passive) deform the six basic sentences, and several others relate them to each other. The complexity goes much farther, but this is enough to suggest that a number of grammatical processes are required to generate the initial sentence and that its structure is moderately involved. Moreover, a reader will not

---

[2] Each set of brackets encloses the constituent indicated by its superscript label. The notation is equivalent to a tree diagram. Symbols: S = Sentence, Adv = Adverbial, V = Verb, Part = Particle, PP = Prepositional Phrase, P = Preposition, NP = Noun Phrase, D = Determiner, N = Noun, Nuc = Nucleus, VP = Verb Phrase, Adj = Adjectival.

understand the sentence unless he grasps the relations marked in the deep structure. As it draws on a variety of syntactic resources, the sentence also activates a variety of semantic processes and modes of comprehension, yet in brief compass and in surface *form* that radically permutes *content*.

I choose these terms wilfully: that there are interesting grounds here for a form-content division seems to me quite certain. Joyce might have written, "I gazed up into the darkness. I saw myself as a creature. The creature was driven by vanity. The creature was derided by vanity." Or, "Vanity drove and derided the creature I saw myself as, gazer up, gazer into the darkness." Content remains roughly the same, for the basic sentences are unchanged. But the style is different. And each revision structures and screens the content differently. The original sentence acquires part of its meaning and part of its unique character by resonating against these unwritten alternatives. It is at the level of sentences, I would argue, that the distinction between form and content comes clear, and that the intuition of style has its formal equivalent.[3]

Sentences play on structure in still another way, more shadowy, but of considerable interest for criticism. It is a commonplace that not every noun can serve as object of every verb, that a given noun can be modified only by adjectives of certain classes, and so on. For instance, a well-defined group of verbs, including "exasperate," "delight," "please," and "astound," require animate objects; another group including "exert," "behave," and "pride," need reflexive objects. Such interdependencies abound in a grammar, which must account for them by subcategorizing nouns, adjectives, and the other major classes.[4] The importance of categorical restrictions is clearest in sentences that disregard them—deviant sentences. It happens that the example from Joyce is slightly deviant in this way: in one of the underlying sentences—"Vanity derided the creature"—a verb that requires a human subject in fact has as its subject the abstract noun "vanity." The dislocation forces the reader to use a supplementary method of interpretation: here, presumably he aligns "vanity" (the word) with the class of human nouns and sees vanity (the thing) as a distinct, active power in the narrator's psyche. Such deviance is so common in metaphor and elsewhere that one scarcely notices it, yet it helps to specify the way things happen in the writer's special world, and the modes of thought appropriate to that world.

I have meant to suggest that sentences normally comprise intricacies of form and meaning whose effects are not the less substantial for their subtlety. From this point, what sorts of critical description follow? Perhaps I can direct attention toward a few tentative answers, out of the many that warrant study, and come finally to a word on critical theory. Two samples must carry the discussion; one is the final sentence of "The Secret Sharer":

> Walking to the taffrail, I was in time to make out, on the very edge of a darkness thrown by a towering black mass like the very gateway of Erebus—yes, I was in time to catch an evanescent glimpse of my white hat left behind to mark the spot where the secret sharer of my cabin and of my thoughts, as though he were my second self, had lowered himself into the water to take his punishment: a free man, a proud swimmer striking out for a new destiny.

---

[3] I have argued the point at length in "Generative Grammars and the Concept of Literary Style," *Word*, 20 (Dec. 1964), 423–439.

[4] Chomsky discusses ways of doing this in *Aspects of the Theory of Syntax*, Chapter 2.

I hope others will agree that the sentence justly represents its author: that it portrays a mind energetically stretching to subdue a dazzling experience *outside* the self, in a way that has innumerable counterparts elsewhere in Conrad. How does scrutiny of the deep structure support this intuition? First, notice a matter of emphasis, of rhetoric. The matrix sentence, which lends a surface form to the whole, is "# S # I was in time # S #" (repeated twice). The embedded sentences that complete it are "I walked to the taffrail," "I made out + NP," and "I caught + NP." The point of departure, then, is the narrator himself: where he was, what he did, what he saw. But a glance at the deep structure will explain why one feels a quite different emphasis in the sentence as a whole: seven of the embedded sentences have "sharer" as grammatical subject; in another three the subject is a noun linked to "sharer" by the copula; in two "sharer" is direct object; and in two more "share" is the verb. Thus thirteen sentences go to the semantic development of "sharer," as follows:

1) The secret sharer had lowered the secret sharer into the water.
2) The secret sharer took his punishment.
3) The secret sharer swam.
4) The secret sharer was a swimmer.
5) The swimmer was proud.
6) The swimmer struck out for a new destiny.
7) The secret sharer was a man.
8) The man was free.
9) The secret sharer was my second self.
10) The secret sharer had (it).
11) (Someone) punished the secret sharer.
12) (Someone) shared my cabin.
13) (Someone) shared my thoughts.

In a fundamental way, the sentence is mainly *about* Leggatt, although the surface structure indicates otherwise.

Yet the surface structure does not simply throw a false scent, and the way the sentence comes to focus on the secret sharer is also instructive. It begins with the narrator, as we have seen, and "I" is the subject of five basic sentences early on. Then "hat" takes over as the syntactic focus, receiving development in seven base sentences. Finally, the sentence arrives at "sharer." This progression in the deep structure rather precisely mirrors both the rhetorical movement of the sentence from the narrator to Leggatt via the hat that links them, and the thematic effect of the sentence, which is to transfer Leggatt's experience to the narrator via the narrator's vicarious and actual participation in it. Here I shall leave this abbreviated rhetorical analysis, with a cautionary word: I do not mean to suggest that only an examination of deep structure reveals Conrad's skillful emphasis—on the contrary, such an examination supports and in a sense explains what any careful reader of the story notices.

A second critical point adjoins the first. The morpheme "share" appears once in the sentence, but it performs at least twelve separate functions, as the deep structure shows. "I," "hat," and "mass" also play complex roles. Thus at certain points the sentence has extraordinary "density," as I shall call it. Since a reader must register these multiple functions in order to understand the sentence, it is reasonable to suppose that the very process of understanding concentrates his attention on centers of density. Syntactic density, I am suggesting, exercises an important influence on literary comprehension.

Third, by tuning in on deep structures, the critic may often apprehend more fully the build of a literary work. I have already mentioned how the syntax of Conrad's final sentence develops his theme. Consider two related points. First, ''The Secret Sharer'' is an initiation story in which the hero, through moral and mental effort, locates himself vis à vis society and the natural world, and thus passes into full manhood. The syntax of the last sentence schematizes the relationships he has achieved, in identifying with Leggatt's heroic defection, and in fixing on a point of reference—the hat—that connects him to the darker powers of nature. Second, the syntax and meaning of the last sentence bring to completion the pattern initiated by the syntax and meaning of the first few sentences, which present human beings and natural objects in thought-bewildering disarray. I can do no more than mention these structural connections here, but I am convinced that they supplement and help explain an ordinary critical reading of the story.

Another kind of critical point concerns habits of meaning revealed by sentence structure. One example must suffice. We have already marked how the sentence shifts its focus from ''I'' to ''hat'' to ''sharer.'' A similar process goes on in the first part of the sentence: ''I'' is the initial subject, with ''hat'' as object. ''Hat'' is subject of another base sentence that ends with ''edge,'' the object of a preposition in a locative phrase. ''Edge'' in turn becomes object of a sentence that has ''darkness'' as subject. ''Darkness'' is object in one with ''mass'' as subject, and in much the same way the emphasis passes to ''gateway'' and ''Erebus.'' The syntax executes a chaining effect here which cuts across various kinds of construction. Chaining is far from the only type of syntactic expansion, but it is one Conrad favors. I would suggest this hypothesis: that syntactically and in other ways Conrad draws heavily on operations that link one thing with another associatively. This may be untrue, or if true it may be unrevealing; certainly it needs clearer expression. But I think it comes close to something that we all notice in Conrad, and in any case the general critical point exemplified here deserves exploration: that each writer tends to exploit deep linguistic resources in characteristic ways—that his style, in other words, rests on syntactic options within sentences (see fn. 3)—and that these syntactic preferences correlate with habits of meaning that tell us something about his mode of conceiving experience.

My other sample passage is the first sentence of Dylan Thomas' ''A Winter's Tale'':

> It is a winter's tale
> That the snow blind twilight ferries over the lakes
> And floating fields from the farm in the cup of the vales,
> Gliding windless through the hand folded flakes,
> The pale breath of cattle at the stealthy sail,
>
> And the stars falling cold,
> And the smell of hay in the snow, and the far owl
> Warning among the folds, and the frozen hold
> Flocked with the sheep white smoke of the farm house cowl
> In the river wended vales where the tale was told

Some of the language here raises a large and familiar critical question, that of unorthodox grammar in modern poetry, which has traditionally received a somewhat facile answer. We say that loss of confidence in order and reason leads to dislocation of syntax, as if errant grammar were an appeal to the irrational. A cursory examination of deep structure in verse like Thomas', or even in wildly deviant verse like some of Cummings', will show the matter to be more complex than that.

How can deviance be most penetratingly analyzed? Normally, I think, in terms of the base sentences that lie beneath ungrammatical constructions. Surface structure alone does not show "the river wended vales" (line 10) to be deviant, since we have many well-formed constructions of the same word-class sequence: "machine made toys," "sun dried earth," and so on. The particular deviance of "the river wended vales" becomes apparent when we try to refer it to an appropriate underlying structure. A natural one to consider is "the river wends the vales" (cf. "the sun dries the earth"), but of course this makes "wend" a transitive verb, which it is not, except in the idiomatic "wend its way." So does another possibility, "NP + wends the vales with rivers" (cf. "NP + makes the toys by machine"). This reading adds still other kinds of deviance, in that the Noun Phrase will have to be animate, and in that rivers are too cumbersome to be used instrumentally in the way implied. Let us assume that the reader rejects the more flagrant deviance in favor of the less, and we are back to "the river wends the vales." Suppose now that "the vales" is not after all a direct object, but a locative construction, as in "the wolf prowls the forest"; this preserves the intransitivity of "wend," and thereby avoids a serious form of deviance. But notice that there is *no* transformation in English that converts "the wolf prowls the forest" into "the wolf prowled forest," and so this path is blocked as well. Assume, finally, that given a choice between shifting a word like "wend" from one subclass to another and adding a transformational rule to the grammar, a reader will choose the former course; hence he selects the first interpretation mentioned: "the river wends the vales."

If so, how does he understand the anomalous transitive use of "wend"? Perhaps by assimilating the verb to a certain class that may be either transitive or intransitive: "paint," "rub," and the like. Then we will take "wend" to mean something like "make a mark on the surface of, by traversing"; in fact, this is roughly how I read Thomas' phrase. But I may be wrong, and in any case my goal is not to solve the riddle. Rather, I have been leading up to the point that every syntactically deviant construction has more than one possible interpretation, and that readers resolve the conflict by a process that involves deep and intricately motivated decisions and thus puts to work considerable linguistic knowledge, syntactic as well as semantic.[5] The decisions nearly always go on implicitly, but aside from that I see no reason to think that deviance of this sort is an appeal to, or an expression of, irrationality.

Moreover, when a poet deviates from normal syntax he is not doing what comes most habitually, but is making a special sort of choice. And since there are innumerable kinds of deviance, we should expect that the ones elected by a poem or poet spring from particular semantic impulses, particular ways of looking at experience. For instance, I think such a tendency displays itself in Thomas' lines. The construction just noted conceives the passing of rivers through vales as an agent acting upon an object. Likewise, "flocked" in line 9 becomes a transitive verb, and the spatial connection Thomas refers to—flocks in a hold—is reshaped into an action—flocking—performed by an unnamed agent upon the hold. There are many other examples in the poem of deviance that projects unaccustomed activity and process upon nature. Next, notice that beneath line 2 is the sentence "the twilight is blind," in which an inanimate noun takes an animate adjective,

---

[5] See Jerrold J. Katz, "Semi-sentences," in Jerry A. Fodor and Jerrold J. Katz, eds., *The Structure of Language* (1964), pp. 400–416. The same volume includes two other relevant papers, Chomsky, "Degrees of Grammaticalness," pp. 384–389, and Paul Ziff, "On Understanding 'Understanding Utterances,' " pp. 390–399. Samuel R. Levin has briefly discussed ungrammatical poetry within a similar framework in *Linguistic Structures in Poetry* (The Hague, 1962), Chapters 2 and 3.

and that in line 5 "sail" takes the animate adjective "stealthy." This type of deviance also runs throughout the poem: Thomas sees nature as personal. Again, "twilight" is subject of "ferries," and should thus be a concrete noun, as should the object, "tale." Here and elsewhere in the poem the division between substance and abstraction tends to disappear. Again and again syntactic deviance breaks down categorical boundaries and converts juxtaposition into action, inanimate into human, abstract into physical, static into active. Now, much of Thomas' poetry displays the world as process, as interacting forces and repeating cycles, in which human beings and human thought are indifferently caught up.[6] I suggest that Thomas' syntactical irregularities often serve this vision of things. To say so, of course, is only to extend the natural critical premise that a good poet sets linguistic forms to work for him in the cause of artistic and thematic form. And if he strays from grammatical patterns he does not thereby leave language or reason behind: if anything, he draws the more deeply on linguistic structure and on the processes of human understanding that are implicit in our use of well-formed sentences.

Most of what I have said falls short of adequate precision, and much of the detail rests on conjecture about English grammar, which at this point is by no means fully understood. But I hope that in loosely stringing together several hypotheses about the fundamental role of the sentence I have indicated some areas where a rich exchange between linguistics and critical theory might eventually take place. To wit, the elusive intuition we have of *form* and *content* may turn out to be anchored in a distinction between the surface structures and the deep structures of sentences. If so, syntactic theory will also feed into the theory of *style*. Still more evidently, the proper *analysis* of styles waits on a satisfactory analysis of sentences. Matters of *rhetoric,* such as emphasis and order, also promise to come clearer as we better understand internal relations in sentences. More generally, we may be able to enlarge and deepen our concept of literary *structure* as we are increasingly able to make it subsume linguistic structure—including especially the structure of deviant sentences. And most important, since critical understanding follows and builds on understanding of sentences, generative grammar should eventually be a reliable assistant in the effort of seeing just how a given literary work sifts through a reader's mind, what cognitive and emotional processes it sets in motion, and what organization of experience it encourages. In so far as critical theory concerns itself with meaning, it cannot afford to bypass the complex and elegant structures that lie at the inception of all verbal meaning.

DISCUSSION QUESTIONS

1. Explain how tracing a surface structure back to deep structure illuminates the style of a specific author.

2. In your own words explain how examining the deep structure of the sentences from "The Secret Sharer" elucidates the intuitions felt, but not supported directly, by the surface structure.

3. How does the examination of deep structure help one to understand unorthodox grammar in the surface structure? Trace one of the unorthodox grammatical sentences in an E. E. Cummings poem from surface structure back to deep structure.

---

[6] Ralph Maud's fine study, *Entrances to Dylan Thomas' Poetry* (Pittsburgh, 1963), describes the phenomenon well in a chapter called "Process Poems."

ACKNOWLEDGEMENTS

For specific permission to reprint the articles in this anthology we are grateful to the living authors and to these publishers.

National Society for the Study of Education. For Kenneth G. Wilson, "The History of the English Language" ["The English Language: Past and Present"], pp. 109–132; and Richard Venezky, "Linguistics and Spelling," pp. 264–274. Both articles reprinted with permission from *Linguistics in School Programs*, Sixty-ninth Yearbook of the National Society for the Study of Education, Part 2, edited by Albert H. Marckwardt (Chicago: University of Chicago Press, 1970).

National Council of Teachers of English. For Karl Dykema, "Where Our Grammar Came From," *College English* 22 (1961): 455–465. Copyright © 1961 by the National Council of Teachers of English.

Speech Association of America. For W. Nelson Francis, "Revolution in Grammar," *Quarterly Journal of Speech* 40 (1954): 299–312; and Charles V. Hartung, "The Persistence of Tradition in Grammar," *Quarterly Journal of Speech* 48 (1962): 174–186.

Technology Review. For Benjamin Lee Whorf, "Science and Linguistics." Reprinted with permission from *Technology Review* 42 (1940): 229–230, 247–248. Copyright © 1940 by the Alumni Association of the Massachusetts Institute of Technology.

National Council of Teachers of English. For Noam Chomsky, "The Current Scene in Linguistics," *College English* 27 (1966): 587–595. Copyright © 1966 by the National Council of Teachers of English.

Indiana University Press. For "Knowledge of Language," pp. 32–49, from *Modern Linguistics: The Results of Chomsky's Revolution*, by Neil Smith and Deirdre Wilson, © 1979 by Neil Smith and Deirdre Wilson. Reprinted by permission of Indiana University Press.

Journal of English Linguistics. For John Algeo, "Tagmemics: A Brief Overview," *Journal of English Linguistics* 4 (1970): 1–6.

MIT Press. For "Phonology," chapter 6, pp. 70–71, 79–96, 99–104, in *Linguistics: An Introduction to Language and Communication*, by Adrian Akmajian, Richard A. Demers, and Robert M. Harnish. Copyright © 1979 by The MIT Press. Reprinted by permission of The MIT Press, Cambridge, Massachusetts.

Georgetown University Press. For George Lakoff, "Humanistic Linguistics," in *Georgetown University Round Table on Languages and Linguistics, 1974*, edited by Francis P. Dineen, S.J. (Washington, D.C.: Georgetown University Press, 1974), pp. 103–117. Copyright © by Georgetown University.

Basic Books. For George A. Miller, "Nonverbal Communication," *Communication, Language and Meaning*, pp. 231–241. Copyright © 1973 by Basic Books.

American Psychological Association. For Roger Brown, "Development of the First Language in the Human Species," *American Psychologist* 28.2 (1973): 97–106. Copyright © by the American Psychological Association. Reprinted by permission.

W. H. Freeman and Company. For Breyne Arlene Moskowitz, "The Acquisition of Language," *Scientific American* 239.5 (1978): 92–110.

Basic Books. For Edward S. Klima and Ursula Bellugi, "Teaching Apes to Communicate," *Communication, Language and Meaning,* pp. 95–106. Copyright © 1973 by Basic Books.

University of Texas Press. For E. Bagby Atwood, "*Grease* and *Greasy:* A Study of Geographical Variation," *The University of Texas Studies in English* 29 (1950): 249–260. Reprinted by permission of the University of Texas Press.

Johnson Reprint Corporation. For John L. Fischer, "Social Influences on the Choice of a Linguistic Variant," *Word* 14 (1958): 47–56. Reprinted by permission of Johnson Reprint Corporation.

University of Alabama Press. For Harold B. Allen, "*The Linguistic Atlas of the Upper Midwest* as a Source of Sociolinguistic Information," in *James B. McMillan: Essays in Linguistics by His Friends and Colleagues,* © 1977, The University of Alabama Press. Reprinted by permission.

Georgetown University Press. For Bruce Fraser, "Some 'Unexpected' Reactions to Various American-English Dialects," in *Language Attitudes: Current Trends and Prospects,* edited by Roger W. Shuy and Ralph W. Fasold (Washington, D.C.: Georgetown University Press, 1973), pp. 28–35. Copyright © by Georgetown University Press.

Cambridge University Press. For Anthony S. Kroch, "Toward a Theory of Social Dialect Variation," reprinted from *Language in Society* 7 (1978): 17–36, by permission of Cambridge University Press. Copyright © 1978 by Cambridge University Press.

Holt, Rinehart and Winston. For "Black English," pp. 117–133, from *Man's Many Voices: Language in its Cultural Context,* by Robbins Burling. Copyright © 1970 by Holt, Rinehart and Winston, Inc. Reprinted by permission of Holt, Rinehart and Winston.

Cambridge University Press. For Roger D. Abrahams, "Black Talking on the Streets," reprinted from *Exploration in the Ethnography of Speaking,* edited by Richard Bauman and Joel Sherzer, 1974, pp. 240–262, by permission of Cambridge University Press. Copyright © 1974 by Cambridge University Press.

Mouton Publishers. For Mary Ritchie Key, "Linguistic Behavior of Male and Female," *Linguistics* 88 (1972): 15–31.

Linguistic Society of America. For Robin Lakeoff, "Language in Context," *Language* 48 (1972): 907–927. Copyright © by the Linguistic Society of America.

Linguistic Society of America. For Dwight L. Bolinger, "Truth is a Linguistic Question," *Language,* 49 (1973): 539–550. Copyright © by the Linguistic Society of America.

University of Alabama Press. For Sidney Greenbaum, "Some Verb-Intensifier Collocations in American and British English," *American Speech* 49.1–2 (1974): 79–89.

National Council of Teachers of English. For Robert C. Pooley, excerpts from *The Teaching of English Usage,* 2nd ed., 1974, pp. 173–174, 201–209. Copyright © 1974 by the National Council of Teachers of English.

National Council of Teachers of English. For Elaine Chaika, "Grammars and Teaching," *College English* 39 (1978): 770–783. Copyright © 1978 by the National Council of Teachers of English.

Harvard Educational Review. For Kenneth S. Goodman and Yetta M. Goodman, "Learning about Psycholinguistic Processes by Analyzing Oral Reading," *Harvard Educational Review* 47 (1977): 317–333. Copyright © 1977 by President and Fellows of Harvard College.

John Wiley and Sons, Inc., Publishers. For Johanna S. DeStefano, "Language and Reading," pp. 125–144, in *Language, the Learner, and the School.* Copyright © 1979 by John Wiley and Sons.

National Council of Teachers of English. For Kellogg Hunt, "Early Blooming and Late Blooming Syntactic Structures." in *Evaluating Writing: Describing, Measuring, Judging,* edited by Charles R. Cooper and Lee Odell, pp. 91–107. Copyright © 1977 by the National Council of Teachers of English.

McQuade, Donald A. For Donald C. Freeman, "Linguistics and Error Analysis: On Agency," pp.

143–150; and Joseph M. Williams, "Non-Linguistic Linguistics and the Teaching of Style," pp. 24–36. In *Linguistics, Stylistics, and the Teaching of Composition* (Department of English, University of Akron: n.d.). Copyright © 1979 by Donald A. McQuade. Reprinted by permission of the editor, Donald McQuade.

National Council of Teachers of English. For Dennis Baron, "Non-Standard English, Composition, and the Academic Establishment," *College English* 37 (1975): 177–183. Copyright © 1975 by the National Council of Teachers of English.

National Council of Teachers of English. For Ricardo Garcia, "A Linguistic Frame of Reference for Critiquing Chicano Compositions," *College English* 37 (1975): 184–188. Copyright © 1975 by the National Council of Teachers of English.

The University of Wisconsin Press. For Bernard Spolsky, "Contrastive Analysis, Error Analysis, Interlanguage, and Other Useful Fads," *The Modern Language Journal* 13 (1979): 250–257. The University of Wisconsin Press. Copyright © The Board of Regents of the University of Wisconsin System.

Teachers of English to Speakers of Other Languages (TESOL). For Edna Acosta-Belén, " 'Spanglish': A Case of Languages in Contact." Reprinted from *On TESOL 75: New Directions in Second Language Learning, Teaching and Bilingual Education,* edited by Marina K. Burt and Heidi C. Dulay, pp. 151–158. Copyright © 1975 by Teachers of English to Speakers of Other Languages, Washington, D.C. Reprinted with permission of the publisher and Edna Acosta-Belén.

Florida FL Reporter. For Thomas Kochman, "Social Factors in the Consideration of Teaching Standard English," in the special copyrighted anthology issue of the *Florida FL Reporter* entitled *Linguistic-Cultural Differences and American Education* 7.1 (Spring-Summer 1969): 87–88, 157; Alfred C. Aarons, Barbara Y. Gordon, and William A. Stewart, eds.

National Council of Teachers of English. For Mitford Mathews, "The Freshman and His Dictionary," *College Composition and Communication* 6 (1955): 187–190. Copyright © 1955 by the National Council of Teachers of English.

Appleton-Century-Crofts and Prentice-Hall. For Albert H. Marckwardt, "The New Webster Dictionary: A Critical Appraisal," *Readings in Applied English Linguistics* (1964), pp. 476–485. Copyright © 1958, 1964 by Appleton-Century-Crofts; 1980 by Prentice-Hall and Harold B. Allen.

Encounter Ltd. For R. W. Burchfield, "On That Other Great Dictionary . . . and the American Language," *Encounter* 48.5 (May 1977): 47–50. Copyright © by Encounter Ltd.

Linguistic Society of America. For Archibald A. Hill, "Laymen, Lexicographers, and Linguists," *Language* 46 (1970): 245–258. Copyright © by the Linguistic Society of America.

Babel and the editor-in-chief, Dr. György Radó. For Thomas J. Creswell, "Usage in Contemporary American Dictionaries." Reprinted with permission from *Babel* 23.1 (1977): 23–28. Published by Akadémiai Kïadó. Copyright © 1977 by Fédération Internationale des Traducteurs.

American Name Society. For Francis Lee Utley, "The Linguistic Component of Onomastics," *Names* 11 (1963): 145–176.

University Presses of Florida. For John Algeo, "Semantic Names: The Kind of Meaning," chapter 6 in *On Defining the Proper Name,* University of Florida Humanities Monograph #41. Copyright © 1943 by University of Florida Press.

University of Texas Press. For Archibald A. Hill, "Poetry and Stylistics," Chapter 5, pp. 41–52, in *Constituent and Pattern in Poetry,* University of Texas Press, 1976. Copyright © 1976 by Archibald A. Hill. Reprinted by permission of the University of Texas Press.

W. W. Norton and Company, Inc. For Paul Kiparsky, "The Role of Linguistics in a Theory of Poetry." Reprinted from *Language as a Human Problem,* pp. 233–245, edited by Einar Haugen and Morton Bloomfield, with the permission of W. W. Norton and Company, Inc. Copyright © 1973, 1974 by the American Academy of Arts and Sciences.

National Council of Teachers of English. For Richard Ohmann, "Literature as Sentences," *College English* 27 (1966): 261–266. Copyright © 1966 by the National Council of Teachers of English.

INDEX

Boldface numerals indicate page limits of an article by the author named in the entry.

A NOTE ON THE TYPE

The text of this book was set in Times Roman, a VIP version of a Linotype face. Times Roman was designed by Stanley Morison for *The Times* (London), and first introduced by that newspaper in 1932.

Among typographers and designers of the twentieth century, Stanley Morison has been a strong forming influence, as typographical adviser to the English Monotype Corporation, as a director of two distinguished English publishing houses, and as a writer of sensibility, erudition, and keen practical sense.

In 1930 Morison wrote: "Type design moves at the pace of the most conservative reader. The good type-designer therefore realises that, for a new fount to be successful, it has to be so good that only very few recognise its novelty. If readers do not notice the consummate reticence and rare discipline of a new type, it is probably a good letter." It is now generally recognized that in the creation of Times Roman Morison successfully met the qualifications of this theoretical doctrine.

Typography design by Karin Gerdes-Kincheloe.

This book was composed by Monotype Composition Co., Baltimore, Md. Printed and bound by R. R. Donnelley & Sons, Harrisonburg, Va.